THE
ULTIMATE
CROSSWORD
WORD-PHRASE
FINDER

THE ULTIMATE CROSSWORD WORD-PHRASE FINDER

A Unique Source
for Cruciverbalists

Philip J. Sayles

The Ultimate Crossword Word-Phrase Finder: A Unique Source for Cruciverbalists

Published by Wheatmark
610 East Delano Street, Suite 104
Tucson, Arizona 85705 U.S.A.
www.wheatmark.com

International Standard Book Number: 978-1-60494-172-2
Library of Congress Control Number: 2008935789

Preface

This first edition of what may be a one of a kind crossword puzzle dictionary contains approximately one hundred forty-four thousand words that make up approximately forty-three thousand crossword phrases and some more commonly used single words. These entries have been compiled over a period of ten to twelve years dating back to the late nineties. This all started as a reference for the author's personal use and not with any intent to creating a new and different crossword dictionary, at least not at the onset. Initially, I kept a small notebook and, as it grew, I transferred it to the computer; ultimately, it has grown into a two hundred and twenty plus page dictionary of crossword phrases. This is something that is new and different to the crossword world. The usual crossword dictionary deals as a reference for single word clues, but to my knowledge, none concentrate on crossword phrases in the manner that this book does. This book is for the astute cruciverbalist (someone who enjoys or creates crossword puzzles) who is determined to complete each and every crossword puzzle.

This reference will be useful to the novice and the expert alike. Novices will use the resource frequently as they cut their teeth on increasingly more challenging puzzles. More experienced cruciverbalists will use the book to find a single answer that provides the breakthrough to fill in that last unsolved corner where "Kampuchea coin" intersects with "River in southwest Zimbabwe." Hopefully, this reference will allow all users to move up the ladder of crossword difficulty that makes our shared addiction so enjoyable.

Many of the phrase clues have been entered once as it was originally written in the crossword puzzle and a second time with the noun or verb being listed first in alphabetical order. Example:

Within a stone's throw: near
Stone's throw, within a: near

Public hall: lyceum
Hall, public: lyceum

The purpose was to make it possible to find a particular clue regardless of how the phrase would be worded in a given crossword puzzle. To make searching easier, concentrate on looking up the phrase as it is written; then if that fails, search using the second option.

There will be instances wherein you may not find the exact answer you are looking for, but your search may give you a hint as to what the correct answer may be.

My initial intent was to confine this dictionary to crossword phrases (clues), but as time went on, I started adding the more commonly used single-word clues, which minimizes the need to reference a second dictionary.

Anyone who is familiar with crossword puzzles has experienced the use of words that have had the spelling skewed to fit the puzzle. I included some misspelled entries, along with the correct spelling, especially if the misspelled word occurred on more than one occasion.

Throughout the dictionary, you will find a two-or-more-word phrase with one word <u>underlined</u> and no apparent answer. The underlined word within the phrase is the answer you are looking for. Example:

Clue: holly _____
Answer: holly <u>wreath</u>

Clue: seventh _____ stretch
Answer: seventh <u>inning</u> stretch

You will also find multiple-word phrases with no underlined word (s) or accompanying answers and in these instances the answer lies with any one or more of the words within the phrase depending upon a given crossword puzzle. The same applies with the names of persons throughout the dictionary in that either the first or last name may be the answer you are looking for.

References to foreign issues are common in today's crossword puzzles. The more common languages and locations referenced are Africa, British, English, French, France, German, Greek, Italian, India, Indian, Spain, and Russia. In these instances, you will find that many clues making reference to these foreign places will be listed under their respective headings, and for the most part, there will not be a second listing elsewhere, regardless of how the phrase is worded.

Other common headings are dance, fabric, goddess, music/musical, mythical Norse, Polynesian, rivers, Shakespearean, Spanish, wines, and many more. Again, entries under these headings (and others) will most likely not be found elsewhere in the dictionary.

Tips for solving crossword puzzles

1. Above all else, be open-minded in interpreting the clue. For example, the clue "shot" could be an adjective, a verb, or a noun. To a large degree, the difficulty of a puzzle is determined by the phrasing of a clue. To prompt the answer "divine," an easier puzzle might give "heavenly" as a clue, a medium puzzle could prompt "locate water," while a tough puzzle might supply a clue like "see the future." A good crossword editor takes puzzles submitted by contributors and changes the clues to adjust the difficulty and, therefore, the entertainment value of a puzzle.

2. Larger puzzles have themes, sometimes indicated with a title, pertaining to the longer horizontal and vertical answers. The theme is sometimes sequential pieces of a quote but can also be answers centered on a common focus like presidents, sports, or literature. The answers are often puns and occasionally share an unusual syntactic substitution such as using the number "4" to replace the letters "for" in an answer ("comfortable" becomes "com4table") or "2" to replace the letters "to."

3. Tense matters. If the clue is written in the past tense, the answer is in the past tense. If the clue ends in "ing," the answer must agree. Editors are never sloppy about the agreement between clues and answers.

4. Take advantage of plurals. If the clue is plural, so is the answer. You can almost always fill in the last letter of the answer as "s," the exception being Latin roots such as atrium/atria.

5. Use answers containing common letters. There aren't many "j" words in crossword puzzles ("raja" comes to mind). I've often seen the clue "jai_____," but I've never seen the clue "___ alai." At the other end of the spectrum, there are lots of "e" words—"ete" (French for "summer") and "eero" (first name of architect "Saarinen") are obscure but commonly used crossword answers because of the combination of common letters. If a "q" does happen to surface, it is almost always followed by "u" in both vertical and horizontal answers ("Qatar" is the only exception that readily comes to mind).

6. If the clue ends with a question mark, then it is some sort of play on words. These add to the enjoyment of the puzzle by adding humor and difficulty and by forcing the solver to be open-minded and clever.

7. Foreign language answers can be prompted in several ways. "Tia" (Spanish for "aunt") could be tipped off as "Aunt: Sp" or "Juan's aunt" or "Toledo aunt."

8. If the clue contains an abbreviation, then the answer probably does, too. For example, "IRS employee" could be "CPA," and "ABA member" could be "atty," and "NCO" could be "sgt."

A

AAA offering: Route
Aage Haugland, for one: basso
A bit too intrusive: nosy
A distance from land: offshore
A foremost painter: Rubens
"A Law unto Itself"
The "A" list: elite
A twist of fate
"A votre santé": French toast
A Washougal: vulture
A way to drink whiskey: neat
A way to walk: on air, on water
Aardvark snack: ant
ABA member: attorney, att.
Abaca: hemp
Abacus: slab, cupboard
Abacus piece: bead
Abaddon: pit, hell
Abaft: aft, after, astern, behind
Abalone: Awabi, ormer, sea ear
Abalone in Channel Island: ormer
Abalone (British deal): ormer
Abalone eater: otter
Abalone fancier: otter
Abandon the truth: lie
Abate: ease, ebb, lessen, wane
Abbe: priest
Abbess: spiritual
Abbot: Dom
Abbot, female: abbess
Abbr. at the bottom of the page: cont.
Abdicate: quit, leave, relinquish
Abdomen, relating to the: celiac
Abdominal: odious, celiac
Abduct: kidnap
Abductor, tabloid: alien
Abdul-Jabbar's alma mater: UCLA
Abdul, Paula: music
Abecedarian: tyro, novice, amateur, learner,
    initiate, neophyte
Abel, Elie: newsman
Abel's birthplace: Eden
    brother: Cain, Seth
    father: Adam
    mother: Eve
    slayer: Cain
Aberdeen kid: lad
Aberdeen native: Scot
Aberdeen River: Dee
Aberration: mania, wrong
Abeyance: cold storage, rest, inertness
Abhorrence: hatred
Abigail's brother: David
    husband: David, Nabal
    mother: Amasa
    son: Chileah
Abiosis: without life
Abject fear: horror
Abject one: worn
Able to feel or perceive: sensitive
Able-bodied: fit, hale, hardy, lusty

"Abner" creator: Al Capp
Abner's father: Ner
Abnormal animal: freak
Aboard ship: asea
Abodes, cliffside: aeries
Abode, craggy: aerie
Abode, lofty: aerie
Abode, urbane: condo
Abominable: nasty
Abominable snowman: yeti
Abou Ben Adhem had one: dream
Abounding in trees: sylvan
Abounds: teems
About: as to, anent, around, or so, circa
About, data wise: circa
About face: turn, reverse, reversal, turnabout,
    volte-face
About half of us: women, men
About in memos: In re
About to fall: tottering, wobbling
About to happen: imminent
About that time: circa
About 22 degrees: NNE
Above, poet's: o'er
Above the horizon: risen
Aboveboard: lawful
Ab ovo: from day one, beginning
Abraham's brother: Haran, Nahor
        concubine: Hagar
        father: Terah
        grandfather: Nahor
        son: Isaac, Medan, Shuah, Midian,
            Zimran, Ishmael
        wife: Sarah
        earlier name: Abrams
Abrams, Creighton: commander, gen.
Abrasive material: emery
Abridged: elided
Abridged, not: Uncut
Abridged, perhaps: edit
Abrupt in speech: blunt
Abrupt movement: jolt, jerk
Abruzzi bell town: Atri
Absalom's sister: Tamar
Abscess duct: fistula
Absence of oxygen: anaerobic
Absent of quantity: zero
Absorbs, as a loss: eats
Absorbs effortlessly: osmoses, osmosis
Abstergent, use a: lave
Abscam, agency that created: FBI
Absent without leave: AWOL
Absentee ticket holder: no show
Absentminded murmur: huh
Absolute: utter
Absolute minimum: none
Absolutely necessary: integral
Absolution targets: sins
Absorb, as cost: eat
Absorbed: in to, ate, rapt
Absorbedly: raptly
Absorbent application: talc
Absorbs: digests
Abstain from: forgo, forego

Abstract being: esse
Abstract, it may be: art
Abstractionist, Swiss: Klee
Absurd talk: bosh
Abu Dhabi and Dubai, for two: emirates
Abu Dhabi: emir
Abundance, in: plenty, galore
Abundantly supplied: replete
Abuse verbally: revile
Abusive names: epithets
Abyss: chasm, ravine, void
Abyssinian weight: kasm
Abzug, Bella: feminist
Academic finery: regalia
Academic growth: ivy
Academic specialty, pursued an: majored
Academic term: semester
Acapulco affirmative: si si
A/C amount: Btu
A/C supply: elec.
Accelerando (in music): faster
Accelerator bit: ion
Accented, not: atonic
Accents: brogues
Accentuated period: era
Acceptance of what comes: fatalism
Accepted practice: custom
Accepting customers: open
Accepting one: a bidder
Access code: user ID
Access shaft: adit
Accessible, makes: opens
Accessible, most: nearest
Accident: mishap
Accident ahead indicator: flare
Accident, small: mishap
Accidentally: by chance
Accolades: kudos
Accommodations, share: double up
"Fait accompli"
Accomplice, unwitting: pawn
Accomplish a lot: get far
Accord: unison
Accord, bring into: attune, atone
Accord maker: Honda
"According to Hoyle": kosher
According to key: tonal
Accordion component: reed
Account, detailed: report
Account insurer: FDIC
Account, prolonged: litany
Accounting acronym: LIFO, FIFO
Accounting agency: GOA
Accounting inspection: audit
Accounting entry: debit, credit
Accounting time: year-end
Accouter: equip
Accoutrements: gear, attire, apparel
Accrued interest: earned
Accumulate: amass
Accuracy, deviation from: error
Accusatory exclamation: aha
Accused's need: bail
Accustom: inure

Accustom to hardship: inure
Accustomed, most: inure
Ace beater: trump
Ace, in bridge: honor
Aces, at times: ones
Acheron: Hades, river
Achieve: earn
Achieve harmony: agree
Achieved greater proportions: grew
Achilles's companion: Patroclus
        father: Peleus
        lover: Briseis
        mother: Thetis
        slayer: Paris
        victim: Hector
Achilles story: Iliad
Achromatic color: grey, gray
Achy spot: sore
Acid brandy: lace
Acid in milk: lactic
Acid in protein: amino
Acid in soap: oleic
Acid neutralizer: alkali
Acid taste, having a: sour
Acid testing paper: litmus
Acid type: amino, nitric
Acid-tongued: tart
Ack-ack: flak
Acknowledge a greeting: nod
Acknowledge defeat: yield, concede
Acology, science of: remedies
Acolyte: assistant, fan, helper, novice
Acomia: baldness
Acquainted, get: meet
Acquainted, got: met
Acquiesce: admit, agree, allot
Acquired, just: new
Acquired kin: in-laws
Acquires, as a debt: incurs
Acquires by work: earns
Acre native: Israeli
Acrisius's daughter: Danae
        slayer: Perseus
Acrobat originator: Adobe
Acrobatic feat: nip up
Acrobat's hose: tights
Acrobats might meet, where: midair
Acronym kin: acrostic
Acropolis: citadel
Act affectedly: mince
Act, amazing: feat
Act as chairperson: preside
Act as host: entertain
Act exaggeratedly: emote
Act, in Acts: doest
Act like a coquette: flirt
Act of deception: scam
Act properly: behave
Act servile: kowtow
Act subdivision: scene
Act worried: pace
Acted like Niobe: wept
Acting class: drama
Acting group: cast

Acting award: Obie
Acting with force: vehement
Action site: arena
Action word: verb
Actionable wrong: tort
Activate a pager: beep
Active one: esse, doer
Activity, needless: ado
Actor, bad: ham
Actor in a crowd: extra
Actor, overdoing: ham
Actor's résumé items: roles
Acts badly: emotes
Acts on a preference: opts
Actual: true, real
Actual being: esse
Acutely perceptive: keen
A.D.: anno Domini
Ad astra per aspera
Ad award: Clio
Ad for the lovelorn: personal
Ad spiel: hype
Ad writer's honor: Clio
Adage: maxim
Adage-spouting detective: Chan
Adak native: Aleut
Adam Bede: Novelist
Adams, Ansel: photography
Adam's apple came from, where: Eve
Adam's arboretum: Eden
Adams, Edie: musician
Adam's grandsons: Enus, Enas, Enoch
Adam's Home: Eden
       sons: Abel, Cain, Seth
       wife: Eve
Adamson lioness: Elsa
Adamson's, joy, pet: Elsa, lion
Add, as to batter: stir in
Add comments to: annotate
Add explanation to: annotate
Add highlights: dye
Add nutrients: enrich
Add on: append
Add oxygen: aerate
Add to the heap: pile on
Add to the mixture: blend in
Add vitamins to: enrich
Adda city: Lodi
Addams, Chas Samuel: cartoonist
"Addams Family" cousin: Itt
       manservant: Lurch
Added one's two cents: chimed in
Added stipulation: and
Adderley, Nat: Jazz player
Addict: user
Addis Ababa denizen: Ethiopian
Addison's partner: Steele
Additional ones: others
Additional quantity: more
Additionally: too, also, and, more
Address, gave an: orated
Address part: zip, zip code
Address phrase: "care of"

Address, president's: "Fellow American"
Address term: sir
Adds to: supplements
Adds to unnecessarily: pads
Adds up: counts
Adds up to: equals
Ade, George: humorist
Aden country: Yemen
Aden native: Yemeni
Adept athlete: ace Andean
Adherent: fan, IST
Adhesive, powerful: epoxy
Adhibit: affix, use
Adieu, somewhere else: ciao
Adipose: fatty
Adit: duct, way, access shaft
Adjective: modifier
Adjournment, in law: continuance
Adjuration: oath, plea
Adjust a camera: focus
Adjust against: rearrange
Adjust beforehand: preset
Adjust slightly: tweak
Adjust the tires: realign, realigned
Adjust to: orient
Adjustable border: hem
Adjutant: aide, helper
Adjutant bird: stork
Ad lib: wing it
Ad libber's asset: wit
Admetus's father: Pheres
       wife: Alcestis
Admin. head: gov., CEO
Admiral, kind of: rear
Admiral's charge: fleet
Admire oneself: preen
Admirer: beau
Admirer's response: ooh
Admirer's sound: ooh
Admires: esteems
Admit defeat: eat crow
Admit into membership: initiate
Admonition to spot: stay, sit
Adobe: clay, mud, silt, tile
Adobe adobe, perhaps: casa
Adolescent affliction: acne
Adolescent blight: acne
Adonis's slayer: boar
Adonijah's brother: Amnon, Absalom, Chileab
       father: David
       mother: Haggith
       slayer: Benaiah
Adopt a clause: espouse
Adore opposite: detest
Adored one: idol
Adoree, Rene: French actress
Adorn, richly: jewel
Adorned: graced
Adorned, richly: jeweled
Adornment, glittering: tiara
Adornment, male: beard
Adornment, sparkling: diadem
Adornment, without: bare
Adriatic port: Bari

Adriatic resort: lido
Adriatic town: Bari
Adroit: deft
Adroit eluder: evader
Ads, skip the: zap
Adult: grown, elder
Adult filly: mare
Adult German male: Herr
Adult grigs: eels
Adulterate: debase
Adults only, for: X-rated
Adumbrate: dim, darken, sketch
Advanced cautiously: edged
Advanced course: seminar
Advantage: plus, edge
Advantage of, take: avail
Advent: coming
Adventure: gest, geste
Adventure, merry: lark
Adventure tales: yarns
Adventurous: daring
Adventurous, more: gamier
Adventurous rogue: Picaro
Adverb: modifier
Adversarial: insert
Adverse fate: doom
Advertent: attentive
Advertiser's plan or sketch: layout
Advertising award: Clio, Cleo
Advice (old style): rede
Advice, piece of: tip
Advice, take: heed
Advice, took: heeded
Advice, word of: tip
Advisor, venerable: elder
Adytum: shrine, inner sanctum
Aeneas's companion: Achates
　　　father: Anchises
　　　mother: Venus, Aphrodite
　　　son: Lulus, Ascanius
　　　wife: Creusa, Lavinia
Aeolus's daughter: Alcyone, Halcyone
　　　father: Poseidon,
Aerial navigational system: Teleran
Aerialist's insurance: net
Aerie: nest
Aerie builders: eagles
Aerie newborn: eaglet
Aeriform liquid: gas
Aerobatic maneuvers: loops
Aerope's husband: Atreus
　　　lover: Thyestes
　　　son: Menelaus, Agamemnon
Aerosol output: spray
Aesculapius' daughter: Hygeia, Panacea
　　　father: Apollo,
　　　slayer: Zeus, Jupiter
　　　teacher: Chiron
　　　wife: Epione
Aeson's brother: Pelias
　　　son: Jason
Aesop specialty: fable
Aesopian finale: moral
Aesopian loser: hare

Aesopian smart aleck: hare
Aesop's also ran: hare
Aesthetic quality: good taste
Affable: mild, suave
Affair: liaison, matter
Affaire de coeur: love affair
Affaires d'honneur: duels
Affect: impact
Affect dramatically: upend
Affect emotionally, in a way: scar
Affect strongly: stir
Affected adversely: hurt
Affected manners: airs
Affectedly cute: too-too
Affectedly shy: demure
Affectionate touch: caress
Afferent: sensory
Affiche: poster
Affirm solemnly: assert
Affirm with confidence: aver
Affirmations: yeas, yeses
Affirmative, terse: yep
Affix a brand to: sear
Afflicted: stricken
Affliction: woes, banes
Affluent one: yuppie
Afghan borders: fringes
Afghan oass: Khyber
Afghan prince: amir, emir
Afghani currency: pul
Aficionado: fan
Afore: ere
A-frame: chalet
Africa explorer: Burton
Africa, Out of: movie
African antelope: gnu, nyala
African-Arabian Sea: Red Sea
African conflict, major: Boer War
African equine: zebra
African expanse: Sahara
African fox: asse
African game dish: eland
African garden hose: jembe
African gazelle: admi
African hardwood tree: shea
African lake, large: Chad
African menace: tsetse
African native: Tchad, Ibo
African plain: Savanna
"African Queen" author: Forester
African serpent: asp, mamba
African grassland, open: veldt, veld
African village: Sted
African wild sheep: arui
Africa's Sierra Leone
Afrikaner: boar
Afrikaner's rifles: Roers
Aft: astern
After all: considering
After awhile: later
After dinner: postprandial
After dinner drink: cognac
Aftereffects, lasting: scars
Aftermath: wake

Afternoon drink place: teahouse
Afternoon snooze: siesta
Aftershock: tremor
After swim need: towel
Afterword: epilog, commentary
Again: anew, renovo
Again and again: often
Again as new: refresh
Against: anti
Against adversity: uphill
Against the clock: in haste, race
Against the law: illicit
Against the sun: counterclockwise
Agalloch: aloes
Agana's island: Guam
Agassi, Andre: tennis
Agatha Christie title: dame
Agave: Century Plant
Agee, James: writer
Agee, Tommie: baseball
Agency (1941): OPA
Agency with eagle logo: USPS
Agency with many schedules: IRS
Agenda: program, schedule
Agenda, part of an: item
Agent (Fed): G-man, T-man
Agent of the comics: Abie
AGFA rival: Hodak
Aggravating problem, minor: hassle
Aggregate amount: all
Aggregate of two: sum
Aggressive personality: type A
Agile: lithe
Agitated state: snit
Agnus Dei
Agoraphobia, e.g.: fear
Agrapha saying: logia
Agree: jibe
Agree silently: nod
Agree with: side
Agree with, as sentiments: echo
Agreeable idor: aroma
Agreed silently: nodded
Agreement: unity
Agreement, allies': pact
Agreement, as sentiments: echo
Agreement between nations: entente
Agreement, finalized: deal
Agreement, indicate: nod
Agreement, international: entente
Agreement, private: yes, sir
Agreement, Versailles: oui
Agreement, words of: So am I
Agrees: jibes
Agrippina, to Nero: Mater
Agrippina's son: Nero
Agronomist's study: soil
Agronomy, study of: agriculture
Aguscate: avocado
Ahab & company: whalers
Ahab's daughter: Athalie
　　　father: Omri
　　　kingdom: Israel
　　　wife: Jezebel

Ahaggar Mountains locale: Sahara
Ahasta luego
Ahaz's kingdom: Judah
    son: Hezekiah
    wife: Abi
Ahaziah's father: Ahab, Joram, Jehoram
    kingdom: Judah, Israel
    mother: Jezebel, Athaliah
    sister: Jehosheba, Jehosobeath
Ahead of, at sea: afore
Ahead of schedule: early
Ahinoam's father: Ahimaaz
    husband: Saul, David
    son: Amnon
"Aida": opera
Aida composer: Verdi
"Aid and Abet"
Aided a con: abetted
"Aide-de-camp"
Aiello, Danny: actor
Aigner, Etieme: designer
Aigrette: egret
Aikon, Conrad: poet
Ailurophile's love: cats
Aim, took: zeroed in
Aim toward: head
Aimed: pointed
Air around a fen: miasma
Air, bad: Smog
A/C amount: BtuA/C supply: electric
Air France destination: Orly
Air, in music: arioso
Air mover: fan, wind
Air mystery, e.g.: aura
Air of the Olympian gods: Aether
Air or heaven, to a poet: ether
Air passage: duct
Air-crafted enclosure: nacelle
Aircraft guidance system: SHORAN
Aircraftman, British: erk
Air current device: bellows
Aired anew: reran
Aires or Taurus, e.g.: signs
Airline: Aer Lingus
Airline capacity: seats
Airline employee: pilot, copilot
Airline name, former: Braniff
Airline with King David lounges: El Al
Airplane part: aileron, flap, rudder, pylon
Airplane trip, short: hop
Airport: drome, aerodrome
Airport fluid: deicer
Airport pickup: rental
Airport porter: skycap
Airport queue: cab
Airport rentals: autos, cars
Airport runway: tarmac
Airport screening org.: TSA
Airport summons: page
Airports:
    Atlanta: ATL, Hartsfield
    Chicago: ORD, O'Hare, Midway
    Dallas: DFW
    Denver: DEN

    Detroit: DTW
    Las Vegas: LAS
    Los Angeles: LAX
    Miami: MIA
    New York: JFK, EWR, LGA
    Phoenix: PHS
    San Francisco: SFO
    St. Louis: STL
    Washington: DCA, IAD, BWI
    Paris: ORLY
Airports, major: hubs
Air pressure unit: millibar
Air rifle, small: BB gun
Air show stunt: loop
Airtight: seal, sealed
Air traffic control system: Teleran
Air traffic control need: radar
Airwick target: odor
Airy: ethereal, thin
Ait, on the Seine: ile
Aix angel: Ange
Ajaccio's island, to natives: Corse, Corsica
AKC certificate notation: breed
Akin, Claude: actor
Al Capp character: Abner
Al fresco: outdoor
Jai alai
Alabama flower: goldenrod
Aladdin monkey: Abu
Aladdin prince: Ali
Aladdin villain: Jafar
Aladdin's benefactor: Genie
    servant: Genie
Alamagordo's county: Otero
Alameda: mall, promenade
Alamo alternative: Avis, Hertz
Al a pan, played: piped
Alar: winglike, wing-shaped
Alarm: dismay
Alarm bell: tocsin
"Alas": woe is me
Alas, to Aries: Helas
Alaska discoverer: Vitus, Bering
Alaska glacier: Muir
Alaska island: Adak
Alaska liquor: hoochinoo
Alaska, once known as: territory
Alaska peak: Denali
Alaska purchaser: Wm. Seward
Alaskan army base: Haines
Alaskan island: Attu
Alaskan liquor: hoochinoo
Alaskan native: Aleut
Alaskan wear: anorak
Alb: vestment
Alb wearer: priest
Alba, Jessica: actress
Albacore: tuna
Albanian currency: lek
Albee, Edward: playwrite
Albert jewelry: watch Chain
Albert pottery: terra-cotta
Alberta native: Cree
Albinoni, Tomaso: composer

Albright, Lola: actress
Albright, Madeleine birthplace: Prague
Alcohol, rubbing: ethanol
Alcohol, tobacco, and firearms org.: ATF
Alcott girl: Meg
Alcott, Amy: actress
Alcove: niche
Alder tree, Scot: arn
Aldo, Ray: actor
Alecto was one: Furia
Aleichem, Sholom: writer
Alejandro, Rey: conductor
Alembicate: distill
Alencon product: lace
Aleppo grass: johnson
Aleppo stone: agate
Aleppo's home: Syria
Aleppo's land: Syria
Alert, suspiciously: wary
Aleta, son of: Arn
Aleut language: Inuit
Aleutian island: Attu, Atka
Alewife: fish, herring
Alex Haley novel: Roots
Alexander and Peter: tsars
Alexander, Shana: journalist
Alexandria Pharos: the Pharos of Alexandria
Alfonso, Maria Conchita
Alfonso's queen: Ena
Alfresco: out of doors
Alfresco, opposite of: indoors
Algae: seaweed
Alger, Horatio: author
Algerian seaport: Oran
Algology, study of: algae
Algonquian spirit: manito
Algonquin abode: tepee
Alhambra room: sala
Ali, Muhammad: boxer
Alibi contraction: wasn't
Alibi, like a good: iron clad
Alice's balladeer: Arlo
Alice's cat: Dinah
Alice's chronicler: Arlo
Alien: exotic
Alien, chatty: Alf
Alien expt.: INS
"Alien" kid: Newt
Aliens, for short: ETs
Alien's spacecraft: UFO
Alignment, in: true
Alimentary canal: intestine
Alimony getters: exes
Alkalies of India: Rehs
All, in combo: omni
All better: cured
All ears: nosy
All gone: eaten up, used up
All integers or real numbers: infinite set
"All Kidding Aside"
All knowing: omniscient
All or nothing, between: some
All purpose truck: ute, utility
All smiles: radiant

All there: sane
All together: en masse
All thumbs: inept
All worked up: agog
Allay pain: soothe
Alleges: claims
Allegorical deck: tarot
Allegro, far from: lento
Allen, Fred: comic
Allen, Woody: actor, director
All-encompassing abbr.: etc
Allende, Isabel: novelist
Allergic reaction: rash
Alleviate: ease, rid
Alexel Karenin's wife: Anna
Alley machine: pinsetter
Alley Oop's girl: Oola
        locale: Moo
        kingdom: Moo
        ride: Dinny
        weapon: club
Alliance: bloc
Allie's pal: Kate
Allied by nature: akin
Allies agreement: pact
Alligator: caiman
Alligator pear: avocado
Allman Bros.: band
All-nighter, pull an: cram
Allot: mete
Allotted amount: ration
Allotted piece of work: stine
Allow to use: lend
Allowance for waste: tret
Allowance, separation: palimony
Alloy of silver and gold: asem
Alloy of silver and tin: pewter
All-powerful: mighty, supreme
All-season: yearlong
Allude to: cite, refer to, refer
Alluring siren: Lorelei
Ally's opposite: foe
Alma mater, (007): Eton
Almanac tidbit: fact
Almodovar, Pedro: director
Almond confection: paste
Almond liqueur: amaretto
Almond, Marc: "Of Soft Cell"
Almost bubble: simmer
Almost (in poems): nigh
Almost never: once
Alms, ask for: beg
Alms box: arca
Alms man: donee
Aloe vera
Aloeus's father: Neptune, Poseidon
        mother: Canace
        son: Otus, Ephialtes
        wife: Iphimedia
Alone in Lyons (France): seul
Alonson, Maria Conchita
Aloof: Iicy
Alou, Jesús: baseball
Alou, Matty: baseball

Alou, Moises: baseball
Aloud: spoken
Alouettes, par exemple: oiseaux
Alpaca cousin: vicuna, llama
Alpert, Herb: trumpeter
Alpha Centauri:
Alpha counterpart: omega
Alpha opposite: omega
Alpha plus one: beta
Alphabet five: vowels
Alphabet soup letter: noodle
Alphabet string: stu
Alphabetic quintet: aeiou
Alphabetic symbol of yore: rune
Alphabetizer's omission: the
Alphabets, like old: rune, runic
Alpine climber: Alperstein
Alpine crest: arête
Alpine dance: gavotte
Alpine dress: dirndl
Alpine goat: ibex
Alpine herdsman: Senn
Alpine heroine: Heidi
Alpine moppet: Heidi
Alpine plant: edelweiss
Alpine province: Tyrol
Alpine region: Tyrol
Alpine ridge: arête
Alpine shelter: hospice
Alpine snow field: Neve, Firn
Alpine Wind: Bise
Alps Locale: Europe
Alps Mont Blanc
Already assembled: prefab
Also: too
Also not: nor
Also ran: loser
Alsop, Stewart: writer
Alt, Carol: model
Altair or Antares: star
Altar boy: acolyte
Altar constellation: Ara
Altar curtain: riddel
Altar end: apse
Altar end of the church: apse
Altar exchange: I dos, vows
Altar in the sky: aura, Ara
Altar platform: predella
Altar screen: reredos
Altars, Latin: Aras, Arae
Altdorf's canton: Uri
Alter ego
Alter to make better: amend
Alteration site: hem
Altercation, brief, heated: set to
Alternative to nothing: all
Altitude measure: feet
Altman, Robert: director
Alula: spurious wing
Always (poet): e'er
Alysheba's mother: mare
Amahs serve, where: orient
Amandine, Sole
Amaretto flavor: almond

Amaryllis family member: agave
Amas follower: amat
Amateur pro Ted Mack
Amateur sports org.: NCAA
Amatol ingredient: TNT
Amazement, fill with: awe
Amazon rain forest: selva
Amazon River mouth: para
Amazon source: Peru
A.M. (part of): ante
Ambassador from the Vatican: nuncio
Ambergris source: whale
Ambiguous, not: clear cut
Ambler, Eric: novelist
Ambrosia of immortality: Amrita
Ambulance worker: EMT
Ambush: trap
Amebas have one: cell
Ameche, Don
Amend maker: atoner
Amenhotep's god: Aton
Amenity, motel: ice
Amerada acquirer: Hess
American aloe: century plant
American day begins, where: Guam
American education reformer: Mann
AKC certificate notation: breed
"American Idol" number: solo
American Mexican: gringo
American naval hero: Oliver Perry
American omegas: zees
American suffragist: Catt
American sunfish: roach
American symbol: eagle
AmerInd: Ute
AmerInd of Canada: Cree
Ames Bros.: music
Ames, Ed: musician, actor
Amex rival: NYSE
Amin, Idi: deposed leader
Mes amio
Amis, Kingsley: writer
Amish community project: barn
Amish, for one: sect
Amish pronoun: thou
Ammo wagon: caisson
Ammonia compound: amines
Sal ammoniac (ammonium chloride)
Ammunition box: bandoleer
Ammunition chest: caisson
Ammunition wagon: caisson
Amneris's rival: Aida
Amnesiac's lack: recall
Amoeba center: nuclei
Amoebas have one: cell
Among the clouds: aloft
Amorist: lover
Amorous archer: Cupid
Amorous look: ogle
Amorous murmur: coo
Amorphous mass: blob
Amorphous mineral: opal
Amos, amas, amat
Amos, Tori: musician

Amount mean: average
Amount of electrical output: wattage
Amount of medicine: dose
Amount realized: intake
Amount, slight: trace,
Amount to make do with: less
Amount, token: sop
Amount, unmeasured: any
Amounts to nothing: null, worthless
Ampere, Andrea: Fr. physicist
Ampersands: ands
Amphibian, tailed: newt, salamander
Amphibian, tailless: toad
Amphion, son of: Zeus
Amphitheater: bowl, arena, coliseum, stadium
Amphitheater level: tier
Amtrack train: Acela
Amulet, pharaoh's: scarab
Amuse to the max: slay
Amusement, respectful: awe
Amusing behavior: drollery
Amusing sorts: wits
Amusing way (in a): drolly
Amygdala: basil ganglia, tonsil
Amy's sister: Meg
An awful lot: loads, oodles
An era, the end of: legend's retirement
An organized society: polity
Anabaptist Simons: Menno
Anabaptist sect: Amish
Analysis, type of: vector
Analysis concerns: ids
Analyze a sentence: parse
Analyze grammatically: parse
Ananias, for one: liar
Anarchist's goal: chaos
Anathema: hate
Anathema to Serge: lint
Anatolian capital: Ankara
Anatomic canals: venae, vena
Anatomical holder: sac
Anatomical network: retia, rete
Anatomical passage: iter
Anatomical ring: areola
Anatomical sac: vesicle
Anatomical tissue, of an: telar
Ancestor of edomites: Esau
Anchises' son: Aeneas
Anchor, lift: sail
Anchor: moor
Anchor, heaviest: bower
Anchor, small: kedges
Anchorages: portst
Anchored, not: adrift
Anchors aweigh
Ancient: age old
Ancient alphabetic symbol: rune
Ancient Andean: Inca
Ancient ascetic: Essene
Ancient Asia: Nede
Ancient barbarian: Goth
Ancient box: cist
Ancient Briton: Celt
Ancient Campanian: Oscan

Ancient Celt: Gaul
Ancient celtic priest: druid
Ancient center of philosophy: Athens
Ancient chariot: essed, led
Ancient Chinese: Seres
Ancient city: Albalonga
Ancient city near Carthage: Utica
Ancient city of Asia Minor: Ilion
Ancient city of Bithynia: Nicaea
Ancient colonnade: stoa
Ancient cosmetic: kohl
Ancient cross: tau
Ancient document: lapyrus
Ancient drink: morat
Ancient Egyptian: copt
Ancient empire: Inca, Median, Hittite,
     Persian, Cissyrian, Anthenian
Ancient English kingdom: Wessex
Ancient Ethiopian capital: Meroe
Ancient European area: Gaul
Ancient female warrior: Amazon
Ancient France: Gaul
Ancient French kingdom: Navarre
Ancient Greek: Spartan
Ancient Greek city: Elis, Sparta
Ancient Greek city native: Argive
Ancient Greek colony: Ionia
Ancient Greek country: Elis
Ancient Greek deity: Pan
Ancient Greek dialect: Ionic
Ancient Greek god of war: Wres
Ancient Greek headdress: polos
Ancient Greek magistrate: Epnor
Ancient Greek portico: stoa
Ancient Greek vessel: alabastrum
Ancient harp: lyre,
Ancient Icelandic literature: eddic
Ancient Italian family: Este
Ancient Jewish ascetic: Essene
Ancient Jewish judicial council: Sanhedrin
Ancient Jewish mystic: Essene
Ancient keepsake: relic
Ancient Kingdom: Wessex, Ghor, Ghur,
     Cumbria, Shu, Hora
Ancient language: Latin
Ancient mariner: Noah
Ancient meeting place: Agora
Ancient monument: sphinx, obelisk, pyramid
Ancient musical instrument: lute
Ancient mystical script: rune
Ancient ointment: nard
Ancient Olympic site: Elis
Ancient people of Eastern Europe: Getae
Ancient Persian: Mede
Ancient Persian neighbor: Mede
Ancient Peruvian: Inca
Ancient Phoenician seaport: Tyre
Ancient physician: Galen
Ancient poetry collection: epos
Ancient portico: stoa
Ancient potato farmer: Inca
Ancient queen: Cleopatra
Ancient region of Palestine: Judea
Ancient Roman awning: velarium

Ancient Roman chariot: biga
Ancient Roman coin: denarius
Ancient Roman "noon": XII
Ancient Roman soothsayer: augur
Ancient Roman theater: odea
Ancient royal forest: Dean, Sherwood
Ancient Scandinavians: Norse
Ancient scroll: papyri
Ancient serf: esne, helot
Ancient ship: birume
Ancient sin city: Sodom
Ancient slave: Esne
Ancient South American native: Inca
Ancient story: myth
Ancient strongbox: arca
Ancient tale: saga, epic, myth
Ancient theater: odium
Ancient time: eld
Ancient tome: codex
Ancient town: Africa: Zama,
     Armenia: Dwin, Tvin
     Greece: Abae, Opus,
     Italy: Elea, Luna, Cumae
Ancient wine jug: olpe
"Ancient," word form for: paleo
Ancient writing: rune
"And another thing": also
And not: nor
And others: et al
And so forth: etc.
And so on: etcetera, etcetera
"And so to bed"
And then some: in spades
Andean bird: condor
Andean forage grass: ichu
Andean tuber: oca
Anderson, Hans Christian: author
Anderson, Loni: actress
Andes capital: Quito
Andes empire: Inca
Andes plant: oca
Andes ruminant: alpaca, llama
"San Andreas fault"
Andre's affirmative: oui
Andress, Ursula: actress
Androcles's pal: lion
"Androcles and the Lion" setting: arena
Androcles's friend: lion
Android's lack: emotion
Andromache's husband: Hector
     son: Astyanax, Molossus
Andromeda's father: Cepheus
     husband: Perseus
     mother: Cassiopeia
     rescuer: Perseus
Titus Andronicus
Andy Capp's wife: Flo
Andy Gump's wife: Min
Andy's radio pal: Amos
Anecdote collection: ana
Anemone holders: vases
Anesthetize, in a way: gas
Anet, Claude: French novelist
Angel of the highest order: seraph

Angelic instrument: harp
Angelica's father: Galaphron
　　　　husband: Medoro
　　　　lover: Oriando
Angelou, Maya: poet
Angel's favorite sign: SRO
Angels of the highest order: seraphim
"Angkor Wat" (Cambodia): temple
Angler with pots: eeler
Angler's basket: creel
Angling leader: snell
Anglo-Saxon laborer: esne, helot
Anglo-Saxon letter: edh
Anglo-Saxon money: ora
Anglo-Saxon Serf: esne, helot
Angora goat fabric: mohair
Angrily: irately
Angry, is extremely: seethes
Angry look: glower
Angry, make: enrage
Angry, really: raving, livid
Angry, very: livid, raving
Angstrom, Anders: Swedish physicist
Angular home: A-frame
Angular script (type): Ronde
"Angus Dei"
Anima theorist: Jung
Animal behavior, study of: ethology
Animal fat: lard, suet
Animal leash: tether
Animal life: fauna
Animal, long-clawed: badger
Animal park: zoo
Animal pelt: pelage
Animal, performing: seal
Animal restraint: tether
Animal rights org.: PETA
Animal shelter: sty, stable, barn, pen
Animal stomach: craw
Animal track: spoor
Animal, tusked: boar
Animal variety: breed
Animal welfare org.: SPCA
Animated: alive
Animated character: toon
Animation frames: cells
Anisette relative: ouzo
Anjou: pear
Ankara native: Turk
Ankle bone: tarsus, talus
Ankle-high shoe: gaiter
Ankle, of an: tarsal
"Anna and the King of Siam"
"Anna Taught in Siam"
"Annabel Lee" poet: Poe
Annan, Kofi: U.N. Sec
Annapolis grad: ens., ensign
Annapolis newcomer: plebe
Annapurna's country: Nepal
Anne Nichols hero: Abie
Annealing oven: lehr
Annelid worm: leech
Annex: ell
Annexes: adds on, ells

Annie, for one: orphan
Annie Oakley: pass, free ticket, markswoman
Annie's pooch: Sandy
Announced strikes: umped, umpped
Annoy continually: harass
Annoy incessantly: drive crazy, drive buggy
Annoying insect: mite, gnat
Annoying, more: peskier
Annoying runt of a person: twerp
Annual exam: medical
Annual list: ten best, Xmas
Annual purchase: calendar
Annuls: voids
"Per annum"
Anoint: anele
Anoint as part of last rites: anele
Anoint, old style: anele
Anoint with oil: anele
Anon, sooner than: ere
Anon's companion: ever
Anonymity's opposite: fame
Anonymous litigant: doe
Another, in Argentina: otra
Another name: alias
Another suitor: rival
Another time: again
Another time: again
Anouk, Aimee: actress
Anquilliform one: eel
Ansel Adams's tool: camera
Answer a judge: plea
Answer an argument: rebut
Answer back: retort, respond
Answer on quiz: true, false
Answer, toady: yes
Answer with attitude: sass
Answers a charge: pleads
Ant: emmet
Ant, crop-chomping: atta
Ant genus: Eciton
Ant horde: army
Ant, leaf-cutting: atta
Antagonism: enmity, inimical
Antarctic cape: Adare
Antarctic explorer: Byrd, Ross
Antarctic ice shelf: Ross
Antarctic sea: Ross
Antarctic volcano: Erebus
Ante meridiem (full form of a.m.)
Ante up: pay
Anteater, spiny: echidna
Antediluvian: old, aged, fogy, hoary, passé,
　　　age-old
Antelope: eland, nyala, gnu, oribi, impala,
　　　kudu, saddaby
Antelope, African: nyala
Antelope, Chinese: goral
Antelope, female: doe
Antelope, maned: gnu
Antelope, mountain: chamois
Antelope of puzzledom: eland
Antelope, ox-like: eland
Antelope, sable: sasin
Antelope, striped: bongo

Antenna: aerial, feeler, rabbit ears
Antenna, TV type: Yagi
Antenna type: UHF
Anthem, sacred: motet
Anthemis nobilis: chamomile
Anthology: omnibus
Anthony Eden's earldom: Avon
Anthony, Marc
Anthony the Roman: Marc
Anthracite or lignite: coal
Anthropologist's concern: custom
Anthropomorphize: humanize
Anti-antis: pros,
Anti-art artist: dadaist
Anti-Brady Bunch: NRA
Antic: dido
Anticipate: await
Anticipation, fearful: dread
Anticipatory times: eves
Anti-discrimination agency: EEOC
Antietam General: Lee
Antigone's brother: Polynices, Polyneices
　　　father: Oedipus
　　　mother: Jocasta
　　　sister: Ismene
　　　uncle: Creon
Antilochus's father: Nestor
　　　friend: Achilles
　　　slayer: Memnon
Antiope's father Asopus
　　　husband: Lycus, Theseus
　　　queen of: Amazons
　　　son: Zehtus, Amphion, Hippolytus
Antipasto morsel: olive
Anti-pellagra: vitamin
Anti-prohibitionist: wets
Ars antiqua
Antiquarian's adjective: rare
Antique drink mixer: krater
Antiquity: yore
Antiquity, in antiquity: eld, elder
Antithesis of aweather: alee
Antithetical: polar
Antitoxin: sera
Antler branches: tines
Antler points: prongs
Antlered ruminant: deer
Antler's prongs: tines
Antoinette lost hers: tete
Antony's friend: Caesar
　　　lover: Cleopatra
　　　wife: Octavia
Antonym of feral: tame
Anu's Daughter: Nanai
Anvil, small: teest
Anxiety, feel: dread
Anxious, be: fret
Any goddess: deity
Any woman: she
Anything: noun
"Anything but that"
"Anything else"
Anything puzzling: crux
Anything remote: forane

Anything spiral: helix
Aoki, Isao: Japanese golfer
AP rival: UPI
Apache leader: Cochise
Apache weapon: bow
Apartment dweller, often: lessee
Apartment in Soho: flat
Apartment mgr.: supt.
Apartment, owned: condo
Apartment ownership, kind of: condo
Apartment, took an: rented, leased
Apartment, trendy: loft
Apathetic: lanquid
APB datum: AKA
Ape: lar
Ape or Parrot: Imitate
Ape, Signing: Koko
Ape-like: simian
Apennine eruptor: Etna
Apennines site: Italy
Aperture: hole
Aperture, small: vent
Apex covering: eip
Apex, on the: atop
Apex ornament: finial
Aphorism: adage
Aphorisms, certain: sutras
Aphrodite's, father: Zeus
      goddess of: love
      mother: Dione
      Roman equivalent: Venus
      son: Eros
Apian way, for one :relent
Apogee: farthest point in orbit
Apogee's opposite:perigee
Apocalyptic tunes: The Four Horsemen
Apollo: Helios, Phoebus
Apollo and Hermes: gods
Apollo's birthplace: Delos
      beloved: Cyrene, Daphne
      father: Zeus, Jupiter
      games: Olympic
      god: Sun
      mother: Leto, Latona
      oracle site: Delphi
      priestess: Oracle
      sister: Diana, Artemis
      son: Ion, Orpheus
      temple site: Delphi
Apologizes, humbly: eats crow
Apothecary's measure: dram, dose
Apothecary's weight: dram
"A pox upon thee: fie
Appalling person: terror
Apparatus distillation: alembic
Apparatus, dyeing: ager
Apparatus, heating: etna
Apparatus, hoisting: jack
Apparatus, planetarium: orrery
Apparition: ghost, spirit, phantom
Appeal, type of: snob
Appeal, urgent: plea
Appealing, most: cutest
Appear in court: testify

Appear to be: seem
Appearance: mien, aspect
Appearance, brief: cameo
Appearance, short: cameo
Appears ominously: looms
Appears to be: seems
Appellation: name
Bon appétit
Appetite, Build a: Whet
Appetite Stimulus: Aroma
Appetizer: Pate
Appetizer, Spanish restaurant: tapa
Appia, Via (Roman route): Iter
Applause: ovation
Applause, burst of: round
Applause, round of: hand, ovation
Apple cider girl: Ida
Apple Goody: pie
Apple name: Ida
Apple of one's eye: pet
Apple or pear: pome
Apple product: Mac, iPod, cider
Apple seed: pip
Apple site, famous: Eden
Apple-polish: fawn, toady, kowtow
Apples and pears: pomes
Appliance: unit, range, stove,
Applicant's offering: résumé
Applied, as pressure: everted
Applied sweetener: candied
Apply a layer to: coat
Apply a mudpack: daub
Apply, as pressure: exert
Apply crudely: daub
Apply plaster: ceil
Appointed time: hour
Appointment, keep a: meet
Appoints: names
Apportioned cards: dealt
Appraisal determination: value
Appraise: rate, value
Appreciate: savor
Appreciation, show: clap
Appreciative sounds: oohs
Apprehensive feeling: antsy
Apprised of: in on
Approach: near, verge on
Approach, as a disclosure: lead up to
Approach for a loan: hit up
Approach the summit: ascend
Appropriate: co-opt
Approval, seal of: cachet
Approval, show: clap
Approx. no.:est.
Approximately: or so
Approximation, words of: or so
April addressee: IRS
April Fools' baby, for one: Aries
April need: CPA
Apron wearer: maid, mom
Apse locale: basilica
Apt papal name: Pius
Apterous opposite: alar
Aptitude: head

Aptitude, having: talented
Aquafina: Evian (French mineral water)
Aquamarine: aqua, blue, beryl
Aquamarine mineral: beryl
Aquarium denizen: skate
Aquarium favorite: tetra
Aquarium fish, tropical: scalare
Aquarium, freshen: aerate
Aquarium process: aeration
Aquarium, tend the: aerate
Aquarius constellation: Cetus
"Aquarius" musical: Hair
Aquarius tote: ewer, pitcher, bucket
"The Age of Aquarius"
Aquarius tote: ewer
Aquarius vessel: ewer
Aquatic fun lover: otter
Aquatic organism, primitive: algae
Aquatic resort: spa
Aquatic shocker: eel
Aquila star: altair
Aquiline: steed
Aquilo star: Altair
Aquino, Corazin: Philippines leader
Eleanor of Aquitaine
Arab chieftain's domain: emirate
Arab lateen: rigged vessel: dshaw,
dhow
Arab prince: emir, rani
Arab republic, to Rivera: Siria.
Arabesques are performed on: one leg
Arabian Caliph: Hasan
Arabian garment: aba, abas
Arabian kettle drum: atabal
"Arabian Nights Ali Baba"
"Arabian Nights" bird: roc
"Arabian Nights" hero: Sinbad
Arabian peninsula monarchy: Oman
Arabian sailboat: dhow
Arabic robe: aba
Arachnid: mite, tick
Arachnid, stinging: scorpion
Arafat, Yasir: PLO leader
Aral, for one: sea
Arami's friend: Porthos
Arapaho foe: Ute
Arbison, Roy: singer
Arboreal endangered plant: elm tree
Arboreal quaker: aspen
Arboretum, first: Eden
Arbors: bowers
Arcade amusement: video games
Arcade foul: tilt
Arcade game: pin ball
Arcade name: Atari
Arcaro, Eddy: Jockey
Arch, pointed: ogee
Arch style: lancet
Arch support: insole
Archaic companion: fere
Archaic interjection: fie
Arched recess: apse
Archeologist's find: fossil, ruins, stele, idol
Archeologist's site: digs, ruins

Archer, amorous: Cupid
Archer, Ann: actress
Archer, legendary: Wm. Tell
Archer, mythical: Eros
Archibald, Nate: basketball
Archie Bunker, like: biased
Archie and Jughead: teens Archie's dimwitted
        pal: Moose
Archimedes shout: eureka
Archimedes' tool: lever
Archipelago components: islands
Archipelago dot: isle
Archipelago part: isle
Architect, noted: Pei
Architect's info: specs
Architectural column support: socle
Architectural construction: tectonic
Architectural curves: hances
Architectural edge: arris
Architectural pier: anta
Architectural pilaster: anta,
Architectural space: pediment,
Architectural order: ionic
Architectural style: Tudor
Architecture (like Moorish): ornate
Archives: annuals
Arctic abode: igloo
Arctic bird: tern
Arctic bovine: musk ox
Arctic explorer: Peary
Arctic gravel mound: pingo
Arctic inhabitant: Aleut
Arctic Ocean part: Kara Sea
Arctic wasteland: tundra
Arden, Elizabeth: xosmetics
Arden, Eve: actress
Ardently: eagerly, madly
Ardor: zeal
Area between hills: vale
Area, large defined: region
Area near the net: forecourt
Are in Taxco: estan
Arena: stadium, stadia
Ares' sister: Eris
Arezzo's river: arno
Argentina legend: peron
Argentine cowboy: gaucho
Argentite or cinnabar: ore
Arguable: moot
Argue against: refute
Argue for: urge
Argued, easily: tenable
Argyle item: sock
Aria singer: diva
Aria, usually: solo
Ariadne's father: Minos
        husband: Theseus
        home: Naxos
        mother: Pasiphae
Arid: dry, sere
Aries month: April
Arikara: Ree
Arises from: stems
Aristaeus's father: Apollo

mother: Cyrene
son: Actaeon
wife: Autonoe
Aristocracy: elite
Aristocrat: noble
Aristocratic address: milady
Aristotle Onassis
Arithmetic mean: avg.
Arithmetic term: divisor, LCD
Arithmetic verb: add
Arizona observatory: Lowell
ASU rival: UCLA
Arizona tourist stop: petrified forest
Ark, man with the: Noah
Arkansas range: Ozarks
Arkansas resort: hot springs
Arkin, Adam
Arkin, Allen: actor
Arlen, Harold: composer
Arm bone: ulna, radius, humerus
Armadillo: apara, 'apar
Armani, Giorgio: designer
Armchair companion: ottoman
Armed bodies: forces
Armed forces: military
Armed hostilities: war
Armed struggle: war
"Armed to the teeth"
Armless egyptian: asp
Armor, body: mail
Armor-breaking weapon: mace
Armored dinosaur: Ankylsaur
Armored god: Ares
Arms agreement: pact
Arms, it has long: ape
Arms position: akimbo
Armstrong, Louis: jazz great
Armstrong, Neil: astronaut
Armstrong, "Satchmo": Louis
"Up in arms"
Army address: Sir, APO
Army base: post, fort, billet
Army doc: medic
Army duds: khaki
Army food: rations
Army instrument: bugle
Army mollusk: octopus
Army mule, for one: mascot
Army station: post
Army supply officer: dime-master
Army wheels: jeep
Arne, Thomas: composer
Arnold Ziffel, notably: pig
Arnold Ziffel's home: sty
Arnold's role: Conan
Aroma, faint: sniff
Aromatic chemical: ester
Aromatic compound: ester
Aromatic cosmetic liquid: Bay rum
Aromatic flavoring: anise
Aromatic herb: anise, hyssop
Aromatic herb in tea: mint
Aromatic plant: chia
Arose: came up, got up

Around: or so
Around (in dates): circa
"I Get Around"
Arp, Jean (or Hans): painter
Arp's art: dada
Arrange: rig, assort.
Arrange bricks: lay
Arrange by types: sort
Arrange in advance: pre-set
Arrange in rows: tier
Arrange in sequence: sort, seriate
Arrangement: set up, array, format
Arrangement of things, pleasing: harmony
Array of numbers: matrix
Arrive at: reach
Arrive unexpectedly: blew in
Arrived era, Andre: adieu
Arrived era, Roma: farewell
Arrogant: vain
Arrogant person: snob
Arrow poisons: inec, upas, urari, ince, curare,
        curari
Arrowsmith's wife: Leora
Arroyo: wadi
Arroz con pollo ingredient: rice
Art category: genre
Art class wear: smock
Art colony site: Taos
Art deco icon: Erté
Art deco illustrator: Erté
Art deco names: Erté, Arp
Art gum, for one: eraser
Art, modern: Dada
Art movement: Dada
Art museum specialist: restorer
Art object: curio
Art of boxing: pugilism
Art of convincing: suasion
Art school: academy
Art work, type of: etching
Artaxerxes composer: Arne
Artemis's companion: Aura
Artemis's twin brother: Apollo
Artery, large: carotid Artful dodger, like a: sly
Arthurian heroine: Elaine
Arthurian isle: Avalon
Arthurian times: yore
Arthur's Foster brother: Kay
        home: England
        island paradise: Avalon
        resting place: Avalon
Arthur's wizard: Merlin
Artichoke middle: heart
Article of commerce: ware
Article teaser: blurb
Article written by Freud: er
Artifact: curio, relic, legacy, rarity
Artifice: hoax, ploy, ruse, wile, craft, feint,
        guile, skill
Artificial, as pearls: faux
Artificial channel: sluice
Artificial water passage: sluice
Artificially formal: stilted
Artisan's furnace: kiln

Artist inventor: Morse, Samuel
Artistic word: oeuvre
Artistic work: oeuvre
Artist's degree: BFA
Artist's lifework: oeuvre
Artist's material: gesso
Artist's medium: oils
Artist's paint holder: palette
Artist's plaster: gesso
Artist's rental: loft
Artist's space: loft
Artist's studio: atelier
Artist's topper: beret
Artsy: crafty
Aru Island, formerly: Aroe, Arroe
As a friend, in French: en ami
As a matter of course: routinely
As a precaution: incase
As a result: ergo
"as a rule": ergo
As being: qua
As far as: up to
As found: in situ
"As if I care"
As if in a trance: dazedly
As it happens: live
"Such as it is"
"As It were"
As long as it lasts: duration
As mentioned: idem
As much as: up to
As of: from
As of now: to-date
As opposed to Pizzicato: Arco
As regards: anent
As soon as: when
As too much: impose
As well: too
As well as: also, too
Asana practitioner: yogi
Ascend higher: soar
Ascend to a height: soar
Ascertain:learn
Ascot: tie
Asdic relative: sonar
Asgard denizen: god
Asgard group: Aesir
Ashes cache: urn
Ashley's mom: Naomi
Ashram dweller: Hindu
Asia begins here: Urals
Asia Minor, region of: Ionia
Asia start: Urals
Asian capital: Hanoi
Asian celebration: Tet
Asian desert: Gobi
Asian export: tea
Asian goat antelope: serow
Asian holiday: tet
Asian humped ox: zebu
Asian illness: flu
Asian inland sea: Aral
Asian monk: lama,
Asian mountain dwellers: Kurds

Asian nomads: Kurds
Asian ox: zebu,
Asian princess: Rani
Asian royalty: Rani
Asian sea: Aral
Asian, southeastern people of: Hmong
Asian sultanate: Brunei
Asian water lily: lotus
Asian weight unit: tael
Asian wild sheep: argali, urial
Asian women's quarters: oda
Asia's shrunken sea: Aral
Asiatic primate: loris
Asiatic tree, tall: acles
Asimov creation: I, Robot
Asimov, Isaac: sci-fi writer
Ask a question: pose
Ask about: query
Ask for ID: card
"Ask Dr. Ruth"
Ask too much: impose
Asked ardently: pled
Askew in England: agee
Asks for aims: begs
Asmara loc.: Eth.
Asner, Ed: actor
Asparagus unit: spear
Aspen sight: ski lift
Aspen wear: après-ski
Assail: beset
Assam silkworm: eria, eri
Assayer's material: ore
Assembled, already: prefab
Assembly of the clergy: synod
Assent, pious: amen
Assert positively: aver
Assertive, rudely: pushy
Assign one's share: allot
Assigned work: task
Assist in malfeasance: abet
Assist in wrongdoing: abet
Assistance, without: solo, alone
Assistant: aide, second
Assistant lecturer: Aushilfslehrer
Assuages pain: eases
Assumed as fact: given, posited
Assumed manners: airs
Assuming airs: uppity
Assuming, most: meekest
Assured vigor: elan
Assyrian sky god: Anat
Astaire, Fred: actor
Asteroid, largest: Ceres
Asteroid, near earth: Eros
"Asteroids" game creator: Atari
Astolat lily maid: Elaine
Astonished cry: wow
Astor, Brooke: philanthropist
Astral altar: Ara
Astringent: acid, keen, sour, tart
Astrologer's tool: zodiac
Astrologer of yore: magi
Astronaut base: earth
Astronaut concern: g force

Astronaut's ade: tang
Astronaut's ferry: LEM
Astronaut's wear: G-shirt
Astronomer, ancient: Ptolemy
Astronomer, warly: Galileo
Astronomer's delight: clear night
Astronomer's instrument: sextant
Astronomer's sighting: nova,
Astronomer's time period: eon
"ASU" rival: UCLA
Aswan dam site: Nile
At a distance: afar, away, above, aloof
At an angle: tilted, slanted
AT&T park ballplayers: Giants
At any point: ever
At any time: ever
At bay: treed, cornered
At fruition: ripe
At full speed, as a ship: a main
At hand: near
At large: free
At no time: never
At no time, in Bonn: nie
At once: PDQ, stat
At once, to the bard: anon
At random: about, anyhow, anyway
At that place, Latin: illi
At the same time: together
At the table: seated
At the tiller: aft
At the time, poetically: ne'er
At this time: now
Ate hungerly: wolfed
Ate on the run: bolted
Atelier: studio, workshop
Atelier item: easel
Athapaskan: Hupa
Athena, name for: Alea
Athena's domain: wisdom
    breastplate: egis
    father: Zeus
    rival: Sparta
    symbol: owl
Athenian market place: Agora
Athenian orgy cry: evoe
Athens of America: Boston
Athen's "T": Tau
Athletic sort: jock
Athletic star: pro
Anthony the Roman: Marc
Atlantic crosser: SST, Nina
Atlanta arena: omni
Atlanta, capturer of: Sherman
Atlanta universities: Emory, Georgia Tech
Atlantic inlet: Delaware Bay
Atlantis proprietor: NASA
Atlas's brother: Prometheus
    daughter: Hyads, Hyades, Pleiades, Atlantides
    father: Lapetus
    mother: Clymene
    race: Titan
    wife: Pleione
Atlas abbr.: terr.

Atlas dot: isle
Atlas filler: maps
Atlas or Prometheus: Titan
ATM code: pin
Atman: soul
Atmosphere: air, aura
Atmosphere, like the upper: rarefied
Atmospheric condition: climate
Atom kin: aero
Atom, charged: ion
Atom fragment: ion,
Atom home: molecule
Atom splitting: fission
Atomic arsenal: nukes
Atomic bomb code: little boy, big boy
Atomic or stone: age
Atreus's brother: Thyestes
   father: Pelops
   mother: Hippodamia
   slayer: Aegisthus
   son: Menelaus, Agamemnon,
     Pleisthenes
   wife: Aerope
Attach: tie
Attachment, sticky: Post-it
Attack a castle: siege
Attack from every angle: beset
Attack on all sides: beset
Attack opposite: retreat
Attack, prolonged: siege
Attack, sneak: ambush
Attack snidely: sniped at
Attack, sudden armed: sortie
Attack, surprise: raid,
Attack verbally: assail, snip at, sail into
Attack vigorously: assail
Attack warning: red alert
Attains maturity: ripens
Attempt: effort, essay, try, aim, seek
Attempted: essayed
Attendance: gate
Attendant: usher, clerk
Attention: ear
Attention getter: ahem, gavel, hey, psst
Attention, lavish: dote,
Attention, pay little: gloss over
Attention, with full: raptly
Attention-getter: scream,
Attention-getting cough: ahem
Attentive: all ears
Attentiveness, showed: sat up
Attic: garret
Attic accumulation, perhaps: junk
Attic end: gable
Attic, small: garret
Attica township: Demes
Attila (for one): Hun
Attila follower: Hun
"Attila the Hun"
Attila's faithful: Huns
Attire, formal: tux
Attire (dressing): heels
Attired: clad
Attired, elegantly: chic

Attired ,splendidly: arrayed
Attitude: tone
Attitudes: mindsets
Attorney, future exam of: LSAT
Attorney degree: LLB, LLM, LLD
Attractive device: magnet
Attractive guy: hunk
Auber's operatic heroine: Manon
Au courant: upon, aware
Au vin, coq : French chicken dish
Auction action: nod
Auction buy: lot
Auction competition: bidding
Auction goer: bidder
Auction handout: paddle, number
Auction off: re-sold, re-sell, sell
Auction site: eBay, uBid
Auctioneer's cry: sold
Audacity: nerve
Audience: ear
Audience accolade: bravo
Audience clamor: encore
Audio: visual
Audio antiques: hi-fis
Audio partner: video
Audiometer inventor: Bell
Audiophile's concern: tone
Audition: try out
Audition hope: role
Audition tape: demo
Auel, Jean M.: writer
Auel heroine: Ayla
Auger, Uses an: Bores
Aught or Naught: Nil, Zero
Augment: Add
Augur: Bode, Seer, Oracle
Augury: Omen
Augustus, for one: Emperor
Auld Lang: Syne
Auld Lang Syne: yore
Auntie Em's state: Kansas
"Auntie Mame"
Au pair: nanny
Aura: halo
Aura, unnatural: eeriness
Aureate: gilt, gold
Auricle: ear
Auricle: ear
Auric's creator: Ian
Aurora borealis
Aurora locale: sky
Aurora (other): Eos
Aurora, to Plato: Eos
Aurora's domain: dawn, east
Baba au ruhm
Aushilfslehrer: assistant lecturer
Aussie cockatoo: arara
Aussie girl: Sheila
Aussie hopper: roo
Aussie ratite: emu
Aussie rocker: ACDC
Austen heroine: Emma
Austen novel: Emma
Austin, Jane: writer

Austin title: Emma
Austin Powers' assets: mojo
Austin, Tracy: tennis
Australian capital: Canberra
Australian desert lizard: moloch
Australian eucalyptus: yate
Australian peaks, to natives: Alpen
Australian rock: Ayers (former name for
  Uluru)
   Australian tribal hut: miamia
Australia's national gem: opal
Australis and borealis: auroras
Authentic: true
Authenticated: valid
Authenticating mark: seal
Author, spooky: Poe
Author, uncredited, for short: ghost
Author, well known: anon
Authority: say so
Authority, final: say so
Authority (misuse): power trip
Authorized stand-in: proxy
Author's concern: plot, title,
Author's need: plot
Author's payment: royalty
Auto body woe: rust, dent, mar
Auto, classic: REO, Packard
Auto engine, powerful: Hemi
Auto insurance, type of: no fault
Auto making a comeback: repo
Auto parts store: NAPA
Auto quintet: tires
Auto race (long distance): Enduro, endurance
Auto registration datum: VIN
Auto rod: axle
Auto safety device: air bag, seat belt, lap, belt
Auto safety feature: crumple zone
Autobahn hazard, wintry: eis
Autobiography, certain: memoir
Autocrat: tsar, czar, ruler
Autogiro feature: rotor
Autographed: inscribed
Automatic introduction?: semi
ATM builder: NCR
ATM code: PIN
ATM necessity: PIN number
ATM user's password: PIN
Automatons: robots
Auto racing city, famous: Lemans
Auto racing family: Unser
Autumn leaves, like: sere
Autumn moon: harvest
Autumn sign: Libra
Autumnal hue: rust
Vol-au-vent:French menu item
Avail oneself of: use
Available: to let
Available, in a way: on sale
Avakian, Aram: director
Avalon, Frankie: musician
Avant opposite: après
Avatar of Vishnu: Rama
Ave, ave follower: sir
"avec" (opposite of): sans

Avedon, Richard: photographer
Avena sativa: oat
Avenger king: Tara
Average guy: joe
Average, just: so-so
Averages: par, norm
Avers: states
Rara aves,
Avian ballet role: swan
Avian chatterbox: macaw
Avian compartment: pigeonhole
Avian, earthbound: emu
Avian excavator: Coal Mynah
Aviary mimic: myna
Aviary resident: bird
Aviation marker: pylon
Aviator of Vishnu: Rama
Aviators, tabloid: ETs
Aviator's test: solo
Avifauna
Avignon's river: Rhone
Avoid ignorance: learn
Avoids adroitly: evades, eludes
Avon, the Bard of
Aw shucks: heck
Await action: pend
Awaited: abided
Awaits judgment: pends
Awaits: bides, pends
Awake, wide: alert
Award, commercial: Clio
Awkward stupid person: lout
Awkwardly: clumsily
Awareness, kind of: self
Aware of: on to
Away from home: a field
Away from the wind: alee
Awesome: rad
Awful: horrid, beastly
Awful, simply: horrid
Awoke: aroused, come to
AWOL nabbers: MPs
Axe cousin: adze
Axe handle: haft
Axe, small: hatchet
Axel, performed an: leapt
Axe-like tool: adz, adze
Axel securer: U-bolt
Aye, aye follower: sir
Ayla's creator: Jean Auel
Ayn or Sally: Rand
Ayn's shrugged: Atlas
Ayres, Lew: actor
Azine and acridine: dyes
Aztec emperor: Montezuma

B

"B" movie crook: yegg
Baa's companion: moo
B & B, part of: med
Ali Baba
Baba au rhum

"Babe" star: pig
Babe's place: sty
Babies, Beanie
Babies do it: teethe
Babilonis, Tia: skater
"Baby Baby, Ooh"
Baby carriage: pram
Baby elephant: calf
Baby equine: foal
Baby food: pap, puree, Pablum
Baby grand: piano
Baby kiss, notably: photo op
Baby shower gift: layette
Baby sit: mind, tend
Baby sitter, long-term: nanny
Baby sitter, often: teen
Baby sitter's bane: imp
Baby soother: talc
Babylon mountain: Ararat
Babylonian abode of the dead: Aralic
Babylonian deity: Luan
Babylonian earth mother: Ishtar
Babylonian god of heaven: Bel
Babylonian goddess: Aya, Nina
Babylonian hero: Etana
Baby's big first: steps
Baby's company: Gerber
Bacall, Lauren: actress
Bacardi: rum
Baccarat alternative: faro
Baccarat score, top: nine
Bacchanalia: orgy,
Bacchanals, cry of: evoe
Bacchic cry: evoe (riotously drunk)
Bach contemporary: Handel
Bach instrument: organ
Bach was one: organist
Bach opus: Fugue
Bacharach, Burt: songwriter
Bachelor of letters degree: Litt B
Back again: fro, returned
Back bitter: molar
Back burner, put on the, maybe: heat
Back, front and Scotland: yards
Back in the navy: stern
Back out: renege
Backpack: hike, load, camp
Backpack contents: gear
Back streets: alleys
Back to normal: itself
Back when: ago
Backcourt man: guard
Backer: sponsor
Backslide: lapse
Back-forty measurement: acre
Back's counterpart: forth
Backspace through: erase
Backup fuel supply: oil reserve
Backward direction, in a: astern
Backwards, go: regress, reverse
Backwoodsman: hick, rube, swain, yokel,
　　rustic, bumpkin
Backyard community: ant hill
Backyard griller, maybe: dad

Bacon contemporary: egg
Bacon, et, al,: essayists
"BLT" base: bacon, lettuce, tomato, toast
Bacon on the hoof: pig
Bacon slice: rasher
Bacon, thin slice of: rasher
Bacteriologist culture: agar
Bacterium: aerobe
Bad actor: ham
Bad air: smog
Bad beginning: mal
Bad cholesterol: LDL
Bad custom: cacoethes
Bad cut: gash
Bad doings: evil
Bad ems, German spa
Bad end, very: doom
Bad habit: vice
"Bad hair day"
Bad headache: migraine
Bad, hopelessly: abysmal
Badlands: wilds
Bad legislation: dysnomy
Bad luck, bring: jinx
Bad, more than: evil
Bad mouth: dis, malign
Bad move, really: folly
Bad note: counterfeit bill
Bad place to be lead: astray
Bad review: pan
Bad sign: omen
Bad temper: spleen
Bad thing to bear: grudge
Bad throat sound: rale
Bad time for Julius: Ides
Bad to the Bone: Evil
Baden-Baden, e.g.: spa
Badge, marshall's: star, shield
Badger: nag
Badgered: baited
Badger-like animal: ratel
Badgers of Bari (Italy): Tassos
Badges: IDs
Badly: lily
Badminton stroke: lob
Badminton target: net
Baer, Max: boxer
Baez, Joan: singer
Baffling thing: enigma
Bag (large): tote, valise
Bag, open-topped: tote
Bag or tote: purse
Bag, perfumed: sachet
Bag, redolent: sachet
Bagel center: hole
Bagel flavor: onion
Bagel partner: lox
Bagel shop: deli
Bagel topper: lox
Bagel type: sesame
Bagel's kin: bialy
Baggage handler: porter, red cap, sky, cap
Bagging fibers: istles
Bagnold, Enid: writer

"Bah": fie
Bahai origin: Iran
Bahamas group: Indies
Bahamas naval base: Mayaguana
Bahamas resort: Nassau
Bahamian capital: Nassau
Bahrain or Kuwait: Gulf state
Bahrain VIP: emir
Bail out: rescue, aid, eject
Bailed out: aided
Bailiwick: area, sphere
Baird, Cira or Bil: puppeteer
Baiul, Oksana: skater
Baiz, Amy
Baja bash: fiesta
Baja cheer: salud
Baja girl: chica
Baja Ms.: Srta
Baja Mrs.: Sra
Baja opposite: alta
Bake pottery: fire
Bake, ready to: risen
Baked-potato garnish: chives
Bakehead: rail, stoker
Bake-off figure: chef
Baker, Anita: musician
Baker's mixture: batter
Bakery come-on: aroma
Bakery emanation: aroma
Bakery lure: aroma
Bakery treat: éclairs
Baking chamber: oven
Baking pit: umu
Baking powder: leaven
Baksheesh: tip
Balaam's rebuker: ass
Balance: scales, inane
Balance part: beam
Balance provider: ATM,
Balance unsteadily: teeter
Balancing bar: beam
Balbo, Italo: Italian politician, aviator
Balcony scene swain: Romeo
Balcony section: loge
Bald head: dome
Bald spot covering: toupee, sod
Balder, god of: light, peace
Balder's father: Odin
Baldwin, Alec: actor
Baldwin brother: Alec
Balearic port: Palma
Baleen source: Whale
Bales, make: hay
Bali Hai
Balin, Ina: actress
Ball game starter: anthem
Ball girl, tennis: Deb
Ball gown fabric: tulle
Ball of fire: dynamo
Ball of yarn: clew
"Ball" partner: Arnaz
Ballad ending: e'er
Ballad step: pas
Ballad writer: poet

Ballard, Kay:
Ballerina knee bend: plie
Ballerina painter: Degas
Ballerina, prima: étoile
Ballerina strong point: toe
Ballerina support: barre, bar
Ballerina's practice bar: barre
Ballesteros, Seve: golf
Ballet bend: plie
Ballet costume: tutu
Ballet dance: adagio, pantomime
Ballet duet: adagio
Ballet leap: jete
Ballet movement: plie, chasse
Ballet music: opera
Ballet, popular: swan lake
Ballet pose, one-legged: arabesque
Ballet shoe: toe shoe
Ballet turn: pirouette
Balloon, kind of: hot air
Balloonist's necessity: hot air
Ballot, kind of: absentee
Ballot marks: exes
Ballpark figure: guess, stat, ump
Ballpark, in the: close
Ballpark, makeshift: sandlot
Ballpark nosh: frank
Ballroom dance: samba, rumba, tango
Balls with lids: eyes
Ball-shaped cheese: edam
Balustrade: railing
Ballyshannon estuary: Erne
Balm: lotion
Balm, natural: aloe
Balm of the Bible: nard
Balsam or resin: Tolu
Balthazar, e.g.: magus
Baltimore bard: Poe
Baltimore suburb: Essex
Balustrade: rail, fence, railing
Balzac, Honore: writer
"Bambino," the: Ruth, Babe
Bambi's aunt: Ena
Bamboo: cane
Bamboo muncher: panda
Bamboo stalk: cane
Bamboo sugar: silica,
Bamboolike grasses: reeds
Bamboozle: con, bilk, dupe, fool, gull
Ban: lon
Banal, beyond: inane
Banal, more: triter
Banana Boat song: Dayo
Banana oil, e.g.: ester, lacquer
Banana, Polynesian: fei
Banana stalk: stem
"Banana, Top"
Banana-like fruit: plantain
"Bananas" name: Woody
Banca or waka: canoes
Band: stripe
Band crew member: roadie
Band event (brass): parade
Band together: ally

Bandage, stretchy: ace
Banded stones: agates
Bando, sal: baseball
Bandwagon: fad, chic, mode, rage
Bandy words: argue, spar
Bane of grain: ergot
Bane of pvts: sgts
Banff lake: Louise
Bang: slam
Bang down: slap, slam
Bangkok cash: bahte, bahts
Bangkok coin: att
Bangkok native: Thai
Bang-up job, it does a: TNT
Bang-up result?: dent
Banishment, prolonged: exile
Banister post: newel
Banjo's cousin: uke
Bank agreements, some: escrows
Bank assessments: carrying charges
Bank dep.: acct.
Bank deposits, of a sort: silt
Bank holding: lien
Bank job: heist
Bank of France: Rive
Bank of the Tiber: ripa, riparian
Bank offering: home loan, loan, CDs
Bank take-back: repo
Bank to bank, walked: waded
Bank window initials: FDIC
Banker's box: till, safety
Banking center: Zurich
Banking center, big: Zurich
Banking convenience: ATM
Bankroll: fund, wad
Bankrupt: ruin. Broke, belly up
Banks are liquid, its: Wabash
Banner, narrow: pennon
Banquet finale: dessert
Banquet host: emcee
Banshee cry: wail
Bantam crest: comb
Bantu language: Zulu
Bantu people: Zulu
Baptism and Others: Rites
Bar at the dinner table: oleo, butter
Bar choice, raw: oyster
Bar code, read a: scan
Bar fruit: lime
Bar legally: estop
Bar mitzvah reading: Torah
Bar mixture: tonic
Bar of soap: cake
Bar order: usual
Bar order, expensive: round
Bar passer: attorney, abbr. atty.
Bar patron: toper
Bar preparation: salad
Bar sing-along: karaoke
Bar, type of: piano
Bara, Theda: actress
Bara's nickname: vamp
Barbarian: Hun, vandal, Conan
Barbarian leader: Attila

"Barbarian, the, Conan"
Barbarous one: ogre
Barbary pirate: corsair
Barbary state: Tunis, Algiers, Morocco, Tripoli
Barbecue buttinskies: ants
Barbecue extra: keg
Barbecue tidbit: rib
Barbershop call: next
Barcelona bed: cama
Barcelona boy: niño
Barcelona uncle: tio
Bard or minstrel: poet
Bard river: Avon
Bard title, start of: alls
Bard work: tale
Bard's baddie: Iago
    collection: sonnets
    contraction: e'er
    prince: Hal
    teen: Romeo
Bard's bathe, where the: Avon
Bard's palindrome: e're
Bard's wife: Anne
Bare, more: emptier
Barefoot, walks: pads
Barely: just
Barely beat: nip, nose out
Barely enough: scant
Barely sufficient: scant
Barely visible: wee
Barely win, just: nip
Barenboim, Daniel: pianist-conductor
Bargain event: sale, fire sale
Bargain hunter's bonanza: closeout
Bargain hunter's scene: yard sale
Bargain hunts: shops
Bargain prices, at: on sale
Bargain, terrific: buy
Bargain, type: plea, buys, haggle
Bargained: dealt
Bargains: twofers, buys, deals
Barge in on
Barge route: canal
Baritone, above a: tenor
"Bark up the wrong tree"
Barkin, Ellen: actress
Bark's bottom: keel
Barley brew: ale
Barley used in brewing: malt
Barn area: loft, stall
Barn dance, seat at a: bale
Barn loft: haymow
Barn raising group: Amish
Barn topper: vane
Barnes, Djuna: writer
Barnes partner: Noble
Barnhardt, Sarah: actress
Barnyard honker: goose
Baron Von Richthofen
Baroness Karen Isak
Baronet's title: sir
Baronet's wife: dame
Baroque composer: Bach
Baroque great: Bach

Baroque manner, in a: ornately
Baroque painter: Rubens
Baroque style: rococo
Baroque style, in: ornately
Barrack's bane: snorer
Barracuda: spet
Barrel business: cooperage
Barrel maker: cooper
Barrel part: stave, band
Barrel, small: keg
Barrel spigot: spile
Barrett, Angela
Barrett of gossip: Rona
Barrett, Rona: writer, columnist
Barrette: clasp, clip
Barrie captain: Hook
Barrie character: Tinkerbell
Barrier: Gate
Barrier, type of: sonic
Barriers, surmountable: hurdles
Barrister's concern: law
Barrooms: pubs, bars
Barry, Dave: writer, humorist
Bart Simpson's bartender: Moe
Bart Simpson's bus briver: Otto
Bart Simpson's sister: Lisa
Bartender's tool: opener
Barter about: deal for
Bartholdi masterpiece: Statue of Liberty
Bartlett's entries: Quotes
Bartok, Bela: composer
Barton, Clara: nurse, Red Cross
Bart's dad's dad: Abe
Bart's mother: Marge
Bart's sister: Maggie, Lisa
Baruch, Bernard: financier
Baruch's father: Neriah, Zabbai
    occupation: scribe
Bas-relief
Basalt source: lava
Base for beer: malt,
Base in baseball: bag
Base melody: taps
Base, return to: tag up
Base, secret: lair
Baseball club: bat
Baseball divisions: innings, leagues
Baseball family name: Alou
Baseball feature: seam
Baseball practice hit: fungo
Baseball players:
    Agee , Tommie
    Alou, Jesus
    Alou, Matty
    Alou, Moises
    Bando, Sal
    Blue, Vida
    Cabell, Enos
    Gehrig, Lou
    Gooden, Dwight
    Hershiser, Orel
    Hodges, Gil
    Maglie, Sal
    McGuire, Mark

    Musial, Stan
    Oliva, Tony
    Ryan, Nolan
    Speaker, Tris
    Staub, Rusty
    Tiant, Luis
    Vincent, Fay
    Williams, Ted
Baseball scoreboard letters: R, H, E
Baseball VIP: mgr
Baseball's hot corner: third
Basel's river: Rhine
Basement sink: wash tub
Basement stuff: store
Basenji, for one: dog
Bashful: coy, red
Basic assumption: given
Basic idea: gist
Basic principle: tenet
Basie, Count: band leader
Basil sauce: pesto
Basilica area: nave, apse
Basilicas (part of): apses
Basin craft, perhaps: yacht
Basinger, Kim: actress
Basket fiber: istle, raffia
Basket, kind of: picnic
Basket, make a: score, weave
Basket making: slath,
Basket making fiber: raffia
Basket material: osier
Basket throw: shot
Basket weave: natte
Basket weaving grass, Mexican: otate
Basket willow: osier
Basketball, father of: Nia Smith
Basketball hoop: rim
Basketball players:
    Archibald, Nate
    English, Alex
    Holman, Nat
    Irving, Julius
    Malone, Moses
    Olajuwon, Akeem
    Reed, Willis
    Unseld, Wes
Basketball throw: shot
Basketball timer: shot clock
Basket-making fiber: raffia
Basmath's father: Solomon
Bass in a glass: ale
Bass, like a: low
Basso: base singer, operatic singer
Basso Cesare: Siepi
Bassoon's cousin: oboe
Bassoon's kin: oboe
Basswood tree: linden
Baste: tack
Basted: tacked, sewn
Bastille Day season: Ete
Bat eyelashes, for example: flirt
Bataan people: Itas
Bates establishment: motel
Bath accessory: loofa

Bath décor: tile
Bath powder, uses: dusts
Bath sponge: loofa, loofah
Bathe: lave, wash, soak
"Bather's" painter: Renoir
Bathrobe fabric: terry
Bathroom item: mat, towel
Bathsheba's husband: Uriahs
Batik, did: dyed
Batman alias: Wayne
Batman and Robin: duo
Batman creator: Kane, Bob
Batman's garb, part of: cowl
Batman's home: Gotham
Baton: wand
Baton, wield a: twirl
Bator, Ulna
Battalions, grp, of: regt, regiment
Battalions, group of:regiment
Battenberg's river: Eder
Batter ploy: bunt
Battering tool: ram
Batter's change of mind: check swing
Battery, kind of: solar
Battery, lithium-ion
Battery powered: cordless
Battery, restart: jump, charge
Battery terminal, like one: anodal
Battery terminals: anodes, posts
Battery units: volts, amps
Battery word: volt
Batting posture: stance
Battle of Endor fighters: Ewok
Battle of nations: war,
Battle site of 1836: Alamo
Battle sites: arenas
Battle tactic: siege
Battleship, famed: Iowa
Battleship of 1898: Maine
Bauble: doodad
Baucis's husband: Philemon
Bauxite giant: Alcoa
Baxter, Anne: actress
Baxter, Les: orchestra leader
Bay doc: vet
Bay of Biscay
Bay state: Massachusetts
Bay transport: water taxi
Bay window: oriel
Bayed: ululated
Baylor, Elgin: NBA
Baylor University location: Waco
Bayou cooking: Creole
Bayou dweller: Creole
Bayou stew: gumbo
Bays and chestnuts: horses
Be a gourmand: eat
Be a role model: inspire
Be a thespian: act
"Be all's partner": end all
Be an accomplice: abet
Be an omen: bode
Be an omen of: portend
Be anxious: fret

Be concerned: care
Be curious: inquire
Be entitled to: earn
Be evasive: hedge
Be footloose: rove, roam
Be frugal: stint
Be gone (old style): avaunt
Be impatient: snap
Be in a sticky situation: adhere
Be in accord with: agree
Be in stitches: laugh
Be more durable: out last
Be my guest: please do
Be next to: abut, up next
Be of use to: avail
Be on the lookout: abet
Be overattentive, as a waiter: hover
Be rile with: teem,
Be rueful: feel sorry
Be seen among moguls: ski,
Be short with: snap at
Be sincere: mean
Be taught: learn
Be undecided: pend
Be unwilling: demur
Be useful: avail
Be without: lack, need
Beach alternative: pool
Beach bottles letters: SPF
Beach cover up: tide
Beach hut: cabana
Beach, Lies on the: Tans, Suns
Beach Need: Dingy
Beach Scavenger: Gull.
Beach Vehicle: Dune buggy
Beach Washer: Tide
Beachcomber's Find: Jetsam
Beachgoer's Shade: Tan
Bead, Tube-shaped: Bugle
Beaded Footwear: Mocs
Beads at a Mass: Rosary
Beads on Blades: Dew
Beagle: Snoopy
"Beale Street Blues"
Be all and end all: some, pith, root, soul, total,
    whole
Beam: joist
Beam above door: lintel
Beam, bright: laser
Beam, construction: I-bar, T-bar, girder,
    timber
Beam, high-tech: laser
"Beam me up"
Beamed: smiled
Bean, broad: fava
Bean curd: tofu
Bean for sprouts: mung
Bean hull: pod
Bean, Roy: judge
Bean, nutritious: soy
Bean, Orson: actor
Bean town: Lima
Bean, type: urd, fava
Beanery drink: java

Beanery handout: menu
Bean-filled treat: burrito
Beanie Babies
Beans or peas: legumes
Beantown: Boston
Beantown team: Sox, Red Soxs
Bear Bryant's school: Alabama
Bear, Cato's: Ursa
Bear, dangerous: Kodiak
Bear down: press
Bear, Gentle: Ben
Bear in the sky: Ursa
Bear, injured by a: mauled
Bear, Pliny: Ursa
Bear skin, maybe: rug,
Bear, story book: Papa
Bear witness: attest, testify
Beard, neaten a: trim
Beard, type of: goatee
Bearded grass: darnel
Bearer's boss: bwana
Bearing: mein
Bearing, gets ones: orient
Bearings, provide: orient
Bearish times: dips, downturn
Bear-like: ursine
Bear-like beast: panda
Bearnaise and birdelaise: sauces
Bearnaise sauce ingredient: shallot
Bear's advice: sell, buy
Bear's pad: lair, den
Bear up: endure
Beast, mythical: centaurs
Beast, shaggy: yak
Beat: flog
Beat a retreat: run
Beat around the bush: hedge
Beat badly: drub
Beat it: lam, scram
Beat soundly: thrash
"Beat the clock" activity: stunt
Beat, Walk the: Patrol
Beaten Way: Path
Beatle Bailey's pal: Plato
Beatle bride: Yoko,
Beatles' meter maid: Rita
Beatnik's instrument: bongo
Beaton, Cecil: photographer
Beatrice's admirer: Dante
Beats, barely: nips
Beats the odds: wins the lottery
Beattle, Ann: author
Beatty, Ned: actor
Beat up: battered
Beau monde: fashionable folks
Beautiful and graceful girls: peris
Beautiful landscape, like a: scenic
Beautiful, make: adorn
Beautiful Nile queen: Nefertiti
Beautiful woman, most: Helen
Beautiful young man: Adonis
Beauty contest: pageant
Beauty packs: mud
Beauty pageant prize: tiara

Beauty pageant VIP: judge
Beauty parlor sound: snip
Beauty's swain: Beast
Beauty salon offering: facial
Beauvais department: Oise
Beaver, baby: kit
Beaver, kind of: eager
Beaver young: kits
Beaver skin: pelt
Beaver's dad: Ward
Became known: got about
Became less hirsute: shaved
Became less intense: ebbed, abated
Became threadbare: wore, worn
Became too big for: outgrew
Because of this action: Hereto
Becker actor: Otoole
Becker boomers: Aces
Beckett's homeland: Eire
Beckoned: bidden
Become accustomed: inure
Become adept to: master
Become apparent: emerge
Become, at last: end up
Become boring: pall
Become emeritus: retire
Become exhausted: run out
Become fond of: take to
Become frayed: worn, wears
Become keyed up: tense
Become liable: incur
Become more unfavorable: worsen
Become popular: catch on
Become serious: sober
Become skilled at: master
Become solid: set
Become tense: tauten
Become very pale: blanch
Become very thin: emaciate
Becomes clear: dawns
Becomes weary: jades
Bed accessory: sham
Bed and breakfast: inn
Bed, bloke's: doss
Bed canopy: tester
Bed choice: king, queen
Bed, light: cot
Bed of coal: seam
Bed, potential: sofa
Bed, rough: doss
Bed, straw: pallet
Bede, Adam
Bedouin attire: aba
Bedouin head wrap: cord
Bedouin leader: sheik
Bedroom community: exurb
Bedroom noise: snoring, alarm
Bedroom piece: bureau, dresser, chest
Bedroom racket: snore
Bedroom slipper: mule
Bedside noise: alarm
Bedspreads: coverlets
Bedstead, light: cot
Bedtime story: tale

Bee batteries: stings
"The Bee Gees"
Bee sounds, made: droned
Bee, stingless: drone
Beef designation: prime
Beef, half a: side
Beef up, as a battery: recharge
Beefy bovine: steer
Beehive: apiary
Beehive state: Utah
Beehive state flower: sego
Beehive state jock: Ute
Beehive state native: Ute
Beekeeping: apiculture
Beelines: direct routes
Beelzebub: Satan
Beer base: malt
Beer can opener: tab
Beer choice: lager, draft, light
Beer foam: barm
Beer, spring: Bock
Bee-related: apian
Beersheba citizens: Israelis
Beery, Noah
Bees, group of: colony, swarm
Beet or carrot: root
Beet product: sugar
Beet-faced: florid
Beethoven, like: deaf
Beethoven piece: opus
Beethoven symphony: Ninth
Beethoven's birthplace: Bonn
Beethoven's "Für Elise"
Beethoven's "Moonlight" Sonata
Beethoven's Third: Eroica
Beethoven's work: Eroica, Sonata
Beetle: dor, car, scarab
Beetle Bailey dog: Otto
Beetle Bailey's boss: Sarge
Beetle, Tut's sacred: scarab
Before a jury: on trial
Before birth: prenatal
Before, briefly: til, until
Before dinner nibbles: canapés
Before, in combo: pre, ante
Before long: anon
Before now: ere
Before this time: erenow, ago
Before, to Byron: ere
Beg pardon: ahem
Bega, Lou: Latin music
Beget: sire
Begger's cry: alms
Begin a journey: set forth
Begin again: restart
Begin earnestly, as winter: set in
Begin the betting: ante
Beginner: novice, amateur, layman, tyro,
    rookie
Beginning: nascent
Beginning at: from
Beginning, the very: outset
Beginning too soon: jump the gun
Begins co-nobelist: Sadat

Begins to appear: dawns
Begrudge: envy
Begum's spouse: Agha
Behave bullishly: buy
Behavior, ethical: decency
Behavior modification technique: hypnosis
Behavior, quirky: tic
Behavior, type of: normal
Behavioral patterns: modes
Behavioral sci: psych
Behind, at sea: aft
Behind behind you, the: derriere
Behind schedule: late
Behind the times: passe
Behind time: late
Beiderbecke, Bix: jazz name
Beijing name: Mao
Being: esse, entity
Being, actual: esse
Being hauled: in tow
Being, metaphysical: entia
Being, spanish: ente
Being, to Brutus: esse
Belabor: assail
Belfast: Maine
Belfry sounds: peals
Belgian resort: spa
Belgian sleuth: Hercule Poirot
Belgium Sleuth: Poirot
Belgrade citizen: Serb
Belgrade resident: Serb
Belief: tenet, ism
Beliefs, collection of: mythos
Believer in God: theist
Belittling look: sneer
Bell, deep: gong
Bell, Claiborne: senator
Bell Tower: steeple
"For Whom the Bell Tolls": Hemingway novel
Bell warning: tocsin
Bella Abzug, for one: feminist
Bellhop, call to a: front
Bellicose deity: Ares
Bellis bailiwick: law
Bellman's call, often: taxi
Bellow, Saul: writer
Bell-shaped hat: cloche
Belly dance instrument: oud
Belly dancer clackers: zills
Belly up, go: flop, fail
Bellyache: moan, gripe
Belly flop: dive
'"Dion and the Belmonts"
Belmont Stakes, 2/3 of: mile
Belong: inhere
Belong to me: mine
Belongs to us: ours
Beloved ones, in Belfast: cheris
Below par, it's always: birdie, eagle
Belt clip-on: pager, cell
Belt holder: loop, shot glass,
Belted, biblically: smote
Belt-like sharpener: strop
Beluga delicacy: roe

Bemoan: regret, deplore
Bemuse: at sea
Ben & Jerry's rival: Edy
Ben Hur route: Iter
Ben Jonson works: Odes
Bench mark: norm, normal
Bench, hard: pew
Bench rapper: gavel
Benchley classic: Jaws
Benchmark test: litmus
Benchwarmer: reserve
Bend gracefully: arch
Bend the elbow: drin
Bend the mind: think
Bend to one side: lean
"Fender bender"
Benders: jags, sprees, tears
Bending easily: lithe
Bends: arches
Knee bends
Nota bene
Beneath one's dignity: infradig
Benedictine title: Dom
Benefactors: donors
Benefit: sake
Benefit, be of: avail
Benefit, extra: gravy
Benefit from a mistake: learn
Is of benefit: avails
Benefit, job: perk
Benefits, colloquially: perks
Benet, Stephen Vincent
Benny, Jack: comic
Bent out of shape: warped, irate
Benz, Karl: Auto pioneer
Beowulf drink: mead
Beowulf: epic
Bequest recipient: legatee
Berber's home: Algeria
Bereft of looks: shorn
Beret covers it: tete, head
Beret filler: tete (French head)
Bergen, Edgar: ventriloquist
Bergen's dummy: Charlie McCarthy,
    Mortimer Snerd
Berger, Erna: soprano
Bergman, Ingrid: actress
Bergonzi, Carlo: tenor
Bering Sea bird: auk
Bering Sea native: Aleut
Berkeleianism, founder: Berkeley
Berkeleianism, system: idealism
Berland, Terri: actress
Berlin bride: frau
Berlin cash: euro
Berlin sausage: wurst
Berliner: ich, bin, ein
Bermuda grass: doob
Bern river: Aare
Bernese mount: alp
Bernhardt, Sarah: stage actress
Bernice's brother: Agrippa
    father: Herod
    husband: Polemo

lover: Titus, Vespasian
Bern's river: Aare,
Berra, Yogi: baseball
Berry, Noah: actor
Berry stem: cane
Bert, the Cowardly Lion: Lahr
Berth, kind of: upper
Berth preference: lower
Beseech: pray, beg, press
Beset: assail
Beside: along
Besides: else
Besides oneself: agog
Besmirch: smear
Bessemer-converter owners: steel makers
Best friend, man's
Best medicine: TLC
Best of all worlds: utopia
Best possible: ideal
Bestial hideaway: lair
Bestow honor upon: adorn
"Bet a Million" financier: Gates, Bill
Bet, make a: lay, wager
Beta carotene
Beta following: gamma
Betamax maker: Sony
Bete noire: bane, ogre
Betel palm: arecas
Beth's sister: Meg
Beth and Jo's sister: Amy, Meg
Bethuel's daughter: Rebekah
    father: Nahor
    mother: Milcah
    uncle: Abraham
Betrays: rats on
Bettelheim, Bruno: psychologist
Better than stereo: quad
Betti, Ugo: playwrite
Bettie, Ann: author
Betting, begin the: ante
Betting factor: odds
Betting game: faro
Betting spot: casino
Between all or nothing: some
Between gigs: idle
Betz, Carl: actor
Beurre bosc, for one: pear
Beverage, delicious: nectar
Beverage, dinner: wine
Beverage, warming: cocoa
Beverages in a sale: ales
"Beware the Ides of March"
Bewilders: dazes
Bewitch: hex, enamor
Beyond approach: squeaky clean
Beyond banal: inane
Beyond racy: lewd
Beyond rad: awesome
Beyond the limit: ultra
Beyond the usual: ultra
Beyond unconventional: outre
Beyond zealous: rabid
Bi + one = tri
Bialy's kin: bagel

Bias, free from: fair
Bias, kind of: gender
Bias, without: fair
Biathlon weapon: rifle
Biblical birthright seller: Esau
Biblical boatman: Noah
Biblical book: Isaiah
Biblical city: Sodom, Accad
Biblical dancer: Salome
Biblical garden: Eden
Biblical giant: Anak
Biblical grain measure: omer
Biblical hero: Gideon
Biblical high priest: Eli
Biblical hunter: Nimrod
Biblical judge: Gideon
Biblical king: Onri, Hiram, Herod, Josiah,
    Saul
Biblical kingdom: Sheba
Biblical matriarch: Sarah
Biblical measure: omer
Biblical miracle site: Red Sea
Biblical mount: Sinai
Biblical mountain: Ararat, Sinai
Biblical name: Enos
Biblical name for Syria: Aram
Biblical ointment: nard
Biblical patriarch: Enos
Biblical physician: Asa
Biblical placing society: Gideon
Biblical plant: hyssop
Biblical prophet: Isaiah, Nahum
Biblical proposition: unto
Biblical queen land: Sheba
Biblical strongman: Samson
Biblical tower: Babel
Biblical twin: Esau
Biblical two-by-two Craft: ark
Biblical weed: tare
Biblical witch's home: Endor
Bibliography word: alia
Bibliothecal org.: ALA
Bicep, brandish ones: Flex
Bicker: argue
Bicycle, two-seater: tandem
Bid adieu: past, part
Bidding site: eBay, sale, auction
Bidding, start the: open
Biddy: hen
Biddy's bailiwick: nest
Bien aime
Bien aime: darling
Bien, muy
Bien opposite: mal
Big Apple stadium: Shea
Big band era
Big bang producer: Nitro, TNT
"Big bang theory"
Big Bend flora:cacti
Big Bend state: Tennessee
Big Bertha birthplace: Essen
Big Bird: rhea
Big Bird's street: Sesame
Big blue: IBM

Big bother: hassle
Big Brother creator: Orwell
Big buildup: hoopla
Big business-related: corporate
Big casino: ten
Big Deal: 'So What'
Big Dipper: ladle
Big Dipper bear: Ursa
Big Dipper constellation: Ursa Major
Big Dipper neighbor: Draco
Big family: clan
Big foot's cousin: yeti
Big galoot: ape
Big gulp: swig
Big horn: tuba, ram, sheep
Big leagues: majors
Big money in India: crore (ten million)
Big name in blocks: Lego
Big palooka: ape
Big pieces: chunks
Big pileup: logjam
Big promos: ballyhoos
Big purveyor of language lessons: Berlitz
Big shot: VIP, honcho
Big Sky state: Montana
Big sports event: bowl game
Big steel town: Gary (Ind.)
Big Sur, California
Big ticket item
Big wheel's wheels: limo
Big-eared pachyderm: African elephant
Bigger than big: huge, humongous
Bigger's detective: Chan
Biggers, Earl Derr: novelist
Biggin's content: coffee
Bigot, of a sort: racist
Big-time celebration: gala
Bike and bridle, e.g.: path
Bike or trike: cycle
Bike, ride a: cycle
Bike seat: saddle
Bike, secure the: padlock
Bike's backrest: sissy bar
Bike's cousin: moped
Biker's rest: sissy bar
Biking, go: pedal
Bikini, e.g.: atoll
Bikini event, once: "A" test
Bikini or thong: swimwear
Bilbo's home: Shire
Bilge water: rot
Bilked (gets): overpays
Bilko, Sarge
Bilko's name: Ernie
"Bill and Coo"
Bill, for short: inv., stmt
Bill of fare: menu, program
Bill of sale: title
Bill tack-on: rider
Billed, not get: prepay
Billiard bounce: carom
Billiard shot: bricole, carom
Billiard stroke shot: masse
Billiard strokes: masses

Billiard's preliminary: lag
Billy Blanks exercise system: trebo
Billie joe, ode to
Billings hours: MST
Billini opera: Norma
Billion (one) years: an eon
Billion, in combogiga
Billionth, in combo: nano, giga
Billow: wave, surge
Billowing garment: cape
Billows of smoke: plumes
Bill's movie buddy: Ted
Bill topper: star
Billy and the kids: goats
Billy Budd's captain: Vere
Billy Joel's instrument: piano
Binary base: two
Binary digit: zero, bit
Binary digits, possible: ones, zeros, bits
Binary system elements: ones, zeroes
Binchy, Maeve: writer
Bind legally: oblige
Bind with cord: lash
Bing center: cherry pit, pit
Bingo kin: keno
Bio, last: obit.
Bio of, wrote a : profiled
Biography: vita
Biological determinate: gene
Biology categories: genera, genus
Biology gel: agar
Biology grouping: genus
Biondi, Matt: swimmer
Bionic woman: cyborg
Biotin: vitamin H
Birch kin: alder
Birch tree: alder
Birchbark craft: canoe
Bird, artic: auk
Bird, Australian: emu
Bird beak: nib
Bird, Bering Sea: auk
Bird, combo form: avi
Bird crop: craw,
Bird expert: Audubon, John James
Bird extinct: moa, dodo
Bird, fabulous: roc
Bird, fast-running flightless: rheaBird feather:
    pinion
Bird, fly-catching: pewee
Bird, hieroglyphics: ibis
Bird, Irene's: dove
Bird, largest: ostrich
Bird, marsh: stilts
Bird, nonflying: dodo, emu
Bird of Egypt, sacred: Ibis
Bird of June: peacock
Bird of Minerva: owl
Bird of myth: roe, roc
Bird of paradise
Bird of prey: raptor
Bird of the vane's mate: pea hen
Bird of wonder: phoenix
Bird or fruit: kiwi

Bird or person: biped
Bird, out-back: emu
Bird, passerine: vireos
Bird, rare: oner
Bird, razor-billed: auk
Bird, shore: rael
Bird, swamp: sora
Bird, tropical: toucan
Bird, weird-sounding: loon
Birdelaise: sauce
Bird-feeder staple: seed, suet
Birdie, ruin a: par
Birds, collectively: aves
Birds, for the: avian
Birds, of: avian
"Birds of a feather"
Birds of ill: omen
Birds, to Brutus: aves
Bird's waxlike swelling: care
Birds, weird-sounding: loons
Bireme mover: oars
Birth: origin
Birth, of: natal
Birth veil: caul
Birthday cake must: wish
Birthday number: age, years, yrs.
Birthmark: nevis, nevi
Birth-related: natal
Birthright seller: Esau
Birthright seller of Genesis: Esau
Birthstone; Sunday: topaz
        Monday: pearl
        Tuesday: ruby
        Wed.: amethyst
        Thurs: sapphire
        Friday: cat's eye
        Saturday: diamond
Birthstone; Jan.: garnet
        Feb.: amethyst
        Mar.: jasper
        Apr.: diamond
        May: agate
        June: emerald
        July: onyx
        Aug.: sardonyx
        Sept.: sapphire
        Oct.: opal
        Nov.: topaz
        Dec.: ruby
Birthstone after sapphire: opal
Biscotti flavor: anise
Bishop domain: diocese
Bishop hat: miter
Bishop symbol of office: crosier
Bishoprics: sees, diocese
Bishop's bailiwick: see
Bishop's break: schism
Bishop's chair: throne
Bishop's chimere: robe
Bishop's headgear: miter, mitre
Bismarck opponent: Beust
Bisque and miso: soups
Bisset, Jacqueline: actress
Bistro: café

Bistro VIP: chef
Bit controller: rein
Bit for Fermi: atom
Bit of chicanery: wile, ruse
Bit of current: amp
Bit of glitter: sequin
Bit of gossip: tale
Bit of reality: dose
Bit of scripting: line
Bit of serendipity: fluke
Bit of silent acting: charade
Bit of wisdom: axiom
Bit of wood: chip
Bite, had a: ate, snacked
Bite, just a: taste
Bite, least likely to: tamest
Bite, playful: nip
Bite, quick: nosh
Bites san teeth: gums
Biting, disposition to: mordacity
Bitingly funny: wry
Biteless bridle: hackamore
Bitten by an insect: stung
Bitterly cold: glacial, frigid
Bitterly pungent: acrid
Bittern cousin: egret
Bitterness: rancor, gall
Bivouac: camp
Bivouac sight: tent
Bivouacked: encamped
Bizet opera: Omar
Bjorn, Borg: tennis
Black: ebon
Black and blue: livid
Black bears town: Orono
Black bird: rook, jack daw, daw, starling
Black bird, European: meri, mari
Black bird, southern: ani
Black cat, maybe: omen
Black cuckoos: anis
Black current cordial: cassis (French wine)
Black death: plague
Black, deep: inky
Black diamond: coal
Black earth: mold
Black eye: shiner
Black Friday mo.: Nov.
Black garnet: melanite
Black gem: onyx
Black gold carrier: pipe, pipe line
Black-hearted: evil
Black Hills regions: Dakotas
Black hole, once: star
Black, lustrous: raven
Black magic: voodoo
Black magic, of: occult
Black mark: demerit, smut
Black market: smut
Black numbers, little: dresses
Black Panther Party founder: Seale
Black plague: bubonic
Black Sea port: Odessa
Black shade: sable, jet
Black sheep: scapegrace

Black suit: club, spade
Black tea: pekoe, bohea
Blacken: tarnish, ink
Blacken with heat: char
Blacker: inkier
Blackflag target: pest
Blackford Oakes org.: CIA
Blackguard: knave
Blackjack table staple: shoe
Blackjack (weapon): cosh
Blackmail: extort
Blackmailer's words: or else
Blackmore heroine: Doone
Blacks out: faints
Blacksmith's block: anvil
Blackstone's forte: magic
Blackthorn: sloe
Blackthorn fruit: sloe
Blade of yore: snee
Blair, Bonnie: skater
Blake, Amanda: actress
Blake, Eubie: composer, pianist
Blalock, Jane: golf
Blame: onus
Blameless: innocent
Blameworthy: culpable
Blanc, Mont
Blanch: steam
"Carte blanche"
Blanched, become: etiolate
Blandishment: flattery, enticement
Bland, hardly: savory
Bland page: fly leaf
Blanda, George: football
Blandly urbane: suave
Blank space: gap
Blank tapes: erase
Blanks a tape: erases
Blarney stone site: Eire
Blasé: jaded
Blass, Bill: designer
Blast from the past: oldie
Blast the ears: deafen
Blast-furnace fuel: coke
Blast-furnace input: ore
Blatant: overt
Blaze up: flare,
Blazer ornament: button
Blazing and vanishing star: nova
Blazing mound: pyre
Blazing up: afire,
Blazoning arms: heraldry
Bleach: bluing
Bleach bottle: jug
Bleached out: pale, faded
Bleacher creature: bum
Bleachers, like: tiered
Bleaching vat: kier
Bleak: dismal
Bleak and forbidding: austere
Blend: mix, fuse, meld, mingle
Blender setting: puree
Blender, used a: pureed
Blending: fusions

Blessed event: sneeze
Blessing, timely: boon
Blight, adolescent: acne
Blight on the landscape: eyesore
Blind alley: impasse, dead-end
Blindness, word: alexia
Bliss, kind of: wedded
Bliss, to Buddhist: nirvana
Blissful setting: Eden
Blissful spot: Eden
Blissful state: Nirvana
Blister: bleb
Blister, cause of a: rub
Blister or scrape: sore
Blitz: air raid, red dog
Blizzard maker: snow
Bloated: gouged, swollen
Blob: dollop
Blockbuster: movie, hit
Block head: oaf, dolt
Block legally: estop
Block of ice on a glacier: serac
Block of stamps: pane
Block surrounding: street
Blockage: logjam
Blocks, big name in: Lego
Blocks passion: impedes desire
Bloke: man, fellow, chap
Bloke, polite: gent
Bloke's streetcar: tram
Bloke's "you bet": right o
Blond, pale: ash
Blond shade: ash
"Blondie" kid: Elmo
Blood component, watery: sera, serum
Blood deficiency: anemia
Blood flow blockage: clot
Blood of the gods: ichor
Blood pigment:-heme
Blood runs cold, its: reptile
Blood bank deposit: serum, sera, platelets,
     plasma
Bloodletting creature: leech
Bloody Mary ingredient: vodka
Bloom, Claire: actress
Bloomer, Amelia: feminist
Bloomer, late: aster
Blossom, shaggy: dahlia
Blossom, starts to: buds
Blot: blotch, splotch
Blot out: efface
Blotches of color: mottles
Blotter heading: AKA
Blotter spot: desk
Blotto: drunk, soused, pie-eyed
Blouse: top
Blouse, long: tunic
Blouse, loose: middy
Blouse part: yoke
Blouse trim: lace
Blouse with sailor collar: middy
Blouse-like garment: tunic
Blow away: awe
Blow hard: gust

Blow off steam: vent
Blow one's own horn: brag
Blow ones stack: erupt
Blowgun projectile: dart
Blowouts, big: bashes
Blows away: erodes, awes
Blows gently: wafts
Blowtorch pro: welder
Blowtorch, use a: weld, heat, thaw
Blow up: enlarge
"BLT" base: toast, tomato, lettuce, bacon
Blubber: sob, fat
Blue Anais Mountains
"Am I Blue?"
Blue chip initials: IBM, ATT
Blue chip, noted: IBM
"Blue Dahlia" star: LaddBlue, deep: indigoes,
    endigoes
Blue dye: anil , woad
Blue flower: speedwell
Blue Grotto island: Capri
Blue Grotto isle site: Capri
Blue Hen State: Delaware
Blue hues: azures, aquas, ajans, teals
Blue moons, like: rare, rarity
Blue pencil: edit, cut, trim, emend
Blue pencil mark: caret
Blue penciler: editor
Blue pigment: bice
Blue print: cyanotype
Blue sight from space: Earth
"Blue Tail Fly" singer: Ives
Blue toon character: smurf
Blue, Vida: baseball
Blue whale kin: sei
Bluebonnet state: Texas
Blue-fin of the sea: tuna
Bluegrass instrument: autoharp
Bluejackets, fellow: shipmates
Bluenose: prig, prude, square
Blue-pencil: edit, cut, trim, emend
Blue-pencil mark: caret
Blue-penciled: edited
Blue-ribbon beer: Pabst
Blues, mild case of the: blahs
Blues or Bruins: Six (NHL teams)
Blues or folk groups: jug bands
Blues Street: Beale
Bluish green: aqua
Bluish white element: zinc
Blunder, social: faux pas
Blunders: goofs
Blunt blade: epee
Blunt manner, in a: starkly
Blurbs: ads
Blushrelative: rouge
Blustery: raw
Blyth or Miller: Ann
Blyton, Enid: writer
BMT's cousin: IRT
Boadicea was their queen: Iceni
Board game: pachisi
Ouija board
Board sticker: dart

Board, thick: plank
Board with a thumb hole: palette
Boarded up: shut, nailed
Boarding house guest: lodger
Boarding points: bus stops
Boarding school: prep
Boast: crow
Boast about: brags, vaunts
Boast, start a famous: veni
Boat: prau, proa
Boat, clumsy: ark
Boat crane: devit
Boat, fishing: dogger
Boat, flat: scow
Boat, flat bottom: dory
Boat front: bow, prow
Boat, garbage: scow
Boat hoist: davit
Boat in "Jaws": Orca
Boat, light: wherry
Boat, Malayan: proa, prahu
"Boat, missed the": lost out
Boat, narrow: dory
Boat, old: tub
Boat planking: strake
Boat, pleasure: sloop
Boat, portable: canoe
Boat, racing: scull
Boat repair place: dry dock
Boat runway: ramp
Boat, secure a: moor
Boat trailer: wake
Boat with a message: aviso
Boater: hat
"Boating" painter: Manet, Edourard
Boating pronoun: her
Boats for felines: catamarans
Boats, Malay: proas, praus, prahus
Boatswain's signal: pipe
Bob: nod
Bob Cratchit's job: clerk
Bob Hope forte: adlibbing
Bobbsey twin: Nan, Bert
"Bobby sox"
Bob's road buddy: Bing
Bobwhites: quails
Boca Raton, Florida
Bocho Series: L.A. Law
Bodes: augurs
Bodily disorder or disease: ailment
Bodoni bold: typeface
Body: soma
Body behind the front: air mass
Body builder: genes
Body builder's mantra: no pain no gain
Body cleaning spot: car wash, spa
Body: comb. Form: somat, somato
Body of mystical teaching: cabala
Body relative: anatomic
Body trunk: torso
Body, upper: torso
Bog: fen, marsh, morass, muskeg
Bog dirt: peat
Bog down:

Bog down: impede
Bog fuel: peat
Bogart, Bacall: actress
Bogging down: miring
Boggling painting: op art
Boggy lowland: fen
Boggy wasteland: moor
Bogs down: mires
Bogus butter: oleo
Bogus, not: real
Bohemian: arty
Bohemian dance: polka
Bohemian, more: artier
Bohemian, most: artiest
Bohr's study: atom
Boil, almost: scald
Boil, bring to a: heat
Boil slowly: stew
Boitana, Brian: skater
Bojangles, emulates: taps
Bold and self-assured: assertive
Bold enough, is: dares
Bold look: leer
Boldly attempt: dare
Boldly resisting: defiant
Boldness in battle: valor
Bolero composer: ravel
Bolívar, Senor Símon
Bolivian export: tin
Boll weevil
Bologna Boniface: Oste
Bologna eight: otto
Bolshevik leader: Lenin
Bolshevism founder: Lenin
Bolt holder: nut
Bolt together: elope
Bomb shelter: abri
Bombay attire: sari
Bombay Mr.: Sri
Bombay weight: ser
Bombeck, Erma: writer
Bon Jovi, Jon: rocker
"Bon mot": clever remark, witty remark
Bon opposite: mel
Bon voyage party: send-off
Bona fide: true
Bonanza state: Montana
Bonbon center: fondant
Bond buyer's concern: yield
Bond investor's concern: yield
Bond passed him in 2007: Aaron
Bond rating: AAA
Bondage, symbol of: yokes
Bondi, Beulah: actress
Bonding material: glue, mortar
Bondman: vassal
Bondsman: slave
Bone, bred in the
Bone comb. form: oste
Bone dry: arid, sere
Bone, heal a: mend
Bone in a cage: rib
Bone, little: ossicle
Bone marrow: medulla

Bone of contention: issue
Bone, organic basis of: ossein (protein in bone)
Bone tissue: marrow
Bone-china name: Spode
Bones, curved: ribs
Bones of contention: issues
Bonet, Lisa: actress
Bonet role: Denise
Bonfire residue: ash, cinders
Bonheur, Rosa: artist
Bonita, la isla
Bonjour, mes amis
Bonn connector: und
Bonn refusal: nein
Bonn title: herr
Bonnie Raitt: singer
Bonny miss: lass
Bonus: extra
Bony fish, large: mola
Boobock, baby: owlet
Booby hatch: can, jug
Booed: jeered
Booed and hissed
Book abstracts: précisBook after Philemon: Hebrew
Book binder's tool: awl,
Book binding device: trindle
Book binding leather: roans
Book, by the: legal
Book category: genre
Book checks: audits
Book, fact: almanac
Book genre: how to
Book jacket ad: blurb
Book jacket feature: bio
Book jacket parts: flaps
Book holder: rack
Book ID: ISBN
Book illustration: plate
Book, large heavy: tome
Book lover: bibliophine
Book of Norse myth: Edda
Book of records: liber
Book of words: thesaurus
Book page: folio
Book, part of: page, leaf
Book reference: atlas
Book reviewer, for short: CPA
Book sheath: forel
Book size: quarto
Book, world: atlas
Bookbinder's need: glue
Bookbinding leather: roan
Bookbinding material: vellum
Bookie's list: morning list
Bookie's numbers: odds
Bookish type: nerd
Books expert: CPA
Books, hit the: study, read
"Books, one for the"
Books with meat: tomes
Bookworm, high school: nerd
Boole: mathematician

Boomboxplatters: CDs
Boombox sound: stereo, blare
Boomerang thrower: Aborigine
Boon: blessing
Boone, Daniel: pioneer
Boonies: sticks
Boor: yahoo, oaf, cad
Boorish person: churi
Boosley, Elaine: comic
Boost the price: marks up
Boot camp attendee: recruit, enlistee
Boot, felt: pac
Boot jingler: spur
Boot liner: felt, pac
Boot uppers: vamps
Booted: shod
Bootlegger, Bugsy the: Moran
Bootlick: fawn
Bootnose of hockey: Abel
"Das Boot"
Boots, high: wader,
Boot-sole protector: hobnail
Booty: loot, swag
Booty, seek: maraud
Booze, butts, and bullets org.: ATF
Boozehound: sot,
Bop on the head: conk
"Teeny bopper"
Bordeaux bunch: grapes
Bordeaux wine: claret
Borden's weapon: axe
Border: line
Border, adjustable: hem
Border, heraldic: orle
Border patrol org.: INS
Border station: checkpoint
Bordered on: verged
Border's on: abuts
Bore out: proved
"Aurora borealis"
Borealis and australis: auroras
Boreas' beloved: Orithyia
    brother: Notus, Hesperus, Zephyrus
    father: Astraeus
    mother: Eos
    son: Zetes, Calais
Bored: jaded
Bored response: yawn
Boredom: ennui
Boredom, express: sigh
Boredom, sign of: yawn
Borges, Jorge Luis
Borgnine, Ernest: actor
Boring: tiresome, pall, dry, ho hum
Boring and dull: blah
Boring, become: pall
Boring, get: pall
Boring performance: snoozer
Boring place: rut
Boring tool: augur
Boring (heavy) tool: trepan
Boris refusal: nyet
Boris turndown: nyet
Born: nee

Born earlier: eldist, older
Born there: native
Born yesterday: naïve
Borneo ape: orang
Borneo island: java
Borneo swinger: orang
Borneo's archipelago: Malay
Borodin opera: Prince Igor
Borodin prince: Igor
Borrow, let: lent
Borrow permanently: mooch
Borrower carries it: debt
Borrower's limit: credit line
Borscht base: beet
Borscht belt bits: schticks
"Borstal Boy" author: Behan
Bose: pear
Boss: employer
Boss, horrible: ogre
Boss, slangily: cheese, big cheese
Bossa Nova cousin: Samba
Bossy's milieu: lea, meadow
Bossy's offspring: calf
Boston Harbor jetsam: tea
Boston NHLer: Bruin
Boston-to-DC region: northeast
Botanical garden display: flora
Botanical outcast: weed
Both hands: bi-manual
Bother, big: hassle
Bother continually: harass
Botherations: fusses
Bothersome person: twit
Bottle rocket path: arc
Bottle top: neck
Bottled drink: soda pop
Bottled spirits: genies
Bottles, water: carafes
Bottom edges: hems
Bottom feeder: carp
Bottom, hit: spank
Bottom line: sum, net, hem, seam
Bottom of the barrel: dregs
Bottom-of-the-barrel action: scrape
Bottomless gulf: abyss
Bottomless depth: abyss
Botts dots, space between: lane
Boucle or crewel: yarn
Bough: limb
Bought and sold: dealt, traded
Bought, just: unused, new
Boulevard liner: elms, trees
Bounce, infield: hop
Bouncer, emulate a: eject
Bound back: echo
Bound, further: limit
Boundary line: edge
Bounded: leapt
Bounden: obligated
Bounder: cad, rat
Bounding gait: gallop
Bounding main: ocean, sea, at sea, on the ocean
Bounty captain: Bligh, William

Bouquet: odor
Bouquet, small: nosegay
Bourbon street vegetable: okra
Bourgeoisie tax: third estate
Boutros' successor: Kofi
Bovary, Emma
Bovary title: Madame
Bovine baby: calf
Bovine, beefy: steer
Bovine bunch: herd
Bovine mouthful: cud
Bovine name: Elsie
Bovine treat: salt lick
Bow and scrape: fawn
Bow application: rosin
Bow Bells native: cockney
Bow, Clara
Bow, Karla: actress
Bow, made a deep: salaamed
Bow opposite: stern
Bow, respectful: salaam
Bow treatment: rosin
Bowdoin College locale: Maine
Bowed line: arc
Bowie's last stand: Alamo
Bowl: arena, stadium
Bowl for maple sap: rogan
Bowl or ship: vessel
Bowl, soup serving: tureen
Bowler: hat, felt hat
Bowler's and pitcher's goals: strikes
Bowling alley name: AMF
Bowling feature: brim
Bowling group: league
Bowling lane button: reset
Bowling piece: nine pin, pin
Bowling or penny: lane
Bowling site: lane, alley
Bowling targets: pins, ten pin
Bowl-shaped strainer: colander
Bowman, Isaiah: geographer
Bowman's wood: yew
Bows and scrapes: kowtows
Bowser's brand: alpo
Bowser's pal: fido
Box: encase
Box component: seat
Box, expensive: loge
Box for bucks: till
"Idiot box"
Box top piece: tab
Box up: encase
Boxcars game implement: dice
Boxcars, in dice: sixes
Boxer: pugilist
Boxer Laila: Ali,
Boxer, maybe: pet
Boxers:
    Ali, Muhammad
    Dempsey, Jack
    Foreman, George
    Frazier, Joe
    Guerrero, Pedro
    Hearns, Thomas

    Holmes, Larry
    Holyfield, Evander
    Hoya, Oscar Dela
    LaMotta, Jake
    Leonard, Sugar Ray
    Louis, Joe
    Marciano, Rocky
    Moore, Archie
    Spinks, Leon
    Tunney, Gene
    Tyson, Mike
Boxer's knockout punch: kayo
Boxer's move: jab
Boxer's quest: title
Boxing weapon: fist
Boxing win: TKO, kayo
Boxy vehicle: van
"Atta boy"
Boy king: Tut
Boyfriend: beau
Boys in the hood: bros
Boys, small: tads
Boys Town site: Omaha
Bracelet, kind of: armlet
Bracelets, some: IDs
Bracket type: ell
Brackish: salty
Brackish liquid: brine
Bradbury, Ray: sci-fi writer
Bradley, Ed: TVname
Bradley, Omar: general
Brady's Bill opposer: NRA
Braga, Sosia: actress
Braid, narrow: cornrow
Braids: plait, ravel
Brain bit: lobe
Brain covering: dura
Brain flash: idea
Brain membrane: pial
Brain messenger: nerve
Brain test: EEG
Brain wave: idea
Brain wave rec.: EEG
Brainiac: egghead, pundit, highbrow
Brainstorm: idea
Brainstorming goal: idea
Brainy gang: Mensa
Brainy society: Mensa
Brainy thoughts: ideas
Brake, kind of: disc
Brake element: brake shoe
Brake pad: shoe
Brake, tap the: slow
Bramble: shrub, brier, bush
Branch off-shoot: twig
Branch headquarters: nest
Branch of deer family: antler
Branch of learning: ology
Branch of mechanics: statics
Branch out, they: limbs
Branches: boughs
Branches of knowledge: fields
Branchlike parts: rami
Brand for browser: alpo

Brand name: label
Brandish ones biceps: flex
Brandy: eau-de-vie, eaux-de-vie
Brandy, fine: cognac
Brandy, good: cognac
Brandy, like good: aged
Brandy of Nashville: Moe
Brandy-based drink: stinger
Brash songster: Ray
Brass Component: Zinc
Brass, low: tuba
Brass tacks: realities
The brass, for short: mgmt
Brat: demon
Brat's christmas present: coal
Brat's opposite: angel
Bratty, is: acts up
Brauhaus tune: polka
Braunschweiger, e.g.: Liverwurst
Brave manner, in a: boldly
Bravery: valor
Braves greeting, in Oaters: how
Bravo: ole
Rio Bravo
Braxton, Toni: singer
Bray, start of a: hee
Brayer, used a: inked
Brazen: immodest
Brazen, more: nervier
Brazil state: Bahia
Brazilian dance: samba
Brazilian macaw: arara
Brazilian plain: campo
Brazilian resort: Olanda
Brazilian state: acre, para
Brazilian soccer great: Pele
Brazilian woman, married: senhora
Brazilian woman's title: senhora
Brazil's emperor's name: Pedro
Bread: moola
Bread, egg-rich: challah
Bread, Middle Eastern: pita
Bread need: yeast
Bread, reuben: rye
Bread, Southern: pone
Bread, twice baked: rusk
Bread with tabooed: pita
Break a leg: good luck
Break a promise: renege
Break away: secede
Break bread: ate, eat
Break down: weep
Break free: escape
Break in continuity: saltus,
Break in the action: lull, hiatus
Break into: snap
Break of commandment: covet
Break one's silence: speak
Break out: erupt
Break protector: cast
Break, short: breather
Break the record of: top
Break the rules: cheat, flout
Break time, maybe: ten

Break up: rend, disband
Breakaway group: sect
Break-dance music: rap
Break down: weep, sob
Break-even amount: cost
Breakfast fare: cereal, toast
Breakfast nook: dinette
Breakfast order: hotcakes, pan cakes
Breakfast roll: bagel
Breastplate: armor
Breastplate, Athena's: egis
Breath cessation: apnea
Breath, convulsive: gasp
Breath, deep: sigh
Breath freshner: mint
Breath, out of: winded
Breathalyzer test flunker: sot, drunk
Breathe hard: gasp, puff, pant, heave
Breather: lung, lull
Breathing device: scuba
Breathing, pause: caesura
Breathing room: leeway
Breathing, smooth: lene
Breathing tube: snorkel
Breathless: awed
Breckenridge, Myra:
Breeze, gentle: zephyr
Breeze, make a: fan
Breezed through: aced
Breeze's big brother: gust
Breezy greeting: ciao
Breezy send off: tata
Brest beam: rai
Breton, for one: Celt
Brew tea: steep
Brew, weak: near beer
Brewer, Teresa: pop music
Brewer's grain: malt
Brewer's oven: oast
Brewer's plant: hop
Brewery fixture: oast
Brian Boru's land: Eire
Brian Song star: Caan
Briars: thorns
Bribe to a disc jockey: payola
Bribe: sop
Bribe, small: sop
Bribery, open to: venal
Brick carrier: hod
Brick holder: hod
Brick, mud: adobe
Brick, unfired: samel, adobe
Brick worker: mason
Brickell, Edie: pop music
Bricks, arrange: lay
Bricks, harden: fire
Bridal chest: trousseau
Bridal notice word: nee
Bridal veil material: tulle
Bridal wreath shrub: spirea
Bridalveil Falls park: Yosemite
Bridegroom: man
Bride's portion: dowry
Bride's walk: aisle

Bridesmaid opposite: usher, groom
Bridesmaids, many a: sisters
Bridge between electrodes: arc
Bridge bidder, perhaps: north
Bridge builder: engr
Bridge card, highest ranking: Ace
Bridge champion: Oswald, Jacoby
Bridge contract, defeats a: sets
Bridge coup: slam
Bridge defeat: set
Bridge guarder, memorable: troll
'Bridge on the River Kwai"
Bridge phrase: I Pass
Bridge position: north, south, east, west
Bridge quorum: four
Bridge seat: north, south, east, west
Bridge strategy: finesse
Bridge support: pier
Bridge system: goren
Bridge tactic: preemptive bid
Bridge towers: pylons
Bridge-like card game: skat
Bridges, Beau: actor
Bridges, Lloyd: actor
Bridle, biteless: hackamore
Bridle part: rein, bit, blinder
Brie coating: rind
Brief altercation: set to
Brief but vigorous fight: set to
Brief communication: note
Brief last writes: obits
Brief moment: split second
Brief moment of time: trice
Brief promotional prose: blurb
Brief remainder: memo
Brief romance: affair
Brief stay: stop over
Briefcase closer: hasp
Briefer: terser
Bright and early
Bright beam: laser
Bright object: star
Bright ring: halo
Bright star: sun, Vega
Bright star of Lyra: Vega
Bright stars: novae
Bright, too: glare, gaudy
Bright, unusually: apt
Bright, very: glittery, apt
Bright-eyed and bushy-tailed: alert
Brightness measure: IQ test
Brighton buggy: pram
Brigitte's brainstorm: idee
Brigitte's friend: amie
Brilliant achievement: eclat
Brilliant stroke: coup
Brillo rival: SOS
Brimming over: full
Bring about: win, beget, cause, create, draw in
Bring around: hook, sway, turn, convert, win over
Bring back: renew, recall, recoup, return
Bring bad luck: jinxs
Bring charges: arraign

Bring dishonor upon: shame
Bring down: bag, hew, drop, fell, raze, floor, level, shoot
Bring forth: elicit, bear, beget, yield, create, invent
Bring forward: adduce, submit, tender, unveil, advance
Bring home: earn
Bring in: pay, net, win, draw, earn, fetch
Bring in, as earnings: makes
Bring in the sheaves: reap, harvest
Bring into accord: attune
Bring into agreement: align
Bring into court: arraign
Bring into existence: create
Bring into harmony: attune
Bring off: effect, finish, rescue, execute, realize
Bring on oneself: incur
Bring out: cull, elicit, educe, utter
Bring pressure to bear: arm-twist
Bring to a near boil: scald
Bring to bay: tree
Bring to bear: exert, use
Bring to light: detect, find, trace
Bring to maturity: rear
Bring to mind: recall, evoke
Bring to pass: cause, do
Bring to ruin: undo
Bring together: mix, unite, herd, join, link, yoke, amass, integrate
Bring together: muster, unite
Bring together again: reunite
Bring under control: harness, tame
Bring up: moot, rear, raise, broach, teach, train
Brings tears to your eyes: onions
Brinkley, Christie: model
Brinks, chronological: eves
Briny: saline
Brisbane native: Aussie
Briseis' lover: Achilles
Bristle, stiff: seta
Bristle-like parts: aristas
Bristles, of: setal
Bristles with: teems
Bristly organ: setae, seta
Brit, early: Celt
Britain's Churchill Downs: ascot
British alphabet ender: zed
British apartment: flat
British baby carriage: pram
British blackjack: cosh,
British bomber grp.: RAF
British bye: tata
British café: tea room
British car, expensive: jag, rolls
British chap: bloke
British colony (near Spain): Gibraltar, Gib
British colony: shire
British cry: I see, I say
British elevator: lift
British FBI: CID
British flick: kinema, kineme
British football: rugby

British gallery: tate
British garden: kew
British golly: i say
British hero: Nelson
British hoodlum: yob
British import from Chile: nitre
British lexicon, noted: OED
British lampoon: satirize, satirise
British lunchroom: tea shop
British machine gun: Sten
British medical journal: Lancet
British Museum's Elgin Marbles
British nanny: au pair
British navigational aid: Decca
British Navy: HMS
British nobleman: baronet, baron, vis
British pantry: spence
British philosopher: Russell
British phrase: I say
British physicist: Paul Dirac
British poet: Byron
British political party: Tory
British pop: pater, paterfamilias
British potato chip: crisps
British prep school: Eton
British racer: Jackie Stewart
British record co.: EMI
British ref. work: OED
British rule in India: Maj, Raj
British sailor: limey, tar
British sand hill: dene
British school: Eton
British "sees eye to eye":grees
British smell: odour
British supper dish: hotpot
British tar: limey
British tavern: pub
British tenant farmer: crofter
British time: GMT, GST
British truck: lorres
British trunk: boot
British water closet: loo
British weight: stone
Briton, ancient: Celt
Brits, early: Saxon
Brit's phrase: I say
Britt, Mai: actress
Brittany port: Brest
Brittle material: glass
Broad at Heathrow: emplane, enplane
Broad-footed: platypod
Broad street: Avenue
Broadband connection type: DSL
Broadcast while happening: live
Broad-chested: husky
Broad-mouthed container: jar
Broad-topped ridge: loma
Broadwalk extension: pier
Broadway award: Tony
Broadway backer: angel
Broadway opening: debut, act one
Broadway score: seat
Broadway's "Miss Saigon"
Brobdingnagian: huge, giant, jumbo, hulking,

immense, mammoth, massive
Broccoli bit: floret
Brock, Lou: baseball
"Brockovich, Erin"
Broderick, Matthew: actor
Brogan or buskin: shoe
"London broil"
Broke a contract: reneged
Broke bread: ate
Broke off: ended
Broke out: escaped
Broken: asunder
Broken in: tame,
Broken, not: working, useable, intact
Broken bone stabilizer: splint, cast
Broker business: realty, stocks
Broker's group: NASD
Bronco QB: Elway
Bronson, Chas.: actor
Bronte, Charlotte: writer
Bronte, Emily: writer
Bronte's governess: Eyre
Bronte sister: Emily, Anne
Bronte star: Emily
Bronx cheer: boo, hoot, jeer, razz, taunt,
     catcall, raspberry
Bronze coating: patina
Bronze component: tin
Bronze, metal in: tin
Bronze, to Brutus: aes
Brood, they are inclined to: hens
Brooding bunch: hens
Brooding place: nest
Broods over: frets
Brook, small: rill
Brook sound: babble, gurgle
Brooklyn end: ese
Brooklyn, a Tree grows in
Brooks, Mel: director
Broom companion: mop
Broom, Hilda: comic witch
Broom of twigs: besom
Broom rider: hag, witch
Brosnan's role: Bond
Brother: friar, monk, fra
Brother at: arms: ally
Brother or ladder, kind of: step
Brotherhood since 1869: Elks
"I am my brother's keeper"
Brought about: did
Brought forth: educed
Brought in the wind: tacked
Brought to court: arraigned
Brouhaha: fuss, ado, melee, row
Broun, Heywood: journalist
Brown: mocha
Brown and simmer: braise
Brown and white porgy: scup
Brown bagger?: wino
Brown coal: lignite
Brown, dark: sepia
Brown, light: ecru
Brown, dull: drab
Brown ermine: stoat

Brown, Helen Curly
Brown Kiwi: Roa
Brown, Leroy: musician
Brown paper, strong: kraft
Brown pigment: sienna, umber
Brown, reddish: auburn
Brown, Rita Mae: novelist
Brownest: tannest
Brownie: elf
Brownie nuts: walnut
Brownish gray: taupe, dun
Brownish orange: tawny
Brownish purple: puce
Brownish shade: sepia, rust
Browns, as mushrooms: sautés
Browse: netsurf
Browse, these days: netsurf
Browser site: mall, net, Web
Browser's delight: mall
Browser's ID: dog tag, Email address
Brubeck, Dave: jazz
Bruce Lee's art: kung fu
Bruce's ex: Demi
Bruckner, Anton: composer
Bruin's bases: lairs
Bruit: noise, din, rumor
Bruited: noised
Brunch favorite: quiche
Brunched: ate
Brunei head of state: sultan
Brush off: whisk
Brush, wields a: paints
Brush wolf: coyote
Brushed a dog: groomed
Brusque: tart, curt
Brussel-based org.: NATO
Brut: sec
Brute, et tu
Brute strength: muscle
Brutus's belly: alvus
Brutus spoke it: Latin
Bryant, Anita: music
Bryce Canyon state: Utah
BTU kin: cal., calorie
Bubble, almost: simmer
Bubble up: foam
"Bubble wrap"
Bubbly, make: aerate
Bucephalus: steed
Buck back: aroo
Buck heroine: Olan
Buck of the woods: stag
Buck or stink ending: aroo
Buck passer: ATM
Bucket handle: bail
Bucket of bolts: crate
Bucket of song: oaken
Bucket of suds: brew
Buckets, like some old: oaken
Buckle, as lumber: warp
Bucks: male, ones, males, moola, smackers
Bucktoothed dummy: snerd
Buckwheatgroats: kasha
Bucolic: rural

Buddhist, bliss to: nirvana
Buddhist in nirvana: arhat
Buddhist practice: Zen
Buddhist scripture: sutra
Buddhist shrine: stupa
Buddhist spirit: Mara
Buddhist who has attained nirvana: arhat
Buddhism, type of: Zen
Buddy: compadre, pal, chum
Buddy, kind of: bosom
Buenos Aires
Bueno's opposite: malo
Buffalo, forest: anoa
Buffalo grass: grama
Buffalo hockey pro: Sabre
Buffalo Pea: Plum,
Buffalo, small: anoa
Buffalo wings: fingerfood
Buffaloes: snows
Buffet, hit the: eat
Bug: wiretap
Bug repellant: deet
Bugged out: left
Buggy terrain: dunes
Bugle, yellow: iva
Bug's beverage: spider cider
Bugs bunny voice: Blanc
Bugs the bootlegger: Moran
Build an appetite: whet
Build, as a monument: erect
Build assets: save, accrue
Build castles in the air: dreams
Build onto: add
Builder's choice: site
Builder's knot: clove hitch
Building: edifice
Building certificate: permit
Building expansion: ell
Building lot: site
Building material: adobe
Building, round: yurt, silo
Building, subsidiary: annex
Building unit: lot
Builds on: adds
Buildup, big: hoopla
Built up, not: rural
Bulb gas: argon
Bulbs, pungent: onions
Bulfinch specialty: myth
Bulgaria's capital: Sofia
Bulgarian coin: leva,
Bulged the eyes: goggled
Bulges out: swells
Bulk: heft
Bull dog cousin: pug
Bull dog backer: Eli
Bull fighter: torero, matador, picador
Bull fighting red cloth: muleta
Bull run victors: rebs
Bull, sign of: Taurus
Bull to Bear, Went from: Fell
Bulletproof Screen: Mantlet, Mantelet
Bullets: Ammo
Bullet-size: Caliber

Bullet-train, East Coast: Acela
Bullfight, of Barcelona: corrida
Bullfighter: torero
Bullishly, behave: buy
Bullock, Sandra: actress
Bulls (like some): papal
Bulls noise: snort
Bully: hector, meany, meanie, braggart,
      heckler
Bulrush: sedge
Bulrush, large: tule
Bum around: roam
Bumble: err, error
Bumble Bee offering: tuna
Bumbler: oaf
Bumbling: inept
Bummed out: sad
Bump along: jounce
Bump hard: jar
Bump on the back of the heel: akropodion
Bump or knot: node
Bump, ski slope: mogul
Bumpkin: hick, oaf
Bumpy, hardly: even
Bunauel, Luis: actor, director
Bunch of flowers: nosegay, nose joy
Bunched closely: huddled
Bunches and bunches: a lot
Bundle, grain: sheave, sheaf
Bundle of straw: sheaf
Bundle maker: baler
Bungalow: casita
Bunk or futon: bed
Bunker: trap, sand trap
Bunker tool: rake
Bunko squad concern: fraud
Bunsen burner locale: lab
Buntline, Ned: writer
Bunyan's blue ox: Babe
Buoyed up: elated
Burbank, Luther: horticulturist
Burden, heavy: onus, load
Burden of proof: onus
Burdened: laden
Burdens: onuses
Burdensome: taxing
Bureau: agency
Bureaucrat, subordinate: satrap
Bureaucrat's delight: red tape
Burg, icy: Nome
Burger go-with: Coke, cola, onion
Burger mate: cola
Burger side: slaw, fries
Burglar's key: loid
Burglar's take: loot, haul
Burglar's tool: jimmy
Burgle: rob
Burgoo and pepper pot: stew
Burgundy buddies: Amis, Amish
Burial place: charnel
Burke, Delta: actress
Burkina Faso neighbor: Ghana
Burlap fiber: jute
Burmese girl: mima

Burmese native: Mon
Burmese religion: Buddhism
Burn plastic: spend
Burn, purposely: sear
Burn slower: gloib
Burn soother: aloe
Burn to cinders: char
Burned and looted: rioted
Burned up the highway: sped, tore
Burner, type of: bunson, etna
Burner for aromatic sticks: censer
Oat burner
Oat burner: horse
Burning desire results: arson
Burning, not: unlit
Burning pile: pyre
Burning the midnight oil: work late
Burnoose wearer: arab
Burnout cause: stress
Burns, Robert: poet
Burns the surface of: sears
Burnt out: jaded
Burnt up: irate, angry
Burrito base: tortilla
Burrito covering, perhaps: salsa
Burrito kin: tamale
Burrough, Edgar Rice
Burrow, Abe: writer
Burrow, rabbit's: warren
Burrowing animal: mole, vole
Burrowing beast: wombat
Burrowing rodent: agoutis
Burst forth: erupt, irrupt
Burst inward: irrupt, implode
Burst of applause
Burst of laughter: peal
Burstyn, Ellen
Burton, Tim: director
Bus route: line
Bus, small: jitney
Buscaglia , Leo: writer
Busch, Mae: old movies star
Buses: Coaches
Bush and Taft, once: Elis
Bushel unit: peck
Bushmiller, Ernie: cartoonist
Bushwhack: trap, ambush, assail, attack
Business class: typing
Business day start: open
Business, do: deal
Business, doing: open
Business enclosure: SASE
Business magazine: Inc.
Business mailing: direct marketing
Business man, powerful: baron
Business man's bonus: perk
Business now, in: open
Business of folding: origami
Business salutation: sir
Business suffix: ltd, inc.
Business suit accessory: tie tack
Buskin or brogan: shoe
Buster Brown's dog: Tige
Busy place: zoo

Butcher's leavings: offal
Butler, Artie: composer
Butler, called the: rang
Butler, fictional: Rhett,
Butler's woman: O'Hara
Butte kin: mesa
Butter, bogus: oleo
Ersatz butter
Butter, ersatz: oleo
Butter, Indian: ghee
Butter, kind of: cocoa
Butter, made with: rich
Butter rating: grade A
Butter up: woo
Butterbean: lima
Buttercup genus member: anemone
Butterfingered: clumsy
Butterfly, move like a: flit
Butterworth or Wiggs: Mrs.
Buttinskies, barbecue: ants
Button alternative: cuff link, zipper, snap
Button blades: epees
Button, kind of: panic
Button, replace a: sew
Buttonhole: waylay, accost
Buy by mail: order
Buy gas: tank up, fill up
Buy stuff: shop
Buyer's caution: as is
Buyer's concern: as is, price
Buys, so to speak: falls for
Buzz: hum
Buzzed: whirred
Buzzing about: astir
Buzz's capsule-mate: Neil
Bwana helper: bearer
Bwana, in India: sahib
Bwana trip: safari
By and by: anon
By and large: all told, broadly, en masse,
 mainly
By dint of hard work
By fits and starts
By heart: rote
By itself: apart
By jove: egad, I say
By oneself:
By oneself: alone
By the book: legal
Bygone: olden
Bygone despot: tsar
Bygone player: hi-fi
Bygone rulers: shahs
"Let bygones be bygones": forgive
Byrnes, Edd: actor
BYU locale:-Utah, Hawaii
Byway: lane
Byzantine object of worship: ikon, icon

C

"C", to Einstein: speed of light
C-worthy?: fair

Caan, James: actor
Cab, grab a: hail
Cabal group:cell
Caballeros roam, where the: llanos
Cabbage concoction: slaw
Cabbage, curly: kale
Cabbage, fermented: kraut
Cabbage salad: slaw
Cabbage seed: colza
Cabbage tree: palm
Cabell, Enos: baseball
Cabin boy: sailor
Cabinet Dept. since 1977: Energy
Cable add-on: HBO
Cable car: telpher
Cable channel: ESPN, USA
Caboodle partner: kit
Cabot, Sebastian: explorer
Cached: hid
Cacophony: din, noise
Cacti, spineless: mescals
Cactus defense: spine
Cactus drink: tequila
Cactus, type of: cholla
Cad: roue
Caddies, many include: tea sets
Caddoan Indian: Pawnee
Cadence, rhythmic: lilt
Cadge: beg, bum
Cadmus' daughter: Ino, Agave, Semele,
 Autonoe
  father: Agenor
  sister: Europa
  victim: dragon
  wife:Harmonia
Cads, Camagiiey: Cuban heels
Cad's rebuke: slap
Caduceus org.: AMA
Caesar or nicoise: salad
Caesar or Waldorf: salad
Caesarian trio, start of: veni
Caesar's accusatory words: et tu
Caesar's bad day: Ides
  behold: esse
  being: esse
  boast, part of: I saw
  book: scroll
  concern: curae
  conquest: Gaul
  day: diem
  farewell: vale
  garb: toga
  ground: terra
  hyway.: Iter
  hail: ave
  "I am": sum
  land: terra
  law: lex
  "now": nunc
  partner: Coca
  penultimate words: et tu
  project: forum
  pronouncement: 'I came"
  "this": hoc, soc

 trio, one of: vidi
 troops: legion
 "X": ten
 year: annum
 worst day: Ide
Caeser, Louise: actress
Café: bistro
Café attraction: aroma
Café au lait
Café con leche: coffee with milk
Café cup: tasse
Café feature, maybe: awning
Café, word with: noir
Cage, Nicholas: actor
Cager's coup: jump shot
Cager's goal: hoop
Cagers, some: guards
Caine or Law role: Alfie
Cain's ma: Eve
Cain's parents: Adam and Eve
Caisson laborer: sandhog
Cajun county: parish
Cajun veggie: okra
Cake, custard-filled: gateau
Cake pan type: bundt
Cake, raisin: baba
Cake, rich: torte
Cake, ring-shaped: bundt
Cake type: bundt
Caked-on dirt: crud
Cake-like cookie: bar
Calabrian town: Acri (Ancient Italy)
Calamitous: tragic
Calcareous colonizers: coral
Calculate: add
Calculated risk: gambit
Calculating: shrewd
Calculations, preliminary: estimates
Calculator, early: abacus, abaci
Calculator key: clear
Calcutta attire: sari,
Calderon, Erma: author
Caldwell, Erskine: writer
Caledonia, ancient: Scotland
Calendar or chant: Gregorian
Calendar box: day
Calendar square: day
Calf-length pants: capris
Calf-roping event: rodeo
Calf's place: leg
Calhoun, Rory: actor
Calico's comment: meow
Calico printing: teer
Baja California
California border lake: Tahoe
California county: Alameda
California flag symbol: bear
California mountain range: Sierra Nevada
California redwood: sequoia,
California theme park: Marine World
Cal Tech rival: MIT
California wine region: Sonoma
California-Nevada lake: Tahoe
California's Fort Ord

California's Los <u>Gatos</u>
California's motto: eureka
California's <u>Muir</u> Woods
Caligula's nephew: Nero
Caliph, Arabian: Hasan
Call for: need. Require, entail
Call forth: evoke
Call it a night: retire
Call list: phone bill
Call out: cry
Call to a bellhop: front
Call together: muster
Cala lily plant name: arum
Callas, Maria: opera
Called (archaic): yelept
Called off: cancel
Called the butler: rang
Called to arms, once: alarum
Called up: evoked, phoned, paged
Calligraphy medium: ink
Calligraphy aid: fountain pen
Calligraphy's fine points: nibs
Calling company: Avon
Calliope's sister: Erato
Calloway, Cal: band leader
Calls for: involves, requires
Calls to mind: evokes
Calm: lull
Calm, kind of: unease
Calmly: coolly
Calms: sedates, lulls
Calories, high in: fat
Calories, loaded with: rich
Calories, 252: FTU
Calpurnia's attire: stola
Calypso beloved: Ulysses, Odysseus
      Island: Ogygia
Calyx part: sepal
Camaguey cads: Cuban heels
Cambodia exile: Lon Nol
Cambodia money: riels
Cambodia's Lon <u>Nol</u>
Cambrian, for one: era
Cambridge academics: Dons
Cambridge rival: Oxford
Cambridge student nickname: can tab
Cambridge University: MIT
Came across as: seemed
Came closer: neared
Came down with: had
Came forth: emerged
Came later: ensued
Came out even: tied, balanced
Came to a point: narrowed, tapered
Came to terms: agreed
Came unraveled: frayed
"<u>Then</u> Came You"
Camel cousin: llama
Camelot character: Enid
Camelot denizen: Enid
Camelot lady: Enid
Camelot's magician: Merlin
Camelot's royal: King Arthur
Camels, did some: skated

Camembert cousin: brie
Cameo, maybe: role
Cameo material: onyx
Cameo stone: onyx
Camera accessory: zoom lens, flash
Camera diaphragm: iris
Camera letters: SLR (single-lens reflex)
Camera perch: tripod
Camera setting: f-stop
Camera, swing the: pan
Camera type: SLR
Cameron, Diaz: actress
Cameroon seaport: Duala
Camo wearer: hunter
Camp cook's fuel: sterno
Camp, kind of: base
Camp Lejeune truant: AWOL
Camp, make: bivouac
Camp Swampy dog: Otto
Campaign: crusade
Campaign concern: issue
Campaign event: debate
Campaign preoccupation: image
Campaign topic: issue
Campaign tactic: smear
Campbell, Joseph forte: myth
Campbell, Glen: country music
Campbell, Neve: actress
Camped out: tented
Camper, maybe: van
Campers, for short: RVs
Campfire glower: ember
Campground initials: KOA
Camping, goes: roughs it
Campo cousins: llanos
Campus area: quad
Campus figure: prof
Campus hangout: quad
Campus house: frat, dorm
Campus pad: dorm
Camus, Albert: writer
Camus colleague: Sartre
Can opener: pull tab
Canaanite god: mot, baal, molech, moloch
Canada Dry product: soda
Canada prov.: PEI
"Canadian Bacon" lead: Alda
CFL <u>Grey</u> Cup
Canadian law enforcer: RCMP
Canadian oil co.: Esso
Canadian police: Mounties
Canadian television network: CBC
Candidate (most have one): slogan
Canal city: Venice
Canal mule: Sal
Canal of song: Erie
Canal, old barge: Erie
Canal sight: barge
Canal to the Red Sea: Suez
Canapé topper: roe, paste
Canary relative: serin
Canasta play: meld
Cancel: undo
Cancel a debt: write off

Cancel, as a mission: abort
Cancel out: negate
Canceled: null, voided, ended
Cancun toast: salud
Candia: crete
"Candid <u>Camera</u>"
"Candid Camera" man: Funt
Candid, more: franker
Candid quality: openness
Candidates, chooses from the: elects
Candidates, often: debaters
Candied item: yam
Candle amount: age
Candle: taper
Candle cord: wick,
Candle holder: sconce
Candle ingredient: tallow
Candle lover: moth
Candle, make: dip
Candle (one) represents: age
Candle, small: votive
Candle wax: paraffin
Candlelight: flame
Candlepins: bowling
Candles: tapers
Candle's light: glow
Candy and cookies: snacks
Candy bar ingredient: nougat
Candy, chewy: nougat
Candy, creamy: fondant
Candy, hard: drop
Candy Mogul B. H.: Reese
Candy shape: bar, cane
Candy sheet: bark
Candy striper: aide
Canea citizen: Cretan
Canea's island: Crete
Canetti, Elias: writer
Canine accessory: flea collar, collar
Canine condominium: kennel
Canine cry: yip, yelp
Canine cuspid (tooth): dog
Canine doctrinaire: dogmatist
Canine, jowly: pug
Canine of primers: spot
Canine pals do it: wag
Canine registry: AKC
Canine related-dental
Canine sleuth: Asta
Canine warning: growl, snarl
Canines, acquire: teethe
Canis aureus: jackal
Canis Major cynosure: Dog Star
Canister: jar
Canned: fired, axed
Canned fish: tuna
"Cannery <u>Row</u>"
Cannes' cash: franc
Cannes' cleric: abbe
Cannes' confidantes: amies
Cannes' meal course: roti
Cannes' season: ete
Cannes' wine: aile
Cannoli filling: ricotta

Cannon attachments: ades
Cannon booms: salvos
Cannon, Dyan: actress
Cannon shots: volleys
Cannon type: loose,
Canoe, go by: paddle
Canoe or raft: boat,
Canoe, rough: dug out
Canoe wood: birch
Canoeist's danger: rapids
Canon competitor: Ricoh
Canonical hour: nones
Canonized one: saint
Canoodle: spoon
Cans: tins, fires
Can't be done: not possible
Can't stand: detest, hate, despise,
Canteen initials: USO
Canter: lope
Canterbury can: tin
Canterbury locale: Kent
Canticle, performed a: intoned
Cantina offering: tamale
Cantina snack: taco
Cantor, Eddie: actor
Cantor, Eddie wife: Ida
Canute's foe: cree
Canvas cover: tarp
Canvas holder: easel
Canvas item: tarp
Canvasser, noted: Gallup
Cap: beret, tam,
Cap brim: visor
Cap material: ice
Cap, nerdy: beanie
Cap ornament: tassel
Cap visor: bill
Cap, visored: kepi
Capable of: up to
Capable of movement: motile
Capacitance unit: farad
Cape, fearsome: horn
Cape fox: asse
Cape Kennedy platform: gantry
Cape Kennedy rocket: Apollo
Cape, long: mantle
Cape of N. Honshu: Oma
Cape Town coin: Rand
Cape wavers: matadores
Caper: antic
"Per capita": Each
Capital, provide: back, loan, fund
Capitalize on: use
Capitals, (State):
    Alabama: Montgomery
    Alaska: Juneau
    Arizona: Phoenix
    Arkansas: Little Rock
    California: Sacramento
    Colorado: Denver
    Connecticut: Hartford
    Delaware: Dover
    Florida: Tallahassee
    Georgia: Atlanta

    Hawaii: Honolulu
    Idaho : Boise
    Illinois: Springfield
    Indiana: Indianapolis
    Iowa : Des Moines
    Kansas: Topeka
    Kentucky: Frankfort
    Louisiana: Baton Rouge
    Maine: Augusta
    Maryland: Annapolis
    Massachusetts: Boston
    Michigan: Lansing
    Minnesota: St Paul
    Mississippi: Jackson
    Missouri: Jefferson City
    Montana: Helena
    Nebraska: Lincoln
    Nevada: Carson City
    New Hampshire: Concord
    New Jersey: Trenton
    New Mexico: Santa Fe
    New York: Albany
    North Carolina: Raleigh
    North Dakota: Bismarck
    Ohio: Columbus
    Oklahoma: Oklahoma City
    Oregon: Salem
    Pennsylvania: Harrisburg
    Rhode Island: Providence
    South Carolina: Columbia
    South Dakota: Pierre
    Tennessee: Nashville
    Texas: Austin
    Utah: Salt Lake City
    Vermont: Montpellier
    Virginia: Richmond
    Washington: Olympia
    West Virginia: Charleston
    Wisconsin: Madison
    Wyoming: Cheyenne
Capital of Angola: Luanda
Capitol feature: dome, rotunda
Capitol hill runner: page
Capone foe: IRS, FBI
Capone's nemesis: Ness
Capote, Truman: writer
Capp, Andy
Capp's hyena: Lena
Capp's pub order: ale
Capp's quaff: ale
Capri: isle
Capri pants: calf-length
Capricorn: goat
Capri's, for one: pants
Caps on the Clyde: tams
Capshaw, Kate: actress
Capsize: keel over, turn over
Capsule, maybe: dose
Captain, crazed: Ahab
Captain Morgan: rum
Captain's shout: avast, ahoy
Captain's superior: major, maj.
Captive of Paris: Helen
Capuchin monkey: sai

Car dealer's deal: demo
Car dealer's option: lease
Car, dilapidated: crate
Car gauge extreme: empty
Car glass, like: tinted
Car loan: debt,
Car pioneer: Ranson Olde
Car protector: alarm
Car starter: ignition
Car stopper element: brake shoe
"Car Talk" network: NPR
Car trunk item: tool kit, spare
Cara, Irene
"Cara Mia"
Carafe's cousin: ewer
Caravan maker: Dodge
Caravan stop: oasis
Caravel, famous: Pinta
Caraway liqueur: kummel
Carbine: rifle, sten
Carbohydrate (tasty): pasta
Carbohydrate, type of: starch
Carbon-based: organic
Carbon compound: enol
Carbon deposit: soot,
Carbon dioxide, frozen: dry ice
Carbon 14 job: dating
Card collection: hand, deck
Card combination: ten ace
Card combo: pair
Card for fortune: tarot
Card game: loo, war
Card game authority: Hoyle
Card game, bridge-like: Skat
Card game cry: gin
Card game for three: Skat
Card game for two: écarté
Card game guru: John Scarne
Card game of yore: taroc, tarok
Card game, outwitted in a: euchred
Card game (three-handed): Skat
Card, kind of: index
Card, pictorial: tarot
Card played, like a: face up
Card player, cheating: sharper
Card player's call: gin
Card, predictive: tarot
Card raising event: auction
Card sharks: gamblers
Card, set of: hand, deck
Card spot: pip
Cardboard drink container: carton
Carder's demand: ID
Cardholder, in a sense: hand
Cardinal direction: east
Cardinal, like a: crested
Cardinal point: east,
Cardinal's cap monogram: STL
Cardiology concern: heart, aorta
Cardiologist's insert: stent
Cards, apportioned: dealt
Cards, mystical: tarots
Card-table misplay: renege
Carefree: blithe

Carefree walk: amble
Careful notice: heed
Careful, persistent effort: diligence
Carefully: warily
Carefully selected: well chosen
Caressed clumsily: pawed
Cargo: lading, lade
Cargo afloat: flotsam
Cargo cast overboard: jetsam
Cargo loader: stevedore
Cargo unloader: stevedore
Cargo plane: air taxi
Cargo space: hold
Caribbean attraction: Aruba
Caribbean resort: Aruba
Caring: heedful
Carioca's home: Rio
Cariou, Len: actor
Carmel, crème: flan
Carmel, like: gooey
Carmel-custard sweet: flan
Carmelite saint: Theresa
"Carmen" setting: Seville
Carmichael, Ian: actor
Carnaby Street locale: Soho
Carnival: fair
Carnival city: Reo
Carnival ride: carousel
Carnival sideshow locale: Midway
Carnivore, tame: cat,
Carnivore, weasel-like: marten
Carnivore's delight: T-bone
Carnivore's diet: meat
Carnivore's mouth: maw
Carnivorous aquatic mammal: otter
Carotene, beta
Carousing: on a tear
Carp, colorful: koi,
Carpathian range: Tatra, Tatre, Tatry
Carpenter joint: miter, mitre
Carpenter, Karen: musician
Carpenter tool: adze
Carpenter's friend: walrus
Carpenter's gap maker: spacer
Carpenters or harvesters: ants
Carpenter's wood pin: dowel
Carpentry kit item: adze
Carpe diem
Carpet fiber: istle
Carpet, India: agra
Carpet measurement: area
Carpet thickness: pile
Carpetbagger: swindler
Carpeting, type of: wall-to-wall
Carpet-maker's fiber: istle
Carp-like fish: bream
Carport kin: garage
Carr, Caleb: writer
Carr, John Dickson: writer
Carr, Vikki: musician
Carrere, Tia: actress
Carriage: shay, landau
Carriage, horse-drawn: surrey, hansom
Carriage, one-horse: shay

Carriage, small: fiacre
Carriage with fringe on to: surrey
Carried along: borne
Carried, as by the wind: borne
Carried away: taken
Carried off: taken
Carried on: ranted
Carried through on: did
Carrier pigeon: messenger
Carries a mortgage: owes
Carries out: does
Carries wearily: lugs
Carrington series: dynasty
Carrion feeders: hyenas
Carrot: beet: roots
Carrot family plant: anise
Carrot-top: redhead
Carry a Grudge,: Sore
Carry awkwardly: lug
Carry current: hot
Carry off: take, remove
Carry on: rant, rage
Carry on a lot: rave
Carry on a trade: ply
Carry out, as a task: execute
Carry out item: trash
Carry tales: tattle
Carry wearily: lug
Cars, some: wagons
Carson, Kit: frontier man
Carson, Rachel: biologist
Cart, two-wheel farm: tumbrel
Cart, heavy, low: dray
Cart, strong: dray
Cartagena cheer: Ole
Carte blanche
Cartel: bloc
Carter, Dixie: actress
Carter, Jimmy Earl: ex-president
Carter, Nell: actress
Cartesian leader: Rene
Carthage neighbor: Utica
Cartilage injury: tear
Cartographer's book: atlas
Carton opener: cutter, box knife
Cartoon apparition: Casper
Cartoon bear: Yogi
Cartoon character, myopic: Magoo
Cartoon chipmunk: Dale
Cartoon dog: Astro, Ren
Cartoon flapper Betty: Boop
Cartoon frame: cel, cell
Cartoon mice: Eek, Meek
Cartoon pup: Ren
Cartoon series: Jem
Cartoon shriek: eek
Cartoon skunk: Lepew
Cartoon vamp: Betty Boop
Cartoon woodpecker: Woody
Cartridge filler, often: ink
Caruso , Enrico: musician, tenor
Craved poled: totem
Carver: graver, engraver
Carvey, Dana: comic

Car-wheel lock: boot
Casa component: sala
Casa division: sala
Casa material, perhaps: adobe
Casa room: sala
Casaba: melon
Casaba tether: vine
Casablanca pianist: Sam
Casals's instrument: cello
Casanova type: roué
Casbah (kasbah) native: Arab
Cascade Range locale: Oregon
Cascade volcano: Shasta
Case for small items: etui
Case in point: example
Case of pins and needles: etui
Casement: window
CaseyDr. Ben
Cash advances: loans
Cash cache: tills
Cash, causally: moola
Cash giver: ATM
Cash, needing: broke, short
Cash source: ATM
Cash substitute: IOU, credit
Cash-back deal: rebate
Cashes in: redeems
Cashmere kin: mohair
Casino action: bet, gamble
Casino, big: ten
Casino employee: dealer, pit boss
Casino figure: dealer
Casino game: keno, poker, faro
Casino maximum: limit
Casino supply: dice, chips, decks
Casino surveillances camera: eye in the sky
Cask: tub, vat, tun, barrel
Cask, small: keg
Cask stopper: bung
Caspian Sea tributary: Ural
Cassatt, Mary: painter
Casserole staple: rice
Cassette, copy a: dub
Cassidy, Hop along: Boyd
Cassini or Vidou: Oleg Cassini, Oleg: designer
Cassio's mistress: Bianca
Cassis-flavored wine: Kir
Cassowary kin: emu, rhea
Cast a shadow: shade
Cast a vote: opt
Cast about: strewn
Cast off from the body: egest
Cast out: banish
Cast, something to: die
Castaway refuge: isle
Casting about, one who's: angler
"The Castle" author: Kafka
Castle defenses: barbicans
Castle, Irene: dancer
Castle, kind of: sand,
Castle that danced: Irene
Castle wall: parapet
Castle with many steps: Irene
Castles, as in chess: rooks

Castor's brother: Pollux, Polydeuces
    constellation: Gemini
    father: Zeus, Tyndareus
    mother: Leda
    sister: Helen
    slayer: Idas
Castro amigo: Che
Casual eatery: bistro
Casual promenader: stroller
Casual talk: confad
Casual wear: chinos
Casually: idly
Cat, breed of: rex
Cat burglars requisite: stealth
Cat, fat: hale
Cat or goat: angora
Cat, patchwork: calico
Cat scanners?: vets
Cat, tail-less: manx
Cat, tortoise-shell: calico
Cat treat: catnip,
Cat, tufted-ear: lynx
Cat, working: mouser
Catamaran feature: sail
Catamount: puma, mountain lion
Catapult, medieval: onager
Catatonic state: coma
Catawba: wine, river, Indian
Catcall: jeer, boo
Catch a wave: surf
Catch flies: shag, swat
Catch fly balls: shag
Catch for speeding: tag, nab
Catch on something: snag
Catch sight of: espy, notice
"Catch some rays"
Catch the perp: nab
Catch-all category: misc
Catch-all phrase: et al
Catches on: gets
Catchphrase, teen: as if
Categories, creative: genres
Cater for: feed
Caterer's brewers: urns
Caterer's supply: urns
Caterpillar, destructive: web worm
Caterpillar hairs: setae
Caterpillar, kind: tent
Caterpillars, some: tractors
Caterwaul: yowl, meow
Cates, Phoebe: actress
Cathedral center: nave
Cathedral city: Ely
Cathedral instrument: organ
Cathedral part: nave, aspe
Cathedral Town, famous: Ely
Cather, Willa: writer
Cathode opposite: anode
Catholic devotion: novena
Catholic publication: ordo
Catholic tribunal: Rota
Catilope: Organ
Catena: Series
Catkins, they have: willows

Cato's bear: Ursa
Cato's "I love": amo
Cat's do it: shed
Cat's-eye kin: agate
Cat's paw: dupe, pawn
Cattails, thick with: reedy
Cattle: kine
Cattle breed: Angus, devon
Cattle call award: role
Cattle country: range
Cattle drive tool: goad, lasso
Cattle herds: droves
Cattle, hornless: Angus
Cattle pen: kraal
Cattle prod: goad
Cattle, raise: ranch, breed
Cattle shed: hemmel
Cattle stall: crib
Cattle thieves: rustlers
Cattle town, old: Omaha
Cattlemen: rovers
Catty remarks, made: sniped
Caucasian, a: Osset
Caucasus Aryan: Osset
Caucuses: primaries
Caught in a web: snared
Caught in the act: nailed
Caught red-handed: seen
Caught stealing: out
Cauldrons: vats
Caulking, apply: seal
Cause: agent
Cause and effect law: karma
Cause as a consequence: entail
Cause as a result: entail
Cause friction: chafe
Cause havoc: wreak
Cause of distress: bane
Cause of mischief: bane
Cause of trysts: Apollo
Cause of, Was the: Led to
Cause Serious Injury to: Maim
Cause Surfeit: Cloy
Cause to be Immobile: Stun
Cause to Buy and Sell: Whipsaw
Cause to Exist: Engender
Caustic Quality: Vitriol
Caustic Solution: Alkali
Caution: Warn, Care
Cautious, Less: Rasher, Braver
Cautious Person's Concern: Risks
Cavalry Issue: Saber
Cavalry Solider: Lancer
Cavalry Weapon: Lance, Saber
Cavalryman, European: hussar
Cavalryman sidearm: saber
Cave: grot, grotto
Cave denizen: bat
Cave, perhaps: den, lair
Cave, small: grotto
Cave sound effect: echo
Cave, study of: speleology
"Caveat emptor"
Caveman from Moo: Oop

Cavernous opening: caw
Caverns, Virginia: Luray
Caves in: relents
Caviar, finest: beluga
Caviar fish: beluga
Caviar source: shad
Cavity detector: X-ray
Cavity in a rock: vug
Cavort: prance
Cawdor title: thane
Cayee, Edgar: psychic
Cays: coral reef, isle
Cayuse: horse
Cayuse controller: rein
CBS founder: Paley
CD contents: Data
CDs (some): IRAs
Cease all action: end
Cease fire: truce
Cease to be seen: disappeared
Ceasor, Sid: actor
Cedar or pine: conifer
Cede: yield, grant,
Ceiling, arched: vault
Cel character: toon, cartoon
Celeb, metro: divas
Celeb ox: Anoa
Celebrate, opposite of: mourn
Celebration, big-time: gala
Celebration, of a: sestal
Celebration ritual: toast
Celebratory poem: ode
Celeb's ox: Anoa
Celery piece: stalk
Celeste's mate: Babar
Celestial: devine
Celestial altar: Ara
Celestial bear: Ursa
Celestial being: angel
Celestial ellipse: orbit
Celestial equator: meridian
Celestial teacher: Taoist
Celine, Dion: singer
Cell feature: bar
Cell habitants: nuns
Cell messenger: RNA
Cell nuclei substance: DNA
Cell phone processors: CBs
Cellar, briefly: bsmt
Cellar choice: wines
Cellar content: wine, salt
Cellar, in the: last
Cellar, salt: shaker
Cellist's direction: arco
Cellist's need: resin
Cello kin: viola, viol
Cells' predecessors: CBs
Celt: Geal, Gaul, Scot
Celt language: Gaelic
Celtic minstrel: bard
Celtic Neptune: Ler
Celtic sea god: Ler
Celts, to Romans: foes
Cemeteries, early: catacombs

Cenozoic, for one: era
Censor, in a way: bleep
Censor's sound: bleep
Censorious speech: tirade
Censors: bans, bleeps
Censor's target: smut
Census information: stat
Centauri, Alpha
Center: nuclei, hub
Center of a roast: honoree
Center of great activity: loci
Center point: focal, foci
Center, start for: epi
Centering point: node
Centerpiece: epergne
Centesimi, (100): lira
Central: inner
Central American rebel: Contra
Central court: atria
Central Park sight: Hansom
Centurion moon: luna
Centurion's route: Iter
Centuries, untold: eons
Cen. fraction: yrs.
Century Plant: agave
Century, Twelfth: medieval
CEO carrier: limo
CEO extra: perk
CEO transport: limo, BMW
Ceramic ware, translucent: porcelain
Ceramic's clay box: sagger, saggar
Ceramicist's sieve: laun
Cere: wax
Cereal, made of: oaten
Cereal disease: ergot (fungus)
Cereal grass: ragi
Cereal spike: ear
Cerebellum section: lobe
Ceremonial chamber: kiva
Ceremonial departure: congee
Ceremonial dinner: seder
Ceremonial fire: pyre
Ceremonial parade: cavalcade
Ceremonial pole: totem
Ceremonial splendor: pageantry, pomp
Ceremony, ghostly: exorcism
Ceremony, solemn: rite
Certain aphorisms: sutras
Certain chorister: alto
Certain compound: isomer
Certain computer program: tutorial
Certain driver: pile
Certain driveways: oval
Certain electrode: anode
Certain polygons: isogons
Certain Pyrenees inhabitant: Basque
Certain refuge: imigre
Certain school objectives: obedience
Certain something: aura
Certain takeoffs: jatos
Certain Tuscans: Sienese
Certainly: to be sure
Certificate feature: seal
Certificate to build: permit

Cerulean, somewhat: bluish
Cervante's hero: Quivote, Quixote
Cervine male: stag
Cervine surname: Deer
Cessations: halts
C'est la vie
Chachi's beloved: Joanie
Chad Toucher: Niger
Chadic language: Sokoro
Chad's capital: N'Djamena
Chafe places: sores
Chafe severely: gall
Chafer: rub, abrade
Chagall, Marc: painter
Chain dance: Conga (Cuban)
Chain mail: armor,
Chain of hills: ridge
Chain of stations: network
Chain reaction pioneer: Fermi
Chain, type of: daisy
Chair bottom material: cane
Chair, comfy: recliner
Chair, in a: seated
Chair, is the: heads
Chair, lounge: chaise
Chair material: wicker
Chair name: Eames
Chair or collar type: wing
Chair part: splat
Chair, type of: Morris
Chair-back Piece: Slat
Chaired: Headed
Chairperson, Act as: Preside
Chalcedony: Agate
Chalcedony, Reddish-brown: Sard
Chalcedony Varieties: Quartz, Sards
Chalcidice mountain: Athos
Chaldean oracle: seer
Chalet backdrop: alps
Chalet feature: eave
Chalice, christian: grail
Chalice of medieval legend: grail
Chalice veil: aer
Chalk talk: lecture
Chalk target: pool cue
Chalked item: cue
Chalky mineral: talc
Challenged, is sibilantly: lisps
Challenging: hard
Chamber, kind of: echo
Chamber music: sonata, da camera
Chamonix's Mont Blanc
Champagne bottle: split
Champagne bottle size: magnum
Champagne bucket: icer, cooler
Champagne cocktail: mimosa
Champagne, dry: sec
Champagne glass: flute
Champagne go-with: caviar
Champagne holder: flute
Champagne orange drink: mimosa
Champagne quantity: split
Champagne word: brut
Champignons: mushrooms

Champing at the bit: antsy, eager
Champion of a cause: paladin
Champleve: inlaid, enameled work
Chan, Jackie: actor
Chance: hap
Chance, having a good: odds on
Chance, not a
Chancel cross: rood
Chances: odds
Chances, like some: slim
Chancy: iffy
Chandelier pendants: prisms
Coco Chanel:
Coco Chanel: designer
Chaney, Lon: actor
Chang, Michael: tennis
Change: vary
Change address: move
Change color: dye
Change, continuous: flux
Change drastically: mutate
Change for the better: amend
Change genetically: mutate
Change into bone: ossify
Change one's locks: dye
Change, place for: coin purse
Change slowly: evolve
Change the constitution: amend
Change the position: reset
Change the wording: amend
Change, violent: upheaval
Change text: emend
Changeable: fickle
Changed the tires around: rotated
Changed to suit: adapted
Changes, as a signal: modulates
Presto chango
Channels 2–13: VHF
Channel marker: buoy
Channel surf: zap
Chant or calendar: Gregorian
Chant rejoiner: ah so
Chanteus Piaf, Edith
Chantey subject: Sea
"Chantilly Lace" (50s Song)
Chanting sounds: oms
Chanting words: mantra
Chants: in tones
Chan-Tucker smash: Rush Hour
Chanukah, for one: feast
Chaos before creation: abyss
Chaos, utter: havoc,
Chaos's daughter: Nox, Nyx, Gaea
    son: Erebus
Chaotic, made: Messed Up
Chap: guy
Chap, British: bloke
Chap, scurrilous: cad
Chap, ungentlemanly: cad
Chap, well-bred: gent
Chapeau: hat
Chapeau, certain: beret, tam
Chapeau place: Tete
Chaperones: duennas

Chaperoned girl: Deb
Chaplin in-law: O'Neill
Chaplin (Mrs.): Oona, Paulette
Chapter heading: rubric
Chapter in history: era
Character: nature
Character assassination in print: libel
Character, inherent: nature
Character of people: ethos
Character, of a sedate: staid
Characteristic deposition: nature
Characteristic, exist as a: inhere
Characteristic quality of sound: timbre
Characterize in words: depict
Charades, play: mime
Charcoal grill: hibachi
Charge ahead: lunge
Charge for a hand delivery: ante
Charge for bucks: ATM fee
Charge it: owe
Charge, standard: base rate
Charge with: entrust
Charged atom: ion
Charged for: billed
Charged with gas: aerated
Charges, fixed: fees
Charges, prefer: sue
Chariot end: eer
Charisse, Cyd: actor
Charity festivity: gala
Charlatan: faker
Charles, et al:tunas
Charles, Cyd: dancer
Charles, Nora
"Charlie Chan"
Charlie Chan: detective
Charlie, for one: Tuna
Charm: amulet, enamor, fetish, disarm, allure,
     appeal, talisman
Charm, good luck: amulet
Charm, having a sophisticated: debonair
Charmed arde: coterie
Charming scene: idyll
Charon's boat: ferry
Charon's ferry scene: Styx
Charon's river: Acheron
Charred: burnt
Chart type: bar graph
Charter: rent, lease
Charteris character: saint
Charybdis: whirlpool
Charybdis' partner: Scylla
Chase away: rout
Chase flies: shag
Chase, Ilka: actress
Chased: hunted
Chased the puck: skated
Chasm: yawn, deep cleft, gorge, abyss
Chaste: vestal, pure
Chastity symbol: unicorn
Chat: rap
Chat, slangily: rap
Chatter, like some: idle
Chatter, type of: idle

Chatterbox, avian: magpie, macaw
Chatterbox, self-centered: popin jay
Chattered: prated, yak, gab
Chatty feline: siamese
Chatty pets: mynas
Chatty starling: myna
Chaucer creation: tale
Chaucer offering: tale
Chaucer piece: tale
Chaucer pilgrim: Yeoman
Chauvenist's crime: sexism
Chavez, Cesar: Labor Union
Cheap: junky, for a song
Cheap and showy: brassy
Cheap booze: rot gut
Cheap cheroot: stogie
Cheap smoke: stogie
Cheap wheels: moped
Cheap whiskey: Red Eye
Cheapen: devalue
Cheapskate: picker
Cheat: flam, scam, con
Cheat a bit: fudge
Cheat out of money: swindle, con
Cheat sheets: cribs
Cheated: bilked
Cheating card player: sharper
Check: arrest
Check cashing need: ID's
Check endorser: payee
Check entry: amount
Check for accuracy: vet, audit, edit
Check for errors: proof
Check for prints: dust
Check in: arrive
Check mark: tick
Check off: mark
Check out: case
Check recipient: payee
Check registry entry: amount
Check the accounts of: audit
Check writer: signer, payer
Checked items: baggage
Checked out: eyed
Checker move: twist
Checking for fraud: auditing
Checking out: eying, leaving
Checkout ID: UPC
Checkout scan: UPC
Checks out: vets
Checkup, final: autopsy
Cheech and Chong: costars
Cheech's partner: Chong
Cheek: nerve
Cheek dampener: tear
Cheekier: balder
Cheeky: brass
Cheer, theater: bravo
Cheer, type of: Bronx
Cheerful: perky
Cheerful mode, in a: jovial
Cheerful tune: lilt
Cheerio: ta-ta
Cheers: skoal, salud, root, toast, rahs

Cheers for toreros: oles
Cheese, ball-shaped: edam
Cheese by-product: whey
Cheese cake, name in: Sara, Sara Lee
Cheese cake, piece of: gam
Cheese coating: rind
Cheese, chunk of: slab
Cheese, creamy white: brie
Cheese , crumbly: feta
Cheese, crusty: brie
Cheese dip: fondue
Cheese, dutch: edam
Cheese, goat: feta
Cheese, gourmet: bleu
Cheese, italian: asiago
Cheese, mild creamy: muenster, munster
Cheese, mold-ripened: brie
Cheese, moldy: bleu
Cheese, often grated: romano
Cheese, party tray: brie
Cheese, sharp: romano
Cheese, shredded: grated
Cheese snack: nacho
Cheese, soft: brie, ricotta
Cheese, upscale: brie
Cheese, wax-coated: edam
Cheesy snacks: nachos
Cheesy Welch-dish: rarebit
Chef's formula: recipe
Chef's phrase: ala
Chekhov, Anton: writer
Chekhov heroine: Anya
Chemical analysis aids: reagents
Chemical compound: isomer, ester
Chemical dye: eosin
Chemical ending: ase
Chemical salt: iodate, niter
Chemical suffix: ene
Chemist burner: etna, bunson
Chemistry chart figure: atom
Chemistry lab item: pipette, petri dish
Chenille item: robe
Chennai's home: India
Cherbourg cherub: angel
Cherbourg church: Eglise
Cherchez la femme
Cheroot, cheap: stogie
Cherries, dark red: bings
Cherry color: cerise
Cherry, sour: morello
Cherrystone, e.g.: clams
Chess master, Russian: Tal
Chess piece: rook, bishop, queen, king
Chess piece, lowest ranking: pawn
Chess player, top: master
Chess player's word: mate
Chess turn: move
Chess win: mate, check mate
Chest muscles: pecs
Chest or closet wood: cedar
Chest protector: rib cage
Chesterfield or Utser: coat
Chesterfield part: sleeve
Chestnut hull: bur

Cheviot or merino: wool
Chevron shape: vee
Chevron weave: herringbone
Chewable stick: gum
Chewbacca's friend: Han
Chewing gum base: chicle
Chews out: tells off, scold
Chews the scenery: emotes
Chewy candy: nougat
Chewy roll: bagel
Chewy treat: caramel
Chi follower: PSI
Chi, Tai
Chi chuan, Tai
Chiang Kai-shek
Chianti: wine
Chianti, e.g.: vino,
Chianti go-with: pasta
Chic: smart, style
Chic beach resort: Lido
Chic getaway: spa
Chic, not: passe
Chicago trains: els
Chicago's planetarium: Adler
Chicaneries: wiles,
Chicanery, bit of: ruse
Chicanery, pieces of: wiles
Chichén Itzá man: Mayan
Chicken chow mein
Chicken feed: mash
Chicken herb: sage
Chicken, little: bantam
Chicken Little's mother: hen
Chicken liver appetizer: rumaki
Chicken Kiev
Chicken male: capone
Chicken style: Kiev
Chicken, turned: ran
Chicken wire: mesh
Chicken, young: fryer
Chick-pea plant: cicer
Chicle product: gum
Chief: main
Chief god of Memphis: Ptah
Chief Olympian: Zeus
Chief transport: canoe
Chief's advisor: elder
Chiefs people: tribe
Chiefly: mainly
Chieftain's plaid: kilt
Chiffon: gauze
Chiffon, like: sheer
Chignon: bun
Chihuahua chapeau: sombreros
Chihuahua chum: amigo
Child, kind of: only
Childhood game: tag
Childlike person: naif
Chileab's father: David
        mother: Abigail
Chili add-in: carne
Chili bean: kidney, pinto
Chili con carne
Chili consideration: hotness

Chili pepper dip: salsa
Chili powder spice: cumin
Chill in the air: nip
Chill out: relax
Chilled out: calm
Chilling effect, they have a: cold snap
Chills: ague
Chilly and damp: raw
Chimera's father: Typhon
        mother: Echidna
Chimney in Paisley: lum
Chimney nesters: storks
Chimney deposit: smut, soot
Chimney pipe: flue
Chimney shaft: flue
Chimp's cousin: orang
Chin feature: clefts
China, English: Spode
China, fine: bone
China, in polo's time: cathay
China mountain range: alai
China river: Tarim
China's largest river: Chang
China's Mississippi: Yangtze
Chinese aborigine: Meo
Chinese, ancient: Seres
Chinese antelope: goral
Chinese (comb. Form): sino
Chinese counting device: abacus
Chinese dollar: yuan
Chinese divination book: Iching
Chinese dumpling: wonton
Chinese dynasty: Han, Chou, Sun, Ming
Chinese ethnic group: Han
Chinese exercise system: tai chi
Chinese faction: Tong, Ming
Chinese food General: Tso
Chinese fruit: litchi
Chinese fruit tree: litchi
Chinese home: junk, sampan
Chinese, in prefixes: sino
Chinese mountain range: Alai
Chinese or Toulouse chaser: goose
Chinese pan: wok
"Chinese Parrot" sleuth: Chan
Chinese philosophy: Tao
Chinese porcelain, fine: Ming
Chinese province: Honan
Chinese sauce: soy
Chinese secret society: Tong
Chinese society: Tong, Ming
Chinese soup: wonton
Chinese taxi: rickshaw, ricksha
Chinese temple: pagoda, taa
Chinese veggie: bok choy
Chinese warehouse: hong
Chinos, e.g.: pants
Chip companion: dip
Chip container: kitty, pot
Chip dip: salsa
Chip maker: Intel
Chip off the old block: son
Chip off the old urn: shard
Chip source: potato

Chipmunk, cartoon: Dale
Chipmunk pouch: cheek
Chipmunk, singing: Alvin
Chipmunk snack: acorn
Chipped: nicked, hacked
Chipped in: helped
Chips & dips: snacks
Chips in a chip: antes
Chip's partner: fish
Chisel kin: adz
Chisholm Trail end: Abilene
Chit letters: IOU
Chitchats: gabs
Chivalrous deed: gist, gest
Chivalrous, most: bravest
Chive relative: leek
Chloe's love: Dap
Chlorination victim: alga, algae
Chloroform kin: ether
Cho, Margaret: comedian
Chocolate dessert: mousse
Chocolate dip: fondue
Chocolate, ersatz: carob
Chocolate, "good": dark
Chocolate, imitation: carob
Chocolate maker: godiva
Chocolate source: cacao
Chocolate substitute: carob
Chocolate tree: cacao
Chocolatier's device: mold
Choice: option
Choice, flexible: any
Choice of options: menu
Choice word: nor
Choices, top: a list,
Choir accompanier: organ
Choir leader: cantor
Choir leaders, pertaining to: cantorial
Choir platform: riser
Choke or joke: gag
Choler: ire
Cholla: cacti
Chomped down: bit
Chomsky, Noam
Chong, Rae Dawn: actress
Choose a successor: anoint
Chooser, can't be a: beggar
Chooser's word: those
Chooses from the candidates: elects
Chop: hew
Chop chop to chaucer: apace
Chop, kind of: karate
Chophouse choice: rib-eye
Chopin, Frederic: composer
Chopin opus: etude
Chopin piece: eludes, etudes
Chopin's birthplace: Poland
Chopped down: felled
Chopper saves at sea, abbr.: ASR
Chopper's destination: helipad
Chopping skill: karate
Chopping veggies: dicing
Chord, type of: triad
Chores: odd jobs

Chorister, certain: alto,
Chorus girl: dancer, chorine
Chorus leader: choragus
Chorus platform: riser
Chosen few: elite
Chou Enlai: China leader
Chow mein additive: MSG
Chowder: soup
Chowder ingredient: oyster, clam
Chowder tidbit: clam, oyster
Chowed down greedily: ravened
Bok choy:
Bok choy: Chinese cabbage
Christian chalice: grail
Christian missionary: apostle
Christiania today: Oslo
Christie (do a): ski
Christie, Agatha: author
Christie, Agatha, title: dame
Christie Brinkley, emulate: pose
Christie, Julie: actress
Christie Sleuth: Poirot
Christies, do: ski
Christmas and Easter: islands, holidays
Christmas, in Roma: Natale
Christmas item: yule log
Christmas, period before: advent
Christmas present, brat's: coal
Christmas tree choice: balsam
Chrome start: mono
Chromosome occupant: gene
Chromosome part: gene
Chromosome passenger: gene
Chronicles: annals, tales
Chronological brinks: eves
Chronology error: prolepsis
Chronometer: clock,
Chrysler building feature: spiral
Chrysler model, old: DeSoto
Chuan, Tai Chi
Chubby: plump, obese
Chuck: toss
Chuckle: chortie
Chuckwagon chow: grub
Chukker's game: polo (period of play)
Chunkier: pudgier
Church aisle finisher: apse
Church alcove: apse
Church altar site: apse
Church assistant: deacon
Church calendar: ordo
Church collection: alms
Church council: synod
Church court: rota
Church dignitary: prelate
Church dissenter: heretic
Church doctrine: dogma
Church doctrine, flouter of: heretic
Church donation: tithe
Church event: bingo
Church figure: rector, elder
Church instrument: organ
Church law: canon
Church members, certain: Anglican

Church of England: Episcopal
Church official: bishop
Church offshoots: cults
Church parking place: pew
Church part: apse, altar, nave
Church party: social
Church reading: Psalm
Church reading desk: lectern
Church rite: Mass
Church room: sacristy
Church stipend: prebend
Church topper: spire
Churchill gesture: vee
Churchill successor: Eden
Churlish person: boor
Churn, part of: dasher
Churn up: roil
Chutist's need: rip-cord, chute
Chutzpah, full of: brash
CIA forerunner: OSS
Ciao: ta-ta
Cicada: locust
Cicatrix: scar
Cicero's robe: toga
Cider-sweet girl: Ida
C'est la vie
Cigar, fine: Havana
Cigar, long: Corona
Cigar, mild: Claro
Cigar shape: terete
Cigar, tapering: Corona
Cinco de Mayo event: fiesta
Cinder: ash
Cinema award: Oscar
Cinema dog: Asta
Cinemax rival: HBO
Cinnamon bun
Cinnamon bark: cassia
Cinnamon candles: red hots
Cinnamon goody: bun
Circle, bright: halo
Circle combining form: gyro
Circle dance: hora
Circle, flattened: ellipse
Circle, numbered: dial
Circle of colors: areole
Circle of flowers: lei
Circle of lights: halo
Circle or tube: inner
Circle segment: radii
Circle size: area
Circle, squashed: oval
Circle, tiny: dot
Circle, wee: dot
Circuit: loop
Circuit, one: lap
Circular band of foliage: lei
Circular current: eddy
Circular tent: yurt
Circular water container: basin
Circumference-to-diameter ratio: PIS
Circumnavigator: mage plan
Circumvent: avert
Circus arena: ring, tent

Circus barker: seal
Circus concessionaire: grifter
Circus crowd noise: ooh
Circus maxmus racers: chariots
Circus routine: act
Circus team: Barnum and Bailey
Cire perdue: metal casting, lost wax
Loc cit: footnote abbr.
Citizen: voter
Citizen of note: Kane
Citizen, ordinary: civilian
Citizen's arrest
Citizen's concern: government, govt.
Citizen's rights: voting
Dual citizenship
Citrus Bowl site: Orlando
Citrus drink: ade
Citrus fruit: ugle
Citrus hybrid: tangelo
Citrus peel: zest
City: burg
City area: up town
City building: tenement
City environs: exburgs
City folk: urbanites
City, major: capital
City manager's degree: MPA
City map: plat
City near Sparks: Reno
City of art: Florence
City of canals: Venice
City of lights: Paris
City of seven hills: Rome
City on the Adda: Lodi
City on the Arkansas: Tulsa
City on the Mohawk: Utica
City on the Moselle: Metz
City on the Tiber: Rome
City on the Truckee: Reno
City or copy at a newspaper: desk
City square: plaza
Civet, lesser: rasse
Civet relative: genet
Civet secretion: musk
Civic concern: crime
Civil rights org.: ACLU
Civil War lady of song: Lorena
Civil wrong: tort
Clackers, belly dance: zills
Claiborne, Liz: designer
Claim: aver, profess, assert
Claim on property: lien
Claimed as one's own: staked
Claims: dibs
Claims on property: liens
Claims to be true: alleges
Claire, Ina: actress
"Claire de Lune" composer: Debussy
Clairvoyance: ESP, seer
Clam genus: mya
Clammy: dank, humid, damp
Clamor, loud: din
Clampett, Elly May: character
Clampett portrayer: Ebsen

Clan subdivision: sept
Clancy hero Jack: Ryan
Clannish: tribal
Clans (of): tribal
Clan's emblem: totem
Clanton's, one of the: Ike
Clanton's, (Ike) foe: Earp
Clap of thunder: peal
Clapboard: siding
Clapper's place: bell
Clapton, Eric: actor, guitarist
Clapton classic: Layla
Clapton of Layla: Eric
Clapton's instrument: guitar
Clarinet kin: oboe
Clarinet vibrator: reed
Clarion blast: tantara
Clark, Ramsey: Sec of State
Clark, Robin: writer
Clark's partner: Lewis
Clash of arms: war
Clash, they often: egos
Clasp tightly: clench
Clasp toward the center: infold
Class: ilk
Class ender: bell
Class period: hour
Class, skip a: cut
Classic auto: REO, Packard
Classic language: Latin
Classics, like many: unread
Classic muscle car: GTO
Classic prefix: neo
Classic stories: epics
Classic with Achilles: Iliad
Classical poet: Ovid
Classical start: neo
Classical villain: Iago
Classified: want ad, labels
Classified items: ads
Classify: assort, label
Classroom sound: psst
Classy spread: pates
Clatter: din
Claudius "I": ego
Claudius's son: Nero
Claudius's son-in-law: Nero
Claudius successor: Nero
Clausewitz's emphasis: tactics
Claw: nail
Claw badly: maul
Clay and lime: marl
Clay and sand: marl
Clay box used in ceramics: sagger, saggar
Clay, lump of: clod,
Clay nodule: eagle stone
Clay, old: ali
Clay softening: malaxage
Clay, shape: model, mold
Clay used in ceramics: kaolin
Clayey earth: loom
Clay pigeon game: skeet
Clay pigeon hurler: trap
Clay-target sport: skeet

Clean energy source: hydro
Clean house: vacuum, dust
Clean, make: purify
Clean, one way to come: bathe
Clean slate: tabula rasa
Clean slate, with a: anew
Clean the deck: swab
Cleaned a diskette: deleted, erased
Cleaned the board: erased
Cleaner scent, often: pine
Cleaners, took to the: bilked
Cleaning targets: dust bunnies
Cleaning, thorough: scrubbing
Cleanse: purify
Cleanse of impurities: purge
Cleanse, to a poet: lave
Clear and understandable: lucid
Clear as mud: vague
Clear away: erase, remove
Clear of odors: air out
Clear on things: undeluded
Clear plastic: Lucite
Clear sky: ether
Cleared for takeoff: de-iced
Clears out, slangily: gits
Cleek: hook, one iron
Clefts: rima
Clemons, Samuel: Twain
Cleo player: Liz
Cleopatra's attendant: Iras, Charmian
     brother: Ptolemy
     cause of death: asp
     lover: Anthony, Marc, Caesar, Julius
     needle: obelisk
     river: Nile
     undoing: ssp
     wooer: Marc
Clergy assembly: synod
Clergy member's home: deanery
Clergy, not: laity
Clergyman: curate
Clergyman, certain: vicar
Clergyman's residence: manse
Clergyman's wear: tippet
Cleric, minor: deacon
Cleric of Cannes: abbe
Clerical attire: alba
Clerical hat: biretta
Clerical tunic: albs
Cleveland suburb: Berea
Clever, be: out fox
Clever maneuver: ploy
Clever, pretty: shrewd
Clever ploy: ruse
Clever remark: quip, bon mot
Clever saying: mo
Clever tactic: ploy
Cleverer, be: outfox
Cleverist: wiliest, niftiest
Cliborn, Van: pianist
Click beetle: elater, dor
Click on item: icon
Click "send": Email
Client mtg.: appt.

Cliff dwelling: aerie
Cliff dwelling, now: ruin, ruins
Cliff of Maui: Pali
Cliff, rugged: crag
Cliffs: bluffs
Cliffside abode: aerie
Climax beginning: anti
Climb a rope: shin, or shim
Climb up: ascend, clamber
Climber: scaler
Climber's challenge: alps
Climber's need: toe hold
Climber's tool: ice ax
Climbing devise: ladder
Climbing maneuver: rappel
Climbing palm: rattan
Climbing plant: liana, woodbine
Climbing spike: piton
Climbing vine: wisteria
Clinch a deal: ice
Clinched hand: fist
Cline, Patsy: music
Clingy cures of yore: leeches
Clingy seedpod: bur
Clinic or spread: Mayo
Clink or cooler: jail
Clio's sister: Erato
Clio awards contenders: ad men
Clip wool: shear
Clipped sheep: sheared
Cliques: sets
Clive Cussler hero: Pitt
Cloak, hooded: domino
Cloak, one-piece: toga
Cloak, Roman: toga
Clobber: bash
Clobbers, biblically: smites
Clockface: dial
Clock master: Thomas Seth
Clock, type of: cuckoo
Clockmaker: horologist
Clockwise: Deasil, Dexral, right-handed
Clockwork, word with: like
Clod buster: hoe
Clog cousin: sabot
Cloisonné component: enamel
Cloister dweller: nun
Cloistered: nun
Clomped: trod
Clorinda's beloved: Tancred
     father: Senapo
     guardian: Arsete
     slayer: Tancred
Close: nigh
Close, as drapes: drew
Close at hand: nearby
Close by: at hand
Close by, like anything: not far
Close call: near miss
Close companion: pal
Close falcon eyes: seel
Close, Glenn: actress
Close star: sol, sun
Close tightly: seal

Close to extinction: scarce
Close with a bang: slam
Closed, securely: sealed
Closed-mouth person: clamClose-fitting dress:
    sheath
Close-fitting hat: toque
Closeout: sale
Closer, came: neared
Closer to retirement: older
Closes in: nears
Closet items: hangers
Closet need: rod
Closet freshener: sachet
Close-tie: bond
Closing document: deed
Closing notice?: obit, (obituary)
Cloth dealer: draper
Cloth line: seam, hem
Cloth measurer: ells
Cloth, scraps of: rags
Clothes horse: model
Clothes line?: seam
Clothes presser, crude: sad iron
Clothes, provide with: tog
Clotheshorse, use a: air dry
Clothespress: armoire, wardrobe
Clothier's concern: fit
Clothing: togs, garb
Clothing caveat: hand wash
Clothing consumer: moth
Clothing decorations: bead work
Clothing fabric: serge, acetate
Clothing for newborns: layette
Clothing material, stretchy: lycra
Clothing, nonuniform: nufti
Clothing reenforcer: gusset
Cloud formation, low-altitude: stratus
Cloud fragment: wisp
Cloud, in England: grey
Cloud layer: strata
Cloud of gas or dust: nebula
Cloudburst: rain
Cloudless nights, like: starry
Clouds, among the: aloft
Clouds, fleecy white: cirri, cirrus
Clouds, high: cirrus
Clouds , interstellar: nebula
Clouds, low drifting: scud
Clouds, low-lying: fog
Clouds, mass of: bank
Clouds racing by: scuds
Clouds, thin: wisps
Cloud-seeding compound: iodide
Cloudy: dim
Clouseau's title, abbr.: Insp
Clouseau's valet: Koto
Clover, dried: hay
Clown character: Bozo
Clown, medieval: jester
Clown's need: wig
Cloy: excess, glut
Cloying: tread
Club at a course: iron, wood
Club car: lounge

Club in a bag: iron
Club, short, heavy: cudgels
Club stint: gig
Club, type of: glee
Club-like weapon: mace
Clucker: hen
Clucking sounds: tsks
Clue, drop a: hint
Clue, small: hint
Clueless: asea,
Clueless about, not: in on, aware
Clues: keys
Clump of grass: tuft, tuffet, tussock
Clump of hair: tuft
Clumsy: inept, gawky, oaf
Clumsy as an ox: inept
Clumsy sort: klutz
Clunk: thud
Cluster bean: guar
Clutch: grab
Clutch member: egg
Clutchers, condor's: talons
Cluttered, less: barer
Cluttered room: rat's nest
Clymene's father: Oceanus
        husband: Lapetus
        mother: Tethys
        son: Atlas, Epimetheus, Prometheus
Coaching, get: train
Coach's responsibility: team
Coal: ember, gleed
Coal, bed of: seam
Coal, brown: lignite
Coal deposit: seam
Coal, kind of: cannel
Coal measure: ton
Coal scuttle: hod
Coal seam: bed
Coalition: boc, union
Coals (hot): embers
Coarse grass: reed
Coarse hair: bristle
Coarse hominy: samp (corn mush)
Coarse humor: ribald
Coarse lacework: macramé
Coarse sand: grit
Coast: shoreline
Coast along: glide
Coastal area: tide land
Coastal city: port
Intra-coastal waterway:
Coastline features: cays
Coat, expensive: fur
Coat hanger, makeshift: hook, nail, peg
Coat of arms: crest,
Coat, type of: ulster, pea
Coat with flour: dredge
Coat, woman's short: topper
Coated metal: terne
Coated with metal: plated
Coated with wax: cerated
Coating, metal: plate
Coating, non-rust: zinc
Coating of ice: rime

Coating, protective: mastic
Coating, thin: film
Coax: induce
Cobalt violet: thistle
Cobb, Lee: actor
Cobbler's punch: awl
Cobbler's tool: awl
Cobra kin: mamba
Cobweb, make: spin
Coca, Imogene: comic
Cochise: Apache
Cockamamie: inane
Cockatoo, Aussie: Arará
Cocked hat: tricorn
Cockney's expectation: 'ope
Cockney's optimism: 'ope
Cockpit button: eject
Cockpit info: alt
Cocktail, creamy: grasshopper
Cocktail ingredient: liquor
Cocktail seafood: oyster
Cocktail setting: piano bar
Cocktail, Scotch: Rob Roy
Coco, James: actor
Cocoa source: cocoa
Coconut exporter: Fiji
Coconut fiber: coir
Coconut meat, dried: copra
Coconut pulp: copra
Cocoon dweller: larva
Cod kin: hake
Coda's place: end
Code: crypto, zip, area, bar
Code dot: dit
Code, put in: encipher
Code word: genetic, alfa
Coder's mistake: software bug
Codger's queries: Ehs
Cody costar: Oakley
Coe, David Allan:
Coe, Sebastian: runner
Coen, Joel: director
Coercion, obtained by: extort
Coercion, without: freely
Coffee break treat: roll
Coffee container: urn
Coffee cup, big: mug
Coffee cup holder: zare
Coffee cup, small: demitasse
Coffee, diner: joe, java
Coffee emanation: aroma
Coffee, flavor: sweeten
Coffee, high-grade: mocha
Coffee house order: mocha, espresso, latte
Coffee keeper: thermos
Coffee liqueur: Tia Maria
Coffee, really bad: mud
Coffee shop: café
Coffee time: break
Coffee to go necessity: lid
Coffee variety: iced, decaf, reg
Coffee with milk: café con leche
Coffin stand: bier
Coq au vim

Coq au vin
Cogitate (with one): chew
Cogito ergo sum
Cognition, content of: idea
Cohesive group: unit
Coif: hairdo
Coif, frizzy: afro
Coiffure: hairdo
Coiffure, elegant: updo, chignon
Coil about: loop
Coil around: loop
Coil of yarn: hank, skein
Coin anagram: icon
Coin, dummy: slug
Coin of Riga, old: lat
Coin of the realm: species
Coin, old Indian: Anna
Coin slot word: insert
Coin, worthless: sou
Coincide: overlap
Coins, science of: numismatics
Coins specialist: numismatist
Colada, pina
Colander kin: sieve
Cold, (as an old house): drafty
Cold and wet: dank
Cold and windy: raw
Cold abode: igloo
Cold, bitterly: glacial, frigid
Cold blooded: heartless, cruel, brutal, callous,
    ruthless, pitiless
Cold comfort, they offer: ice bags
Cold, dry wind: mistral
Cold feet: timidity, fear
Cold-hearted: stony
Cold, kept: iced
Cold place: Artic, Arctic
Cold shoulder: shun
Cold snap, no mere: Ice Age
Cold spell: snap
Cold symptoms: rheumy
Cold temperature, very: absolute zero
Cold War agency: TASS
Cold War competition: arms race
Cold War principle: USSR
Cold War org.: KBG
Cold wind: bise
Cold winds do: bite
Cold cuts seller: deli
Coldness: iciness
Cole, Natalie: music
Cole Ridge setting: Xanadu
Cole Ridge's mariner, like: ancient
Coleman, Ornate: jazz
Coleridge character: ancient mariner
Coleridge setting: Xanada
Coleridge's daughter: Sara
Coles, Chas: dancer
Coliseum, now: ruins
Coliseum site: Rome
Collage creature's need: paste
Collapse, in a weary way: plop
Collapsing, keep from: prop up
Collar attachment: leash

Collar controller: stay
Collar, kind of: eton, flea, ruff
Collar, Elizabethan: ruff
Collar, flatfoot's: arrest
Collar insert: stud
Collar, pleated: ruff
Collar stiffener: stay
Collar, type of: flea
Collateral, it can be used for: asset
Colleague: peer, pal, chum
Collect in abundance: amass
Collected abundantly: raked in
Collected reminiscences: ana
Collected sayings: ana
Collection bus.: repo
Collection, eclectic: olio
Collection, haphazard: olio
Collection of anecdotes: ana
Collection of fauna: zoo
Collection of gifts: loot
Collection of points, in math: loci
Collection of sayings: ana
Collection, scout: badges
Collection, varied: olio
Collective bargainers: unions
Collective knowledge: lore
Collector: gleaner
Collector, obsessive: pack rat
Collector of stamps: philatelist
Collector's coup: set
Collects: gleans
Colleen: Irish girl, lass
Colleen's home: Erie
College credit: unit, hour
College organization: sorority
College stat: GPA
College study: major
College treasurer: bursars
College VIP: prexy, dean
College World Series home: Omaha
Collegian's jacket: blazer
Collie, fictional: Las
Collie, Terhune: Lad
Collier: mine
Collie's charge: sheep
Collie's, like some: bearded
Collins, Phil: music
Colloidal extract of algae: agar
Colloquial intensifier: Sam Hill
Colloquially benefits: perks
"Eau de Cologne"
Cologne crowd: Drei(3)
Colonel Blimp: fogy, tory, fossil, mossback,
    fuddy-duddy
Colonel Mustard game: Clue
Colonial ruler: viceroy
Colonnade, ancient: stoa
Colonnade, Greek: stoa
Colonnade lineup, sometimes: elms
Colony member: ant,
Colony, type of: penal
Color, bright: loud
Color, drab: dun
Color, hints of: tinges

Color to dye for: henna
Color T-shirts: tie dye
Color, vivid: magenta
Colorado Mount: Oso
Colorado tree: aspen
Coloration: hue
Coloratura Mills: Erie
Coloratura Mills: aria
Coloratura's offering, perhaps: aria
Colorfast, wasn't: bled
Colorful carp: koi
Colorful, far from: drab
Colorful fish: tetra
Colorful, not: drab
Coloring sticks: crayons
Colorless: wan
Colors, circle: areole
Colors, delicate: tints
Colossal: epic, hugh, vast, immense
Colossal beast: behemoth
Colossal one: Titan
Coltrane's instrument: sax
"Columbo" star: Falk
Columbus home: Ohio
Columbus ships: Nina, Pinta, Santa Maria
Column: pillar
Column in a wall: pilaster
Column, rightmost: ones
Column structure: portico
Column, type of: ionic
Comaneci, Nadia: gymnast
Comb content: honey
Comb creation: part
Comb producer: bees
Comb, type of: rattail
Comb with a wire brush: card
Combat accessory: battle scarf
Combat for two: duel
Combine: mix, harvest
Combine resources: pool
Combine with water: hydrate
Combined effect, enhanced: synergy
Combo: band
Combo, small: trio
Comb-plate organ: ctene
Combustible material: tinder
Combustible pile: pyre
Combustion, undergo: burn
Come across as: seem
Come after: ensue
Come afterward: ensue, follow
Come around: awake
Come back: respond, return
Come back to win: rally
Come before: antecede, precede
Come down hard: rain, pour, teem
Come forth: emanate, emerge
Come from behind: rally
Come in third: show
Come into view: emerge
Come next: follow, on deck
Come off as: seem
Come off in pieces: peel
"Come on, get real"

Come out even: tie, balance
Come to a boil: seethe
Come to a conclusion: end
Come to a halt: cease, stop
Come to pass: happen
Come to terms: agree
Come to understand: see
Come together: merge, meet
Come unglued: rage
Come unstitched: ravel
Come up short: fold
Comeback: rejoin, rejoiner , retort, answer
Comeback, makes a: rallies
Comedian: card
Comedian, colorful: red button
Comedian forte: humor
Comedian, one-named: Sinbad
Comedy, silly: farce
Come-on: tease, teaser
Comes down a bit hard: sleets
Comes out in drops: exudes
Comes to a decision: opts
Comes to a point: tapers
Comes to office: accedes
Comes to maturity: ripens
Comes with: brings
Comet competitor: ajax
Comet discoverer: Halley
Comet: Hale Bopp
Comet cloud: coma
Comet envelope: coma
Comet head: coma
Comet rival: Ajax
Comet to ancients: omen
Comet's gaseous cloud: coma
Comfort: solace
Comfortable, warmly: snug, cozy
Comforter stuffing: eider
Comfy: cozy
Comical, absurdly: zany
Comic book heroes: X-Men
Comic hero, Incredible: Hulk
Comic book thud: bam
Comic "Bea Lillie"
Comic conjurers: Penn and Teller
Comic device: double talk
Comic ghost: Casper
Comic pooch: Odie
Comic penguin: Opus
Comic possum: Pogo
Comic strip bark: arf
Comic strip caveman: Oop
Comic strip dog: Otto
Comic strip moppet: Lulu
Comic strip queen: Aleta
Comic strip prince: Arn
Comic strip viking: Hagar
Comic strip warrior: Conan
Comic's stock and trade: humor
Coming out: debut
Coming to a point: tapered
Coming to light: emergent
Coming up: next
Comintern founder: linen

Command: decree
Command decision: say so
Command, level of: echelon
Command, nautical: alast
Command to a new knight: arise
Commanded: bade, led
Commandeer: usurp
Commander's eight bells: noon
Commandment, break of: covet
Commandments peak: Sinai
Commando assignment: raid
Commando attack: raid
"Commedia dell' arte"
Commencement: advent
Commend: laud
Commend highly: cite
Commends loudly: hails
Comment, despondent: alas
Comment, mocking: gibe
Comment to the audience: aside
Comments to, add: annotate
Commercial award: Clio
Commercial cat name: Morris
Commercial soot: Lampblack
Commercial stoppage: embargo
Commercially popular: hot
Commiserator's word: alas
Commit a faux pas: err, error
Committee: panel
Committee, type of: ad hoc
Common ancestor, having a: akin
Common article: the
Common contraction: I've
Common expression: idiom
Common iliac artery
Common level: par
Common market initials: EEC
Common phrase: idiom
Common practice: usage
Common preservative: salt
Common query: how
Common Solar Design: Sunburst
Common Type Size: Pica
Commonplace: trite
Commonsense: wit
Commotion: to do
Communion vessel: pyx
Communication, brief: note
Communication Satellite: Comsat
Communicator's using Yerkish: apes, chimps
Communique: message
Communities, like some: gated
Community club: Rotary,
Community fellows: menfolk
Community, outlying: exburg
Community type: gated
Commuter's home, in short: burb, burg, exurb
Commuter line: rail, el
Commuting cost: fare
"Como esta usted"
Compact: disc, treaty
Compact filler, perhaps: rouge
Compact heap, small: wad
Compact machine gun: uzi

Companion: cohort
Companion, archaic: fere
Companion, close: pal
Companion, kind of: boon
Companion of aah: ooh
Companionship, lacking: lonely
Company: firm
Company for the baby: Gerber
"The Company": CIA
Comparable: akin
Comparative ease, periods of: let ups
Comparative ending: ier
Comparative phrase: as to
Compare: liken
Comparison shopper: pricer
Comparison word: than
Comparisons: similes
Compass needles: magnets
Compass plant: rosinweed
Compass point: nebe
Compass, use a: orient
Compassion, felt: cared
Compassionate: humane
Compassionate letters: TLC
Compel: must, make
Compelled, was: had to
Compete at auction: bid
Competence, with: ably
Competently: ably
Competitions: rivalries
Competitor: entrant, foe
Competitor, Universal: MGM
Compilation: ana, digest
Complacently: smugly
Complain bitterly: rail, jaw, berate, scold
Complaining sort: whiner
Complains: laments, repine, rail
Complete: plenary, whole
Complete disaster: fiasco
Complete failure: fiasco
Complete reversal: U turn
Complete wreck: total
Completed: done
Completed, in Caen: fini
Completed without error: aced
Completely: in to to, in total
Completely convinced: sold
Completely full: satiated
Completely inoperative: kaput
Completely unfamiliar: alien
Completely wreck: total, ruin
Complex, has a: Oedipus
Complex, not: simple
Complexion, dark: olive
Complexion problem: acne, oiliness
Compliant ones: sheep
Compliant, too: meek
Complicated, not as: easier
Complimentary: free
Complimentary ticket: pass
Comply with: obey
Component: part, unit
Component piece: part, unit
Comportment: mien

Compos mentis: sane
Compose: indite, pen,
Composed: serene, penned
Composer's concern: tempo
Composite picture: mosaic
Composition: opus
Compositions, like some: choral
Composition for two: duet
Composure: aplomb
Composure under fire: poise
Compote fruit: pear
Compound, double-bound: enol
Compressed earth: pisé
Compressed lumps: wads
Compressed, more: denser
Compresses, in computerese: zips
Comprise: embody
Compulsive: driven,
Computer abbr.: DOS
Computer acronym: GIGO, ROM, ASCII
Computer add-on: modem, printer, scanner
Computer chip maker: Intel
Computer code: ASCII
Computer connection, kind of: Wi-Fi
Computer correspondence: Email
Computer datum: bit
Computer document: file
Computer drive: CD Rom
Computer, explanatory: tutorial
Computer fodder: data
Computer game, early: long
Computer glitch: bug
Computer, Kubrick's: HAL
Computer image bits: pixels
Computer language: Ada, APL, Basic, Java,
    Lisp, Perl, ALGOL, COBOL, Pascal,
    Fortran
Computer network: system
Computer network, restricted: intranet
Computer operating system: Unix
Computer pioneer: IBM,
Computer phone link: modem
Computer pointer: cursur
Computer pro: tech
Computer problem: bug, virus
Computer procedure: algorithm
Computer screen flashing spot: cursor
Computer screen image: icon
Computer shortcut: macro
Computer term: ROM
Computer 2001: Hal
Computer type choice: font
Computer whiz: nerd
Comrades: cohorts
Comrades in arms: alley
Comstock bonanza: lode
Comstock Lode state: Nevada
Con: anti
Con artist may go by it: alias
"Chile con carne"
Con does, sometimes a: time
Con game: sting, bunco
Con man's accomplish: shill
Con man's trick: scam

Con men: shills
Conan the Barbarian
Conceal: hide, veil
Conceal, cover to: bury
Concealing garment: burka
Concealment, wait in: lurk
Concede defeat: say uncle
Conceited, more: vainer
Conceited smile: smirk,
Conceive: ideate, originate
Concentrated: dense
"Concentration" puzzle: rebus
Conception, mental: image
Concern, feel: care
Concerned, be: care
Concerning: regarding, inre, as to
Concert ending: ile
Concert extender: encore
Concert goof: odium
Concert hall: odea, odeum
Concert proceeds: gates, gate
Concert windup: finale
Concerto: opus
Conciliation, settle by: mediate
Conciliatory act: apology
Conciliatory offering: sop
Concludes one's case: rests
Concluding clause: apodosis
Concluding section: epilog
Conclusion, in: thus
Conclusion, ultimate: end-all
Concoct: brew
Concoction, herbal: tea
Concrete foundation: slab
Concrete reenforcer: rebar
Concrete smoother: trowel
Concur: assent
Concurrence: assent
Condensed wrapup: recap
Condescend to give: deign
Condiment, Bombay: chutney
Condiment origin: mustard seed
Condiment, red: paprika
Condition, undesirable: malady
Conditional release: parole
Conditions: ifs
Condo builder: developer
Condo luxury: sauna
Condominium, canine: kennel
Condon, Eddie: jazz name
Condor clutchers: talons
Condor nest: aerie
Condor's digs: aerie
Conducive to peace: irenic
Conducive to tranquility: restful
Conduct a meeting: hold
Conduct oneself inconspicuously: efface
Conduct, rules of: ethics
Conductance measure: MHO
Conductance unit: mho
Conductor: maestro
Conductor's baton: wand
Conductor's wand: baton
Cone: anagram

Cone bearer: larches
Cone maker: pine tree
Cone, sno: summer treat
Cone-bearing tree: yew, pine
Cone-shaped shelter: tepee
Conestoga: wagon
Confection, almond: paste
Confection, fancy: bonbon
Confection, nutty: nougat
Confectioner's creation: hard candy
Confederate president: Davis
Confederate soldier: reb
Confer: bestow, dub
Confer holy orders on: ordain
Confer honors on: awards
Confer knighthood: dub
Conference: parley
Conference site (1945): Yalta
Confess: avow
Confessor's list: sins,
Confidence, had: relied
Confidence, have: rely
Confidence, lacking in: timid
Confidence trick: ruse
Confident, over: smug
Confidentially: entre-nous
Conflagration: fire
Conforming to reality: true
Confound it: darn, dang, drat
Confront, solicit: accost
Confrontation, type of: face-to-face
Confucius "The Way": Tao
Confuse: bemuse
Confused: "at sea", addled
Confusion descriptor: utter
Confusion, mental: fog
Confusion, tumultuous: melee
Confusion, widespread: havoc
Congeal: jell, set, gel
Congeniality: niceness
Congenitally joined: adnate
Conger chasers: eelers
Congers: eels
Congo's former name: Zaire
Congressional agcy: GAO
Congressional candidate's goal: seat
Congressional consideration: acts
Conical home: tepee, wigwam, yurt
Conical shelter: tepee, wigwam, yurt
Conjecture: opine
Conjectured: surmised
Conjoined parts: adnexa
Conjunctive: brae
Conman's hoax: scam
Connect: attach
Connect up: link
Connected up: linked
Connecticut tableware: Bristol crystal
Connecticut tourist mecca: mystic
Connecting devise: adapter, link
Connection, without a: apart
Connections: ins
Connective, negative: nor
Conniptions: say so, fits

Conniving: sly
Conniving one: schemer
Conqueror, l066: Norman
Conquistador fighter: inca
Conquistador's quest: Mrs., oro
Conrad Aikon: poet
Conrad's Lord <u>Jim</u>
Conreid, Hans: actor
Con's utterance: nay
Conscience: superego
Conscientious one's duty: moral obligation
Conscious being: ego
Conscious of, be: sense
Consecrate: anoint, bless
Consent, gave: acceded
Consequence: result
Consequence, unlucky: tough break
Consequently: ergo
Conservative opening: ultra
Consider: deem
Consider in detail: examine
Considers to be: deems
Consistent with reality: true
Consociate: unite
Consommé: soup
Consonants, soft: lenses
Conspicuous: salient
Constantine the Great's mother: Helena
Constantly, to a poet: e'er
Constellation near Scorpios: Ara
Constellation illustration: star chart
Constellation in a night sky: Orion
Constellation Lepus: Hare
Constellation, Palindromic: Ara
Constellation, Rigel's: Orion
Constellation with a belt: Orion
Constitution change: amendment
Constrained, as speech: stilted
Constriction in the body: stenoses
Constrictor, tropical: boa
Construction area: site
Construction beam: I beam
Construction lift: hoist, crane
Construction site creation: scaffolding
Construction spot: site
Consultant, manual: user
Consume totally: use up
Consumer: user, buyer
Consumer goods: mdse
Consumer lure: rebate, sale
Consumer's org.: BBB
Consumer protection org.: BBB
Consumers report employee: rater
Contain: hold
Container: can, box, crate, pail
Container, broad-mouthed: jar
Container, cylindrical: barrel
Container for food preservation: jar
Container, open: tub
Container, shallow: tray
Container's weight: tare
Containing air: pneumatic
Containing borax: boric
Containing carbon: organic

Containing copper: cupric
Containing fire: igneous
Containing gold: dore
Containing iron: ferric
Containing silver: lunar
Containing slag: drossy
Containing tin: stannic
Contaminant free: pure
Contempt, word of: pish
Contemptible: base
Contemptible fellow: cad
Contemptible, fine: scorn
Contemptibly small: measly
Contemptuous action: indignity
Contend for superiority: vie
Contended: vied
<u>Nolo</u> contendere
Contends in court: sue
Content of cognition: idea
Contented sigh: aah
Contented sound: purr
Contents of snippy retorts: sass
Contest, elimination: spelling bee
Contest submission: entry
Continent divider: sea, ocean
Continent, smallest: Eur, Europe
Continental cash: euro
Continental pref.: Amero
Continental currency: Euro
Contingent on, was: hinged
Continue: go on
Continued: resumed
Continued story: serial, series
Contort: writhe
Contract, broke a: reneged
Contract language, overlooked: fine print
Contract principle: signee
Contract, secure: land, seal, deal
Contract section: clause
Contract, sign a: ink
Contract term: hereby
Contraction: tie
Contraction, common: hadn't
Contraction in an alibi: wasn't
Contractor's figures: bid
Contradictory statement: paradox
Contrary condition: war and peace
Contrary emotion: love and hate
Contrary to fact: untrue, lie
Contribute: kick in
Contributing element: factor
Contribution, creative: idea
Contribution, initial, of a sort: ante
Contribution receivers: donees
Control, bring under: harness, tame
Control, kind of: dual
Control, out of: amok
Controlling position: driver's seat
Controls, like some: dual
Controversial documentarian: Moore
Controversial points: issues
Convenes: meets, sits
Convent: abbey
Convent head: abbott, abbess

Convention handout: name tag
Convention wear: name tag
Conversant with: adept
Conversation, informal: chat
Conversation piece: phone
Convertible quintet: tires
Convex lens, like a: toric
Convex molding: ovolo, ovoli
Conviction, with: adamantly
Convinced, completely: sold
Convincing: cogent
Convoy chaser: U-boat
Convoys: fleets
Convulsive breath: gasp
Cook aid: recipe
Cook book Aunt:Erma
Cook, cookie: baker
Cook in a wok: stir
Cook in butter: sautee
Cook in embers: roast
Cook in oil: fry
Cook meat in closed pot: braise
Cook pot: olla
Cook slowly: braise, stew
Cook slowly in liquid: braise
Cookbook page: recipe
Cookbook phrase: add-in
Cooked on a griddle: ala plancha
"Cooked to a <u>turn</u>"
Cookie, cake-like: bar
Cookie cook: baker
Cookie, grab a: nosh
Cookie jar theft: raid,
Cookie maker: Famous Amos
Cookie Man: Amos
Cookie quantity: batch
Cookie sheet-full: batch
Cookie that debuted in 1912: Oreo
Cookie, type of: bar
Cookie, upscale: scone
Cookies and candy: snack
Cooking direction: braise
Cooking mixture: batter
Cooking oil: canola
Cooking style: ala provencal
Cooking, what's: menu
Cooking wine: sherry, marsala
Cookout area: patio, yard
Cookout, Polynesian: luau
Cook's contest: bake off
Cook's covering: apron
Cook's file: recipe
Cook's in butter: sautés
Cook's in embers: roasts
Cook's in fat: sautés
Cook's lure: aroma
Cook's name: Stu
Cool: neato
Cool fabric: linen
Cool, most: grooviest
Cool place: shade
"<u>Way</u> cool"
Cooler: jail, stir
Cooler, low-tech: fan

Cooling-off period: détente
Coolio's genre: rap
"In a Coon's age"
Co-op owner: stockholder
Cooper hero: Hawkeye, Deerslayer, Pathfinder
Cooperative group: cartel
Coopertown concern: baseball
"Cop a Plea"
Cop show vehicle: prowl car, patrol car
Copacetic: A-OK
Cope: fend
Coped: made do
Copenhagen amusement park: Tivoli
Copenhagen native: dane
Copied: emulated
Copied a drawing: traced
Copier, fix a: un-jam
Copier of old: scribe
Copies: mimics, apes
Copious: ample
Copland, Aaron: composer
Copland ballet: Rodeo
Copper and zinc: brass
Copper coin: penny, cent
Copper crust: patina
Copper engraving: mezzotint
Copper film: patina
Copperfield's girl: Dora
Copper-zinc alloy: similor
Cop's lure: sting
Cops run them down: tips
Copter, early: gyro, (giro)
Copter kin: gyro
Copy: repro
Copy a cassette: dub
Copy a drawing: trace
Copy, close: replica
Copy cat: aper
Copy, fix: emend, trace
Copy the example of: copy
Copyist: scribe
Copyright kin: patent
Coq au vim
Coquette, act like a: flirt
Coquettish: coy
Coral creation: atoll
Coral formation: palus, cay
Coral habitat: sea
Coral island: atoll, cay
Coral reef: atoll,
Coral reef, ring-shaped: atoll
Coral ridge: reef
Coral sea inlet, large: Papua
Coral spot: cays, reef
Coral worm: palolo
Corazon, Aquino:Phillippine leader
Cord cloth: rep
Cord, stretchy: bungee
Cord, strong: twine
Cordage fiber: sisal, jute, istle
Corday's victim: Marat
Cordelia's dad: Lear
Cordero, angle: jockey
Cordero's attire: silks

Cordial, black current: cassis
Cordial, less: icier
Cordial way, in a: warmly
Cordons bleus: bird, chefs
Corduroy ridge: rib, wale
Cordwood measure: stere
Coretta's husband: Martin Luther King
Corfu coins: oboli,
Corgi: welsh dog
Cork locale: eire
Corker: lulu
Corn beef sandwich: Reuben
Corn bin: crib
Corn bread: pone
Corn bread loaf: pone
Corn chip dip: salsa
Corn chip flavor: nacho
Corn, fixes: pops
Corn flour: pinole
Corn, ground: meal
Corn holder: husk, cob, ear
Corn husk, stuffed: tamale
Corn kin: bunion
Corn lily: ixia
Corn meal cakes: hush puppies
Corn meal mush: samp
Corn peel: husk
Corn product: salad oil, meal, ethanol
Corn tassel: silk
Cornball: trite
Corncracker state: Kentucky
Cornell, Ezar: college founder
Corner piece (chess): rook
Corner, secluded: nook
Corner, sharp: angle
Corner stone abbr.: estab.
Corner the market: co-empt, co-emption
Cornered: at bay
Cornfield cry: caw
Cornfield menace: crow
Cornfield sight: ear
Cornfield sound: caw
Cornfield weed: darn
Cornhusker city: Omaha
Cornice decoration: dentil
Corning brand: Pyrex
Cornish Hamlets: Trefi
Cornmeal mush: polenta
Cornstalk tip: tassel
Cornstarch brand: Argo
Cornucopia: horn
Coronado's quest: oro(gold)
Coronet: crown, tiara
Corot, Jean: Fr. painter
Corp biggie: CEO
Corp. money manager: CFO
Corpsmen: medics
Habeas corpus
Corrals: paddocks, pens
Correct: proper
Corrections, make: emend
Correctly pitched, in music: on key
Correspondence, stampless: EMail
Correspondent: pen pal

Correspondent, friendly: pen pal
Corresponding fluid: ink
Corrida clamor: ole
Corrida cry: ole
Corrida sight: toro
Corrida victim: el toro
Corrigenda, list of: errata
Corroded: ate, rusted
Corroded, as by acid: ate
Corrodes,: eats away, rots away
Corrosive chemical: acid
Corsages, football: mums
Corset, tighten: lace
Corsica island: Elba
Cort, Bud: actor
Corte's foe: Aztec
Corundum variety: emery
Corvine: crow, ravine
Cosmetic, ancient: kahl, kohl
Cosmetic brand: Avon, Coty, Mary Kay
Cosmetic name: Olay
Cosmetic, use: make up
Cosmic cycle: eon
Cosmic force: tao
Cosmonaut's insignia, old: CCCP
Cosmonaut's lab: Mir
Cosmopolitan: urbane, urban
"Cosmos" host: Carl Sagan
"Cosmos" producer: Carl Sagan
Cossack, usually: Slav
Cost as much as: run to
Cost of leaving, perhaps: fare
Cost of repairs: upkeep
Cost, slangily: damage
Costa de Sol City: Malaga
"Costa del Sol"
Costa Rican, any: tico
Costa Rican peninsula: Osa
Costello's partner: Abbott
Costumer head: Edith
Cote dweller: dove
Cote sound: bleat, baa
Coterie: charmed circle
Cotillion: prom, dance, ball
Cotillion honoree: deb
Cotillion venues: ballrooms
Cottage, alpine: chalet
Cotton, Joseph: actor
Cotton fabric: muslin, pima, lisle, gingham
Cotton fabric (fine): batiste, chambray, susi
Cotton fiber knots: neps
Cotton gin name: Eli
Cotton, handfuls of: wads
Cotton jersey: balbriggan
Cotton or increase: mather
Cotton or linen: fabric
Cotton pods: bolls
Cotton, raw: bolls
Cotton seeder: gin
Cotton, shirtmaker's: pima
Cotton substitute: acetate
Cotton thread, strong: lisle
Cotton to: like
Cotton, un-ginned: seedy

Cotton-pickin contraption: gin
Cottonwood: popular
Couch: daybed, settee
Couch potato fare: tv dinners
Cough, attention-getting: ahem
Cough drop: lozenge
Cough drop flavor: anise
Cough, polite: ahem
Cough-soother: troche
Could a fooled me: had no idea
Couldn't do better: superb
Coulomb, one, per sec.: amp.
Council, tribal: elders
Countenance: visage
Counter change: tips
Counter offer: soda
Counter, type of: Geiger
Counterclockwise: levo, levorotatory
Countercurrent: eddy
Counterfeit, inferior: ersatz
Counterfeited: forged, fake, bad, pseudo
Counterfeiter catcher: T-man
Countermands: overrides
Countess husband: earl
Countess title: lady, madam
Counting device: abacus
Counting everything: in all
Counting intervals: ten
Counting-out starter: eeny
Countless: myraid
Countrified: rural
Country: nation
Country address: RFD, Rte
Country club instructor: pro
Country estate: manor, villa
Country folks, naïve: yokels
Country home: villa
Country house: manor
Country, in the: rural
Country parson: vicar
Country road: lane
Country, wild: bush
Country yokel: rube
Country's core: heartland
Count's eqivalent: earl
Coup: oust
Coup de grace
Coup de tat
Coup for Goren: slam
Coup participant: plotter
Coup plotter: junta
Coup, stage a: usurp
Coup target: etat
Coupe coating: car wax
Couples-only ship: ark
Coupling devise: yoke
Couple, half a: Mrs.
Couplet creator: poet
Coupons, cut:clip
Coupons, use: redeem
Coupon-user's amount: rebate
Courage, pretense of: bravado
Courage, slangily: guts
Courage under fire: valor

Course: way, grainy
Course activity: golf
Course club: iron, wood,
Course, first: soup, salad
Course of action: plan
Course of travel: route
Course yell: fore
Court, pertaining to: aulic
Court: date, woo
Court barrier: tennis net
Court, brought to: arraigned
Court, central: atria
Court conference: sidebar
Court cry: oyez, oyer
Court divisions: nets
Court, intermediate: appellate
Court of justice: tribunal
Court offense: foul
Court order: writ, rise
Court postponement: stay
Court pseudonym: Roe, Wade
Court ranking: seed
Court statement: plea
Court "thing": res
Court VIPs: judge, DAs
Courted a ticket: sped
Courtesy envelope: SASE
Courthouse ritual: oath
Courtroom bargain: plea
Courtroom proceeding: trial
Courtroom testimony, like: oral
Courtyard: atrium
Courtyard, interior: atria
Cousin of nerd or wimp: twerp
Cousteau, Jacques Yves: sea explorer
Cousteau's invention: scuba
    island: Iles
    sea: Mer
Couture start: haute
Couturier's initials: YSL
Covent garden highlight: aria
Cover completely: bury
Cover crop: legume
Cover the walls: paper
Cover to conceal: bury
Cover with concrete: pave
Cover with a hard coat: encrust
Cover with a net: enlace
Cover with metal: plate
Coverage, kind of: media
Covered passageway: arcade
Covered with water: awash
Covering, external: skin, tarp
Coverlet: spread
Covet: envy
Cow: browbeat
Cow catcher: lasso
Cow owner, noted: O'Leary
Coward, Noel: playwrite
Coward's lack: nerve
Cowboy activity: ranching
Cowboy beat: range
Cowboy boss: rancher
Cowboy charge: herd

Cowboy meets: rodeos
Cowboy movie:: oater
Cowboy shout: whoa
Cowboy Star, old: Lash Larue
Cowboys: buckaroos
Cower, in fear: quail, wince
Cowhand's nickname: Tex
Cow-headed goddess: Isis
Cowhide puncher: awl
Cowl, wearing a: hooded
Cowpoke, singing: oatly
Cows: daunts
Cow's bellow: bawl
Cows mouthful: cuds
Cows of India, like: sacred
Cox, Courtney: actress
Coyly, acts: flirts
Cozumel coin: peso
Cozy, get: nestle
Cozy, more: homier
Cozy retreat: nest
Cozy seat: lap
CPA record: acct.
CPA's sum: amt.
Crabs (moves like): sidle
Crack of dawn: sun up
Crack squad: a team
Cracked: rimose, ajar, gaped
Cracked and redden: chap
Cracked, in a sense: ajar
Cracker shape: animal
Cracker spread: pate
Cracker topper, fancy: caviar
Crackerjack: whiz
Crackle's colleague: snap
Cracks in volcanoes: vents
Cracow native: polish
Craft of WW ll: U-boat
Craft partner: art
Craft, slow moving commodious: ark
Craftier: wilier
Crafty: sly, artsy
Crafty expedient: ruse
Crafty move: ruse
Crafty person: artisan
Craggy hill: tor
Cram into the overhead: stow
Cram, reason to: exam
Crammed together: dense
Cramped: narrow
Cramped, not as: roomier
Cramps: spasm
Cranberry condiment: sauce
Cranberry growing site: bog
Crane: hoist
Crane, boat: davit
Crane, ship: davit
Crane cousin: heron
Crane-arm part: gib, jib
Crane's home, at times: marsh
Cranial nerve: radix
Cranky, act: grump, grumpy, whine
"Nook and cranny"
Cranston, Alan: senator

Craps table two: snake eyes
Cratchit's, bob, job: clerk
Crate: jalopy, box
Crate part: slat
Cravat: scarf, necktie, tie, ascot
Craven, Wes: actor
Crawford, Cindy: model
Crawl, did the: swam
Crawl out of one's skin: molt
Crawl with: teem, rife
Crawl space: pool
Crayon drawing: pastel
Crazed captain: Ahab
Craziness, symbol of: loon
Crazy about: into, adore
"Crazy as a loon"
Crazy eight's cousin: uno
Crazy Horse: Sioux
Crazy Horse foe: Custer
Crazy Horse tribe: Oglala
Crazy way, in a
Crazy, in a way: madly
Crazy, word with: like
Cream de la crème: elites
Cream enhancer: aloe
Cream-filled roll: éclair, cannoli
Cream of tartar: argol
Cream Puff: éclair
Cream-sauce base: roux
Creamy cocktail: grasshopper
Creamy color: ivory
Create knotted lace: tat
Creation of puzzles: enigmatology
Creative atoner: make-up artist
Creative categories: genres
Creative contribution: idea
Creative spark: idea
Creative thinker: idea man
Creative works: arts
Creator of impressions:aper
Creator of puzzles: enigmatologist
Creature, malodorous: pole cat
Creature of Nepal, elusive: yeti
Creature, simious: ape
Creatures: beings
Creche figures: magi
Credit, gives: ascribes
Credit report blot: lien
Credit union user: member, employees
Credit, unlimited: blank check
Creed, Nicene
Creek: rill
Creek bed, dry: coulee
Creeping grass: zoysia
Creeps upon: nears
Crème caramel: flan
Cremona name: amati
Creole state Acadian: Cajun
Creole veggie: okra
Creole treat: jambalaya
Crepe suzette
Crepes cousin: bini
Crepes relatives: blintees
Crept: edged

Crept away: slunk
Crescent moon ends: horns
Crescent-shaped: luna, lunate
Crest, bantam: comb
Crest, ones sharing a: clan
Crest site: coat of arms
Crested bird: jay, cardinal
Crests or ridges, to a zoologist: crista, crestae
Crete Mountain: Ida
Crete Sea: Aegean
Cretin: idiot, oaf, boob, clod, dolt, dope,
     fool, lout, dumbo, dummy, half-wit,
     numskull, simpleton
Creusa's father: Priam,
       husband:Aeneas
       mother: Hecuba
       son: Ion, Ascanius
Crevasse pinnacle: serac
Crevice: rift
Crew cut, gives a: crops
Crew member: bos'n, hand, oarsman
Crewel or boucle: yarn
Crewmate of Uhura: Sulu
Crew team tool: oar
Cri de coeur
Cricket club: bat
Cricket position: ons
Cricket segments: overs
Cricket team: eleven
Cried noisily: bawled
Cries at a circus: ohs
Cries of praise: hosannas
Crime, help in a: abet
CSI test sire: DNA lab
Crime solving factor: DNA
Crime syndicate: Cosa Nostra
Crimes, high: treason
Criminal attorney: defender
Criminal game: clues, clue
Criminal gang: mob
Criminal, vicious: thug
Criminals, in the station house: perps
Crimson tide home: Alabama
Crinkle fabric: crepes
Crisis point: head
Crisp or Tarantino: Quentin
Criss Angel, for one: magician
Crist, Judith: author, critic
Criterion: std., standard, rule
Critic, kind of: art
Critical hospital area: ICU
Critical juncture: crunch time
Critical point: key issue
Critical success: éclat
Criticize harshly: slam, scathe
Criticize severely: blister, scathe
Criticize, sharply: rap, slam
Critic's handout, sometimes: rave
Critics "Siskel and Ebert"
Crius' father: Uranus
       mother: Gaea
       son: Astraeus
Crocheted item: bootee, dolly
Crock: olla

Crockery: china
Crockett of folklore: Davy
Crockett, Davy: frontier man
Crockett's last stand: Alamo
Crocus bulb: corm
Croesus' desire: more
       kingdom: Lydia
Croiz de Guerre: French mil. decoration
Cromwell, Oliver: revolutionary
Cromwell's nickname: Ironsides
Cronyn, Hume: actor
Crook, "B" movie: yegg
Crooked: askew
Crooked, made: bent
Crooner's tune: ballad
Crop, bird: craw
Crop duster: aviator
Crop units: rows, acres
Crop, worldwide: rice
Crop-chomping ant: atta
Croquet court: lawn
Croquet hoops: wickets
Crosby, Stills, Nash, and Young
Cross, Amanda: mystery writer
Cross, ancient: tau
Cross at risk: jaywalk
Cross, chancel: rood
Cross in a church: rood
Cross paths: meet
Cross to bear: onus
Cross, type of: tau
Cross-barred pattern: plaid
Crossbeam: trave, traverse
Crossbow bolt: arrow,
Cross-country runner: harrier
Crossed, as a stream: forded
Cross-reference: index
Crossword design: grid
Crossword diagram: grid
Crotchety one: coot
Crouches: stoops
Crouches in fear: cowers
Croupier's tools: rakes
Crow, one with a: prier
Crow, time to: sun up, sun rise
Crowd, a (maybe): three
Crowd around: mob,
Crowd control cop's directive: move along
Crowd for Caesar: III
Crowd, huge: mob scene
Crowded: packed
Crowded in: thronged, trooped
Crowded, more: busier
Crowding in, go: trooping, thronging
Crowds, like some: ugly, unruly
Crowd-scene actor: extra
Crown and scepter: regalia
Crown, wears a: reigns, rules
Crown wearers: king, queen
Crown, wore the: reigned
Crown: coronet, tiara, diadem
"Triple Crown"
Crowning point: acme
Crow's cousin: oriole

Crow's nest cry: ahoy
Crucial qualifier: acid test
Crucial time: crisis
Cruciate ligament spot: knee
Crucified: rood
Crude bed, in Britain: doss
Crude bed, in Soho: doss
Crude clothes presser: sad iron
Cruder: rawer
Crudities: raw
Cruel dude: meanie
Cruel tyrant: Nero
Cruelty, delight in: sadism
Cruise, go on a: set sail
Cruise setting: ocean
Cruise ship: liner
Cruise ship fare: passage, passenger
Cruise shop woes: mal de mer
Cruise stop: Nassau, POC (port of call), isle
Cruise worker: steward
Cruising place: main drag
Cruller's kin: donut
Crumbles: rots, decays
Crumbum: heel
Crumpet companion: tea
Crumple: wad, wad up
Crumpled up: wadded
Crunch targets: abs
Crunchy fair fare: kettle corn
Crunchy sandwich: BLT
Crunchy stalk: celery
Crusade: quest
Crusader's stronghold: acre
Crush: quell
Crushed grapes: trod, trodden
Crushed underfoot: trod
Crusher, jungle: boa
Crust, it's below the: mantel
Crustacean's claw: chela
Crusted over: caked
Crusty roll: kaiser
Crux: nub
Cry about: bemoan
Cry, astonished: wow
Cry, audibly: sob
Cry, awed: wow
Cry, chilling: shriek
Cry from a sty: oink
Cry, gloating: oho
Cry, harsh: caw
Cry, mournful: alas
Cry of alarm: oh no
Cry of affirmation: yes, yea
Cry of bacchanals: evoe
Cry of delight: whee
Cry of disdain: pooh, pah, pish
Cry of disgust: fie, pah
Cry of dismay: yipe
Cry of woe: alas
Crying shame: pity
Cryptologist's concern: codes
Crystal containing stone: geode
Crystal gazer: seer
Crystal, like some: leaded

Crystal, natural: snow
Crystal, six-sided: snow flake
Crystalline alkaloid: aricin
Crystalline compound: amide
Crystalline gem: iolite, iolete
Crystalline hydrocarbon: tolans
Crystal-lined stones geodes
Crystallize: jell
"CSA" defender: reb
"CSA" monogram: reb, rel
C-3PO and R2-D2: robots
C to C musically: octave
"CTRL" neighbor: ALT
Cub Scout group: den
Cub Scout leader, sometimes: den mother
Cuba, to Castro: isla
Cuban dance: cha cha
Cuban dance tune: rumba
Cuba's "this": esta
Cubbyhole: nook
Cube inventor: Rubik
Cubed, two: eight
Cubic meter: stere
Cubicle filler: desks
Cuchulain's father: Lug, Lugh, Lugus
    foe: Medb, Maeve
    kingdom: Ulster
    mother: Dechtire
    son: Conlaoch
    victim: Conlaoch
    wife: Emer
Cuckoo, tropical: ani
Cuckoopint plant: arum
Cuckoos, black: anis
Cuddle: nestle
Cuddle up: canoodle
Cudgel one's brain: rack
Cue stick, prepares a: chalks
Cue the cast: prompt
Cuff, kind of: rotator
Cugat specialty: rumba
Cuisine, Far East: Thai
Cuisine, kind of: haute, ethnic
Cuisine, spicy: creole
Cuisine start: haute
Cuisine, Tex-Mex:
Cuke: cucumber
Culbertson, Ely: bridge
Cul-de-sac: alley
Culp, Robert: actor
Mea culpa
Cult: sect
Cultivate: raise, till
Cultivation (capable of): arable
Culture character: athos, ethos
Culture media: agar
Culture revolution figure: Mao
Culture, start for: agri
Cultured fellow: gent
Cum laude modifier: magna
Cumin or mint: herb
Summa cum laude
Cummerbund: sash
Cummerbund site: waist

Cummings, Alan: actor
Cummings creation: sonnet
Cumulus lead-in: alto
Cunning, most: wiliest
Cuomo, Mario: politician
Cup, big: mug
Cup, café: tasse
Cup holder: saucer
Cup, holy: grail
Cup or pay ending: ola
Cupbearer of the gods: Hebe, Ganymede
Cupboard: hutch
Cupboard, dutch: kas
Cupel, use a: test, (small porous cup)
Cupid: amor, Eros, putto, cherub
Cupid counterpart: Eros
Cupidity: greed
Cupid's beloved: Psyche
    brother: Anteros
    father: Hermes, Mercury
    mother: Venus, Aphrodite
    title: Dan
Curate: clergy
Curative salts: epsom
Curative treatment: therapy
Curdle: clabber
Curd's companion: whey
Cure: remedy
Cure meat: smoke, salt
Cure-alls: panaceas,
Cured, in a way: smoked
Cures of yore, clingy: leeches
Cures, T. S.: writer
Curie discovery: radium
Curing agent: salt
Curiosity: oddity
Curious, be: inquire
"Curious George" author: Rey
Curl or lock: tress
Curl, unruly: cowlick
Curler's need: ice, stone
Curler's playing area: rink
Curley-leaf cabbage: kale, cole
Curley's Friend: Moe
Curling iron, uses a: crimps
Curling target: tee
Curls: ringlets
Currency exchange premium: agio
Currency, temporary: script
Current, bit of: amp.
Current chasers: events
Current choice: AC DC
Current, circular: eddy
Current conductor: anode
Current craze: rage
Current favorite: rage
Current letters: AC DC
Current, make: up date
Current, powerful: whirlpool
Current rage: fad
Current restrictor: diode
Currie's daughter: Irene, Eve
Currie's discovery: radium
Currie's partner: Ives

Curry comb target: mane
Curse word (old): fie
Cursor mover: mouse
Curt: abrupt
Curtain call, takes a: bows
Curtain fabric: ninon, sheer, lace, etamine, chintz
Curtain holder: tie back, rod
Curtain material, notable: iron
Curtain trim: tassels, pom pom
Curtain type: tieback
Curtaining: voile
Curtis, Jamie Lee: actress
"Bell curve"
Curve, double: ogee
Curve, enclosed: ellipse
Curve in geometry: conic
Curve, switchback: ess
Curved bones: ribs
Curved line: arc
Curved path: arc
Curved planking (vessel): sny
Curving inward: concave
Cushion, long narrow: bolster
Cushion, small: pad
Cush's son: Seba
Cushy job: plum,
Cuss words: oaths
Cussler hero: Pitt
Custard: flan
Custard apple: ates, papaw, papayo
Custard desert: éclair, flan
Custard, like: eggy
Custard-filled cake: gateau
Custodian's need: key
Custom: wont, usage
Custom charge: duty
Customary function: role
Customary observance: rite
Customer: buyer, patron
Customer, after a sale: owner
Customer, hack's: fare
Customize: adapt
Customs target: smuggler
Cut and paste: edit
Cut and ran: fled
Cut and run: flee
Cut down: hew
Cut from the same cloth: akin
Cut in thirds: tri-sect
Cut in two: saw
Cut into tiny pieces: mince, dice
Cut, previously: sawn
Cut quickly: snip
Cut short: curtail, clip, crop, trim, abort
Cut some slack: ease
Cut to fit: trim
Cut trees for lumber: log
Cuticle site: finger nail, toe nail
Cutlass or scimitar: swords
Cutlasses' kin: epee
Cutlery, piece of: utensil
Cutlets, prepare: bread
Cuts a notched ridge: pinks

Cuts back: pares
Cuts for friars: tonsures
Cuts off, in a way: boycotts
Cuts short: bobs
Cutting remark: barb
Cutting tool: adz, axe, knife, saw
Cuttlefish defense: ink
Cuttlefish ink: sepia
Cuttlefish kin: octopi
Cuttlefish pigment: sepia
Cutup: prankster
Cuzco builder: Inca
Cuzco locale: Andes, Peru
Cuzco (Peru): Inca
Cyanotype: blue print
Cyaxeres, King, was one: Mede
Cybernetics founder: Wiener, Norbert
Cyberspace, enters: logs on
Cyberspace junk mail: spam
Cyberspace letters: AOL
Cyberspace locales: webs
Cyberspace message: Email
Cyberspace Note: Email
Cyberspace visitor: user
Cycles: pedals
Cycle part: phase
Cycle starter: tri
Cyclists:
        Armstrong, Lance
        Lemond, Greg
Cyclotron: atom smasher
Cyclotron item: ions, protons
Cycnus's father: Ares, Mars
        slayer: Heracles, Hercules
Cygnet's father: cob
Cygnet's parents: swans
Cygnus star: Deneb
Cylindrical container: barrel
Cynical, make: jade
Cypress growth: knee
Cyprinoid's fish: dace
Cyrano's despair: nose
Cyrus, Billy Ray: country music
Cyrus conquest: Lydia, Media, Babylon
        daughter: Atossa
        father: Cambyses
        son: Cambyses
Cyrus' realm today: Iran
Cyst, harmless: wen
Cyst, superficial: wen
Czar: tzar
Czar, terrible: Ivan
Czarist aristocrat: Boyar
Czar's order: ukase
Czeck capital: Prague

D

Da capo Aria
Da Gama, Vasco: explorer
"Da" opposite: nyel, nyet
Da or ja: yes
D'Artagnan prop: Epee

"Daba, Aba Honeymoon"
Dabbling duck: teal
Dactyl: toe
Dactyl gram: fingerprint
Dad, gift for: tie
Dada collectibles: Arps
Dada founder: Arp
Dadaism founder: Arp
Daddy Warbuck's ward: Annie
Daffy trademark: lisp
Dagger companion: cloak
Dagger, old: snee, dirk
Dagger, wavy: kris
Dagwood's dog: Daisy
Dagwood's neighbor boy: Elmo
Dah partner: dit
Dahl, Arlene: actress
Daily charge: rate
Daily section: op-ed
"Daily Planet" reporter: Kent
Dainty: elfin
Daiquiri flavor, familiar: banana
Daiquiri ingredient: rum
Dairymaid, Hardy's: Tess
Dais prop: lectern
Daisy, Michaelmas: Aster
Daisy or volcano: Shasta
Daisy Mae Scraggs
Daisy Mae's friend: Abner
"Upsy daisy"
Dakota dialect: Teton
Dakota resident, noted: Ono
Dalai Lama
Dalai Lama city: Lhasa
Dali, Salvador: painter
Dallas cager: Mav
Dalmatian's accumulation: spots
Daly, Tyne: actress
Dam, small: weir
Damage, severe: havoc
Damage superficially: mar
Damage to, do: impair
Damaged, easily: frail
Damascene's land: Syria
Damascus, from: Syrian
Damayanti's beloved: Nala
Dame Myra Hess
"Dame Yankee" temptress: Lola
Damone, Vic: musician
Damper: soggier, wetter
Dam's partner: sire
Damsel: maiden, maid
Damsel rescuer: hero
Danae's father: Acrisius
        lover: Zeus
        son: Perseus
Danaus' brother: Aegyptus
        daughters: Danaids, Danaides
        father: Belus
        founder of: Argos
        grandfather: Neptune, Poseidon
Dance about: prance
Dance all night: party
Dance band: combo

Dance, Brazilian: samba
Dance, chain: conga
Dance, circle: hora
Dance clumsily: balter
Dance, colonial: minuet, reel
Dance, Cuban: cha cha, conga
Dance, fiery: flamenco
Dance for two: tango
Dance, formal: ball
Dance: gym: hop
Dance, half of a: cha
Dance inline: conga
Dance, Israel: hora, horah
Dance, Jaffa: hora
Dance, joyous: hora, horah
Dance, Latin: cha-cha
Dance, Latin music: Salsa
Dance, luau: hula
Dance, medieval: estample
Dance move: step, glide
Dance of the 30's: Lindy
Dance or paint: war
Dance or paint: war
Dance, Scottish: reel
Dance site: disc
Dance spot: disco
Dance, stately: pavane
Dance step: pas
Dance, storytelling: hula
Dance studio wear: tights
Dance wear: tutu
Dance wildly: gyrate
Dancer, disco: go go
Dancer, seven veil: Salome
Dancer's asset: grace
Dancer's partner: dasher
Dances in the grass: hulas
Dances, regal: proms
"Dances with Wolves"
"Dancing Queen" singers: Abba
Dandelion, finally: puff ball
Dandy: fop
Danger: risk, peril
Danger signal: alarm, flare
Dangerfield persona: loser
Dangerous feat: stunt
Dangerous gas: radon
Dangerous loop: noose
Dangerous, not: safe
Dangerous tide: rip
Dangle a carrot: tempt
Dangler, tempting: carrot
Dangles: lolls
Daniel landed in one: den
Danish island: Aero
Danish measure: alen
Danish seaport: Odense
Danish weight: eser
Dank place: dungeon
Danke, in Dijon: merci
Danny's "Taxi" role: Louie
Danseuse: ballerina
Danson, Ted: actor
Dante's beloved: Beatrice

birthplace: Florence
daughter: Antonia
death place: Ravenna
party: Guelph, Blanchi
patron: Scala
teacher: Latini
wife: Gemma
work: Inferno, Commedia, Paradiso,
    Vita Nuova, Purgatorio
year: anno
Danza, Tony:actorDaphne turned into this
tree: laurel
Dapper: sporty
Dapper, more: nattier
Dappled: pied, piebald, motley
Dappled, as a horse: pied
Dare alternative: truth
Daring deed: feat
Daring exploit: gest
Daring feat: stunt
"Dark, a shot in the"
Dark continent: Africa
Dark, poetically: ebon
Dark, totally: unlit
Dark yellow: ochre
Darkens in the sunlight: tans
Darker: bedim
Dark-haired lad: brunet
Darkness: pall
Darkness, end of: esses
Darkness prince: Satan
Darkroom image: photo, X-ray
Darkroom solution: toner, fixer
Darn it: sew
Darned things: sewed
Darrow, Clarence: atty
Dart about: flit
Dart away: scoot
d'Artagnan's creator: Dumas
d'Artagnan prop: epee
Dartboard locale: pub, bar
Darth Vader Attire: cloak
Darth Vader, once: Jedi
Darth Vader side: Empire
Darth Vader son: Luke
Darth's daughter: Leia
    real name: Anakin
Darting stinger: wasp
Dartmouth College location: Devon,
    Hanover, New Hampshire
Darwin's ship: Beagle
Syr Darya
"Das Kapital" author: Marx
Dash: elan
Dash off: hie
Dash widths: ens
Dashboard gadget: tach
Dashiell contemporary: Erle
Dashiell's peer: Erle
Dashing: rakish
Data, dig for: delve
Data, enter: type
Data holder: CD ROM
Data, misrepresent: skew

Data speed unit: baud
Data storage unit: byte
Date abbr.: BCE
Date maker: palm
Date palm locale: oases, oasis
Dating, stop: drop
Dateless: stag
Daughter of the moon: Nokomis
Daughter of the night: Nemesis
Daughter's brothers: Sons
Dauntless: Heroic
Daven: Couch
Davenport: Sofa
Davenport, Lindsay: tennis
Davenport resident: Iowan
David hid from soul, where: Engesi
King David's grandfather: Obed
David's son: Solomo
    target: Goliath
    wife: Abigail
Davis, Geena: actress
Dawbar, Pam: actress
Dawdle around: loiter
Dawdled: tarried
Dawn goddess: Aurora, Eos
Dawn Horse Epoch: Eocene
Dawn, Of the: Eoan
Rae Dawn Chong
"Dawson's Creek" extra: teen
Day blindness: nyctalopia
Day mein: fluorescent paint
Day of atonement: Yom Kippur
Day one: onset
Day-to-day deterioration: wear
Day, to Jose: dia
Daybreak deity: Aurora
Daybreak, in verse: morn
Daydream: wish, fantasy
Daydreamer, fictional: Mitty
Daydreams: reveries
Daylight Savings Time ends: October
Days long ago: yore
Day's march: etape
"Days of yore"
Daytime drama: soap
Dazed, with "out": zoned
Dazzled: wowed
DC fundraiser: PAC
DC lobby: PAC
De-camp, aide-
De, coup de grâce
De, crème de menthe
De, eau de cologne
De, esprit de corps
De, Ile de France
De, nom de guerre
De, nom de plume
De, pas de deux
Dead center, hit: nailed
Dead duck: goner
Dead man's hand, part of: aces
Dead Sea document: Scroll
Dead Sea feeder: Jordan
Dead Sea fortress, historic: Masada

Dead-ball era, The
Deaden, as in acoustics: damp, dampen
Deadline, past: late
Deadlock: tie, even, stall mate
Deadly poison: bane
Deafened ears, fell on: dinned
Deal, a better: cheaper
Deal in: sell
Deal prelude: ante
Deal, sealing a: clinching
Deal, type of: done
Deal with: handle, cope
Dealer, seller: trader
Dealer's wheels: demo
Dealing a mighty blow: smiting
Dealmaker, expert: closer
Dealt with adversity successful: coped
Dealt with an issue: coped
Dean, Silas: diplomat
Dear in Italy: cara
Dear in Venice: cara
Dearer, as memories: fonder
Death Valley rarity: rain,
Deathlessness: immortality
Debatable: moot
Debate issue: topic
Debate, lively: cross fire
Debate topic: issue
Debated: argued
Debauchee: roué
Debonair: urbane, suave
Debt, get out of: repay
Debt instrument, informal: IOU
Debt letters: IOU
Debt securities: liens
Debts securer: lien
Debts, unpaid: arrears
Debussy music: Etude
         sea: mer
         subject: mer
         work: "La Mer"
Debutante's bow: curtsy
Decade, memorable: era
Decadent: effete
Decades, important: eras
Decaf brand: Sanka
Decant: pour
Decapod, edible: shrimp
Descartes' concern: "I am"
Decathlon units: events
Decay, like a tree of old: dote
Decay or decline: ebb
Decayed swamp matter: peat
Decaying bog moss: peat
Decays: rusts, rots, spoils
Deceit, skillful: guiles
Deceitful: two-faced
Deceitful cunning: wile
Deceiver: beguiler
Deception: hoax
Deception, act of: scam
Deception, artful: ploy
Deceptive scheme: set up, feint, scam
Decide: opt

Decide, as a judge: rule
Decide, unable to: torn
Decides, (as by a jury): rules
Decision alteration: change of heart
Decision, comes to a: opts
Decision, make a: opt
Decisions, sometimes: hasty
Decisive, be: opt
Decisive win: rout
Decisively important: fateful
Deck, allegorical: tarot
Deck, clean the: swab
Deck cleaner: mop
Deck foursome: Aces
Deck hands: crew
Deck posts: bitts, ship post
Deck the halls: festoon
Deck the halls syllables: las
Decked. They may be: halls
Decks out: arrays
Declaim: orate, recite
Declaim wildly: rave
Declamation, loud, bombastic: harangue
Declare: aver
Declare frankly: avow
Declare illegal: gag
Declare invalid: annul, void
Declare openly: avow
Declare positively: aver
Declare to be true: affirm
Declare untrue: deny
Declared: avowed
Decline in value: sag
Decline or decay: ebb
Decline, period of: ebb
Decline politely: beg off
Decline to vote: abstain
Declined: slid
Decorate anew: redo
Decorate cupcakes: ice
Decorate excessively: ornate
Decorated leather: tooled
Decorated tin-ware: tole
Decorates richly: gilds
Decoration, flower-shaped: rosette
Decoration, intricate: detail
Decoration suggestion: color scheme
Decorative interlaced lines: tracery
Decorative mat: doily
Decorative material: art
Decorative needle case: etui,
Decorative pouring vessel: ewer
Decorative trinket: gew-gaw
Decorous, stiffly: prim
Decrease, gradually: wane
Decreased bit by bit: dwindles
Decreases intensity: wanes
Decree: fiat, ordain
Decree, formal: edict
Decree, royal: fiat, edict
Decreed: ruled
D-Day beach: Omaha
Dedicatory poem: ode
Deduces: infers

Dee, Joey: pop singer
Dee, Kiki: pop singer
Dee, Ruby: actress
Dee, Sandra: actress
Deed, chivalrous: gist
Deed, daring: feat
Deed holders: owners
Deeds, like some: in escrow
Deejay's disc: demo
Deem appropriate: see fit
Deep bell: gong
Deep blue: indigo
Deep blue dye: anil
Deep bow: salaam
Deep breath: sigh
Deep discount event: clearance sale
Deep down: inside
Deep drink: swig
Deep fissure: abyss
Deep hole: pit
Deep knee bends
Deep repugnance: hate
Deep sea explorer: diver
Deep sleep: sopor, coma
Deep space mission: probe
Deep water: sea
Deep well: Artesian
Deep-bodied herring: shad
Deeply absorbed: rapt
Deeply engrossed: rapt
Deeply felt: intense
Deep red gem: garnet
Deep-seated feeling of rancor: grudge
Deep-seated: inbred, inborn, innate, settled,
         inherent
Deep-six: toss, trash
Deep space mission: probe
Deep-voiced lady: alto
Deer: roe, napu
Deer head: rein
Deer, large grayish: Milu
Deer (male): stag, buck, hart
Deere contest: tractor pull
Deere's vehicle: tractor
Def Jam genre: Rap
De facto: actually
Defeat: set
Defeat, at bridge: set
Defeat, concede: say uncle
Defeat, disperse in: root
Defeat, more than just: crush, shellac
Defeat soundly: shellac, trounce
Defeat, utterly: thrash, romp
Defeats a bridge contract: sets
Defeats a wrestler: pins
Defeats by guile: outwits
Defective: flawed
Defendant's answer: plea
Defendants, legally: rei
Defendant's ploy: alibi
Defense ditch: moat
Defense mechanism: denial
Defense org.: NATO, SAC
Defense system initials: SAC

Defensive fortifications: ramparts
Defiant reply: never, no way
Defined, less: vaguer
Definition basis: meaning
Defoe, Daniel: writer
Defoe castaway: Crusoe
Defoe hero: Crusoe
Defraud: bilk, cheat
Defy gravity: levitate
Degraded: abased
Degree in mathematics: nth
Deighton, Len: writer, author
Deity: God
Deity, Native American: Great Spirit
Deity of creation: Brahma
Deity of destruction: Siva
Deity of sustenance: Vishnu
Deity of the Quran: Allah
Deity, Phoenician: Baal
Deja vu
Dejected: glum, morose
Dejection, expressing: sighing
Dekes: feints
Tierra del fuego
Del. neighbor: Ins.
Dela Mare, Walter: writer
Delaney, Kim: actress
Delay by deception: stall
Delay, not: act, now
Delay, temporary: deferral
Delay the process of: retard
Delay, without: ASAP, a pace
Delays: lags
Dele undoer: stat, stet
Delemare, Walter: Eng poet, novelist
Delete the files: erase
Deleted items, oft.: spam
Delhi address: sri
Delhi coin: rupee
Delhi domestic: amah
Delhi dude: Indian
Delhi honorific: Sri
Delhi melody: raga
Delhi sir: sahib
Delhi title: sri
Deli crepes: blini
Deli loaf: rye
Deli lunch: hero
Deli order: sub
Deli salmon: lox
Deli sandwich: hero
Deli scale word: tare
Deli unit: lbs
Delibes opera: Lakme
Delicate: lacy
Delicate colors: tints
Delicate, physically: frail
Delicious dish: viand
Delicious drink: nectar
Delight, filled with: enrapt
Delight in: enjoy
Delight in cruelty: sadism
Delighted in: like, adore
Delineate: etch, draw, outline

Delinquent GI: AWOL
Deliver a keynote: orate
Delivery necessity: labor
Delivery person (old time): ice man
Delon, Alain: actor
Delphi oracle: priestess
Delphi figure: oracle
Delphi prognosticator: oracle
Delphic datum: sign
Delphi's god: Apollo
Delta preceder: gamma
Delt's neighbor: abs, pecs
Deluded: led on
Delve deeply: root
Demagnetize, as a tape: erase
Demand, peremptory: ultimatum
Demands: exacts
Demeanors: miens
Demille genre: epic
Demille production: epic
Demimonde members: courtesans
Demolished: razed
Demonstrate: prove
Demonstrates connections: relates
Demonstrates fallibility: errs
Demure: chaste, prim
Demure manner, in a: coyly
Demure, most: coyest
Demure way, in a: coyly
Den: lair
Den furniture: day bed
Den sleeper: sofa bed, day bed
Dendrite's partner: axon
Dendrite's place: neuron
Denebola's constellation: Leo
Denizen of Sherwood Forest: Robin Hood
Denmark leader: Dee
Dennis's dog: Ruff
Denny's competitor: IHOP
Denominations: sect
De novo: again
Dense, less: sparser
Dent: bung, mar, ding
Dent, minor: ding
Dental filling: amalgam, inlay
Dentist drill: bur
Dentist plea: open wide
Dentist's test: oral exam
Deny: gainsay, naysay
Department store container: show case,
    display case
Departures: adieus
Depend on: hinge, rely
Depict by drawing: limn
Depilatory brand: Nair
Depletes: saps
Deployment, period of: tour
Nom de plume
Deportment: mien
Deposit: set, lai
Deposit, river: silt
Deposition, characteristic: nature
Depository for goods: storage
Depot: station

Depp, Johnny: actor
Depraved: bad, evil
Depression Era agency: WPA
Deprivation, type of: sensory
Deprive of authority: dethrone
Deprived, as of happiness: bereft
Depth, bottomless: abyss
Depth charge target: U-boat, sub
Depth charges: ash cans
DePutti, Lya: silent film actress
Deputy sheriff: bailiff
Derby or boater: hat
Derby or pillbox: hat
Derby setting: Epsom
Derek, Bo: actress
Derelict: remiss
Deride: sneer
Derisive shouts: hoots, hah
Derive benefit from: profit
Dern, Bruce: actor
Dern, laura: actress
Dernier cri: the latest thing
Derogatory, insinuatingly: snide
Derrick: hoist
Dershowitz, Alan: attorney
Dervishes: fakirs
Dervish's faith: Islam
Desalination byproduct: sea salt
DesCartes, Rene: math
Descend a cliff: rappel
Descend upon: assail
Descendent, direct: scion
Descendent or heir: scion
Describe grammatically: parse
Desdemona's enemy: Iago
    husband: Othello
    slayer: Othello
Desensitize: inure
Desert anomaly: oasis,
Desert denizen: sand rat
Desert description: arid
Desert dweller: Arab
Desert formation: dune
"Desert Fox": Rommel, Erwin
Desert gully: wadi
Desert of Asia, high: Gobi
Desert lake: mirage
Desert, Mongolian: Gobi
Desert mount: dromedary (camel)
Desert near Sinai: Negev
Desert nomad: Arab
Desert phenomenon: mirage
Desert plant: agave, yucca
Desert refuge: oasis, oases
Desert safari: caravan
Desert sight: mirage, dune, oasis
Desert terrain: sand
Desert valley, certain: wadi
Desert wind, hot: simoom
Deserted: forlorn
Deserter classification: AWOL
Deserves: merits
Deserving a slap,: fresh
Desiccated: sere

Design description: spec
Design device: stencil
Design in relief: cameo
Design linchpin: motif
Design on fabric: batik
Designated driver, like a: sober
Designated recipient: heir
Designated specifically: earmarked
Designated successor: heir
Designed for offices: ergonomic
Designer: "Giozgio Armani"
Designer label name: Dior, Levi
Designer water source: Evian
Designs: motifs
Desirable street: easy
Desire, intense: yen
Desired: lusted
Desired, just as: ideal
Desirous look: leer
Desk feature, old: ink well
Desk, raised: ambo
Desktop: PC
Desktop symbol: icon
Desolate: barren
Desolate, most: starkest
Desperado, like a: lawless
Desperado's fear: posse
Despondent comment: alas
Despot: tyrant, tsar, tzar, ogres
Despot, bygone: tsar
Despotic: bossy
Dessert, deep-dish: pie
Dessert, frozen: sherbet, sorbet
Dessert menu items: cakes, pies
Dessert, non-filling: Jell-O
Dessert of stewed fruit: compote
Dessert pastry: éclair, pie
Dessert, rich
Dessert, rich: mousse
Dessert trolley: cart
Dessert wine: sauterne
Destined to unhappy end: doomed
Destiny, unhappy: doomed
Destitute person: pauper
Destroy one's self-confidence: abash
Destroys: kills, ruins
Destruction, wide: havoc
Destructive: ruinous
Destructive bug: borer
Destructive caterpillar: web worm
Destructive current: El Nino
Destructive prowler: vandal
Destructive spree: rampage
Detailed account: report
Detective: sam spade
Detective, adage-spouting: Chan
Detective, orchid-loving: Wolfe
Detectives check them: clues, alibis
Detectives, for short: PIs
Detector, kind of: motion
Deteriorated: spoilt
Deterioration, day-to-day: wear
Determine by chance: cast lots
Determine value: assess

Determine who brakes in billiards: lag
Determiner of wind direction: Coriolis force
Detested thing: anathema
Detonation stuff: tetryl
Detour around: by pass
Detroit athlete: Tiger, Lion, Red Wing
Detroit dud: Edsel
Detroit's nickname: Motown
De Triomphe, Arc
Deus ex machina
Deuterium discover: Urey
Une, deux
Devastate: ruin
Develop: arise, evolve
Develop in the mind: gestate
Develop slowly: evolve
Developed, fully: ripe, adult
Developer's layout: plot
Developing bit by bit: gradual
Development, stage of: phase
Develops into: becomes
Devers, gail: track
Deviate, as a rocket: yaw
Deviation: anomaly
Deviation from accuracy: error
Device, dramatic: aside
Device to restrict current: diode
Devil fish: manta, ray
Devil-may-care: gay, rash, wild, rakish
Devine, Andy: actor
Devine, Wm.: actor
Devious maneuver: ploy
Devious one: sneak
Devoid of feeling: apathetic
Devoid of vegetation: barren
Devonshire county seat: Exeter
Devoted to schoolwork: studious
Devotee: buff
Devotee's suffix: ist
Devoted: fan, ist
Devotion, deep: ardor
Devotion, object of: idol
Devotion, regard with: adore
Devoutly religious: pious
Devoutly wish: pray
Dewlap: jowl
Dey, Susan: actress
Dhow sailor, typically: Arab
Diadem: tiara
Diabolical: evil
Diacritical mark: tilde
Diagnostic image: scan
Diagonal pattern: twill
Diagonal spar: sprit
Diagram: chart
Diagram a sentence: parse
Dial tone:
Dialect, highlands: Erse
Dialogue, bit of: line
Dialogue, platonic: Crito
Dial-up device: modem
Diameter halves: radii
Diametrically opposed: polarized
Diamond apparel: mitt, uniform

Diamond club: bat
Diamond corner: base
Diamond cover: tarp
Diamond, fabulous: hope
Diamond feature: hardness
Diamond judges: umps, jewelers
"Diamond Lil"
Diamond, Neil: music
Diamond org.: MLB (baseball)
Diamond ploy: bunt
Diamond point: base
Diamond port: Antwerp
Diamond stat: fouls, RBI, ERA
Diamond shape: baguette
Diamond side: facet
Diamond thief: steal
Diamond weight: carat
Diamonds in Raul's deck: oros
Diamonds or clubs: suits
Diana's headpiece: coronet
"Dianna" singer: Anka
Diapason, use a: tune
Diaphanous: sheer
Diarist, prolific: Pepys
Diary: log
Diary keeper: Pepys
Diary lock: hasp
"Diary of a Mad Housewife"
Diary opener: Dear
Diatom, e.g.: alga
Diatribe: rant
Diaz, Cameron: film star
Dice: mince
Dice, rigged the: loaded
Dice spots: pips
Dice throw: roll
Diciembre, after: enero
Dick and Jane dog: Spot
Dick Tracy's wife: Tess
Dickens-based musical: Oliver
Dickens box: Sydney carton
Dickens, Boz
Dickens character: Dora
Dickens's Mr. Drood: Edwin
Dickensian moppet: Tiny Tim
Dickinson, Angie: actress
Dickinson, Emily: writer
Dickinson, Emily birthplace: Amherst
Dictation pro: steno
Dictation taker: steno
Dictatorial bosses: ogres
Dictionary: lexicon
Dict. entry: def.
Did dock work: laded, loaded
Did laps: swam,
Did livery work: shoed
Did nothing: loafed
Did once: used to
Did skin diving: snorkeled
Did some batiking: dyeing
Did some camels: skated
Did something with: used
Did spectacularly on: aced
Did well: thrived, prosper, aced

Didactical mark: breve
Didn't dillydally: acted
Didn't draw a card: held
Didn't follow: led
Didn't go together: clashed
Didn't have: taken
Didn't just check: mated
Didn't know when yet: TBA
Didn't pass: failed
Didn't spoil: kept
Dido's brother: Pygmalion
   father: Belus, Mutton
   husband: Acerbas, Sichaeus
   lover: Aeneas
Dieci meno sette: tre
Diego, Don, masked: Zorro
Die's down: wanes, abates
Diet, kind of: balanced
Diet, starvation: fast
Dietary need: iron
Dieter of rhyme: sprat
Dieter's portion: less
Dieter's repast: salad
Diets extreme: fasts
Difference: other
Difference, shade of: nuance
Difference, subtle: nuance
Difficult duty: onus
Difficult, not: easy, painless
Difficult situations: binds, dilemma
Difficult to grasp: intangible
Diffident: shy
Diffusion: osmosis
DiFranco, Ani: singer
Dig deep: delve
Dig for data: delve
Dig in: eat
Dig in the earth: grub
Dig into: delve
"Dig into the files"
Digestive aid: antacid
Digestive juice: bile
Digging, keep: deepen
Digit, familiar: toe
Digit, large: big toe
Digit, largest: nine
Digital alternative: analog
Digital readout: LCD
Digital watch readout: LCD, LED
Digits, having: toed
Digress: ramble
Digs in the earth: grubs
Dijon pal: ami
Dik-dik cousin: gnu
Dilapidated: old
Dilapidated car: crate
Dilemma part: horns
Dilettantish: arty
Diligence: care
Dill seed: anet
Dillard, Annie: writer
Dillon, Matt: Marshall
Dillon, Melinda: actress
Dilly: lulu

Dillydally: tarry
Diluted: cut, thinned, watery, watered
Diluted, not: pure
Dim, make: blear
Dimension, third: depth
Diminish: ebb, abate
Diminish in intensity: abate ebbs
Diminutive, more: tinier
Diminutive tom: thumb
Dinah's brother: Levi, Simeon
   father: Jacob
   mother: Leah
Dinar earner, perhaps: Iraqi
Diner: eater, car
Diner and a movie: date
Diner check: tab, bill
Diner chow: eats, hash
Diner coffee: joe
Diner freebie: jelly, ice water, water
Diner side dish: slaw
Diner sign: neon
Diner special: hash
Diner's choice: entree
Diner's companion: wine
Diner's gaffe: hiccup
Diner's options: menu
Dinesin, Isak: writer
Dinesin's cont.: Afr.
Dinesin's continent:Africia
Ding-a-ling: nut, kook, yo-yo, flake, loony,
  wacko, nitwit, weirdo, lunatic
Dingbat: kook
Dinghy propeller: oar
Dingier and grubbier: grimier
Dinned: clamored
Dinner beverage: wine
Dinner course: entree
Dinner, do: cook
After dinner mint
Dinner, one pot: stew
Dinner, take out for: treat
Dinner ware: china
Dinny's rider: Oop
Dinosaur bone: fossil
Dinosaur genus: ceratops, ceratopsian
Dinosaur trap: Tar, (pit)
Dinsmore, Elsie: author
Diocese: see
Diogenes: cynic
Diogene's prop: lamp
Diomedes's father: Ares, Mars, Tydeus
   foe: Aeneas, Hector
   slayer: Hercules
   victim: Rhesus
Dion, Celine: music
Dione'sdaughter: Venus, Aphrodite
   father: Oceanus
   lover: Zeus
   mother: Tethys
Dionysian reveler: satyr
Dior, Christian: designer
Dioscorea Bulbifera: yams
Dioscuri twins: Castor, Gemini, Pollux
Dioscuri twins' father: Zeus, Tyndareus

   mother: Leda
   sister: Helen
Dip: salsa
Dip in broth: sop
Diploma: degree
Diploma holder: alumni
Diploma word: arts
Diplomat: consul, envoy
Diplomat, kind of: career
Diplomatic etiquette: protocol
Diplomatic maneuvering: finesse
Diplomat's asset: tact
   forte: tact
   need: tact
Dipper, big: ladle
Dipper, old time: groud
Dipper's dish: fondu
Dips in broth: sops
Dipsomaniac: sot
Direct descendant: scion
Direct, nautically: conn
Direct opposite: inverse
Direct route: beeline
Directed: bade
Direction finder: map
Direction indicator: vane, arrow
Direction of, in the: toward
Direction reversal: U-turn
Director's electrician: gaffer
Dirks, old: snees(daggers)
Dirt, caked-on: crud
Dirt remover: soap
Dirty: grungy
Dirty old man: lecher
Dirty politics: sleaze
Dirty spot: smudge
Disadvantage: snag
Disagreeable person: pill
Disagreeable task: onus
Disagreement: spat
Disagreement, in: at odds
Disappear gradually: fade
Disappoint, more than: appall
Disapproval, shows: boos
Disapproval, sound of: boo, Bronx cheer
Disaster, complete: fiasco
Discard: shed, drop, dump, junk
Discard carelessly: dump
Discern: know
Discernment: taste, senses
Discharge: emit
Discharged trough the pores: egested
Disciple of Paul: Erastus
Discipline, exercise: yoga
Disciplined, not: lax
Disclose info. Anonymously: leak
Disclosed: avowed, stated
Disco dancer: go go
Discomfort: pain
Discomfort, dull: ache
Disconcert: faze
Disconnect: unplug, uncouple
Discordant, as in music: atonal
Discount event: sale

Discount event, deep: clearance sale
Discourteously: rudely
Discover, as an idea: hit on
Discover suddenly: hit on
Discreet, not be: blab
Discrimination basis: age
Discuss again: rehash
Discussion group: panel
Discussion, place for: forum
Disdain, expresses: tuts
Disdain, show: sneer
Disease carrier: germ, virus
Disease carrier, rod-shaped: E. coli
Disentangle: undo
Disgrace: infamy
Disguised, not: overt
Disguises: cloaks, masks, wigs
Disgust, cry of: fie
Disgusting: odious, foul
Deep-dish pie
Dish of a dish: plate
Dished out, in a way: ladled
Dishes, clear: bus, bused
Dishing out: ladling
Dishonorable man: cad
Dishonorable ones: cads
Dishrag, like a: limp
Dishwasher phases: cycles
Disinclination to exertion: sloth
Disincline: averse
Disk content: data
Disk, metal: gong
Diskette, cleaned a: deleted, erased
DJ's countdown list: top ten
Dislike intensely: loathe
Dislikes: loathes
Dislikes and then some: abhors
Dislodge from a chair: unseat, get up
Disloyal: untrue
Dismal: grim
Dismal cry: yowl
Dismal, more: drearier
Dismay: appall
Dismay, words of: oh no
Dismiss lightly: pooh pooh
Dismounted: alit
Disney site: Epcot
Disney, Walt Elias
Disney's "Little Mermaid": Ariel
Disorder, total: chaos
Disorder, utter: chaos
Disorderly: rowdy
Disorderly disturbance: fracas
Disorderly outburst: to do
Disparaging remarks: slurs
Disparaging, slyly: snide
Disparate: unequal
Dispatch boat: aviso
Dispense with: waive
Disperse in defeat: rout
Displacement unit: cuin
Display case: vitrine, curio
Display clearly: evince
Display, flashy: pomp

Display in public: stage
Display, majestic: pomp
Display of bad temper: scene
Display of courage: manifestation
Display of disinterest: yawn
Display of oils: art show
Display of sympathy: farce
Display, put on: array
Display, stately: pomp
Displaying aplomb: cool
Displaying shock: agape
Displeasure, show: groan
Disposal input: orts
Disposed of: rid
Disposition, have a: tend
Disposition to biting: mordacity
Dispossession, wrongful: ouster
Dispute: row
Dispute settler: arbiter
Disqualify: bar
Disquiet: unrest, unease
Disrepute, fall into: incur dishonor
Disrespect: insult
Dissipated one: roue
Dissolute one: roue
Dissolved substance: solute
Dissolve: melt
Dissuade: deter
Dissuaded, not to be: adamant
Distance: mileage
Distance across: width
Distance around: girth
Distance between pillars: span
Distance between wing tips: span
Distance from base: lead, lead-off
Distance from land: offshore
Distance measure: mile
Distant: shy, far
Distant past: yore
Distant runner: miler
Distilled Walker: Hiram (whiskey)
Distinct thing: entity
Distinction, subtle: nuance
Distinctive air: aura
Distinctive doctrine: ism
Distinctive stretch: era
Distinctive style: elan
Distort a story: slant
Distort, as data: skew
Distorts, as test results: skews
Distress, cause of: bane
Distress, deep: woe
Distress, grievous: woe
Distress, in Dijon: Misere
Distress signal: SOS, flare
Distressing (more): direr
Distribute proportionally: allot
Distribution of favors: patronage
DC subway: Metro
District, London: Mayfair
District of Ancient Palestine: Samaria
Disturbance: pother, bother
Disturbance, disorderly: fracas
Disturbance, noisy: riot, fracas

Disturbing emotion: anger
Dit counterpart: dah
Ditch, big: moat
Ditch, defense: moat
Dither, in a: agog
Dits and dahs: code
Ditty: song
Diva Maria Callas
Diva: prima donna
Diva Maria's lover: Ari
Diva Rose Ponselle
Diva song: aria
Divan: sofa
Dive: swoop
Dive, as a whale: sound
Dive, fancy: gainer
Dive, like a: sleazy
Dive sound: splash
Diver, raucous: loon
Divergence: split, difference, gaps
Divergence, wide: gulf, gap, parting,
     deviation, digression
Diver's milieu: sky, sea
Diver's need: air
Diver's position: pike
Diver's weapon: speargun
Diverse, made: varied, varies
Dives, some: headers
Divide in two parts: bisect
Divide into two camps: polarize
Divided Asian country: Korea
Dividend earner: share
Divider, road: median
Divides in three: trisects
Divine being: god, deity
"Divine Comedy": poem by Dante
Diviner: oracle
Diving Bell inventor: Eads
Diving Bird: Grebe
Diving bird, large: loon
Diving duck: auk
Diving position: tuck
Diving, type of: sky
Diving woe: bends
Diving worry: bends
Divining device: rod
Divining rod, use a: dowse
Divisible by two: even
Divisible by two, not: odd
Division or disunion: schism
Division word: into
Divorce capital, once: Reno
Dix, Dorothea: reformer
Dixon, Willy: blues
Dizzy duo: Zees
Dizzy, Get: Reel
Dizzying gallery fare: op art
Dizzying genre: op art
DJ's supply: CDs
DNA and RNA: acids
DNA component: gene
DNA synthesizer: lab
Do a farrier's work: shoe
Do a favor for: oblige

Do a parental job: raise, rear
Do a takeoff: ape, mimic
Do away with: abolish, rid, destruct
Do better than: outdo, one-up
Do, biblically: doth
Do business: deal, sell
Do dinner: cook
Do followers: re mi
Do likewise: ape
Do museum work: curate
Do nothing: idle
Do oneself well: prou
Do perfectly: ace, nail
Do postal work: sort
Do quickly: expedite
Do re mi: moola
Do scut work: toil
Do something with: use
Do the math: add
Ne'er do well
Dobbin's comments: neighs
Dobbin's dish: nosebag
Dobbin's domicile: stable
Dobbs, Lou: CNN
Doc, Grumpy, Happy: dwarves
Doc of the bay: vet
Doc prescribes them: meds
Dock: bob
Dock work, did: laded, loaded
Dock worker's org.: ILA
Dock Walloper: longshoreman
Doc's friend: Grumpy
Doctor Seuss pachyderm: Horton
Doctoral requirement: theses, thesis
Doctorate exam: oral
Doctorow book: Ragtime
Doctor's clue: symptom
Doctrine: dogma, ism, tenet, creed
Doctrine, distinctive: ism
Doctrine that is accepted: belief
Document, closing: deed
Document (pre-license): permit
Dodge model, old: Omni
Does and cows: shes, females
Does a takeoff: apes
Does likewise: apes
Does not exist: isn't
Does something: acts
Does target practice: aims
Does the cancan: kicks
Does the trick: avails
Does well: excels
Doesn't fold: stays
Doesn't go on: halts
Doesn't hesitate: acts
Doesn't present objectively: slants
Doesn't stay: goes
Hors d'oeuvre
Dog ancestor: wolf
Dog, barkless: basenji
Dog, black-tongued: chow
Dog bowl bits, maybe: orts
Dog, chocolate: Lab
Dog, comic strip: Otto

Dog command: heel, sit
Dog, curled tail: Akita
Dog days in Dijon: Ete, Aug.
Dog, dosed a: wormed
Dog, "Great": Dane
Dog, head: alpha
Dog, Hungarian: puli
Dog in Garfield: Odie
Dog in Oz: Toto
Dog, Japanese: Akita
Dog of film: Asta, Otto
Dog or turkey: trot
Dog, short-legged: corgi
Dog show concern: gait
Dog show org.: AKC
Dog star: Sirius
Dog, stray: cur, mutt
Dog tag: ID
Dog, Welsh: corgi
Dogged little pest: flea
Doggedness: persistence
Doggerel: verse
Doggie bag item: ort
Doggie catcher: riata, lasso
Dogies: orphans
Dogma: tenet, ism
Dog-paddled: swam
Dogpatch denizen: Lil Abner
Dogpatch resident: Abner
Dogpatch denizen: Lil Abner
Dogpatch verb: ain't
Dog's family tree: pedigree
Dog's name, popular: Rex
Dog's portion, poor: none
Dogsled puller: team
Dog team runner: musher
Doily: napkin
Doing a jig saw puzzle: piecing
Doing as told: obeying
Doing business: open
Doing well: acing
DOJ org.: FBI
Dojo blow: karate chop
Dojo sport: karate
Dojo teaching: karate
Doldrums, in the: sad
Doling out: meting
"Be a doll and …"
He's a doll: Ken
Doll, Hopi: kachina
Doll party dinnerware: tea set
Doll, Raggedy: Ann
Doll, Topknot: Kewpie
Dollop: glob, lump, dab, gob
"Doll's House" author:Ibsen (Henrik)
Dolly and her clones: ewes
Dolly user: red cap
Dolly Woods loc.: Tenn.
Dolphin kin: orca,
Dolphin, predatory: orca
Dolphin, young: calf
Dolt: oaf
Domain: realm, lands
Dome: cupola

Dome, kind of: geodesic
Domed home: igloo
Domed recess: apse
Domed structure: cupola, rotunda, vault
Domestic establishment: ménage
Domesticated, not: feral, wild
Domesticated polecat: ferret
Domestic's word: ma'am
Domicile: res. Residence
Domicile, have a: reside
Domicile, secondary: pied-a-terre
Domineering: imperial
Domingo, Placido: tenor
Domingo song: aria
Anno Domini
Dominion: empire
Domino: tile
Domino, Fats: singer
Domino feature: hood
Domino spots: pips
Don Diego, masked: Zorro
Don Juan: Lothario
Don Juans: roues, romeos
Dona:lady, madam
Donald Duck nephew: Huey
Donat, Robert: actor
Donation: alm
Donations, poor box: alms
Done, Donne's: o'er
"Done to a turn"Done, to Donne: o'er
    (French)
Done with: over
Donkey: ass, neddi, neddy
Donkey cry: bray
Donkey, Dresden: esel, (Germany)
Donne's "done": o'er
"Don't bother": skip it
"Don't dele": stet
Don't just seem: are
"Don't look so glum": cheer up
Don't split these: hairs
Donut, douse a: dunk
Donut, enjoy a: dunk
Donned garment, easily: slip on
Donne's "done": o'er
Doogie Howser, MD
Doomsayer's sign: omen
Doomsday book money: ora, orae
Lorna Doone novel
Doonesbury drawer: Garry Trudeau
Door: portal
Door column: anta
Door ding: dent
Door fastener: hasp
Door frame: sash
Door frame side: jamb
Door mat, use a: wipe
Door that's not a door: ajar
Door topper: lintel
Doorbell, response to a: it's open, enter
Doorman's ornament: epaulette
Doozie: lulu, pip
Dorcas, emulates: sews
Dore, Gustavo: illustrator

Doris' brother: Nereus,
     daughter: Nereids
     father: Oceanus
     husband: Nereus
Dorm covering: ivy
Dorm denizens: coeds
Dorm dwellers, some: coeds
Dorm sharer: roomie
Dorm tenant: co-ed
Dormant: latent
Dormant stage (in a): latent, asleep
Dormouse: lerot
Dorothy's dog: Toto
Dory mover: oar
Dory's need: oar
Dos alternative: unix
Dos, notes after: res.
Dos Passos book: "U.S.A."
DOS runner: PC
Dosage units: pills, drams, CCs
Dossier: file
Dossier list: aliases
Dostoyevsky masterpiece: The Idiot
Dot-om alternative: org.
Dots in the river: Islets
Dotty: daft
Dotty game piece: domino
Double: twin
Double agent
Double agent: mole, spy
Double curve: ess, ogee
Double bond compound: enol
Double dagger: diesis
Double Dutch item: rope
Double entendre: ambiguity
"Double Fantasy" singer: Ono
Double helix: DNA
Double layer: two-ply
Double or twin: bed
Double reed instrument: oboe
Double-reeded instrument: oboe
Double standard:unequal
Double take, does a: reacts
Double play, half of a: one out
Double vision: diplopia
Double-breasted: overlapping
Double-breasted jacket: reefer
Double-cross: betray
Doubleday, Abner: baseball pioneer
Double-dealer: gyp, cheat, knave, conman
Double-dealing: fraud, deceit, chicane
Double-dealing spy: mole
Double-domed: egghead, high-brow
Double-note drum beat: flam
Doubles: ringers, images
Double-talk: bosh, bunk, hokum, hooey
Mrs. Doubtfire
Doubtful, more: iffier
Doubting Thomas: skeptic
Douglas, Kirk: actor
Douse a donut: dunk
Dove alternative: camay
Dover and Gibraltar: straits
Dove's aversion: war

Dove's home: cote
Dovetail: fit, mesh
Dovetail component: tenon
Ne'er do well
Dow uptick: gain
Dow-jones figure: avg
"Down and Out in Beverly Hills"
Down and out: poor, needy
Down and out sorts: paupers
Down counterpart: across
Down east state: Maine
Down home: folksy
Down in the dumps: moping
Down mood: blahs
Down partner: out
Down pat, had: knew
Down the drain: wasteful
Down the tube: shot
Down Under cutie: koala
Down Under native: Maori
Down Under one: Aussie
Down Under rockers: AC/DC
Down, upside: invert
Downwind: lee ward, alee
Down with: has
Down-at-the-heel: seedy
Downcast: morose
Downed a sub: ate
Downey, Roma: actress
Downgrade: demote
Downhill fast, go: ski
Downpour: rain, shower, spate
Downpour, heavy: deluge
Downpour, torrential: deluge
Downright: really, utterly
Downs, Epsom: race track
"Ups and downs"
Downstage: out front
Downward leap: plunge
Downward measurement: depth
Downward movement of air: katabatic wind
Downy fungi: mold
Dowry, of a: dotal
Doyle, Arthur Conan: author
Doze: nod, drowse, nap
Dr. Ores' music: rap
Drab color: dun
Drachma's successor: Euro
Dracula girl: Mina
Dracula sometimes: bat
Draft agency: SSS
Draft animal: oxen, mule
Draft letters: SSS
Draft, second: rewrite
Draft status: on tap
Draftee, new: GI
Drafting pattern: template
Draft-worthy: One A
Drag around: tote
Drag behind: tow
Drag race participant: car
"Dragnet" org.: LAPD
Dragon, dispatch a: slay
Dragon of puppetry: Ollie

Dragon of song: Puff
Dragon, perhaps?: tattoo
Dragon roll ingredient: eel
Dragon slayer: George
Dragon's breath: fire
Drain cleaner: lye, Drano
Drain of color: etiolate
Drain of resources: sap
Drainers and strainers: colanders
Drake, fake: decoy
Paul Drake creator: Erie
Drake's ship: The Golden Kind
Dram (1/60 of): minim
Drama award: Obie
Drama, daytime: soap
Drama, Japanese: Noh
Drama section: act
Drama set to music: opera
Dramatic base: plot
Dramatic conflict: agon
Dramatic device: aside
Dramatic intro: ta da
Dramatic snippets: scenes
Dramatic, wildly: lurid
Dramatics, turn on the: emote
Dramatis personae: casts, parts, roles, actors,
     actresses
Drank: toped
Drank hastily: gulped down
Drapes, close: drew
Dravidian language: Telugu, Tamil
Draw a likeness: depict
Draw a line in the sand: dare
Draw a picture: describe
Draw back: cringe, recede
Draw forth: elicit
Draw on: use, tap
Draw out: elicit
Draw to a close: end
Draw upon: tap
Draw water: pump
Draw with a laser: etch
Drawer fresheners: sachets
Drawer handle: knob, pull
Drawer oddments: socks
Drawing: map
Drawing, depict by: limn
Drawing power: allure
Drawing room: salon
Drawls and twangs: accents
Drawn-out, more: longer
Drawn tight: taut
Draws back: shies
Dread: cocked one: Rasta
Dreadful: dire
Dreadful, really: dire
Dreadlock one: Rasta
Dreadlock wearer: Rasta
Dream: aspire
Dream acronym: REM
Dream of: aspire
Dream on: no way
Dream or moon attachment: scape
Dream phenom: REM

Dreaming, maybe: asleep
Dreamland, in: asleep
Dreamlike: surreal
Dreams: ideals
Dreary and despondent: glum
Dreary in Yorkshire: dree
Dredged matter: silt
Dreg's: lees
Drei minus zwei: ein
Drench: embrue, imbrue, soak
Drenched, not quite: damp
Drenched through: soaking
Dresden denial: nein
Dresden donkey: esel
Dresden's river: Elbe
Dress accessory: sash
Dress, close-fitting: sheath
Dress down: reprimand, berate
Dress, dressy: lace, lacy
Dress fussily: preen
Dress material: rayon, tricot
Dress panel: inset
Dress part: yokes, bodice
Dress, sleeveless apron-like: pinny
Dress, slinky: sheath
Dress trim: piping
Dress with no waist: shifts
Dressed: clad
"Dressed to the <u>nines</u>"
Dresser fussy: fops
Dresses: frocks
Dress in: dons
Dressing down: tirade
Dressing gown: kimono
Dressing room, use a: try on
Dressmaker cut: bias
Dressy event: gala
Drew a blank: forgot
Drew forth: evoked, educed
Drew near: came
Drew on: used
Drew out: educed
Drew up: shrank, planned, sketched
Dribble: bounce
Dried clover: hay
Dried coconut meat: copra
Dried up: sere
Drier than extra sec: brut
Dries off: towels
Driest: serest
Drift: trend
Driftwood bringer: tide
Drill for penetrating rock: borer
Drill through: pierce
Drilled through: pierced
Drillmaster: instructor
Drink alcoholicbeverages: imbibe
Drink coolant: ice
Drink daintily: sip
Drink, deep: swig
Drink, delicious: nectar
Drink heartily: swig
Drink, iced: tea, ade
Drink known for its curative powers: elixir

Drink mixer, antique: krater
Drink of the gods: nectar
Drink, plantation: julep
Drink, safe to: potable
Drink, stiff: belt
Drink, stimulating: bracer
Drink, syrupy: julep
Drink tea, perhaps: sip
Drink with crumpets: tea
Drink with scones: tea
Drink with sushi: sake
Drinker: toper
Drinker's say: hic
Drinker's sound: hiccup
Drinking bout: jag, spree
Drinking cup: tankard
Drinking mug: toby
Drinking problem, minor: age
Drinks for bar regulars: usual
Drinks heavily: topes, souses
Drinks in: absorbs,
Drinks in excess: topple
Drinks of gods: nectars
Drinks to: toasts
Drinks, wee: drams
Drip catcher: bath mat
Drip-dry fabric: nylon
Dripping wet: sodden
Dripping with sarcasm: snide
Drive a semi: haul
Drive against: ram
Drive away: shoo, leave
Drive back: repel
"They Drive by <u>Night</u>"
Drive forward: impel
Drive out: eject,
Drive, prepares to: tees up, shifts
Drive, quick: spin
Drive-in employee: carhop
Drive-in server: carhop
Drivel, sentimental: goo
Driven snow, <u>as</u> <u>pure</u> <u>as</u> <u>the</u>
Driven, was: rode
Driver, certain: pile
Driver, Minnie: actress
Driver's concern: blind spot
Driver's perch: tee
Driver's warning: honk
Drives back: repulses
Drives forward: impels, propels
Drives out: rousts
Driveways, certain: oval
Driveway material: asphalt
Driveway type: asphalt
Driving aid: tee
Driving force: urge
Drogheda locale: Eire
Droll: wry
Dromedary, e.g.: camel
Drone: hum
Drone or worker: bee
Droned: hummed
Drones home: apiary

Drooping plants: nutant
Droops: sags, wilts
Drop a clue: hint
Drop a glass: smash
Drop from the team: cut
Drop in on: see, visit
Drop in the mailbox: send
Drop, salty: tear
Droplets, flower: dew
Droplets, form: dew, bead
Droplets, salty: tears
Dropouts second chance: GED
Dropped a line: wrote
Dropped in importance: paled
Dropped off?: nodded, dozed
Drops down suddenly: dips, plops
Drops in the air: mists
Drops in the slot: mails
Drops off: wanes,
Drops out of a hand: folds
Drove a nail obliquely: toed
Drowse off: nod
Drowsy, become: nods
Droxie alternative: Oreo
Dru, Joanne: actress
Drudge: slog
Drug agency: DEA, FDA
Drug buster: narc
Drugstore cowboy: ogler
Druid: celt, robot, priest
Druids and shamans: priests
Drum, fifer's: tabor
Drum, Indian: tabla (Indian percussion
    instrument)
Drum, kind of: ear, bass, kettle
Drum kit, part of a: snare
Drum major's hat: shako
Drum sound: roll
Drumbeat, double note: flam
Drums, as fingers: taps
Drums, jungle: tom-tom
Drums, powwow: tom-tom
Drunk: blotto, souse
Drunk as a skunk: oiled, bombed
Drunken utterance: hic
Drury Lane composer: Arne
Dry and withered: sere
Dry, as champaign: sec
Dry, as wine: sec
Dry by heat: bake
Dry champaign: brut
Dry creek bed: coulee
Dry goods: cloth
Dry gulch: arroyo
Dry gully: arroyo
Dry Italian wine: Soave
Dry, more: serer
Dry off: towel
Dry out: parch
Dry run: trial
Dry, very: brut
Dry watercourse: wadi
Dryden works: essays
Drying apparatus: oast

Dryly humorous: wry
Dryope's husband: Andraemon
    sister: Iole
"DST" ends: October
Diable, Ile du
Plat du jour
Dubai VIP: emir
Dubious honesty, of: shady
Dublin dish: Irish stew
Duck, dabbling: teal
Duck (dead): goner
Duck foot: web
Duck hunter's lure: decoy
Duck, male: xrake
Duck or hue: teal
Duck's kismet: evades destiny
Ducks, phony: decoys
Ducks, sea: eiders
Ducommun, Elie: journalist
Dude, cartoon: Daffy
Dude, cruel: meanie
Dude, durango: hombre
Dude, vain: fop
Dudgeons (high): ire
Dudley's gal pal: Nell
Duds: garb, apparel
Duds, throw out the: cull
Due for payment: owing
Due process proceeding: trial
Duenna: chaperon
Dues payer: mem., member
Dues paying group: club
Duet number: two
Duffel filler: gear
Duffer's delight: par
Duffer's goal: par
Duffer's miracle: ace, hole in one
Dugout: canoe
Dugout canoe: pirogue
Dugout, in Dijon : abri
Dugout shelter: abri
Dukakis, Olympia: actress
Duke or count: peer
Duke, Patty: actress
Duke's lady: duchess
Dulcimer cousin: zither
Dull: jejune, ho hum, blah, lethargic
Dull and boring: blah
Dull discomfort: ache
Dull finish: matte
Dull one: dolt
Dull routine: rut
Dull surface: matte
Dull work, like: boring
Dullea, Keir: actor
Dulls: blunts
Dumas dueler: Athos
Dumas refusal: nyet
Dumas senior: pere
Dumas swordsman: Aramis
Dumb: dora
Dumbfound: stun
Dumbfounded, leaves: awes, stuns
Dummkopf: ass, oaf

Dummy, bucktoothed: snerd
Dummy coin: slug
Dummy (protest): effigy
Dump: jilt
Dump so to speak: jilt
Dump truck fillers: loaders
Dumpling, Chinese: wonton
Dumpling go-with: stew
Dumpster: bin
Dumpster locale: alley
Dumpster output: odor
Duncan's slayer: Macbeth
Dundee, Angelo: boxing trainer
Dundee citizen: Scot
"Dundee", for one: Aussie
Dundee refusal: nae
Dunderheads: morons
Dune buggy kin: ATV
Dungeon objects: irons
Dunk, item to: tea bag
Dunkin, Isadora: dancer
Dunne, Irene: actress
Duodecimal: twelfths
Duplicate: ditto
Duplicate copy: repro
Duplicate , exact: twin, clone
Duplicate, of an exact: clonal
Duplicates, for short: repros
Durable: well made
Durable, be more: outlast
Durable paper: manila
Durable, prove: wear
Durango coin: peso
Durango dude: hombre
Durante, Jimmy: comic, movie
D'Urberville girl: Tess
Durbin, Dianna: actress
Durer supplies: acids
Durham-Yorkshire river: Tees
During: while, amid
Duryea, Dan: actor
Dusk to poets: een
Dusseldorf donkey: esel
Dusseldorf iron: eisen (German)
Dust bowl refugee: okie
Dust bunny particle: mote
Dust collector: rag
Dust devil: eddy
Dust, kind of: cosmic
Dust particle: speck
Dust speck: mote
Duster, kind of: crop
Dusting powder: talc
Dusting target: crop, furniture
Dutch airline: KLM
Dutch boy: Hans Brinker
Dutch cheese: Edam
Dutch cheese town: Edam
Dutch city: "The Hague," Ede, Breda
Dutch coin, once: guilder
Dutch colonist: Boer
Dutch cupboard: Kas
Dutch government seat: The Hague
Dutch master painter: Vermeer

Dutch or brick: oven
Dutch painter, 17th century: Steen
Dutch philosopher: Spinora
Dutch pottery: delft
Dutch pottery city: Delft
Dutch town: Ede
Dutch treat: Gouda
Dutch underground: Holland Tunnel
Dutra, Olin: golf
Duty, difficult: onus
Duty or pride, word with: civic
Duville, Shelly: actress
Dvork, Antonin: composer
Dwarf of folklore: troll
Dwarf with glasses: Doc
Dwarf plant: bonsai
Dwarf tree: bonsai
Dwarfs: Doc, Grumpy, Sleepy, Happy
Dwarf's cousin: gnome
Dweeb: nerd, geek, wimp, twerp
Dwell: inhabit
Dwell on: harp
Dwell on anger: stew
Dwell permanently: reside
Dwell upon: stress, ponder
Dwellers on the Bering Sea: Aleuts
Dwelling, conical: wigwam, teepee
Dwelling mistake: hovel
Dwelling, prehistoric: cave
Dwelling, Taos: adobe
Dwells: inhabits
Dwelt: lived
D.D.E's command: ETO
    rival: A.E.S.
    successor: JFK
Dworkin, Andrea: writer
Dye: pigment
Dye compound: eosin
Dye container: vat
Dye, hair: henna, henra
Dye ingredient: aniline
Dye, kind of: azo
Dye, rose-colored: eosin
Dye-yielding shrub: añil
Dynamic lead-in: aero
Dynamic, prefix for: aero
Dynamo part: armature
Dynasty noted for porcelain: Ming

E

"E" to Einstein: energy
Each one: every
Eager: agog
Eager and willing: ready
Eager, extremely: keen
Eager, obviously: agog
Eager, plus: avid
Eagle aspirer: Boy Scout
Eagle plus two: par
Eagle, shore: erne
Eagle, type of: erne, bald
Eagle, white-tailed: erne

Eagle's lair: aerie
Ear bone: incus
Ear dangler: hoop
Ear, of the: aural
Ear part: kernel, cob, lobe
Eared sealed: otary
Earhart, Amelia: aviator
Earl Grey, e.g.: tea
Earle's sea bank: sande dune
Earlier: prior, ago
Earlier form of a word: etyman
Earlier in time, be: antedate
Earliest known inhabitant: aborigine
Early afternoon: two
Early Brits: Saxons, Picts
Early calculators: abaci
Early cemeteries: catacombs
Early course additive: salad oil, dressing
Early English money: ora
Early Greek: Ionian
Early Iroquois foes: Eries
Early jazz: bop
Early life: youth
Early Mexican: Aztec
Early modern human: cro-Magnon
Early movie theater: penny odean, nickel
    odean
Early physician: Galen
Early stage: onset
Early time in life: tender age
Earmarks: tags
Earn: get
Earn, as interest: yield, accrue
Earned: merited
Earned, not: undue
Earp's cohort: Doc
Earring, small: stud
Ears, all: nosy
Earth bound?: atlas
Earth color: ocher, tan, umber
Earth feature: tilt
Earth goddess: Erda
Earth, in combo: geo
Earth inheritor: meek
Earth mover: dozer
Earth neighbor: Venus
Earth orbit (one): year
Earth orbiter: moon
Earth orbiter of yore: mir
Earth, packed: hard pan
Earth, parcel of: acres
Earth, to Pliny: terra
Earth science: geology
Earth-shaped: oblate
Earth star: sol, sun
Earth tone: umber
Earthbound avians: emus
Earthenware fragment: shard
Earthenware pot: olla
Earth's is elliptical: orbit
Earth's reflectiveness: albedo
Earthshaking: profound
Earthy color: tan, ocher, umber
Earthy deity: Geb

Earthy deposit: marl
Earthy lump: clod
Earthy pigment: ochre
Ease, ill at
Ease, ill at: nervous
Ease of mind: peace
Ease up: slacken
Easel partner: palette
Eases: allays
Eases the way: smooths
Easily argued: tenable
Easily damaged: frail
Easily handled, as a ship: yar
Easily influenced: malleable
Easily misled: gullible
Easily overwrought: nervous
Easily provoked: irascible
Easily split mineral: mica
Easily swayed: amenable
Easily taught: apt
East Chadic: Kera,
East Coast bullet train: Acela
East India palm: nipa
East Indian sailor: lascar
East Indies vine: odel
"East of Eden" brother: Cal, Caleb
East, to Pedro: Este
"East Wind" deity: Eurus
Easter Parade Ave.: Fifth
Easter (pre-Easter): lent, lenten
Eastern Church images: ikons
Eastern marketplace: bazaar
Eastern path: Tao
Eastern philosophy: amir, Taoism
Eastern region: Shinto
Eastern servant: amah
Eastern staple: rice, pita
Eastern title: Aga
Eastman's invention: camera
Easy as ABC
Easy as ABC
Easy care fabric: dacron
Easy chair: Morris
Easy does it: careful
Easy going: unhurried, relaxed
Easy marks: saps, suckers
Easy pace: amble
Easy target: sitting duck
Easy walker: ambler
Easy way out: door
Easy win: romp
Eat beaver-style: gnaw
Eat grass: graze
Eat hungrily: wolf
Eat one's words: retract
Eat soup impolitely: slurp
Eat sumptuously: feast
Eat up a storm: pig out
Eat your heart out: yearn
Eatery, casual: bistro
Eatery, informal: deli
Eatery, NYC: deli, sardis
Eating alcove: dinette
Eating away: corroding, eroding

Eating, combo. form: iatro
Eating guards: bibs
Eating, start: dig in
Eats formally: dines
Eats, supplied the: catered
Eau Claire
Eau de Grace
Eau-de-vie: brandy
Eaves dropper: rain, spy
Eavesdrop: spy
Eban, Abba
eBay competitors: bidders
eBay milieu: Web
eBay transaction, often: resale
Ebb and flow: tides
Ebb and flow, relating to: tidal
Ebb, lowest: nadir
Ebbs: wanes
Ebenezer's oath: bah
Ebert, Roger: critic
"Ecce Homo" painter: Titian
Eccentric: outre, dotty, odd, daft, batty
Eccentric person: kook
Ecclesiastic's residence: deanery
Ecclesiastical assembly: synod
Ecclesiastical desk: ambo
Ecclesiastical month: elul
Ecclesiastical vestment: alb
Ecce Homo
Ecdysiast's forte: disrobing (stripper)
Echo: resound
Echo, for one: nymph
Echoing taboo: no no
Eclectic collection: olio
Eclipse, to an ancient: omen
Eclipse, kind of: lunar, solar
Eclipse phenomenon: corona, shadow
Eco, Umberto: writer
Eco-friendly feds: EPA
Eco-friendly org.: EPA
Eco worry: ozone
Ecole attendee: élevè
Ecole des Beaux-arts
Economic upturn: boom
Economy class: couch
Economy indicator: GNP
Economy, support the: spend
Economy yardstick: GNP
Ecru: tan, beige
Ecto opposite: endo
ECU issuer: EEC
Ecuador bug: mosquito
Ecumenical council site: Lyons
Edberg, Stephen: tennis
Eddie's cop character: Axel
Eddy: swirl
Edelweiss, where it grows: alps
Edenburg boys: ladies
Eden's tree: fig
Eden's wear: fig leaf
Eder, Shirley: columnist
Ederle, Gertrude: swimmer
Edge: verge, brim, rim
Edge past: sidle

Edges sideways: sidles
Edible: food
Edible decapod: shrimp
Edible mollusk: cockle
Edible roots: yams, carrots, onion
Edible tuber: ola, oca
Edict: fiat
Edison, Thomas: inventor
Edison rival: Tesla
Edison's home: Menlo Park
Edit menu option: undo
Edited, not: uncut
Editing, improve by critical: emend
Editing, does film: dubs
Editor, at times: omissionary
Editorial "keep": stet
Editorial notation: stet
Editorial symbols: carets
Editor's command: stet
Editor's mark: caret
Editor's notes: dele
Editor's order: stet
Edmonton gridders: Eskimos
Edomites ancestor: Esau
Ed's readings: mss
Edsel was one: flop
Educated, formally: schooled
Education reformer, American: Mann
EEC currency: Euro
Eel, ferocious: moray
Eel, large marine: moray
Eel, young: grig
Eerie feeling: déjà vu
Eerie writer: Poe
Eerie get-together: séance
Eeyore's outburst: bray
Efface: erase
Effect: result
Effervescence: gaseous
Effervescence, lacking: flat
Efficient: able
Efficiency expert's goal: order
Effigies: idols
Effluvium, emit: reek
Effort, kind of: team
Effort (Latin): nisus
Effort, put forth: exert
Effortless pace: lope
Effrontery: gall
Egg cell: ovum
Egg desert: flan
Egg drink: flip, nog
Egg Foo young
Egg fooyung
Egg fu young
Egg on: abet, goad, urge
Egg producer: ovary
Egg rating: Grade A
Egg white: glair
Eggar, Samantha: actress
Egghead: genius
Egg-laying mammal: anteater, echidna,
     platypi, platypus
Eggnog enhancement: nutmeg

Eggnog time: yule, noel
Eggnot topper: nutmeg
Egg-rich bread: challah
Eggs roll, when: Easter
Egg-roll time: Easter
Egg-shaped: oval, ovate, ovoid
Eggy dessert: flan
Ego companions: ids
Ego Ibutyhiending: IST
Egoist: snob
Egret: wader
Egyptian, armless: asp
Egyptian beetle: scarab
Egyptian burial jar: canopic
Egyptian Christian: Copt
Egyptian cobra, small: asp
Egyptian cotton: sak
Egyptian cross: ankh
Egyptian dancing girl: Al'me
Egyptian dog-headed ape: Aani
Egyptian edifice, massive: pyramid
Egyptian god: Ptah
Egyptian god of music: bes
Egyptian goddess: isis
Egyptian headdress creature: asp
Egyptian king, first: Menes
Egyptian life symbol: ankh
Egyptian lizard: adda
Egyptian, many: Arabs
Egyptian monument: obelisk
Egyptian native: Copt
Egyptian sacred bird: ibis
Egyptian scared bull: apis
Egyptian singer: Alme
Egyptian sun god: Aten, Atmu
Egyptian symbol of life: ankh
Egyptian temple: karnak
Egyptian temple site: Luxor
Egyptian underworld god: Osiris, Serapis
Eight ball rod: cue stick
Eight bells, commander's: noon
Eight binary digits: byte
Eight bits: byte
Eight furlongs: one mile
Eight, group of: octet
Eight, in Aachen: acht
Eight, in Ecuador: ocho
Eight ounces: cup
Eight (pref): octo
Eight quarts: peck
1836 battle site, memorial: Alamo
1860 initials: CSA
1865 yielder: Lee
Eighth day, occurring every: octal, octan
Eighth of a byte: bit
Eighth of a mile: furlong
Eighth planet: Neptune
Eine kleine Nachtmusik
Einstein's birthplace: Ulm
Einstein's continuum: space-time
Eisenhower's command: ETO
     rival: A. E. S.
     successor: JFK
Eject: oust, spew

Ekberg, Anita: actress
El cheapo: low-priced
El Dorado: legendary land
El Dorado loot: oro (gold)
El Greco's city: Toledo
Elaborate pretense: charade
EL AL destination: Israel
Elan: verve
"Ere I saw Elba"
Elbow: prod, joint
Elbow grease: toil
Elbow room: leeway, space
Elcar, Dana: actor
Elder statesman: cato
Elderly, somewhat: oldish, tribal
Elderly person: oldster
Elderly's facility: assisted living
Eleanor's husband: Henry ll, Franklin
Electa's sibling: Orestes
Electee's first act: oath
Election night event: exit poll
Election, part two of an: run-off
Election committee: caucus
Electorate: voters
Electors: voters
Electra's brother: Orestes
     father: Agamemnon
     husband: Pylades
     mother: Clytemnestra
     sister: Iphigenia
Electric bridge: arc
Electrical atmosphere: aura
Electrical bypass: shunt
Electrical discharge: spark
Electrical flashes: sparks
Electrical interference: static
Electrical output, amount of: wattage
Electrical phenomena: surge
Electrical unit: MHO, OHM, watt, volt, Amp
Electrician, director's: gaffer
Electrician's tool: amp meter, volt meter
Electrified particles: ions
Electrode bridge: arc
Electrode, certain: anode
Electrolysis atoms: ions
Electromotive unit of force: volt
Electron, free: ion
Electron, high-speed: beta
Electron part: module
Electron tube, kind of: triode
Electron tube gas: xenon
Electronic control system: servo
Electronic data processing: EDP
Electronic device: maser
E-filing recipient: IRS
Electronic instrument cabinet: console
Electronic reminder: beep
Electronic surveillance: wire tap
Electronics big name: Sony
Electrons, free: ions
Elects: chooses, opts, prefers, votes
Elegant: dressy, chic
Elegant coiffure: chignon
Elegant shop: salon

Elegant writer: poet
Elegantly attired: chic
Element "53" compound: iodide
Element "54": xenon
Element, silver-white: cobalt
Element units: atom
Element, uplifting: helium
"Elementary, my dear Watson"
Elephant, baby: calf
Elephant boy: Sabu
Elephant drivers: mahouts
Elephant eater: roc
Elephant, exiled: rogue
Elephant gone amok: rogue
Elephant keeper: mahout
Elephant owner: raja, rajah
Elephant party: GOP
Elephant, storybook: Babar
Elephant tooth: tusk
Elevate to high position: exalt
Elevated seat: perch
Elevator button: up, down, floors
Elevator music: ear candy
Elevator routes: shafts
Elevenses treats: scones (mid-morning snack)
Eleventh grade exam: PSAT
Eleventh Greek letter: lambda
Elf: sprite, pixie
Elf size: wee
Elfman, Danny: composer
Eliab's brother: David
    daughter: Abihail
    father: Helon, Pallu
    son: Abiram, Dathan
Eliada's father: David
    son: Rezon
Elicit: educe
Elicit a chuckle: amuse
Elicited by devious means: wormed
Eligible: fit
Elimination contest: spelling bee
Eliot, T. S.: playwrite
Eliot's Bede: Adam
Eliot's Jenny antidotes, e.g.: cat
Eliot's Miser: Marner
Eliphaz's father: Esau
    mother: Adah
    son: Teman
Elisheba's brother: Nahshon,
    father: Amminadab
    husband: Aaron
    son: Abihu, Nadab, Eleazar, Ithamar
Elite: "A" list
Elite alternative: pica
Elite, bigger than: pica
Elite league: ivy
Elite police team: swat
Elixir seeker: alchemist
Elizabeth of cosmetic fame: Arden
Elk: wapiti
Elliott, Missy: music
Ellipses: ovals
Ellipsis component: dot
Ellipsoidal: oval

Elliptic: ovoid
Elman, Mischa: violinist
Elmer Fudd voice: Mel Blanc
Elmer Gentry's wife: Cleo
Elmer's contented cow: Elsie
Elongated fish: gar
Eloquent speaker: orator
Els, Ernie: golf
Elsie farm: dairy
Elves, king of: Oberon
Elves, malicious: goblins
Elvis' birthplace: Tupelo
Elvis' daughter: Lisa
Elude the Tag: Slide
Elusive creature of Nepal: yeti
Ely, Ron: actor, Tarzan
Ely of Tarzan: Ron
Em to Dorothy: aunt
Email abbr.: AOL
Email, nuisance: spam
Email provider: AOL
Email senders: PCs, users
Email server, big: AOL
Email, unwelcome: spam
Emailed a duplicate: CCed
Emailer's need: modem
Emanating from stars: stellar
Emanation: emit, aura
Emanation, subtle: aura
Emanation, unseen: aura
Embankment, protective: berm
Embankment, river: levee
Embark on a journey: set out
Embarkation location: pier
Embarrassed, not: unabashed
Embarrassing mistake: botch
Embassy implant: bug
Ember, glowing: coal
Embers, finally: ash
Emblem: logo
Emblem, embossed: seal
Emblem, royal: regalia
Embossed art: relief
Embossed emblem: seal
Embrace, as a cause: espouse
Embrace, tight: bear hug
Embroider: sew
Embroideries, some: crewels
Embroiders, maybe: lies
Embroidery silk: floss
Embroidery thread: floss
Embru: drench
Emcee stand: dais
Emerald island: Erie, Eire
Emerald Isle: Ireland
Emerald measure: carat
Emerald's mineral: beryl
Emergency action system: triage
Emergency floaters: life raft, life jacket
Emergency, kind of: dire
Emergency light: flare
ER picture: X-ray
ER practice: CPR
Emerging: nascent

Emerging magma: lava
Emeril's word: bam
Emeritus, become: retire
Emerson opus: essay
Emerson, Ralph Waldo: author
Eminem's genre: rap
Eminent: noted
Eminent concert pianist: Van Cliburn
Emirate, Persian Gulf: Qatar
Emit a scent: redolent
Emit coherent light: lase, laser
Emit effluvium: reek
Emit vapor: steam
Emitting light: aglow
Emmet: ant
Emmy's kin: Obie
Emollient-producing plant: aloe
Emollient yielder: aloe
Emoluments: salaries
Emotion, contrary: love and hate
Emotion, disturbing: anger
Emotion, without: dryly
Emotional outburst: scene
Emotional projection: empathy
Emotional request: plea
Emotional shock: trauma
Emotionally distant: aloof
Emotionally stirring: heartwarming
Empathize: grok
Emperor: tsar
Emperor after Claudius: Nero
Emperor Augustus' great, great-grandson:
    Nero
Emperor before Trajan: Nerva
Emperor Galba's successor: Otho
Emperor Selassie: Haile
Emperor, suicidal: Nero
Emphatic (be): stress
Emphatic request: demand
Empire builder: Maya, Inca
Empire state capital: Albany
Employee: earner
Employees, new: tyros, novice
Employers: users
Employment summary: resume
Emporium, rural: general store
Empress, really: awe, wow
Empty, in math: null
"Empty nester"
Empty out: delete
Empty places: spaces
Empty the bilge: bail
Empty-headed: stupid
Emulate a bouncer: eject
Emulate a critic: rate
Emulate Bryan: Orate
Emulate Dorcas: sew (Dorcas Society)
Emulate Hammer: rap
Emulate Oprah: host
Emulate Swift: satirize
Emulated Miss Daisy: rode
Emulates a kestrel: swoops
Emulates a teapot: whistles
En masse: together

En point: a tip
Ente en pointe
Enameled metal: tole
Enchiladas garnish: salsa
Encircle: gird, wreathe
Enclitic contraction: it'll
Enclose within walls: mure, mures
Enc. for a response: SASE
Enclosure, muddy: sty
Encourage: abet
Encourage strongly: urge
Encrusted: caked
Encumbrance: lien
Encyclopedia medium: CD ROM
End of shutdown: reopen
End of the day event: sunset
End of the Earth: pole
End to be attained: goal
End-blown flute: recorder
Endearing closing: love
Ended a layoff: rehired
Ending for dance: arama
Endless phenomenon: time
Endo, opposite of: ecto
Endor fighters, battle of: Ewoks
Endorse: okay, support
Endorser, check: payee
Endorser's need: pen
Ends up with: nets
Endure longer: out last
Energetic, nimbly: spry
Energetic, not as: wearier
Energetic one: doer
Energetic people: dynamos
Energy: pep, vim,
Energy, ebullient: vim
Energy, lose: tire,
Energy units: ergs, mev, rad
Eng. honor: OBE
Engage: hire
Engage in: wage
Engage in a contest: vie
Engage in ransacking: rifle
Engaged in war: waged
Engagement, brief: gig
Engine compartment: cab
Engine cover: hood
Engine disks: cams
Engine housing: nawelle, pod
Engine option: hemi, diesel
Engine, powerful: turbo, jet, turbojet
Engineer award: OBE
Engineering detail: spec.
England, Church of: Episcopal
England (S.W. region): Cornwall
English, Alex: basketball
English askew: agee
English art gallery: Tate
English baby carriage: pram
English biscuits: scones
English cathedral city: Ely
English cattle breed: devon
English channel: BBC
English Channel feeder: Seine

English Channel port: Dover
English Channel spot: Wight
English Channel wwimmer: Gertrude Ederle
English chap: Brit
English china: Spode
English county: shire
English daisy: gowan
English designer: Casion, Wm.
English dramatist: Peele
English duchy Top: York
English dynasty: York
English farewell: ta-ta
English "FBI": CID
English garden: kew
English historical region: Essex
English horn: cor
English law: soke
English model, noted: Twiggy
English noblewoman: Milady
English novelist: George Eliot
English pantry: spence
"English Patient, the" setting: Sahara
English privy: loo
English professor: don
English reference book: OED
English sand hill: dene
English shrine: stoa
English streetcar: tram
English sweet: treacle
English tavern: pub
English valley: dene
English wasteland: heaths
English woodland: weald
Engrave: etch
Engraving in relief: cameo
Engrossed: rapt
Engrossed, deeply: rapt
Engrossed with: in to
Enhance, not: detract
Enhanced combined effect: synergy
Enhancement, land of: faery, fairy
Enigmatology: creation of puzzles
Enjoy a puddle: slosh
Enjoy, as a benefit: reap
Enjoy, really: relish
Enjoy the pool: swim, dive
Enjoyed: savored
Enjoyed oneself: grooved
Enjoyment, keen: zest
Chou Enlai: Chinese leader
Enlightenment, spiritual: satori
Enlivens: vivifies
Ennoblement in Peru: sublimation
Ennui: boredom
Eno, Brian: music producer
Enoch's angel: Uriel
Enormously: vastly
Enos's father: Seth
        grandfather: Adam
        grandmother: Eve
        uncle: Abel, Cain
Enough, formally: enow
Enough, more than: plethora
Enough to Omar: enow

Enough, wasn't: ran short
Enpower: enable
Enrapture: ravish
Enrique Iglesias' father: Julio
Ensign in Othello: Iago
Ensnaring scheme: scam
Entebbe's land: Uganda
Entanglement: morass
Enter again: rekey
Enter data: key
Enter the picture: appear
EnterpriseCaptain: Picard
USS Enterprise
Enterprise (USS) officer: Uhura
Entertain lavishly: regale
Entertainer, one-name: cher
Enthralled: rapt, agog
Enthused about: big on
Enthused, far from: blasé
Enthusiasm: oomph, vim
Enthusiasm, and then some: mania
Enthusiasm, extreme: mania
Enthusiasm plus: mania, zeal
Enthusiasm, with: avidly, oomph
Enthusiastic follower: fan
Enthusiastic review: rave
Entice: tempt
Enticement: bait
Entire extent: gamut
Entire range: gamut
Entitle to, be: earn
Entr.: acte
Entrance court: atria
Entrance, curved: arch
Entrance, shaft: adit
Entranced: rapt
Entre nous: between us
Entreat: beg, sue
Entreaty: plea
Entreaty, make an: urge
Entry endorsement: visa
Entry in red: debit
Entry level job
Entry permit: visa
Entryway, graceful: arch
Entwine: enlace
Enumeration abbreviation: etc.
Enumerator's finish, briefly: et al
Enunciation problem: lisp
Envelope: wreathe
Envelope abbr.: attn, att
Envelope, courtesy: SASE
Envelope, padded: mailer
Envelope, silky: cocoon
Envious, in Bonn: brio
Environment: milieu
Environment group: Greenpeace
Environment science: ecology, ecol
Environmental prefix: eco
Environs: area
Envoy: legate
Enya's music: new age
Enzyme ending: ase
Enzyme secretion: saliva

Enzyme suffix: ase
Ephemeral heavenly blaze: nova
Ephron, Nora: writer, director
Epic chronicle: saga,
Epic hero, Russian: Igor
Epic journey: odyssey
Epic of Troy: Iliad
Epic poem: epopee, epode, epos
Epic poetry writer: epopee
Epidermal opening: pore
Epidermis aperture: stoma
Epilates': giant
         brother: Otus
         father: Aloeus, Poseidon
         mother: Iphimedia
         slayer: Apollo
Épinard: spinach
Episode, first: pilot
Epistles writer: Paul
Epoch, geologic: eocen
Epochs: ages, eons, eras
Eponymous Utah tribe: Ute
Epopee: poem
Epps, Omar: actor
Epsilon followers: aeta
Epsom Downs: race track
Equal billing, get: costar
Equalfooting, on: at par
Equal, in Epinal: Egal (France)
Equal partner's cut: half
Equal to the task: able
Equal-angle figure: isogon
Equality State: Wyoming
Equator segment: arc
Equatorial constellation: Cetus
Equestrian maneuver: Caracole
Equine, long-eared: ass
Equine pest: gnat
Equine sound: neigh
Equinox month: Sept
Equip anew: refit, rearm
Equip again: refit, rearm
Equipped with a tiller: steerable
Equitable: fair
Equitable, least: unfairest
Equitably: fairly
E pluribus unum
ER pictures: X-rays
Era of Good Feelings
Era, the end of an: legends retirement
Eradicate: uproot
Erase: efface, delete
"Ere I Saw Elba"
Erelong: anon
Ergo: hence, hense
Eric the Red, son of: Leif
Ericson, Leif: navigator
Eris's brother: Ares, Mars
         daughter: Ate
         goddess of: strife, discord
         mother: Nox, Nyx
Eritrea's capital: Asmara
Ermine, brown: stoat
Ermine in summer: stoat

"Ernani": opera
Ernie's friend: Bert
Ernie's pal: Bert
Ernst, Max: painter
Eros in Rome: love, amour
Erosion, remove by: ablated
Erotic: sexy
Errand runner: gofer, legman, page
Errare humanum est
Erratic move: zig
Errors: errata, mistakes
Errors, like some: dumb
Ersatz butter
Ersatz butter: oleo
Erstwhile Turkish dignitaries: beys
Erte's art: Dada
Erte's field: art deco
Erudite: well-read
Erudite person: scholar
Erwin, Stu: actor
Esau's country: Edom
Esau's father-in-law: Elon
Escapade, carefree: lark
Escapades: larks
Escape, as through a crevice: seep
Fast escape: lam
Escape, hasty: lam
Escape hatch: exit
Escaped adroitly: eluded
Escapee: evader
Escargot: snail
Eschew getting up: sleep in
Escort to a seat: usher
Escort, without an: solo, stag
Escorted by: with
Escorted off: led away
Escritoire: desk, table
Escutcheon border: orle
Eskimo: AmerInd
Eskimo boat: umiak, oomicik
Eskimo boot: mukluk
Eskimo canoe: kayak
Eskimo of films: Nanook
ESL, part of: Eng.
Esoteric: arcane
Esposito, Phil: hockey
Esprit: morale
Esprit de corps
Essay byline: Elia
Essayist, famous: Elia
Essayist's pseudonym: Elia
Essen article: der
Essence: inner, soul, nubs, gist, pith
Essential: innate, vital
Essential character: nature
Essential part: piths
Essential perfume: attar
Essential point: gist
Established fact: given
Established practice: usage
Established rule: axiom
Estate, country: villa
Estate, feudal: fief
Estate, freehold: allod

Estate house: manor
Estate or time, kind of: real
Estate recipient: heir
Estate sharer: coheir
Estated, but needy: land poor
Esteemed one: idol
Estefan, Gloria: music
Ester of guanosine: GTP
Ester start: poly
Estes, Simon: baritone
Estevez, Emilido: actor
Estrada, Erik: actor
Estrange: alienate
Estuary: ria, inlet
Et cetera relative: and so on
Et labora, oro
Étagère feature: shelf
Eternal: ageless
Eternal city: Rome
Eternal shape: triangle
Eternally: eer
Eternity has, what: no end
Ethel's friend: Lucy
Ethereal: airy
Ethical standards, indifferent: amoral
Ethically neutral: amoral
Ethiopia's capital: asmara
Ethiopia's ruler: Haile Selassie
Ethiopian lake: Tsana
Ethiopian prince: Ras
Ethiopian title: Ras
Ethnic group, Chinese: Han
Ethnic group, of an: racial
Etiquette guru: Emily Post
Etna's island: Sicily
Etonian dad: Pater
Etouffee Ingred.: Craw daddy
"ET Tu" time: Ides
Etude composer: Chopin
Etui contents: pins
Eucalyptus eater: koala
Eucalyptus tree: yate
Eucharist plate: paten
Eucharistic plate: paten
Euclid or plate: Greek
Euler, Leonhard: physics, math
Euphonium relative: tuba
Euphoria: elatum
Euphoric, more: happier
Euphrates, it joins the: Tigris (river)
Eurasian expanse, vast: steppe
Eurasian range: Alai, Ural
Eureka: a ha
Euripides drama: medea
Europa's brother: Cadmus
         father: Agenor, Phoenix
         husband: Asterius
         lover: Zeus
         sons: Minos, Sarpedon
Europe's boot: Italy
European alliance: NATO
European apple: Sorb
European country: Eire
European dormice: Loirs, Loire

European eagle: ern
European fish dish: turbot
European flatfish: brill, turbot
European lake: Onega
European mountains: Ural, Alps
European nomad: Hun
European resort: Riviera
European Smoker: Etna (Volcano)
"ETO" Head: D. D. E. (Eisenhower)
Europe's longest river: Volga
Eurydice lover: Orpheus
Euterpe's sister: Erato
"Eva Luna": (Allende book)
Evader: fleer
Evades: ducks, eludes, avoids
Evaluates: weighs
Evander's father: Hermes, Mercury
    mother: Carmenta, Carmentis
    son: Pallas
Evangelists: apostles
"Even as we speak": now
Even exchange: trade-off
Even in movement: steady
Even once: ever
Even one: any
Even so: yet
Even though: albeit
Even up: align, tied
Evening: dusk
Evening event: soiree, sunset
Evening, evian: soir, soiree
Evening gala: soiree
Evening gown fabric: satin
Evening gown material: taffeta
Evening out: date
Evening party: soiree
Evening reception: soiree
Evening repast: dinner
Evening song: vesper
Evening, this: tonight
Evening wear: pj's
Evenly split: in two
Evens, Gil: jazz composer
Event, dressy: gala
Event, inexplicable: miracle
Event, traumatic: crisis
Eventually: in time
Ever, to Byron: e'er
Everest guide: Sherpa
Everest view: Nepal
Evergreen: cedar
Evergreen, ornamental: paths
Evergreen scent: pine
Evergreen, somber: yew
Evergreen State: Washington
Evergreens, like some: piny
Everhart, Angie: model
Everlasting: perpetual
Everlasting, once upon a time: eterne
Everly Bros: music
Evers partner: anon
Evert, Chad: actor
Evert, Chris: tennis
Every: each

Every day layer: hen
Every, in Eboli: ogni
Every Rx abbr.: OMN
Every seven days: weekly
"Everybody Hurts" Group: R.E.M.
Everybody in Bonn: alle
Everybody's opposite: no one
Everyone, to Etienne: tout lemonde
Everything Considered: In All
Everything, it means: omni
Eve's home: Eden,
    husband: Adam,
    son: Abel, Cain, Seth
Evian: spa
Evian evening: soir, soiree
Evidence of text change: erasure
Evidence, provides: adduces
Evidence, show: prove
Evidence, strong sort of: DNA
"Do no evil"
Evil eye: hex
Evil for evil, return: retaliate
Evil hypnotist of fiction: Svengali
Evil spell: curse
Evil spirit: demon
"Evil Woman" Org.:ELO
Evils, like one of two: lesser
Evinced: shown
Evinces curiosity: asks
Evinrude, ole: inventor
Evita's husband: Juan
Evolutionary link: ape man
Ewe or mare: she, female
Ewell, Tom: actor
Ewer: jug
Ewe's home: cote
Ewok's home: Endor
Exacerbated, most: angriest
Exact, to a brit: spot on
Exact copy: clone
Exact duplicate, of an: clonal
Exact in measuring: precise
Exact restitution: avenge
Exacting (too): fussy
Exaggerated claims, make: oversell
Exaggerated promotion: hype
Exaggerator's suffix: est
Exaltation in verse: ode
Exam, annual: medical
Exam, big: midterm, final
Exam, doctorate: oral
Exam, face to face: oral
Exam for HSjuniors: PSAT
Exam, long-answer: essay
Exam option: true, false, yes, no
Exam question, type of: essay, oral
Exam results: scores, grades
Examine: scan
Examine with care: peruse, case
Examined by sight: perused
Example, typical: epitome
Exams, some: midterm
Exasperate: vex
Excavate further: deepen

Excavator, avian: coal mynahs
Excedrin ingredient: aspirin
Exceed in firepower: outgun
Except if: unless
Except on the condition: unless
Except that: unless
Except when: unless
Exception to the rules: anomalies
Excess of solar over lunar years: epact
Excess publicity: hype
Excessive: ultra
Excessive fluid accumulationedema
Excessive pride: hubris
Excessively: wide, steeply, too, unduly
Exchange, even: trade-off
Exchange for cash, perhaps: redeem
Exchange for fast cast: hock, pawn
Exchange premiums: agis, aqios
Exchange rate: market
Exchange rate, lower: devalue
Exchange verbal blows: spar
Excited: agog
Excited, feel: tingle
"I'm so Excited"
Exciting: heady
Exciting, not: tame, dull
Exclaiming over: aahing
Exclamation: egad
Exclamation of disgust: pah, drat, yuck
Exclamation of surprise: yipe
Exclamation, old-time: egad
Exclusive: only
Excursion: junket, tour, outing
Excuse me: ahem, oops
Excuse, trumped-up: pretext
Excuse, lame: cop out
Excuses: outs
Excuses, like some: lame. Sad
Execute perfectly: ace, nail
Exec: Mgr, CEO, CFO, COO
Exec, slangily: suit
Executive incentive: bonus
Executor's concern: estate
Exemplar of blindness: bat
Exemplar of innocence: lamb
Exemplar of lightness: feather
Exercise, Chinese: tai chi
Exercise discipline: yoga
Exercise, gentle: yoga
Exercise, kind of: isometric
Exercise, mild: yoga
Exercise place: gym, spa
Exercise series: reps
Exercise system: yoga
Exercise system, Chinese: tai chi
Exercise units: reps
Exert: strain
Exes are made, where many: Reno
Exhale audibly: sigh
Exhaust: tire, sap, use up, wear down
Exhaust problem: emission
Exhausting routine: rat race
Exhausting walk: slog
Exhibition location: booth

Ex home owner: seller
Exigency: need
Exile, certain: émigre
Exile, place of: Elba
Exiled elephant: rogue
Exiled Roman poet: Ovid
Exist as a characteristic: inhere
Exist as a group: are
Existence: esse
Existence in Latin xlass: Esse
Bane of one's existence
Existing: in esse
Existing in one from birth: innate
Exit ramp site: motel, hotel
Ex machina, dues
Exodus author: Uris
Exodus character: Ari
Exodus hero: Ari, Nora
Exodus name: Ari
Exorcist's quarry: demon
Exotic: foreign
Exotic farm bird: emu
Exotic flower: orchid
Exotic island: Bali
Exotic vacation spot: Bali
Expand the family, in a way: adopt
Expanse of land: tract
Expansive: wide
Expatriation, those forcing: banishers
Expected: due
Expected anytime: due
Expected to arrive: due
Expecting any time: due
Expedite: hasten
Expedition: trek
Expel: oust, evict,
Expel by legal process: evict
Expenditure: out lay
Expense account: perk
Expense accts., like some: padded
Expensive bar or pub order: round
Expensive box: loge
Expensive, not so: less
Expensive pub order: round
Experience, severe: ordeal
Experience, trying: ordeal
Experience, type of: hands on
Experienced person: veteran
Experiencing jitters: edgy
Experiencing pressure: under the gun
Experimental: new, untested
Experimentation station: chem lab, lab
Expert: pro, maven, pundit, guru, ace
Expert, as in language: maven
Expert dealmaker: closer
Expert in fabrication: liar
Expert on stars and spars: sailor
Expert, revered: guru
Expertise, showing: adept
Expertise, sphere of: area
Explanation introducer: idest
Explanation to, add: annotate
Expletive: oath
Expletive, mild: egad, gosh, drat, darn

Explicit, least: vaguest
Exploding star: nova
Explodes in anger: lashes out
Exploit: use, feat
Exploit, daring: gest
Exploit, notable: gesti
Exploited laborer: peon
Explorer, Eric the Red: Vasco da Gama
Explorer need: map
Explorer, polar: Byrd
Explorer, 16th century: Cortez
Explorer's sketch: map
Explosion: blast
Explosive, blasting: TNT, Tonite
Explosive devise: mine, petard
Explosive liquid: nitro
Export or import: trade
Expose as false: debunk
Exposed to the world: bared
Exposes to view: opens
Expound at length: orate
Express: put
Express a view: opine
Express an idea: opine
Express approval: endorse
Express boredom: sigh
Express curiosity: ask
Express disapproval: boo
Express forcefully: assert
Express great happiness: rejoice
Express grief: sob
Express, not an: local
Express opposition: object
"Express, Oriental"
Express positively: assert
Express scorn: sneer
Express words by letter: spell
Expresses disdain: tuts
Expressing dejection: sighing
Expression: phrase
Expression, common: idiom
Expression of displeasure: scowl
Expression of evil intent: threat
Expression of puppy love: arfs
Expression of wariness: phew
Expression, unwelcome: leer
Expression, villainous: sneer
Expressionless: dead pan
Expressions: idioms
Expressway: belt, rte
Expunged: erased, deleted, effaced
Extend over: span
Extend "time": renew
Extend wide: yawn
Extended family: kin
Extends over: spans
Extension: renewal
Extensive, extremely: vast
Extent, to any: at all
External covering: skin, tarp
External layer: skin,
Extinct bird: moa, dado
Extinct kiwi relative: moa
Extol: laud

Extort money from: bleed, con, scam
Extract flavors by boiling: decoct
Vanilla extract
Extraordinary power: brute strength
Extras: pluses
Extraterrestrial, TV: Alf
Extravagant party: bash
Extreme: dire
Extreme mental distress: anguish
Extreme, most: utmost
Extreme poverty:penury
Extremely: very
Extremely eager: keen
Extremely extensive: vast
Extremely happy: in orbit
Extremely heavy rains: torrential
Extremely modest home: hut
Extremely scanty: exiguous
Extremely unconventional: weird
Extremely unkind: harsh
Exxon brand: Esso
Exxon Valdez, for one: tanker, oiler
Eyas's home: nest
Eye at the end of a lariat: honda
Eye coating: sclera
Eye, comb. form: ocul, oculo
Eye doctor's lens: optics
Eye for an eye, for instance: revenge
Eye glass: monocle
Eye glasses, informally: specs
Eye, in Versailles: oeil
Eye inflammation: stye
Eye lashes: cilia, ciliam
Eye layer: uvea
Eye liner: Kohl
Eye membrane: cornea
Eye nuisance: stye
Eye opener: alarm
Eye part: cornea, iris, uvea
Eye protector: lash, lid
Eye ridge: brow
Eye signal: wink
Eye, red-eye steak
Eyed, sloe: dark-eyed
Eye to eye, see: agree
Eye tricking poster: op art
Eyeball-bending drawing: op art
Eyebrow shape: arch, arc
Eyelet: grommet
Eyelets, used: laced, tied
Eyelid woes: styes, sties
Eye-popping pictures: op art
Eyes amorously: ogles
Eyes, of the: ocular
Eyesore, urbane: slum
Eyewash acid: boric

F

"F" in f-stop: focal
F.A.M. Members: masons
Fa follower: sol
Fab four name: Paul, Ringo, John, George

Faberge eggs recipient: tsar (Russian)
Faberge product: egg, Easter egg
Fable: legends
Fable ender: moral
Fable loser: hare
Fable part: moral
Fable writer: Aesop
Fabled longhaired beauty: Rapunzel
Fable's lesson: moral
Fabric: textile
Fabric, angora: mohair
Fabric, clingy: knit
Fabric coloring method: tie-dye
Fabric, cool: linen
Fabric, crinkled: crepes
Fabric, drip-dry: nylon
Fabric, easy care: Dacron
Fabric, evening gown: satin
Fabric, flax: linen
Fabric from cork: Irish linen
Fabric fold: pleat
Fabric, fuzzy: felt
Fabric, gauzy: tulle
Fabric, glazed: chintz
Fabric, glittery: lame
Fabric, glossy: sateen, satin
Fabric, man-made: Dacron
Fabric, mesh: net
Fabric, net: tulle
Fabric, net-like ornamental: lace
Fabric, nubby: linen
Fabric, openwork: lace
Fabric, ornamental: lace
Fabric, party: net,
Fabric, pillow: percale
Fabric, plaid: tartan
Fabric, quick drying: nylon
Fabric, robe: terry
Fabric roll: bolt
Fabric, rough: burlap
Fabric sample: swatch
Fabric, sheer: organza, voile
Fabric, sheet: percale, muslin
Fabric, soft, ribbed: faille
Fabric, sporty: plaid
Fabric, stretch: lycra
Fabric, stretchy: knit
Fabric, string: poplin, khaki
Fabric stuffing: batt
Fabric, sturdy cotton: nankeen
Fabric surface: nap
Fabric, thin plain-weaved: batiste
Fabric, tie: rep
Fabric, tough: denim, khaki
Fabric, twilled: silesia
Fabric, uniform: chino
Fabric, upholstery: damask, velour
Fabric with a glazed finish: cire
Fabric, waxy-patterned: moire
Fabric, wool: tweed
Fabric, woolen: worsted
Fabrication expert: liar
Fabulist, French: Jean de La Fontaine
　　Greek: Aesop

　　Roman: Phaedrus
　　Russian: Ivan Krylov
Fabulous diamond: hope
Fabulous time: blast
Façade: veneer, surface, front
Face cover: veil, mask
Face facts: get real
Face, make a: mug
Face the target: aim
Face to face exam: oral
Face with stone: revet
Face, wry: moue
Faced on: fronted
Face-down: prone
Face-powder base: talc
Faces the target: aims
Facetious: droll, jocular
Facetious tribute: roast
Facial communicator: smile
Facial powder: talc
Facilitate: aid, aide
Facing: toward, lining
Facsimile copy: reprint
Fact: truth
Fact book: almanac
Fact fudger: liar
Faction: ring, gang, bloc, sect, wing side
De facto: in fact
Ipso facto: in itself
Factoid: tidbit
Factory assembled: prefab
Factory-built structure: prefab
Facts and figures: data
Facts, odd: trivia
Fad: novelty
Fade away: evanesce
Faded: drab
Fads and crazes: styles
Fail,: flunk
Fail big time: bomb
Fail to tip: stiff
Fail to utilize: waste
Failing that: else
Fails to be: isn't
Fails to pay: defaults
Failure, complete: fiasco
Failure, temporary: lapse
Failure, total: dud, bust
Failure, utter: bust
"Faint Heart Ne'er Won"
Faint smell: whiff
Faint trace: tinge, hint
Faint-hearted: timorous
Faints with pleasure: swoons
Fair amount: half
"Fair Deal" pres.: HST, Truman
Fair-minded: just
Fair, more: blonder
Fair offering: ride
Fair share: half
Fairway clumps: divots
Fairway lumps: divots
Fairway wood: brassie
Fairway wreckers: mole

Fairy, kind of: tooth
Fairy tale abode: palace
Fairy tale brother: Grimm
Fairy tale brute: ogre
Fairy tale figure: gnome
Fairy tale queen: Mab (Eng. literature)
Fairy tale heavy: ogre
Fairy tale word: once, upon
Fairylike being: peri (mythological figure)
Faithful's response: amen
Fake: mock, bogus
Fake drake: decoy
Fake it: act
Fake leather: vinyl
Fake, not: true, real
Fake out: deke
Fake out, on the rink: deke
Fake pill: placebo
Fake sword, maybe: prop
Fakir's income: alms
Fa la link, on a musical scale: sol
Falana, Lola: actress
Falco, Edie: actress
Falcon, small: kestrel
Falcon's home: aerie
Fall back: lag, ebb, revert
Fall back function: reset
Fall back or spring forward: resets
Fall back strategy: plan B
Fall fete: halloween
Fall guy: patsy, sap
Fall in folds: drape
Fall into disrepute: incur dishonor
Fall lead-in: prat
Fall off: abate
Fall planting: tulip
Fall sound: clunk
Fall, start to: tip
Fall upon: assail
Fallaci, Oriana: writer
Fallen apart, as plans: gone awry
Fallen log cover: moss
Falling ice: sleet
Falling star: meteor
Falling-out: spat, rift
Falling-out, minor: tiff
Falls back: ebbs, lags
Falls into disuse: lapses
False alibi, furnish with a: abet
False claims, spread: smear
False front: act, guise
False hope, given: led on
False, prove: belie
False step: stumble
False swearing: perjury
False witness: liar
Falsetto: high-pitched (voice)
Falsetto, sing in: yodel
Falsify: fudge
Falstaff Prince: Hal
Falter: waver
Falter at the finish: fade
Famed Atlantic xrosser: Nina
Famed lexicon, abbr.: OED

Famed Russian mystic: Gregory Rasputin
Familiar author: anon
Familiar digit: toe
Familiar saying: adage
Familiar threat: or else
Familiar with: upon
Familiarize: orient
Family, big: clan
Family, extended: kin
Family friction, source of much: in-law
Family history: lineage
Family Hominidae: man
Family Isoetaceae: Isoetes
Family, large: tribe
Family of frogs, large: ranid
Family pet: canine
Family problem: feud
Family supporter: breadwinner
Family tree entry: surname
Family treasure: album
Family Ulmaceae: trema
Famine counterpart: feast
Famished: unfed
Famous apple site: Eden
Famous Atlantic crosser: Nina
Famous boast, start a: veni
Famous caravel: pinta
Famous Christian: Dior
Famous fabulist: Aesop
Famous fawn of film: Bambi
Famous last word: amen, et tu
Famous lemon: Edsel
Famous triangle: Bermuda
Famous wizard: Merlin
Fan blade: vane
Fan (disgruntled): heckler
Fan fave: idol
Fan letdown, temporarily: tie
Fan mail recipient: idol
Fan of, a big: into
Fan produced periodical: zine
Fan spreader: peacock
Fanatic feeling: zeal
Fancy confection: bonbon
Fancy flapjack: crepe
Fancy hair net: snood
Fancy, more than: regal
Fancy shop: salon
Faneuil Hall locale: Boston
Fanfare, mock: ta da
Fannie-Mae offering: loan
Fans, like some: avid
Fan-shaped: alary
Far and wide: all over, everyplace, everywhere
Far afield: astray
Far away: remote
Far East cuisine: Thai
Far from allegro: lento
Far from colorful: drab
Far from deliberate: rash
Far from enthused: blasé
Far from fleet: poky
Far from fresh: trite
Far from jumpy: sedate

Far from polite: rude
Far from terra firma: at sea
Far right of a highway: slow lane
Fare in a shell: taco,
Fare reductions: diets
Fare well: prosper
Farewell: adios, adieu, bye bye
Farewell, forum: vale
Farewell, Italian: addio
Farewell, London: ta ta
Farewell, western: Adios
Farfel's master: Nelson
Farfetched: absurd, dubious, doubtful, fishy, strained, unlikely
Far-flung: distant, remote, outlying, wide, widespread
Farinaceous: mealy
Farm: grange
Farm, kind of: organic
Farm agency: USDA
Farm animals: live stock
Farm bleater: goat, sheep, ewe
Farm enclosure: sty, pen
Farm feed: forage
Farm fowl, fixed: capone
Farm horse: dobbin
Farm teams: minors
Farm worker: hand
Farmer's assoc: grange
Farmer's place: dell
Farming, Good for: Arable
Farming, Suitable for: Arable
Faro Dealer's Box: Shoe
Farrier's Tool: Rasp
Farrier's Work , Do a: Shoe
Farsi, where to hear: Iran
Farthest point: apogee
Fashion: style
Fashion accessory: hat, gloves
Fashion, first name in: Yves
Fashion line: hem,
Fashion, name in: Dior
Fashion status symbol: label
Fashionable: dressy
Fashionable beach resort: lido
Fashionable folks: beau, monde
Fast break: meal
Fast food joints: pizzerias
Fast food option: to go
Fast decision: hunger strike
Fast lane user: roue
Fast message: telegram, Email
Fast runner in slow film: blur
Fast ski run: schuss
Fast sled: luge
Fast talk: jive
Fast talked: snowed, jived
Fast time, for some: Ramadan
Fast transport: jet
Fasten down a tent: peg
Faster, got to go: rushed
Faster than largo: adagio
Fastidious: neat
Fasting (period of): Lent

Fast-talk: snow, jive
Fat cat: nabob, plutocrat
Fat cats: haves
Fat cat's friend: Odie
Fat cat's victim: Odie
Fat Man was one: A-bomb
Fat of geese: axungia
Fat solvent: ether
Fate: kismet
Fate, adverse: doom
Fateful date: Ides
Fateful day: Ides
"Fatha" Hines: Ear., Earl
Father of basketball: Nai Smith
Father of a princess: Roi
Father of geometry: Euclid
Father of medicine: Hippocrates
Father of modern astronomy: Copernicus
Father of modern China: Dr. Sun Yatsen
Father of nuclear physics: Rutherford
Father of science fiction: Jules Verne
Father Time's tool: scythe
Fathers, single: priests
Fathomless: unplumbed
Fatigue: bore
Fatigue, yield to: sat
Fatima's descendant: Agha
Fatima's husband: Ali
Fatt, Lester: guitarist
Fatty: adipose
Fatty compound: lipid
Fatty tissue: suet
Fatty tissue tumor: lipoma
Fatuous: inane, sappy
Fatuous, mindless: inane
Faucet: spigot
Faucet hookup: hose
Faucet word: hot, cold
Faulkner's bundren: anse
Fault, find: nag
Fault phenomenon: quake
Faultfinder: nag
Avifauna
Fauna's go-together: flora
Faunus's grandfather: Saturn
    son: Acis, Latinus
"Faust" author: Johann Goethe
"Faust" character: Devil
Faux pas: blunder, slip, error, gaffe
Favor: resemble
Favorable mention: plug
Favorable, most: optimal
Favored: liked
Favorite at a ball: belle
Favorite son
Favorite son: known man
Favoritism: bias
Fawcett, Farrah: actress
Guy Fawkes Day
Fawn, famous, of film: Bambi
Fawning in attitude: servile
Fawning, target of: idol
Fax predecessor: telex
Fazed, not: undaunted

FBI acronym: AKA
FDR dog: Fala
    mother: Sara
    father: James
    wife: Eleanor
Fe, commonly: iron
Fear, extreme: horror
Fear, overwhelming: panic
Fear, sudden: alarm
Fear, tremble with: quake
Fearful anticipation: dread
Fears, like some: idle
Fearsome Cape: Horn
Fearsome warrior: Julu
Feat, daring: stunt
Feast: repast
Feather adhesive: tar
Feather an arrow: fledge, fletch
Feather, large: plum, plume
Featherbrained: inane
Feathers, fluff: preen
Feathers, glue for: tar
Feather's partner: fuss
Feathers, showy: plume
Feathery neck ware: boa
Feathery scarves: boas
Featured passages: solos
Feckless: inept
Fed a line: cued
Fed. buyer: CSA
Fed. retirement ID: SSN
Federated: allied
Fedora: hat, felt hat
Fedora feature: brim
Feds concern: economy
Feed: fatten
Feed, as a fire: stoke
Feed lines to: cue
Feedback, give: react
Feedback, offer: reply
Feeder: tributary
Feeder feature: perch
Feeding time cry: meow
Feel: palpate
Feel anxiety: dread
Feel at home: belongs
Feel badly about: rue
Feel certain: know
Feel concern: care
Feel excited: tingle
Feel grateful: owe
Feel ones way: grope
Feel or perceive, able to: sensitive
Feel sorry for: regret
Feel sympathy for: ache
Feeler, put out a: test
Feeling: vibe
Feeling blue: sad, low
Feeling, fanatic: zeal
Feeling, gloomy depressed: angst
Feeling low: glum
Feeling of insecurity: angst
Feeling of uneasiness: qualms

Feeling, overall: mood
Feeling, scary: fear
Feeling, vague: sense
Feeling, without: numb
Feels annoyed: resents
Feet container: yard, shoe
Feet, having: pedate
Feet of clay: weakness
Feet, on both: erect
Feet, slangily: dots
Feign: act
Feign illness: malinger
Feints: jokes, jukes, hoax
Felis pardalis: ocelot
Feliciano, Jose
Felician College site: Lodi
Feline, chatty: Siamese
Feline, North American: lynx
Feliz Año Nuevo: Happy New Year
Fell on deafened ears: dinned
Fell softly: plop
Fellow: guy, boy
Fellow bluejackets: shipmates
Fellow, contemptible: cad
Fellow, cultured: gent
Fellow, dissolute: roué
Fellow feeling: agape, concern, empathy,
    rapport, affinity, kindness
Fellow, insignificant: twerp
Fellow, loutish: lug
Fellow, stupid: dolt
Fellow, vain: fop
Felon, foster a: abet
Felt boots: pacs
Felt certain: knew
Felt compassion: cared
Felt grateful: owed
Felt hat: fedora
Felt sorry about: rued
Felt sorry for: pitied
Female antelope: doe
Female fete: hen party
Female gallinaceous bird: hen
Female honorific: Mrs.
Female lobster: hen
Female merino: ewe
Female octopus: hen
Female pheasant: pea hen
Female principle: yin
Female prophet: seeress
Female ruff: ree
Female ruler: empress
Female saint: ste
Female sandpiper: ree
Female servant: maid
Female squirrel: doe
Female vampire: lamia
Female voice (lowest): alto
Female warrior: Amazon
Female water spirit: nixie
Feminine ending: esse
Feminine principle: yin, anima
Feminine pronoun: her
Femme fatale: siren, dangerous woman

Femme fatale Negri: Pola
Femme fatale Negrillo: Pola
Fence groundwork: posthole
Fence picket: pale
Fence steps: stiles
Fence supplier: cat burglar, burglar
Fenced goods, like: stolen
Fencer's shout: touché
Fences: wall, pens in
Fence's ware, like a: stolen
Fencing cry: en garde
Fencing move: lunge
Fencing, piece of: epee
Fencing stance: en garde
Fencing technique: lunge
Fencing term: touche
Fencing weapon: epee, foil
Fend off: stave, repel
Feng shui
Feral quality: wildness
Ferber, Edna: writer
Fergie's Daughter: Bea
    duchy: York
    first name: Sarah
    husband: Andrew
Ferment: unrest
Ferment, in a: rage
Fermented liquid: alegar
Fermenting agent: yeast
Fermions, they're compared to: bosons
Fern, future: spore
Fern leaf: frond
Fern parts: root, stem, frond
"Fernando" group: Abba
Fernando, Rey
Ferns, class of: agamae
Ferocious eel: moray
Ferocious fly, when doubled: tse (tsetse)
Ferrara, Abel: director
Ferrer, Jose: actor
Ferry or wherry: boat
Ferry, run a: ply
Fertile surface layers: top soil
Fertility goddess: Astarte, Ishtar
Fertilized ovum: zygote
Fertilized plant seed: oospore
Fertilizer: guamo, dung, marl
Fertilizer compound: urea
Fertilizer ingredient: niter, potash
Fertilizer, like some: marly
Fertilizer, loamy: marl
Fervent: ardent
Fervent appeal: plea
Fervent aspiration: ideals
Fervent wish: hope
Fervor: ardor, zeal
Fescues or zoysia: grasses
Festive downpour: confetti
Festive log: yule
Festive night: eve
Festivities, pre-drink: toasts
Festoons: adorns, swag, lei
Feudal estate: fief
Feudal laborer: esne

Feudal lord: liege
Feudal peasant: serf
Feudal privilege: soke
Feudal servant: serf
Feudal slave: esne
Feudal tenant: vassal
Feudal underling: serf
Feudal vassals: lieges
Fever: ague
Fever, malaria: ague
Feverish: hectic
Few and far between: sparse
Fez: hat
Fez dangler: tassel
Fez wearer: Turk
Fibber: liar
Fibber, bragging: istle
Fibber plus: liar
Fiber, carpet-maker's: istle
Fiber cluster: nep
Fiber, cordage: sisal
Fiber knot: nep
Fiber, man-made: rayon, nylon
Fiber plant: sunn (hemp), jute
Fiber, rope: hemp, jute
Fiber source: legume, bran
Fiber, spandex:lycra
Fiber spun into yarn: noil
Fiber, strong: bast, bast fiber
Fiber, synthetic: orlon
Fiber, tough: hemp
Fiberglass bundle: batt
Fiber-rich grain: oat
Fibers, bagging: istles
Fibula neighbor: tibia
FICA number: SSN
Fiction: prose
Fiction, type of:sci-fi
Fictional: untrue
Fictional archeologist: Amelia Peabody
Fictional Butler: Rhett
Fictional captain: Nemo
Fictional collie: Las
Fictional daydreamer: Mitty
Fictional governess: Eyne
Fictional Heep: Uriah
Fictional newswoman: Lois
Fictional pirate: Jack Sparrow
Fictional plantation: Tara
Fictional rabbit: Peter
Fictional sheparddess: Bo Peep
Fictional spy: Matt Helm
Fictional work: novel
Fiddle, like a: fit
Fiddle, classic: strad
Fiddle de dee
Fiddle, fat: viol
Fiddle with: tinker
Fiddle-faddle: rot, bosh, bull, bunk, nuts,
    fudge, bunkum, humbug
Fiddle, valued: Strad (Stradivarius)
Fiddle with: toy, adjust
Fiddles with a guitar: strums
Fiddlesticks: nonsense

Fiddling despot: Nero
Fiddling with: toying
Bona fide: true
Fidel's pal: Che
Fidgeting: antsy
Fido's front feet: forepaws
Fido's pal: spot
Fido's scrap: ort
Fido's snippets: ort
Fie relative: tut
Fief: estate, domain
Field fungoes: shags (baseball)
Field mouse: vole
Field of action: arena
Field of knowledge: sphere
Field protector: tarp
Field worker: farmer, ref, umpire
Fields, Totie: comic
Fiend: ogre
Fiendish: evil
Fierce mother: tigress
Fierce flyer of lore: roc
Fierce warrior: Maori
Fiery: ardent
Fiery dance: flamenco
Fiesta bands: mariachis
Fiesta décor: piñata
Fiesta item: piñata
Fiesta music: mariachi
Fifer's drum: tabor
Fifi's date: ami
Fifth day of Kwanzaa: nia
Fifth of twelve?: May
Fifth sign: Leo,
Fifty- fifty: even
Fig-filled treat: Newton
Fight card listing: event
Fight, fixes the: rigs
Fight memento, perhaps: scar
Fight, prepare for: spar
Fight, ready to: armed
Fighting fish: betta
Fights, big: wars
Figment, not a: real
Figure, final: total
Figure of speech: trope, idiom, metaphor,
    aporia, simile, litotes
Figure of speech, symbolic: metaphor
Figure out: get, solve
Figured out: got, solved,
Figurehead's place: bow, prow
Figures, check the: ogle, audit
Figures, stock: ratio
Figurine, valuable: jade
Fiji capital: Suva
Fiji neighbor: Samoa
Filament, metal: wire
Filbert: nut
Filbert tree: hazel, hazel nut
Filch: rob
Filch, old style: nim
File: queue
File label: tab
File stand-in: icon

Filing concerns: taxes
Filipino cutlass: barong
Fill: sate
Fill a pipe: tamp
Fill beyond full: sate
Fill cavities with mortar: grout
Fill, more than: sate
Fill the hull: lade
Fill the lungs: inhale
Fill the tank: fuel up
Fill to the gills: sate
Fill to the max: sate
Fill with: imbue
Fill with amazement: awe
Fill with fizz: aerate
Fill with love: enamor
Filled the hold: laded
Filled with delight: enrapt
Filled with wonder: awed
Fillets a fish: bone, clean, debone
Fill-in hires: office temp, temp
Fillings: inlays
Fillings, dental: inlays
Fill-ins: subs
Fills with Horror: Appals
Fills Space: Exists
Fills with Reverence: Awes
Fill up: sate
Filly, adult: mare
Film award: Oscar
Film festival site: Cannes
Film, kind of: cult
Film, like some: X-rated
Film, low-budget: B movie
Film noir, for one: genre
Film princess: Leia
Film projection: image
Film rating grp.: MPAA
Film segment: clip
Film set: scene
Film set light: klieg
Film set workers: grip
Film spectaculars: epics
Film speed: ASA
Film splicing machine: editor
Film, word with: noir
Filming technique: slo mo
Filmmaker's locale: lot
Filmy:Gossamer
Filter: leach
Filter in: seep
Filthy deposits: crud
Filthy lucre: cash, loot, pelf, bread, bucks,
    dough, moola, riches, moolah
Filthy money: lucre
Filthy rich: lucre
Finagled: wangled
Finagler's concern: angles
Final: exam
Final authority: say so
Final checkup: autopsy
Final deed: envoi
Final figure: total
Final Four org..: NCAA

Final metamorphic stage: adult
Final passage: coda
Final short story: obit
Final word: epilog
Finalize: seal
Finally: at last
Financial aid concern: need
Financial average: Dow
Financial burden: debt
Financial hub, Swiss: Zurich
Financial magazine: Inc.
Financial wiz: CPA
Financially solvent: afloat
Finch: serin
Finch, small: linnet
Find a new tenant: re-let
Find contemptible: scorn
Find out: learn
Find out about: hear, learn
Find pleasure in: enjoy
Find practical: use
Find seats: usher
Find suddenly: hit on
Finder's fee: reward
Finds a buyer: sells
Finds fault: crabs, carps
Fine brandy: cognac
Fine fabric from cork: Irish linen
Fine fettle, in: tip top: well
Fine, impose a: ameree, amerce
Fine mist, reduce to a: atomize
Fine point: nicety, detail
Fine porcelain: limoges
Fine print type size: agate
Fine spray of liquid: haze, mist
Fine steed: Arabian, Arab
Fine woolen fabric: saxony
Finery: regalia
Fine-tune: adjust
Fingal's cave island: staffa
Finger Lakes, largest of the: Seneca
Finger paint: daub
Fingerling: naming
Fingerprint: latent, clue
Fingerprint ridge: whorl
Finger's: names
Finish a "J": dot
Finish among the first three: place
Finish line marker: tape
Finish lines: tapes
Finish the course: eat
Finish third: show
Finish, very close: photo finish
Finished up: ended
Fink, play the: rat on
Finland neighbor: Russia
Finn Air competitor: SAS
Finnish bath: sauna
Finnish first name: Eero
Finn's pal: Sawyer
Fir, fragrant: balsam
Fire, ceremonial: pyre
Fire chief's foe: arsonist
Fire cracker part: fuse

Fire god, Roma: Vulcan
Fire, feed the: stoke
Fire pile: pyre
Fire, slangily: axe, can
Fire, start a: ignite, kindle
Firearm discharge, simultaneous: salvo
Firearm type: rifle, pistol, revolver
Firecracker part: fuse
Fired clay, made of: earthen
Fired up: eager
Firedog: andiron
Firefighting aid: anadow
Firefly cousin: glowworm
Fireplace: grate
Fireplace ashes: residue
Fireplace shelf: hob
Firepower, exceed in: out gun
Fireproof mineral: asbestos
Fireside: hearth
Firewood units: steres
Fire-works: petards
Firm grasp: grip
Firm, make: stabilize
Firm up: set, tone, jell, gel
Firma, terra
Firmament: sky
Firmed up: set
Firmness: solidity
Firth of Clyde, island in the: Arran (Scotland)
First American in space: Glenn
First arboretum: Eden
First century emperor: Nero
First coed college (U.S.): Oberlin
First course: soup, salad
First creature off the ark: raven
First episode: pilot
First estate: clergy
First gear: low
First grade fare: ABDs
First in importance: primary
First killer: Cain
First king of England: Egbert
First lady: Eve
First lady of scat: Ella
First light: sun up, dawn
First magnitude star: Vega
First name in art: Mona
First name in classic cars: Alfa
First name in cosmetics: Estee
First name in hostelry: Leona
First name in jazz: Ella
First name in lexicography: Noah
First name in mystery: Agatha
First name of horror: Lon
First of all: Adam, primo
First on the scene: Adam
First organ donor: Adam
First place: Eden
First quarter tide: neap
First sign , the: Aries
First state: Delaware
First strategy plan: plan A
First stringers: "A" team
First to second, go from: shift

First version: draft
First voyage: maiden
First aid plant: aloe
First-stage rocket: booster
Fiscal period: year
Fischer win: mate, check mate
Fish balancer: fin
Fish basket: creel
"Fish Called Wanda, A"
Fish, carp-like: bream
Fish commercially: troll
Fish, cyprinoids: dace
Fish dish, European: turbot
Fish-eating mammal: otter, bear
Fish, elongated: gar
Fish exhibition: ocean, ocean area, oceanaria
Fish, fighting: betta
Fish, fresh water: darter
Fish , future: roe
Fish groups: schools
Fish, in a way: dap
Fish, kettle of: awkward situation
Fish lander: gaff
Fish, large: bigeye
Fish, large aquarium: skate
Fish, large scaled ocean: porgy
Fish, like some: bony
Fish, long-nosed: gar
"Fish Magic" artist: Klee
Fish, marine: robalo
Fish net: trawl
Fish, ocean: hake, tuna
Fish, pilot: remora
Fish, pointy-snouted: skate
Fish, prepared: boned
Fish, raw, dish: sushi
Fish roe: ova
Fish sauce:
Fish, scaleless: eel
Silvery fish: shad
Fish, small: minnow
Fish, small silvery: smelt
Fish spear: gig, trident
Fish tail: slue
Fish tempter: lure, bait
Fish, thin sliced: sashimi
Fish trap: eelpot, weir
Fish type: peto, mero, wahoo, sey
Fish, walleye: pike
Fish with a net: trawl
Fish-eating duck: smew
Fished with a baited line: trolled
Fished with pots: eeled
Fisher, Carrie: actress
Fisher, Ham: cartoonist
Fisherman: eeler
Fishes from a boat: trolls
Fishhook connector: snell
Fishhook, large: gaff
Fishhook, like a: barbed
Fishhook line: snell
Fishhook line, short: snell
Fishing basket: creel
Fishing boat: dogger, dory

Fishing float: bob, bobber
Fishing fly, feathered: herp
Fishing lures: jigs, flies
Fishing place: bank, lake, pier, pond, river, ocean, sea,
Fishing reel: pirn
Fishing rod: pole
Fishing tool, heavy: set line
Fishing vessel: smack
Fissile rock: shale
Fisson opposite: fusion
Fissure: rift
Fissure, deep: abyss
Fist, make a: clench
Fists: dukes
Fit for a king: regal
Fit for highness: regal
Fit for the job: able
Fit, kind of: retro
Fit of pique: snit
Fit of shivering: ague
Fit to be drafted: One A
Fit to be tied: irate
Fit to cut the mustard: able
Fit to market: salable
Fit to perform: able
Fit together: nested
Fit well: mesh
Fit within: nested
Fitting manner, in a: duly
Fitzgerald, Ella: music
Fitzgerald's poet: Omar
Five, comb. form: penta, pent
Five, group of: pentad
Five hundred sheets: ream
Five or nine digit number: zip, zip code
Five-sided figure: pentagon
Five-year period: luster, lustre, lustrum
Five-year plan empire: USSR
Nine to fiver
Fix, as a copier: un-jam
Fix, as an election: rig
Fix boundaries: define
Fix firmly: implant, embed
Fix potatoes: mash, peel
Fix the eyes on: look, ogle
Fix the outcome: rig
Fix up an old house: rehab
Fixe, Idée
Fixed: stable, set, repaired
Fixed a table: laid, set
Fixed an interest rate: locked in
Fixed charge: set rate
Fixed farm fowl: capone
Fixed up building: rehab
Fixes dishonestly: rigs
Fixes the fight: rigs
Fixes up: rehabs, repairs
Fizz, lack: flat
Fjord: inlet
Fjord locale: Norway
Fjord port: Oslo
Flag: banner
Flag down: hail

Flag features a beehive, it's: Utah
Flag, naval: ensign
Flag pole topper: eagle
Flair: talent, elan, knack
Flair for music: ear
Flairs: knacks
Flake, slangily: weirdo
Flake off: peel
Flaky: daft
Flaky material: mica
Flaky sesame confection: halva
Flambeau: torch
Flambeau relative: cresset (oil lamp)
Flamboyant surrealist: Dali,
Flame, put out a: snuff-out
Flamenco accolade: ole
Flamenco shout: ole
Flamenco dance shout: ole
Flaming meal: flambé
Flanagan's flock: boys
Flanders of fiction: Moll
Flapjack chain: IHOP
Flapjack, fancy: crepe
"Flapper" follower: era
Flared: gored
Flashback experience: relive
Flash, brief: gleam
Flash flood: spate, rush, deluge, torrent, burst, float
Flash of lightning: bolt
Flash on and off: blink
Flashed: glinted
Flashes: glints
Flashes, electrical: sparks
Flashes of light: glints
Flashes on and off: blinks
Flashing lights: strobes
Flashlight carrier: usher
Flashy: loud, snazzy
Flashy displays: pomps
Flat: off key
Flat boat: barge
Flat bread of india: chapati
Flat paper: lease
Flat replacement: spare
Flat space: room
Flat broke: hard up
Flatfish, European: brill
Flatfoot: cop
Flatfoot's collar: arrest
Flatten at the poles: oblate
Flatten circle: ellipse
Flatter: fawn
Flatter, in a way: ape
Flatterer: toady
Flattery: oil, compliments
Flat-topped elevation: butte, mesa
Flat-topped hill: butte, mesa
Flat-topped rise: butte, mesa
Flaubert heroine: Emma, Bovary
Flaubert work: "A Simple Soul"
Flavor enhancer: Msk, Msg
Flavor, tangy: mint
Flavors: tangs

Flawless: ideal
Flax fabric: linen
Flax filament: harl
Fledging: bird
Flee: elope, escape
Flee hastily: lam
Flee, unable to: at bay
Fleece seeker: Jason
Fleece, soft, silky: alpaca
Fleecing operation: bunko
Flees to the JP: elopes
Fleet, far from: poky
Fleet, part of a: vessel, ship
Fleeting: brief
Fleeting flash: glint
Fleeting traces: wisp
Fleetwood: Mac
Fleming, Ian: author
Fleming, Rhonda: actress
Fleur-de-lis
Fleur-de-lys
Flexibility, show: adapt, bend
Flexible choice: any
Flexible mineral: mica
Flick, old style: nim
Flicker: wag
Flickertail State: N. Dakota
Flickertail State city: Fargo
Flier, takes a: risk
Flier with Cupid: Comet
Fliers, retired: SSTs
Flies, caught: shagged
Flight formation: echelon
Flight panel: FAA
Flight routes: arcs
Flight segment: riser
Flight shortened: tail wind
Flight to escape danger: hegira, hejira
Flightless bird: emu, moa, ratite, rhea
Flights, some: stairs
Flighty maneuver: flit
Flighty, not: sedate
Flimsier: cheaper
Flimsy: gossamer
Flimsy paper: tissue
Fling with force: hurl
Flint: rock
Flint or quartz: silica
Flint, worked: flaked
Flintlock musket: fusil
Flintstones creator: Hanna
Flip chart stand: easel
Flip comment: head, tails
Flip flop: sandal, U-turn, waver, reverse, tong
Flip through: scan, skim, leaf
Flips out: freaks
Flirt: lead on, dally
Flirtation: idyll
Flits about: gads, darts
Float: buoy
Float away: bob
Float downriver: waft, tube
Float for Finn: raft
Float in a pool: natant

Float like a cork: bob
Float, not: sink,
Float, warning: buoy
Floating fragrances: aromas
Floating haven: ark
Floating leaf: pad
Floating log, spin a: birl,
Floating platform: raft
Floats along: bobs, drifts, tubes
Floats gently: wafts, bobs
Floats on the breeze: wafts
Flock: bevy
Flock mom: ewe, hen
Flock together: troop
Flood insurance?: stilts
Flood prevention structure: dike, levee
Flood residue: mud
Floodgate: sluice
Floods, protect from: embank
Floods the market: glut
Floor: awe
Floor beam: joist
Floor covering: matting, tile
Floor for good: kayo
Floor mat, japanese: tatami
Floor protector: mat
Floor sample: demo
Floor tile material: PVC, ceramic
Flop: dud
Floppy: diskette
Floppy content: data
Floppy taker: PC
Flops down: sprawls
Flora or fauna: bista
Flora partner: fauna
Floral attraction: odor
Floral display: spray
Floral motif: fleuron
Floral neckwear: lei
Florence river: Arno
Florentine or Venetian: Italian
Florentine poet: Dante
Florid: red
Florida port: Tampa
Florida race track: Hialeah
Florida's first golf course: Sarasota
Florimel's husband: Marinel
Flo's coworker: Vera
Flotsam and jetsam
Flour, coat with: dredge
Flour holder: bin
Flour or sugar: staple
Flour, prepare: sift
Flourish: wield
Flouter of church doctrine: heretic
Flow like lava: ooze
Flow like sap: ooze
Flow out: emanate, issue
Flow regulator: cock, gate, valve
Flow slowly: ooze
Flowers:
    January: carnation
    February: primrose
    March: violet

    April: daisy
    May:Lily of the Valley
    June: rose
    July: sweet pea
    August: gladiolus
    Sept.: Aster
    Oct.: dahlia
    Nov.: chrysanthemum
    Dec.: Holly
Flower adornment: lei
Flower and weeds: plants
Flower bed: plot
Flower droplets: dew
Flower, exotic: orchid
Flower girl: hippie
Flower holder: stem, vase
Flower named for a turban: tulip
Flower oil: attar
Flower parts: pistel, petal, sepal, anther,
    anther, stamen, ament, stalk, stigma
Flower petal oil: attar
Flower planting: bed
Flower plot: bed
Flower product: nectar
Flower-arranging art: ikebana
Flowering shrub: oleander
Flowering tree: mimosa
Flowerless plant: fern, moss, lichen, liverwort
Flowers: geum
Flowers, circle of: lei
Flowers in a vase: spray
Flower-shaped decoration: rosette
Flowery kingdom: China
Floyd, Pink
Flu shot results: immunity
Flu strain: asian
Flu symptom: fever, ague, chill, ache, malaise
Fluctuate repeatedly: yo yo
Fluency: ease
Fluff a line: err.
Fluff, as hair: tease
Fluff feathers: preen
Fluffy scarf: boa
Fluid accumulation, excessive: edema
Fluid rock: magma
Fluid, vital: plasma
Flurry: ado
Flurry, kind of: snow, ado
Flush with: even
Flustered: abashed
Flustered, not: calm
Flute cousin: oboe
Flute, high-pitched: piccolo
Flute player: piper
Flute, small: piccolo
Flutter, as eyelashes: bat
Fluttered: waved
Fly as a unit: swarm
Fly catcher: web
Fly, hazardous: tsetse
Fly high: soar,
Fly in the ointment: bane
Fly off the shelves: sell
Fly quickly: flit

Fly, small: gnat
Fly, to a spider: prey
Fly trap, maybe: web
Fly-catching bird: pewee
Flyer: aviator, pamphlet
Flying, capable of: volant
Flying fish: gurnard
Flying fox: bat
Flying greats: aces
Flying group: USAF
Flying horse: pegasus, hippogriff
Flying island: laputa
Flying lemur: colugo
Flying nuisance: gnat
Flying off the shelves: red hot
Flying prefix: aero
Flyleaf: page (blank)
Flytrap: web
Focal point: loci
Foch, Nina: actress
Focus group: eyes
Focus, lose: blur
Fodder grass: hay
Fodder, horse: oats
Fodder structure: silo
Fog, thin: mist, haze
Fogg's creature: Verne
Foil: stymie
Foil kin: epee
Foist oneself on others: impose
Fold, gather in: shirr
Folding business: origami
Folds: pleats
Folds, arranged in: draped, pleated
Folger's Mrs. Olsen
Foliage: leaf
Folio page: recto,
Folk art dolls, like: nested
Folk dance shoe: clog
Folk song mule: Sal
Folk stories: lores
Folk wisdom: lore
Folklore creatures: goblins
Folklore meany: ogre
Folklore sprite: elf
Follett, Ken: writer
Follow: ensue
Follow, as advice: act on
Follow behind,: in tow, lag
Follow closely: lag, shadow, tail
Follow immediately: ensue
Follow in pursuit: chase
Follow in sequence: ensue
Follow relentlessly: shadow, dog
Follow unobserved: tail
Followed: traced, trailed, tailed
Followed the law: belted up, buckled up
Follower, enthusiastic: fan
Following, immediately: next
Follows intently: dogs
Foment: incite
Fond, too: dating
Fond desire: wish
Fond, is overly: dotes

Fond widths: ens
Fonda, Henry: actor
Fontanne's husband: Lunt
Fontanne's partner: Lunt
Food additive: MSG, agar
Food: aliment
Food and drink: repast
Food basic: staple
Food cookers: pots, pans
Food cooler: fridge
Food decoration: rosette, rossette
Food fancier: epicurer, epicure
Food from Tara: poi
Food, health: tofu
Food, heavenly: manna
Food item: viand
Food, like some: ethnic
Food list: menu
Food lover: epicure
Food, miracle: Manna
Food on a Stick: kabob
Food or music, kind of: soul
Food org.: USDA
Food preservation container: jar
Food preserver: salt
Food processor setting: chop, puree
Food, put up: can
Food scrape: ort
Food, soft,: pap, pab
Food steamer: wok
Food store: deli
Food source: market
Food, supplies: caters
Food thickener: agar
Food tray: salver
Food wrap: cello (cellophane), foil
Foofaraw: ado, fuss
Fool, pompous: ass
Fooled, was: bit
Foolish: inane, daft, silly
Foolish, less: wiser
Foolish mistake: boner
Foolish plus: inane
Foolish talk: prate
Foolishness: nonsense
Fool's attire: motley
Fool's gold: pyrite
Foot pedal, used a: treadled
Foot: pes
Foot, comb. form: pedi
Foot levers: pedals
Foot pound: stomp
Foot, slangily: tootsy
Foot the bill: treat, pay
Foot warmers: socks
Football play: down
Football, british: rugby
Football compliment: eleven
Football corsages: mums
Football field: grid, gridiron
Football flight: spiral
Football formation: huddle
Football pass: spiral
Football names:

Blanda, George
Levy, Marv: coach
Shula, Don: coach
Swann, Lynn: NFL
Williams, Doug: QB (NFL)
Football, spongy, type of: nerf
Footfall: step
Footless: apod, apodal, inept
Footlights: stage
Foot-like part: pes
Footlocker: trunk
Footloose, be: rove, roam
Footman: lackey
Footman's attire: livery
Footnote abbr.: eral, et al, loc cit
Footnote datum: page
Footnote, make a: cite
Footnote word: idem
Foot-pound: stomp
Foot-pound relative:erg
Footprint: track, impression, mark
Footrest: ottoman
Foot's a column: adds
Footwear insert: shoe tree
Footwear, tragic: buskins
Footwear, wooden: sabots
Foo Young, Egg
For adults only: X-rated
For all to see: overt
For example: such as
For fear that: lest
For pickup: to go
For shame: tut
For some time: awhile
For sure: really
For the asking: free
For the birds: avian
For the most part: meanly, largely, generally,
    typically
For the time being: now, pro tem, currently,
    at present
For two in music: a duet
"For what reason": why
"For Whom the Bell Tolls"
FYI notes: memos
Foray, made a: raided
Foray, sudden: raid
Forbes rival: Inc.
Forbes, Steve: Forbes Mag. CEO
Forbidden: taboo
Forbidden perfume brand: Tabu
Forbidden thing: no no
Force: dint, coercion, duress
Force a bill through: ramrod
Force apart: pry, cleave
Force oneself on others: impose
Force open: pry, cleave
Force out: oust
Force, unit of: dyne
Force, use: make, impel
Force through: ramrod
Force to leave: route
Force, type of: brute
Force was with him, the: Yoda

Forced fee for freedom: ransom
Forceful: cogent
Forceful person: dynamo
Ford, Glen: actor
Ford, Harrison: actor
Fore opposite: aft
Foreboding: fear
Forefront: van guard, head, lead
Forehead: brow
Forehead cover: bangs
Foreign missions: legations
Foreign student study: ESL
Foreign wool particle: moit
Foremost: premier
Forensics: debating
Foreordain: destine
Foreshadow: bode
Forest buffalo: anoa
Forest clearing: glade
Forest denizen: deer
Forest edges: treelines
Forest near tundra: Taiga
Forest ox: anoa
Forest resource: timber
Forest space, open: glade
Forest, subartic: Taiga
Forest wildcat: lynx
Forested: sylvan
Foretell: augur
Foretelling: omen
Foretold: boded
Forever: aye
Forever, practically: eons
Forever, seemingly: ages
Forever to Keats: eterne
Forever in verse: e'er
Forger's nemesis: T-Man
"Forget" a word: elide
Forget it: no dice, no way, no soap
Forgets a letter: elides
Forgiving, becoming more: relent
Forgot to include: omitted
Fork lift platform: pallet
Fork or spoon: utensil
Fork over: spend, pay
Fork part: prongs, tine
Forked out: paid
Form a thought: ideate
Form an opinion: deem
Form notions: ideate
Form, of a: model
Form of parchisi: ludo
Formal and sanctimonious: churchy
Formal agreement: debate
Formal argument: debate
Formal, artificially: stilted
Formal attire: tux
Formal ball: cotillion
Formal court order: writ
Formal dance: ball
Formal decree: edict
Formal document: writ
Formal head wear: top hat
Formal introduction: debut

Formal order: decree
Formal paper: thesis
Formal procedure: rite
Formal prohibition: ban
Formal, somewhat: dressy
Stiffy Formal: prim
Formality: rite
Formally chooses: anoints
Formally educated: schooled
Formally known as: nee
Formally, long ago: erst
Formally, once: erst
Formally precise: prim
Former: one time, quondam
Former airline name: Braniff
Former capital of Japan: Nara
Former government heroine agency: ICC
Former nuclear agency: AEC
Formerly, formerly: erst, once
Formic acid producer: ant
Formicary: nest
Formicary member: ant
Formosa: Taiwan
Formosa island group: Matsu
Forms a gully: erodes
Forms a thought: ideals
Forms a union: federates
Formula math: algebra
Forsake a lover: jilt
Forsaken: lonely
Forseti's father: Balder
"Forsyte Saga" heroine: Irene
Fort, like many: walled
Fortas, Abe: jurist
Forth, sallies
Forth, salles: sets out on a trip
Forthright, not: sly, lied
Forthright, wasn't: lied
Fortification outwork: tenail
Fortified like Jericho: walled
Fortified stronghold: castle
Fortified wine, a: port
Fortify: arm
Fortress tower: turret
Fortune: hap, fate
Fortune holder: cookie
Fortune recipient: heiress
Fortune teller: seer, tarot
Fortune teller card: tarot
Fortune teller deck: tarot
"48 Hours" lead: Nolte
Forty-two gallons of oil: barrel
Forty winks: catnap
Forum farewell: vale
Forum garb: toga
Forum hello: ave
Forum site: Rome
Forum wear: toga
Forward: bold
Forward, not: shy
Forward or reverse: gear
Fossey, Dian: naturalist
Fossey's friends: apes
Fossil fuel: oil, coal

Fossil resin: amber, copal
Foster a felon: abet
Foster (author) subject: Swanee River
Foster river: Swanee
"Foucault's Pendulum" author: Eco
Fought with swords: dueled
Foul mood: snit
Foul-tasting: rancid
Foul-ups: snafus
Foul weather overshoe: galosh
Found, as: in situ
Found, as a relic: dug up
Foundation garment: corset
Foundling: waif
Fountain, Pete: Jazz
Fountain measure: scoop
Fountain nymph: naiad
Fountain, Roman: Trevi
Fountain treat: shake, malt
Four Corners state: Utah
Four couples: octet
Four flush: con
Four-footed pal: pet
Four-footed romeo: tomcat
Four pairs united: octet
Four quarters: year, dollar
Four roods: acre
Four score: eighty
Four seasons: year
Four Seasons in Valencia: Año
Four, set of: tetrad
Four-star review: rave, accolade
Four-bagger: homer
Four-in-hand: tie
Four-in-hand straps: reins
Four-sided figure: rhomb, square
Fourteen-line poem: sonnet
Fourth dimension: time
Fourth estate: journalism, press
Fourth estate grp.: UPI
Fourth person: Abel
Fourth planet: Mars
Fowl (small): bantam
Fox, baby: kit
Fox, female: vixen
Fox, flying: bat
Fox mate: vixen
Fox, Redd: actor
Foxhole: abri
Foxy ladies: vixens
Foyer: hall, lobby, entrance, vestibule
Fracas: tassel, riots
Fraction of a rupee: paisa
Fractious: testy
Fracture finder: X-ray
Fragile, it may be: ego
Fragments, pottery: shards
Fragrance: aroma
Fragrance, floating: aromas
Fragrant: olent
Fragrant compound: ester
Fragrant fir: balsam
Fragrant, make: embalm
Fragrant oleoresin: elemi

Fragrant resin: elemi
Fragrant rootstock: orris
Fragrant wood: cedar
Frame of mind: mood, morale
Framework of bars: grate
France, bank of: Rive
France, long ago: Gaul
Francis, Kay: actress
Franck, Cesar: composer
Franc's successor: Euro
Frank: honest
Frank, Anne: diarist
Frank, Herbert saga: "Dune"
"Frankenstein" author: Shelley
Frankenstein gofer: Igor
Frankenstein servant: Igor
Frankenstein's Igor: lab assistant
Frankfurter: hot dog, red hot, weiner
Franklin, Aetha: music
Franklin and Hupp Comet: cars
FDR agency: OPA
Franklin's flier: kite
Frankness: openness
Frat event: keg party
Frat letters: epsilons
Frat member, future: rushee
　　Frat party garment: toga
Frat party order: keg
Frat recruiting event: rush
Frat Z: aeta
Fraternal member: Elk
Fraternity letter: rho, eto, taus, zeta, beta,
　　kappa, eta, theta, psi
Fratianne, Linda: skater
Fraud, check for: audit
Fraud, checking for: auditing
Fraud, obtain by: scam
Fraudulent operation: scam
Fraught with uncertainty: risky
Fraulein "no": nein
Frau's spouse: Herr
Frayed, become: worn, wears, wore
Frazer, Joe: boxer
Freaks out: goes ape
Fred Astaire's sister: Adele
Freddy Krueger's street: Elm
Free conditionally: parole
Free electron: ion
Free from bias: fair
Free from vanity: modesty
Free press: comp, complimentary
Free ride, in sports: bye
Free spirits, place for: open bar
Freedom, in slogans: lib
Free-for-all: melee,
Freehold estates: allods
Freelancers enclosure: SASE
Freeman, Mona: actress
Frees of: rids
Freeway, get on the: merge
Freeway lacks: tolls
Freeze over: ice up
Freight rider: hobo
Freight shipment, best rate: car lot

Freight weight: ton
Freighter capacity: tonnage
Freighter hazard: berg
Freighter load: cargo
Freighter, way of the: shipping lane
French affirmative: oui
French airport: Orly
French air raid shelter: abri
French aits: iles
French "alone": seul
French American dialect: Acadian
French annuity: rente
French article, feminine: une
French article: une, les
French artist: Degas
French assent: uui
French autoracing mecca: Lemans
French "bad": mal
French bagpipe: musette
French ballerina: etoile
French "be": etre
French being: etre
French bench: banc
French beverage: pernod
French butcher shop: etal
French cake: gateau
French card game: ecarte
French children: enfants
French city known for silk: Lyon
French city near England: Calais
French city, war-ravaged: Stlo
French cleric: abbe
French coastal region: Riviera
French coin (old): sou, denier, fau, teston
French company: CIE
French composer: Chas Gounod
French cop: flic
French cup: tasse
French currency: franc, euro
French dance, formal: bal
French danke: merci
French date: ami
French "dear: cherie, cher
French "distress": misere
French dog: chien
French "done": oer
French doors, like: paned
French dramatist: Moliere
French dugout: abri
French eatery: bistro
French "equal": egal
French equivalent of inc.: cie
French exclamation: voila
French "eye": oeil
French faith: foi
French farewell: adieu
French fat: gras
French father: pere
French "file": liasse
French film: cine
French film award: Cesar
French floor: etage
French fresh: frais
French friend: ami

French gesture: shrug
French GI: poilu
French girl: mlle
French girlfriend: ami, amie
French "good": bien, ben, bon
French goodnight: bonsoir
French hat: chapeau
French head: tete
French heavenly being: ange
French "help": amot
French " here": ici
French holy woman: ste
French home: tory
French honey: cherie
French "I" verb: etre
French impressionist: Renoir
French island: iles
French "isn't that so": nestcepas
French "ja": oui
French king: Roi
French "land": terre
French landmass: ile
French landscape painter: Corot
French Landscapist: Corot
French Leader: Tete
French legion headgear: kepi
French legislature: Senat
French liqueur: Pernod
French lily: lis
French love: amor
French "mad": fou
French "manor": chateau
French map dot: ile
French Marshal, 1744: Saxe
French "Me": Moi
French meadow: pre
French "melted": fondu
French menu item: vol-au-vent, vol-de-vent
French menu phrase: ala
French milk: lait
French "mine": amoi
French miss: Mlle, elle
French monarch: roi
French month: mai, aouts
French morning: matin
French mother: mere
French museum: Louvre
French "name": nom
French negative: non
French neighbor: Germany, Luxemburg, England
French night: nuit
French nightclub: boite, bistro
French "no": non
French noble: doc, duc
French nose: nez
French novelist: Anet, Claude
French one: une
French Oregon: ÉtatFrench "our": notre
French quotation mark: guillemet
French painter: Renoir, Corot
French pal: ami
French pate: tete
French perfume center: grasse

French "permission": oui
French philosopher: Rousseau
French pirate: Lafitte
French plural article: les
French political unit: État
French port: Lehavre
French possessive pronoun: ses
French Postimpressionist: Henri Rousseau
French pronoun: mes, lui, toi
French purchase: Achat
French range: Alpes
French recreation area: parc
French red: medoc
French refusal: non
French region: Alsace
French resort city: Nice
French restaurant: bistro
French revolutionary: Marat
French river: Somme, Seine, Isere
French romance: amour
French royal house: Capet
French royal title: duc
French schnoz (nose): nez
French school: école, lycée
French sea: mer
French season: emi, ete
French seasoning: sel
French senior: pere
French "she": elle, ella
French shepard: patre
French shout: viola
French si: oui
French silk: soie
French single: une
French "some": des
French soul: ame
French soup: potage
French spa: Evian
French "SRTA": SSTs, Mlle
French star: etoile
French state: etats, etat
French stoneware: gres
French street: rue
French summer: ete
French sweetheart: cherie
French "thanks": merci
French "there": voila
French "these": gore
French "they": ils
French thirst-quencher: eau
French "this": afi
French "three": trois
French title: Mlle
French "to be": etre
French "to love": aimer
French topper: beret
French tower: eiffel
French "tres bien": very good
French turndown: non
French TV network: RTF
French Uncle: Em
French "very": tres
French "vigilant": alerte
French vineyard: cru

French water: eau
French weapon: arme
French well: bien
French White House: Élysé
French wine: vin
French wine-growing area: Alsace
French "with": avec, chez
French "without": sans
French woman: Colette
French "word"mot
French words: mots
French "yes": oui
French "you": vous
French-American dialect: Acadian
Frenchman or Spaniard: Espagnol, Espanola
Frenzied state: amok, manic
Frenzy: rage, mania, spree
Frenzy, in a: amok
Frenzy of publicity: hype
Frequency unit: kHz
Frequent, not very: rare
Frequent visitors: habitués
Frequently: often, oft
Frequents: haunts
Fresco base: gesso, mural
Fresh: lippy, sassy, minty
Fresh, far from: trite, stale
Fresh, get: sass
Fresh growth: sprig
Fresh start:
Freshly painted: wet
Freshman course word: intro
Fret: fuss
Freud article: der
Freud colleague: Adler
Freud contemporary: Adler
Freud Rival: Adler, Alfred Adler
Freud to himself: ach, ich
Freudian focus: dream
Freudian trio, one of a: ego
Freud's daughter: Anna
Freud's friend: Adler
Freud's topic: ego, ids
Friar: monk
Friar cuts: tonsures
Friar Tuck quaff: ale
Friars Club officials: abbots
Friar's title: Fra
Friction, cause: chafe
Friction easer: oil, grease
Friday, sometimes: pay day
Friday's creator:Defoe
Fridge, old: ice box
Fridge, raid the: nosh
Fridge stick: oleo
Friend (in the hood): bro
Friend never met: penpal
Friend of d'Artagnum: Athos
Friend of Freud: Adler
Friend of Threepio: Artoo
Friendly: warm
Friendly advice: tip
Friendly correspondent: penpal
Friendly, looks: smiles

User friendly
Friends and neighbors: kith
Friends, nice: amis
Friends pronoun: thee
Friends to Juan: amigos
Friendship: liking
Friendship, kind of: platonic
Fries, future: spud, potato
Fries lightly: sautés
Fries, maybe: side (dish)
Fries or slaw: side (dish)
Frig, old: ice box
Frig, raid the: nosh
Frig stick: oleo, butter
Frigate bird: ioa, iwa, alcatras
Frighten a fly: shoo
Frightened: trepid, warned
Frightened, visibly: ashen
Frighteningly unnatural: eerie
Frills, with: ruffed
Frilly, more: lacier
Frilly trim: ruffle
Friml, Rudolph: composer
Fringe area
Fringe benefit: plus, perk
Frisée and chicory: endives
Frisk about: romp, prance, caper
Fritter away: blow, spend, waste, consume,
   squander
Fritter away time: loaf
Frittering: wasting
Fritz to himself: ich
Fritz turndown: nein
Fritz's sigh: ich
Frodo's friend: Sam
Frog genus: rana
Frog haven: pond
Frolic: gambol
Frolic boisterously: romp
Frolics: romps
From a time: since
From birth: natal
From Damascus: Syrian
"From here to eternity": ever
From Maine: eastern
From Munich: German
From now on: hence, any more
From Oslo: Norse
From square one: anew
From the top: again
From the USA: Amer, American
Frome, Ethan: fictional writer
Front, false: façade
Front feet, Fido's: forepaws
Front page boxes: ears
Frontier, once: west
Frontier outpost: fort
Frontier settlement: outpost
Frontier town, like a: rowdy
Fronton cheers: oles
Fronton word: jei, jai
Frosh's digs: dorms
Frost, touch of: nip
Frostbitten: numb

Frost's concern: meter
Frosty coating: rime, hoar
Frosty eyes: coals,
Frosty treat: smoothie
Froths: spumes
Frozen, become: ice up
Frozen carbon dioxide: dry ice
Frozen dessert: sorbet
Frozen food case name: Sara Lee
Frozen plain: tundra
Frugal, be very: eke
Frugal, most: sparest
Frug's kin: Watusi
Fruit, brownish: fig
Fruit or bird: kiwi
Fruit desert: tart,
Fruit drink: ade, cider
Fruit, fuzzy: kiwi
Fruit, hollow: fig
Fruit, late summer: pear
Fruit, lumpy: pear
Fruit, one-celled: iomentums
Fruit pastry: pie, tart
Fruit ripener: ethene, ethylene
Fruit seeds: pips
Fruit skin: peel
Fruit source: orchard
Fruit, sticky: figs, dates
Fruit, yellow: papaya
Fruition, at: ripe
Frutti, tutti
Fry lightly: sauté
Fry quickly: sauté
Fry up, as onions: sauté
Frying medium: lard, oil
Fudd, Elmer Voice: Mel Blanc
Fuddy-duddy: fogey
Fuel-carrying ship: coaler
Fuel ferry: coaler
Fuel, fossil: oil, coal
Fuel from bogs: peat
Fuel provides, what: energy
Fuel rating: octane
Fuel source: coal mine
Fuel supply, backup: oil reserve
Fuel valve: intake
Fuentes, Carlos: sriter
Fugard's "A Lesson from Aloes"
Fugitive's flight: lam
Fugue composer: Bach
Fugue master: Bach
Fulfilled a promise: kept
Full: sated, satiate
Full amount: total
Full, completely: satiated
Full disclosure, made: aired
Full force: brunt
Full grown: adult
Full house indicator: SRO
Full house letters: SRO
Full house sign: SRO
Full, in: id est
Full moon or half-moon: phase
Full of chutzpah: brash

Full of gunk: mucky
Full of holes: leaky
Full of prickles: brambly
Full of spunk: feisty
Full of vigor: lusty
Full to excess: glut, satiate
Full volume, play at: blast, blare
Full deck, shy of a: loco, nuts
Full-fledged: ripe, adult, grown, mature, total, genuine, grown-up
Full-length tunic: caftan
Fullness: plenum, satiety
Full-scale: total, all-out, complete
Full-strength: pure
Fully: to the hilt
Fully developed: ripe, adult
Fully extended: taut
Fulton's power source: steam
Fumble: grope
Fumble for words: haws
Fume: seered
Funambulist's tool: rope
Function, customary: role
Function properly: work
Functions: uses
Functions, various: uses
Fund, kind of: index, mutual
Fundamental ingredient: basic, basis
Fundamentals (basic): ABCs
Fundraiser: telethon
Fundraiser, popular: car wash, raffle
Fundraiser, often: gala, benefit
Fundraising dinner unit: plate
Funds, furnish the: endow
Funeral item: pyre, dirge,
Funeral oration: euloge, eulogy
Fungi, downy: mold
Fungus disease: rot, mold, rust, scab, smut, ergot, tinea, blight, mildew
Fungus, downy: mold
Funicello, Annette: Mouseketeer
Funk, go into a: sulk
Funk, in a: blue
Funnel-shaped: conic
Funnel-shaped flower: petunia
Funny Buzzi: Ruth
Funny, in a way: odd
Funny person: riot, card
Funny remark: gasser
Fur, dark: sable
Fur, popular: lapin, ermine, mink
Fur, royal: ermine
Fur trader: voyageur
Fur trading mogul: Astor
Fur tycoon: Astor
Fur, valuable: ermine, mink
Fur-bearing animal: nutria
Furious, make: enrage
Furlong fractions: feet
Furnace cap., abbr.: BTUs
Furnace duct: flue
Furnace tender: stoker
Furnish the funds: endow
Furnish with a false alibi: abet

Furniture buildup: dust
Furniture Chain, Swedish: IKEA
Furniture mover: caster
Furniture relocator: mover,
Furniture style: Adam, Empire, Shaker, Bauhaus, Federal, Mission, Colonial, Georgian, Queen Ann, Chippendale
Furniture wood: cedar, teak, oak, maple, cherry
Furrow maker: hoe, plow
Furry stole: boa
Furry wrap: stole
Furs, royal: ermine
Further bound: limit
Further delay, without: now
Furtive: sly
Furtive glimpse: peek
Furtive sound: psst
Furtive whisper: psst
Furtiveness: stealth
Furze genus: ulex (shrub)
Fuse: lighting aid: amadow
Fuse ore: smelt
Fuse rating: amps
Fuse word: amp
Fusilli's shape: spiral (fired round)
Fuss in a Shakespeare title: ado
Fuss with makeup: primp
Futile: otiose
Futon or bunk: bed
Future bks: MSS
Future flower: bud, seed
Future frat member: rushee
Future fries: spud
Future officer: cadet
Future resident: intern
Future school members: roe
Future, toward the: ahead
Future visiting need: time machine
"Futureworld" name: Yul
Future-minded investment: ira
Fuzzy, get: blur

G

Gab or slug ending: fest
Gabor, Ava: actress
Gabor, Zsa Zsa: actress
Gabs and gabs: yaks
Gad: rove
Gad's brother: Asher
     father: Jacob
     mother: Zilpah
     son: Eri, Ezbon, Haggi
Gaea's children: titans
Gael pop star: Enya
Gael republic: Erie
Gaelic: Erse
Gaelic pop star: Enya
Gaelic tongue: Erse
Gagarin, Yuri: qstronaut
Gaheris's brother: Gareth, Gawain
     father: Lot

     mother: Margawse, Morgause
     uncle: Arthur
Gaiety: mirth
Gail, Max: actor
Gainsay: deny
Gait, bouncy: skip, trot
Gait, bounding: gallop
Gait, slow: trot, amble
Gait, unhurried: lope
Gaiters: spates
Gaius's garb: toga
Gal of song: Sal
Gala, evening: soiree
Gala occasion: ball
Galahad's mother: Elaine
Galahad's title: sir
Galahad's weapon: lance
Galatea's beloved: acis
Galaxy unit: star
Galaxy shape: spiral
Galaxy, type of: spiral
Galba, he overthrew: Otho
Galba, ruler before: Nero
Galbraith's subj.: econ, economy
Galen, emulates: heals
Galena: ore
Galileo's home: Pisa, Italy, Tuscany
Galileo's muse: Urania
Galindo, Rudy: skater
Galleon: ship
Galleon cargo: oro, ore
Galleon need: spar, sail
Galleon type: caravel
Gallery: arcade.
Gallery event: art sale
Gallery fare, dizzying: op art
Gallery, kind of: peanut
Galley, ancient: bireme, trireme
Galley drudge: rower
Galley mover: oars
Galley slave: rower
Galley slave tool: oar
Galley with two oar banks: bireme
Galley with three oar banks: trireme
Gallic airport: Orly
Gallic gesture: shrug
Gallico, Paul
Gallimaufry: olio
Gallinaceous bird, female: hen
Gallivant: room, gad
Galloon: orris
Galloped away: cantered
Galloping gourmet: kerr
Galoot, big: ape, oafs
Galumph: plod
Galvanize: arouse
Galvanizing metal: zinc
Gama, vasco da: explorer
Gambler's card game: faro
Gambling game: faro, keno
Gambling stakes: antes, pot
Gamboling place: lea
Gambrinus invention: ale, beer, lager
Game delay: rain date

Game divided into chukkers: polo
Game for: up to
Game, go after: hunt
Game hunter's trip: safari
Game, mechanical: pinball
Game of strategy: chess
Game outing: safari
Game plan: idea
Game played with counters: nim
Game ragout: salmi (game stew)
Game show host: emcee
Game show prize: trip
Pregame show
Game trap: gin
Game with mallets: polo
Games of chance: lotteries
Gametes: ova
Gamut: range
Gamy, slightly: off, foul, rank
Gance, Abel: director
Gandhi's bane: violence
Gandhi's foe: Raj
Gandhi's title: Mahatma
Gandolfini costar: Falco
Gang, criminal: mob
Ganges, steps to the: ghat
Gangsters gals: molls
Ganoid fish: gar
"Elmer Gantry"
Ganymede's abductor: Zeus, Jupiter
        brother: Ilus
        father: Tros
        function: cupbearer
Gap: hiatus
Gap, narrow the: gain
Garage content: auto
Garage event: sale
Garage job: tune-up, lube
Garage sale words: as is
Garage squirter: oil can
Garand or Mauser: rifle
Garbage bin output: odor
Garbage receptacle: ash can
Garbanzo or pinto: bean
Garbo, Greta: actress
Garbo's homeland: Sweden
Garcon's yes: oui
Garden dormouse: lerot
Garden green: chard
Garden hose crimp: kink
Garden hose (plastic): PVC
Garden of Genesis: Eden
Garden party: fete
Garden path: alley
Garden soil: loam, loom
Garden spot: yard
Garden State: New Jersey
Garden State city: Camden, NJ
Garden structure: gazebo
Gardener, Erle Stanley: writer
Garfield guy: Jon
Garfield's housemate: Odie
        middle name: Abram
        patsy: Odie

        pooch: Odie
Garfunkel, Art: music
Gargamelle's son: Gargantua
Gargoyles, like: ugly
Garish: loud
Garish light: neon
Garland: anadem, swag, bay, lei
Garland of yore: anadem
Garlic juicer: press
Garlic mayo: aioli
Garlic section: clove
Garlicky dish: scampi
Garment, billowing: cape
Garment, concealing: burka
Garment, down: vest
Garment, goose down: vest
Garment, high priests: ephod
Garment, hybrid: skort
Garment, long, loose: muumuu
Garment, long-sleeved: caftan
Garment, loose outer: cloak, robe
Garment maker: tailor
Garment, sleeveless: aba, vest
Garment, sheik's: aba
Garment, unisex: tee, sarong
Garne, John Nance: vice pres.
Garner, Erroll: composer, jazz pianist
Garr, Teri: actress
Garret: attic
Garrulous: chatty
Gas burner: jet
Gas, buy: tank up
Gas, charged with: aerated
Gas, dangerous: radon
Gas, flammable: ethane
Gas in bulbs: argon,
Gas, ionized: plasma
Gas, kind of: leaded
Gas made by lightning: ozone
Gas plant's family: Rue
Gas pump option: diesel, octane
Gas, pungent: ammonia
Gas, rare inert: xenon, neon, radon
Gasbag: talkative
Gascon headgear: beret
Gaseous element: xenon, neon
Gaseous fuel: ethane
Gaslight and big band: eras
Gasp of delight: ooh
Gasthaus: inn
Gastropod, marine: murex
Gastropod's movement: snail's pace
Gate: exit
Gate, farm: stile
Gate, starting: post
Gatehouse cry: halt
Gates,Phoebe: actress
Gather: reap, harvest
Gather and arrange: collate
Gather and bind, as grain: sheave
Gather bit by bit: glean
Gather dust: sat
Gather opinions: poll
Gather slowly: glean

Gather together: amass
Gathering: crowd
Gathering dust: idle
Gator Bowl site: Florida
Gaucho locale: llano
Gaucho roams, where: pampas
Gaucho's domain: pampas
Gaucho's rope: riata
Gaucho's weapon: bola
Gaudy sign: neon
Gaudy trimming: glitz
Gauge face: dial
Gauge, utility: gas meter
Gaul gold: aurum
Gaul conqueror: Caesar
Gaul invader: Caesar
Gauls, to Romans: foe
Gaunt: angular, slim, lean
Gauguin's island: Tahiti
Gauze weave: leno
Gave a hand: dealt, aided
Gave a leg up: helped
Gave a nasty look: leered
Gave an address: orated
Gave an opinion: said
Gave back: repaid
Gave conditionally: lent
Gave consent: acceded
Gave false hopes to: led on
Gave in: caved
Gave orders: bossed
Gave no stars to: panned
Gave rise to: bred, spawned
Gave some to another: shared
Gave stars to: rated
Gave up: ceded
Gayle's sister: Lynn
Gaze, hard: steely
Gaze upon: behold
Gazes dreamily: moons
Gazelle: goa, dorcas
Gazelle, African: admi
Gazelle hound: saluki
Gazpacho: soup
Gdansk Province city: Gdynia
Gear: cog
Gear tooth: cog
Geared up: got ready
Geary, Cynthia: actress
Geddes, Norman Bel: designer
Gee: uh-huh
Gee, it precedes: haw
Geeky: unhip
Geese, flock of: skein
Geezer: codger
Gehrig, Lou: baseball
Geiger, Hans: inventor
Geisha's accessory: obi, fan
Geisha's attire: kimono
Geisha's place: Japan
Geisha's tie: obi
Geisha's zither: koto
Geller, Uri: Psychic
Gem, blue-white: zircon

Gem, deep red: garnet
Gem, jet black: onyx
Gem of a small part: opal
Gem, porous: pearl
Gem, relief-carved: cameo
Gem, round: pearl
Gem State: Idaho
Gem surface: facet
Gem, Sydney: opal
Gem, Yellow-brown: tigereye
Gemini Drink: Tang
Gemini Half: Twin
Gemini Rocket: Agena
Gemini star: Castor, Pollux
Gemma Donati's spouse: Dante
Gemologist's weight: carat
Gem's plane: facet
Gemsbok (Gemsbuck) cousin: Eland
Gemstone, Australian: Opal
Gemstone, mount a: set
Gemu Gefa Native: Ethiope
Gendarme's schnoz: nez
Gene processing: splicing
Gene Siskel: critic
Genealogists' pursuits: lineages
Genealogy chart: tree
Genealogy diagram: tree
General address: sir
General, Antietam: Lee
General Arnold's nickname: Hap
General assembly: Diet, Plena, Plenus,
    Congress, Parliament
General decoration: star
General drift: trend
G.M. navigation system: OnStar
General or king: leader
GPexpertise: anat, anatomy
General surface: facet
General vicinity: area
Generally believed: reputed
Generally speaking: as a rule
Generator: dynamo
Generator part: rotor
Generic: no name
Generosity: largesse
Generous: shares
Generous, be: treat
Generous, hardly: tight-fisted
Generously: amply, nobly
Genes, alter: splice
Genesis: birth
Genesis city: Sodom
Genesis hunter: Esau
Genesis locale: Eden
Genesis name: Eve, Adam
Genesis setting: Eden
Genesis son: Enos
Genetic abbr.: RNA, DNA
Genetic blueprint: DNA
Genetic designer monogram: RNA
Genetic double: clone
Genetic messenger: RNA, DNA
Genetic pioneer: Mendel
Genetic sequence: RNA

Genetically engineered: cloned
Geneva has one: soft G
Genghis Kahn
Genghis Kahn was one: Mongol
Genie portrayer: Eden (Barbara)
Genie's dwelling: lamp
Genoa export: Salami
Genre: ilk, ilk, ild
Genteel: urbane
Gentle: kind
Gentle exercise: yoga
Gentle pace: trot
Gentle person: lamb
Gentle slope: glacio, rise
Gentle stroke: putt
Gentle touch: caress
Gentle treatment: TLC
Gentleman, Mexican: caballero
Gentleman, no: cad
Gentleman suitor: swain
Gentlemen opposite: cad
Gentles: tames
Gently persuaded: coaxed
Gents: men
Genuine: real
Genuine nuisance: pest
"Geodesic Dome"
Geographical div.: zone, terr.
Geologic epoch: Azoic, Eocnen, Hadean,
    Archean, Miocene, Permain
Geological deposits: sinter
Geological division: era
Geological divisions: Lias, Liassic
Geological formation: volcano, mecca, mesa
Geological sample: core
Geological time unit: epoch
Geometric abstract: op art
Geometric curves, certain: parabolas
Geometric figure: cube
Geometric finding: area
Geometric pattern: fractal
Geometry calculation: area
Geometry, father of: Euclid
Geometry pioneer: Euclid
Geometry problem: area
Georga Segal (emulate): sculpture
George Axelrod play: VII Year Itch
George Elliot's "Adam Bede"
Georgetown athlete: Hoya
Georgia peach: Ty Cobb
Georgian Bay's locale: Ontario
Geothermal spout: Geyser
Geraint's thigh protector: tuille
Geraint's wife: Enid
Gerard ter Borch
Gerbera or shasta: daisy
Gerda's husband: Frey
Germ cell: spore
Germfree: sterile
German abode: Haus(home)
German achtung: attention
German admiral, ill-fated: Spee
German, adult male: Herr
German alas: ach

German alpine pasture: alm
German, ancient: Teuton
German and: und
German area: Saar
German article: der, ein, das, und
German "at no time": nie
German "attention": achtung
German Beer, dark: Bock
German bride: frau
German coal region: Saar
German coins, old: talers, thalers
German conjunction: und
German connector: und
German denial: nein
German district: Ruhr, Saar
German donkey: esel
German "east": ost
German empire: Reich
German envious: brio
German "et": und
German "everybody": alle
German "exclamation": ach
German "expletive": ach
German "from": von
German hoe: hacke
German "home": heim
German honor: ehre
German hurry: eilen
German "i": ich
German ice: eis
German ice cream: eis
German "illumination": licht
German import: Audi
German industrial city: Trier
German industrial park: Saar, Essen
German "is": ist
German lament: ach
German mountains: Zollern, Hotzenwald
German "Mr.": Herr
German "Mrs.": Frau
German nickname for Helena: Leni
German "no": nein
German "of": von
German "one": ein, eine
German "over": uber
German "pass": reichen
German physicist: Ohm, Georg
German "please": bitte
German port: Emden
German "possibly": etwa
German POW camp: Stalag
German prison camp: Stalag
German pronoun: ich
German quacker: ente
German "rather": segal
German rover: ens
German refusal: nein
German sausage: wurst
German sigh: ich
German surrealist: ernst
German "thanks": danke
German "the": der
German "three": drei
German thunder god: Donar

German "to be": etre
German " to himself": ich
German toast: prosit (drinking toast)
German "tree": baum
German tribal district: Gaue
German turndown: nein
German undertow: sog
German "us": uns
German valley: Ruhr
German wife: frau
German "with": mit
German "you bet": jawohl
Germane: akin
German's honor: ehre
Germany has had three: Reichs
Germany, Italy, and Japan: axis
Germfree: sterile
Geronimo: Apache
Gershin, Gina: actress
Gershom's (Gershon) father: Levi
Gershwin, Ira: lyricist
Gershwin lass: Bess
Gertrude's husband: Claudius
Gertrude's son: Hamlet,
Gervaise's daughter: Nana
Gesture: sign
Get a lode of this: ore
Get a grip on: grasp
Get a move on: hie
Get a taste of: try
Get along: manage
Get around: skirt
Get around a foe: outflank
Get away from: escape
Get back: recoup, regain, return, reconnect
Get back for: avenge
Get better: heal
Get by coercion: extort
Get by effort: earn
Get coaching: train
"Get cold feet"
Get cozy: nestle
Get equal billing: costar
Get even for: revenge
Get fresh: sass, mouth off
Get fuzzy: blur
Get going: start
Get gussied up: preen
Get heavier: gain
Get hold of: obtain
Get in the way: impede
Get in touch with: contact
Get introduced: meet
Get lost: bug off
Get melodramatic: emote
Get moving: stir
Get off the beaten path: stray
Get off the dime: act
Get off the fence: opt
Get off the metaphorical fence: opt
Get one's goat: annoy, pester
Get price wise: brings
Get ready: prep
Get ready to move: pack

Get real: as if
Get really upset: fume
Get rid of the suds: rinse
Get ripe: age
Get serious: knuckle down
Get sleepy: drowse
Ger smart: wise up
Get some air: inhale
Get steamed up: fume
Get stuck: bog down
Get taller: grow
Get tangled: mat
Get the better of: one up
Get the drift: see
Get the message: see
Get the move on: hie
Get the news: hear, hears
Get the point: see
Get together: mixer, reunion
Get underway: go, leave, start, begin
Get up on: mount
Get used to: adapt
Get well: heal
Get well treatment: rehab
Get wider: flare
Get wind of: smell
Get word of: heard
Getaway: escape, trip
Getaway, chic: spa
Gets a load of: eyes
Gets melodramatic: emotes
Gets one's bearings: orient
Gets one's goat: irk
Gets rid of: ruts
Gets stuck: jams, lodges
Gets through to: reaches
Getty, Estelle: actress
Getty Museum setting: Malibu
Getty vessel: oiler
Gettysburg General: Meade
Getz genre: jazz
Getz, Stan
Ghost: spirit
Ghost, comes as a: haunts
Ghost or city: Casper
"Ghost" writer: Ibsen
Ghostly ceremony: exorcism
Ghostly meeting: séance
Ghostly noise: moan, boo
GI address: APO
GI, delinquent: AWOL
GI dinner: MRE
GI entertainer: USO
GI from Down Under: Anzac
GI hangout: USO
GI (part of): govt., issue
GI ration: dog biscuit
Giant, evil, hideous: ogre
Giant hero of yore: Ott
Giant, man-eating: ogre
Giant of myth: titan
Giant, one-eyed: Cyclops
Giant stele:Obelisk
Giant's Causeway locale: Northern Ireland

Gibbon: ape
Gibbs, Marla: actress
Gibe at: jeer, twit
Gibraltar landmark: rock
Gibson, Althea: tennis
Gibson ingredient: gin
Gibson, Mel: actor
Giddy happiness: glee
Gide, Andre: writer
Gift-giving time: Yule
"Gift of the Magi"
Gift, small: treat
Gift tag word: for
Gift to a diva: roses
Gig gear: amp
Gigantic: big, huge
Giggle: titter
Giggle, part of a: hie
Giggle, snide: sniggle
Gigi's boyfriend: Ami
Gigi's gloves: gants
Gilbert, Melissa: actress
Gilbert and Sullivan princess: Ida
Gilded: gold, golden
Gimlet garnish: onion
Gimler's larger cousin: auger
Gimmick: ploy
Gin fizz flavor: sloe
Gin flavoring: sloe
Gin mill: bar, pub, dive, joint, saloon
Gin fizz, sloe
Ginger cookies: snaps
Ginger follower: ale
Gingerbread house visitor: Hansel
Gingham alternative: calico
Gin maker's first name: Eli
"Ginnie Mae"
Ginnie or Fannie: Mae
Ginsburg, Ruth Bader: jurist
Ginseng kin:udo
Ginseng plant: udo
Ginza (Tokyo) money: yen
Ginza purchase: obi
Giraffe-like animal: okapi
Girder insert: rivet
Girl at a ball: belle
Girl, chaperoned: Deb
Girl from Baja: chicano, chica, chicana
Girl from Guatemala: chica, chicana
Girl in peril: Pauline
Girl of song: Lola
Girlfriend, special: inamorata
Girls having a ball: debutants
"Les Girls"
Gish, Lillian: actress
Gist: nub
Give a clue about: let on
Give a hand: clap, aide
Give a home to: adopt
Give a hoot: care
Give a leg up: boosts
Give a ticket: fine, cite
Give an edge to: hone, whet
Give and take: banter, exchange, repartee,

trade-off
Give alms: aids
Give another title: rename
Give, as a handicap: spot
Give as an example: cite
Give, as time: devote
Give attention to: heed
Give away everything: blab, talk
Give comfort: cheer
Give consent: accede
Give credit: loan
Give great joy: elate
Give in: relent, cave, cave in
Give into the pressure: buckle under
Give it a go: try
Give medicine: dose
Give off: exude, emit
Give off steam: boil
Give one's all: tries hard
Give or take: about
Give out sparingly: dole
Give power to: enable
Give proof of: attest
Give the boot to: oust
Give the cold shoulder: shun
Give the impression: seem
Give the meaning of: define
Give the raspberries to: jeer at
Give the right to: entitle
Give the thumbs down: nix
Give way: yield
Give zero stars to: pan
Given an "X" to: rated
Given false hope: led on
"On any given Sunday"
Given in to gravity: droop
Given to wandering: errant
Given up: forgone
Gives a heads-up: alerts
Gives a leg up: elevates
Gives a mighty heave: hurl
Gives alms: airs, air
Gives back: reacts, returns
Gives birth to: spawns
Gives credit: ascribes
Gives in the middle: sags
Gives one's consent: accedes
Gives permission: lets, OKs, okays
Gives some slack: loosens
Gives succor: aids
Gives the slip: evades
Gives up land: cedes
Giving an edge to: honing
Giza river: Nile
Giza (Egypt) structure: pyramid
Gizmo: doodad, gadget, doo hickey
Gizzard: craw
Glacial breakup result: ice fall
Glacial deposit: moraine, eskar, esker
Glacial deposit, valuable: placer
Glacial element: serac
Glacial groove: stria, striae
Glacial hills of Iowa: Pahas
Glacial ice: serac

Glacial pinnacle: serac
Glacial ridge: esker, serac
Glacial ridge: var.: asar, osar
Glacier upper part: neve
Glade setting: forest
Gladiator's greeting: ave
Glamorous: exotic
Glance, lascivious: leer
Glance of concern: leer
Glance or look: gander
Glance over: skim, scan
Gland, type of: pineal, adrenal
Glare protector: visor
Glasgow children: oyes
Glasgow, Ellen: writer
Glasgow no: nae
Glasgow turndown: nae
Glass, broken pieces: shards, sliver
Glass bulb, small: ampule, ampoule
Glass: comb. Form: hyal, hyalo
Glass container bottle
Glass cookware: Pyrex
Glass, heat resistant: silex
Glass ingredient: silica
Glass, looking: mirror
Glass, resembles: vitric, vitrum
Glass , square of: pane
Glass, tough: Pyrex
Glass Variety: opaline
Glass vial (small): ampul, ampule, ampoule
Glassmaker: Rene Lalique
Glassmaker's material: frit
Glassware, lab: flask, beaker, retort
Glaswegian's cap: tam
Glaucus's beloved: Scylla
        father: Minos, Sisyphus
        mother: Merope, Pasiphae
        son: Bellerophon
Glaudini, Lola: actress
Glazes: ices
Glazed finish: cire
Glazier's goop: putty
Glazier's unit: pane
Gleaner: collector
Glee club music, like: choral
Glenn, John: astronaut
Glib: facile
Glib, overly: pat
Glib speech: patter
Glide by: elapse
Glider's place: porch
Glimmering: idea
Glimpse from afar: espy
Glimpses: espies
Glissaded: slid, glide
Glistens, it: dew
Glitter, bit of: sequin,
Glitterati member: celeb
Glittering: beady
Glittering adornment: tiara
Glittery fabric: lame
Glittery rock: mica
Gloating: smug
Gloating cry: oho

Glob: dollop
Glob ending: ule
GPS display: Rte, Map
Global warming?: détente
Globe substitute: atlas, map
Globetrotting, went: toured
"Glom onto"
Gloomier, even: sullener
Gloomy: saturnine, sour, dour
Gloomy atmosphere: pall
Gloomy depressed feeling: angst
Gloomy guy: gus
Gloomy mood, in a: sullen
Glop: goo
"Gloria in excelsis dio"
Glorify: exalt, extol
Gloss target: eye lids, lips
Glossed term: lemma
Glossy: sleek
Glossy effect: sheen
Glossy fabric: sateen, satin
Glossy fabric finish: cire
Glove alternative: muff, mitt
Glove leather: hid, kid
Glove part: palm, finger
Glow: aura
Glow, mystical: aura
Glow, rosy: flush
Glowing, as embers: red hot
Glowing embers: coals
Gluck, alma: soprano
Glue for feathers: tar
Glue, kind of: epoxy
Glue on: affix
Glues tight: cements
Glut: sate
Gnats cousin: midge
Gnaw at: nibble,
Gnawed, appearing: erose
Gnome: elf, troll
"Go a step further"
Go after game: hunt
Go against Galahad: tilt
Go against God: sin
Go-ahead: lead, OK, nod, say so
Go around, as an issue: skirt
Go ashore: debark
Go astray, in thought: err, error
Go at it: argue
Go backwards: reverse, regress
Go belly up: fold, fail
Go between: liaison, agent
Go beyond: pass
Go crowding in: troop
Go dead: stall, conk out
Go down the tubes: tank, fail
Go downhill fast: ski
Go fast: zoom, speed
Go for broke: do or die
Go for it: try
Go for the gold: vie, pan
"Go Great Guns"
Go headlong: rush
Go, in Glasgow: gae

Go into a funk: sulk
Go it alone: solo
Go left or right: turn, veer
Go off: detonate
Go off at an angle: veer
Go off the deep end: snap
Go off course: yaw
Go on: continue
Go on the lam: flee
Go one better: top
Go one's way: wend
Go out of business: fold up, fold
Go over, as a hurdle: clear
Go over big: wow
Go over proofs: edit
Go over the edge: snap
Go over the same ground: interate
Go postal: rage
Go public with: air
Go quickly: zip, speed, hie
Go round and round: spin
Go sideways: slue
Go sky high: soar
Go slowly: plod
Go swiftly: hie, scud, scoot
Go team: rah
Go to: attend
Go to earth: hide, lie, doggo
Go together, didn't: clashed
Go two ways: part
Go undercover: spy
Go wild over: flip
Go with the flow: adapt
Goal: aim, end
Goat, alpine: ibex
Goat, female: doe
Goat, Himalayan: tahr
Goat, mountain: ibex
Goat noise: bleat
Goat nut: jojoba, pignut
Goat type: nubian, nebian
Goat, wild: ibex
Goat-boy of fiction: Giles
Goathair garment: aba
Goatish look: leer
Goat-man deity: Pan
Gobbled up: eaten, scarfed
Gobi: Desert
Gobi, like a: Arid
Goblet, Scottish: Tass
God, Amenhotep's: Aton
God (Delphi's): Apollo
God depicted in pyramids: Osiris
God, in Hebrew text: Adonai
God, Moslem: Allah
God, Nile sun: Aton
God, not a: mortal
God of fire: Vulcan
God of love: Amor
God of Memphis, Chief: Ptah
God of north winds: Boreas
God of passion: Eros
God of resurrection: Osiris
God of the east wind: Eurus

God of war: Ares, Odin
God, Pharaoh: Eros
God, roguish, goatish: SatyrGod, solar: Horus
God, thunder: Thor
God, Wednesday: Odin
God, winged: Eros
Goddess: deity
Goddess, charming: Grace
Goddess, cow-headed: Isis
Goddess, Egyptian: Isis
Goddess, fertility:Astarte, Ishtar
Goddess, harvest: Ops, Ceres
Goddess, jealous: Hera
Goddess, Nile: Isis
Goddess of abundance: Ops
Goddess of agriculture: Ceres
Goddess of beauty: Venus
Goddess of criminal folly: Ate
Goddess of dawn: Eos, Aurora
Goddess of discord: Eris, Eros
Goddess of earth: Gaea, Erda, Geb
Goddess of fate: Nom
Goddess of flowers: Flora
Goddess of forest: Diana
Goddess of healing: Eir, Iaso
Goddess of the hunt: Diana
Goddess of love (beauty): Aphradites
 (Roman): Venus
 (Greek): Eros
Goddess of mischief: Ate
Goddess of moon: Selene, Artemis, Luna,
 Diana
Goddess of nature, minor: Nymph
Goddess of Niflheim: Hel
Goddess of night: Nox
Goddess of peace: Irene
Goddess of plenty: Ops
Goddess of rainbow: Iris
Goddess of rashness: Ate
Goddess of retribution: Ate
Goddess of spring: May Queen
Goddess of strife: Eris
Goddess of sun: Sol, Apollo, Aten
Goddess of the chase: Diana
Goddess of the hunt: Diana
Goddess of the moon: Selene
Goddess of underworld: Hades
Goddess of victory: Nike
Goddess of wisdom: Athena, Minerva
Goddess of witchcraft: Hecate
Goddess, Parthenon: Athena
Goddess, Roman grain: Ceres
Goddess, Semite love: Astarte
Goddess statue: Idol
Goddess to Nero: Dea
Goddess, vindictive: Hera
God-fearing: pious, devout, faithful, reverent,
 religious
Godiva's title: lady
Gods: deities
Godzilla's city: Tokyo
Godzilla's foe: Rodan
Godzilla's land: Japan
Godzilla's target: Tokyo

Goes along with: humors
Goes back in business: reopens
Goes back to see: revisits
Goes berserk: freaks out
Goes by: passes, elapses
Goes camping: roughs it
Goes for pizza, say: eats out
Goes furtively: sneaks
Goes head to head: vies
Goes higher: soars
Goes kaput: fails
Goes over big: wows
Goes postal: loses it
Goes to law: sues
Goes to the bottom: sinks
Goes to the polls: votes, elects
Goethe, Johann: writer
Goethe opus: Faust
Goethe or Grass title: Herr
Goethe play: "Stella"
Goes out of business: folds
Go-getter: retriever
Gogh, Vincent Van: painter
Gogol, Nikolai: writer
Going around: orbiting
Going nowhere fast: in a rut
Going on: doing
Going out: ebbing
"Going" rate, the: fare
Going steady: pinned
"Gold Bug" author: Poe
Gold coin: double eagle
Gold, containing: auric
Gold, derived from: auric
Gold digger: miner
Gold fish: carp
Gold holder: pot
Gold leaf: gilding, gilt
Gold measure: karat
Gold medal org.: IOC
Gold purity measure: karat
Gold record: hit
Gold related: auric
Gold rush town: nome
Gold rush starter: nugget
Gold seeker's target: lode, mother lode
Gold, to Gauis: aurum
Gold unit: karat
Gold weight: karat
Gold, went for the: vied
Golda Meir: Israeli PM
Goldberg, Rube: cartoonist
Golden anniversary: fifty
Golden café, e.g.: idol
Golden finish: ager
Golden fleece, Jason's
"Golden Fleece" ship: Argo
"Golden Hind" captain: Drake
Golden idol: orfe
Golden rule preposition: unto
Golden sherry: oleroso, oleoresin
Golden, some are: eagles
Golden State: California,
Golden State wine city: Napa

Golden touch, royal with a: King Midas
Golden treasure seeker: Jason
Golden-ager: elder, senior, ancient, retiree, old-timer
Golden apples guardian: Ithun, Ithunn
Goldfinger, Auric
Goldilock's victims, one of: Papa
Goldrush starter: nugget
Golf appurtenance: tee
Golf club figure: pro
Golf coup: ace, hole-in-one
Golf course: fairway
Golf course by the sea: links
Golf holes, unplayed: byes
Golf taps: putts
Golf trophy, international: Ryder Cup
Golfers:
    Ballesteros, Seve
    Blalock, Jane
    Dutra, Olin
    Els, Ernie
    Ochoa, Lorena
Golfer's cleek: irons
Golfer's expert: pro, ace
Golly: gosh
Gomer's group: Marines
Gomez's hairy cousin: Itt
Gondola, ply a: pole
Gondolier's home: Italy
Gondolier's road: canal
Gong: bell
Goober: peanut
Good buy: find, deal
Good cholesterol: HDL
Good for nothing: idler, lowlife
Good grief: my word, my gosh
Good, in Guatemala: bien
Good judgment: prudence, level-headed, common sense
Good jumper: kangaroo, roo
Good look: eyeful
Good looker: eyeful
Good luck charm: amulet
Good luck symbol: mascot
Good mouser: owl, cat
Good natured: jovial, genial
Good natured banter: jost
Good night (French): bonsoir
Good old days: yore
Good or bad, neither: either
Good or bad sign: omen
Good physical health: vigor
Good quality: asset
Good smell: aroma
"In on a good thing"
Good working order: useable
Goodall subject: ape
Goodbye (Latin): vale
Goodbye, say: part, leave
Goodbye to Galius: vale
Gooden, Dwight: baseball
Goodies, oldies but
Goodly number, a: many
Good-natured kidding: raillery

Goodness: virtue,
Good-tempered: amiable,
Goody, goody: prude, prug, prig
Goodyear icon: Blimp
Gooey mixture: glop
Goofball: bozo, weirdo, yo-yo
Goofier: zanier
Goofy one: nut
Google, Barney
Google rival: Yahoo
Goolagong, Evonne: tennis
Goolagong rival: Everett
Goombah: pal
Gone from the coop: flown
"Goosebumps" author: R. L. Stine
Goose egg: nil, nada, zero
Goose genus: anser
Goose, Grenoble: oie
Goose kin: swan
Goose, nonaquatic: nene
Goose, wild: brant
Goose down garment: vest
Goosefoot: salsola
Gopher State: Minnesota
Gorbachev (Mrs.): Raisa
Gordon, Ruth: actress
Gore: Tex
Goren coup: slam
Gorey, Edward: illustrator
"Gorilla in the Mist"
Gorp item: raisins, peanuts, nuts
Gospel author: Luke, St. Luke
Gossamer: ethereal
Gossans: iron hats
Gossip: jaw
Gossip, bit of: tale
Gossip, like some: catty
Gossip morsel: tidbit
Gossip, scandalous: dirt
Gossip tidbit: item
Gossip unit: item
Gossiper's delight: scandal
Got acquainted: met
Got along: fared
Got fit: tuned up
Got in debt: owed
Got off the dime: acted
Got on, time wise: latened
Got paid: earned
Got ready: geared up
Got the gold: won
Got the suds out: rinsed
Got to go fast: rushed
Got underway: began, started
Got wind of: heard
Got wind to: smelt
Gotcha: aha
Gotham: Nick
"Gotta Be Me, I've"
Gouda alternative: Edam
Gouda cousin: Edam
Gouged piece of turf: divot
Goulash or slumgullion: stew
Gounod, Chas: Fr. composer

Gounod ppera: Faust
Gourd: Pepo
Gourd family fruit: melon
Gourd instrument: maraca
Gourd, maybe: Dipper
Gourd-shaped rattle: maraca
Gourmand, be a: eat
Gourmand course: entrée
Gourmand's delight: eating
Gourmand's malady: gout
Gourmet delicacy: snail
Gourmet mushrooms: morels
Gourmet, galloping: kerr
Gourmet's asset: palate,
Governess Jane (fictional): Eyre
Government by a minor: Regency
Govt. dept.: Bur.
Government form: regime
Government in power: regime
Government security: T-Bill
Govt's. workplace overseer: OSHA
Gown, dressing: kimono
Gown (evening) fabric: taffeta
Goya's duchess: Alba
Goya's home: Spain
GPS display: Rte, Map
Grab a cab: hail
Graceful: tactful
Graceful girl: sylph
Graceful rhythm: lilt
Graceland icon: Elvis
Graceless guy: boor
Gradation: nuance, ablaut
Grade school break: recess
Grade school org.: PTA
Grade (top): "A" plus
Grades (K-12): elhi
Gradient: slope
Gradual assimilation: osmosis
Gradual slope: glacio
Gradually decrease: wane
Gradually waste away: erode
Grad., certain: alumna
Grad. school: univ
Graduate's prize: sheep skin
Graf: Spee
Graffiti writer: Vandal
Graft, to, in a way: in arch
Grafted, (in heraldry): ente
Grafting twig: cion, scion
Craggy abode: aerie
Graham, Katherine: publisher
Graham, Otto: NFL
Graham who galloped: kerr
Grail descriptor: Holy
Grain-based diet: macrobiotics
Grain beard: awn
Grain bristle: arista
Grain bundle: sheaf
Grain bundles: sheaves
Grain container: bin
Grain fiber: awn
Grain, fiber-rich: oat
Grain file: wheat index

Grain for grinding: grist
Grain, hulled: groats
Grain rot: ergot
Grain spike: ear
Gram start: epi
Grammar class: gender
Grammar task: parse
Grammatical case: dative
Grammatical study: syntax, gerund
Grammer, Kelsey: actor
Grammy category: pop
GTO, part of: Gran
Granary, often: silo
Grand Bahama Islands
Grand Canyon site: Mesa
Grand Coulee Dam
Grand ending: ule
Grand in scale: epic
Grand in scope: epic
Grand Prix Racing
Grand, quite: epic
Grand total: sum
Grand tour site: Europe
Grande, Rio
Grandee: noble, don
Grandeur: pomp
Grandfather, sometimes: exempt
Grandiloquent: bombastic
Grandiose: epic
Grandma's malady: ague
Grandmother, Russian: babushka
Grandpa's rumble seat
Grandparents (of): aval
Grandson, perhaps: iii
Grandstand cry: defense
Grange, Harold: "Red" (football)
Granite or quartz: rock
Granny: knot
Granola kin: muesli
Granola morsel: oat
Grant: cede, subsidies
Grant, Amy: music
Grant approval: let, OK
Grant territory: cede
Granted: ceded
Grant's home: Ohio
Grant's, Cary, birthplace: Bristol
Grape, dried: raisin
Grape sugar: dextrose
Grapefruit look-alike: pomelo, shaddock
Grapefruit mishap: squirt
Grapefruit relative: pomelo, shaddock
Grapes, crushed: trod
Grapes, pulpy: uvas
Grapevine, the: word of mouth
Graph part: axis
Graphic image: icon
Graphic, lo res
Graphite, remove: erase
Graphite remover: eraser
Grappler's grip: half nelson
Grasp, firm: grip
Grasping: avid
Grasping device: tongs

Grass beard: awn
Grass, clump of: tuft
Grass clump: tussock
Grass, creeping: zoysia
Grass, leaf of: blade, sprig
Grass of greens: bent (golf course greens)
Grass or Goethe title: Herr
Grass, put down: sod
Grass, reedlike: gama
Grass stalk: reed
Grass, tough: zoysia
Grass, unit of: blade
Grass variety: zoysia
Grasshopper: katydid, locust
Grasshopper rebuker: ant
Grassland: lea, swards, prairie
Grass skirt accessory: lei
Grassy area: yard, lawn
Grassy expanse: lea
Grassy field: meadow
Grassy plant: sedge
Grassy shoulder: berm
Grate: rasps, grille
Grate upon: rasp, jar
Grateful, feels: owes
Gratia dei
Grau, Shirley Ann: writer
Grave matter: bones
Gravel mound, artic: pingo
Gravel ridge: osar, eskers, ose
Graven image: idol
Graves, Peter: actor
Gravity, defy: levitate
Gravity, given in to: droop
Gravity powered vehicle: sled
Gravity studier: Newton
Gravity, yield to: sag
Gravy bowl: boat
Gravy, on the menu: jus
Gravy tidbit: giblet
Gravy's kin: sauce
Gray, Asa: botanist
Gray brown: taupe
Gray, Erin: actress
Gray head: lee
Gray igneous rock: syenite
Gray, neutral: dun
Gray, orin
Gray, pale: dun, ash
Gray rock: slate
Gray, Thomas, works: odes
Gray with age: hoary
Gray, Zane: writer
Gray-headed: hoar
Graze part: brush
Grazing land: range
Grazing matter: grass
Grease cutter: soap
Grease gun target: axel, zerk
Greasier: oilier, fattier
Greasy marks: smears
Great achievement: feat
Great ball of fire: star,
Great bear: Big Dipper, Ursa Major,

constellation
"Great Caesar's ghost": egad
Great distance, a: afar
"Great" dog: Dane
Great lake, shallowest: Erie
Great many: gobs, lots
Great numbers: myriads
Great pretenders get them: oscars
Great receiver: Rice, (NFL)
Great reviews: raves
Great shape, in: trim, fit
Great skill, with: adroitly
Great Wall location: Asia
Great work: opus
Greater extent, to a: more so
Greater omentum: caul
Greatest quantities: maxima, maximum, most
Grecian goat cheese: feta
Grecian theater: odea
Ode on a Grecian Urn
Greed: lust, avarice
Greed's cousin: envy
Greedy: ovid, rapacious
Greedy one: pig
Greedy sorts: pigs
Greek, ancient: Spartan
Greek architectural order: Doric
Greek architecture, order of: ionic
Greek bit: iota
Greek cheese: feta
Greek city, ancient: Sparta
Greek city-state: Sparta
Greek colonnade: stoa
Greek column, type of: Doric, ionic
Greek consonants: betas
Greek contest: agon
Greek counterpart of Mars: Ares
Greek crosses: taus
Greek dialect: Aeolic, Eolic, Doric
Greek discordia: eris
Greek Dodecanese island: Cos
Greek drink: ouzo
Greek "E": epsilon
Greek, early: Ionian
Greek getaway: Isle
Greek god: Zeus
Greek god of dead: Hades
Greek god of earth: Gaea, Geb
Greek god of light: Apollo
Greek god of love: Eros
Greek god of moon: Artemis
Greek god of poetry: Apollo
Greek god of sea: Poseidon, Nereus
Greek god of sun: Apollo, Sol
Greek god (two-faced): Janus
Greek god of war: Ares
Greek god of wind: Aeolus
Greek goddess of agriculture: Demeter
Greek goddess of wisdom: Athena
Greek gero: Ajax, Odysseus
Greek horseshoes?: omega
Greek island: IOS, Crete
Greek letters: pis, mus, omega, rho, tau, iota,
    alpha, beta, gamma, delta, epsilon zeta, eta,
    theta, kappa, lambda, sigma, phi, chi, pse,

omega
Greek market: agora
Greek Mercury: Hermes
Greek met Greek, Where: agora
Greek name for Greece: Hellas
Greek or Roman: classical
Greek "P": rho
Greek peak: Ossa
Greek poet: Sappho, Psappho, Pindar
Greek portico: stoa
Greek restaurant staple: gyro
Greek sea: Aegean
Greek salad cheese: feta
Greek salad ingredient: feta
Greek salad topper: feta
Greek "second": beta
Greek sorceress, Media
Greek style contest: agon
Greek "T": tau
Greek tense, abbr.: aor
Greek theater: odeon
Greek town square: agora
Greek underground: ELAS
Greek vowel: iota
Greek war god: Ares
Greek wheeler-dealer: Ixion
Greek wines: retsinas
Greek winged monster: harpy
Greek "X": chi
Greek "Z": zeta
Greek Zorba, the
Green: lime, Nile
Green Beret org.: USMC
Green, Brian Austin: actor
Green card org.: INS
Green egg layer: emu
Green eggs' mate: ham
Green film: patina
Green Gable girl: Anne
Green Gable kid: Anne
Green Hornet's alter ego: Reid
Green Hornet valet: Kato
Green mineral: jade
Green Mountain state citizen: Vermonter
Green, not: ripe
Green parrot: kea
Green Party's road: Natures Way
Green pod: okra
Green prefix: eco
Green quartz: prose, prase
Green rust: patine
Green science: ecology
Green seed: pea
Green, shade of: pea, moss
Green stone: jade
Green superhero: Hulk
Green wool on clay sheep: Chia
Green card holder: alien
Greenhorn: tyro, novice
Greenhouse kin: hotbed
Greenhouse tray: flat
Greenhouse vine: smilax
Greenish blue: aqua
Greenish brown: hazel

Greenish melon: casaba
Greenland base: Etah
Greenland military base: Thule
Greenland settlement: Thule
Greenspan, Alan: economist
Greenspan stat: GNP
Greensward: turf
Greer, Garson: actress
Greet formally: bow
Greet the master: wag
Greet warmly: hug
Greeted: hailed
Greeted, as a dog: wag
Greeted the moon: bayed
Greeting: ciao
Greeting, breezy: ciao
Greeting (forum): ave
Greeting, warm: embrace
Greeting with a bow: salaam
Gregarious, far from: asocial
Gregg expert: steno
Gregorian chant
Gregorian songs: chants
Grendel's foe: Beowulf
Grenoble goose: oie
Grenoble's river: Isere
Gretsky milieu: Ice
Grey, Joel: actor
Grey (Lady): tea
Grey Cup org.: CFL (football)
Griddle cake: hotcake, pancake, flapjack
Gridiron conference: huddle
Gridiron gain: yardage
Gridiron option: pass, run, punt
Gridiron play: down
Gridiron stat: tds, yds
Gridiron unit: team
Gridlocked: stuck
Grief, poetic: dolor
Grier, Rosy: football (NFL)
Grieved: wept
Grieves loudly: moans
Grievous distress: woe
Griffith, emile: boxer
Grigs, adult: eels
Grill (car) cover: bra
Grill (charcoal): hibachi
Grills: asks, cooks, interrogates
Grimace: moue, face
Grimace, pouting: moue
Grimm character: ogre
Grimm creation: ogre
Grimm heavies: ogres
Grimm heroine: Gretel
Grimm youngster: Hansel
Grimy: sooty, dirty, dusty, soiled
Grin, kind of: wry
Grin, smug: smug
Grinch creature: Seuss
Grind down: file
Grind, maybe: hone
Grind one's teeth: gnash
Grind teeth: gnash
Grinder, spice: pestle

Grinding grit: emery
Grinding machine: lathe
Grinding tool: miller
Grinding wheel substance: emery
Grip, loosen a: ease
"Get a grip on"
"Get a grip on: grasp
Gripe: complaint
Gripe meekly: whine
Gripping device: clamp
Gris, Juan: Spanish painter
Gris-gris: charm, spell, amulet, fetish
Grisham, John: novelist
Grisham Works: novels
Grissom, Gus: astronaut
Grit: sand
Grit for grinding: emery
Grits: hominy
Groan associate: moan
Groan causer: pun
Groaner maybe: pun
Groats, buckwheat: kasha
Grocery store (urbane): bodega
Grog base: rum
Grommet: eyelet
Groom: hostler, ostler
Groom, is a: weds
Groomed, well: soigné, soignée
Groove, narrow: stria
Groove on: dig
Grooved on: dug
Groovy: fab
Gross: crass
Gross, Arye: actor
Gross minus tare: net
Grotesque: bizarre
Grotesque waterspout: gargoyle
Grotto: cave
Groucho's brother: Harpo
Grouchy: cranky, snap
Grouchy person: crab
Ground breaker: hoe, spade, shovel, plow, harrow
Ground cavity: pit, cav
Ground corn: meal
Ground cover: sod
Ground grain: grist
Ground, higher: upland
Ground, low: marsh
Ground swell: surge
Groundbreaking person: hoer
Grounded planes: SSTs
Groundhog (noted): Phil
Groundless: idle
Grounds: basis
Grounds for a suit: tort
Groundskeeper: caretaker
Groundwork for a fence: posthole
Group, as a: en masse
Group, as of beauties: bevy,
Group by twos: paired, pair off
Group, cohesive: unit
Group of ants: colony
Group of geniuses: Mensa

Group of related things: schmear, schmeer
Group of seven: septets, heptads
Group of toads: knot
Group of two: dyad
Group of whizzes: Mensa
Group, offshoot: sect
Group protest participant: rioter
Group, select: A list
Group, splinter: sect
Group sum in series: subtotal
Groupies: fans
Grouping: array
Grouping, impressing: array
Grouping, large impressive: array
Groups together: lumps
Grove: copse
Groves, city: parks
Grow abundantly: run riot
Grow dark: laten
Grow gradually: accrete
Grow incisors: teethe
Grow together: accrete
Grow toward evening: laten
Grow up: mature
Grow weary: sag, tire
Grow wheat: farm
Growing media: peat, agar
Growing on a trellis: latticed
Growing out: enate, enation
Growing season beginning: spring
Grown up: adult
Grows molars: teethes
Grubby guy: slob
Grudge, hold a: resent
Grumpy mood: snit
Grungier: cruddier
Grunion catcher: smelter
G-suit letters: NASA
GTO, part of:Gran
Guacamole or hummus:chickpea
Guacamole tossed overboard: dip in the ocean
Guadalajara girlfriend: amiga
Guadalupe grocery: bodega
Guanaco's cousin: llama
Guarantee: insure, warrant
Guarantee a pension: vest
Guarantee to work: surefire
Guard: sentry
Guard duty, do: watch
Guard, on ones: alert, leery
Guard, put on: alert, alarm, warn
Guardhouse: brig,
Guardian charge: ward
Guardian spirit: lar
"Guarding Tess"
Guardsman, royal: Exon (A British
    Guardsmen Regiment)
Guatemala fashions:
Gudrun's wife: Alti, Etzel, Sigurd, Siefgied
    father: Hetel
Queen of Olympus: Hera
Guerrero, Pedro: boxer
Guerrica painter: Picasso
Guess: reckon

Guess, hazard a: opine
Guessed: figured
Guesstimate phrase: or so
Guest, paying: lodger
Guests, many: house full
Guests, unwanted: bores, ants
Guevara, Ernesto: Cuban revolutionist
Guevara, Ernesto: Che
Guffaw: laugh
Guggenheim specialty: art
Guide, Everest: Sherpa
Guides: leads, directs
Guides under the strings: frets
Guiding principle: credo
Guiding standards: ethos
Guide-lines, umpire: rules
Guido, Reni: Italian painter
Guile: cunning, sly
Guiliani, Rudy: NYC mayor
Guilty feeling: remorse
Guinea pig: cavy
Guinevere's love: Lancelot
Guinness, knighted: Alec
Guinness, Sir Alec: actor
Guitar connection: amp
Guitar gadget: capo
Guitar, kind: steel, elec, acoustic
Guitar, mini: uke
Guitar player's device: capo
Guitar, slangily: axe
Guitar sound: twang
Guitar, type of: acoustic, electric
Gujarat garb: sari,
Gulager, Clu: actor
Gulch: Arroyo
Gulch, steep: Arroyo
Gulf of Tonkin River: Red
Gulf War missiles: scuds
Gulf, yawning: chasm
Gulfport's neighbor: Biloxi
Gulfs: chasms
Gull: easy mark
Gull relative: tern
Gull, small: tern
Gullet: maw
Gullible one: sap
Gulls or snows: dupes
Gully, desert: wadi
Gully, dry: Arroyo
Gully, forms a: erodes
Gulp: swig
Gulp down: chug
Gum: lac
Gum (arabic) tree: acacia
Gum up: ruin
Gumbo ingredient: okra
Gumbo veggy: okra
Gums: ulla
Gumshoe, comic: Dick Tracy
Gumshoe's assignment: case
Gumshoe's quest: motive
Gun, long-barreled hunting: roers
Gung ho: eager
Gung ho about: into

Gunk, full of: mucky
Gunnysack material: burlap
Gunpowder igniter: spark, flint
Gunshots: enfilades
Gunsmith: armorer
Gunwale port: Thole
Gurkha knife: kukri
Guru practice: yoga
Guru's title: yogi
Gush forth: spew
Gush out: spew, flow
Gush over: rave
Gusher product: oil
Gushes forth: spews
Gussied up, get: preen
Gusto: elan
Gut feeling, more than a: knew
Guthrie, Arlo: music
Guttersnipe: gamin
Guy, attractive: hunk
Guy, average: joe
Guy Fawkes Day
Guy, informal: fella
Guy like Hamlet: Dane
Guy, lowdown: heel
Guy who's all thumbs: lout
Guys' partners:-dolls, gals
Guys who finish last, like: nice
Guzzle: swig
Guzzle, not: sip
Gwendolen's husband: Locrine
Gym: phys ed
Gym dance: hop
Gym iteration: rep
Gym shoe: sneaker
Gymnasts:
    Comaneci, Nadia
    Korbit, Olga
Gymnast's feat: kip
Gymnast's horse: pommel
Gymnast, like a: lithe
Gymnastics apparatus: pommel
Gymnast's goals: tens
Gymnast's stickum: rosin
Gymnast's goal: ten
Gypsum painting surface: gesso
Gypsum type: selenite
Gypsy gent: Rom, rye
Gypsy man: Rom, rye
Gypsy "pack": tarot
Gyrate: whirl, spin
Gyro holder: pita
Gyro pocket: pita
Gyro shell: pita
Gyroscope pioneer: hexed

H

H+ = <u>ion</u>
Haakon's Vll son: Olaf
Habakkuk: prophet
Habeas corpus: writ
Haberdashery item: tie clip

Habit: rut
Habit, bad: vice
Habitat: ecosystem
Habitat for humanity: Earth
Habits, bad: vices,
Habitual: rote, usual
Habitual practice: usage
Habitually: often
Habituate: enure, inure
Hacienda: casa
Hacienda chamber: sala
Hacienda halls: salas
Hacienda housewife: señora
Hack: cab, axe, slash
Hackman, Gene: actor
Hacks: hews
Hack's customer: fare
Had a colt: foaled
Had a good cry: wept
Had a turn: went
Had charge of: led
Had down pat: knew
Had in mind: meant
Had it coming: entitled
Had leftovers: ate in
Had occasion for: needed
Had one's say: opined
Had some precipitation: rained, snowed
Had the acquaintance of: knew
Had trotters: dined(pigs feet)
Had words: squabbled
Haddock, young: scrod
Hadrian home: villa
Hadrian's hello: ave
Hag: old woman, crone, beldam
Hagar's daughter: Honi
Hagatna's former name: Agana
Hagen, Uta: actress
Haggard: worn
Haggard, Merle: singer
Haggle back and forth: dicker
Haggling topic: cost, price
Hagiography subject: saint
Hagman role: Ewing
Hag's cry: fie
Hag's laugh: cackle
Hahn, Otto: physicist
Hai, Bali
Haifa's native: Israel
Haifa's place: Israel
Haik wearer: Arab
Haiku and sonnet: poems
Haiku composer: poet
Hail, hit with: pelted
Hail (in Rome): ave
Hailed on: pelted
Hair apparent: wig
Hair application: dye
Hair, coarse: seta
Hair curler: iron
Hair cut, layered: shag
Hair cut, short: bob
Hair dye: henna, henra
Hair foundation: scalp

Hair, hank of: tress
Hair, long: mane
Hair, lost: bald, molted
Hair net, fancy: snood
Hair ointment: pomade
Hair piece: wig, wiglet, toupee, fall
Hair piece, long: fall
Hair removal name: neet
Hair ringlet: tress
Hair rinse: henna
Hair, store-bought: wig
Hair style: updo, afro, coif, punk
Hair style, high: afro
Hair style, spiky: punk
Hair, thick mass of: mop
Hair tint: rinse
Hair treatment: perm
Hairdo: coif
Hairdo holders: gel
Hairdo, over-size: afro
Hairdo, punk: mohawk
Hairdo, severe: knot
Hairdo, short: bob
Hairdo style, spiky: punk
Hairdo, upswept: pompadour, pouf
Hairlike cell growth: cilia
Hairline problem: fracture
Hairpiece in full: periwig
Hair-protecting kerchief: do rag
Hair-raising: eerie, scary, spooky
Hair-raising brand: Rogaine
Hair-raising place: nape
"Hairspray" mom: Edna
Hairy: hirsute, virile
Hairy humanoid: yeti, Sasquatch
Hairy insect: bee
Hairy twin: Esau
Haitian summer: Ete
Hajj destination: Mecca
Halbein, Hans: painter
Halcyone's father: Aeolus
        husband: Ceyx
"Hale and Hearty"
Hale, Nathan: patriot
Haleakala's isle: Maui
Helena, German nickname for: Leni
Haley, Alex: writer, author
Half: demi
Half A couple: Mrs.
Half a fly: tse,
Half a mo: jiffy
Half a score: decade, ten
Half and half: one
Half of a table game:Ping (Pong)
Half, prefix for: demi,
Half the integers: even
Half-asleep: dozy
Half-baked, it may be: idea
Half-cocked: rash, brash, reckless, foolhardy,
        imprudent
Half-free servant: serf
Half-grown: young
Half, in combo: demi
Halfhearted: tepid,

Half-moon tide: neap
Half-pint: cup
Half-shell item: oyster
Half-witted: dull, slow, moronic, backward,
        imbecile, imbecilic
Halk wearer: Arab
Hall, kind of: town
Hall (public): lyceum
Hallowed-out fruit: gourd
Halloween décor: cobweb
Hall's, gus org.: CPUSA
Halo: nimbus
Halos, of sorts: auras,
Halt, bring to a: stymy, stymie
Halt, come to a: end, stop
Halvah base: Sesame
Halves of quarters: bits
Ham, Mia: soccer
Ham insert, often: clove
Ham it up: emote
Ham hocks, e.g.: soul food
Ham holders: rye
Ham on rye
Ham on stage: emoter
Ham portion: slice
Ham, smoked: cured
Haman's adversary: Esther
Hambletonian, participates in the: trots
Hambletonian entrant: trotter
Hamelin character: piper
Hamelin pest: rat
Ham-handed: inept, clumsy, gauche,
        bumbling, all thumbs
Hamilcar conquest: Spain
        home: Carthage
        son: Hannibal
        surname: Barca
Hamilton notes: tens
Hamilton-Burr competition: duel
Hamilton's prov.: Ontario, Ont.
Hamlet: Dane
Hamlet portrayer: Olivier
Hamlet smelled, what: a rat
Hamlet star: L. Olivier
Hamlet "trouble": esse
Hamlet's love: Ophelia
Hamlet's oath: fie
Hamlet's realm: Denmark
Hamlet's title: prince
Hamlet's was bare: bodkin
Hamlin (Harry) series: L.A. Law
Hamlisch, Marvin: composer
Hammarskjold, Dag
Hammed it up: emoted
Hammer for stakes: maul
Hammer, kind of: claw
Hammer, meeting: gavel
Hammer part: claw, peen
Hammer, wield a: nail
Hammered home: instilled
Hammered in: nailed
Hammerhead kin: mako, tiger, white, sharks
Hammer's creator: spillane
Hammett detective: Ned Beaumont

Hammett Falcon: Maltese
Hammett gumshoe: Sam Spade
Hammett's hound: Asta
Hammock, enjoy a: loll
Hammock, hang in a: loll
Ham's brother: shem
Ham's "Consider It Done": Wilco
Han or Ming: dynasty
Hand delivery, charge for a: ante
Hand, gave a: dealt
Hand holder: wrist
Hand, menacing: fist
Hand over: entrust, give
Hand shuttle, use a: tat
Hand, slangily: mitt
Hand, sleight of
Hand, upper: in control
Hand warmer: muff
Hand with an attitude: fist
Handbag name: Gucci
Handball point: ace
Handbook: vade mecum, guide
Handel, George: composer
Handfuls of cotton: wads
Handicrafter: artist
Handkerchief, large: bandana
Handle: wield, see to
Handle an order: fill
Handle problems: cope
Handle roughly: maul, paw
Handle, to Hadrian: ansa
Handle with care: wield
Handled with skill: finessed
Hand-over-mouth reaction: gasp
Hands on hips: akimbo
Hands out: issues
Hands-on workplace: lab
Handsome man: Adonis
Handwriting: script
Handwriting, kind of: Spencerian
Handy: of use
Handy abbr.: etc.
Hang around: loiter
Hang down: droop
Hang glide: soar
Hang fire: pend
Hang five: surfHang in a hammock: loll
Hang in there: persist
Hand loosely: drape
Hang of it: knack
Hang on: last
Hang on to: keep
Hang ten: surf
Hanger-on: leechHanging beds: hammocks
Hanging ornament: tassel
Hanging plant: fuchsias
Hanging roots tree: banyan
Hangout, thief's: den
Hang's fire: pends
Hangs in folds: drapes
Hangs ten: surfs
Hank Ketcham's Dennis e.g.: menace
Hank of hair: tress
Hankering: yen, itch

Hanna, Daryl: actress
Hannarskjold, Dag: UN secretary
Hannibal's challenge: Alps
Hannibal's route: Alps
Hanoi New Years: Tet
Hanover's wife: Frau
Han's Arp genre: Dada
Hansoms for hire: cabs
Haphazard: randon
Haphazard collection: olio
Happen again: ensue
Happen, made: caused
Happen next: ensued
Happen to: betide, befall, befell
Happens, as it: live
Happens next: ensues, recur
"Happily ever after"
Happiness, perfect: bliss
Happy associate: Doc
Happy, extremely: in orbit
Happy feeling: joy
Happy, less than: annoyed
Happy loser: dieter
Happy rumble: purr
Happy shout: wow
Happy tunes: lilts
Happy's pal: Doc
Harangue: tirade, rant
Haran's brother: Abraham
    daughter: Iscah, Milcah
    father: Terah, Shimei
    son: Lot
Harasses recruits: hazes
Harbor, safe
harbor, safe: haven
Harbor sight: tug
Hard: effortful
Hard and fast rules: laws
Hard as a rock: stony
Hard bench: pew,
Hard but easily breakable: crisp
Hard candy, piece of: sourball,
Hard copy error: typo
Hard facts: info
Hard hand defense: karate
Hard roll: bagel
Hard seat: pew
Hard stuff: booze
Hard to climb: steep
Hard to come by: rare, sparse
Hard to find: rare
Hard to swallow, it can be: pill
Hard top: sedan
Hard volcano glass: obsidian
Hard work: toil
Harden: inure, anneal
Harden, as clay: bake
Harden brick: fire
Hardest to come by: rarest
Hardly bland: savory
Hardly bumpy: even
Hardly generous: tight-fisted
Hardly gentlemanly: rude
Hardly irrational: level-headed

Hardly look good: dire
Hardly thrilling: blah
Hardly verbose: terse
Hardly vibrant: drab
Hardly wordy: terse
Hardness scale: mohs
Hard-nosed: harsh
Hardship, accustom to: inure
Hardy lass (heroine): Tess
Hardy, Ollie: comic
Hardy, Thomas: author
Hardy's dairymaid: Tess
Hardy's pal: Laurel
Harebrained: inane
Harebrained prank: caper
Harem jewelry: anklets
Harem head: sultan, pasha
Harem room: oda
Harem woman, enslaved: odalisque
Mata Hari
Harlem theater: Apollo
Harley, to some: hog
Harmful: evil
Harmful thing: bane
Harmless: innocuous
Harmless fib: white lie
Harmless lie: fib
Harmles, render
Harmless, render: Defuse
Harmonia's daughter: Ino, Agave, Semele,
    Autonoe
    father: Ares, Mars
    husband: Cadmus
    mother: Venus, Aphrodite
    son: Polydorus
Harmonize: attunes
Harmony: concord
Harmony, achieve: agree
Harness: yoke
Harness part: bite, rein, blinder, hame
Harness up: hitch
Harold Grange: "Red"(football)
Harold's (King) capital: Oslo
Harp inventor, Parisian: Erard
Harp kin: lyra,
Harp, old Greek: lyre
Harp on: nag
Harper, Tess: actress
Harper's Bazaar cover illustrator: erte
Harper's Ferry state: W. Va.
Harps on: nags
Harriman, Pamela: ambassador
Harrington, Padraig: PGA, pro golf
Harris honorific: Brer
Harris, Lou: pollster
Harrison, Rex: actor
Harrow boy's mother: mater
Harrow's rival: Eton
Harsh: mean, hard, grim
Harsh criticism: flak
Harsh light: glare
Harsh or severe: stern
Harsh rule: tyranny
Harsh sounding: raspy

Hart, Bret: writer
Hart, Doris: tennis
Hart, Moss: playwrite
Harte, Bret: author
Hartford competitor: Aetna
Hartford logo: elk
Hart's mate: Hind
Hartman, Lisa: actress
Hartman, Phil: actor
Harvest goddess: Ops, Ceres
Harvest the crops: pick, reap, glean
Harvesters or carpenters: ants
Has a higher standard: outranks
Has an effect on: impacts
Has an outstanding figure: owes
Has coming: earns, due, deserve
Has down pat: knows
Has legs, so to speak: lasts
Has markers out: owes
Has no presence: isn't
Has the con: steers
Has to: must
"Has 1001 uses"
Hasenpfeffer, for one: stew
Hasenpfeffer ingredients hare
Hash out differences: argue
Hash, served: slung
Rosh Hashana
Rosh Hashanah
Hassle: nag
Hassle, minor: spat
Hassles a debtor: duns
Hassocks: poufs
Hasta luega, amigo
Hasten: hie, run
Hasty escape: lam
Hasty outline: sketch
Hat: topper, fez
Hat attachment: vail
Hat, bell-shaped: cloche
Hat, close-fitting: toque
Hat, cocked: tricorn
Hat designer: Milliner
Hat, jaunty: beret, tam
Hat or umbrella tree
Hat, rakish: fedora
Hat, slangy: lid
Hat, snap brim: fedora
Hat, straw: leghorn
Hat, tall military: shako
Hat, ten-gallon: Stetson
Hat tied under chin: bonnet
Hat, woman's: toque
Hatch, escape: exit
Hatch, Orrin: senator
Hatched, it may be: plan
Hatcher, Teri: actress
Hateful: odisus
Hatfield clan chief: Anse
Hatfield to a McCoy: enemy
Hatha yoga
Hatred: odium
Hatter's tea guest: Alice
Haughty manner: airs

Haughty one: snob
Haughty type: snob
Haugland, Aage, for one: basso, bass
Hauled, being: atow
Hauler, low-tech: ox cart
Haulers, strong: oxen
Haunches: rumps
Haunting sound: moan
Hausfraus exclamation: ach
Hautboy: oboe
Have a desire for: feel like
Have a disposition: tend
Have a few: imbibe
Have a go at: try
Have a hunch: intuit
Have a loan from: owe to
Have a metal coating: plated
Have an ax to grind
Have an effect on: impact
Have an inkling: sense
Have being: are
Have confidence in: rely
Have down cold: know
Have high hopes: aspire
Have in hand: own, possess
Have in mind: intend
Have it made
Have on: wear
Have one's say: opine
Have rapport: relate
Have reciprocal effect: interact
Have second thoughts: hedge
Have the nerve: dare
Have thoughts: ideate
Haven, floating: ark
Having a common ancestor: akin
Having a rounded roof: domic,
Having a sophisticated charm: debonair
Having a will: testate
Having aged less: younger
Having aspirations: aspire
Having coffee, say: on break
Having existence: being
Having flaps for hearing: eared
Having many meanings: polysemy
Having masculinity: virile
Having momentous consequences: fatal
Having more pizzazz: snazzier
Having no drawbacks: ideal
Having no get-up-and-go: inert
Having quick intelligence: clever
Having sequins: beaded
Having teeth: dentate
Having the means: able
Having the right stuff: able
Having threads: filar
Having three parts: trinary
Havoc: mayhem
Hawaii county seat: Hilo
Hawaiian acacia: koa
Hawaiian attire: muu muu
Hawaiian carving: tiki
Hawaiian crow: nene
Hawaiian flowers: lehua, hibiscus

Hawaiian fish food: luau
Hawaiian flow: lava
Hawaiian goose: nene
Hawaiian islands:
    Big Isle: Hawaii
    Friendly Isle: Molokai
    Garden Isle: Kauai
    Gathering Isle: Oahu
    House of the Sun: Haleakala
    Mystery Isle: Niihau
    Pineapple Isle: Lanai
    Valley Isle: Maui
Hawaiian island, second largest: Maui
Hawaiian lizard fish: ulae
Hawaiian port: Hilo
Hawaiian salutation: Aloha
Hawaiian seafood, informally: mahi
Hawaiian state bird: nene
Hawaiian timber: koa
Hawaiian tree: koa
Hawaiian valediction: aloha
Hawaiian veranda: lanai
Hawaiian wreath: lei
Hawaii's highest peak: Mauna Kea
Hawick hillside: brae
Hawk: sell, vend
Hawk: elanet, falcon
Hawk, fish eating: osprey
Hawk, like a: taloned
Hawk, nestling: eyas
Hawk, Olympian: ares
Hawk, slim: kite
Hawke, Ethan: actor
Hawkeye portrayer: Alan Alda
Hawkeye State: Iowa
Hawk's arena: omni
Hawk's nest: aerie
Hawn, Goldie: actress
Hawser: rope
Hawser, used a: roped
Hawthrone's home: Salem
Hay: fodder
Hay fever cause: pollen
Hay holder: loft
Hay portion: bale
Hay storage unit: bale
Hayes, Helen: actress
Hayes, Isaac: music
Hayloft locale: barn
Haymarket Square event: riot
Haymarket Square figures: strikers
Hayseed: hick, rube
Hayseed humor: corn
"Haystacks" painter: Monet
Hazard a guess: opine
Hazard, what to: guess
Hazards: risks, dangers, dares
Hazardous: unsafe
Hazardous fly: tsetse
Hazelnut: filbert
Haze-over: mist
Hazzard County deputy: Enos
HBO receiver: TV
He is parted from his money: fool

He asked for more: Oliver
He clubbed 61 in 1961: Maris, Roger
He had a golden touch: Midas
He had an Irish Rose: Abie
He rules often: Hoyle
He wanted more: Oliver
He who hesitates is lost
Head and shoulder sculpture: bust
Head cover: hair, cap, tam, do rag
Head dog: alpha
Head, in Montreal: tete
Head, in the: mental
Head of hair, thick: mane
Head of the brewery?: foam
Head of the clast: icono
Head over heels: in love
Head sets, to hams: ears
Head squeeze: nelson
Head support: neck
Head to head, goes: vies
Head wrap: dorag,
Head wreath: anadem
Headache: hassel
Headache, bad: migraine
Headache type: sinus
Headdress, pope's: miter, mitre
Headdress, royal: tiara
Headed for: bound, bound for
Head 'em off, place to: pass
Headgear: turban, cap, tam, beret
Headgear, french legion: kepi
Headgear, gascon: beret
Headgear, tasseled: fez
Headland: ness
Headlights, low: dims
Headlong: rush
Headlong, go: rush
Headquarters: base
Headmaster's cousin: rector
"Heads or tails": call-it
Headsets, to hams: ears
Heads-up, gives a: alerts
Headwaters: source
Headway, makes: gains
Headwear maker: hatter
Headwear, heavenly: halo
Heal a bone: mend
Healing succulent: aloe
Health club staffers: masseurs
Health food: tofu, carob, kelp, yogurt
Health plan outgo: copay, premium
Healthy and sound: hale
Healthy minded: sane
Healthy, robustly: hale
Healthy upstairs: sane
Heaps kudos on: lauds
Hear a case: try
Hear clearly: get
Hear visually: lip-read
Heard the alarm: woke, wakened
Heart, by: rote
Heart chambers: atria
Heart of the matter: gist, grux
"Deep in the Heart of Texas"

Heart or essence: pith
Heart outlet: aorta
Heart parts: atria
Heart printout, for short: ECG, EKG
Heart stimulant: adrenalin
Heartaches: woes
Hearten to: heed
Heartfelt: deep
Hearth: grate
Hearth lights: embers
Hearth need: log
Hearth tool: poker
Heartily recommend: swear by
Heartrending: sad
Hearts and spades in bridge: major suit
Heart-shaped: cordate
Hearty enjoyment: zest
Hearty's partner: hale
"Hale and hearty"
Hearty laugh: yuk, roar
Heat, of: caloric
"The heat is on"
Heat headliner: O'Neal
Heat, kind of: solar
Heat (pref.): pyr
Heat to a boil: scald
Heated discourse: tirade
Heated martini: Hot Gibson
Heath-covered wasteland: moor
Heathen: pagan
Heathen gods: idols
Heathens, infidels: pagans
Heather locale: moor
Heather (where it grows): moor
Heather habitat: moor
Heather's role on Melrose place: Amanda
Heating apparatus: oast, kiln, oven, etna
Heating pipe: duct
Heats up: warms
Heave, mighty: hurl
Heaven, prefix meaning: urano
Heaven or air, to a poet: ether
Heavenly: devine
Heavenly altar: ark
Heavenly being to Pierre: ange
Heavenly beings: angels
Heavenly food: manna
Heavenly headwear: halo
Heavenly highlight: aura
Heavenly hunter: Orion
Heavenly, just: divine
Heavenly prefix: urano,
Heaven's above: skies
Heaven's, comb. form: urano
Heavier, get: gain
Heaviest anchor: bower
Heavy boot: tome
Heavy boring tool: trepan
Heavy burden: onus
Heavy club: bat
Heavy drinker: taper
Heavy feel: heft
Heavy fliers: geese
Heavy gold chain: rope

Heavy hammer: sledge
Heavy hydrogen discoverer: Urey (Harold)
Heavy lifter: crane
Heavy, low cart: dray
Heavy metal band: AC/DC
Heavy rainfall: spate, downpour, deluge
Heavy reading: tomes
Heavy stone: buhr
Heavy thread: lisle
Heavy, very: leaden, ponderous
Heavy volume: tome
Heavy weight: con
Heavyhearted: sad
Heavyweight sport: sumo
Hebrew: Semite
Hebrew for day: yom
Hebrew god: Yahweh
Hebrew grain measure: omer
Hebrew judge: Eli
Hebrew letter: yod, teth, alef, resh, aleph
Hebrew letter, first: alef, aleph
Hebrew lyre: asor
Hebrew measure: omer
Hebrew month: Elul, Adar
Hebrew patriarch: Jacob
Hebrew prophet: Isaiah, Isiah, Obadiah
Hebrew scroll: Torah
Hebrides island: Iona
Hebrides isle: Iona
Heche, Anne: actress
Heckle: razz
Heckler's weapon: tomato
Hectic place: zoo
Hector and Priam: Trojans
Hecuba's daughter: Creusa, Polyxena,
        Cassandra
    father: Dymas
    husband: Priam
    son: Paris, Hector, Helenus, Troilus,
        Deiphobus, Polydorus
Hedda Gabler author: Ibsen
Hedge, neaten the: clip, trim
Hedged: evaded
"Hee Haw" host: Owens
Heels: cads
Heels, blocky: wedges
Heels, it has two: loaf
Heels, thin: stilettos
Heep, Urilah: writer
Heep's and Bathsheba's husband: Uriahs
Heflin, Van: actor
Hegel, Georg Wilhelm: philosopher
"Heidi" author: Spyri
"Heidi" hairpiece: brade
Heidi's peak: alp
Height, it means: arco
Height, to a cager: asset
Heinlein's genre: sci-fi
Heir or descendent: scion
Heirlooms: relics
Hejaz native: Saudi
Held in: pent
Held responsible: blamed
Held sway: rule, reigned

Held up: delayed
Helen, abductor of: Paris
Helen of Troy
Helena rival: Estee
Helen's abductor: Paris
Helen's mother: Leda
Helen's place: Troy
Helga's husband: Hagar
Helio, daughter of,: Eos
Helio's sister: Eos
Helium, like: inert
Helix: spiral
Helix (double): DNA
Hellenic H: eta,
Hellenic letter: rho
Hellman's attic content: toys
Hello (forum): ave
Helm: tiller
Helm, Matt: detective
Helmet, kind of: pith
Helmet, pith: topi, hat
Helmet, visored: armet
Helm's position: alee
Help in wrongdoing: abet
"Help Me Rhonda"
Help pay: defray
Help the hood: abet
Help to do wrong: abet
Help, unexpected: manna
Helped out: obliged
Helper, briefly: asst.
Helpful tip: hint
Helping: portion
Helping (serving) of ice cream: dollop
Helpless: unable
Helsinki native: Finn
Helvetica, for one: font
He-Man (like a): macho
Hematite: ore
Hematite yield: iron
Hemidemisemiquaver: note (music's 64th note)
Hemingway handle: Papa
Hemingway sobriquet: Papa
Hemispherical roof: dome
Hemp product: rope
Hem's partner: haw
Hen: biddy
Hen: layer
Hence: ergo
Hengist's brother: Horsa
Henie, Sonja: skater
Henley, Beth: writer
Henley, Don: music
Henley essential: oar
Henley pullers: oars
Henley's claim to fame: regatta
Hennery: coop
Hennins lookalikes: steeples
Henri's ait: Ile
Henri's art school: Ashean
Henri's land mass: ile
Henri's pals: amis
Henri's refusal: non

Henri's yes: oui
Henry Ford's only son: Edsel
Henry fifth triumph (site of): Agin Court
Henry, a famous: eighth, VlII
Henry Vl found it: Eton
Henry VlII last wife: Catherine Parr
Henry VIII's house: Tudor
Henry VlII's six wives
Henry's two of six: Annes
Hen's home: roost, coop
Henson creation: muppet
Hentoff, Nat: columnist
Heparin target: clot
Hepburn, Audrey: actress
Hepburn nickname: Kate
Hepplewhite products: settees
Her kettle restored youth: medea
Hera's son: Ares
        husband: Zeus
Heracles's captive: Iole
Heraldic bearing: orle
Heraldic border: orle
Heraldic crosses: taus
Heraldic green: vert
Heraldic wreath: orle
Herb, aromatic: anise
Herb for taddies: catnip
Herb, kitchen: oregano
Herb masher: pestle
Herb of wisdom: sage
Herb or guru: sage
Herb teas: tisanes
Herbal brew: tea
Herbal concoction: tea
Herbal infusion: tea
Herbal soother: tea
Herbal tea choice: rosehip
Herbalist's generosity ?: thyme sharing
Herbert, Frank saga: Dune
Herbivore, huge:hippo
Herbivores, human: vegans
Hercule's creator: Agatha
Hercules fought, serpent: Hydra
Hercules' TV spinoff: Xena
Hercules victim: Hydra
Herd follower: nomad
Herd orphan: dogie
Here, in French: Ici
Hereafter, the: kingdom come
Hereditary: lineal
Hereditary rider: dynast
Heredity unit: gene
Here's partner: now
Hermit: loner
Hermit's sine qua non: solitude
Hero: deli sandwich, sub, hoagie
Hero at Roncesvalles: Roland
Hero birthplace: Deli
Hero purveyor: Deli
Hero sandwich: torpedo, hoagie
Hero, war: ace
Hero, where to find a: deli
Hero's act: deed
Hero's horse: steed

Hero's journey: quest
Hero's suffix: ism
Hero's tale: epic, saga
Herod's daughter: Salome
        father: Antipas, Antipater
        kingdom: Judea, Judaea
        mother: Cyprus
        son: Herod, Joseph, Pheroas, Phasaelus
Heroic: epoc
Heroic events, series of: epos
Heroic exploit: deed
Heroic poem: epos, epic
Heroic tale: saga
Heroin, slangily: scag
Heroine Jane Eyre
Heroism, tale of: saga
Heron: bittern, egret, wader
Heron kin: ibis
Herr in Madras: sri
Herr spouse: Frau
Herr von Bismarck, Otto
Herring: sprat
Herring, certain: shad
Herring, deep-bodied: shad
Herriot, e.g.: met, opera
Herriot, for one: vet
Herr's abode: haus
Herr's date: Fräulein
Herr's wife: Frau
Hersey's town: Adano
Hershey competitor: Nestle
Hershiser, Orel: baseball
He's a doll: Ken
He's always on the move: nomad
He's big overseas: Ben (London clock bell)
He's tickled: Elmo
Hesitate, doesn't: acts
Hesitate, not: act
Hesitation sound: er
Hess, Hermann: novelist
Hess, Myra: pianist
Heston's org.: NRA
Hex halved: tri
Hey: yoo hoo, psst
Heyerdahl, Thor: explorer
Heyerdahl's Kon Tiki
Hi, bye: ciao
HI or AK (once): terr. (Hawaii or Alaska)
Hibachi residue: ashes
Hibachi site: porch
Hibernate: den
Hibernate, place to: lair, den
Hibernate relative: aestivate, estivate
Hibernates: dens
Hibernia language: Erse
Hid away: stashed
Hidden: ulterior, covert, cloaked
Hidden microphone: bug
Hidden obstacle: snag
Hidden valley: glen
Hide: hole up
Hide a message: encode
Hide in the shadows: lurk
Hide: hair link: nor

Hideaways: dens, retreats
Hideous creature: ogre
Hideous monster: ogre
Hideout: lair
Hides (bundles of): kips
Hideyoshi's castle site: Osaka
Hiding: cloaking
Hiding place: cache
Hieden, Eric: skater
Hieroglyphics: Egyptian
Hieroglyphics bird: Ibis
Hieroglyphic stone: Rosetta
Hi-fi component: amp
High boots: waders
High crimes: treason
High desert of Asia: Gobi
High dudgeon: ire
High hopes, have: aspire
High in calories: fat
High IQ society: Mensa
High king's hill: tara
High male voice: alto
High mark: a plus,
"High Noon" marshall: Kane
High note: ela (el a)
High note on sheet music: ledger lines
High pH solution: alkali
High priest, biblical: Eli
High priest garment: ephod
High rank: eminence
High ranking Hindu: Rajah
High regard: esteem
High roller: gambler, spender wastrel
High school bookworm: nerd
High school equivalency test: GED
High school exam: PSAT
High school, private: academy
High school reading: Iliad
High schooler learning paper: GED
High sign: nod, tip, wink, alarm, signal
High society: Beaumont's
High speed electron: beta
High spirits: gaiety, glee, elan, levity
High time: noon
High up: aloft
High velocity, of: supersonic
High volume: loud
High waistline: empire
High-altitude phenomenon: jet stream
Highbrow type: snob, arty
Highchair wear: bib
High-class tie: ascot
Higher court, he seeks a: appellant
Higher ground: upland
Higher position, in a: over
Higher power, takes to the: cubes
Higher priced: marked up
Higher standard, has a: outranks
Highest in excellence: supreme
Highest point: zenith, top most
Highest ranking bridge card: Ace
Highest stage: acme
Highfalutin one: snoot
High five, give a: slap

High-grade: cull
High-grade coffee: mocha
Highland dance: fling
Highland girl: lass
Highland group: clan
Highland lake: Loch
Highland negative: nae
Highland tongue: Erse
Highland units: clans
Highlander: gael, scot
Highland dialect: Erse
High-level employee: exec
Highlights, ad: dye
Highlights, they can create: dyes
Highly rated: four-star
High-minded, more: nobler
High-pitched flute: piccolo
High-pitched sound: shrill, treble
High-pitched voice: treble
High-powered: driven, strong, dynamic
High-powered megaphone: bull horn
High-rise Units: Condos
High-spirited: bold, brash, fiery, jolly, jaunty
High-spirited girl: Hayden
High-strung: edgy, taut, hyper, jumpy
Hightail it: flee, ran
Hightailed it: scat, ran
High-tea finger food: scone
High-tech pointers: lasers
High-tech scan: MRI
Highway alerts: flares
Highway cones: pylons
Highway hulk: semi,
Highway interchange sights: motels
Highway parade: convoy
Highway rumbler: semi
Highway's far right: slow lane
Hike: tramp
Hike, long: trek
Hike, not just a: trek
Hike, take a: tramp
Hike trail: path
Hike, tough: trek
Hiker's problem: blister
Hill, Benny: comic
Hill, chain of: ridges
Hill companion: dale
Hill, flat top: butte
Hill, high, craggy: tor
Hill, high pointed: tor
Hill, small natural: knoll
Hill, woody: holt
Hillary's 1953 conquest: Everest
Hilary, Edmund
Hillary, Edmund's Title: sir
Hillock: knoll
Hills, area between: vale
Hills, broad-topped: lomas
Hill's opposite: dale
Hillside, Hawick: brae
Hillside, Scottish: brae
Hilltop: rise
Him, to Colette: lui
Himalayan beast: yak

Himalayan cedar: deodar
Himalayan goat: tahr
Himalayan guide: Sherpa
Himalayan holy men: lama
Himalayan humanoid: yeti
Himalayan kingdom, landlocked: Nepal
Himalayan land: Nepal
Himalayan legend: yeti
Himalayan peak: Everest
Himalayan plant: atis
Himalayas' home: Asia
Himmel preceder: ach
Hinder the growth of: stunt
Hindi kin: Urdu
Hindmost: rear
Hindu: Rama
Hindu attire: sari
Hindu caste members, certain: Teli
Hindu cousin: Urdu
Hindu cymbals: tal
Hindu destroyer: Shiva
Hindu god: Shiva
Hindu guitar: sitar
Hindu, high-ranking: Rajah
Hindu holy pilgrimage: yatra
Hindu honorific: sri
Hindu incantation: mantra
Hindu kingdom: Nepal
Hindu loincloth: dhoti
Hindu melodic patterns: ragas
Hindu mendicant: fakir
Hindu, most: Asian
Hindu "Mr.": sri
Hindu musical works: ragas
Hindu mystic writing: tantra
Hindu mystics: yoga's, yogis
Hindu peasant: Ryot
Hindu priest: Brahman
Hindu priestly caste: Brahman
Hindu prince: Rajah, Raja, Maharaja
Hindu princess: Rani
Hindu queen: Ranee, Rani
Hindu royalty: Rani, Ranee
Hindu sacred river: Ganges
Hindu sage: swami
Hindu scripture: Veda
Hindu social classes: castes
Hindu statesman: Nehru
Hindu taboo: beef,
Hindu teacher: swami, swani, guru
Hindu title: sri
Hindu tune: raga
Hindustani: Urdu
Hines, Carl: pianist
Hines, Earl Fatha: pianist
Hinges on: depends
Hingis, Martina: tennis
Hingle, Pat: actor
Hint at: suggest, allude
Hint, useful: tip
Hints of color: tinges
Hip bone section: ischia
Hip-hop music: rap
Hip-hop star: Puff Daddy

Hip-knee connection: femur, thigh
Hippie attire: beads
Hippie greeting: peace
Hippie's digs: pad
Hippie's garment, like: tie dyed
Hippie's home: pad
Hippo's home: zoo
Hippodrome: arena
Hire: employ, engage
Hire a lawyer: sue
Hire, fill-in: office temp, temp
Hired, just: new,
Hired muscle: goon
Hireling: menial
Hirsch, Judd: actor
Hirsute, became less: shaved
Hirt, Al: trumpeter
Hi's comic strip wife: Lois
His and hers: theirs
His dragon was killed by Cadmus: Ares
His name may ring a bell: Pavlov
His nibs: big shot
His pad's the pond: frog, toad
His patron is St. Crispin: cobbler
His towel partner: hers
Hispania, half of: Haiti
Hispanic: Latino
Hispaniola country: Haiti
Hispaniola, por ejemplo: isla
Hiss: spit, boo
Hissed at: jeered
Historian's concern: past
Historian word: ago
Historic Memphis street: Beale
Historic shrine: Alamo
Historic times: ages
Historical novel: saga
Historical Parks: Rosa
Historical period: age, epoch, era
Historical records: acts, annals
History: past
History book topic: era
History question: when
History, special time in: era
History warehouse: museum
History repeats, what: itself
Hit bottom: spank
Hit counterpart: miss
Hit dead-center: nail
Hit hard: swat, smack
Hit it off: click
Hit on the head: conk, cosh
Hit or miss: smack
Hit sign: SRO (standing room only)
Hit the books: study, read
Hit the bottle: tope
Hit the brakes: slow, stop
Hit the buffet: eat
Hit the ceiling: rage
Hit the hay: retire, slept, turn in, crash
Hit the road: leave
Hit the wrong key: err, typo
Hit up for payment: dun
Hit with hail: pelted

Hitch, as a horse: tie up
Hitch, made a: tied
Hitchcock's favorite direction: NNW
Hitcher's hope: ride
Hitching post: altar
Hi-tech, perhaps: modern
Hitler was one: paranoic, paranoiac
Hitler's architect: speer
Hitting the right notes: on key
HMO Staffer: RN, MD, LPN
Ho Chi Minh City, once: Saigon
Ho hums: blahs
Ho preceder: heave
Hoagies: subs
Hoarfrost: frost, rime
Hoax: gag
Hobbit's home: shire
Hobbling: lame
Hobby ender: ist
Hobby knife: X-Acto
Hobby shop buy: kit
Hobby shop inventory: kits
Hobby, slangily: bag
Hobo fare: stew
Hoboes ride, what: rails, trains
Hockey buff: rink rat
Hockey feint: deke
Hockey players:
    Esposito, Phil
    Kavalex, Alexel
    Orr, Bobby
Hockey team: skaters
Hocus pocus
Hodgepodge: olio, hash
Hodges, Gil: baseball
Hoe, in Heidelberg: hacke
Hoedown honey: Gal
Hog, kind of: road
Hog, young: shoat
Hogan, Paul role: Dundee
Hogan dweller: Navajo
Ms. Ima Hogg
Hogwarts lesson: spell
Ho-hum feeling:apathy, ennui
Hoisting machine: winch, crane, gin, pulley
Hoists: lifts,jacks, heft
Hokkaido native: Ainu
Hokkaido port: Muroran
Holbein, Hans: painter
Holbrook, Hal: actor
Hold a grudge: resent
Hold a session: sit
Hold an opinion: deem
Hold back: reserve
Hold close: hug
Hold contents: cargo
Hold dear: cherish, value, treasure
Hold down a job: earn
Hold fast: adhere
Hold, filled the: laded
Hold firm: resist
Hold forth: orate
Hold gently: cup, cradle
Hold hands, pay to: ante

"Hold it", (Spanish): alto
Hold off for: await
Hold on: cling
Hold on tight: cling
Hold one's own: cope
Hold onto: retain, keep
Hold out: endure
Hold sway: reign
"Hold the fort"
"Hold the mayo"
Hold, to Titian: tenere
Hold up: rob, detain
"Hold your horses": rein
Holder, anatomical: sac
Holds gently: cups
Holds off for: awaits
Holds on tightly: clings
Holds title to: owns
Holds up: lasts, robs
Holds up well: wears
Hole, deep: pit
Hole reenforcer: grommet
Hole, unintended: leak
Hole up: lay low
Holiday cheer: nog
Holiday décor: wreath
Doc Holiday
Holiday launcher: eve
Holiday lead-in: eve
Holiday number: noel
Holiday quaff: wassail
Holiday suffix: mas
Holidays, celebrate: observe
Holiday's friend: Earp
Holland export: Edam, bulbs
Hollandaise, e.g.: sauce
Holliday's partner: Earp
Hollow: dell, pit
Hollow fruit: fig
Hollow out: bore
Hollow place: pit
Hollow, small: recess
Hollow stone: geode
Holly: ilex
Holly City of the Middle East: mecca
Holly Golightly's creator: Capote
Holly or holm oak: ilex
Holly shrub: ilex
Holly wreath
Hollywood asset: star quality
Holm, Ian: actor
Holm oak: ilex
Holman, Nat: basketball
Holme's cohort: Watson
Holme's home site: Baker Street
Hologram maker: laser
Holt, Tim: western actor
Holy cats!: yipes
"Holy" children, certain: terror
Holy city: Toledo
Holy cow: yipe
Holy cup: grail
Holy image: icon
Holy one: saint

Holy one, female: ste
Holy place: shrine
Holy terror: brat
Holy water receptacle: font
Homage, paid: knelt
Homage, pay: kneel
Hombre's abode: casa
Homburg cousin: fedora
Home, away from: afield
HBO receiver: TV
"Home Alone" kid: Kevin
Home, briefly: res.
Home expert: Martha Stewart
Home, extremely modest: hut
Home, figuratively: hearth
Home finder: realtor
Home, modest: cottage
Home of Machu Picchu: Peru
Home of St. Francis: Assisi
Home of the Ewoks: Endor
Home of the Keydets: VMI
Home on the high: (var.) Aery, aerie
Home port: base
Home, portable: tepee
Home products brand: Avon
Home seller: realtor
Home tele: res., phone
Home trailer: stead,
Home turnover: resale
Home wreckers: termites
Homeboy's turf: hood
Homecoming: return
Homecoming hits: RBIs
Homely: ugly
Homer opus: iliad, epic
Homeric account: saga
Homeric epic: Odyssey
Homeric poem: iliad
Homer's dad: Abe
Homer's instrument: lyre
Homer's penultimate letter: psi
Homes, humble: cabins,
Homes in the sticks: nests
Homes, part of: Huron, Ontario, Mich., Erie, Superior
Homesteader: nester
Homework assignment: report
Homily: sermon
Homo Sapiens: man
Homophone for Edie: Idi
Homophone for seize: sees
Homophone for urn: ern
Homophones of dues: dews
Honcho: kingpin, boss, VIP
Honda rival: Yamaha
Honduras river: Ulua
Hone a razor: strop
Hones: whets, sharpens, edges
Honest: frank, upfront
Honest fellow: Abe
Honest-to-goodness: real, really
Honey badger: ratel
Honey bug: bee
Honey drink: mead

Honey factory: bee hive, apiary
Honey source: nectar
Honey tongued: suave
Honeybee genus: apis
Honeycomb: wax
Honeycomb unit: cell
Honeymoon spot: Niagara
Honeysuckle: vine
Hong Kong home: sampan, junk
Hong Kong illness: flu
Hong Kong port: Macao
Honker, barnyard: goose
Honker, little: gosling
Honky-tonk: dive, joint, hangout, juke, joint, tavern
Honor: fete, esteem
Honor, badge of
Honor: code of, maid of
Honor in style: fete
Honor, Italian style: onore
Honor society letters: phi
Honor with insults: roast
Honor, word of: oath
Honorable: noble
Honoraria: fees
Honorarium: fee
Honorary law deg.: LLD
Honored: feted
Honored one: laureate
Honored with entertainment: feted
Honshu mecca: Ise
Honshu port: Osaka
Honshu shrine center: Ise
Honshu volcano: Fuji
Hooch holder: flask
Hooded Cape: Anabata
Hooded cloak: domino
Hoodlum: yob, yobbo, criminal, gangster, vandal
Hood's Allan-adale
Hood's (Robin) missile: arrow
Hoodwink: gull, deceive, dupe, trick
Hook, fishing: gaff
Hook up with: meet
Hooker's helper: snell, smee
Hook-like parts: unci, uncus
Hooky player: truant
Hool, Moe Dee: rapper
Hoop or stud: earring
Hoople, Maj. Amos
Hoople expletive: egad
Hoops nickname: Shaq
Hoops place: lobe
Hooray for me: ta da
Hooray for one: ta da
Hoosegow: jail, pokey, can
Hoosegow, London: Gaol
Hoosier poet: Wm. Riley
Hoosier state: Indiana
Hootenanny participant: gal
Hoover Dam lake: Mead
"Hop aboard": get on
Hop, skip, jump: verbs
Hope, Bob sponsor: USO

Hope they meet: ends
Hopeless: goner
Hopeless case: goner
Hopelessly bad: abysmal
Hopi dolls: kachinas
Hopi prayer stick: baho
Hopped on: boarded
Hoppers: bins
Hopping mad: livid, fuming
Hops hot spot: oast
Horace "hence": ergo
Horace's poetry: odes
Horae, on of the: Irene
Horas, twenty-four: dia
Horatian work: ode,
Horde: legion, mob, army
Hordeolum: stye
Horizon, above the: risen
Horizon, like the: far, afar
Horizon, maybe: vista
Horizontal support: beam
Hormone producer: gland
Horn, English: cor
Horn, loud: klaxon
Horne, Marilyn: mezzo-soprano
Horned beast: rhino
Horned viper: asp
Hornless cattle: angus
Horny, pref.: kerato
Horoscope, do a: cast
Horrible: grisly
Horror, fills with: appals
Horror film extras: ghouls
Horror film servant: Igor
Horror film street: Elm
Horror, first name of: Lon
Horror flick extras: ghouls
King of horror: Stephen
Horror struck: aghast
Hors d'oeuvres: canape, morsel, appetizer
Hors d'oeuvres, classy: caviar
Horse: cayuse
Horse and buggy user: Amish
Horse, calico: pinto
Horse collar parts: hames
Horse color: dun, dapple gray
Horse, farm: dobbin
Horse, dappled: piebald
Horse drawn cab: hansom
Horse drawn carriage: surry
Horse halter: whoa
Horse handlers: grooms
Horse head: nebula
Horse home: stable
Horse laugh: guffaw
Horse opera: Oater (western movie)
Horse power, add: soup up
Horse race: derby
Horse race position: gate
Horse, reddish: sorrel
Horse, saddle: morgan
Horse shoe part: calk
Horse shoe score: ringer, leaner
Horse shoes, play: toss

Horse, speedy: Arabian
Horse, spirited: steed
Horse, stocky: cob
Horse, thick-set: cob
Horse, warrior's: steed
Horse whip: flog
Horse, wild: bronc, branco
Horse with no wins: maiden
Horseback, on: riding, astride
Horsefeathers: baloney
Horse-drawn carriage: surry, hansom
Horseman's pedal problem: stirrup inertia
Horsemanship school: manege
Horse-racing prize: purse
Horses: equine
Horse's ankle: hock
Horse's family tree: pedigree
Horse's gait: trot, lope
Horses, saddle: mounts
Horses, strutting: prancers
Horseshoer's tool: rasp
Horticulture art: bonsai
Horus's father: Osiris
         mother: Isis
Hose fasteners: garters
Hose holder: garter belt, reel
Hosiery hue: ecru,taupe
Hosiery materials: lisle
Hosiery thread: lisle
Hospital area, critical: ICU
Hospital solution: saline
Hospital unit: bed, ward
Host proposal: toast
Host, Valhalla: Odin
Host with a book club: Oprah
Hostage holder: captor
Hosted the party: treated
Hostel visitors: youths
Hostelry, first name in: Leona
Hostess cake product: Ho Ho
Hostess, famous: Perle Mesta
Hostile armies: foes
Hostile country: enemy
Hostile to: anti
Hostilities, armed: war
Hostilities, lessening: détente
Hot air in Spain: solano
Hot and humid: sultry
Hot and sticky: sweaty, humid
Hot cereal: Farina
Hot crime: arson
Hot desert wind: simoom
Hot dish base: trivet
Hot dish holder: trivet
Hot dog part: skin
Hot dog topping, briefly: kraut
Hot drink: toddy
Hot fudge: sundae
Hot, perhaps: stolen
Hot place to relax: sauna
Hot plate coils: elements
Hot pepper: Tabasco
Hot rods, like some: souped-up
Hot rum drink: grog

Hot rum mixture: grog
Hot sauce: Tabasco
Hot spiced wine: wassail
Hot springs: spa
Hot time in Quebec: été
Hot tub: sauna
Hot tub inlets: jets
Hot tub wood: cedar
Hot under the collar: angry, irate
Hotel accommodations: suites
Hotel employee: valet
Hotel feature, modern: atria
Hotel guest: patron
Hotel lobbies: atria, atrium
Hotel no no: pets
Hotel, quaint: inn
Hotel room, get one: check in
Hotel room opener: key card
Hotel, run-down: fleabag
Hotels, small: inns
Hotfoot it: hie
Hotfoots it: hies
Hothouse cold item: frame
Hot-humid: torrid
Houdini, Harry: escape artist
Hound, sad-faced: basset
Hound's track: scent, odor
Hound's trail: odor, scent
"Like a House Afire"
House annex: garage
House boat: barge
House boat, Shanghai: sampan
House cat perch: sill
House, clean: vacuum, dust
House clearing event: yard sale, garage, sale
House member: Rep., Dem.
"At the House of Chez"
House prefix: ware
House starter: ware
House, summer: gazebo
House, Tijuana: casa
House, upper: Senate
House with a smoke hole: tepee
Houseboat: barge
Houseboat, Shanghai: sampan
Housed troops: billeted
Household: menage
Household god: Lar, Penate
Household member: pet
Household spirit: lar
Housing: shelter
Housing agency: FHA
Housing, inexpensive: Prefab
Housing org.: NHA
Houston Colt 45, today: Astro
Houston Space Center: Johnson
How madmen run: amok
How sardines are packed: in oil
How some are taken: aback
"How stupid of me": duh
How-to book: manual
Howard Hugh's old airline: TWA
Howard, Ken: actor
Howe, Elias: inventor

Howe, to Washington: foe
However: thou, but
Howled: ululated
Howser, Doogie, M.D.
Hoya, Oscar De La: boxer
Hoyle, Edmond: card game authority
Hreidmar's son: Otter
Hubbard's dog had, what: none
Hubbies: men
Hubble, Edwin: astronomer
Hubbub, major: tumult
Hubbubs: ado(s)
Huck Finn creator: Twain
Huck Finn's transport: raft
Huckster's cure-all: snake oils
Hudson (Henry) boat: Half Moon
Hudson Highway, scenic: Storm King
Hudson River fish: shad
Hudson River town: Saratoga
Hudson's guzzle, what: gas
Hue and cry: clamor
Hue, soft: pastel
Huff and puff: gasp, pant
Huff, Kabba the
Huff, In a: irate
Huffman, Dustin: actor
Hug companion: kiss
Huge creature: behemoth, giant
Hugh numbers: myriads
Hugh volume: tome
Hughes, Langston: writer
Hughes, Ted: poet
Hugo contemporary: Dumas
Hugo, Victor: writer
Huitres: oysters
Hula accompaniment: uke
Hula dance fete: luau
Hulking: large
Hulking herbivore: hippo
Hulks pump: iron
Hull bottom: keel
Hull edge: gunwale
Hull, fill the: lade
Hull part: keel
Hull plank: wale
Hull sealant: tar
Hull's bottom:bilge
Hum: whir, lilt
Human being: Adamite
Human eater: ogre
Human herbivore: vegan
Part human, part machine: bionic
Human trunk: torso
Humane org.: SPCA
Humane Society goal: adoptions
Humanoid, hairy: yeti
Humanoid Hobbit foes: Orcs
Humans: bipeds
Humble: demean, menial
Humble homes: cabins
Humbled, meal for the: crow
Humbled, was: ate crow
Humbly apologizes: eats crow
Humboldt city: Elko

Humbolt Bay city, California: Eureka
Humdinger: lulu
Humdrum: blah
Hume, Cronyn: actor
Humidity problem: mildew
Humidor content: cigar
Humiliate: abase
Hummed: ironed, whirred
Hummus holders: pita
Hummus source:chickpea
Humor, coarse: ribald
Humor, hayseed: corn
Humor, like some: wry
Humor, kind of: dry
Humor, perhaps: lie
Humorous, dryly: wry
Humorous play: farce
Humorously: in jest
Humorously sarcastic: ironic
Hums happily: lilts
Hun king: Atli
Hun leader: Attila
Hunan, keemun, etc.: teas
Hunch have a: sense, intuit, feel
Hundred, comb. form:centi, hecto
Hundred smackers: C spot
Hundred weight: CWT
Hung fire: pended
Hung in the sun: aired
Hung onto: kept, held
Hungarian sheepdog: puli
Hunger strike, take part in a: fast
Hungry for more: avid
Hungry in London: leer
Hungry man's slice: slab
Hungry, probably: unfed
Hunk, big: slab
Hunker down: crouch
Hunkers: squats
Hunky-dory: AOK, okay, swell
Hunt, Linda: actress
Hunt and peck error: typo
Hunt for food: prey
Hunt goddess: Diana
Hunt illegally: poach
Hunter: Nimrod
Hunter constellation: Orion
Hunter, Evan: author, writer
Hunter, Tad: actor
Hunter of myth: Orion
Hunter's garb: camo
Hunter's quarry: game
Hunter's trail: spoor
Hunter's wear: camo
Hunting down: tracing, trailing
Hunting gun, long-barreled: roers
Hunting trip: safari
Huntington, Aisne: sculptor
Huntley, Chet:t.v. news
Hupmobile contemporary: REO
Hurl forth: spew
Hurok, Sol: impresario
Hurrah, shout: cheer
Hurricane courses: paths

Hurricane track: path
Hurry: dash
Hurry, in a: fast
Hurry, really: fly
Hurry, to a hausfrau: eilen
Hurry up: hie
Hurst, Fannie: author (Back Street)
Husband, first: Adam
Husband or wife: mate
Hush, as a voice: low
Hush-hush: secret
Hush-hush org.: CIA
Husks: hulls, pods
Husky vehicle: sled
Husky-voiced: hoarse
Hussein, Saddam: Iraq leader
Hut, kind of: thatched
Hutches: pens, cages
Hutchison, Kay: Texas senator
Hutt, Jabba the
Hutton, Lauren: actress, model
Hutton, Ray: INA
Huxtable, Ada: critic
Hybrid garment: skort
Hybrids: crosses
Hydraulic device: ram, jack, lift, pump, brake,
    press, elevator
Hydrocarbon suffix: ene
Hydrogen, (heavy) discoverer: urey
Hydrogen number: one
Hydro-massage facility: spa
Hydro project: dam
Hydrometer scale: brix, baume
Hydrox rival: Oreo
Hydroxlycarbon compound: enol
Hyena's kin: Aardwolf
Hymn of joy: paean
Hymn of praise: paean
Hymn of thanksgiving: te deum, paean
Hyperion's daughter: Eos
        father: Uranus
        mother: Gaea
        sons: Aurora, Selene, Helios
        wife: Theia
Hyphen kin: dash
Hypnotic condition: trance
Hypnotic state: trance
Hypnotist of fiction, evil: Svengali
Hypnotized: under
Hypocritical greeter: glad hander
Hypodermic needle amt.: CCs
Hypothesize: posit
Hypothetical physics particle: quark
Hypothetical protein model: biogen,
    biogenesis
Hysterical fear: panic

I

"I am", to Caesar: sum
"I came" to Caesar: veni
"As if I cared"
"I don't buy that": get real, likely story

"I don't mind at all"
I don't think so: uh uh
I. E. means:idest
"I get it": oho, eureka
"I had no idea"
"I knew it": aha
What "I" is: vowel
"I Robot" writer: Asimov
"I Say old chap"
"I think therefore I am"
"I" to Nero: ego
"I" to Seneca: ego
"I" trouble: egoism
"I wouldn't bet on that"
Iacocca, Lee: auto CEO
Sam I Am
I am so bored: ho hum
Iago's wife: Emilia
Ian, Janis: songwriter
Ibex's peak: alp
Ibis milieu: Nile
Ibis relative: heron, stork
Ibis-headed god: Thoth
IBM competitor: NEC
Ibsen character: Ase
Ibsen, Henrik: dramatist
Ibsen hero: Gynt
Ibsen heroine: Nora
Ibsen's Hedda: Gabler
Ibsen's home: Oslo
Icahn, Carl: financier
Ican treasure: oro (gold)
Icarus, emulate: fly
Ice and rice: solids
Ice burg: Nome
Ice, coating of: rime
Ice, covered with: rimy, rime
Ice cream cone, like an: conical
Ice cream drink: float
Ice cream, fudgy: ripple
Ice cream nut: pecan.
Ice cream serving: dip, cone
Ice crystals: frost
Ice holder: chest
Ice house: igloo
Ice mass:- floe
Ice melter: sun, NaCl, salt
Ice pellets: hail
Ice sheet: floe
Ice, without: straight, neat
Iceboat feature: sail
Iced drink: tea, ade
Ice-fishing need: hole, reel, rod, spear
Ice-free seas: open water
Icelandic literary works: Edda
Icelandic monetary unit: eyrir
Icelandic myth collection: Edda
Icelandic opus: Edda
Icelandic poetry collection: Edda
Icelandic tale: Edda
Icelandic writing: Edda
Ice-T music: rap
Ichabod Crane's beloved: Katrina
ICI on Parle Français

Icing, thin: glaze
Icon: symbol
ICU figures: RNs
Icy burg: Nome
Icy coating: rimes
Icy crystals: rimes
Icy downpour: sleet
Icy remark: brr
Icy treat: snow cone
"I'd rather not": nah
Idaho college town: Boise
Idea, main: gist,
Ideal place: utopia
Idee fixe
Identical: alike
Id companion: ego
ID, kind of: photo, badge
Id's counterpart: ego
Identifies: pegs
Identify a caller: trace
Identify, slangily: peg
Idiot savant: offensive term
Idiotic: daft, stupid
Iditarod terminus: nome
Iditarod vehicle: sled
Idle, be: sit
Idol: Baal
Idol, Billy: singer
Idyllic pasture: lea
Idyllic spot: Eden
If it ain't this, don't fix it: broke
If not: else
"If Roast Beef Could Fly" author: Leno (Jay)
Iffy attempt: stab
Igloo dweller: Inuit, Eskimo
Igneous rock: basalt
Ignorance, avoid: learn
Ignorant: unaware
Ignorant, less: sager
Ignore a diet: eat
Ignores, rudely: snubs
Ignores the trash can: litters
Iguana: lizard
IKEA began, where: Sweden
Ike Clanton's foe: Earp
Ike's command: ETO
Ike's one-time wife: Tina
Ile du Diable
Iliad author: Homes, Homer
Iliad deity: Ares
Iliad locale: Troy
Iliad poet: Homer
Iliad warrior: Ajax
Ilk: sort, each, kind
"I'll take your dffer": deal
Ill-advised: rash, brash, hasty, madcap
Illampu locale: andes
Ill-behaved: bratty
Ill-boding, most: direst
Illegal drinking place: adda
Illegal firing?: arson
Illegal lending: usury
Illegal, make: ban
Illegitimate income, source of: scam

Ill-fated: tragic
Ill-favored: ugly, plain, homely
Ill-humor: spleen
Ill-humored: dour, sour, cross, surly
Illinois enemy: Osage
Ill-mannered one: oaf
Ill-natured: nasty, mean
"Illness as Metaphor" writer: Sontag
Ill-suited: unfit
Ill-tempered one: tartar
Illuminated naturally: sunlit
Illumination, in Berlin: licht
Illumination unit: phot
Ilus' father: Tros
        grandson: Priam
        mother: Callirrhoe
        son: Laomedon
Illusion, kind of: optical
Illusory display: op art
Illusory painting: op art
Illustrated material: art
Illustration of a moral: object lesson
Illustrious: famed
I'm so bored: ho hum
Image: icon
Image receiver: retina, film
Imagination, without: aridly
Imaret: inn
Imbibe slowly: sip
Imelda's addiction: shoes
Imitation: faux, mimicry
Imitator: mimicer, mimer
Immature: callow
Immature newt: eft
Immature raptor: owlet, eaglet
Immeasurable time: eon
Immediate successor: heir
Immediately following: next, right after
Immense: vast, huge
Immerse: soak
Immerse briefly: dip
Immerse for cleansing: bathe
Immigration factor: quota
Imminent(be): impend
Immobile, cause to be: stun
Immodest: brazen
Immodest look: leer,
Immune, make: vaccinate
Immunologist's concern: antigen
Impact, sign of: dent
Impact, sudden: jolt
Impaneled one: juror
Impart: instill
Impart information: cues one in
Impart knowledge: educate
Impassive: stolid
Impatient, be: snap
Impatient cluck: tsk
Impatient one's query: when
Impediment: bar
Impelling action: urge
Impend: loom
Imperfection: flaw
Imperial officer: palatine

Imperial or parkay: oleo
Imperial sovereignty: empire
Impermeable substance: caulking
Impersonator's work: apery
Impertinent, be: sass
Impertinent person: snit
Impervious to light: opaque
Implore: prae, plea, beg, pray
Implored: pled
Impolite sound: burp
Import duties: tariff
Importance, dropped in: paled
Importance, first in: primary
Important decades: eras
Important, decisively: fateful
Important, is: matters
Important, most: paramount, key
Important period of history: era
Importune: ply
Impose a tax: assess
Impose on: use
Imposing residences: villas, manor, estate
Impossible to understand: clear as mud
Imposter: faker,
Impractical: mad
Impregnable: secure
Impresario Hurok: Sol
Impress: wow
Impress deeply: awe
Impresses: awes
Impressing grouping: array
Impression, give the: seem
Impression, make a lasting:
Impressionist's skills: apery
Impressions, creator of: aper
Impressive organization: array,
Imprints firmly: etches
Imprison: immure, confine
Imprisonment: durance
Imprisonment, reason for, once: debt
Improbable wish: dream
Impromptu: ad lib
Impromptu jazz performance: jam session
Improper, slightly: racy
Improve, as skill: hone
Improve by editing: emend
Improve by experience: season
Improve with age: mellow
Improvise: ad-lib, wing it
Improvise musically: vamp
Imprudent decision: unwise
Impudent: brash
Impudent, more: sassier
Impudence: gall, audacity
Impulse: urge
Impulse, natural: urge
Impulse transmitter: axon
Impulsive: rash
Impulsive, too rash
Imus, Don: tv, radio
In a blunt manner: starkly
In a chair: seated
In a cheerful mode: jovial
In a contemptible manner: meanly

In a cordial way: warmly
In a dither: agog
In a fitting manner: duly
In a fog: dazed
In a foul mood: sour
In a frenzy: amok
In a huff: piqued, irate
In a hurry: fast
In a lather: soapy
In a little while: anon
In a masterful manner: adeptly
In a row: linear
In a sluggish way: idly
In a snit: mad
In a tangle: afoul
In a tizzy: agog
In a while: anon
In addition: too, also, and
In alignment: true
"In and of itself"
In any case: at least
In any event: rain or shine
In between: limbo
"In-box" contents: Emails
In business now: open
In case: lest
In conclusion: thus
In dire need of gas: empty
In disagreement: at odds
In disorder: messy
In disposed: ill
In due time: anon
In fine fettle: well
In force: valid
In full: idest
In full view: overt
In good order: neat
In good working order: useable
In great shape: trim, fit
In isolation: alone
In it for the money: pro
In jig time
In lieu of
In medias res
In no time: soon
In nothing flat: pronto
In perpetuity: ever
In place of: for
In profusion: galore
In progress: begun
In question: at issue
In regard to: anent
In reserve: aside, apart
In search of: after
In situ: as found
In that case: if so
In that place: therein
In the altogether: bare
In the ballpark: close
In the cellar: last
In the country: rural
In the course of: amid
In the dark: unaware
In the direction of: toward

In the file: on record
In the flesh: nude
In the head: mental
In the know: hip, aware
In the lead: ahead, winning
In the least: at all
In the main: mostly
In the manner of: ala
In the open: overt
In the proper manner: duly
In the raw: nude, bare
In the same manner: alike
In the same place: ibid, ibidem
In the slightest degree: at all
In the short time: anon
In the wake of: after, behind
In the wrong way: badly
In theory: ideally
In unison: as one
In vain: futile
In vino veritas
In vogue: mod
In what manner: how
In what way: how
In whatever way: how
Inaction: stasis
Inactivity, period of: calm
Inadvertent mistake: slip
Inadvisable action: no no
Inamorata, inamorato: beau, dear, flame,
    honey, lover, steady
Inane: dumb, silly, empty
Inattentive, utterly: out to lunch
Inaugural words: oaths
Inaugurate: open, start
Inauguration: open
Inauguration highlight: oath
Inca country: Peru,
Inca empire, once: Peru
Incan treasure: oro(gold)
Incantation: spell,
Incapacitate: hog-tie
Incendiarism: arson
Incense burner: censer
Incense-producing resin: myrrh
Inch along: creep
Inch forward: ease
Inch fractions: mils
Inch multiplier: feet
Incisive remark: mot
Incite: sic, egg on
Inclination: trend
Inclination, strong: yen
Incline: ramp
Incline to one side: list
Incognita, terraIncome, provide with: endow
Income source: job
Incomplete: sketchy
Icon, sluggishness: snail
Inconclusive, as a jury: hung
Incongruities, some: ironies
Inconsequential amount: iota
Inconsistent quality, of: iffy
Incorrect (pref.): mis

Increase sharply: soar
Increase, sudden: surge
Incriminating information: dirt
Incumbent, beat a: unseat
Indecent: lewd
Indecision, show: shrug
Indefinite number: some, few, many
Indefinite person: anyone, any body
Indefinite response: perhaps
Indehiscent fruit: key, nut, pepo, berry, grain,
    grape, melon, achene, loment, samara
Indent key: tab
India alkalies:REHS
India attire: sari
India flatbread: chapati
India ink
India master: sahib
India Mr.: sri
India Mystic: fakir
India (northwest) native: Punjabi
India nurse: ayah
India pink city: Jaipur
India prince: Raja, Rajah
India prince or king: maharaja
India region: Goa
India water vessel: lotas
India weight: ser
Indian appellation: sri
Indian attire: sari, saree
Indian bread: nan, naan, chapati
Indian bread ingredient: corn
Indian butter: ghee, ghi
Indian buzzard:Tesa
Indian, Caddoan: Pawnee
Indian chief: sachem
Indian coastal region: Malabar
Indian coin: rupee
Indian coin, old: anna
Indian corn: maize
Indian corn strain: dent
Indian drum: tabla
Indian dwelling: wigwam, tent
Indian emperor (1600): Akbar
Indian fabric, light: madras
Indian flat bread: naan
Indian food item: dal
Indian honorific: sahib
Indian instrument: sitar, vina, sarod, tabla,
    tamura
Indian language grp.: Siouan
Indian leader: Cochise
Indian lentil dish: dal
Indian memorial post: Xat
Indian menu item: dal
Indian music: raga
Indian nurse: ayah
Indian nursemaid: amah
Indian Ocean inlet: Red Sea
Indian peasant: Ryot
Indian pony: Cayuse
Indian prince: Raja, Rana, Rajah, Maharaja
Indian princess: Rani, Begum, Ranee
Indian, Quechua: Inca
Indian round bread: naan

Indian royalty: rani
Indian ruler: raja
Indian rupee, 1/100th of a: paisa
Indian shrine site: Agra
Indian social system: caste
Indian, Sonoran: SeriIndian tea: assam
Indian title of respect: pandit
Indian title of respect, once: sahib
Indian tourist city: Agra
Indian weight unit: ser, cash, pank, pice, powe, rati, tank
Indian wrap: sari
Indiana Jones quest: ark
Indians (Arizona): Papago, Apache, Pima, Hopi, Hano
Indians (Bolivian): Uro
Indians (Canadian): Cree
Indians (Dakota): Teton, Sioux, Ree, Ojibwa
Indians (Delaware): Lenape
Indians (Hudson Bay): Cree
Indians (Manitoba): Cree
Indians (Nebraska): Pawnee, Otoe
Indians (Nevada): Paiute
Indians (New York): Oneida, Seneca, Onondaga
Indians, Nez Perce
Indians (Ohio): Erie
Indians (Oklahoma): Osage, Pawnee
Indians (Plains): Otoe, Caddo, Pawnee, Comanche
Indians (Pueblo): Zuni, Hopi
Indians (Shoshonean): Ute
Indians (Sioux): Oteo, Otoe
Indians (S. American): Inca
Indians (Southwestern): Ute, Apache, Paiute
Indians, Venezuelan: Caribs
India's "Father of the Nations": Gandhi
India's Jawaharlal: Nehru
Indicate agreement: nod
Indication of approval: show of hands
Indifferent: blasé
Indifferent to ethical standards: amoral
Indifference, total: innui
Indigenous: native
Indignation, righteous: wrath
Indigo bush: dalea
Indigo dye: anil
Indigo plant: anil
Indira's father: Nehre
        son: Rajin
Indirect suggestion: hint
Indistinct: blury
Indistinct, become: blur
Indivisible numbers: primes
Individual: self, person, unique
Individualist: loner
Indo-European people member: Jat
Indolent manner, in an: glib
Indonesian island: Aru, Aroe, Arroe, Bali
Indoor missiles: darts
Induced by entreaties: urge
Inducement, stereotypical: carrot
Inductance, unit of: henry
Indulge: pander to, dote

Indulge in voguing: pose
Indulge to excess: pamper, dote
Indulgent bout: spree
Industrial gem: bort
Industrial Japanese city: Osaka
Industry magnate: Czar
"Industry" motto, state with the: Utah
Industry, plus: toil
Ineffective: otiose
Inelegant solution: kludge
Inept one, socially: nerd
Inequitable: unfair
Inescapable outcome: fate
Inescapable fate: doom
Inevitability: fate
Inexpensive cigar: stogy
Inexperienced: new, novice
Inexperienced mascot?: Green Giant
Inexperienced sailor: lubber
Infamous box: Pandora's
Infamous lady: Godiva
Infantry camp: Etape
Infer: deduce
Inferior by comparison, looks: pales
Inferior counterfeit: eratz
Inferior substitute: eratz
"Inferno" author: Dante
Inferno chronicler: Dante
Infield bounce: hop
Infield protector: tarp
Infiltrator: spy
Infinitesimal: tiny
Infirmities: ills
Inflammatory beginning: anti
Inflatable item: ego, balloon
Inflation, key factor in: air
In-flight features: meals
In-flight info.: ETA
Influence: sway
Influence, special: clout
Influenced, easily: malleable
Influences: affects
Info-gathering mission: recon
Infomercial brand, old: Ginsu
Informal: casual
Informal conversation: chat
Informal debt instrument: IOU
Informal eatery: deli
Informal guy: fella
Informal head cover: do rag
Informal language: slang
Informal luncher: brown bagger
Informal wear: tee, T-shirt
Information: data
Information agency: USIS
Information communicated: advice
Information highway: net
Information, incriminating: dirt
Information packed: newsy
Information, piece of: datum
Information, small piece: snippet
Informative: newsy
Informed about: on to
Infraction: breach

Infrequency: rareness
Infrequently: rarely, seldom
Infuse: imbue
Infuse with color: imbue
Ingénue's quality: naivete
Ingenuity: wit, skill
Inges, William: playwrite
Ingot: bar
Ingram, David: explorer
Ingredient, fundamental: basic, basis
Ingress: entry
Inhabit a house: reside
Inhabitant: dweller
Inhabitant, earliest known: Aborigine
Inhabitant, original: native
Inherent: innate
Inherent character: nature
Inheritance: dower
Inheritance factor: gene
Inheritance unit: gene
Inheritor: legatee
Iniquitous place: den
Initial contribution: ante
Initials, royal: HRH
Initiation practice: rite
Injunction, issue an: enjoin
Injure a toe: stub
Injury aftermath: scar
Injury memento: scar
Injury, minor: bruise
Injury to, cause serious: maim
Injustice: raw deal
Ink ejector: octopi
Ink partner: pen
Ink shooters: octopi, octopus
Inking pad: dabber
Inkling: clue
Inkling, have a: sense
Inland sea: Aral
Inlet, narrow: ria
Inlet, quiet: cove
Inmost part: core, pith, heart, center, depths, kernel marrow, nucleus
Inn with stout drinks: tap house
Innate: inborn, inbred
Innate skill: talent
Inner city concern: slum
Inner coating: lining
Inner core of organs: medulla
Inner-self: anima, soul
Inner-urban assn.: NUL
Innisfail: Eire
Innkeeper: hotelier
Innocent mischief, quest for: lark
Innocent, prove: clear
Innsbruck locale: Tyrol
Innsbruck's province: Tyrol
Innuendo: hint
Inoperative, completely: kaput
In-port merchandise ship: bum boat
Inquiry word: who, when, what
Inquiring sound: ehs
Inscribe indelibly: etch

Inscribed pillar: Athel
Inscribed tablet: stele
Inseam measure: length
Insect antenna: feeler
Insect colony: hive
Insect eater: toad, frog
Insect egg: nit
Insect, hairy: bee
Insect, night flying: luna moth
Insect not found in Antarctica: ants
Insect, plant-sucking: aphid
Insect resin: lac
Insect, shrill: cicada
Insect, social: ant, bee
Insect stage: imago, pupa
Insect, wood: tick
Insecticide: DDT
Insecurity, feeling of: angst
Insensitive, make: numb
Insert mark: carets
Insert pointers: carets
Inserted gores: paneled
Inserts fraudulently: foists
Inside information, bits of: tips
Insight, keen: acumen
Insight, lacking in: obtuse
Insignificant: mere
Insignificant fellow: twerp
Insignificant item: trivia
Insignificant part: iota
Insignificant person: twerp
Insignificant trifle: fico
Insincere: glib
Insinuate: hint
Insinuatingly derogatory: snide
Insist emphatically: aver
Insist upon: stipulate
Insists: avers
Insolvent, legally: bankrupt
Insomnia indicator: bags
Inspect the joint: case
Inspected surreptitiously: cased
Inspections, like some: on site
Installments: episodes
Instance: case
"Instead of" word: lieu
Instilled forcefully: drubbed, futile
Instinct, kind of: gut
Instinctive feeling: vibe
Instruction period: lesson
Instructional: how to
Instrument, angelic: harp
Instrument made from granadilla: oboe
Instrument, seven-pedal: harp
Instrument, wailing: sax
Insulation material: mica
Insulation measurement: R-value
Insult: dis
Insults, yells: jeers
Insurable event: death
Insurance claim: loss
Insurance giant: lloyds
Insurance grp: HMO
Insurance scheme: arson

Integer, least positive: unit
Integers, half the: even
Intellectually acute: keen
IQ test name: Binet
Intelligence test pioneer: Binet
Intelligible, make: clear up
Item with a thumbhole: palette
Intense, became less: ebbed
Intense desire: yen
Intense fear: dread
Intense look: stare
Intense suffering: agony
Intense training program: crash course
Intensity, with great:
ICU units: CCs
Inter alia
Interest, accrued: earned
Interest amount: PCT
Interest charges, avoid: pay in full
Interest, type of: self
Interfere: meddle
Interior courtyard: atria
Interior design: décor
Interjection, archaic: fie
Interjection of distaste: fie
Interjections, mild: ahs
Interlaced: wove
Interlacing of rope: knot
Intermediate (pref): mes
Intermediate court: appellate
IRS employee: CPA, ACCT
International agreement: entente
IBM competitor: NEC
International linear units: meters
International org.: UNESCO
International treaty, 1947: GATT
International understanding: entente
Internet fan: user
Internet hookup: modem
Internet insult: flame
Internet search engine: Yahoo
Internet suffix: org
Interpol headquarters: Lyon
Interpret: read
Interpret tea leaves: read
Interrogate: quiz
Interrupt: cut in, barge in
Interrupter's word: ahem
Interruption: gap
Intersect: meet
Intersected: met
Intersection points: nodes
Interstate division: lane
Interstate sign: gas, food
Interstellar cloud: nebula
Interstices: spaces, gaps
Interval of eight diatonic degrees: octave
Intervene: step in
Interview, kind of: exit
Intertwine: weave
Intervals of rest: respites
Intestinal fortitude: grit, guts, nerve spirit
Intestine: comb. form: ileo
Intimidate: cow

Intimidation, use: coerce
Intolerant one: racist, bigot
Intoxicating: heady
Intra-coastal waterway
Intrepid: bold
Intricate decoration: detail
Intricate tracery design: moresque
Intrinsically: per se
Intrigue: scheme, plot
Introduction: proem, lead-in
Introduction bit: prolog
Intro, dramatic: ta da
Intro, maybe: opening remarks
Intro to physics: meta
Intrusive, a bit too: nosy
Intuit: grok
Intuit knife: ulv
Intuition: vibe
Intuition, more than: ESP
Inundation, sudden: avalanche
Invalidate: void, vitiate
Invasion date: D-Day
Invasions: raids
Inveighed against: railed
Invent, as a word: coin
Invention precursor: idea
Inventive, was more: lied
Inventor's document: patent
Inventor's friend: patentor
Inventor's protection: patent
Inventor's quest: patent
Inventor's spark: idea
Inventor's specialty: idea
Inventory abbr.: mdse
Inventory, dept. Store: mdse
Inventory word: mdse
Inverness native: Scot
Inverness part: cape
Inverno month: Enero
Inversion problem: smog
Investigates deeply: delve
Investigation aids: clues,
Investigative measure: wiretap
Investment, future-minded: IRA
Investment return: yield, gain
Investor's concern: Dow
Investor's hope: gain,
Investor's insurance: hedge
Invests with a gift: endues
Invigorating: brisk
Invigorating medicine: tonic
Invisible emanation: aura
Invisible substance: gas
Invitation addendum: RSVP
Invited: bade, asked
Invoice number: amount, amt
Invoice stamp: paid
Invoke misfortune: curse
Involuntary movement: reflex
Involving risk: dicey, dangerous
Iodine source: kelp
Ion source: atom
Ionized gas: plasma
Iota: bit, jol, spot, whit

IOU note: chit, marker
Iowa commune: Amana
Ipanema person: girl
Ipanema's city: Rio
Iphicles brother: Heracles, Hercules
      mother: Alemene
      son: Iolaus
Ipso (facto) meaning: itself
IQ, informally: brains
High IQ group: Mensa
Iran, formerly: Persia
Iran religion: Bahá'í
Iranian religion: Bahá'í,
Iranian shrine city: Meshed
Iraqi port: Basra
Irascible: anger, angry, gruff
Irate: steamed
Ireland alias: Erin
Ireland island: Aran
Ireland, name for: Erin, Eire
Ireland, poet's: Erin
Ireland's Blarney Stone
Ireland's largest county: Cork
Irene's bird: dove
Iridescent jewel: opal
Iris (European): orris
Iris center: pupil
Irish: Celtic
Irish fairy folk: shee
Irish Gaelic: Erse
Irish island group: Aran
Irish mother of gods: Danu
Irish overcoat: ulster
Irish playwright: Shaw
Irish Port: Sligo,
Irish Rose's love: Abie
Irish Spring alternative: Dial
Irish sweetheart: gra
Irish tongue: Gaelic
Irish wailer: banshee
Irish writing system, old: ogam
Irksome one: gadfly
"I, Robot"writer: Asimov
Iron: press, smooth
Iron, bars of: ingot
Iron coats: rust
Iron: combo. Form: ferro
Iron for one: element
Iron hats: gossans
Iron holder: holster
Iron output: steam
Iron oxide: rust
Iron pumper's pride: abs, pecs
Iron, source of: or
Iron works: foundry
Ironic: wry
Ironical taunt: sarcasm
Ironically: wryly
Iron-rich meat: liver
Irons, Jeremy: actor
Iroquois enemies: Erie
Iroquois people: Seneca
Irrational, hardly: level-headed
Irrational motives: urges

Irregular stone foundation: rip rap
Irregularly notched: erose
Irritable, more: testier
Irritate by rubbing: chafe
Irritated, easily: testy
Irritated state: snit
Irritating nocturnal sound: snore
Irving, Amy: actress
Irving, Julius: basketball
Irving, Washington: writer
Is a groom: weds,
Is a poor loser: sulks
Is about to take place: impends
Is entitled to: earns, earned
Is for them: are
Is important: matters
Is, in Avila: esta
Is, in German: ist
Is, in Segovia: esta
Is, in Spanish: esta
Is in the running: vies
Is inclined: tends
Is of benefit: avails
Is of use: avails
Is off base: errs
Is operational: works
Is sibilantly challenged: lisps
Is situated: lies
Is the right size: fits
"Is that all right": okay
"Is that so": do tell
Is unable to: can't
Is very thrifty: ekes
Isaac's father: Abraham
      mother: Sarah
      son: Esau
      wife: Rebekah
Ishmael's captain: Ahab
      leader: Aga Kahn
      mother: Hagar
      people: Arab
Is in glass: mica
Isis' beloved: Osiris
      brother: Osiris
      father: Geb
      husband: Osiris
      mother: Nut
      son: Sept, Horus
Islam, adherents of: Moslem, Muslim
Islam holy city: Mecca
Islamic chieftain: emir
Islamic god: Allah
Islamic greeting: salaam
Islamic judge: qadi
Islamic prince (var.): Emeer
Islamic scripture: Koran
Islamic sect: Shia, Sufi, Sunni, Shiite, Sufism,
    Ismaili, Wahhabi
Islamic teacher: Mulla
Islamic unity: AIAI (Al-Itihaad al-Islamiya)
Island area: lagoon
Island attire: sarongs
Island, exotic: Bali
Island, like an: insular

Island near Corsica: Elba
Island of exile: Elba
Island of two states: Ellis
Island, off shore: cay
Island range: atolls
Island, ring-shaped: atoll
Island, romantic: Bali
Island, small: ait
Island, small, low: cay
Island strings: ukulele
Islas Malvinas: Falkland Islands
Isle of exile: Elba
Islet: ait, cay, key
Ismalli's leader: Aga Kahn
Isn't any more: was
"Isn't that a bit much"
Isolation, in: alone
Isolde's love: Tristan
Israel airline: El Al
Israel dance: hora
Israel-Jordan lake: Red Sea
Israel leader: Ehud Barak
Isreal tribe: Asher
Israeli desert: Negev
Israeli gun: uzis
Israeli native-born: Sabre, Sabra
Israeli seaport: Eilat
Israel's language: Hebrew
Issue a summons: cite
Issue an injunction: enjoin
Issue forth: emanate
Isthmus land: Panama
ISU location: Ames, Iowa
Be "it": seek
It blows off steam: geyser
It bugs people on the phone: tap
It can be carried: torch
It can be hard to swallow: pill
It can be hot: tip
It can clean our soles: mats
It can't be cloned: snowflake
It can't be grown: money tree
It closes on Sunday: amen
It could be under the kettle: trivet
It covers Congress: C-SPAN
It divides to multiply: ameba, amoeba
It does a bang-up job: TNT
It doesn't hold water: sieve
It flows past Florence: Arno
It gets the lead out: eraser
It goes overboard: anchor
It glistens: dew
It has a ball at the circus: seal
It has a low pH: acid
It has a photosphere: sun
It has an uphill battle: Coho
It has long arms: ape
It has the spirit: cask
It has two heels: loaf
It haunts the Himalayas: yeti
It holds the line: reel
It hooks big fish: gaff
It increases your dough: yeast
"It is not fair"

It lets off steam: kettle
It makes jelly jell: pectin
It makes scents: attar
It may be a king or queen: sheet, card
It may be airtight: alibi
It may be below deck: cabin
It may be cured: ham
It may be defended by a scholar: thesis
It may be found in a trunk: sap
It may be fragile: ego
It may be good or bad: karma
It may be half-baked: Idea
It may be hatched: plan
It may be humble: abode
It may be keen: eyesight
It may be light or grand: opera
It may be lost: temper
It may be on the house: lien
It may be on the range: home
It may be on the staff: clef
It may be passed from father to son: gene
It may be posted: bail
It may be pushed around": cart
It may be rattled: saber, cage
It may be read: palm
It may be rigged: mast
It may be slung: mud
It may be struck: pose, deal
It may be tapped at sea: SOS
It may be tidy: sum
It may be uncontrollable: urge
It may be upper or lower: case
It may be used for collateral: asset
It may become bald: tire
It may come in spots: tea
It may exist among thieves: honor
It may follow a dot: com, edu
It may get rattled: saber
It may lead to a suit: tort
It means everything: omni
It means image: icono, iconic
It might be enough: once
It might be framed: art
It might be true or not: rumor
It might give you chills: flu
It might threaten a king: rook
It might turn over a new leaf: rake
It needs refinement:
It often splits: amoeba
It opens many a door: knob
It pulls a bit: rein
It remains in Pandora's box: hope
It sank in Havana Harbor: Maine
It sometimes needs boosting: morale
It spreads the dough: rolling pin
It springs eternal: hope
It towers over Taormina: Etna
It underlies the finish: base coat, primer
It was once wild: West
It was raised by Paul Revere: alarm
It works according to scale: map
Italian abode: villa
Italian auto: Fiat, Lancia, Ferrari, Maserati,
    Alfa Romeo, Lamborghini

Italian Avenues: promenades
Italian cheese: Asiago
Italian cooking tomato: roma
Italian bowling game: bocci, boccie, bocce
Italian desert: spumoni
Italian family, princely: este
Italian farewell: addi
Italian hero ingredient: genoa salami
Italian hot spot: Etna
Italian island: Elba, Capri, Ischia, Lipari,
    Sicily, Aeolian, Capraia
Italian lady: donna, signora, signorina
Italian leader: duce
Italian marble city: Carrara
Italian menu word: alla
Italian 'milk': latte
Italian mountain range: Alps, Etna
Italian noble: conte
Italian noble family: Este
Italian noble surname: Este
Italian or spaniard: Latino
Italian "our": nostra
Italian palace city: Asolo
Italian party: festa
Italian physicist: Volta
Italian pockets: Tascas
Princely Italian family: Este
Italian resort: lido, Abano, Capri, Sorrento
Italian road: strada
Italian romance: amore
Italian sendoff: ciao
Italian skies: cieli
Italian smoker: Etna
Italian sonnet's coda: sestet
Italian specialty: pasta
Italian staple: pasta
Italian "stop it": basta
Italian street: via, corso
Italian town, literary: Eboli
Italian verse form: terze, rima
Italian weight: libra, oncia
Italian wine center: Asti
Italian wine city: Asti
Italian wine, dry: Soave
Italian wines: Soaves
Italian woman of rank: donna
Italian writer: Eco
Italic feature: slant
Itches: yens
Itchy skin problem: tinea (ringworm)
Itea: willow
Items in black: assets
Items of business: agenda
Items of property: assets
Items on an actor's resume: roles
Items to be attended to: agenda
Ithaca king: Odysseus
Ithamar's father: Aaron
Itinerary word: via
Ito, lance: judge
It's a moneymaker: mint
It's a positive thing: anode
It's a wrap: saran
It's academic: moot point

It's always below par: birdie, eagle
It's among thieves, in proverb: honor
"It's an ill wind"
Its banks are liquid: Wabash
It's before a landing: riser, step
It's better than sorry: safe
It's blood runs cold: reptile
It's below the mantle: core
It's capital is Beauvais: Oise
It's cut and dried: hay
It's days are numbered: calendar
It's definitely not good: evil
Its first is for fools: April
It's for suckers: straw
It's for two, in song: tea
It's good to meet them: needs
It's hung out to dry: wash
It's icon is a lightbulb: idea
It's in development: embryo
It's kept by a keeper: inn
It's left of zero: star
It's legally wrong: tort
It's motto is "Industry": Utah
It's never in neutral: ion
It's no soft serve: ace
It's north of Java: Borneo
It's not a sure thing: gamble
It's not nice to fool her: Mother Nature
It's not to one's credit: debit
It's often raised: havoc
It's often smashed: atom
It's on an embarrassed face: egg
It's pressed for cash: ATM
It's raised on a farm: silo
It's read at the table: menu
It's seen in anger: red
It's sometimes certified: mail
Its sweet on sweets: icing
It's taken while waiting: order
Itty bitty: teensy
Iturbi, Jose: conductor
Ivan's tea kettle: samovar
Ivanov, Lev: Russian dancer
"I've Gotta Be Me"
Investor's site: AMEX
Ivey, Judith: actress
Ivory: off-white
Ivory Coast gulf: Guinea
Ivy clump: tod
Izmir people: Turks

J

Jabber: pratt
Jabber away: natter
Jack, in cards: knave
Jack London's setting: Yukon
Jack, no-fat: Sprat
Jackanapes: ape, brat, fool, monkey
Jacket, double-breasted: reefer
Jacket, goose downed: parka
Jacket, hooded: parka, anorak
Jacket, kind of: mao, pea, nehru

Jacket, like some: tweedy, suede
Jacket part: peplum
Jacket, short: eton, bolero, reefer, nehru
Jacket, sports: balzier
Jacket top: hood
Jacket, waist-length: eton
Jacket, winter: parka,
Jackie's second: Ari Onassis
Jackpot games: lottos
Jackson Hole backdrop: Tetons
Jackson, Kate: music
Jackson, Samuel: actor
Jacob, Irene: actress
Jacob's brother: Esau(twin)
     brother:in-law: Laban
     father: Isaac
     son: Asher, Aser, Gad, Judah
     twin: Esau
     wife: Leah, Rachel
Jacoby, Oswald: bridge
Jacques Chirac's world: monde
Jacques in song: Brere, Frere
Jacque's pal: ami(French)
Jade: cloy, sate
Jade worker: carver
Jaffa dance: hora
Jaffe, Rona: writer
Jag: rip
Jagged edge: erose
Jagged rock: crag
Jagger, mick: music
Jaguar cousin: ocelot
Jaguar's prey: tapir
Jahan was one: shah
Jai, alai: pelota
Jaipur princes: Rani
Jalopy: heap
Jam ingredient: cars
Jam in tightly: cram, wedge
Jam or pickle: mess,
Jamaican dance: reggae
Jamaican drink: rum
Jamaican dude: mon
Jamaican export: rum
Jamaican music: reggae, ska
Jambalaya, e.g.: stew
Jambalaya item: prawns
James Bond, like: suave
James, Etta: soul singer
James, P. D.: writer
James's brother: John, Jesus, Joses
     cousin: Jesus
     father: Zebedee
     mother: Mary, Salome
James Joyce novel: Exiles, Ulysses
Jamie Lee's mom: Rita
Jammed: wedged
Jammed together: dense
Jane Austen title: Emma
Jane, to Tarzan: mate
Janeway, Eliot: economist
Janeway's, Captain, ship: Voyager
Jangles: clangs
Janis, Ian: music

Janitor's need: keys, mop, pail, rag
Jannings, Emil: actor
Janowitz, Tama: writer
January birthstone: garnet
Japan: Nippon
Japan Buddhism: Zen
Japan capital, once: Kyoto
Japan "Temple City": Kyoto
Japanese aborigine (native): Ainu
Japanese American, first generation: issei
     second generation: nisei, sansei
Japanese appetizer: sushi
Japanese apricot: ume, umeboshi
Japanese bed: futon,
Japanese capital until 1868: Kyoto
Japanese cartoons: anime
Japanese cedar: sugi
Japanese celery: udo
Japanese tea ceremony
Japanese city, industrial: Osaka
Japanese clog: geta
Japanese coin: yen
Japanese consort: geisha
Japanese dance-drama: Noh
Japanese delicacy: eel
Japanese diver: ama
Japanese dog: akita
Japanese drama: Kabuki, Noh
Japanese entertainer: geisha
Japanese feudal lords: daimios
Japanese feudal warrior: samurai
Japanese flower arranging art: ikebana
Japanese floor mat: tatami
Japanese fry pan: ros
Japanese gateway: torii
Japanese honorific: san
Japanese island: Bonin
Japanese legislature: diet
Japanese martial arts: kendo
Japanese mat: tatami
Japanese menu veggie: udo, urd
Japanese mercenary: ninja
Japanese money: yen
Japanese mushroom: enoki
Japanese national park: Aso
Japanese painter: Kano Tanyu
Japanese pearl diver: ama
Japanese salad plant: udo
Japanese soup: miso
Japanese religion: Shinto
Japanese reply: ah so
Japanese robe: kimono
Japanese soup: miso
Japanese straw mat: tatami
Japanese tea ceremony
Japanese teahouse mat: tatami
Japanese Temple City: Kyoto, Nagano
Japanese tender: yen
Japanese theater: Kabuki, Noh
Japanese title: san,
Japanese verse: haiku
Japanese volcano: Fuji
Japanese warrior: samurai
Japanese "yes": hai

Japan's divine emperor: Tenno
Jar, cookie
Jar, mouthy: olla
Jargon: argot, cant, patois
Jarrett, Ned: NASCAR
Jarring to the eyes: harsh
Jarvik creation: artificial heart
Jason's ship: Argo
Jason's vessel: Argo
Jason's wife: Media, Tedea
Jauntier: perkier
Jaunty and stylish: pert
Jaunty hat: beret, tam
Jaunty lid: tam, beret
Jaunty rhythm: lilt
Java, it's north of: Borneo
Jawaharlal, India's: Nehru
Jaws of menace: shark
Jazz and rap: malay
Jazz, early: bop
Jazz, first name in: Ella
Jazz form: bebop
Jazz genre: bop
Jazz instrument: sax
Jazz melody:riff
Jazz performance, impromptu: jam, session
Jazz player: kid ory
Jazz style: bop, bebop
"Jazz's" home: Utah
Jazzy job: gig
Jazzy refrain: riff
Je ne sais quoi
Jealous olympian: Hera
Jeannie portrayer: Eden, Barbara
Jeans name: Levi
Jedi Ally: Ewok
Jedi Ally, furry: Ewok
Jedi knight trainer: Yoda
Jedi master: Yoda
Jeer at: gibe, heckle
Jekyll's alter ego: Hyde
Jekyll's servant: Poole
Jello ring: mold
Jells: thickens, sets
Jelly fish: medusa
Jelly, meat, tomato: aspic
Jelly thickener: pectin
Jelly, used to make: pectin
Jellystone bear: Yogi
Jellystone denizen: Yogi Bear
"Jeptha's Vow" painter: Opie
Jerk, involuntary: spasm
Jerk the knee: react
Jerk, type of: knee
Jerked away: shied
Jerking away: shying
Jerks up and down: bobs
Jerry-built: shoddy, shoddily
Jet forth: spurt
Jet route: lane
Jet set: elite
Jethro Tull
Jets, they may be filled with: spas
Jet-set jets: Lear, SST

Jet-setter's need: Visa
Jetson boy: Elroy
Jetson dog: Astro
Jett, Joan: rock music
Jetty: pier, quay
Jewel of the Nile
Jeweler's magnifier: loupe
Jewelry box: chest
Jewelry, fake: glass, paste
Jewelry mineral: zircon
Jewett, Sarah Orne
Jewish ceremonial: seder
Jewish feast: seder
Jewish folklore figures: golems
Jewish month: Adar
Jewish month after Adar: Nisan
Jewish mourning period: Saiva
Jewish mystic, ancient: Essene
Jewish prayer: kaddish, Aleinu
Jewish scripture: Torah
Jewish teacher: rabbi
Jewish title of honor: Gaons
Jezebel's spouse: Ahab
JFK carrier: TWA
JFK site: "LST"
Jiffy: sec
Jigger: tot
Jigsaw puzzle, did a: pieced
Jigsaw puzzle, doing a: piecing
Jillian, Ann: actress
Jim Baker org.: PTL
Jimmy Carter's home: Plains, Ga.
Jimmy, apply a: pry
Jingle: poem
Jipijapa hat: Panama
Jitters, experiencing: edgy
Jo's sister: Amy, Beth
Job benefit: perk
Job description, colorful: blue collar
Job, entry level
Job for a thief: heist
Job, hold down a: earn
Job holder: earner
Job hunter: drifter
Job, more than a: career
Job, out of a: fired, idle
Job particular, briefly: spec.
Job seeker's hope: offer
Jobs creates them: Apples, Macs
Job's daughter: Keziah, Jemimah
      father: Issachar,
      friend: Bildad, Zophar, Eliphaz
Jockeys:
    Arcaro, Eddie
    Shoemaker, Willie
Jockey brakes: reins
Jockey, kind of:disc
Jockey, often: loser
Joel, Billy: music
Joey: dee
Joey's mom: kangaroo
Johan was one: shah
Johanna Sebastian Bach
John Dickerson Carr

JFK carrier: TWA
JFK site: "LST"
John, in Aberdeen: Ian
John, in Ireland: Sean
John, in Russia: Ivan
John Irving: protagonist
John starter: Demi
John, Welsh form of: Evan
Johnnycake: pone
Johnny Reb
Johnson, Artie: comic
Johnson, Ben: writer
Johnson, Don: actor
Johnson, Lyndon B.: president
Johnson, Osa Helen: explorer
Johnson, Samuel: lexicographer
Joie de vivre: elan
Join film: splice
Join forces: allied
Join on: add
Joined by a treaty: allied
Joining sound tape: splicing
Joins in: adds
Joint, low: knee
Joint, seedy: dive
Joint, shabby: dive
Joint shape: tee
Joint, troublesome: knee
Joist: beam
Jokang temple site: Lhasa
Joke: yuk
Joke, as a: in fun
Joke response: ha ha
Joke, tell a: regale
Jokesters: wags
Jolie, Angelina: actress
Jollity: fun
Jolly Roger: flag, ensign
Jolly Roger's part: skull
Jolt: zap
Jon Bon Jovi: music
Jonathan: apple
Jonathan Swift works: satires
Jones, Catherine Zeta
Davy Jones's Locker
Jones, Indiana, quest: ark
Jones of the Deep: Davy
Jones, Quincy: music
Jones, Tom: fiction
Jong, Erica: writer, feminist
Jongg, Mah
Jonson, Ben works: odes
Joplin's music: rag
Jordan River terminus: Dead Sea
Jorge's mouth: Boca
Jo's sister: Amy, Beth
Josh: rib, kid
Joss stick: incense
Jostles: pushes
Jot in a log: note, notate
Jottings: notes
Joule fraction: erg
Journal item: entry
Journal, online: blog

Journey, begin a: set forth
Journey, continue a: push on
Journey, embark on a: set out
Journey for the self-centered: ego trip
Journey, hero's: quest
Journey, long: odyssey
Journey, self-indulgent: ego trip
Journey stage: leg
Jousting weapon: lance
Jovi, Jon Bon
Jowly canine: pug
Joy, give great: elate
Joy ride: spin
Joy, unbounded: glee
Joyce, James novel: Exile, Ulysses
Joyce's Molly: Bloom
Joyce's nation: Eire
Joyous dance: hora, horah
Joyous outburst: paean
JP, part of: justice, peace
JPEG Alternatives: GIFs
Juan's father: padre
      land: tierras
Judd, Naomi: singer
Judea King: Herod
Judge: deem, find, hear, rate, rank
Judge's chambers: in camera
Judge's knocker: gavel
Judges' meeting: banc
Judge's order: writ, remand
Judge's seat: bench
Judge's state?: soberni
Judge's wear: robe, gown
Judgment, await: pend
Judgment, good: sense
Judgmental reviewer: critic
Judgments, make: deem
Judicial assembly: court
Judicial cover-up: robe
Judicial document: writ
Judicial order: gag, writ
Judicial order, restrain by: enjoin
Jug: ewer
Jug band instrument: kazoo, bottle,
      washboard, stovepipe
Jug or cooler: jail
Jug, vase-shaped: ewer
Jug with wide spout: ewer
Juice the grapefruit: ream
Jujitsu relative: karate
Julep garnish: mint
Mint julep
Juliet's guy: Romeo
Julius Caesar role: Cato
Jullian, Ann
July sign: crab
Jumble: olio
Jump for joy: exult
Jump, kind of: ski
Jump, made: startled
Jumped over: vaulted, omitted
Jumper's cord: bungee, rip
Jumping craze: bungee
Jumpy, far from: sedate

Jun, in Athens: Hera
Junction line: seam
June 6, l944: D-Day
June bug:dor
June celebrant: grad
June honoree: grad, dad
Jung, Carl Gustav
Jungfrau: alp
Jungian term: anima
Jungle bird: toucan
Jungle crusher: boa
Jungle, from the: wild
Jungle journey: trek
Jungle noise: roar
Jungle queen: Sheena
Jungle ruff: mane
Jungle scavenger: hyena
Jungle squawker: toucan
Jungle vine: liana
Jung's inner-self: anima
Junior, maelstrom: eddy
Juniper bush: savin(Eurasian evergreen)
Juniper satellite: Europa
Junk Email: spam
Junk food: snacks
Junk mail, like: unread
Junk, reduce to: total
Junk yard hue: rust
Juno in Athens: Hera
Juno devotee: Roman
Juno to Socrates: Hera
Juno's Greek counterpart: Hera
Junta: regime
Jupiter orbit, nearest point in orbit: periapsis
　　　farthest point in orbit: apoapsis
Jupiter's mother: Ops
　　　neighbor: Mars
　　　wife: Juno
Jurassic Park actress: Dern
Jurist: Abe Fortas
Juror, presumably: peer
Jurors, list of possible: venire
Jury, before a: on trial
Jury decision: verdict, rule
Jury duty, summoned for: paneled
Jury members: peers
Jury, select a: impanel
Jury, was on a: sat
Just: mere
Just a bit: tad
Just a little: dab, tad
"Just a sec"
Just about: nearly
Just acquired: new
Just around the corner: near
Just as desired: ideal
Just as i thought: aha
Just average: so-so
Just barely win: nip
Just bought: unused, new
Just hired: new
Just like: as if
Just made: fresh
Just made it: got by

Just OK: so-so
Just out: new
Just perfect: ideal
Just right: ideal,
"Just the Facts" follower: ma'am
Just touch: abut
Justice, symbol of: scales
Justice, type of: poetic
Jutland Port, northern: Aalborg

K

Kabba the Huff
Kabul language: Afghani
Kabuki kin: Noh
Kachina carver: Hopi
Kachina doll maker:Hopi
Kael, Pauline: film critic
Kafka, Franz: writer
Kafka heroine: Olga
Kahn, Agha
Kahn, Genghis was one: Mongol
Kahn, Madeline: actress
Kahuna's hello: aloha
Kahuna's spud: taro
Kahyyam, Omar
Kal Kan rival: Alpo
Kalahari, like the: Arid
Kalb, Marvin: journalist
Kampala land: Uganda
Kampuchea coin: riel, sen (Cambodia)
Kanaka's wreath: lei
Kanga's creator: Milne
Kangaroo court: mock court
Kangaroo kid: joey
Kangaroo, large: euro, wallaroo
Kangaroo or koala, e.g.: marsupial
Kangaroo, young: joey
Kant, Immanuel: philosopher
Das Kapital
Kapitan's command: U-boat
Kaplin, Caba (Cabe): comic
Kappa Kappa Gamma member: Coed
Kappa preceder: iota
Kaput: shot
Kaput, goes: fails
Karachi languages: Urdu
Karamazov, Ivan
Karan, Donna: designer
Karate's cousin: kung fu, judo
Karate level: dan
Karate school: dojo
Kareem's alma mater: UCLA
Karenina, Anna
Karl Marx's associate: Engels
Karloff, Boris: actor
Karlovy Vary (for one): spa
Karnack neighbor: Luxor,
Karolyi, Bela: gymnast coach
Karpov forte: chess
Karpov's turn: move
Karst features: sinkholes, fissures, caves
Kartvelian people: Imer

Kasbah native: Arab
Kate's pal: Allie
Katmandu language: Nepali
Katy-did:locust, grasshopper
Kaunas native: Balt (Lithuania)
Kavalex, Alexei: hockey
Kay Thompson heroine: Eloise
Kayak kin: umiak, coracle
Kaye, Danny: comic, actor
"Kazaam" star: O'Neal
Kazan, Elia: director
Keach, Stacy: actor
Keanu character: Neo
Keat's contemporary: Byron
Keat's subject: urn
Keaton, Diane: actress
Kebab bed: pilaf
Kebab holder: skewer
Ked competitor: Avia
Kedge: light anchor
Keel, type of: even
Keemun, hunan, etc: teas
Keen: avid
Keen insight: acumen
Keen, it may be: eyesight
Keene, Carolyn: author
Keenly desirous: eager
Keenness of insight: acumen
Keep an appointment: meet
Keep an eye on: tend
Keep back: rein, rein in
Keep company with: hobnob
Keep digging: deepen
Keep down: oppress
"Keep", editorial: stet
Keep fit: jog
Keep from collapsing: prop up
Keep from happening: avert
Keep greedily: hog
Keep out of sight: lie low, hide
Keep perusing: read on
Keep time: clap
Keeps pursuing: dogs
Keeps score: tallies
Keepsake, ancient: relic
Keepsake holder: locket
Keepsake: relic, token
Kefauver, Estes: senator
Keg, straight from the: on tap
Kegler's game: bowling
Kegler's locale: alley
Kegler's number 5: kingpin
Kegler's target: pin, ten pin
Keitel, Harvey: actor
Kelep: ant
Kellerman, Faye: writer
Kelly, Gene: dancer
Kelp component: iodine
Kelly, Walt comic
Kelly, Walt comic: Pogo
Kemo Sabe's friend: Tonto
Kendall, Kay: actress
Kennedy Library architect: Pei
Kennel feature: run, runway

Kenny Roger's hit: "Lucille"
Keno kin: lotto
Kent, Rockwell: painter
Kentish Freedman: laet
Kentucky abutter: Ohio
Kentucky Blue Grass: poa
Kentucky College: Berea
Kentucky Derby prize: Roses
Kentucky legend: Boone
Keokuk's state: Iowa,
Kepler, Johannes: planets
Kepler's study: planets
Kept by a keeper: inn
Kept cold: iced,
Kept firmly in mind: held
Kept near shore: waded
Kept safe: guard
Kept secret: hid
Kept up the fire: fed
Kercheval, Ken: actor
Kerchief: scarf
Kerchief, hair-protecting: do rag
Kermit's creator: Henson
Kern, Jerome: composer
Kerosene burner: lantern
Kerr, Deborah: actress
Kerr, Graham: TV chef
Kerry county seat: Tralee
Kesey, Ken: novelist
Kestrel, emulates a: swoops
Ketch cousin: yawls
Ketch kin: yawl
Ketch (Levantine): Saic
Ketcham's, Hank, Dennis: Menace
Kett, Etta: comic
Kettle and Bell: Mas
Kettle, large: caldron,
Kettles of filmdom: Ma and Pa
Kevin Bacon film: tremors
Key factor in inflation: air
Key in again: reenter
Key in the corner: Esc
Key letter: beta
Key lime pie
Key personnel: typist
Key points: nubs
Keyboard instrument: celesta
Keyed up: on edge, tense
Keynote precursor: intro
Keys: inlets
Keystone konstable: kop
Keystone site: arch
Keystone State port city: Erie
Kahn, Agha
Khan, Genghis's people: Mongols
Khaki, like: drab
Khania's location: Crete
Khartoum locale: Sudan
Khartoum's river: Nile
Khayyam, Omar: poet,
Kia crossover vehicle: rondo
Kibei's parent: Issei
Put the kibosh on
Kick in for a hand: ante

Kick, kind of: onside
Kick oneself for: rue
Kickback: recoil, sop, bribe
Kickboxing variation: Tae Bo
Kickoff type: onside
Kicked out: evicted
Kid: twit
Kid around: jive
Kid in "Alien": Newt
Kid who rode Diablo: Cisco
Kiddie-lit author: Seuss
Kidney-shaped: reniform
Kid's block brand: Lego
Kid's brother's clothes, e.g.: hand-me-downs
Kid's classic: Heidi
Kid's question: why
Kids, well-behaved: dolls
Kiel conjunction: und
Kiel location: Germany
Kierkegaard, Soren: philosopher
Kiev's country: Ukraine
Kiki: Dee
Kilgallen panel mate: Cerf
Kilkenny, from: Irish
Kill a bill: repeal
Kill time: idle
Killed: slew,
Killing time: idle
Kilmer, Joyce: actress
Kilmer, Val: actor
Kiln: oven, oast
Kiln, put in a: dry
Kilt wearer's "no": nae
Kilt wearer's refusal: nae
Kilt wearer's son: laddie
Kim, Lil: rapper
Kimono closer: obi
Kimono sash: obi
Kimono wearer: geisha
Kin, acquired: in-laws
Kin of Unaus: Ais
Kin's partner: kith
Kind of apartment ownership: condo
Kind of artist: con
Kind of attack: panic
Kind of badge: merit
Kind of ball or shirt: tee
Kind of bliss: wedded
Kind of brake: disc
Kind of buddy: bosom
Kind of butter: cocoa
Kind of button: panic
Kind of calm: uneasy
Kind of castle: sand
Kind of chamber: echo
Kind of child: only
Kind of cider: hard
Kind of coal: cannel
Kind of computer connection: Wi-Fi
Kind of coverage: media
Kind of diplomat: career
Kind of drum: ear, bass, kettle
Kind of dye: azo
Kind of eau and wasser: agua

Kind of electron tube: triode
Kind of grin: wry
Kind of hall: town
Kind of house or angle: pent
Kind of instinct: gut
Kind of jump: ski
Kind of justice or license: poetic
Kind of kitchen: eat-in
Kind of lemur: potto
Kind of mail: bulk, email
Kind of maniac: ego
Kind of map: relief
Kind of model: avatar
Kind of module: lunar
Kind of needle: darning, hypodermic
Kind of normal: para
Kind of overcoat: raglan
Kind of ox: musk
Kind of pancake: potato
Kind of parliament: rump
Kind of pathway: neural
Kind of pencil: eyebrow
Kind of pepper: bell
Kind of PC screen: LCD, plasma
Kind of pine: knotty
Kind of pine paneling: knotty
Kind of pilot: test, jet, airline
Kind of porch: stoop
Kind of psychology: Gestalt
Kind of pudding: bread
Kind of quiz: pop
King of rabbit: welsh
Kind of reaction: gut
Kind of rich: filthy
Kind of sale: bake, yard, garage, year-end
Kind of sample: DNA
Kind of school club: glee
Kind of sheet: rap
Kind of sofa: sectional
Kind of stool or ladder: step
Kind of store: general
Kind of student: med
Kind of surgery: elective
Kind of symbol: status
Kind of terrier: Welsh
Kind of therapy: chemo
Kind of transport: rapid
Kind of turn: hair-pin
Kind of weight: troy, kilo, gram, dram,
    pound, ounce
Kind of wind: trade
Kind of wound: flesh
Kinda down: eider, sad
Kindergartner: tyke
Kindled: ignited
Kindly: benign
Kine (cow) dine, where: lea
King address: sire
King, Alan: comic
King and queen toppers: Aces
King Arthur's abode: Avalon
King Arthur's advisor: Merlin
King Arthur's island paradise: Avalon
King Arthur's retreat: Avalon

King, Billy Jean: tennis
King, Carol: music
King, cruel: tyrant
King Cyaxeres was one: Mede
King David's grandfather: Obed
King, fit for a: regal
King Herald's capital: Osle
King in a play: Lear
King Lear's daughter: Regan
King marched, where a: Selma
King, Martin Luther: pastor
King Minos's daughter: Ariadne
King, New Testament: Herod
King of elves: Oberon
King of gorillas: Kong
King of Greek myth: Tantalus
King of guilt feelings: Midas
King of Scotland: Macbeth
King of the hill: champ
King of the Huns: Attila
King of the road: hobo
King of TV: Larry
King or queen: monarch
King, Scottish: Macbeth
King size: giant
King, tragic: Lear
"The King": Elvis
King, Vidor: irector
King who abdicated: Edwards
Kingdom, mountain: Nepal
Kingdom, phylum, class
Kingdoms: realms
Kingclip catcher: Eeler
Kings and queens: ruler
King's place: throne
King's ransom: fortune
Kingsley, Amis: writer
Kink's classic: Lola
Kink's song: Lola
Kink's tune of yore: Lola
Kinsley, Ben: actor
Kin-Tiki craft: raft
Kiosk: stand, booth
Kiosk buy: mag, magazine
Kiosk lit.: mag.
Kipling novel: Kim
Kipling, Rudyard: novelist
Kipling's wolf pack leader: Akela
Kipnis, Igor: harpsichordist
Kippur, Yom
Kirghiz range: Alai
Kirk, to Bones: Jim
Kirk's helmsman: Sulu
Kirk, Capt.'s home: Iowa
Kismet: doom, fate
Hare Krishna
Kiss, quick: peck
Kiss target: cheek
Kisses: busses,
Kisses, loud: smacks
Kissin' kin: coz, cuz
Kistler's costume: tutu
Kitchen cacophony: clatter
Kitchen emanation: odor

"Kitchen" ending: ette
Kitchen extension: ette
Kitchen implement: corer, oven
Kitchen, kind of: eat-in
Kitchen pro: chef
Kitchen staple, once: lard
Kitchen topper: lid
Kitt, Eartha: music
Kitty, perhaps: pet, pot
Kitty's bane: flea
Kity-did (sp): locust, grasshopper
Kiwi, brown: moa, gooseberry
Kiwi language: Maori
Kiwi's extinct cousin: Moa
Klee, Paul: Swiss painter
Klein, Anne: fashions
Kleine Nachtmusik, Eine
Klemperer, Otto of music: conductor
Kline, Kevin: actor
Kline, Randy: country music
Klingons or Vulcan, e.g.: alien race
Klondike conveyance: sled
Klondike "Kate"
Klondike territory: Yukon
Klutz: oaf,
Klutz's cry: oh no
Klutz's mutter: oops
Knack: hang of it
Knack, special: art
Knead: rub
Kneaded rubber: eraser
Knee bend, ballerina: plie
Knee bone: patella
Knee, scrapes a: skins
Kneeling bench: prie-dieu
Knickknack: whatnot, curio
Knickknack stand: étagère
Knife brand: X-Acto
Knife expert: cutler
Knife handle: hilt,haft
Knife, hobby: X-Acto, exacto
Knife holder: sheath
Knife, hunting: bowie
Knife, Inuit: ulu
Knife, jungle: machete, bolo
Knife, large: snee
Knife maker: cutler
Knife part: haft, hilt (handle)
Knife, small: shiv
Knight, boastful: Kay
Knight, kind of: errant
Knight, like a: armored
Knight, often: hero
Knight time: yore
Knighted Guinness: Alec
Knighthood, confer: dub
Knight's aides: squires
Knight's armor: mail
Knight's attire: armor
Knight's combat: joust
Knight's girl: maiden
Knight's glove: gauntlet
Knight's journey: quest
Knights, like some: errant, hero

Knights of the realm: sirs
Knights of yore
Knight's quest: grail
Knight's title: sir
Knight's weapon: mace, lance
Knight's wife: dame
Knitter's need: skeins
Knob: node
Knobs, rota table: dials
Knock against: bump
Knock flat: deck
Knock for a loop: cream
Knock gently: tap
Knock, reply to a: it's open
Knockabout: sloop
Knocked firmly: rapped
Knocked off: slew, killed
Knocked, one way to be: silly
Knockout: eyeful
Knocks for a loop: jolts,
Knockwurst go-with: kraut
Knossos site: Crete
Knot: node, neb (fiber)
Knot, kind of: granny
Knot on a tree: gnarl
Knot, ornamental: tie
Knot up: entangle
Knots in cotton fiber: nebs
Knotted lace, create: tat
Knotty: gnarled
Knotty wood: pine
Know basis: need to
Know it all: guru
Know somehow: feel
Knowing look: leer
Knowledge: lore, info.
Knowledge, branches of: fields
Knowledge, collective: lore
Knowledge, traditional: lore
Knowledgeable: versed,
Known, became: got about
Known to be said: on record
Known, very well: famous, famed
Knows how: can
Knuckle under: bow, cave in, obey, yield, give in, submit, succumb
Knucklehead: schmo
Koafs lutzes
Koan discipline: Zen
Koblenz's river: Mosel
Koch's drink: manhattan
Kohl target: eyelid
KoKo's weapon: snee
Koln's (Cologne's) river: Rhine
Komodo dragon's home: Indonesia
Kon-tiki craft: raft
Kon-tiki museum site: Oslo
Kook or snack: nut
Kool and the Gang
Koosh competitor: Nerf
Kopecks (100): ruble
Koppel, Ted: TV
Korbit, Olga: gymnast
Kosher, not: tref

Kosher product wording: pareve
Kournikova, Anna: tennis
Kramden, Alice
Kramden's (Alice) pal: Trixie
Ralph Kramden's wife: Alice
Krantz, Judy: writer
Krazy Kat
Kreskin's claim to game: ESP
Kringle, Kris
Krishna: Hare
Krishna devotee: Hindu
Kroner are spent, where: Oslo
Krono's daughter: Hera
Krueger'sstreet: Elm
Kruger, Otto: actor
Krupa, Gene: drummer
Krupp industry region: Ruhr
Kubla Khan: Mongol
Kubla Khan locale: Xanadu
Kudos, heaps on: lauds
Kudu cousin: eland
Kukla's friend: Ollie, Fran
Kukoc, Toni: basketball
Kupcinet, Irv: TV
Kurosawa, Mr. Akira: director
Kurz, Selma: soprano
Kuwaiti currency: dinar
Kuwaiti leader: emir
Kwajalein and Eniwetok: atolls
Kvetch: doan, moan, complain
Kwanzaa day: Nia
Kwon Do, Tae
Kyoto bed: futon
Kyoto cash: yen
Kyoto Honorific: San
Kyoto Port: Osaka
Kyoto Sash: Obi
Kyrguzstan's mountains: Alai
Kyser, Kay: band leader
Kyushu cutie: Geisha
Kyushu Volcano: Aso

L

La Baheme: Opera
La Brea: tar pits
La Brea deposits: tar
La Brea goo: tar
La différence, vive
La dolce vita
La Douce, Irma
La Farge, John: painter
La femme: elle
La isla bonita
L.A. Law actress: Susan Dey
"La Mer" composer: Debussy
La Mer, land in: ile
La Scala(Milan opera house)
La senorita: ella
"La Source" painter: Ingress
Lab apparatus: tripod
Lab glassware: flask
Lab item: etna

Lab burner: Bunsen, etna
Lab glassware: beaker vial, retort,flask, pipette,
    mortar
Lab instruction?: heel
Lab lackey: Igor
Lab rat's challenge: maze
Lab safety org.: ASPCA, ASCPA
Lab substance: agar
Label, famous: Dior
LaBelle, Patti: music
Labor at: ply
Labor Day telethon grp.: MDA
Labor dept. watchdog: OSHA
Labor org.: ILO, IWW, UAW, CIO
Laborer: toiler
Laborer, feudal: esne
Laborer, medieval: serf
Laborers on the Volga: boatmen
Labor's I. W. Abel
LaBron's org.: NBA
Labyrinth: maze
Lacarre, John: writer
Lace, Homemade: tatting
Lace or ribbon: trim, edging
Lace tips: aglets
Lacewings lunch: aphids
Lacework, coarse: macramé
Lachrymal secretion: tears
Lachrymose: teary, wept
Lack edges, they: spheres
Lack fizz: flat
Lack of inebriation: sobriety
Lack of interest: ennui
Lack iron: anemic
Lack, not: have
Lack quality: junk
Lacked: needed
Lackey: menial
Lacking: sans
Lacking effervescence: flat
Lacking in insight: obtuse
Lacking moisture: dry, arid
Lacking originality: stale
Lacking principle: amoral
Lacking pulchritude: ugly
Lacking rain: arid
Lacking self-confidence: shy
Lacking texture: limp
Lacking, totally: out of
Lacking uniformity: erratic
Lacking vigor: effete
Lacks existence: isn't
Laconian capital: Sparta
Lacoste, Rene: tennis
Lacquer ingredient: resin
Lacto-ovo vegetarian
La Douce, Irma
Ladd, Alan film: Shane
Ladd, Diane: actress
Ladder or brother, kind of: step
Ladder or stool, kind of: step
Ladder rung: spoke, step
Ladies: dipper, gals
Ladies, foxy: vixens

Ladle: dip
Lad's date: lass
Lad's love: lass
Lady Chaplin: Oona
Lady from Toledo: señora
Lady, graceful: sylph
Lady Grey: Tea
Lady Honorific: ma'am
Lady in distress: damsel, maiden
Lady Jane Grey
Lady Macbeth's bane: spot
Lady of Coventry: Godiva
Lady of la casa: mujer
Lady of Portugal: dona
Lady, slangy: dame
Lady of song: Lola
Lady of Spain: Srta., Sra, señora, dona
Lady Swan: pen
Lady with a swan: Leda
Lady, young: maiden
Lady-killer: dude, hunk, roué, stud, playboy,
    seducer
Lady's finger: okra
Lady's man: gent, romeo, roué
Lager of Linz: bier
Lagerfeld, Kay: designer
Lago Maggiore area: Alps
Lago's wife: Emilia
Lagoon: pond
Lagoon border: atoll
Lagoon boundary: atoll
Lagoon enclosure: atoll
Lagoon protector: reef
Lags behind: loiters, trails
Lahar: slide (volcanic)
Lah-di-dah
Lahore nurse: amah
Lahr, Bert: comic
Lahti, Christine: actress
Laid a course: plotted
Laid off: idled
Laid up: ill, ail
Laid-back: cool, breezy, casual, relaxed
Laila of boxing: Ali
Laine, Cleo: music
Laine, Frankie: music
Laird: scot
Laird's accent: burr
    attire: kilts
    daughter: lass
    household: clan
    prefix: mac
Laissez faire
Laissez passer
Lake Erie port: Toledo
Lake for lucky ones: Tahoe
Lake Geneva spa: Evian
Lake in Switzerland: Geneva
Lake or pond: mere
Lake, shallow: lagoon
Lake, monstrous: Ness
Lake Nasser's dam: Aswan
Lakshmi's husband: Vishnu
    son: Kama

L.A. Law actress: Susan Dey
Lalique, René: glassmaker
Lam, go on the: flee
Lama chant: mantra
Lama, Dalai
Lama, Dalai city: Lhasa
Lama song: chant
Lama or friar: monk
Lamarr, Hedy: actress
Lamas, Fernando: actor
Lama's role model: Buddha
Lamb, Chas alias: Elia
Lamb Chop puppeteer: Lewis
Lamb serving: cutlets
Lamb's alias: Elia
Lamb's sound: bleat, blat
Lame excuse: cop out
Lame, make, perhaps: maim
Lament: bemoan, wail
Laments loudly: keens
Lamotta, Jake: boxer
Lamp oil holder: font
Lamp shade support: harp
Lamp resident: genie
Lampoon: parody,satire
Lancaster, Burt: actor
Lancaster, Elsa: actress
Lancaster group: Amish
Lancelot du Lac
Lancelot's love: Elaine
      son: Galahad
Lanchester, Elsa: actress
Land: terrain
Land bound by three oceans: Asia
Land, Edwin: inventor
Land expanse: tract,
Land formation, steep-sided: mesa
Land in water: isle
Land mass of two continents: Eurasia
Land mass, small: islet
Land, minor: Asia
Land of enchantment: New Mexico
Land of enhancement: faery, fairy
Land of nod: sleep
Land of opportunity: USA, Arkansas
Land of the midnight sun: Norway
Land, to Caesar: terra
Land, to Ovid: terra
Land, uncultivated: heath
Landed: alit
Landed class: gentry
Landed estate of a lord: manor
Landed hard: pancaked, plopped
Landed property: estate
Landed property broker: realtor
Landers, Ann: writer
Landfill: dump
Landing, none-to-gentle: thud
Landing place: pier,
Landing strip surface: tarmac
Landlord, be a: let, rent, lease
Landlord need: tenant
Landmarks, some rural: silos
Landon, Alf: politician

Landowska, Wanda: harpsichordist
Landry, Tom: NFL coach,
Lands in "La Mer": iles
Landscape or portrait: art
Landscape, picturesque: scenery
Land-use guidelines: zoning
Lang, Fritz: Director
Auld Lang Syne
Langsbury, Angela: actress
Langtry, Lillie: actress
Language, alien: foreign tongue
Language expert: maven
Language, Pakistan: Urdu
Language ruler: syntax
Language, study of: "ling"
Language suffix: ese
Language varieties: dialects
Language with click: Zulu
Languish: ail, wilt, pine
Lanka, Sri
Lanolin source: wool
Lao Tzu, way of: Tao
Laos locale: Asia
Lap, lost a: stood
LaPerla product: bra
Lapinski, Tara: skater
Lapis Iazuli color: azure blue, azure
Lapone, Patti
Laps, did: swam
Lapse: expire
Laptev, on the: a sea (Laptev sea)
Laptops: PCs
Lapwing, for one: plover
Lardner, ring: Writer
Large African lake: Chad
Large beak bird: Toucan
Large diving bird: loon
Large family of frogs: ranid
Large gathering of people: throng
Large heavy book: tome
Large in combo: macro
Large kettle: caldron
Large lizard: iguana
Large marine eel: moray
Large merchant ships: argosies
Large number: slew
Large prefix: macro
Large ratite: emu
Large scale: epic
Large slipknot: noose
Large volume: tome
Larger part: bulk, most
Larger than life: epic
Large-scale public show: expo
Largest asteroid: ceres
Largest blue: whale
Largest digit: nine
Largest of the Finger Lakes: Seneca
Largo, faster than: adagio
Lariot: lasso, riata
Lark: whim
La Russa finds relief, where: bull pen
Larva's covering: cacoon
Las Palmas

Las Vegas show: revue
Las Vegas star: Wayne Newton
Las Vegas, viva
LaScala home: Milan
      offering: opera, aria
      role: tenore
      setting: Milano, Milan
      song: Aria
LaScala: (Milan opera house)
Lascivious glance: leer
Lascivious look: leer
La señorita: ella
"La Source" painter: ingres
Laser output: beam
Lash down: secure
Lash holder: lid
Lash Larue: cowboy star
Lash out at: assail,
Lash thickener: mascara
Lass, pert: minx
Lasser, Louise: actress
Lassie refusal: nae
Lasso: riata, lariot
Lassoed: roped, noosed
Last bio: obit
Last book of the Torah: Deut
Last box to check: other
Last number: finale
Last of Socrates: omega
Last place finisher: loser
"Last Supper" setting: Milan
Last syllable of a word: ultima
Last word, famous: amen
Last year's beginner, briefly: soph
Last-ditch: Final, Defiant, Ultimate
Lasted well: wore
Lasting aftereffects: scars
Lasting forever: eternal
Lasting impression, make a: etch
Lasting twenty-four hours: daylong
Lat. list ender: et al
Latavia capital: Riga
Latavia native: Lett
Latavia seaport: Riga
Latch Onto: Glom
Late afternoon: four
Late bloomer: aster
Late night flight: red-eye
Late night snack attach: raid
Late summer sign: Virgo
Lately happening: recent
Later: not now
"Later" at the luau: aloha
Later than: after
Lateral measurement: width
Latest news: up date
Lather, full of: soapy
Lather, in a: het up
Lather up: soap
Lathered: sudsed
Latin altars: arae
Latin American music: salsa
Latin clarifier: idest
Latin class, existence in: esse

Latin dance: tango, cha-cha
Latin dance music: salsa
Latin epic: Aeneid
Latin gentlemen: señors
Latin gods: deities, dei
Latin homework, do: parse
Latin "I" verb: esse, erat
Latin "I" word: amat, amas
Latin 101 word: erat
Latin letters: qed
Latin "thing": res
Latin trio: III
Latino trio: III
Latino's language: Español
"Latraviata" composer: Verdi
Latticework feature: slat
Latticework for roses: trellis
Latvian chess great: Tal
Latvian city: Riga
Laudatory speech: eulogy
Laudatory verse: ode
Laugh, derisive: hah, yuk
Laugh, hags: cackle
Laugh Loudly: Bray
Laugh, Make: Amuse
Laugh, Nasty: Hah
Laugh, Raucous: Yuk
Laugh rudely: hee haw
Laugh-a-minute: riot
Laughed loudly: brayed
Laughing: riant, amused
Laughs, lots of: fun
Laughter, burst of: peal
Launch, cancel a: scrub
Launderer's step: sort, fold, iron
Laundry additive: bleach, soap, softener
Laundry batch: load
Laundry challenge: stain
Laundry load: wash
Laundry, prepare the: sort
Lauper, Cyndi: music
Lauper's "She Bop"
Laura Bush's alma mater: SMU
Laurel: fame, award, bog, pig, bay
Laurel, Stan: comic
Lava, flows like: oozes
"La Vie en Rose" chanteuse: Piaf
Lavish attention: dote
Lavish entertainment: fete
Hasta la vista
Law: ordinance
Law breaker: offender, felon
Law breaking costs: fines
Law change: amend
Law (Latin): lex
Law office staffer: paralegal
Law or Caine role: Alfie
Law school subject: tort
"A Law unto Itself"
Law-abiding: decent, duteous, dutiful
Law-breaking costs: fines
Lawless role: Xena
Lawless of Xena: Lucy
Lawn bowling, Italian: Bocci, Boccie, Bocce

Lawn piece: sod
Lawn, tend the: rake, mow
Lawn, tidy the: rake, mow
Lawrence of Arabia ride: camel
Lawsuit cause: libel
Lawsuit, closes a: settles
Lawyer: advocate
Lawyer, briefly: atty.
Lawyer's aide, briefly: para
Lawyer's (future) exam: LSAT
Lawyer's fee: retainer
Lawyer's honorific: esquire
Lawyer's letters: esq.
Lawyer's org.:ABA
Lawyer's thing: res, law
Lay at an angle: lean
Lay brother: oblate
Lay down: put, rest
Lay in wait: lurk,
Lay out a course: plot
Lay waste: ruin, ravage, destroy, desolate
Layer: ply, stratum, strata
Layer, fragile: ozone
Layer of cloth: ply
Layer of holes: ozone
Layer of soil: solum
Layer of tissue: tela
Layered haircut: shag
Layered mineral: mica
Layers, many: hens
Layers of rock: strata
Layoff, end of a: rehire
Layoff tool: axe
Layout choice: font
Layout style: formal
Lazarus, Emma: writer
Lazarus, Mel, comic strip: momma
Laze about: idle, loll
Laze on the beach: bask
Laziness: idleness
Lazing about: idle
Lazy Susan
Lazybones: slouch
LCD, part of: least, liquid
L'chaim and prosit: toasts
Lea and Perrins: steak sauce
Lea ladies, some: ewes
Lead: clue
Lead, as a work group: head up
Lead astray: seduce, corrupt
Lead balloon: dud
Lead car, sometimes: pace, pacer
Lead from the door: see-in
Lead, in the: ahead of, ahead
Lead ore: galena
Lead, took the: starred
Leader, conservative: neo
Leader of kings: Aces
Leader of the flock: pastor
Leader, teen or fad: pre
Leadership position: helm
Lead-in: intro
Lead-in, modem: ultra
Leading: main

Leading man: hero,
Lead-tin alloy: solder, terne, terneplate
Lead-to-gold seeker: alchemist
Leaf collection site: eaves
Leaf-cutting ant: atta
Leaf, floating: pad
Leaf juncture: node
Leaf, one side of a: page
Leaf opening: stoma
Leaf orifice: stoma
Leaf out: buds,
Leaf stalk: petiole
Leaf vein: rib
Leaf-cutting ant: atta
Leafless: bare
Leafless flower stalks: scapes
Leafy shelter: bower
Leafy vine: ivy
League: club
League, kind of: ivy
League of plotters: cabals
"League of their Own"
League with, in: allied
Leah daughter: Dinah
     father: Laban
     husband: Jacob
     sister: Rachel
     son: Levi, Judah, Reuben, Simeon,
        Jebulun, Issachar
Leakley, Louis: anthropologist
Lean against: abut
Lean and muscular: sinewy
Lean and sinewy: wiry
Lean forward: loom, tend
Lean toward: tend, bend, bent
Leander's love: hero
Leaning on: against
Leaning tower city: Pisa
Leans on the horn: blares
Leap aside: dodge
Leap in a tutu: jete
Leap, skater: axel
Lear, Norman: producer
Learn about: read
Learn by memorizing: rote
Learn, quick to: apt
Learn well: master
Learned: erudite
Learned one: savant
Learner, lone: tutee
Learning aide: tutor,
Learning, fixed way of: rote
Learning method: rote
Learning method, mechanical: rote
Learning, monotonous: rote
Learning of the ages: lore
Learning process: rote
Seat of learning
Learnings: lores
Lear's daughter: Goneril
Least: merest
Least chicken: gamest
Least green: ripest
Least involved: easiest

Least likely to understand: densest
Least of the litter: runt
Least positive integer: unit
Least sociable: shyest
Leather: cowhide
Leather band: strap
Leather, bookbinding: roan
Leather, change to: tan
Leather, fake: vinyl
Leather, napped: suede
Leather shoe strips: welts
Leather, soft: suede, kid skin
Leather with a napped surface: suede
Leather, worked as: tooled
Leather working tool: awl
Leathery: tough
Leave a solid state: melt
Leave at the altar: jilt
Leave in a hurry: bolt, decamp
Leave in haste: decamp
Leave no trace: vanish
Leave on base: strand
Leave on the sly: steal-away
Leave out: omit, skip, elide
Leave port: embark
Leave taking: adieus
Leave the dock: sail, embark
Leave the room: step out
Leaven: yeast
Leavening agents: yeasts
Leaves: departs
Leaves a mark: scar
Leaves as is: stets
Leaves at the altar: jilt
Leaves dumbfounded: awes, stuns
Leaves in a bag: tea
Leaves in a lurch: strands
Leaves, loose: pages,
Leaves out: omits, excepts
Leaving home port: moving away
Lebanon's Gemayel: Amin
LeBlanc, Matt: actor
Lebowitz, Fran: comic
Lech's locale: Gdansk
Lecher: roué
Lecherous one: roué
Lectern: ambo
Lecture giver: prof
Lecture room: hall
Lectern: ambo
Lectern's spot: dais
Leda's daughter: Helen
Lee, Brenda: music
Lee, Peggy: music
Lee, Spike: actor, cirector
Lee's org.: "CSA"
Leek's kin: scallions
Leerier, more: warier
Le Fay, Morgan
Left a blank: spaced,
Left at sea: a port, port
Left bank friend: ami
Left bank river: Seine
Left bank solon: senat

Left hastily: decamped, fled
Left in a hurry: fled
Left in the dark: unaware
Left to a tar: port
Left-hand page: verso
Left-handed: inept, clumsy, gauche, awkward,
     dubious
Leftover dish: hash
Leftover matter: residue
Leftovers: dregs
Leftovers, had: ate in
Leftovers packages: doggy bags
Leftward, nautically: levo, aport
Leg joint: knee, hip
Leg on either side: astride
Leg up: boost
Leg up, gave a: helped
Leg wrap-around: puttee
Legacy: estate
Legal aid org.: ACLU
Legal agreement: mise
Legal case: civil suit
Legal claim: droit, lien
Legal fee: retainer
Legal guarantee: surety
Legal matter: res
Legal memo starter: inre
Legal opener: para
Legal offense: crime
Legal precedents, likely: test case
Legal profession: bar
Legal summons: subpoena
Legal thing: res
Legal writ: elegit, subpoena
Legality: validity
Legally binding: valid
Legally block: estop
Legally insolvent: bankrupt
Legally wrong, it's: tort
Legend cousin: myths
Legend, once: acura
Legendary archer: Wm. Tell
Legendary emblem: eagle
Legendary enchantress: Lorelei
Legendary pioneer: Boone, Daniel
Legendary pugilist: Ali
Legendary realm: Atlantis
Legends: lores, myths, tales
Legends, the stuff of: lore
Leggings of leather: chaps
Leggings of sheepskin: chaps
Legislation passer: congress
Legislative lounges: cloak rooms
Legume: pea, bean
Legumes, some: lentils
Leguminous arbor unit: mimosa tree
Leguminous plant fruit: pea
Lehar, Franz: composer
Leia Organa's brother: Luke
     rescuer: Han
Leibovitz, Annie: photographer
Leif Eriksson discovery: Vinland
     father: Eric, Erik the Red
Leinsdorf, Erich: conductor

Leird, Melvin: Sec of Defense
Leis, occasion for: Luau
Leisure time: vacation, weekend
Leitmotif: theme
LeLog Dor
"LEM" lander: NASA
LeMays', Curtis command: sac
Lemon candy: drop
Lemon, famous: Edsel
Lemon, Jack: actor
Lemon law
Lemon-lime Drink: sprite
Lemon or clunker: car
Lemon peel: jest
Lemon verbena: lemon-scented shrub
Lemonade Color: Pink
Lemond, Greg: cyclist
Lemon-like fruit: citron
Lemony taste: tang
Lemur, kind of: potto
Lemur, nocturnal: loris
Lemur's home: tree
Lena's plumbing: hornpipes
Lend a hand: aid
Lender's claim: lien
Lender's recourse: lien
Lending, illegal: usury
Lendl, Ivan: tennis
Length: extent
Length, focal
Length, unit of: feet
Length x width: area
Lenient, not: harsh
Lennon's "Instant Karma"
Lennon's "Ocean Child": Ono
Lennon's, Seanmom: Ono
Lennon's son: Sean
Lens, eye doctor's: optics
Lens, kind of: zoom
Lens maker: optician
Lens opening: iris
Lens, telescope: ocular
Lens, type of: zoom
Lengthwise: endways
Lentil dish: dal
Leo and Paul: popes
Leofric's wife: Godiva
Leona Helmsley for one: hotelier
Leonard, Elmore: writer
Leonine locks: mane
Leopard group: leap
Leopard, old word for: pard
Leopard spots: rozettes
Leo's dozen: zodiac
Leo's son: lionet
Lepidopterist's gear: net
Leporine leaper: hare
Def Leppard: rock music
Leprechaun's land: Erin
Lepton's home: atom
Lerner, Alan Jay: lyricist
Les etats Unis
Lesage hero: Blas
LeShan, Eda: author

Less certain: unsure, iffier
Less defined: vaguer
Less definite: iffier
Less dependent, make: wean
Less distant: nearer
Less likely: rarer
Less rosy: paler
Less sense, making: inaner
Less strict: laxer
Less than diddly: nil
Less than happy: annoyed
Less than ideal: next best
Less than one: nil
Less trusting: leeriest
Lessen the force of: bate, abate
Lesser Civet: Rasse
"Lesser of two evils"
"Lesson from Aloes"
Lesson length: period
Lestat's curfew: dawn
Let fly: hurl
Let go by: pass up
Let happen: allow
"Let it stand", literally: stet
Let off the hook: spare
Let on: pretend
Let out early: paroled, parole
Let slid: neglect
Let slip: tell
Let the cat out of the bag: told
Let up: abated
L'Etat, cest moi
Lethal loop: noose
Lethargy: ennui
Lets off steam, it: kettle
Lets out: alters, releases, paroles, rents
Letter after epsilon: zeta
Letter after zeta: eta
Letter answerer: pen pal
Letter before sigma: rho
Letter chit: IOU
Letter from the teacher: grades
Letter holders, some: PO boxes
Letter of debt: IOU
Letter, open a: unseal
Letter opener: dear, dear sir
Letter sack: mail bag
Letter, semicircular: cee
Letter signoff: regards
Letter slot: drop-box
Letter stroke: sSerif
Letter turner: Vanna (White)
Letterman's bandleader: Paul Shaffer
Letterman's turf: CBS
Letters after rho: sigmas
Letters from Ellas: betas
Letters, like some: newsy, sealed
Letters of the cross: inri, IHS
Letters on the autobahn: BMW
Lettuce, dark green: cos
Lettuce layer: leaf, bed
Lettuce piece: leaf
Lettuce variety: cos, romaine
Levant, Oscar: pianist

Levee: dike
Level: even, flat
Level, common: par
Level in London: rase (Raze or tear down)
Level off: plateau
Level or bevel: tool
Level-headed, more: saner
Levers, foot: pedals
Levertov, Denise: writer-poet
Levi father: Jacob
       mother: Leah
       son: Kohath, Merari, Gershon
Leviathan author: Thomas Hobbes
Levin, Ira: writer, novelist
Levine, James: conductor
Levy, Marv: coach, NFL
Lewis, Carl: runner
Lewis Carroll creature: snark
Lewis, John L. field: labor
Lewis, Shari: puppeteer
Lex Luther (like): Evil
Lexicography, first Name in: Noah
Lexicon, famed, abbr.: OED
Lexington's Rupp is one: arena
LGA posting: ETA
Lhasa location: Tibet
Lhasa Apso: breed of dog
Lhasa Monk: (Dalai) Lama
Lhasa is, where: Tibet
Liable, become: incur
Liable, not: exempt
Women's Liberation
Libation: potion
Libation, seasonal: nog
Liberal, some are: arts
Liberal, somewhat: leftish
Libertines: roues
Libra neighbor: Virgo
Libra's gem: opal
Library ID: ISBN
Library tome: book, atlas
Library stamp: dater
Libretto feature: aria
Lick up: lap
Licorice herb: anise
Licorice-flavored seed: anise
Lie doggo: go to Earth
Lie down: recline
Lie, harmless: fib,
Lie in the weeds: lurk
Lie in wait: lurk
Lie limply: sprawl,
"Lie upon this quiet life"
Lies obliquely: slants
Lieu: stead
Lieutenant general insignia: triple star
"Life and death": dire, critical
Life-changing event: miracle
Life forms: beings
Life guard beat: pool
Life jacket: Mae West
Life of Riley: easy street
Life-size exhibit: diorama
"Isn't life strange"

Life, zest for: elan
Life-impairing substance: poison,
Life-insurance policy plus: cash value
Lifer's dream: release
Lifework, artist: oeuvre
Lift out leakage: bail
Lift passages: shafts
Lifted: hefted
Lifts, as morale: boosts
Ligeia author: Poe
Light: operetta
Light a fuse: detonate
Light anchor: kedge
Light bender: prism, lens
Lightbulb, toon's: idea
Lightbulb filler: argon
Lightbulb gas: argon
Lightbulb measure: watt
Light, circle of: aureole
Light contact in billiards: kiss
Light covering: film
Light, emitting: aglow
Light, flashes of: glints
Light, harsh: glare
Light Horse Harry: Lee
Light house site: cape
Light in a tube: neon
Light in appearance: airy
Light massage: backrub
Light perfume: cologne
Light, powerful: laser
Light refractor: prism
Light saber wielder: JedI
Light science: optics
Light show, natural: aurora
Light source for serenaders: moon
Light, spot of: blip
Light swords: rapiers
Light, timing signal: strobe
Light unit: pyr
Lighten up: smile
Lighter alternative: match
Lighter fluid: butane
Lighter, get: fade
Light-footed: agile
Light-headed: dizzy, faint, giddy, silly
Lighthearted: merry
Lighthouse: Pharos
Lighthouse light: beacon, warning
"The Lighthouse of Pharos"
Lightness, exemplar of: feather
Lightning byproduct: ozone, ion
Lightning, flash of: bolt, streak
Lightning, like: forked, fast, flash
Lightning, shaft of: bolt
Lights, city of: Paris
Lights-out music: tap
Lights-out time: act 1, act one
Lights, type of: northern
Light-sensitive eye part: retina
Ligurian love: amore
Like: akin
Like a bass: low
Like a beautiful landscape: scenic

Like a convex lens: toric
Like a dive: sleazy,
Like a fence's ware: stolen
Like a frontier town: rowdy
Like a good steak: tender
Like a hawk: taloned
Like a knight: armored
Like a log: wooden
Like a March hare: mad
Like a marsh: reedy
Like a naval orange: seedless
Like a new candle: unlit
Like a poindexter: nerdy
Like a requiem: dirgeful, dirge
Like a tableau: posed
Like a tough cookie: stale
Like a trident: tined
Like a wedding cake: tiered
Like a witch eye: evil
Like always: normal, as usual
Like an epinicion: odic
Like an ice cream cone: conical
Like anything close by: not far
Like before: same
Like bleachers: tiered
Like Caspar Milquetoast: timid, submissive
Like car glass: tinted
Like chiffon or organza: sheer
Like extreme opposite: polar
Like folk art dolls: nested
Like French doors: paned
Like guys who finish last: nice
'Like, I get it': duh
Like it was: same
Like James Bond: suave
Like liquid nitrogen: inert
Like lumber: sawn
Like many classics: unread
Like many nuts: salted
Like moccasins: beaded
Like mountain air: rare
Like music without a key: atonal
Like oak trees: gnarled
Like Pan's hoofs: cloven
Like reality, at times: grim
Like so: thus
Like some crowds: ugly, unruly
Like some crystal: leaded
Like some deeds: in escrow
Like some excuses: lam, sad
Like some expense accts.: padded
Like some fans: avid
Like some fears: idle
Like some fertilizer: marly
Like some fish: bony
Like some gossip: catty
Like some inspections: on-site
Like some kisses and bases: stolen
Like some necessities: bare
Like some observations: astute
Like some old buckets: oaken
Like some police cars: unmarked
Like some seats: taken
Like some talk: small

Like some treasures: sunken, buried
Like souffe: eggy
Like, stupid: duh
Like success smells: sweet
Like suffix: -ine
Like sushi: raw
Like teenagers: youthful
Like the north star: polar
Like the sea: briny
Like the universe: vast
Like Thor: Norse
Like tin: rustproof
Like water under the bridge: past
Like wise: ditto, too, same
Like yesterday's news: old hat
Likely: apt
Likelihood ratio: odds
Likewise not: nor
Lillie, Edie: comic
Lilliputian: wee, teeny
Lily maid of Astolat: Elaine
Lily, popular: calla
Lily Tomlin character: Edith Ann
Lily Variety: calla, sego
Lily-white: pure
Lily-livered: sissy, wimpy, craven, yellow,
　　caitiff, chicken
Lima resident: Ohioans
Lima's port: Callao
Limb of the devil: imp
Limburger feature: odor
Lime tree: teil
Lime-flavored cocktail: gimlet
Limerick locale: Erie
Limerick maker, noted: Lear
Limerick name: Ogden
Limerick starter: there
Limerick writer: Ogden Nash, Lear
Limerick's neighbor: cork
Limestone deposit: tufa
Limestone formation: cave
Limestone region: Karst
Limit, beyond: ultra
Limit, pushed to the: taxed
Limit setter: term
Limit, they say is the: sky
Limited: finite, scarce
Limiting boundary: mete
Limo passenger: VIP
Limoges product: porcelain
Limp and soiled, make: bedraggled
Become limp: wilt
"Limp Watch" painter: Dali
Lincoln cabinet member: Chase
Lincoln Center attraction: opera, met
Lincoln, Elmo: actor
Lincoln's state: Nebr.
Lincoln's vice pres.: Hamlin
Lindberg, Mrs. Chas: Anne
Linden, Hal: actor
Line for an audience: aside
Line of cliffs: scarp
Line of defense: Abatis
Line of rotation: axis

Line of symmetry: axis
Line of work: trade
Line, single file: queue
Line, straight: row
Line up: pose
Line up, put in the: use
Lineage: descent
Linear units, international: meters
Lineman's coup: sack
Linen: napery
Linen color: ecru
Linen, pearly: nacre
Linen plant: flax
Linen source: flax
Lines of praise: ode
Lines of travel, regular: routes
Lines on a map: isobars
Lineup ender: etal
Lineup member: suspect
Lineup, picked out of: fingered
Linger: bide
Lingerie item: teddy, camisole, half-slip
Lingerie material: silk
Lingers: dallies
Lingo: jargon
Lingo, breezy: slang
Linguine topper: pesto, pesta
Linguist's concern: usage
Lingus, Aer
Liniments: balms
Link's letters: PGA, LPGA
Link's site: cuff
Link's warning: fore
Lintel companion: jamb
Lion, "Born Free": Elsa
Lion colored: tawny
"Lion King" hero: Simba
Lion group: pride
Lion monkey: tamarin, marmoset
Lionel, for one: train set
Lioness, Adamson's: Elsa
Lionhearted: heroic, bold, brave, heroic
Lion's colleagues: elks
Lion's cub: lionet
Lion's mane: ruff
Lion's roar, where: MGM
Lip cosmetic: gloss,
Lip movement: pucker
Lip Sync
Lipinshi, Tara: skater
Lips, pertain to: labial
Liquefied, by heat: molten
Liquefy: melt
Liquer, sweet: creme
Liqueur enhancer: anise
Liquid: fluid
Liquid asset: cash
Liquid measure, smallest: minim
Liquid nitrogen, like: inert
Liquid part of fat: olein
Liquid reservoir: tank
Liquid scoop: dipper
Liquid, thick: puree
Lisa's dad: Homer

Lisbon loot: Euros
Lisi, Virna: actress
Lisper's problems: ess
Lissome: slim
List, arrange in a: tabulate
List detail: item,
List enders: etc, etat, etal
List, make a: catalog
List of candidates: slate
List of choices: menu
List of corrigenda: errata
List of Names: rota, roster
List of options: menu
List of text mistakes: errata
List of typos: errata
List shortened: etc
Listen: hark
Listen carefully: heed
Listen in: audit
Listen, place to: keyhole
Listen to: heed, obey
Listening device: ear, aid
Listless: logier
Listlessness: ennui
Liszt, Franz: Hungarian composer
Liszt opus: etude
Liszt piece: sonata, etude
Lit by the waiter: flambe
Lit, softly: aglow
Literary collection: ana
Literary conflict: agon
Literary device: simile
Literary genre: satire
Literary initials: RLS
Literary Italian town: Eboli
Literary miscellany: ana
Literary monogram: TSE, RWE, RLS
Literary passage: extract
Literary snippets: ana,
Literary Swiss girl: Heide
Literary works: essays, opu
Literary works, Icelandic: edda
Lithe: slim
Lithium-ion battery
Lithographer, famous: Ives
Lithospheric depression: basin
Litigant, anonymous: Doe
Litmus reddener: acid
Litmus test Nos.: Phs
Litmus test, one: acid, alkali
Litter member: pup
Litterbug: slob
Little Bighorn state: Montana
Little Bighorn victor: Crazyhorse
Little black numbers: dresses
Little bone: ossicle
"Little Caesar" role: Rico
Little consolation: cold comfort
Little Dickson's girl: Nell
Little dipper: Oreo
Little engine verb: can
Little finger: pinkie
Little grimace: moue
Little kid: tad

"Little Lulu"
Little Mermaid: Ariel
Little more than two cups: bra
"Little Red Book" author: Mao
Little shavers: boys, lads
Little Sheba's creator: Inge
"Little Women"author: Alcott
Littoral flier: ern
Liturgical vestment: amice, alb
Live it up: carouse
Lived: dwelt
Liveliness of mind: esprit
Lively: snappy, active
Lively debate: cross-fires
Lively dance: jig, gallop, galop
Lively tune: lilt
Liver secretion: bile
Liver spread: pate
Liverpool chap: Brit
Liverpool lockups: gaols, gools
Livery work, did: shoed
Lives in Las Palmas: Vidas
Livestock source: Corn Belt
Living quarters: apts, apartments
Living thing: being
Livy bear: Ursa
Livy contemporary: Ovid
Livy's "It Was": erat
Livy's road: Iter (Rome)
Livy's year: anno
Lizard, Australian Desert: moloch
Lizard, Egyptian: adda
Lizard (large): iguana, gila
    (small): eft, uma, gecko
Lizard (Old World): agama
Lizard, sand: adda
Llama country: Andes
Llama relative: vicuna, alpaca
LLB exam: LSAT
Lloyd's business: insurance
Lo res graphics
Load to carry: armful
Loaded with calories: rich
Loading dock worker: foreman
Loadmaster's concern: cargo
Loaf ends: heels
Loafer: drone
Loafer decoration: tassel
Loafing: idle
Loamy fertilizer: marl
Loan: lien, debt
Loan abbr.: APR
Loan, apply for a: hit up
Loan, car: debt,
Loan disclosure No.: APR
Loan figure: rate
Loan quarters to:rent
Loan service: pawn shop
Loan shark: usurer
Loan sharking: usury
Loaned money: tided over
Lobbies: foyers
Lobbies, open-air: atria
Lobby call: page

Lobby, DC: PAC
Lobbying grp. org.: PAC
Lobby, open-air: Atrium
Lobe: ear lap
Lobo: wolf
Rio Lobo
Lobos, Los: pop musicians
Lobster claw: pincer
Lobster coral, e.g.: roe
Lobster eating aid: bib
Lobster, female: hen
Lobster house wear: bid
Lobster order: tail
Lobster pot: trap
Lobster tail: seafood
Lobster trap: pot
Loc Tone: rapper
Lo-cal: diet
Local idiom: dialect
Local movie theater: nabe
Locale: area
Locale in a Western: fort
Locate, perhaps: trace
Locate precisely: pinpoint
Located: sited
Locales, unspoiled: Edens
Location technique: GPS
Loch Ness "no": nae
Lock companion: key
Lock components: hairs
Lock horns: oppose
Lock of hair: tress, ringlet
Lock, type of: yale
Locke, John: Eng. philosopher
Locker room speech: pep talk
Lockheed products: jets
'Loco-Motion' Girl: Eva
Locomotive parking: siding
Locomotive switching site: round house
Locusttree: acacia
Lodge: reside
Lodge dwellers: tribe
Lodge, low-cost: hostel
Lodging: staying, inn, motel, hotel
Lodging for troops: billet
Lodging, provide: take in
Loess and loam: soil
Loewe's partner: lLearner
Loft in a barn: haymow
Loft filler: bales, hay
Lofting shot: lob
Lofty: noble, tall, high, cold
Lofty abode: aerie
Lofty, more: nobler
Lofty place: attic
Lofty standard: ideal
Log, festive: yule
Log roll: birl
Log rolling contest: rolea
Log-cutting machine: saw, re-saw
Loggard: slouch
Logger cheat: gypo
Loggerhead: shrike, turtle
Logger's commodity: pulp

Logging area: forest
Logging tool: whip saw
Logical beginning: ideo
Logical loop: vicious circle
Logical start: astro
Logician's conjunction: ergo
Logograph: puzzle, anagram
Lohengrin or tosca: opera
Lohengrin's bride: Elsa
Lois of "Lois and Clark": Teri Hatcher
Loki's daughter: Hel
Loki's victim: Otter
Lombardo, Guy: band leader
Ban-Lon
Lon Nol of Cambodia
London area: Soho
London art gallery: Tate
London bye: tata
London chap: Brit
London district: Mayfair, Soho, Acton, Chelsea, Belgravia
London flag: Union Jack
London gallery: Tate
London garden: Kew
London hoosegow: gaol
London hub: Heathrow
London, Jack, setting: Yukon
London lavatory: loo
London lockup: gaol
London newspaper: Times
London park: Hede, Hyde
London police founder: Robert Peel
London soft-felt hat: trilby
London streetcar: tram
London street edge: curb
London subway: tube
London theatre, "Old": Vic
London underground: subway
London washroom: loo
Londoners: Brits
London's theater, Old;Vic":
Lone learner: tutee
Lone Ranger name: Reid
Lone Star guy: Tex, Texan
Loner: hermit
Long ago: yore, eons
Long beak bird: toucan
Long bouts: sieges
Longbow sound: twang
Longbow wood: yew
Long, collarless robe: kaftan, caftan
Long-distance line: wats
Long-eared equine: ass
Long, easy stride: lope
Long for: yearn, pine
Long green: moolah, dinero
Longhorn: steer
Long inlet: ria
Long lunch: hero
Long March VIP: Mao Zedong
Long, Nia: actress
Long oar: scull
Long in the tooth: aged
Long-horned mythical beast: yales

Long poem, section of a: canto
Long sentence: life
Long steps, take: stride
Long story: saga, novel
Long timber: beam
Long time, a: blood moon, age, ages, eons
"Long Time No See"
Long voyage: odyssey
Long way around: detour
Long way home: detour
Long winded: prolix, wordy
Long winded, not: terse
Long-answer exam: essay
Long-billed wader: ibis
Long-clawed animal: badger
Longdrawn-out: lengthy, endless
Long-faced: solemn
Longfellow "Bell" town: Atri
Longitude unit: degree, minute, second
Long-lasting: durable
Long-nosed fish: gar
Long-nosed ungulate: tapir
Longoria, Eva: actress
Long-pointed weapon: Spear
Longshoreman: dockwalloper
Long-term babysitter: nanny
Look after: tend, see to, care for
Look ahead: plan
Look, angry: frown, glare
Look as if: seem
Look at amorously: ogle
Look, bold: leer,
Look down on: scorn
Look for water: dowse
Look forward: face
Look forward to: await
Look, goatish: leer
Look good on: fit
Look, immodest: leer
Look in on: visit briefly
Look inside: X-ray
Look intently: peer
Look like: seem
Look, nasty: leer
Look obliquely: skew
Look of loathing: sneer
Look or glance: gander
Look out below
Look over: scan, regard, case
Look searchingly: peer
Look, steady: gaze
Look, suggestive: leer
Look to be: seem
Look, unpleasant: leer
Looked as if: seemed
Looked at flirtatiously: doted
Looked the joint over: cased
Looking glass: mirror
Looking scared stiff: ashen
Look-out, be on the: abet
Lookout Men: sentries
Looks: everything link: aren't
Looks friendly: smiles
Looks good on: becomes

Looks inferior by comparison: pales
Looks sleepy: nods
Loom bar: easer
Loom, made on a: woven
Loop, dangerous: noose
Loop, lethal: noose
Loophole-free: ironclad
Loopholes: outs
Loos, Anita: writer
Loose end: detail,
Loose leaves: pages
Loose material, dust: detritus
Loose robe: caftan
Loose rocks at base of slope: scree
Loose threads: lint
Loose-lipped: loquacious
Loosen, as a grip: ease
Loosens: unties, unhooks
Loose-fitting: baggy
Loose-fold under the chin: dewlap
Looting spree: riot
Lopsided: atilt, wry, uneven
Loquacious: talky
Lord, feudal: liege
Lord's table: altar
Lord's wife: lady
Lorelei or Circe: siren
Lorelei's creator: Loos
Lorelei's river: Rhine
Loren, Sophia: actress
Loren's evening: soiree
Lo-Res graphics
Lorre, Peter: actor
"LA Law" Actress: Susan Dey
Lose: mislay
Lose energy: tire
Lose feathers: molt
Lose focus: blur
Lose force: wane
Lose hair: molt, shed
Lose intensity: ebb
Lose interest: pall
Lose it: freak, go ape
Loser, like some: sore
Loser's cry: rats
Loses all hope: despairs
Loses heart: despairs
Loses it: freaks, goes ape
Loses one's memory: blanks out,
Losing athlete's demands: rematch
Losing plan: diet
Losing proposition: diet
Losing schemes: diets
At a loss
Loss due to leaks: seepage
Loss to Cervantes: Perdida
Lost a lap: stood
Lost cause: goner
Lost control: panicked
Lost deliberately: threw
Lost hair: bald, molted
Lost in thought: rapt
Lost strength: enervate
Lot choice: used car

Lotion additive: aloe, lanolin
Lots and lots: slew
Lots of guests:houseful
Lots of laughs: fun
Lots of paper: reams
Lott, Trent: senator
Lotte, Lenya: singer
Lotto information: odds
Lotus-eater: dreamer, escapist, romantic,
    daydreamer, castle-builder
Loud, offensively: balant
Loud and blaring: brassy
Loud and rude: brassy
Loud kisses: smacks
Loud, harsh cry: yawp
Loudness measurement unit: phon
Loudness unit: sone
Louganis, Greg: diver
Loughlin, Lola: actress
Louis XIV, e.g.: roi
Lounge about: loll
Lounge around: loll
Lounge chair: chaise
Lounge lizard: fop, rake, toff, blade, dandy
Lounging slippers: mules
Louse eggs: nits
Lousy review: slam
Lout, like a: oafish, kook, cad,
    yahoo, lug
Loutish fellow: lug, cad, kook, oaf
Louvre, e.g.: musee
Louvre architect: Lescot
Louvre display: art
Louvre entrance designer: Impei
Louvre hanging: art
Louvre's Mona Lisa
Love affair: amour
Love in a gondola: amore, amor
Love, inflame with: enamor
Love, Italian style: amour
Love me: love my dog
Love or hate: emotion
Love personified: amor
Love Portion Number Nine
"Love Story" author: Segal
Love, to Cato: amo
Lovelorn ad: personal
Lovely one: vision
Lover of beauty: esthete
Lover of nature's beauty: esthete
Lover, star-crossed: Romeo, Juliet
Love's destination: lan
Loving: amorous, fond
Low: moo
Low and harsh voice: gruff
Low bow: salaam
Low brass: tuba
Low ground: marsh
Low island: cay
Low joint: knee
Low, Juliette Org.: GSA
Low or High: Tide
Low pH: acidic
Low pitch: down, bass

Low point: nadir
Low priced: el cheapo
Low profile, keep a: hide, lie doggo
Low score: zero
Low voice: murmur
Low water: ebb tide
Low-altitude cloud formation: stratus
Low-budget film: B-movie
Low-cost lodging: hostel
Low-down Guy: Heel
Low-down, The: Facts
Low-fat label word: lite
Low-key persuasion, use: coax
Low-pressure system: cyclone, trough
Lowe, Chad: actor
Lowe, Rob: actor
Lowell, Amy: poet
Lower: nether
Lower classman: esne
Lower in dignity: debase
Lower in status: demote
Lower oneself: kneel
Lower prices: slash
Lower the exchange rate: devalue
Lowered in status: abased
Lowers the beam: dims
Lowest high tide: neap
Lowest point: bottom, nadir
Lowing: mooing
Lowly: menial
Lowly NCO: Corporal, Cpl
Low-lying land: swale, vale
Low-tech cooler: fan
Low-tech hauler: ox cart
Loy, Myrna: actress
Lox locale: deli
Lox surveyor: deli
Lox seller: deli
Lox source: deli
Loyal: true
Loyal, remain: adhere
Loyal subject: liege
LP holder: sleeve
LP material: vinyl
LP speed: RPM
LP spinners: disc jockets, DJs
Letter. addenda: PSS
Luanda is its capital: Angola
Luau attire: muumuu
Luau dish: poi
Luau fare: poi
Luau entertainment: hula
Luau instrument: uke
Lubber's aye: yes
Lubitsch, Ernst: director
Lucas, George: director
Lucerne et Leman: , lakes, lacs
Lucid, most: sanest
"Luck be a Lady"
Pot luck
Luck, to the trish: cess
Luck, type of: dumb
Lucky charm: amulet
"Lucky Jim" author: Kingsley Amis

Lucy of "Kill Bill": Liu
Lucy of nursery rhymes: Locket
Lucyof "Xena": Lawless
Lucy's friend: Ethel
Lucy's Mari do: Desi
Ludicrous: inane
Ludwig, Emil: biographer
Ludwig's lament: ach
Hasta luego
Luftwaffe foe: RAF
Luggage fasteners: hasps
Lugosi, Bela: actor
Lugosi role (1939): Igor
Luigi farewell: ciao
Luigi's love: amore
    romance: amore
    thirst: sete
Luke's teacher: Yoda, Obi-wan
Lull: rest
Lull before a storm: calm
Lumber, like: sawn
Lumber, piece of: board, plank
Lumberjack commodity: log, wood
Lumberjack, fabled: Paul Bunyan
Lumberjack leaving: stump
Luminary: star
Lummox: oaf, lout
Lump of clay: clod
Lump (rounded): nodule, wad
Luna, Eva: Isabel Allende book
Lunacy: madness,
Lunar dark area: mare, maria
Lunar disappearance: moon set
Lunar effect: tide
Lunar new tear: tet
Lunar phenomenon: tide
Lunar, solar year excess: epact
Lunar valley: rill, rille
Lunar vehicle: LEM
Lunch, make: feed
Lunch order: platter
Lunch order, popular: BLT, burger
Lunch, place for: bag
Lunchbox item: thermos
Luncheonette list: menu
Lung feature: air sacs
Lunt, Alfred: actor
LuPone, Patti:
Lurch and sway: careen
Lurching: careening
Lure into illegality: entrap
Lures: tempts, bait, jigs
Lurked: skulked
Luscious: tasty
Lush: sot, drunkard
Lustrous black: raven
Lusty feeling: hots
Lute, type of: mandolin
Luther, Martin: German theologian
Luthor, Lex: character
Luxuries: extras
Luxurious: posh
Luxury: esse
Lap of luxury

Lydian king: Gyges, Croesus
Lying down: prone
Lymphoid tissue: tonsil, adenoid
Lynchpin site: axle
LBJs beagle: Him, Her
Lynx: bobcat
Lyon, Sue: actress
Lyra's bright star: Vega
Lyric poem: epode, ode
Lyrical: poetic
Lysander's beloved: Hermia
Lysol target: germ

M

"M" to Einstein: mass
Ma Bell: telephone monopoly
Ma has a bow for it: cello
Ma, Yoyo: cellist
Maacah father: Nahor, Talmai, Absalom
    husband: David, Jehiel, Machir
    son: Hanan, Abijam, Achish
Ma's guy: Pa
"Mac" rival: PC
Macabre: eerie
Macabre, danse of: dance of death
Macao monetary unit: pataca
Macaw: parrot, arara, ara
Macaw, brazilian: arara
Macaw genus: ara
Macbeth, for one: thane, feudal lord
Macbeth prop: dagger
Macbeth, Lady (what she did): stabbed
Macbeth's burial place: Iona
MacDowell, Andie: actor
Macedonian, ancient capital: Pella
Macedonian city: Edia
MacGraw, Ali: actress
Mach, Ernst: physicist
Machete cousin: bolo
Machiavellian: wily, shrewd, cunning,
    devious, guileful
Deus ex machina
Machine for hoisting: pulley, crane, lift
Machine gun: Sten
Machine gun, compact: uzi
Machine language: binary
Machine shop area: tool room
Machine type: slot
Macho: virile
Machu Picchu dweller: Inca
Machu Picchu founder: Inca
Machu Picchu home: Peru
Mackerel Cousin: Bonito
Mackerel gull: tern
Mackerel, type of: atkam
MacLachlan, Lyle: actor
MacLaine, Shirley: actress
MacLean, Alistar: author
MacPherson, Elle: model
Macrame unit: knot
Mad Hatter prop: cup
Mad, hopping: fuming

Mad, wasn't merely: rage
Madagascar climber: lemurs
Madame Bovary's name: Emma
Madder family member: Ipecac
Made a basket, say: wove, scored
Made a decision: opted
Made a deep bow: salaamed
Made a hitch: tied
Made a home: nested
Made a tapestry: wove
Made a trade: swap
Made a will: testate
Made after taxes: wage, net
Made an attempt:essayed
Made an impression: sank in
Made before taxes: gross
Made catty remarks: sniped
Made chaotic: messed up
Made do: coped
Made full disclosure: aired
Made hands: dealt
Made happen: caused
Made haste: rushed, hurried
Made inroads into savings: dips
Made it happen: saw to it
Made known, sub rosa: leaked
Made of clay: earthen
Made of oak: wooden
Made of (suff): ine
Made on a loom: woven
Made one's jaw drop: awed
Made one's way: wended
Made perpendicular: plumbed
Made possible: enabled
Made sense: clicked, added up
Made slippery: greased
Made the most of: used
Made the scene: came
Made things right: atoned
Made to order: custom, bespoke
Made top honors: aced
Made tracks: hied
Made up for: atoned
Made varsity: lettered
Made with cream: rich
Mademoiselle's date: Ami
    father: Pere
Made-up: bogus, fake, painted, invented
Madison Ave. guys: ad men
Madison Avenue VIP: ad exec
Madmen run, how: amok
Madness: lunacy
Madonna role: Evita, Eva
Madras Herr: Sri
Sierra Madre Mountains
Madre's sister: tia
Madrid coins, former: peseta
Madrid month: Enero
Madrid mother: madre
Madrid, Mrs: SRA, SRI
Madrid museum: Prado
"Ginny" Mae
Mae West accessory: boa
Mae West role: Lil

Mae West wear: boa
Maelstrom: eddy
Mafia bigwig: Capo
Mafia branch chief: Capo
Magazine, business: Inc.
Magazine employee: fact checker
Magazine exhortation: renew
Magazine, fashion: Elle
Magazine issue: vol., volume
Magazine, lurid: pulp
Magazine, science: Omni
Magazine section: roto
Magazine, small business: INC
Magazine stand: rack
Magazine , tech: Byte
Magazine, women's: Cosmopolitan, Cosmo
Magda's sister: Eva
Magellan discovery: Guam
"As if by magic"
Magic, black: voodoo
Magic cure: panacea
Magic Kingdom neighbor: Epcot
Magic medicine: elixir
Magic potion: philter
Magic wand tip: star
Magician, tribal: witch doctor
Magician's prop: wand
Magician's word: presto, poof
Magi's guide: star
Magistrate command: rise
Magistrate, Venetian: doge
Maglie, Sal: baseball
Magma, emerging: lava
Magna cum laude
Magnani, Anna: actress
Magnate: tycoon
Magnate, powerful: titan
Magnet alloy: alnico
Magnet end: pole
Magnetic field strength unit: gamma
Magnetic flux unit: tesla
Magnetic recording: tape
Magnetic unit: tesla
Magnetism, unit of: esu
Magnolia State: Mississippi
Cro Magnon man
Magoni, Lara: skier
Magoo's (Mr.) nephew: Waldo
Magritte, Rene: painter
Taj Mahal
Mahjongg material: tiles
Mahjongg piece: tile
Mahler, Gustav: composer
Maid, far east: amah
Maid, type of: mer, meter
Maiden name: nee
Maiden name indicator: nee
Maidenhair, for one: fern
Mail acronym: SWAK
Mail carrier's org.: USPS
Mail center: GPO
Mail, kind of: fan, bulk, email
Mail related: postal,
Mail, undelivered: nixie

Mail, unwelcome: bills
Mailbox device: chute
Mailer, Norman: writer
Mailer, return: SASE
Mail-motto word: nor, rain, sleet
Main course: entrée
Main dish: entrée, meat
Main idea: gist
Main impact of an attack: brunt
Mainlander's momento: lei
Main point: nub, gist
Main road: artery
Main role: lead
Main route, not a: sideway, detour
Main street, not the: byroad
Main theme: key notes
Main thrust: brunt
Maine college town: Orono
Maine national park: Acadia
Mainframe component: CPU
Maintaining, keep: reassert
Maintenance director: super
Maintenancy: upkeep
Maison maitre: Pere
Maison rooms: salles
Maison story: etage
Maize unit: ear (corn)
Majestic: grand, regal, royal
Majestic display: pomp
Majestic wader: egret
Her Majesty
Lese majesty
Major and minor: scales
Major city: capital
Major constellation: Ursa
Major Hoople: Amos
Major Hoople word: egad
Major oil hub: Tulsa
Major opening: event
Major recording label: Arista
Major, suffix with: ette
Major work: opus
Majorette's art: twirling
Majorette's gait: strut
Make a decision: opt
Make a difference: matter
Make a fast buck
Make a fist: clench
Make a footnote: cite
Make a gaff: err
Make a hole in: pierce
Make a knight: dub
Make a lasting impression: etch
Make a list: catalog
Make a mess of: foul up, blow
Make a move: step
"Make a run for it"
Make a wrong move: err
Make angry: enrage
Make beautiful: adorn
Make before taxes: gross
Make believe: pretend, feign
Make beloved: endear
Make bubbly: aerate

Make changes: alter
Make clear: elucidate
Make cobwebs: spin
Make copies: xerox
Make corrections: emend
Make cynical: jade
Make dim: blear
Make do with: eke
Make eager: whet
Make earnest petition to: pray
Make exaggerated claims: over-sell
Make faces: mug
Make firm: ftabilize
Make fragrant: embalm
Make fun of: derude, deride, tease
Make furious: enrage
Make fuzzy: blur
Make illegal: ban
Make immune: vaccinate
Make impure: taint
Make in Advance: precook
Make indifferent: alienate
Make insensitive: numb
Make irrational: dement
Make judgments: deem
Make keen (appetite): whet
Make lame, perhaps: maim
Make laugh: amuse
Make less dependent: wean
Make like new: restore
Make limp and soiled: bedraggled
Make long stitches:baste
Make manifest: evince
Make merry: revel
Make more useful: enhance
Make numb: deaden
Make one: unite, join
Make over: redo, cede, deed, assign,
          convey, reform, remodel
Make plain: evince
Make pleas on one's knees: pray, beg
Make possible: enable
Make precious: endear
Make restitution for: redress
Make retribution: atone
Make sacred: hallow
Make sharper: whet, hone
Make shore: land
Make simmer: heat
Make small talk: chat
Make smooth: iron, sand
Make sore by rubbing: chafe
Make stronger: beef up
Make sure: check
Make taboo: ban
Make the call: decide
Make the most of: use
Make things happen: act
Make thinner: dilute
Make too much of: overrate
Make too thin: emaciate
Make tracks: hie
Make yawn: bore
Makes a difference: atters

Makes a faux pas: errs, errors, flubs
Makes a screenplay out of: adapts
Makes a shambles of: ruins
Makes a smooth transition: segues
Makes a sound: utters
Makes accessible: opens
Makes an effort: essays
Makes candles: dips
Makes fun of: mocks
Makes headway: gains
Makes obsolete: outdates
Makes one's way: wends
Makes pretty: adorns
Makes sense: clicks, adds up
Makes taboo: ban
Makes tracks: dubs
Makes up for: atones
Makes use of: avails
Makeshift abode: lean-to
Makeshift ballpark: sandlot
Makeshift desk: table, table top
Makeup, fuss with: primp
Makeup, slangily: war paint
Making less sense: inaner
Making no noise: Silent
Making one's way: wending
Malaga moolah: peso
Malaise: blahs
Malamute's load: sled
Malaprop title: Mrs.
Malaria symptom: ague
Malawi, formerly: nyasa
Malay boats: proas, prahus
Malay monetary unit: tical
Malay sailboat: proa, prahu
Malay tribesman: Moro
Malayan isthmus: kra
Malayan wrap: sarong
Mal-de-mer: seasickness
Malden, Karl: actor
Male adornment: beard
Male duck: drake
Male or female: gender
Male pintail: drake
Male swan: cob
Male, vane: FOP
Malevolent: evil
Malicious burning: arson
Malicious elves: goblins
Malicious, slyly: snide
Malicious way, in a: evilly
Mall activity: buying, shopping
Mall activity in Beijing: siaoping
Mall attraction: sale
Mall booth: kiosk,
Mall feature: atrium, cinema
Mall for Plato: Agora
Mall stands: kiosks
Mallard cousin: teal
Mallard genus: anas
Mallet-wielder's sport: polo
Malodor cause: rot
Malodorous: fetid
Malodorous creature: pole cat, skunk

Malone, Karl: NBA player
Malone, Moses: NBA player
Malta cash: lira
Maltase: enzyne
Maltha component: tar
Malt-shop freebie: straw
Mama Cass Elliott
Mama's boy: son
Mame's "bosom buddy": Vera
"Mamma Mia"
Mammal, omnivorous: coati
Mammal, riverine: otter
Mammal, very large: whale
Mammal's coat: pelage
Mammal's flourished, when: escene
Mammal's need: air
"Mammoth Hunters" heroine: Ayla
"Mammoth Hunters" author: Auel
Mammoths roamed, when: ice age
Mammoth trap: tar, tar pit
Man and wife: wedded
Man address as my lord: earl
"I met a man"
Man, but not woman: isle
"A man for all seasons"
Man from Dundee: Scot
Man from Qum: Irani
"Man is not a fly"
Man of many words: Roget
Man of the future: boy
Man of the haus: Herr
Man of La Mancha: Senor
Man of the cloth: cleric, clergy
Man on a date: escort
Man or woman: human
Odd man out
Old Man Flint
"Pac Man fever"
"Man without a Country": Phillip Nolan
Manacle: leg iron
Manage for oneself: fend
Manage, hard to: ornery
Manage OK: cope
Manage somehow: cope
Managed-care Groups: HMOs
Managerie: zoo
Manages: cares, copes
Manassas general: Reno
Manche capital: Stlo
Manchester, Melissa: musician
Mandarin orange variety: satsuma
Mandate: edict, law
Mandates: laws
Mandikova, Hana: tennis player
Mandolin's kin: lute
Mandrill, for one: baboon
Mane, unruly: mop
Edouard Manet: French painter
Maneuver: tactic
Maneuver, devious: ploy
Maneuver slowly: ease
Maneuver, room to: leeway
Maneuver, wily: ploy
Maneuvering room: latitude

Mangel-wurzel: beet, coarse beet
Man-goat deity: faun
Manhattan ingredient: rye
Manhattan region: Bowery
Maniac, kind of: ego
Maniacal act: rave,
Manicurist board: emery
Manifest, become: emerge
Manifest, make: evince
Manila resin: elemi
Manilow, Barry: Musician
Manipulate, dishonestly: rig
Man-made fiber: rayon, nylon, cacron
Mannequin: model, dummy
Manner: mien, mode
Manner, in a hostile: icily
Manner, in a kingly: regally
Manner, in a proper: suitably
Manner of doing: mode
Manners, ease of: poise
Manners maven: Emily Post
Mannheim mister: Herr
Manor: estate
Man-shaped mug: toby
Mansion and grounds: estate
Mantas: ray
Mantis, mimic a: pray
Mantel: ledge, cape
Mantelpiece, wide-spouted: ewer
Mantle, it's below the: core
Mantra chant: oms
Mantra chanter: Dali Lama
Mantra, use: chant
Mantras (Hindu): ism
Mantuan money: lira (Ancient Italian City)
Manual consultant: user
Manufacture's meas.: GPO
Manuscript sender: author
Manvell, Elsa: hostess
Many a slot: mail-drop
Many, great: gobs, lots
Many guests: houseful
Many in combo: ply, poly
Many layers: hens
Many moons: ages
Many-petaled flower: rose
Mao Tse Tung: China
Maori dish ingredient: taro
Maori Te Kanawa: Kiri
Map a course: plot
Map collection: atlas
Map detail: isle
Map feature: inset
Map, kind of: relief
Map making name: Rand, McNally
Map marker: push pins
Map projection: conic, Mercator, polyconic
Map source: atlas
Map within a map: inset
Maple, Marla: Mrs. Trump
Maple sap, collect: tap
Maple sap bowl: rogan
Maple sugar base: sap
Maple tree genus: acer

Mapplethorpe's work: art
Maraschino, to harmonicas: anagram
Marathon unit: mile
Maraud: ravage, raid
Mrs. Marbella: SRA
Marble: rock
Marble block: slab
Marble figure: statice
Marble (playing): immy, taw, mib
     agate, aggies
Marbles, shooting: taw, aggie
Marceau character: Bip
Marceau's everyman: Bip
Marcel Marceau: mime
March comes in like, what: a lion
March date: Ides
     mother: Marmee
     sister: Amy, Beth, Meg
March 15th, e.g.: Ides
March girl, eldest: Meg
March hare, like a: mad
March king: Sousa
March leader, Long: Mao
March Madness Org,: NCAA
March master: Sousa
March time: Ides
Marchers, half-time: band
Marchers, university: band, ROTC
Marching band needs: drums
Marcianos' Label: Guess
Marco Polo's Home: Venice
Marcos, Imelda: Philippines leader
"Mardi Gras"
Mardi Gras follower: Lent
Mare, Walter Dala: writer
Mareno, Rita: actress
Mare's Nest: hoax
Margaret Mead locale: Samoe
Margarita base: tequila
Margin of time: leeways
Margin, tiny: whisker
Maria, Ave
Maria Conchita Alonso
Maria Elena
Maria Eleni
Tia Maria: coffee liqueur
Mariachi gig: fiesta
Mariachi, like: Mexican
Mariachi wear: serape
Mariana island: Guam
Mariana's largest island: Guam
Eva Marie Saint
Marie's companion: Amie
Marie's Seas: Mers
Marina rental: slip
Marinate: soak
Marine deposit: coral
Marine eel: conger
Marine fish: robalo, snook
Marine gastropod: murex
Marine mollusk: whelk
Marine passageway: sea lane
Mariner, ancient: Noah
Mariner, storied: Nemo

Mariner's milieu: sea
Mariner's saint: Elmo
Marine's bulldog: mascot
Marjoram, e.g.: herb
Mark a page: dog-ear
Mark against students: demerits
Mark, authenticating: seal
Mark, black: smut
Mark down: sale
Mark, insert: caret
Mark of Finn fame: Twain
Mark Twain and Saki, for two: pen name
Mark Twain's forte: satire
Mark with spots: mottle
Markdown: sale
Marked: flagged
Marked down: on sale
Marker:,buoy, pen, tack, pin, IOU, debt
Markers out, has: owes
Market: vend, sell
Market, fit to: salable
Market, kind of: mass
Market move, positive: gain
Marketplace: forum, agora (old)
Marketplace, Athenian: agora
Market, type of: flea
Market venues, widening of: ad creep
Marketing partner: sales
Marketplace, eastern: bazaar
Marketplace, Internet: eBay
Markham, Beryl: aviatrix
Markka fraction: permi
Marksman, sneaky: sniper
Marlette comic strip: Kudzu
Marmalade chunks: rinds
Marmee girl, a: Beth
Marmora: sea
Marmoset with black hands: tamarin
Marner, Silas:
Marner contraption: loom
Marquand sleuth: Moto
Marquand title character: Apley
Marquetry: inlay
Marquette, explorer: Pere
Marquis de Sade
Marquis, for one: noble
Marquis, rank above: duke
Marquis, rank below: earl
Marriage, before: nee
Marriage may change some: names
Marriage product: in-laws
Marriage seeker: suitor
Marriage within a group: endogamy
Marriageable: nubile
Married woman's title: Mrs., wife
Marrying men, abbr.: JPs
Mars: comb. form: Areo
Mars's Greek counterpart: Ares
Mars to Plato: Ares
Mars to the Greeks: Ares
Marseillaise composer: Rouget de Lisle
Marseilles "Me": moi
Marseilles Ms: Mlle
Marsh: bog, swamp, fen, morasses, mire

Marsh bird: stilt
Marsh gas: methane
Marsh grass plant: reed, tule, sedge
Marsh growth: reed, reeds
Marsh, like a: reedy
Marsh vapor: miasma
Marshal, Napoleonic: Ney
Marshal of France, 1744: Saxe
Marshal under Napoleon: Ney
Marshal's badge: shield, star
Marshal's band: posse
Marshal's concern: mob
Marshal's problem: mob
Marshy inlet: bayou
Marshy tract: swale
Marsupial, American: possum
Marsupial, badger-size: wombat
Marsupial, milne: roo
Marsupial, small: wombat
Martens: weasels, sables
Martha's Vineyard, for one: resort
Martial art: aikido, karate, judo, kung fu,
        kendo, tai chi, shaolin
Martial arts school: dojo
Martin, Amis: writer
Martin, Pamela Sue: actress
Martin, Steve: actor
Martini, heated: Hot Gibson
Martinelli, Elsa: actress
Martinez, Tino: baseball player
Martini's partner: Rossi
Martinique volcano: Pelee
Martin's auto partner: Aston
Marvin Kalb: journalist
Marvy: fab
Marx Brothers: Harpo, Gummo, Zeppo,
        Groucho, Chico
Marx, Karl: philosopher
"Bloody Mary"
Mary Kay Ash
Mary Kay Cosmetics
Mary Poppins owned one: carpetbag
Mary's husband: Clopas, Joseph, Alphaeus
        sons: Mark, James, Jesus
Mary's pal: Rhoda
Marzipan base: almond
Ma's guy: Pa
Mascagni temptress: Lola
Mascara applicator: wands
Mascara kin: eye liner
Mascara site: lashes, cilia
Mascot, inexperienced: Green Giant
Masculine, extremely: macho
Masculine nor feminine (not): neuter
Masculine possessive: his
Masculine principle: yang
Masculinity, having: virile
Masefield heroine: an
Maserati, Ernesto: auto designer
Maserati rival: Ferrari
Mash: mush, crush, paste, puree
Mashed potato serving: glop
Masher, response to a: slap
Mashhad man: Irani

Masjid: mosque
Mask: hide, veil, blind, cloak
Mask feature: slit
Mask star: Cher
Mason, Marsha: actress
Mason's burden: Hod
Mason's implement: trowel
Mason's (Perry) PI: Drake
Mass, small: wad
Mass, amorphous: blob
Mass of clouds: bank
Mass seating: pews
Mass, shapeless: glob
Mass, unit of: amir
Mass vestment: alb
Massacre: decimate
Massage, light: backrub
Massage place: parlor
Massages: kneads
Massenet opera: Thais
Masses, the: hoi polloi, full
Masseuse employer: spa
Massive reference work: OED
Mast, Thomas: cartoonist
Master, in colonial India: sahib
Master, in Swahili: bwana
Masterful manner, in a: adeptly
Masters: adepts
Master's garb: green jacket
Masters, old: oils
Masthead names: editors
Mastic or copal: resin
Masticate: chew
Mastroianni's milieu: Italia
Mat, decorative: doily
Mat, Japanese: tatami
Mata Hari: spy
Mata of spydom: Hari
Matador foe: el toro
Matador, wound a: gore
Matadors, procession of: paseo
Match both sides by trimming: even up
Match in poker: see
Match pair: set
Matching game: lotto, lottery
Mate type: soul
Alma mater
Dura mater (Brain Covering)
Material design: print
Material, suitable: serge
Material, thin: voile
Maternally related: enate
Math abbr.: lim, log, div, lcm
Math, do the: add
Math proof: theorem
Math proof abbr.: QED
Math proof letter: QED
Math ratio: sine
Math results: sums
Math statement: axioms
Math subject: algebra
Math term: cosine, ratio, LCD
Math, third power: cube
Math with triangles: trig

Mathematical array: matrix
Mathematical grouping, some: tens
Mathematical proposition: theorem
Mathematician, Swiss: Euler
Matinee star: idol
Mating game: chess
Mating time: end of game
Matisse, Henri: painter
Matisse piece: art
Mato Grosso river: Negro, Rio Negro (Brazil)
Matriarch: female, dame, mother, grande dame
Matriculate: join, enter, enroll
Matrix: array, grid
Matter of discussion: issue
Matter of dispute: issue
Matter, unimportant: trivia
Matterhorn: Alps
Matterhorn echo: yodel
Matter-of-fact: dry, plain, prose, prosy, sober, stoic, stolid
Mattress category: firm, king, queen
Mattress problem: sag
Mature, fully: ripe
Maturing agent: ager
Maturity, comes to: ripens
Maudlin: sappy, gushy
Maui cookout: luau
Maui crater: Eke
Mauna Kea: Volcano
Mauna Kea's city: Hilo
Mauna Loa: Volcano
Maurice Ravel favorite: Bolero
Maven: expert
Mavourneen's place: Erin
Mav's foe (NBA): Cavs
Mawish: corny
Maxim or saw: adage
Maximal suffix: -est
Maximum: utmost
Maximum level: cap
Maxwell, Elsa: hostess
May come undressed: salad
"May it not be an omen"
May, Elaine: director
May 17th honoree: St. Pat
Mayberry sot: Otis
Maybes: ifs
Maynard, Ken: cowboy
Mazatlan mister: senor
Maze: snarl, jungle, tangle
Maze traveler: rat
Maze word: start
Mazel Tov: good luck
McBeal, Ally
McCambridge, Mercedes: actress
McCarey, Leo: director
McCarthy, Mary: author
McCay, Winsor: artist
McClellan, George: commander
McClould, Sam: TV actor
McCloud's hometown: Taos
McClure, Darrell: artist
McClure, Doug: actor

McClurg, Bea: actress
McClurg, Edie: actress
McCoy's nickname: Bones
McCrea, Joel: actor
McDonald's founder: Ray Kroc
McEnroe, John: Tennis player
McGuire, Mark: Baseball player
McHale, Kevin: NBA player
McKellen, Ian: actor
McNally's partner: Rand
McShane, Ian: actor
Mdse bars: UPC
Mdse bill: invoice. inv.
Me: myself
"Me" devotee: egoist
"Me" type: egoist
Mead, Margaret: anthropologist
Mead's island: Samoa
Mead's workplace: Samoa
Meadow: lea, mead, park, field
Meadow bird: bobolink
Meadow flower: violet
Meadow mouse: vole
Meadow of France: Pre
Meadow sound: lowing
Meager: bare, lean, slim, thin
Meagerness: sparsity, smallness
Meal: repast, bran, chow, diet, eats
Meal for the humbled: crow
Meal fragment: ort
Meal, in need of a: unfed
Meal opener: oat
Meal or ranch: spread
Meal part: entrée,
Meal, served a: fed
Meal, sumptuous: spread
Meal, zero-star: slop
Mealy mouthed: unsure
Mean: intend, low, par say, base, plan
Mean and nasty: ornery
Mean one: ogre
Mean people: ogres
Meander: loop, rove, wind, snake
Meandering: devious, sinuous, turning
Meaning: aim, end, gist, goal, hint
Meaning of, give the: define
Meaning, shade of: nuance
Meaningful: deep, meaty, pithy, useful
Meaningless: empty, trite, absurd, paltry, stupid
Meaningless words: nonsense
Means: way, jack, mode, funds
Means of entering: access
Mean's partner: lean,
Mean-spirited: low, base, poor, vile
Meantime: interim, interval
Meanwhile: meantime
Meara's partner, once: stiller
Measles type: German
Measly: paltry
Measly problem: itch
Measure: act, law, bill, plan
Measure of national wealth: gnp
Measure off: pace

Measure out: mete, dole
Measures, firewood: steres,
Measuring device: gage, burette, gauge, caliper, meter, sextant
Measurement, lateral: width
Meat and potato dish: stew
Meat curing agent: nitrite
Meat, dried: jerky
Meat fat: lard
Meat garnish: aspic
Meat, iron-rich: liver
Meat jelly: aspic
Meat, low fat: emu
Meat package letters: USDA
Meat, skewer: kebabs
Meat, spicy: salami,
Meat substitute: tofu
Meat, trendy: emu
Meatballs, type of: Swedish
Meatloaf serving: slab
Mecca belief: Islam
Mecca native: Arab
Mecca pilgrimage: Haj
Mecca resident: Saudi
Mechanical game: pinball
Mechanical learning method: rote,
Mechanically enhanced human: cyborg
Mechanics, branch of: statics
Vade mecum: hand book, useful object
Medal or furniture wood: purple heart
Meddlesome, more: nosier
Medea, (he jilted her): Jason
"Medea" playwright: Euripides
Medea sailed on her: Argo
Medea's husband: Jason
Media corp: AT&T
Media excess: hype
Media, kind of: mass
Media star: celeb
In medias res
Mediate: brood
Medical astringent: alum
Medical care group: HMO
MD, familiarly: doc
MD command: stat
Medical discovery: symptoms
Medical insignias: caducei
Medical journal, Bbritish: lancet
Medical plan: HMO
Medical suffix: -oma, -osis,
Medical thriller writer: Robin Clark
Medicated ointment: oleate
Medicinal herb: cardamom, senna
Medicinal orchid tuber: salep
Medicinal plant: tansy, senna
Medicinal potion: elixir
Medicinal root: ipecac, ginseng
Medicine, amt. of: dose, dosage
Medicine, give: dose
Medicine man: shaman
Medicine, of: latric
Medicine, patent: tonic
Medicine tablet: pill
Medico: doc,

Medieval adventure: quest
Medieval barrier: moat
Medieval battle play: siege
Medieval catapult: onager
Medieval clown: jester
Medieval dance: estample
Medieval entertainer: minstrel, bard
Medieval holding: fief
Medieval hymn start: dies
Medieval laborer: serf
Medieval minstrel: goliard
Medieval musician: lutist
Medieval poem: lai
Medieval Scandinavia, pertaining to: Norse
Medieval science: alchemy
Medieval serf: esne
Medieval shield, large: pavis
Medieval slave: serf
Medieval steward: seneschal
Medieval subordinate: vassal
Medieval system: feudal
Medieval tale: gest
Medieval trade union:guild
Medieval weapon: mace
Mediocre: so so
Mediocre writer: hack
Meditation chant: mantra
Meditation guide: guru
Meditation method: tai chi
Meditation practice: Zen
Meditation room: zendo
Meditative discipline: Zen, yoga
Meditative sect: Zen
Mediterranean capital: Tripoli
Mediterranean flower: crocus
Mediterranean fruit: fig, carob
Mediterranean island: Cyprus, Crete, Malta
Mediterranean isle: Corsica
Mediterranean landmark: Etna
Mediterranean spouter: Etna
Mediterranean, to the Romans: Marenostrum
Mediterranean vessel: setee
Mediterranean wind: solano
Medium for Rembrandt: oils
Medium's session: séance
Meerschaum, e.g.: pipe
Meet defiantly: dare
Meet edge to edge: abut
Meet official: timer
Meet segments: events
Meeting: tryst, session
Meeting, conduct a: hold
Meeting guide: agenda
Meeting hammer: gavel
Meeting, hold a: confer, conduct
Meeting minutes: acta
Meeting, pep: rally
Meeting plan: agenda
Meeting program: agenda
Meeting, secret: tryst
Meg components: bytes
Megalomaniac's desire: power
Meg's sister: Beth
Mehitabel's pal: Archy

Meir, Golda: Israel ruler
Mekong native: Lao
Mekong people: Lao
Melancholy: sad, low, woe, blue
Melanesian sarong: sulu
Melange: olio
Melbourne mate: Aussie
Melding game: pinochle
Melee: brouhaha
Mellow, as brandy: age
Mellow, become: age
Mellow, gets: ages
Melmac émigré: Alf
Melmac visitor: Alf
Melodeon: organ
Melodic: arioso, ariose
Melodious: dulcet
Melodrama: play
Melodramatic cry: oho, alas
Melodramatic, got: emoted
Melody: air
Melon: pepo, casaba
Melon, greenish: casaba
Melon pear: pepino
Melon, tropical: papaya
Melrose Place
Melrose Place character: Aman
Mel's diner waitress: Vera, Flo
Melt: thaw, liquefy, soften
Melt, as an icicle: drip
Melt away: vanish
Melt down, as fat: render
Melt ingredient: cheese
Melt together: fuse
Meltdown site: core
Melted, in Marseilles: fondu
Melted together: fused,
Melting-watch artist: dali
Melts together: fuses
Melville book: Omoo
Melville captain: Ahab
Melville's Billy Budd
Melville's inspiration: sea
Member of the masses: prole,
    (proletarian)
Membership, admit into: initiate
Membrane type: mucous
Memento: relic, keepsake, token
Memo acronym: FYI
Memo letters: ASAP. FYI, attn
Memo opener: INRE
Memo starter: FYI
Memoir topic: past
Memorable bridge guarder: troll
Memorable decade: era,
Memorable saying: saw, sawe
Memorable time: epoch, era
Memorial 1836 battle site: Alamo
Memorial post, Indian: Xat
Memory, enjoy a: relive
Memory failure: lapse
Memory, from: rote
Memory glitch: lapse
Memory joggers: lists

Memory lose: amnesia
Memory, missing: amnesia
Memory, recite from: reel-off
Memory, say from: recite
Memory type: ROM, RAM
Memory unit, PC: meg, bit
Memotti title role: Amahi
Memphis's blues street: Beale
Memphis deity: Ptah
Memphis street, historic: Beale
Memsahib's nanny: Amah
Memsahib's servant: Amah
Menacing hand: fist
Menacing sound: grr
Menagerie: zoo
Mend a toe: darn
Mend argyles: darn
Mend, as a bone: knit
Mendacious: untruthful
Mendacious one: liar
Mendacious, was: lied
Mendicant: beggar
Mendicant does, what a: begs
Mendicant's cry: alms
Men-goats of myth: fauns
Menial worker: flunky, peon
Menjou, Adolphe: actor,
Menlo Park inventor: Thomas Edison
Menlo Park name: Thomas Edison
Mennonite group: Amish
Men's store: haberdashery
Mensa data: iqs
Mensa entrance need: IQ test
Mensa people, like: brainy
Mensa stats: IQs
Mental apathy: stupor
Mental block: Rubik's Cube
Mental conception: image
Mental confusion: fog
Mental distress, extreme: anguish
Mental facilities: wits
Mental flash: idea
Mental image: idea
Mental picture: image
Mental spark: idea
Mentally responsive: alert
Mentally sound: sane
Mention indirectly: allude to
Mentioned, as: idem
Menu choice: rare, entrée
Menu highlight: entrée
Menu item: entrée
Menu phrase: a la
Menu section: dessert
Menu word, Italian: alla
Menu words: a la
Menuhin contemporary: stern
Mercator's tome: atlas
Merchandise id: UPC
Merchandise ship, in-port: bum boat
Merchant: dealer, trader
Merchant ship: argosy
Merchant ship officer: mate
Merchant ships, large: argosies

Mercouri, Melinda: actress
Mercury alias: Hermes
Mercury, move like: rotate
Mercury neighbor: Venus
Mercutio's pal: Romeo
Meredith subject: egoist
Merely: solely
Merganser relative: smew
Merger or buy out: deal
Ante meridiem
Meringue, like: eggy
Merino or cheviot: wool
Merino mamas: ewes
Merit award: badge
Merkel, Una: actress
Merlin's forte: magic
Merlot or pinot noir: red, red wine
Mermaid, Disney's: Ariel
Mermaid, movie: Ariel
Mermaid star: Cher
Merman, Ethel: musician
Merope's father: Atlas, Oenopion
     husband: Polybus, Sisyphus
     lover: Orion
     mother: Pleione
     sister: Pleiades
     son: Aepytus, Glaucus
Merrill, Dina: actress
Merrimack or Monitor: warships
Merry king of rhyme: Cole
Merry sound: ha ha
Merry time: lilt
Merry-making: conviviality
Merry's opposite: sad
Merseyside mom: mater(english)
Mertzes tenant: Lucy Ricardo, Ricky Ricardo
Mesa dweller: Hopi Indians
Mesa relative: butte
Mesh, as gears: engage
Mesh fabric: net
Mesh native: Irani
Meshes: nets
Mesmerized: enrap
Mesopotamia, now: Iraq
Mesozoic: era
Mess hall mess: slop
Message, fast: telegram, email
Message for oneself: fend
Message, get the: see
Message, hide a: encoded
Message, secret: code
Message trans system: telex
Message, urgent: wire
Messalina's husband: Claudius
Messed up: bungled
Messenger: herald
Messiah composer: George Handel
Messina sight: Etna
Mess-up: botch, err
Messy, not: neat, tidy
Messy one: slob
Messy person: slob
Messy place: sty
Messy quarters: pig sty, sty

Mesta, Perle: hostess
Met, as an occasion: rose to
Met highlights: aria
Met production: opera
Met solo: aria
Met star: diva
Metaphysical beings: entia
Basal metabolism rate: BMR
Metal coating, have a: plated
Metal decoration: niello
Metal disk: gong
Metal dross: slag
Metal eater: acid
Metal, enameled: tole
Metal fasteners: hasps
Metal in terne metal: tin
Metal, nonrusting: tin, copper
Metal oxidation: rust
Metal pin: rivet, nail
Metal rooster: vane
Metal, silvery: nickel
Metal strand: wire
Metal strip, vertical: stave
Metal, thin: foil
Metal thread: wire
Metal ware, lacquered: tole
Metal ware, painted: tole
Metallic elements: tin, gold, iron, lead
     zinc, barium, cobalt, copper, nickel,
     radium, silver, arsenic, bismuth,
     cadmium, calcium, lithium, mercury,
     sodium
Metallic fabric: lame
Metallic sound: clack, clang, clink
Metalloid element: boron
Metallurgist's materials: ores
Metamorphic rock: slate, gneiss, marble,
     schist, quartzite, soapstone
Metamorphic stage, final: adult
Metaphorical compound: kenning
Metaphorical small distance: atob
Metaphysical being: entia
Metaphysical poet: John Donne
Mete out: allot, dole
Meteorological device: sonde
Meteorological line: isobar
100 meter dash
Meter/gram system: metric
Meter maid, Beatle's: Rita
Meter maid of song: Rita
Meter reading: kwh
Metered wheels: cabs
Method or procedure: system, process
Methuselah, like: old
Methyl orange: azo dye
Meticulous, more: fussier
Iso metric
Metric pound: kilo
Metric prefix: centi
Metric unit: stere, dacare
Metric volumes: steres, stereos
Metrical accent: ictu
Metro: subway
Metro area: cities

Metronome indication: cadence
Metronome setting: tempo
Mettle that earns a medal: valor
Mew: sea gull, cry
Mewmar, Jillie: actress
Tex-mex cuisine
Mexicali matron: senora
Mexicali mother: sra
Mexican basket-weaving grass: otate
Mexican bye: adios
Mexican cactus: peyote
Mexican cheer: salud
Mexican chum: amigo
Mexican condiment: salsa
Mexican cowboy: charro
Mexican "crazy": loco
Mexican dish: tamale
Mexican, early: Aztec
Mexican fast food: taco
Mexican gentleman: caballero
Mexican girl: amiga
Mexican hors d'oeuvre: nacho
Mexican house: casa
Mexican hut: jacal
Mexican lad: nino
Mexican mom: madre
Mexican month: mes
Mexican Mrs.: sra
Mexican Ms.: srta
Mexican muralist: rivera
Mexican native: maya, aztec
Mexican party item: pinata
Mexican, pre-Columbus: Aztec
Mexican shrub: chia
Mexican snack: nacho, taco, tamale,
     tostada
Mexican "that": esa
Mexican "this": esta, este
Mexican time-out: siesta
Mexican tomorrow: manana
Mexican volcano: Popocatepetl
Mexican water: agua
Mexican wrap: serape
Mexican yes: Si
Mexico's Mickey Mouse: Raton
Meyers, Ari: actress
Meyerson, Bess: actress
Mezza-Mezza: soso
Mezzanine: loge
MFA , part of: master
"Miami Vice" cop: Rico
Mica: isinglass
Mice: vermin
Mice feet: paws
Michaelmas daisy: aster
Michelangelo sculpture: Pieta
Michelangelo work: Pieta, David
Michener book: Iberia
Michener opus: Iberia
Mickey Mouse dog: Pluto
Mickey Mouse in Mexico: Raton
Microbiologist's concern: cells
Microbiologist's dish: petri
Microbiology gel: agar

Microbrewer's need: hops
Microbrewery offering: ale
Microfilm sheet: fiche
Microphone, hidden: bug
Microphone word: testing, test
Microscope lens: ocular, optics
Microscope, type of: ion
Microwave setting: thaw
Midas, for one: king
Midas's undoing:greed
Middle Age serf: esne
Middle American country: Cuba, Haiti,
    Belize, Mexico, Panama, Bahamas,
    Grenada, Jamaica, Barbados,
    Dominican Republic, Honduras
Middle ear bone: anvil
Middle-earth creature: ents
Middle-earth denizen: hobbit
Middle East garb: aba
Middle East denizens: semites
Middle East holy city: Mecca
Middle East notable: emir
Middle Eastern bread: pita
Middle Eastern country: Iran, Iraq, Oman,
    Egypt, Qatar, Sudan, Syria, Yemen,
    Cyprus, Israel, Jordan
Middle Easterner: Arab
Middle Kingdom: China
Middle man: arbitrator
Middle of the road: centrist, neutral,
    moderate, impartial, nonpartisan
Middlemost: central
Mid-East coin: dinar
Mid-East gulf: Aden
Mid-East org. PLO
Mid-East peninsula: Sinai
Mid-East potentate: emir, aga
Mid-East ruler, bygone: shah
Mid-East topper: fez
Mid-month date, old: Ides
Mid-month day: ides
Midnight, after: late
Midnight rider: Revere
Midnight teller: ATM
Mid-17th-century date: MDCLI
Midshipman: reefer
Midterm or final: exam
Midway alternative: O'Hare
Midwives, in Ayr: howdies
Air mien
Mies van der Rohe
Miff: rile
Miffed,: sore
Miffed, plus: irate
Might's partner: main
"Mighty as an oak"
Mighty Dog rival: Alpo
Mighty fine: a one
Mighty mite: atom
Mighty swallow sound: gulp
Mick Jagger and mates: Stones (Rolling)
Mike problem: echo
Mikita, Stan:hockey
Milan's moola of old: lira

Milan's nation: Italy, Italia
Mild acid: acetic
Mild, as weather: balmy
Mild creamy cheese: muenster, munster
Mild discomfort: ache,
Mild expletive: gosh, drat, darn
Mild quake: tremor
Mildest: tamest
Mildori, Ito: figure skater
Mile, eighth of a: furlong
Miles away: afar
Miles, Sarah: actress
Miles, Vera: actress
Milestone: event
Military address: APO, FPO, sir
Military base builders: seabees
Military classes: ranks
Military council: junta
Military echelon: rank
Military engineer: sapper
Military forces: armies, navies
Military greeting: salute
Military hat: kepi, shako
Military hat, tall: shako
Military hitch: tour
Military intro, for some: ROTC
Military jacket trim: epaulet
Military muddle: snafu
MP quarry: AWOL
Military salute: salvo
Military school: OCS
Military status: rank
Military student: cadet
Military trim: epaulet
Milk carton phrase: grade A
Milk dispenser: udder
Milk, in Milan: latte
Milk mishap: spill
Milk product: butter, ice cream
Milk source: dairy
Milk sugar: lactose
Milkmaid's milieu: dairy
Milk's acid: lactic
Milky gem: opal
Milky glass: opaline
Milky iridescence, having a: opaline
Milky Way: galaxy
Milky Way, of the: galactic
Milky Way part: star
Mill around: dither
Millennia: eon
Millennium members: years
Miller, Arthur: playwright
Miller, Mitch, instrument: oboe
Miller or Blyth: Ann
Miller, Penelope Ann
Miller's salesman: Loman
Millet, Kate: writer, feminist
Millionaire makers: lotteries
Millions (pref): mega
Milne bear: pogh, pooh
Milne donkey: Eeyore
Milne marsupial: Roo
Milord's spouse: milady

Miltiades victory: marathon
Mime Marceau: Marcel
Mimic a mantis: pray
Mimicry: apery
Mimics: apes, aper
Mimi's refusal: non
Minces: dices
Mind: psyche
Mind, bring to: recall
Mind duller: opiate
"Mind over matter"
Mind reader: psychic
Mind reader gift: ESP
Mind teaser: riddle
Mindanao seaport: Davso
Mindanao volcano: Apo
Mindful: wary
Mindless: inane
Mind's picture: image
Mindy's mate's home: Ork
Mine, coal: pit
Mine car: tram,
Mine entrance: adit
Mine entrance, horizontal: adit
Mine, in Martinique: amoi
Mine, in Nimes: amoi,
Mine operation: oil rig
Mine passage: shaft
Mineral: zircon
Mineral, aquamarine: beryl
Mineral, chalky: talc
Mineral deposit, kind of: placer
Mineral deposits: ores
Mineral, easily-split: mica
Mineral finds: gems,
Mineral, greenish: talc
Mineral, nutritive: iron
Mineral, outback: opal
Mineral, powdery: talc
Mineral, rare: gem
Mineral, reddish: jasper
Mineral, soft: talc
Mineral streak: vein
Mineral that contains metal: ore.
Mineral, trace: zinc
Mineral used in jewelry: zircon
Mineral, valuable: gem
Miner's excavation: stope
Miner's need: TNT
Miner's stake: claim
Miner's trough: sluice
Minerva, in Greece: Athena
Minerva symbol: owl
Mines: diggings
"Ming the merciless"
Ming things: vases
Mini chicken: bantam
Mini container: vial
Mini play: skit
Mini revelation: knee
Mini, smaller than: micro
Miniature tree: bonsai
Minimally: at least
Minimal water: droplet

Minimum number: quota
Minimum-range tide: neap
Miniscule margin: eye lash
Miniseries "Shaka Zulu"
Miniseries shot: cameo
Minister's helper: deacon
Mink, like: furred
Minnelli, Liza: music
Minnesota Fats: pool shark
Minnow relative: dace
Minnow's home: pond
Minoan culture site: Crete
Minor aggravating problem: hassle
Minor cleric: deacon
Minor defect:foible
Minor drinking problem: age
Minor goddess of nature: nymph
Minor hassle: spat
Minor land: Asia
Minor mistake: goof
Minor prophet: Amos
Minor start: Asia
Minor weakness: vice
Minority group: sect
Minos's daughter: Ariadne, Phaedra
        father: Zeus, Jupiter
        mother: Europa
        son: Androgeos
        wife: Pasiphae
        kingdom: Crete
Minotaur's island: Crete
        slayer: Theseus
Minstrel: bard
Minstrel, Celtic: bard
Minstrel song: lai
Minstrel's instrument: lute
Mint family member: oregano
Mint family plant: chia
Mint location: Denver, Philadelphia
Mint master: coiner
Mint or chamomile: tea
Mint or cumin: herbs
Minty quaff: julep
Minus: sans
Minute opening: pore
Minute quantity: atom
Miracle, scene of: Cana
Miracle food: manna
Miracle for a duffer: ace, hole in one
Mirage, often: oasis
Miriam's brother: Aaron, Moses
Miro, Joan: Spanish painter
Mirror, broken, maybe: omen
Mirror use a: preen
Mirth: glee
Misanthropes: haters
"Ain't misbehavin'"
Miscellaneous mixture: olio
Miscellany: olio, ana
Mischa, Elman: violinist
Mischief: antic, prank
Mischief maker: imp
Mischievous: impish
Mischievous activity: prank

Mischievous look: grin
Mischievous sprite: pixie
Mischievous youngster: scamp
Mise-en-scene: set, site, locale, medium,
        milieu, ambient, climate
"Les Miserables"
Misfit, social: dork, nerd
Misfortune, invoke: curse
Misfortune, state of: hardship
Misfortunes: woes
Mishmash: olio
Misleads: deludes
Misplay a grounder: muff
Misprints: errata
Misrepresent data: skew
Miss America host of yore: Ely
"Miss Brooks" star: Eve Arden
Miss Daisy, emulated: rode
Miss in the comics: Peach
Miss, kind of: near
Miss Kitty's barkeeper: Sam
Miss Piggy's word: moi
"Missed the boat": lost out
Missiles, indoor: darts
Missing from action: AWOL
Missing link: ape-man
Missing memory: amnesia
Mission, cancel a: abort
Mission statement: credo
Missionary, Christian: apostle
Mississippi explorer: Joliet
Mississippi river explorer: La Salle
Mississippi river flatboat: barge
Mississippi source: Itasca
Missive: letter
Missouri mountains: Ozarks
Missouri river: Osage
Missouri river feeder: Platte
Missouri team: Rams
Misspeaking cleric: spooner
Misstate: lie
Mist, melt the: defog
Mist or smoke: vapor, haze
Mist over: fog up
Mist, wind-driven: scud
Mistake: errata, goof-up
Mistake, benefit from a: learn
Mistake eliminator: eraser
Mistake, foolish: boner
Mistake, funny: howler
Mistake, inadvertent: slip
Mistake, outrageous: howler
Mistaken, completely: all wet
Mistakes, list of: errata
"Mister Ed" star: Ames
Mistreat: abuse, illuse
MIT grad: engineer, eng.
Mitch Miller's instrument: oboe
Mitchell, Leona: soprano singer
Mitchell mansion: Tara
Miter wearer: priest
Mitigated: eased
Mitre wearer: priest
Mitt, type of: oven, catcher's

Mitterrand's world: monde
Mix together: blend
Mix vigorously: agitate
Mixed bag: olio
Mixed, easily: soluble
Mixer, popular: seltzer
Mixes in: adds
Mixing site: wet bars
Mix-up: snafu
Mix-up, big: snafu
Mixture: melange, olio
Mixture, miscellaneous: olio
Mixture, soft-soggy: glop
Mlle, canonized: ste
Mlle in Mexico: srta
Mme's daughter: mlle
Mob action, unruly: riot
Mob gone wild: riot
Mob leader: don
Mob scene: riot
Mobile-phone area: cell
Mobster's clique: gang
Moby-Dick foe: Ahab
Moby-Dick's pursuer: Ahab
Moccasin: pac
Moccasin cousin: pac
Moccasins, like: beaded
Mock at: jeer
Mock fanfare: ta-da
Mock or knock: deride
Mocking comment: gibe
Mod painting: pop art
Model airplane set: kit
Model, kind of: avatar
Model material: balsa
Model persona: waif
Model plane adornments: decals
Model, very thin: waif
Model, Somalia-born: Iman
Model, to begin with: kit
Model train maker, once: Tyco
Model with one name: Iman
Modeling asset: poise
Modeling media: clay
Models, like: poised
Model's need: agent, glue
Moderated: emceed
Moderately rich: prosperous
Moderates: tempers
Modern art form: Dada
Modern camera, like: digital
Modern day teller: ATM
Modern music player: iPod
Modem pulses: bauds
Modern recorder: TiVo
Modem speed unit: baud
Modem speed word: baud
Modern wall hanging: HDTV
Modern word: baud
Modernize: renovate
Modest home: cottage
Modest person, very: prude
Modicum: iota, bit, tad, dab
Modify, in congress: amend

Module, kind of: lunar
Modus operandi: style, custom, manner, method, system, process
Moe, Tommy: skier
Moe: a stooge
Moe's cohort: Larry
Moe Dee Hool: rapper
Moffo, Anna: opera singer
Moffo solo: aria
"Mogambo" name: Ova
Mohammed Bible: Koran
Mohammed flight: Hegira
Mohammed magistrate: Cadi
Mohammed prayer leader: Imam
Mohammed prince: Amir, Emir
Mohammed's daughter: Fatima
Mohawk River city: Utica
Mohican chief: Uncas
Mohs or Richter: scale
Moh's scale, one on the: talc
Moire: watered silk
Moist finish?: ure
Moisten the roast: baste
Moisten with drippings: baste
Moistly permeates: seeps
Moisture, lacking: dry, arid
Moisture, natural: dew, rain
Moisture, they remove: dryers
Moisturizer ingredient: aloe
Molar collector: tooth fairy
Molasses, in the UK: treacle
Molasses, like: slow
Mold filler: Jello, gelatin
Mold source: spore
Molding, convex: ovolo
Molding, curved: ovolo
Molding, semi-circle: torus
Mold-ripened cheese: brie
Mole run: tunnel
Molecule component: atom
Molecule maker: atom
Molecule, spiral: DNA
Molecule, single-strand: RNA
Mollifies: eases
Mollusk, edible: cockle
Mollusk, garden: slug, snail, oyster
Mollusk gill: ceras,
Mollusk, marine: whelk
Mollusk, tasty: scallop
Mollusks, tentacled: octopi, clams
Molson and others: ales
Molten rock: magma
Molten waste: slag
Mom & pop org.: PTA
Mom & pop company org.: SBA
Moma artist: Paul Klee
Mombasa's land: Kenya
Moment of time, brief: trice
Moment, type of: senior
Momentous time: era
Mom's brother, perhaps: enate
Mona Lisa singer: Nat King Cole
Mona Lisa site: Louvre
Monaco resort: Monte Carlo

Monarch catcher: net
Monarch, future, for one: heir
Monarch, old: tsar
Monarch, Persian: shah
Monarch stand-in: regent
Monarch, tragic: lear
Monastery: priory
Monastery dweller: fra, friar
Monastery head: abbott
Monastery resident: monk, fra, friar
Monastery superior: abbot
Monastic title: fra, rom, dom
Mondays, traditionally: wash day
"Mondo Cane" theme: more
Mondrian, Piet: painter
Monet, Claude: Fr. painter
Monet contemporary: Renoir
Monetary system: silver standard
Monet's "Amor & Psyche"
Money: lucre, gelt
Money box: till
Money case: wallet
Money, filthy: lucre
Money for the poor: alms
Money grubbing: avarice
Money handler: teller
Money, hard: cash, coins
Money holder: wallet, clip
Money hunger: greedy, greed
"In it for the money"
Money in the bank: asset
Money manager: banker, CFO
Money market, upset the: devalue
Money men, corp.: CFOs
Money, owed: debt
Money repository: bank, safe, vault
Moneyed: rich
Money's motto word: unum
"Moneytalks" group: ACDC
Mongkut portrayer: yul
Mongkut's nanny, king: Anna
Mongol conqueror: Genghis Kahn
Mongol dwelling: yurt
Mongol ruler: Khan,
Mongolian desert: Gobi
Mongolian river: Herlen Gol
Mongrel: cur
Mongrel sound: arf, bark, yip
Moniker: name
Moniker, secret: code name
Monitor or Merrimacc: warships
Monitor, type of PC: LCD
Monitor the contents of: censor
Monitored school event: exam
Monk: friar
Monk, Asian: Dali Lama
Monk, Himalayan: Dali Lama
Monk, Lhasa: Dali Lama
Monk, like a: ascetic
Monk, Tibetan: Dali Lama
Monk title in Portugal: bom
Monk, top: abbot
Monkey: macaco, baboon, rhesus
Monkey bar

Monkey business: trickery
Monkey, fierce: baboon
Monkey, lab: rhesus
Monkey, large: howler
Monkey, little: titi
Monkey, South American: iai
Monkey, squirrel-like: marmoset
Monkey with: tamper, toy
"Monkey wrench"
Monkey's prehensile body part: tail
Monk's hood: cowl
Monk's quarters: cell
Monk's title: fra, friar
Monk's trademark: tonsure
Mono, kin of: uni
Monocle: lens
Monogram, inventor's: tae
Monogram, literary: tse, tae
Monogram on cross: IHS
Monogram pt.: init, initial
Monopolize: own, hog
Monopoly card: chance, deed
Monopoly railroad: Short Line
Monopoly token: shoe
Monorail: tram
Monorails, some: els
Monotony: tedium, boredom
Monotony, routine: daily grind
Monotonous learning: rote
Monroe, Earl: NBA
Monsieur, across the pyrenees: senor
Monsieur, in Bonn: serr
Monsieur, in Madrid: senor
Monsieur's affirmative: oui
Monsieur's cake: gateau
Monsieur's island: iles
Monsieur's pate: tete (head)
Monsieur's prop: easel
Monsieur's refusal: non
Monsieur's shout: viola
Monster: ogre
Monster, fire-eating: dragon
Monster, gila
Monster, hideous: ogre
Monster, smog: (godzilla foe)
Monster, man-eating: ogre
Monster, many-headed: hydra
Monster, tabloid: Nessie
Monster-like: ogreish
Monstrous lake: Loch Ness
Mont Blanc, for one: Alp
Mont Blanc range: Alps
Montagues, one of the: Romeo
Montalban, Ricardo: actor
Montand, Wves: actor
Monte Carlo bet: noir
Montenegrin's neighbor: Albanian, Albania
Monteverdi opera: orfeo
Montevideo's country: Uruguay
Montez, Lola: dancer
Montezuma, for one: Aztec
Montezuma's empire: Aztec
Montgomery, Wes: jazz
Month before Nisan: Adar

Month, ecclesiastical: Elul
Month for peridots: Aug
Month, last: ult, ultimo
Month, purim's: Adar
Monthly bill: statement, stmt.
Monticello, for one: estate
Monument, stone: stele
Monumental: epic, elle
Moo companion: baa
Moo goo gai pan pan: wok
Moo shu pork
Mooch: bum, hit on, cadge
Mood, bad: funk
Mood, down: blahs
Mood, grumpy: snit
Mood, in a foul: sour
Mood, in a gloomy: sullen
Mood rings, once: fads
Moods, nasty: snits
Moon, autumn: harvest
Moon condition: phase
Moon-driven phenomena: tides
Moon feature: craters
Moon fish: opah
Moon, full or half: phase
Moon goddess: Diana
Moon, greeted the: bayed
Moon, in poetry: phoebe, orb
Moon mountain area: terra
Moon of Endor citizens: Ewoks
Moon, of the: lunar
Moon or dream attachment: scape
Moon phenomenon: halo
Moon position: phase
Moon ring: halo
Moon shop people: nasa
Moon snail: sharkeye
Moon track: orbit
Moon Unit Zappa
Moon valley: rille
"Moonlight Sonata"
Moons, many: ages
Moonshine: bosh, jake, hokum, bootleg,
     homebrew, hooch
Moonshine apparatus: still
Moonshine holder: jug
Moonshine mixture: mash
"Moonstruck" star: Cher
Moor: heath
Moore, Demi: actress
Moore, Henry: sculptor
Moore octet: reindeer
Moored, not: adrift
Mooring post: bitt
Mooring site: wharf
Mooring, yacht: berth
Mop companion: pail
Mopes: sulks
Moppable body part: brow
Mopped, it's often: brow, deck
Moppet: kid
Moppet, Alpine: Heidi
Moral discourses: sermons
Moral fortitude: fiber

Moral lapses: sins
Moral principles: ethnics
Moral stories, short: parables
Moral values: ethic
Moral weakness: vice
Morales of "Rapa Nui": Esai
Moralist, early: Aesop
Moralist of yore: Aesop
Moralist, smug: prig
Morally corrupt: putrid
Morally strict: austere
Morally wrong: evil
Moran, Erin: actress
Morante, Elsa: novelist
More al dente: rawer
More annoying: peskier
More contemptible: baser
More dense, as fog: thicker
More doubtful: iffier
More drawn-out: longer
More euphoric: happier
More, in Madrid: mas
More indisposed: sicker
More invidious: snider
More knowing: sager
More lofty: nobler
More luxuriant: lusher
More open: airier
More or less: loosely, around, about
More reasoned: saner
More rundown: seedier
More sardonic: wrier
More shrewd: slier
More spectral: eerier
More spiteful: meaner
More streamlined: sleeker
More succinct: shorter
More suggestive: racier
More suitable: apter
More supple: lither
More suspect: fishier
More suspicious: leerier
More than a job: career
More than a snack: meal
More than ask: beg
More than attentive: enrapt
More than confident: cocky
More than disappoint: appall
More than double: trine
More than enough: plethora, plenty
More than fancy: regal
More than fill: sate
More than just defeat: shellac, crush
More than mega: giga
More than most: all
More than one: plural
More than satisfy: grail, sate
More than serious: dire
More than should be: too
More than sometimes: often
More than suggest: urge
More than takes down: pins
More than wants: needs
More than willing: eager

More to some: less
More tricky: cagier
More unctuous: oilier
More unsubstantial: wispier
More uptight: uneasier
More winsome: cuter, charming
Moreno, Rita
Morgan, Dr. (of comics): Rex
Morgan la Faye
Morgan le Fay
Morissette, Alanis: singer
Mork's planet: Ork
Mormon state: Utah
Mormon title: elder
Morn counterpart: Eve
Morning, in the: matinal, matin
Morning, Paris: matin
Mornings: AMS
Moroccan ruler: sultan
Morocco capital: Rabat
Morocco city: fez, fes
Moron, type of: oxy
Morose: sullen
Morrison, Toni: writer
Morse code word: dah
Morse code, three dots: ess
Morse "e": dot
Morse syllable: dah
Morsel: bit
Morsel for a pangolin: ant
Morsel, juicy: tidbit
Mortal: human
Mere mortals
Mortar, go with: pestle
Mortar mate: pestle
Mortar mixer: rab
Mortar tray: hod
Mortarboard: cap
Mortarboard feature: tassel
Mortarboard wearer: grad.
Mortgage: lien, debt, loan
Mortgage (client): appt.
Mortgage, carries: owes
Mortgage holder: debtor
Morticia's cousin: Itt,
Morticia's husband: Gomez
Mortise insertion: tenon
Mortise partner: tenon
Mosaic part: tile
Moscow citadel: kremlin
Moscow park, (var.): Gorki
Moscow poet: Pushkin
Moscow resident: Russian, Idahoan
Moselle (mosel) tributary: Saar
Moselle (mosel) city on the: Metz, Trier
Moses basket: wicker cot, straw cot
Moses's brother: Aaron
     brother-in-law: Hobab
     father-in-law: Jethro
     sister: Miriam
     son: Eliezer, Gershom
     spy: Caleb
     wife: Zipporah
Moses's mountain: Sinai

Moslem beggar: fakir
Moslem call to pray: azan
Moslem commander: Aga
Moslem crusade: jihad
Moslem deity: Allah
Moslem exodus: hegira
Moslem lady of rank: begum
Moslem magistrate: cadi
Moslem priest: imam
Moslem ruler: amir
Moslem sacred book: Koran
Moslem scholar: ulema, ulama
Moslem sect: Shia
Moslem title: aga
Moslem women's quarters: harems
Mosque feature: minaret
Mosque frequenter: arab
Mosque leaders: imam
Mosque priest: imam
Mosque topper: dome
Mosque tower: minaret
Mosque vip: iman
Mosquito genus: aedes
Mosquito net
Mosquito, yellow fever: ades, aedes
Moss, Kate: model
Most accessible: nearest
Most assuming: meekest
"Most beautiful women": Helen
Most beloved: dearest
Most bohemian: artiest
Most capacious: widest
Most chivalrous: bravest
Most concise: terest
Most cool: grooviest
Most daring: boldest
Most desirable: best
Most desolate: starkest
Most distant: remotest
Most emaciated: boniest
Most excellent:peachy
Most extreme: utiose
Most favorable condition: optima
Most frugal: sparest
Most high-minded: noblest
Most icky: gunkiest,
Most important: paramount
Most in need of scratching: itchiest
Most inferior: worst
Most iniquitous: vilest
Most lucid: sanest,
Most of the time: as a rule
Most of the world: oceans
Most pallid: ashiest
Most perceptive: sagest
Most profound: deepest
Most ready: ripest
Most recent: newest
Most reliable: surest
Most serious charge: gravamen
Most singular: rarest
Most uncouth: crudest
Most uncouthly: rudest
Most unusual: rarest

Most up-to-date: newest
Mostel, Abby Zero: actor & comic
Mote: bit, dot, jot, iota, speck
Motel amenity: ice
Motel vacancies: rooms
Motels of yore: inns
Moth: luna
Moth-eaten: ratty
Moth legacy: hole
Moth, move like a: flit
Moth, pale green: luna
Moth repellent: camphor
Mother Bloor: Ella
Mother, dramatic: detat
Mother, fierce: tigress
Mother, native, language: tongue
Mother of Apollo: Leto
Mother of Calcutta: Teresa
Mother of Castor & Pollux: Leda
Mother of Constantine the Great: Helena
Mother of Ishmael: Hagar
Mother of Miles: Mme
Mother of pearl: nacre
Mother of pearl source: abalone, ormer
Mother of Perseus: Danai
Mother of the gods: Ops, Rhea, Cybele
Mother Teresa: nun, saint
Motherly attention: tlc
Mother's relative: enate
Mother's sister: enate
Moth's legacy: hole
Moth's nemesis: flame
Motion detector: sensor
Motion in the ocean: tide
Motion picker-upper: sensor
Motivational guru: Dale Carnegie
Motives: whys, reasons
Motives, irrational: urges
Motley Crue: music group
Motor city gridder: lion
Motor oil can letters: SAE
Motor or mechanism starter: servo
Motorcycle race: enduro
Motorist's irritations: traffic jam, bottle
    neck, bridge toll
Motorist's need: license
Motown's Diana Ross
Mottled marking: dapple
Mottled stone: marble
Motto word on money: unum
Mound: knoll
Mound, blazing: pyre
Mounds, rounded: knolls
Mount Hood state: Oregon
Mount N arodnaya locale: Urals
Mount Olympus resident: Ares
Mount Rushmore sculptor: John Borglum
Mount the soapbox: orate
Mountain air, like: rare
Mountain, Asian: Alai
Mountain, blue Anais
Mountain cat: puma, lion
Mountain climber: iceman
Mountain climbing gear: pitons

Mountain crest: arete
Mountain, European: Alps
Mountain goat: ibex
Mountain home: chalet
Mountain, it moves: TNT
Mountain kingdom: Nepal
Mountain lake: tarn
Mountain laurel: evergreen
Mountain lion: puma
Mountain lookout: crag
Mountain, Moses's: Sinai
Mountain nymph: oread
Mountain of Troy: Ida
Mountain or river: Ural
Mountain pass: col., gap, chat
Mountain pass info.: elev., elevation
Mountain pool: mere
Mountain predator: puma
Mountain range backbone: massif
Mountain range, China: Alai
Mountain refrain: echo
Mountain ridge: arete
Mountain ridge cleft: gap
Mountain route: pass,
Mountain, saw-tooth: Sierra
Mountain topper: glacier
Mountain, Utah: Uinta, Uintaite
Mountaineer's aid: ice ax
Mountaineer's refrain: yodel
Mountainous: craggy
Mountainous north wind: tramontane
Mountains and trees: nature
Mountains, of high: alpine
Mountains, tien shan: alai
Mounts gemstones: sets
Mournful cry: alas
Mouse alternative: track ball
Mouse catcher: owl
Mouse, field: vole
Mouse predator: owl
Mouse relative: vole
Mouse sound: click
Mouse target: icon
Mouselike mammal: shrew
Mouser, good: owl, cat
Mousse alternative: gel
Mousse shaper: mold,
Mouth (carnivore's): maw
Mouth in biology: ora, kisser
Mouth off: rant
Mouth organ
Mouth, zoologist's: ora
Mouthful: bite
Mouthful, bovine: cud
Mouthpiece attachment: reed
Mouth-watering reading material: menu
Move about aimlessly: gad
Move about rapidly: flit
Move about restlessly: gad
Move abruptly: jerk
Move a little: budge
Move a mum: repot
Move a plant: repot
Move away: recede

Move before the king, one: pawn
Move, brilliant: coup
Move effortlessly: glide
Move energetically: hustle
Move, erratic: zig,
Move furtively: sidle, sneaks, creep
Move gingerly: ease
Move in the breeze: sway
Move into a position: put
Move jauntily: bop
Move like ivy: creep
Move like lava: flow
Move like mercury: rotate
Move like sludge: ooze
Move little by little: edge
Move out: vacate
Move per ground control: taxi
Move quickly: dart
Move, real-estate lingo: relo
Move side to side: wag, sway
Move slightly: budge, stir
Move slowly: inch
Move stealthily: edge
Move swiftly: scoots
Move the furniture: rearrange
Move the puck: pass
Move to & fro: wag
Move to the beat: dance
Move, token: gesture
Move toward: near
Move, unable to: inert
Move wearily: trudge
Moved around in confusion: milled
Moved out: vacated,
Moved, really: raced, sped
Moved stealthily: crept
Movement: action
Movement, abrupt: jolt, jerk
Movement, capable of: motile
Movement, even in: steady
Movement, involuntary: reflex
Mover and shaker: doer, VIP
Mover, people: tram, auto, bus, plane,
    train
Mover's challenge: piano
Moves about stealthily: prowls
Moves furtively: slinks
Moves quickly: darts
Moves with short, jerky moves: bobs
Movie based: cinematic
Movie critique: preview
Movie dog: Asta, Benji
Movie effect: matte
Movie frames: stills
Movie genre: horror
Movie house: cinema
Movie industry: Hollywood
Movie mogul: czar
Movie music: theme
Movie need: cast
Movie (one star): dog
Movie part: role
Movie pig: Babe
Movie, popular: hit

Movie rat: Ben
Movie rental need: VCR
Movie reviewer: critic
Movie set clashers: egos
Movie story line: plot
Movie studio: MGM
Movie theater, local: nabe
Movie to be: script
Movie villain: heavy
Movie with a posse: oater
Movie workplace: set
Movie-set clashers: egos
Moving about: astir
Moving right along
Mozambique neighbor: Malawi
Mozart city: Vienna
Mozart opera: Don Giovanni
MP quarry: AWOL
Mr. Peanut feature: monocle
Mr. Peanut accessory: cane
Mr. (plural of): Messrs.
Mr. T: tele, t.v.
Mr. T's group: A-team
Mr. Universe, posing for: flexing
MRI output: scan
Mrs. Muir's beau: ghost
Mrs. Peel's job: avenge
Ms polishers: eds
Ms readers: eds
Mtg: sess
MTV viewer: teen
Mubarek, Hosni: Egyptian ruler
Mubarak's predecessor: Sadat
Much attachment: in as
Much-heard: stale
Much loved: dear
Muchacha, that: esa
Muchacho: nino
Muck: mire, bog, crud
Muckety-muck: VIP, nabob, bigwig,
    fat cat, big shot
Mud, deep: mire
Mud, in Madrid: lodo
Mud protection: galoshes
Mud puppy's cousin: efts
Mud, slung: smeared
Mud, soft: ooze
Mud, thick: mire
Mudder's father: sire
Muddiest: miriest
Muddle through: get by
Muddled situation: snafu
Muddles: mix up
Muddy: miry, sloshy
Muddy enclosure: sty
Muddy the water: roil
Muddy track: rut
Mudpack, apply a: daub
Muezzin's perch: minaret (mosque tower)
Muezzin's religion: Islam
Muffin base: oat, bran
Muffin, hollow: pop over
Muffin man's locale: Drury Lane
Muffin morsel: walnut

Mufti for caesar: toga
Mug, drinking: toby
Mug, man-shaped: toby
Mug shot, find the: identify
Mugger's comeuppance: mace
Muhammad is his prophet: Allah
Muhammad of Shiraz: Ali
Muhammad or Laila: Ali
Muir, John: naturalist
Mrs. Muir's beau: ghost
Mukluk wearer: Inuits
Mulct: scam, fine
Mule, Army, for one: mascot
Mule (folk-song): Sal
Mule or clod: shoe
Mule or ox: beast of burden
Mule sire: donkey
Mule sound: bray
Mullah's text: Koran
Mulligan and Irish: stews
Mulligan, Gerry: musician
Mulligatawny: soup
Multifaceted, they may be: gems
Multiplex fare: movie
Multiplied: bred
Multitude: legion, slew, horde
Mum: dumb
Mumbai dress: sari
Mumbai Mr.: sri
Mumbai wrap: sari
Mumble: slur
Mummies, some: pharaohs
Mummy, maybe: pharaoh
Mummy, famous: Tut
"Mummy" (movie) setting, The: Egypt
Munch masterpiece: "The Scream"
Munchen man of the house: herr
Munchhausen, Italian style: baron
Munchhausen spun, what: yarns
Munchhausen title: baron
Mundane task: chore
Munich, from: German
Munich mister: herr
Munich setting: Bavaria
Munro's pen name: Saki
Munster's pet bat: Igor
A Muppet: Ernie
Muppet drummer: Animal
Muppet eagle: Eam
Muppet, furry red: Elmo
Muppet Grouch: Oscar
"Muppet Show" host: Kermit
Muppet's creator: Hensen
Mural painter: Rivera (Diego)
Mural undercoat: gesso
Murdock, Iris: writer
Murdock, Rupert: media
Murkiness: gloom
Murmur, amorous: coo
Murmur of content: aah
Murmur or sigh: utter
Murmur soothingly: coo, hum
Murmur, sweet: coo
Murmur's, contented: aahs, hmms

Murphy, Audie: actor
"Murphy Brown" show: FYI
Murphy has one: law
Murphy's Alec Foley
Murphy's Law, e.g.: adage
Murray Schisgal play: "Luv"
Muscat country: Oman
Muscat native: Oman
Muscat resident: Omani
Muscat sultanate: Oman
Muscle: tensor, brawn
Muscle, back: lat
Muscle bound: rigid, stiff, wooden
Muscle: comb. Form: myo
Muscle, contract a: flex
Muscle problem: atrophy
Muscle, push-up: pec
Muscle spasm: kink
Muscle, stretching: tensor
Muscle-controlling cell: motor-neuron
Muscovite: mica
Muscovy pref.: Russo
Muscular: build, built
Muscular cell: fiber
Muscular strength: brawn
Muse, Clio: historian
Muse, Erato: poet
Muse, number of: nine
Muse of history: Clio
Muse of poetry: Erato
Muse's domain: art
Muse's father: Zeus
Muse's number: nine
Muse's province: arts
Museum display: diorama, exhibit
Museum manager: curator
Museum, Paris: Louvre
Museum tour guide: docent
Museum work, do: curate
Musharraf's land: Pakistan
Mushroom, gourmet: morels
Mushroom morsel: cap
Musial, Stan: baseball
Music, air in: arioso
Music, be silent: tacet
Music category: newage
Music collectibles: LPs, CDs
Music device: ipod, radio
Music direction: legato, dal segno
Music drama: opera
Music, elevator: ear candy
Music event: concert
Music, flair for: ear
Music genre: coda, rap, soul, punk
Music hall: Odea
Music entertainment: opera
Music, Jamaican: ska
Music, Joplin's: rag
Music, like elevator: piped
Music lover's woe: tin ear
Music maker, small: uke
Music maker, toothed: saw
Music marking: crescendo
Music master: maestro

Music notation: clef
Music or dance: art
Music or food, kind of: soul
Music service, online: Napster
Music player, modern: iPod
Music player, portable: iPod
Music score mark: slur
Music, sheet, words: lyrics
Music synthesizer pioneer: moog
Music, very in: assai,
Music without a key, like: atonal
Musical beat, recurring: ictus
Musical blast from the past: oldie
Musical chord: triad
Musical combo: trio
Musical composition: sonata, etude, aria
Musical direction: tacet, crescendo
Musical drama: opera
Musical ensemble: trio
Musical gig, part of a: set
Musical group: choir, band, rote
Musical group of nine: nonet
Musical instrument (ancient): lute
Musical instrument, kid's: kazoo
Musical interval: octave, tritone
Musical key: A minor, C minor
Musical, lively: tempo, allegro
Musical, long-running: "Annie"
Musical mark: presa, segno
Musical medley: olio
Musical mixture: medley
Musical movement: rondos, adagio
Musical notes: res, fas, las, sol
Musical opus: motet
Musical pace: tempo
Musical passage: arioso, stretta
Musical passage, brisk: allegro
Musical perception: ear
Musical postscript: coda
Musical practice piece: etude
Musical rattle: maraca
Musical ridge: fret
Musical rotation: segno
Musical show: revue
Musical sign: clef
Musical signature: C sharp
Musical slow: lento, adagio
Musical sound: note
Musical study: etude
Musical, somewhat: poco
Musical symbols: sharps, flats
Musical terms: stretta, dal segno
Musical tool: saw
Musical transition: segue
Musical transition, smooth: segue
Musical twice: bis
Musical, from Weber: "Cats"
Musical works: fugue, opus
Musical wrap-up: coda
C to c musically: octave
Musically correct: in key
Musically slowing: ritardando, rit
Musician, medieval: lutist
Musician, theologian: monk

Musician's asset: ear
Musician's job: gig
Musician's org.: ASCAP
Musician's plant: alberts herb
Musketeer (one of): Aramis
Muslim hat: tarboosh
Muslim honorific: aga
Muslim judge: cadi
Muslim leader: sultan
Muslim mystic: sufi
Muslim prayer leader: imam
Muslim ruler: amir, emir, aga, agha,
    ameer
Muslim sign: clef
Muslim spirit: djinn
Muslim title of honor: aga, agha
Muslim's conical cap: taj
Muss: tousle
Muss one's hair, e.g.: tousle
Mussolini, Benito: ruler
Mussolini's son-in-law: Ciano
Must: ought
Mustang or pinto: horse
Mustangs, the: SMU
Mustard family plant: alyssum
Must-haves: needs
Mutant hero: X-man
Mutate: evolve
Mutiny: rebel
Lego mutton: sleeve
Mutton cut: scrag
Mutton dish: ram
Mutual fund fee: load
Mutual fund (kind of): no load
Muumuu accessory: lei
Muy bien, gracias
Muzhik housing: isbas (housing for a Russian
    peasant)
Muzzles: snouts, nose
"My brother's keeper, am I"
"My Cherie Amour"
"My Fair Lady" scene setting: Ascot
"My Gal Sal"
My goodness: gee
My my: tsk,
"My name is Asher Lev"
Myanmar (once): Burma
Myanmar's continent: Asia
Myers, Mike: actor
Myerson, Bess: actress
Myopic cartoon character: Mr. Magoo
Myrna of old films: loy
Mysteries: enigmas
Mysterious: deep, arcane
Mysterious John: Doe
Mysterious sighting: UFO
Mystery: enigma, rune
"Mystery" channel: PBS
Mystery board game: Clue
Mystery novel bane: cyanide
Mystery writer, for short: anon
Mystery writer's award: Edgar
Mystic of India: fakir
Mystical: occult

Mystical cards: tarots
Mystical glow: aura
Mystical script, ancient: rune
Mystical weeper: Niobe
Mystify: bemuse
Mystifying: cryptic
Mystiques: auras
Mythical archer: Eros
Mythical aviator: Icarus
Mythical beast, long-horned: yales
Mythical creature: centaur, satyr
Mythical father of Manannan: Lir
Mythical female warrior: amazon
Mythical giant: titan
Mythical hunter: Actaeon, Orion
Mythical invocation: mantra
Mythical lamp dweller: genie
Mythical man of brass: Talos
Mythical sailor: Sinbad
Mythical serpent: hydra
Mythical strongman: Atlas
Mythical teacher: Cabala
Mythical weaver: Arachne
Mythological tale: legend
Mythomania: liar

N

Sha na na
Na + oh: ion
Nabbed: snared
Nabokov books: "Ada," "Lolita"
Nabors, Jim: actor
Eine kleine nachtmusik
Nada: zip
Nadelman, Elie: journalist
Nadir opposite: zenith
Nah: nope
"Nah"(opposite): yep
Naha native: Okinawan
Nahoor sheep: sna
Nahuatl: Aztec
Nahuatl speakers: Aztecs
Nail barrel: keg
Nail container: keg
Nail obliquely: toe
Nail, thin: brad,
Nailing at an angle: toeing
Nails down just right: ices
Naish, J. Carrol: actor
Naïve: green
Naïve country folks: yokels
Naïve one: babe
Naiveté in Pennsylvania: inexperience
Naja haje: asp
"Naked Maja" artist: Goya
Name a book: title
Name for a cook: Stu
Given name
Name, good (for short): rep
Name for the wind, in song: Maria
Name in bowling allies: AMF
Name in cheese cake: Sara, Sara Lee

Name in cosmetics: Olay
Name in essays: Elia
Name in limerick: Ogden
In name only: titular
Name in small trucks: Tonka
Name on a news story: by line
Name of a thing: noun
Name, one's good: rep
Name that means "true": Vera
Name, to Pierre: nom
Name valedictorian, e.g.: honor
Named: dubbed
Named after: eponym
Namely (Latin): viz, idest, videlicet
Namely: to wit
Names, series of: rota
Names: titles
Names, list of: roster
Nana Oyl's daughter: Olive
Nancy Drew: girl detective
"Nancy Drew" author: Carolyn Keene
Nanna brother: Nergal, Ninazu
        father: Enlil
        husband: Balder
        mother: Ninlil
        son: Utu
        wife: Ningal
Nanny (UK): au pair
Nanny (Bombay, China): amah
Nanny, Mamsahib's: Amah
Nanny, wheels for: pram
Nanny's charge: kid, tyke, child
Nantes notion: idee
Nap, take a: snooze
Napa Valley spread: winery
Napa Valley tanks: vats
Nape knots: buns
Nape of neck: nucha
Nape, thick: shag
Naples island: capri
Naples staple: pasta
Napoleonic marshal: Ney
Napoleonic or Victorian: era
Napoleon's exile site: Elba
Napoleon's fate: exile
Napoleon's island: Elba
Napoleon's punishment: exile
Napoleon's victory site: Lodi
Napped leather: suede
Narcissist's love: ego
Narcissus's admirer: Echo
        father: Ephesus
        flaw: ego
        mother: Liriope
Narcissus, she loved: Echo
Nares: nostrils
Narrative of heroic exploits: saga
Narrow a passage: stenose
Narrow band on a bldg.: listel
Narrow board: lath,
Narrow braid: cornrow
Narrow channel: stria
Narrow down: taper
Narrow groove: stria

Narrow inlet: ria
Narrow street: alley
Narrow strip of silk: maniple
Narrow the gap: gain
Narrow thru-fare: alley
Narrow waterway: strait, canal
Narwhal's tooth: tusk
NASA counterpart: ESA
NASA excursion: EVA
NASA outfit: g-suit
NASA rocket: apollo
NASA scrub: no go
NASA, transatlantic kin: ESA
Nasal openings: nares
Nasal tone: twang
Nash, Ogden: poet
Nash's medium: verse
Nashville attraction: Opry
Nashville music venue: Opry
Nast, Thomas: cartoonist
Nastasa, Ilie: tennis
Nasty laugh: hah
Nasty mood: snit
Nasty shock: jolt
Nasty smile: smirk
Nathan Hale alma mater: Yale
Nation: republic
National bread of Scotland: oatcake
NHL trick: hat
National merit scholarship hurdle: PSAT
National poet: bard
National security agency: DOD
National wealth, measure of: GNP
Native American artist need: Osage brush
Native American deity: Great Spirit
Native American (part): Mestizo, Mestize
Native habitat: patria
Native healer: shaman
Native instrument of peace: pipe
Native metal: ore
Native Nebraskan: Otoe
Native, not: exotic
Native of: -ite
Native on the Bering Sea: Aleut
Native-born Israeli: Sabre, Sabra
Nativity scene: creche
NATO relative: OAS
NATO turf: Eur., Europe
Natterjack: toad
Natural: innate
Natural ability: talent,
Natural balm: aloe
Natural corn holder: husk, cob, ear,
Natural environment: element
Natural gas
Natural gift: talent
Natural height, person's: stature
Natural home: habitat
Natural impulse: urge
Natural light show: aurora
Natural moisture: dew, rain
Natural resin: lac
Natural sticker: cactus, cacti
Naturalist, American: Muir

Naturalist: John <u>Muir</u>:
Naturalist, noted: Darwin
Naturalness: ease
"Nature" channel: PBS
Nature prefix: eco
Nature reserve: park
Nature's coolant: sweat
Naughty, naughty: tsk
Nausicaa's father: Alcinous
      mother: Arete
Nautical adverb: alee
Nautical assent: aye
Nautical danger: reef, sand reef
Nautical hail: ahoy
Nautical half-hour: bell
Nautical mile: knot
Nautical platform: deck
Nautical position: alee
Nautical rope: tye
Nautical steering wheel: helm
Nautical timber: spar
Nautilus captain: Nemo
Nautilus locale: spa, gym
Navajo foe: Ute
Navajo handiwork: rugs
Navajo lodge: hogan
Naval address: FPO
Naval assignment: brig
Naval base: keel,
Naval enlistee: sailor
Naval force: armada
Naval hospital site: bethesda
Navel NCO: CPO
Naval petty officer: yeoman
Naval pronoun: she
Navarro, Jaime: baseball
Nave neighbor: apse
Navel orange, like a: seedless
Navigation (aerial) system: teleran
Navigation aid: deck officer, map, radar
Navigation devise: loran, sonar
Navigation system, GM: OnStar
Navigation system, type of: inertial
Navigational aid, British: Decca
Navigator, Scandinavian: Eric
Navratilova, Martina: tennis
Navy builder: sea bee
Navy construction arm: sea bees
Navy enlistee: gob
Navy NCO: yeoman, CB, CPO
Navy or vanilla: bean
Navy's goat: mascot
Nazimova, Alla: actress
Ne plus: ultra
Ne plus ultra: acme
Neal, Patricia: actress
Near homer: triple
Near shore, kept: waded
Near the ground: low
Nearby: nigh, local
Near-earth asteroid: Eros
Nearest star: sun
Nearest to rotting: ripest
Nearly all: most,

Nearly new: used
Nearly won: placed
Near-sighted: myopia
Neat & smart: natty
Neat as a pin: simile
Neat, make: tidies,
Neaten, as a napkin: refold
Neatened a bed: made
Neatly dressed: dapper
Neatnik opposite: slob
Neatniks, not: slobs
Nebraska river: Platte
Nebraskan, native: Otoe
Necessary, absolutely: integral
Necessitate: entail
Necessities: musts
Necessities, like some: bare
Neck adornment, in one state: lei
Neck & neck: tied, even
Neck of the woods: area
Neck scarf: ascot
Neck skin, pendulous: dewlap
Neck woe: kink
Necklace: chain
Necklace, sweet smelling: lei
Necklace unit: bead
Neckline, plunging: vee
Necktie: cravat
Necktie, broad: ascot
Necktie knot holder: stickpin
Necktie, thin: bolo,
Necktie, western: bolo
Neckwear, fancy: ascot
Neckwear, floral: lei
Neckwear, uncomfortable: noose
Neckwear, wide: ascot
Nee: born
Need to pay: owe
Need to pay the piper: owe
Needing a rubber match: tied
Needing cash: broke, short
Needle case: etui
Needle dropper: pine
Needle fish: gar
Needle hole: eye
Needle, kind of: darning, hypodermic
Needle, ply a: sew
Needle shaped: acerate
Needle source: fir, pine
Needle work, type of: crewel
Needlepoint <u>lace</u>
Needless: undue
Needless activity: ado
Needs straightening: bent
Needs to be brought home: bacon
Neesom, Liam: actor
Nefarious: erse
Nefarious plan: scheme, evil, vile
Nefertiti's god: Aton, Aten
Nefertiti's river: Nile
Negate entirely: erase
Negative-charged atom: anion
Negative connective: nor
Negative correlative: nor

Negative disjunction: nor
Negative link: nor
Negative pole: cathode
Negative prefix: non, dis
Negative sorts: cynics
Negev's big city: Beersheba
Neglects to include: omits, over-looks
Negligee buy: teddy (chemise)
Negligent: lax
Negotiation results: deals
Neighborhood, in the: locale
Neither: nor
Neither good or bad: amoral
Neither masculine or feminine: neuter
Neither-here-nor-there state: limbo
Nelligan, Kate film: "Eleni"
Nemean predator: lion
Neon kin: xenon
Neonate: baby, infant
Nepalese legend: yeti
Nepalese peak: Api
Neptune neighbor: Uranus
Neptune prop: trident
Neptune satellite: Triton
Neptune's kingdom: sea
Neptune's realm: sea
Nerd kin: wimp, twerp
Nerdy: unhip
Nerdy cap: beanie
Nero, Peter: pianist
Nero's advisor: Seneca
Nero's "I": ego
Nero's (Peter) instrument: piano
Nero's successor: Galba
Neruda, Pablo: poet
Nerve: gall
Nerve-cell part: axon, axite
Nerve cells: neurons
Nerve center: hub, core, seat, focus
      heart, locus, capital
Nerve (combo form): neuro
Nerve gas: sarin, soman, tabun
Nerve, have the: dare
Nerve network: rete, retia
Nerve part: axon
Nerves (of): neural
Nervous twitch: tic
Nervous vibration: tremor
Nervously busy: frenetic
Nesselrode, e.g.: pie, frozen pudding
Nessie's hideout: loch
Nessie's home: loch
Nessus' victim: Heracles, Hercules
Nest: aerie
Nest (eagle's): aerie
Nest egg: savings, ira, cache, funds,
      hoard, kitty, stash, assets, reserve
Nest builder, oval: oriole
Nest residents: birds, hornets, wasp
Nesting place: limb, tree
Nestor's father: Neleus
Nestor's kingdom: Pylos
Net notable: Ashe
Net notes: emails

Net thoughts: blog
Netherlands Antilles island: Saba
Netherlands city: Ede,
Netherlands commune: Ede, Breda
Netherworld: pit, hell, abyss, hades,
 sheal, inferno, hellfire,
 underworld
Net-like fabric: mesh
Net-like ornamental fabric: lace
Netting, cover with: enlace
Nettle: irk
Nettle family member: Ramie
Network: system, sys,
Network of veins: rete
Network, type of: neural
Networked units: PCs
Neural contact point: synapse
Neural network: retia, rete
Neuron, part of a: axon
Neuter pronoun: itself
Neutral color: tan, gray, ecru
Neutral, ethically: amoral
Neutral tone: taupe, ecru
Neutron star, rotating: pulsar
Never say never again
Never the less: yet, anyway
Never-ending: eternal
Never-ending story: soap
New age chanteuse: Enya
New age physician, perhaps: holist
New age singer: Enya
New candle, like a: unlit
New car sticker abbr.: msrp
New day, briefly: morn
New Deal agency: CCC
New Deal org.: WPA
New employees: tyros, novices
New England entrée: yankee pot
New England native: yankee
New Hampshire state flower: lilac
New Haven founder: Eaton
New Haven tree: elm
New hires: trainees
New homeowner, probably: debtor
New Jersey fort: Dix
New Mexico art center: Taos
New Mexico flower: yucca
New Mexico resort: taos
New Mexico, to a Mmexican: estado
New, nearly: used
New Orleans cuisine: creole
New Orleans NFL team: Saints
New Orleans sandwiches: po'boys
New pack members: wolf cubs
New plant variety: hybrid
New, prefix: neo
New product div.: r and d
New shoots: sprigs, sprouts
New socialite: deb
New Testament book: Titus, Acts
New Testament king: Herod
New work alliance: OAS
New York attorney: Queens counsel
New York borough: Queens

NYC eatery: deli
NYC landmark: MGS, NYSE
NYC locale: Soho
NYC residences, many: appts.
NYC university: Pace
New York area: Bronx
New York native: Oneida, Seneca
New York port: Oswego
New York (upstate) school: RPI
NYSE morning ritual: opening bell
NYSE rival: AMEX
New York tennis stadium: Ashe
New Zealand miler: Nell
New Zealand native: Kiwi, Maori
New Zealand parrot: kea
Newborn, aerie: eaglet
Newborn clothing: layette
Newcomer: neo
Newcomer, immodest: upstart
Newcomer, society: deb
Newmar, Jillie: actress
News account, small: report
News agency: UPI
News center: bureau
News chief: editor
News follower: Leno
News items, paid: ads
News maker: Lenin
"A nose for news"
News stand: kiosk
News summaries: recaps
News VIP: anchor
Newsboy's cry: extra
Newscast honcho: anchorman
Newspaper name: Herald
Newspaper name, popular: Herald
Newspaper notice: want ad
Newspaper page: oped,
Newspaper paragraph: item
Newspaper people: press
Newspaper section, old-time: roto
Newswoman, fictional: Lois
Newt, immature: eft
Newton fruit: figs
Newton, Isaac title: sir
Newton John, Olivia: music
Newts: eft
Next in line: heir
Next planet after Earth: Mars
Next to: beside
Next to last item in series: penult
Next up: on deck, on tap
Next year's models, prepare for: retool
Nez Perce chief: Joseph
Niacin or thiamine: vitamin b
Niagara Falls cloud: mist
Niagara River source: Erie
Niagara's veil: mist
Nibble: gnaw
Nibbled away: gnawed
Nibbles on: eats
Niblick, for one: iron (golf club)
Niblick or spoon: club, iron (golf)
Nice eye: oeil

Nice friends: amis
Nice, hot time: ete
Nice notion: idee
Nice summer (French): ete
Nice thought: idee
Nicene creed
Niche: recess
Nicholas II: Russian ruler, Romanov
Nichols, Anne, hero: Abie
Nichols, Kyra: ballet
Nick or scratch: mar
Nickelodeon: music box, juke box
Nickname associated with honesty: Abe
Nicknamed: dubbed
Nick's dog: Astra, Asta
Nicosia native: Cypriot
Nicotine cohort: tar
Nicotinic acid: niacin
Niels Bohr units: atoms
Nielsen, Leslie: actor
Nieman, Leroy: artist
Nieuport's river: Yser (also Nieuwpoort)
Niflheim goddess: Hel
Nigerian email, sometimes: scam
Nigerian native: Ibo, Edo
Nigerian people: Edo, Edos, Ibo
Nigerian tribesman: Ibo, Edo
Night attire: robe
Night blindness: nyctalopia
Night club: cabaret, boite, bistro,
 disco
Night club, cheap: joint
Night club number: song
Night club show: revue
Night crawler: bait, worm
Night flight: red-eye
Night flyer: bat, owl
Night flying insect: moth
Night follower: dawn
Night music: lullaby
Night noise: snore
"Night of the iguana"
Night sky constellation: Orion
Night watches: vigils
Nightmare: ordeal, bad dream
"Arabian Nights"
Nightshade relative: tomato
Nightstand earthenware: ewer
Nighttime gift-giver: tooth fairy
Nighttime nuisance: snoring
Nike competitor: K Swiss
Nil, to Francois: rien
Nile bird: ibis
Nile city: Aswan
Nile dam: Aswan
Nile god: Aton
Nile queen: Cleo, Nefertiti
Nile snake: asp
Nile sun god: Aton
Nile wader: ibis,
Nimble, more: spryer
Nimbus: halo
Nimitz, USS
Nin, Anaise (anais): writer

Nine days of devotion: novena
Nine digit info: SSN
Nine, group of: ennead
    music: nonet
Nine instruments, set of: nonet
Nine-to-five cry: TGIF
Nine-to-fiver
Nine voices, set of: nonet
Nine-headed monster: hydra
Nine-sided figure: nonagon
1942 org.: OPA
1960s style: mod
"1984" author: Orwell
Ninety degrees from norte: este
Ninja leader: shogun
Ninnies: geese
"Ninotchka" name: Greta
Nintendo competitor: Sega
Nintendo forerunner: Atari
Nintendo precursor: Atari
Nintendo rival: Sega
Niobe, acted like: wept
Niobe's claim to fame: tears
Nipped: bite
Nipped, in sports: edged
Nipper's co.: RCA
Nippon city, old: Edo
Nirvana buddhist: arhat
Nirvana reacher: arhat
Nitpicks: nags
Nitrogen, containing: azo
Nitroglycerin container: vial
No: uh uh
"No argument here": suits me
No early bird: night owl
No emotion, showing: stoic
No fat Jack: Sprat
No fun at all: onerous
No get-up-and-go, having: inert
No great shakes: so so
No longer fizzy: flat
No longer in vogue: passe
No longer is: was
No longer one-sided: even
No longer pristine: used
No matter what: anyway
No matter which: any
No mere cold snaps: ice age
No more than: only
No need to explain: I get it
No, on the Rhine: nein
No place for witches: Salem
No strings attached, with: freely
No sweat: easy
No, to a Laird (Scot): nae
No, to a lassie: nae
No, to a Russian: nyet
No, to Ivan: nyet
Noah's landfall: Ararat
Noah's son: Shem
Nobel, for one: Swede
Nobility, of: titled
Noble: lord
Noble Ferrara family: Este

Noble, lowest: baron, beron
Noble, more: loftier
Nobleman, Italian: conte
Noblemen: barons, vis, earls
Noble's pride: title
Nobody's fool: smart
No-brainer: easy one, simple, idiot
Nocturnal animal: tapir
Nocturnal lemur: loris
Nocturnal sound, irritating: snore
Nocturnal swimmer: eel
Nod neighbor: Eden Nod off: drowse
Nods or winks: signals
Noel: yule
Nogales nosh: tamale
No-goodnik: bad egg
Bete noire: dislike, hate
Noir opposite:blanc
Noise: din, sound
Noise, fan: rah
Noise, jungle: roar
Noise, making no: silent, mute
Noise, tiresome: din
Noise, traffic-jam: blare, beep, honk
Noise, whining: zing
Noise unit: decibel
Noisy: raucous
Noisy disturbance: riot, fracas
Nol of cambodia: lon
Nolo contendere
Nom de guerre
Nomad, desert: Arab
Nomad tent: yurt,
Nomad's home: tent, yurt
Nonacademic degree: nth
Nonaquatic goose: nene
Nonclergy: laymen
Nonclergy worshipper: laity
Nonclerical: laic
Noncom nickname: sarge
NCO, lowly: cpl
NCO nickname: sarge
Nonconformists: mavericks
None at all: nil
None better: best
None of the above
None too convincing: lame
Non-earthling: alien
Nonfilling dessert: Jello
Non grata at some motels: pets
Nongreen auto: gas hog,
Nonlethal weapon: taser
Nonmetallic element: iodine
Nonnuclear family: niece
Nonpareil: finest, humdinger
Non-picker-upper: slob,
Nonpoetic writing: prose
Nonprofit website suffix: .org
Nonrequired course, take a: elect,
    elective
Nonreturnable, it's: ace
Nonrust coating: zinc
Nonrusting metal: tin, zinc, copper
Nonsense: pah

Nonsense poet: Lear
Nonsense verse writer: Lear
Nonshiny finish: matte
Nonsoap opera: aida
Nonstop: ever
Nonstudio movie: indie
Nonswimming, maybe: wader
Nonuniform clothing: nufti
Nonunion workplace: open shop
Nonverbal okay: nod
Nonverbal welcome: open arms
Noodle, like a wet: limp
Nook: alcove
Nopal: cacti, cactus
Nope: uh uh
Nora Ephron's sister: Delia
Nordic deity: Odin
Nordiques' home: Quebec
Nor'easter: gale
Normal, kind of: para
Normal procedure: business as usual
Norman Vincent Peale
Normlessness, state of: anomie (social
    instability)
Norm's wife ("Cheers"): Vera
Norse god: Hoenir
Norse god of crop: Thor
Norse god of fate: Norn
Norse god of light, peace: Balder
Norse god of mischief: Loki
Norse god of war: Tyr, Odin
Norse god supreme: Odin
Norse goddess of healing: Eir
Norse goddess of love: Freya
Norse goddess of thunder: Thor
Norse goddess of weather: Thor
Norse inscription, old: rune
Norse king: Olaf
Norse literary collection: edda
Norse myths (book of): edda
Norse pantheon: aesir
Norse poem, old: rune
Norse troublemaker of myth: Loki
Norse Zeus: Odin
North American rail: sora
North Atlantic bird: skua
North Carolina college: Elon
North Carolina university: Elon
North Caucasian language: Udic
North Dakota city: Fargo
North forty unit: acre
North of Virginia: Ollie
North Pole product: toys
North Sea tributary: Rhine
North Star: Polaris
North Star, like the: polar
North Star state: Minnesota
North Sumatran region: Achin
North wind, of the: boreal
Northeasterly wind: bora
Northern constellation: Lyra, Draco
Northern Iraqi: Kurd,
North-woods state: Minnesota
Norway airline: SAS

Norway patron saint: olaf
Norwegian goblin: nisse
Norwegian inlet: fjord
Norwegian king: Olaf
Norwegian monarch: Olaf
Norwegian name: Erik
Norwegian playwright: Ibsen
Norwegian queen: Aleta
Norwegian royalty name: Olav, Olaf
Norwegian saint: Olaf
Norwegian toast: skoal
Nose: neb
Nose alert: odor
Nose around: pry, snoop
Nose job: bob
Nose stimulus: odor, aroma, scent
Nosegay: posy, flower
Nosegay holder: vase
Nosegay makeup: flowers, posies
Nosh: eat, snack
Noshed: ate
Nostalgic times: yore
Nostradamus, reputedly: seer
Nostrils: nares
Nostrum: remedy
Nosy, be: pry
Nosy parker: yentas
Not a figment: real
Not a main route: sideway, detour
"Not a pretty sight":
Not pro: anti, con
Not a single one: nary
Not a sole: no one
Not abridged: uncut
Not accented: atonic
Not admit to: deny
Not alert in perception: obtuse
Not all: some
Not allowed: taboo,
Not, also: nor
Not ambiguous: clear cut
Not animal or vegetable: mineral
Not any: nary, none
Not as complicated: easier
Not as cramped: roomier
Not as energetic: wearier
Not as great: less
Not as loose: tauter
Not as many: fewer
Not as relaxed: tenser
Not at all superficial: deep
Not at all well done: rare
Not at risk: safe
Not available: in use
Not be discreet: blab
Not be frugal: waste
Not be rash: go slow
Not being used: idle, on ice
Not black or white: colored
Not bogus: real
Not bold: timid
Not born yesterday: astute, wise
Not broken: working, useable, intact
Not built-up: rural

"Not care a fig"
Not cautious: rash
Not chic: passé
Not clear: opaque
Not clueless about: in on, aware
Not colorful: drab
Not complex: simple
Not conforming to reality: illusory
Not cool: un-hip,
Not dangerous: safe
Not deceived by: onto
Not delay: act
Not deserved: undue
Not difficult: easy, painless
Not disguised: overt
Not domesticated: feral, wild
Not earned: undue
Not easily found: rare
Not edited: uncut
Not e'en once: ne'er
Not embarrassed: unbashed
Not enhance: detract
Not even: odd
Not even one: zilch, none
Not e'en once: ne'er
Not everyone: some
Not exciting: tame
Not fake: true, real
Not final, as a legal decree: nisi
Not fitting: unapt
Not fixed: mobile
Not flat: hilly, uneven
Not float: sink
Not flustered: calm
Not fooled by: onto
Not for everyone: rated R
Not for the scrap heap: usable
Not forthright: sly
Not forward: shy
Not frank: evasive
Not get billed: prepay
Not get renewed: lapse
Not green: ripe
Not going beyond given domains:
        immanencies, immanence's
"Not guilty" is one: plea
Not hard: easy, soft
Not her: you
Not here: absent
Not hesitate: act
Not illicit: legal
Not imaginary:real
Not in a whisper: aloud
Not in any way: no wise
Not in favor: anti
Not in the pink: ill, ail
Not inert, chemically: reactive
Not interfere with: let be
Not just a star: idol
Not keep up: lag
"Not know from Adam"
Not kosher: tref
Not lack: have
Not late: in time

Not lenient: harsh
Not let forget: remind
Not liable: exempt
Not, likewise: nor
Not liquid or gas: solid
Not live: taped
Not look forward to: dread
Not many: few, a few
Not masc.:fem.
Not messy: neat, tidy
Not moored: adrift
Not Mormon, to a Mormon: gentile
Not moving: inert
Not much: scant
Not much liked: unpopular
Not native: exotic
Not now: then, when
Not obliged: exempt
Not obvious: subtle
Not of the cloth: laic
Not often: seldom
Not often seen: rare
Not on the level: askew
Not on the rocks: neat
Not on time: delayed, late
Not one: nary
Not ordinary: special
Not out of bounds: in play
Not over: beneath
Not owing: paid
Not petit: gras
Not plain: ornate
Not polluted: pure
Not qualified: unfit
Not quite: almost
Not quite a run: triple
Not quite drenched: damp
Not quite right: amiss
Not real: false, fake
Not refined: coarse
Not relaxed: tense
Not resist: obey
Not right: wrong, left
Not rural: urbane
Not satisfied: itchy
Not secret: overt
Not seeing eye to eye: at odds, disagree
Not serious: playful
Not shiny: matte
Not sit well: rankle
Not so fast: whoa
Not so hot: luke warm
Not sociable: shy
Not spelled out: tacit
Not spicy: mild, bland
Not square: hip, hep
Not stifling: airy
Not still: moving, wiggling
Not stringent: lax
Not succeed: fail
Not suitable: unapt
Not taken in by: onto
Not taped: live
Not tasteful: tacky

Not that: this
Not that tough: chewable, easier
Not the same: unequal
Not theoretical: handsome
Not there: here, absent
Not this: that
Not tied to: free
Not to be dissuaded: adamant
Not to be trusted: shady
Not too swift: obtuse
Not total: partial
Not touching: apart
Not up yet: abed
Not us: them, others
Not very cool: unhip
Not very hot: tepid
Not very interesting: dry, blah
Not wanting more: sated
Not wanting to fight: dovish
Not waste: use
Not wasted: used
Not well grounded: a sea
Not windward: alee
Not with it: unhip
Not without sacrifice: at a price
Not withstanding: albeit, anyhow, aside
Not worked out: failed
Not working: out of order
"Not worth a sou" (an old coin)
Not worthless: utile, useable
Not worthy of: beneath
Not written: oral,
Not yet expired: valid
Nota bene (call attention to)
Notable curtain material: iron
Notable exploit: gest
Notation, urgent: asap
Notched: eroded
Notched, irregularly: erose
Notched range: sierra
Notched ridge, cuts a: pinks
Notch-edged: erose
Note at work: memo
Note before la: sol
Note, make a: jot
Notebooks, some: laptops
Noted atlantic crosser: nina
Noted blue chip: IBM
Noted canvasser: gallup
Noted model: alt
Noted name in Ecot: Ella
Noted violin maker: Amati
Noted whale-seeker: Ahab
Noted yodeler: tyrolienne, tyroleans
Note-passer's utterance: psst
Notes played together: chord
Notes, second: res
Notes, some: e-mails
Nothing: nada, nihil
Nothing, alternative to: all
Nothing, amounting to: null
Nothing at all: nil, zilch
Nothing, in Nicaragua: nada
Nothing more than: mere

Nothing special: so-so, average
Nothing, to Nogales: nada
"Nothing ventured, nothing gained": adage
Notice, eviction
Notion: idea
Notion, in Nantes: idee
Notion, nice: idee
Not 'neath: o'er
Notorious pirate: Kidd
Notre Dame city: Paris
Notre Dame niche: apse
Notre Dame site: ile
Notus brother: Eurus, Boreas, Zephyrus
        father: Aeolus, Astraeus
        mother Eos
Noun form: plural
Nourished: fed
Entre nous: between ourselves
Nouveau riche: one with newly acquired
    wealth
Bossa nova
Nova follower: Scotia
Novak, Kim: actress
Novel: new, prose
Novel closer: epilog
Novel plantation: tara
Novelist's concern: plot
Novello, Ivor: actor
Novelty: fad
November event: elec, election
November puller: voter
November stone: topaz
November word: vote
Novice: tyro, beginner, rookie,
        neophyte
Novotny, Rene: skater
Now and then: at times, betimes, some-
        times, occasionally
"Now" cause: Era
Now, in navarra: ahora
Now partner: here
Now, to Caesar: nunc
Nowhere near: afar
Nox's brother: Erebus
        daughter: Day, Eris, Light
        father: Chaos
        husband: Erebus
        son: Charon, Hypnos, Thanatos
Nozzle: jet
Nozzle site: hose
NRC predecessor: AEC
NT book: Rev
Nth degree (slangily): max
Nuclear: atomic
Nuclear plant: reactor
Nuclear submarine: *Nautilus*
Nuclear particle: meson, proton, neutron
Nuclear physics bit: atom
Nudge forward: prod
Nugent, Ted: musician
Nuisance: bane
Nuisance email: spam
Nuisance, flying: gnat
Nuisances: pests

Null: zero
Nuke: microwave, zap
Numb, as a foot: asleep
Number, large: slew
Number, Nero's unlucky: XIII
Number of fates: three
Number of muses: nine
Number, round: zero
Number sequence of sums: Fibonacci
Number stamper: dater
Number, top clock: XII
Number two: veep
Number, vast: myriad
Number, voting: quorum
Number, whole: integer
Numbered circle: dial
Numbers: ordinal
Numbers, array of: matrix
Numbers game: bingo, lotto,
Numbers, great: myriads
Numbers, high: myriads
Numbers, indivisible: primes
Numbers, mach: speed ratio
Numbers, minimal: quota
Numbers pro: CPA
Numbers to crunch: data
Numbing dread, sudden: pall
Numbskull: dunce, dolt
Numerical prefix: tri-, octo-
Numero (famous): uno
Numero uno
Numic dialect speaker: Ute
Nuncio's boss: pope
Nunn, Sam: senator
Nun's headgear: veil
Nun's room: cell
Vita novae
Nurse a baby: suckle
Nurse, India: ayah
Nurse, Lahore: amah
Nurse maid: amah
Nurse, oriental: amah
Nurse specialty: TLC
Nursery buy: crib, plant
Nursery rhyme girl: Jill, Bo Peep
Nurse's helpers: aides
Nurse's portion: dose
Nursing degree: msn
Nutritious snack: granola bar
Nurture: rear
Nurtured: reared, foster
Nut brown ale
Nut center: meat
Nut shell: hull
Nut type: lug
Nut pine: pinon, pinyon
Nutmeg State's flower: laurel
Nutmeglike spice: mace
Nutrition, of: dietary
Nutritional abbr.: RDA
Nutritional deprivation: fast
Nutritional legume: peanut
Nutritional regimen: diet
Nutritionist's amounts: RDAs

Nutritious bean: soy
Nutritive mineral: iron
Nuts for drinks: kolas
Nuts, like many: salted
Nutty candy: nougats
Nutty confection: nougat
Nwapa, Flora: novelist
Nye, Bill: science guy
Nye, Louis: comic
Nyet or nah, e.g.: refusal
Nymph (fountain): naiad
Nymph loved by Apollo: Daphne
Nymph pursuers: satyrs
Nymph, Rhine: Lorelei
Nymph, river: nois, naiad, nais
Nymph, sea: nereid
Nymph, water: naiad
Nymph who pined away: Echo
Nymph, wood: dryad

O

Oaf: klutz, boor, bumbler
Oahu patio: lanai,
Oak tree, like an: gnarled
"Mighty as an oak"
Oaks, Randi: actress
Oar, long: scull
Oasis: wadi
Oasis abode: tent
Oasis feature: well
Oasis former: wadi
Oasis sight: camel
Oasis, view from an: dunes
Oatar ruler: emir
Oater: western
Oater action: brawl, shootout
Oater answer: yep
Oater backdrop: mecca
Oater brawl locale: saloon
Oater crew: posse
Oater extras: posse, rioters
Oater reply: yep
Oater salutation: howdy
Oater setting: fort
Oater town: Laramie
Oater's lash la rue
Oates, Warren: actor
Oath, common: I do
Oath, mild: egad, gosh, heck, jeez
Oath, old: pshaw, nerts, fie, egad
Oath, quaint: egad
Oath, Shakespearean: fie
Oath, Victorian: egad
Oat-holder: nose bag
Oaths, like many: solemn
Oats container: feedbag, bin
Oats enthusiast: mare, horse
Oats, Joyce Carol: writer
Oaxaca approval: bueno
Obed's father: Boaz, Ephial, Shemaiah
    mother: Ruth,
     son: Jesse, Azariah

"Oberon" composer: Weber
Oberon, Merle: actress
Obi: sash, kimono
Obi wearer: geisha
Obliquely: askance
San luis obispo
Obi-wan: Jedi
Obi wan Kenobi
Obi-wan's other name: Ben
Obi-wan actor: Alec
Obi-wan portrayer: Alec
Obie contender: actor
Object: demur
Object of adoration: idol
Object of devotion: idol
Object to: mind
Object, venerated: relic
Objections, raise: demur
Objective, ultimate: end
Objects of devotion: idols
Objects thrown overboard: jetsam
Obligation: onus. Debt
Obligation, unwelcome: onus
Oblige: impel
Obliged, not: exempt
Obliquely: askance
Oblong fashion: ovally
Obscene: lewd
Obscure, completely: opaque
Obscure or dark: opaque
Obscure poem: rune
Obscure riddles: enigmas
Observance: rite
Observance, customary: rite
Observance, formal: rite
Observations, like some: astute
Observatory, Arizona: Lowell
Observe: notice, eye, espy
Observe secretly: spy
Observer: noter
Observes secretly: spies
Obsessed whaler: Ahab
Obsession: mania
Obsessive collector: pack rat
Obsessive sailor: Ahab
Obsidian: volcanic glass
Obsolescent conjunction: lest
Obsolete: passe
Obsolete, makes: outdates
Obsolete repro machine: mimeo
Obstacle: snag
Obstacle , hidden: snag
Obstinate one: die hard
Obtain by fraud: scam
Obtain via a shake down: extort
Obtained by coercion: extort
Obviously eager,: agog
O'Casey, Sean: playwright
Occasion for, had: need
Occasion for leis: luau
Occasion, on any: ever
Occident opposite: orient
Occult character: rune
Occupies, as a post: mans

Occupation: line, job
Occupational hazard: risk
Occupied, keep: amuse
Occupy time & space: exist
Occurrence: event
Ocean abysses: deeps, depth
Ocean color: aqua
Ocean crosser: liner
Ocean current, like: tidal
Ocean depth: abyss
Ocean dot: isle
Ocean fish feeder: erne
Ocean flier: erne
Ocean foam: spume
Ocean land: isle, island
Ocean motion: tide
Ocean phenomenon: tide
Ocean trenches: deeps
Oceania republic: Fiji
Oceanic flavoring: sea salt
Oceanic republic: Fiji
Ochoa, Lorena: golfer
O'connor, Una: actress
Ocote or loplolly: pine
Ocrea, part of an: stipula
Octave interval: eighth
Octavia's brother: Augustus
    grandson: Caligula
    husband: Nero, Antony
    tunic: Stola
Octoberfest mug: stein
Octopus, female: hen
Octopus home: lair
Octopus tentacle: arm
Ocular concern: stye, sty
Ocular distress: stye, sty
Odalisque's quarters: serai
O'Day, Anita: music
Odd: uneven
Odd facts: trivia
Odd fellow: codger
Odd jobs creature: Ian
Odd man out
Odds and ends: scraps
Odds numbers: ratios
Ode inspire: urn
Ode, subject of an: urn
Odenburg exclamation: ach
Odets, Clifford: playwright
Odin's hall: Vahalla
Odin's son: Thor, Tyr
Odor, agreeable: aroma
Odor, offensive: olid
Odor, pleasant: aroma
Odorous: olid
Odysseus disguise: beggar
Odysseus temptation: sirens
Oedipus: Rex
Oedipus solved, what: riddle
Of a certain period: eral
Of a time: eral
Of all time: ever
Of an age: eral
Of an ankle: tarsal

Of cities: urbane
Of dubious honesty: shady
Of high mountains: alpine
Of high velocity: supersonic
Of hours: horal
"Seat" of learning"
Of long standing: older, olden
Of no value: useless
Of people: pref: socio, ethno
Of planetary paths: orbital
Of recent origin: new
Of roses and tulips: floral
Of service: utile
Of sound: tonal
Of stone: lithic
Of that kind: such
Of the ear: aural, auditory
Of the first age: primeval
Of the intellect: mental
Of the kidneys: renal
Of the lower intestine: ileal
Of the Milky Way: galactic
Of the nobility: titled
Of the past: older, ago
"Of thee I sing"
Of this kind: such
Of time: eral
Of trees: arboreal
Of weddings: bridal
Of yore: bygone, olden
Off and on: fitful
Off base?: AWOL
Off base, is: errs
Off beat: far out
Off bottom: aweigh
Off course: lost
Off key: flat,
Off one's rocker: daft
Off schedule: late
Off the beaten track: astray
Off the hook: free
Off the mark: afield
Off the street time: curfew
Off the track: afield
Off-beat way, in an: oddly
Off-center type, briefly: ital
Off-color, beyond: lewd
Offended: hurt
Offender, serious: felon
Offends, deeply: hurts
Offense: sin, misdeed
Offensive manner: odiously
Offensive odor: olid, reek, stench
Offensive, Tet: Vietnam War
Offer more money: out bid
Offer tender: hire,
Offering, kind of: floral
Office, famous: oval
Office PC linkup: LAN
Office plus: window,
Office term: tenure
Office, time in: term
Office transmittal: memo
Office user's deal: lease

Office VIP: exec
Officer, future: cadet
Officer, ship's: purser, ens, captain
Official proclamation: ukase
Official records: acts
Official under Nero: Edile
Officially sanctioned: aegal
Off-road transport: ATV
Offshoot group: sect
Off-shore workplace: oil rig
Off-the-wall: outre, wacky
Off-white color: egg shell, ivory
Oft-deleted files: spam
Often clash: egos
Often-overlooked contract language: fine
    print
Oft-grated cheese: Romano
Ogle: eye
Ogres: giants
Oh, shut up: can it
O'Hara, John: writer
O'Hara, Maureen: actress
O'henry forte: irony
O'Henry works, like: ironic
Ohio college town: Kent
Ohm, George: German physicist
Oil alternative: gas, water colors
Oil barrel: drum
Oil, burning: kerosene
Oil container: drum
Oil extractor: pump
Oil holders: cruets
Oil hub, major: Tulsa
"Oil of Olay"
Oil on, puts: anoints
Oil source: olive
Oil spill formation: slick
Oil tar: cruse
Oil target: squeak
Oil tree (C. America): eboe, obeo
Oil-bearing rock: shale
Oil-rich peninsula: Arabian
Oinochoai: olpesOintment: nard
Ointment, ancient: nard
Ointment, aromatic: spikenard, nard
Ointment, biblical: nard
Ointment, medicated: oleate
Okay, but not great: so-so
Okay, but not super: nice
Okay for the queen: right o
Okay in any outlet: ACDC
Okeefe, Georgia: painter
Okinawan port: Naha
Oklahoma "Sooners"
Oklahoma aunt: eller
Okra morsel: pod
Oktoberfest souvenir: stein
Oktoberfest tune: polka
Olajuwon, Akeem: basketball
Old age: elder, eld
Old barge canal: erie
Old car gadget: crank
Old car sound: rattle
Old cattle town: Omaha

"I say old chap"
Old clay: ali
Old coin: florin
Old colony state: Massachusetts
Old cosmonaut's insignia: CCCP
Old curse word: fie
Old desk feature: ink well
Old dominion state: Virginia
Old English bard: scop
Old enough: of age
Old Faithful: geyser
Old-fashion component: rye
Old-fashion toy: rag doll
Old-fashioned ones: fogeys, fogies
Old-fashioned, stylishly: retro
Old hat: dated
"Oldies but goodies"
Old Irish writing system: ogam
Old Kinks song: Lola
Old Line state: Maryland
Old London theater: Vic
Old map initials: USSR
Old masters: oils
Old mid-month date: ides
Old Nippon city: Edo
Old oath: pshaw, nert
Old photo tint: sepia
Old Roman province: Gaul
Old ruler of Venice: doge
Old South, the: Dixie
Old Spice alternative: Afta
Old-style photos: sepias
Old-style type: caslon
Old Testament book: Ezra
Old Testament twin: Esau
Old-time exclamation: egad
Old-time religion, one with that: pagan
Old-time Turkish title: pasha
Old-time warning: alarum
Old timer: quaint
Old tongue: Erse
Old war story: "Iliad"
Old West carriage: buckboard
Old World lizard: agama
Old World mountain: Ural
Olden times: yore
Oldenburg, Cleas: sculptor
Oldest living thing in Middle-earth:
    Treebeard
Old-fashion, rather: dated
Olduvai location: Afr, Africa
O'leary, Hazel: sec of energy
Oleoresin used in plaster-making: elemi
Olfactory lobe's purpose: smell
Olfactory offense: odor
Olfactory organ: nose
Olfactory stimulus: aroma
Olin, Ken: actor
Olin, Lena(Lana): actress
Oliva, Tony: baseball
Olive drab: military uniform color
Olive genus: olea
Olive Oyl's brother: Castor
Olive stuffer: pimento

Olive tree genus: olea
"Oliver Twist" character: Fagin
Oliver Twist, for one: gamine
Oliver's request: more
Ollie's pal: Fran
  partner: Stan
Olmert, Ehud: of Israel
Olsen, Ole: Vaudeville, comic
Olympian, chief: Zeus
Olympian hawk: Ares
Olympian leader: Zeus
Olympian queen: Hera
Olympian quest: medal, gold medal
Olympic chant: USA
Olympic dream: medaling, medalling
Olympic jump: axel
Olympic org.: IOC
Olympic site, original: Athens
Olympic vehicle: luge
Olympus queen: Hera
Olympus inhabitant: Ares
Olympus resident: god
Omani title: emir
Omega opposite: alpha
Omelet ingredient for Julius: ova
Omen interpreter: seer
Omen of, be an: augur, portend, bode
Omen of, was an: presaged
Omigosh: yipe
Ominous bird: raven
Ominous sign: omen
Omitting none: all
Omits: skips, abates
Omits syllables in speech: elides
Omnia vincit amor: love conquers all
Omnipotence: greatness
Omnirange, navig.: VOR
Omnivorous mammal: coati
On any occasion: ever
On behalf of: per, for
On-call device: pager
On deck: next,
On edge: tense, keyed up
"On Golden Pond" bird: loon
On hold, remain: wait
On ice: in reserve
On its way: sent
On le menu roasted: roti
On luego o: hasta
On-off switch, type of: toggle
On one's guard: leery, alert
On open water: a sea
On one's toes: alert, awake
On pins and needles: antsy, edgy
On sabbatical: porto
On social security: ret., retired
On solid ground: ashore
On stage extra: encore
On strike: idle, idled
On tenterhooks: tense, edgy
On terra firma: ashore
On the alert: aware
On the authority of: per
On the ball: sharp

On the bounding main: at sea
On the briny: asea
On the dot: sharp
On the double: presto, stat, pronto
On the fence: wavering
On the fritz: kaput
On the go: active
On the Laptev: asea (Laptev Sea)
On the line: at stake
On the loose: at large
On the money: exact
On the other hand: else
On the qui vive: alert
On the rise: yeasty
On the road: away, traveling
On the train: aboard
On the up & up: legit, legal
On the wane: ebbing
On the way: coming, in route, enroute
On the way out: going
On the whole: mostly, mainly, usually
On this: here on
On time: prompt
On top of: crowning
Onager: ass, wild ass
Onassis name: Ari
Once again: anew
Once and twice: thrice
Once around the sun: year
Once around the world: orbit
"Once bitten, twice shy"
Once in a lifetime: rare
Once meant once, it: erst
Once more: fresh, anew, again
Once named: nee
Once, once: erst
Once owned: had
Once possessed: had
Oncle's mate: tante
One and the other: both
One and only: sole
One at a time link:
One behind the other: tandem
One better, went: topped
One billion, prefix: giga, gigaton
One celled animal: amoeba
One celled fruit: lomentum
One celled plant: algae
One circuit: lap
One coming out: deb,
One concerned with figures: ogler, cpa
One, to conchita: une
One coulomb, per sec.: amp
One devoted to religion: oblate
One for one deal: swap
"One for the books"
"One for the books", for one: idiom
One foot forward: step
One, French: une
  German: ine, eine
  Scot: ane
One giving testimony: eye witness
One horned animal: rhino
One hundred: pref.: hecto

1/100 of an Indian rupee: paisa
120 or 240: volts
One in a million: rare
"One in a million" link
One in Kasparov's corner: rook
One is at home: ump
One issue of newspaper: edition
One lacking wits: dolt,
One litmus test: acid, alkali
One may run it: meet
One moon: planet: earth
One move before the king: pawn
One, no matter what: any
One of a Freudian trio: ego
One of a pair: twin
One of a personal trio: ego
One of a sinkful: dish
One of Caesar's trio: vidi
One of 170 on a trireme: oar
One of ten: toe, finger, pin
One of the twelve: apostle
One of thirteen in a deck: spade, suit
One of those: that
One of three states: liquid, gas, solid
One of twelve: month, hour
One of two evils: lesser
One of two parts: moiety
One of two: either, neither
One of us: you
One often in a fog: Londoner
One on the Moh's scale: talc
One or more: any, some
One or the other: either
One or two (1 or 2): digits
One out to right a wrong: avenger
One playing with a full deck: dealer
One pot dinner: stew
One pref.: uni
One serving a 6-yr term: senator, sen
One side of a leaf: page
One side of an issue: con, pro
One, Spanish: una
One spot: ace
One-time word processor: steno
One to hang out with: best friend
One true thing: fact
One under a mezzo: alto
One way into Rome: Appian
One way or another: somehow
One way to be knock: silly
One way to be taken: aback
One way to begin: anew
One way to come clean: bathe
One way to get closer to home: steal second
One way to protest: sit-in
One way to ride: piggy back
One way to run: scared, amok
One way to start: anew
One who expiates: atoner
One who looks badly: ogler
One who paddles: canoer
One who razes: leveler
One who rebounds: rallier
One who rights a wrong: atoner

One who won't settle down: nomad
One who's casting about: angler
One who's given the third degree: PhD
One with a bag: totter, toter
One with a crow: prier
One with aspirations: hoper
One with old-time religion: pagan
One with the capacity for veracity: liar
One with wanderlust: nomad
O'Neal, Ryan: actor
O'Neal, Tatum: actress
One-armed bandit: slot
One-armed pitcher: ewer
One-eighth of a byte: bit
One-eighty: U-turn
One-horned animal: rhino
One-horse carriage: shay
One-named comedian: Sinbad
O'Neil, Tip: politician
O'Neill, Eugene: writer
O'Neill's, Eugene daughter: Oona
One-legged ballet pose: arabesque
One-liner: gag, joke, quip
One-name entertainer: Cher
One-piece cloak: toga
One-pot dinner: stew
One's good name: rep.
One's in suits: aces
One's pledged fidelity: truth
Ones sharing a crest: clan
One's time, bide
One's way, made: wended
Ones with power: ins
Oneself: numero uno
Oneself, by: solo
One-seventh of una semana: dia
One-sided: biased, uneven, colored,
        partial, unequal, inclined
One-sided, no longer: even
One-sidedness: bias
Oness: unite
One-to-one learner: tutee
One-word def.: syn
Onion cousin: leek, chive
Onion covering: skin
Onion goody: ring
Onion, mild: leek
Onion, type of: shallot, vadalia
Onion-flavored roll: bialy
Onionskin: paper
Online info: FAQ
Online journal: blog
Online music service: Napster
Online note: email
Online travel reservation: eticket
Online zine: emag
Only: merely, sole, mere
"You Only Live Twice"
"Only Time" chanteuse: Enya
Only's partner: one
On-off switch, type of: toggle
Glom onto: seize
Only chance, their
Onstage extra: encore

Onyx relative: agate
Oodles: scads
Oola's guy: oop
Oom-pah instrument: tuba
Oomph: pep, vim, zip, brio, dash, energy
        zest, zing, vigor
Oops: oh no, uh oh
Oop's girl: oola
"Opal" ending: -ine
Opal or topaz: jewel, gem
Opec nations: UAE, Iran, Iraq, Libya,
        Kuwait, Algeria, Nigeria, Indonesia,
        Venezuela, Saudi Arabia
Open a jacket: unzip
Open African grassland: veldt
Open declaration: avowal
Open denunciation: decrial
Open for discussion: moot
Open, force: pry
Open forest space: glade
Open freight car: gondola
Open, hung: gaped, ajar
Open sesame
Open to all: public
Open to bribery: venal
Open up: bloom
Open wide: yawn
Open work fabric: net, lace
Open-air lobbies: atria
Opener: key, tab
Openers, they are good for: keys
Open-handed blow: slap
Opening: vent
Opening, cavernous: caw
Opening, minute: pore
Opening passage: intro
Opening remarks: intro
Opening scene: Eden, act one
Opening, tiny: ostiole
Opening up: unfurling
Open-mouthed, is: gapes
Opens the window: airs, airs out
Open-topped bag: tote
Opera: opus
Opera: "La Boheme," "Le Cogdor"
Opera, borodin: prince igor
Opera box: loge
Opera boy: Hansel
Opera composer: Verdi
Opera, Egyptian: Aida
Opera fare: aria
Opera goddess: diva
Opera headliners, some: divas
Opera highlight: aria
Opera house: La Scala
Opera house boxes: loges
Opera, kind of: soap, opus
Opera-like musical composition: oratorio
Opera, non-soap: Aida
Opera prince: Igor
Opera role: Erda
Opera set in Egypt: Aida
Opera slave girl: Aida
Opera song: aria

Opera star: divi, diva, mimi
Operandi, modus: style, custom, manner,
        method, system, process
Opera's slave princess: Aida
Operatic airs: Ariosi
Operatic dialogues: duets
Operatic highlight: aria
Operatic melody, short: arietta
Operatic prince: Igor
Operatic song: aria
Operatic star: diva
Operating conditions: modes
Operating room, like an: aseptic
Operation, fraudulent: scam
Operational, is: works
Operative: agent
Ophelia's brother: Laertes
        father: Polonius
        love: Hamlet
Opinion: say so
Opinion, form a: deem
Opinion, gave an: said opinion, hold an: deem
Opinion, voice an: say
Opinions, gather: poll
Opole's river: Oder
Opponent of Bismarck: Beust
Opponent, unconquerable: nemeses
Opportunist: user
Opportunities for repentance: sins
Oppose change: stand pat
Opposed: anti
Opposed to: anti
Opposed to aweather: alee
Opposed to intaglio: cameo
Opposed to vacuums: plena
Opposer: defier
Opposing forces: foes
Opposite in direction: converse
Opposite, like extreme: polar
Opposite of celebrate: mourn
Opposite of exo: ento
Opposite of plummet: soar
Opposite of ruddy: wan
Opposite of "supra": infra
Opposite of sur: notre
Opposite of tape: erase
Opposition: flak
Opposition, express: object
Opposition, register: protest
Oppress, old style: peise
Opt out: withdraw
Optic applicator: eye cup
Optic covering: eye lid
Optical device, transparent: lens
Optical illusion: mirage
Option list: menu
Optimum, reach an: peak
Optimistic feeling: hope
Optimistic, more: rosier
Optimistically: rosily
Opulent: lush
"Or" follower: else
"Or" partner: and
Ora pro nobis: pray for us

Oracle's sign: omen
Oral declaration: parol
Oral history: lore
Orange bowl org.: ncaa
Orange box: crate
Orange coating: rust
Orange coconut dessert: ambrosia
Orange drink: Crush
Orange, inedible: Osage
Orange seed: pip
Orange shade: ochre
Orange variety: Naval, Florida
Orange-red stone: sard
Oranges, squeeze: ream
Oranges, Texas: Osage
Oranjestad's land: Aruba
Orate, but not off-the-cuff: read
Oration: ologe
Orator's platform: podium, dias
Orbison, Roy: music
Orbit extreme: apogee, apsis
Orbital point: apsis, apogee
Orbiter, earth: mir, space station
Orbits: circuits
Orca, famed: Shamu
Orchard buy: peck
Orchard unit: tree, bushel
Orchestra funding org.: NEA
Orchestra place: pit
Orchestra's thing: music
Orchid edible: stalep
Orchid rings: leis
Orchid-like flower: iris
Orchid-loving sleuth: Wolfe
Orchid-loving Wolfe: Nero
Order: command
Order about: boss
Order around: boss
Order from on high: decree
Order of business: agenda
Order, sort of: tall
Order to relax: at ease
Order, type of: gag, side
Ordered: bade
Orderly arrangement: array
Orders for dinner: has
Ordinary citizen: civilian
Ore hauler: tram
Ore truck: tram
Oregon, to Yvette: etat (French for state)
Oreo and milk action: dunk
Orestes sibling: Electra
Orfeo ed Euridice composer: Gluck
Org. Unit: sept
Organ, mouth: harmonica
Organ parts: stops, reeds, pipes
Organ, pipe: reed
Organ valve: stop
Organic acid: amino
Organic basis of bone: ossein
Organic compound: ketone, este
Organic division, having: celled
Organism, simple: monad
Organism, small: zoa

Org.: assn.
Organization formed 1941: OPA
Organization, impressive: array
Org. that over-sees fed. spending: GAO
Organza, like: sheer
Organize: plan
Organized society, an: polity
Orgy cry: evoe
Oriental delicacy: sushi
Oriental fabric, rich: brocade
Oriental nurse: amah
Oriental potentate: amir
Oriental servant: amah
Oriental sleuth: Chan
Oriental temple: taa, pagoda
Origami: practice of folding paper
Origami, practice: fold
"Origin of Species" writer: Darwin
Original inhabitant: native
Original matter: ylem
Originality, lacking: stale
"Orinoco Flow" singer: Enya
Orion follower: Sirius
Orion, found in: Rigel
Orion has one: belt
Orion's brightest star: Rigel
Orison, utter an: pray
Orlando attraction: Epcot, Sea World
Orleans heroine: Joan of Arc
Orly plane, once: sst,
Ormandy, Eugene: conductor
Ornament, dainty: diadems
Ornament, hanging: tassel
Ornamental case: etui,
Ornamental container: urn
Ornamental evergreen: paths
Ornamental knobs, small: knops
Ornamental knot: tie
Ornamental mat: doily
Ornamental, more: lacier
Ornamental network: fret
Ornamental pattern: seme
Ornamental trees or shrubs: hollies
Ornamental vessel: urn
Ornamented musical composition: rococo
Ornate, elaborately: rococo
Ornate, too: flashy, florid
Orpah's husband: Chilion
    sister-in-law: Ruth
Orphan, herd: dogie
Orpheus's father: Apollo, Oeagrus
Orpheus played it: lyre
Orr, Bobby: hockey
Orsk's river: Ural
Ortega's other woman: Otra
Ortestes's sister: Electra
Ortrud's victim: Elsa
Ory, Kid: jazz
Osage kin: Omaha
Oscar cousin: Emmy
Oscar night luminary: actor, actress
Oscar nominees: actor, actress
Oscar's roommate: Felix
Oscillates: swings

Oscillating: swinging, asway
Osier: willow
Osiris' sister: Isis
    wife: Isis
Oslo, from: Norse
Osprey kin: erne
Osprey's home: aerie
Ossicle site: ear
Ossified, more: bonier
Ostrich's Aussie cousin: emu
Ostrich's kin: emu, moa
Ostrichlike bird: rhea, moa
OT prophet: Esau
Otary feature: ear
"Othello" villian: Iago
Other sock: mate
Other woman, the: mistress
Others of the same class: etc.
O'toole, Peter
Ottawa chief: Pontiac
Ottawa resident: Ontarian
Ottoman: pouf
Ottoman official: agha, sultan
Ottoman ruler: Bey (governor)
Ottoman title: agha
Oui and da: yeses,
Oui opposite: non
Oui, in New York: yes
Ounce fraction: dram
Ounce or inch: unit,
Our, French: notre
"Our Friend" dog: Pete
"Our Gang" dog: Pete
Our, Italian: nostra
Ours, in tours: notre
Ouse tributary: cam
Oust from power: expel, depose, evict,
    dismiss
Ouster, sudden: coup
Out & out: arrant, utter, sheer
"Out, cat": scat
Out cry: hue
Out flow: issuance
Out for the night: asleep
Out, in baseball: away
Out in the open: overt
Out loud: oral, audibly
Out of a job: fired, idle
Out of bed: astir
Out of bounds, not: in play
Out of breath: winded
Out of commission: kaput
Out of control: amok
Out of date: passe
Out of kilter: disorder
Out of order: amiss
Out of place: inapt
Out of practice: rusty
Out of reach: far, beyond one's reach
Out of shape: unfit
Out of sight: hidden, rad, perdu,
    perdue
Out of style: passe
Out of the country: abroad

Out of the norm: odd,
Out of the question: absurd, no way
Out of the right order: amiss
Out of the sun: shaded
Out of the way: aside
Out of the way place: nook
Out of whack: askew
<u>Veg</u> out: laze around
Outback animal: koala
Outback buddy: mate
Outback cutie: koala
Outback maker: Subaru
Outback mineral: opal
Outbuilding: lean to
Outburst, as of laughter: gales
Outburst, disorderly: to do
Outburst, joyous: paean
Outcast: pariah, nerd
Out-class: excel
Outcome, fix the: rig
Outcome, inescapable: fate
Outcome, inevitable: fate
Outdoor area of house: deck
Outer: ectal
Outer covering, thick: rind
Outer ear: pinna
Outer edge: rim
Outer garment: coat, warp
Outer, in combos.: exo.
Outer limits: edges
Outer space: sky
Outfield, practice in the: shag
Outfit: garb, gear
Outlander: alien
Outlandish: outre
Outlaw foray: raid
Outlaw hunting group: posse
Outlay: cost
Outlet insert: plug
Outlet, okay in any: ACDC
Outline, hasty: sketch
Outlook, upbeat: optimism
Out-of-the-way: rare, remote, distant,
    obscure, removed
Outperform: top
Outpost, frontier: fort
Outpouring: spate
Outpouring, sudden: spate
Outside (combo form): ecto
Outside the norm: atypical
Outstanding amount: debt
Outstanding, as a debt: unpaid, owed
Outstanding figure, has an: owes
Outstretch: reach
Outward aspect: appearance
Outward, not: inly
Outwit, tough to: astute
Outwitted in a card game: euchred
Ouzo flavor: anise
Ouzo ingredient: anise
Oval: ellipse
Oval nest builder: oriole
Oven, annealing: lehr
Oven, brewer's: oast

Oven gadget: timer
Oven, slow: warm
Oven, tobacco-curing: oast
Oven light: pilot
Over: upon, atop
Over act: emote
Over and above: also, as well, beyond,
    besides, as well as
Over and over: oft, often, frequently
Over here, subtle: psst
"Over" in Berlin: uber
Over one's head: deep
Over, pored: examined closely
Over with: past, done
Overadorn: ornate
Overacted: emoted
Overagain: renew, anew
Overall feeling: mood
Overall top: bib,
Overattentive, as a waiter: hover
Overbearing: pushy
Overcharge: soak, gouge
Overcoat, kind of: raglan
Overcoat, long: ulster
Overcome utterly: whelm
Overconfident: smug
Overdecorated: rococo
Overdone: arty
Overexertion, results of: ache
Overfeed: sate, stuff
Overflow: teem
Over-fond, was: doted
Overhaul: refit, repair,
Overhead structure: roof
Overhead, use the: show
Overindulge: binge, dote
Overlapping, to mehta: stretto
Overloads, it prevents: fuse
Overly: too, excess, degree
Overly glib: pat
Overly petty, be: split hairs
Overly prudish one: prig
Overly trusting: naïve
Overnight flight: redeye
Overnight visit: stay
Overpower verbally: shout down
Overpraise: hyped
Overpublished: hyped
Overrefined: effete, prissy
Overrule: veto
Overrun with: rife
Overshadow: eclipse, dwarf
Overshot the puck: iced
Oversight: error
Oversimplified writing: pablum
Oversize hairdo: afro
Overstrung, most: edgiest
Overt: open, public, blatant
Over there: yon, afar, yonder
Over-the-top: extreme, reckless, excessive
Overthrow: depose
Overthrow attempt: coup
Overthrow first base: error
Overtime cause: tie, even

Overture: prelude
Overturn: upend, upset
Overwelcome with flattery: snowed,
    flooded
Overwhelming fear: panic
Overwhelming victory: landslide
Overworked phrase: cliche
Ovid's bird: avis
Ovid wind instrument: ocarina
Owed right now: due
Owens, Jessie: track
Owl's query: who
Owned apartment: condo
Owned item: asset
Owned, once: had
Owned, previously: used
Owner's papers: deed, title
Ownership document: title, deed
Ownership proof: title, deed
Ox, kind of: musk
Ox, legendry: Babe
Ox of Celebes: anoa, goa, noa
Ox, small: noa
Ox, Tibetan: yak
Oxalis plant: oca, sorrel
Oxanadus rockers: elo
Oxen, team of: yoke
Oxen, Tibetan: yaks
Oxen, two: yoke
Oxen, wild: gaurs
Oxford alternative: Aetna
Oxford feeder: Eton
Oxford part: sole, heel, arch, toe
Oxford rival: Cambridge
Oxford river: Thames
Oxford scholarship: Rhodes
Oxford tutor: don
Oxidation of metal: rust
Oxlike antelope: eland
Oxygen, absence of: anaerobic
Oxygen form: ozone
Oxygen thriving organism: aerobe
Oyer & terminer
Oyster, open an: shuck
Oyster, young: spat
Oyster's abode: bed
Oz, Amos: writer
Ozark state: Missouri
Ozem's brother: David
    father: Jesse, Jerahmeel
Ozone no-no: CFCs
Ozymandias's expression: sneer

P

P & q: consonant
Paba part: amino
Pablo Neruda: poet
Pablo "please": por favor
Pablo's girl: amiga
Pace, easy: amble
Pace for Picard: warp speed
Pachyderm, big-eared: African elephant

Pacific island: Oceania, Oceanica,
    Belau, Palau
Pacific ocean discover: balboa
Pacific phenomenon: tsunami
Pacific rim region: asia
Pacing: tempo
Pacino, Al: actor
Pack: load, box
Pack animal: llama, camel, mule, rat
Pack down: tamp
Pack firmly: tamp
Pack members, new: wolf cubs
Pack rat member: Dean, Frank
Pack to capacity: jam
Package destination: address
Package, seal a: tape
Package sealer: tape
Package, type of: care
Packaging weight: tare
Packed away: ate, stowed
Packed it in: quit
Packing a pistol: armed
Packing a punch: potent
Packing a wallop: potent
Packing boxes: trunks
Pac-Man morsel: dot
Pact letters: NATO
Pact member: ally
Pad: mat
Pad or worthy, word with: note
Pad site, perhaps: knee
Pad, type of: lily
Padded envelope: mailer
Paddles: canoes
Paddles, one who: canoer
Paddock: corral
Paddock occupant: mare, foal
Paddock youngster: foal
Paddy crop: rice
Paddy wagon: Black Maria
Padlock adjunct: hasp
Padre's pals: Pedro
Pagan deity: Baal
Pagans of Mindanao: Atas
Page, folded corner: dog ear
Page number: folio
Ope'd page(opened)
Page, Patti: musician
Page size of a book: octavo
Pageant figures: magi
Pageant tipper: crown, tiara
Pageant winner: queen
Pageant winner's accoutrement: tiara
Pages, flip: leaf
Pago Pago locale: Samoa
Pagoda: taa, temple
Pagoda figure: idol
Pagoda sounds: gongs
Pagodas, like: Asian
Paquin, Anna: actress
Pahlavi's domain: Iran
Pahlavi's title: shah
Paid at a sale: less
Paid attention: hearkened, heeded

Paid, got: earned
Paid homage: knelt
Paid news items: ads
Paid performer: pro
Paid work: job
Paige, Satchel: baseball player
Pain in the neck: bane, kink
Pain, sharp: stab
Pained reaction: ouch
Pains: agonize
Paint, apply: coat
Paint layers: coats
Dance or paint: war
Paint polymer: silicone
Paint, poster: tempera
Paint, remove: strip
Paint resin: alkyds
Paint the town red: carouse
Paint undercoat: primer, sealer
Painted, freshly: wet
Painted, in a way: enameled, coated
Painted tin ware: tole
Painter, a foremost: Rubens
Painter of Toledo: El Greco
Painter's application: primer, primer coat
Painter's garb: smock
Painter's ground: gesso
Painter's tool: ladder, brush, easel
Painter's undercoat: gesso
Painting: qeuvre
Painting genre: opart
Painting, illusory: opart
Painting style: opart, genre
Painting the town: on a spree
Painting, wall: fresco, art
Pair split in Vegas: aces
Pair up: match
Pairs, in: dually, duo
Pajama cover: robe
Pajamas topper: robe
Pakistan neighbor: Iran
Pakistan's language: Urdu
Pakula, Alan: director
Pal in Dijon: ami
Pal Joey's penner: Ojana
Pal, kind of: pen
Pal, slangy: bro
Palamedes's brother: Sforza, Achilles
    father: Nauplius
Palapa roofs: thatching
Palatable: edible
Palate: uvula
Palate refreshers: sorbets
Pale: wan
Pale, become very: blanch
Pale blond: ash
Pale, turned: blanched
Pale, very: ash, ashy
"Paleo" opposite: neo
Paleozoic: era
Palermo's island: Sicily
Palermo's locale: Sicily
Palest: wannest
Palestine, ancient region of: Judea

Palestine's "heights": Golan
Palette adjunct: easel
Palette color: umber
Palindrome, bard's: ere
Palindromic address: maam
Palindromic comic dog: Otto
Palindromic constellation: Ara
Palindromic girl name: Ada, Anna
Palindromic interjection: oho
Palindromic Platte River people: Oto
Palindromic preposition: ere
Palindromic sound effect: toot
Palindromist's dogma: tenet
Pallet: skid
Pallid: wan
Pallid, most: ashiest
Palm branch: frond
Palm, climbing: rattan
Palm fiber: tal
Palm genus: areca
Palm leaf: frond
Palm off: fob, foist
Palm readers opener: i see
Palm whack: slap
Las palmas
Palmed off: foisted
Palmer, Betsy: actress
Palmetto state: South Carolina
Palms off: foists
Palms, some: sagos
Palmyra's queen: Zenobia
Palomino prodder: spur
Palpebral on the eye: lid
Paltry: measly
Pampas backdrop: Andes
Pamper: baby
Pampering place: spa
Pamphlet: tract, folder
Pampleteer: Thomas Paine
Pamplona cry: ole
Pamplona pal: amigo
Pamplona runner: toro
Tai pan
Pan y leche, source of: tienda
Panache: elan
Panama Canal city: Colon
Panama or stovepipe: hat
Panama parent: madre
Panamanian dictator: Noriega
Panamanian leader: Omar Torrijos
Panasonic rival: Sanyo
Panay people:ati
Pancake kin: crepe
Pancake, kind of: potato, blueberry
Pancake, thin: blin, blini, blinis,
    crepes, blintz, latke
Pancake chain: IHOP
Pancake order:stack
Pancake, Russian: blinis
Pancreatic enzyme: amylase, lipase
Pane content: stamps
Pandemonium's lack: order
Pandora creator: Hephaestus
Pandora unleashed, what: ills

Pandora's boxful: ills
Pandora's box, it remains in: hope
Pangolin morsel: ant
Panhandle state: Texas
Panic, don't: be calm
Panjim is its capital: Goa
Panorama: view, vista
Panoramic view: vista
Pan's hoofs, like: cloven
Pans in reverse: snap
Pan's opposite: rave
Pansy hybrid: viola
Pansy, small: viola
Pant fashions, passe: capri's
Pantheon, like: domed
Pantheon member: god
Pantheon site: Rome
Panther or puma: feline
Panther people: Eries
Pantomime pastime: charades
Pantry: larder
Capri pants
Pants for air: gasps
Panty hose brand: leggs
Panty hose choice: taupe
Panty hose color: ecru, nude
Panza's parolee: Don Quixote
Papal court: curia
Papal envoy: legate
Papal name: pius
Papal representative: legate
Papal scarf: orale
Paparazzi prey: celeb.
Papas, Irene: actress
Papeete's island: Tahiti
Paper ballot shred: chad
Paper, crinkly: tissue
Paper, durable: manila
Paper fasteners: staples, clips
Paper folding: origami
Paper, formal: thesis
"Paper Lion" actor: Alda
Paper, lots of: reams
Paper measure: quire
Paper mill need: pulp
Paper source: pulp
Paper, thin: tissue
Paperback id: ISBN
Paprika dish: goulash
Papuan port: lae
Papyri: ancient scroll
Papyrus plant: sedge
P & q: consonant
Par excellence: top, prime, premier,
    supreme, foremost
Par plus one: bogey
Parabola: arc
Parabola, like a: arched
Parachute, uses a: bails
Parachuting, avoid: elude descent
Parade, highway: convoy
Parade honoree: hero
Parade sight: float
"Paradise Lost", e.g.: epic

Paradise: Eden, elysium, zion, heaven,
    utopia, nirvana, empyrean
Paradise, bird of
Parallel bands: stria, striae
Parallels the radius: ulna
Paramecium, e.g.: monad
Paramount rival: MGM
Paramour: lover
Paranormal: eerie
Paranormal ability: ESP
Paranormal claim: ESP
Paraoh's god: Aton
Paraphernalia: gear
Parapsychology topic: ESP
Parasite: lice, leech, drone
Parcel of earth: acres
Parched: thirsty
Parching: drying
Parchisi, form of: ludo
Parchment: vellum
Pardon: remit
Pardon, political: amnesty
Pardonnez-moi, monsieur
Parent, informal: mama
Parent, panama: madre
Parent, Seville: padre
Parenteral cephalosporin: tazicef
Paretsky of "Mystery": Sara
Paretsky of "Whodunit": Sara
Paris abducted her: Helen
Paris airport: Orby, Orly
Paris captive: Helen
Paris cop: flic
Paris dance, formal: bal
Paris grid component: rues
Paris museum: Louvre
Paris night: nuit
Paris payment: euro
Paris purchase: achat
Paris river: seine
Paris season: ete
Paris "she": elle
Paris sizzles: ete (summer)
Paris street: rue
Paris subway: metro
Paris thirst-quencher: eau
Paris "to love": aimer
Paris tower: Eiffel
Paris turndown: non
Parish leader: vicar
Parish official, minor: beadle
Parisian author: Byron
Parisian harp inventor: Erard
Parisian papa: pere
Parisian read: elle
Parisian touchdown site: Orly
Parisian way: rue
Parisina's husband: Azo
    lover: Hugo
    slayer: Azo
Park bird: pigeon
Park dwellers, some: campers
Park feature: trail
Park (NYC): Central

Park shelter: gazebo
Parka: anorak
Parka closure: snap,
Park,dining site: picnic area
Parker, Eleanor: actress
Parking lot sign: full
Parking lot party: tailgate
Parking nuisance: meter
Parking place: lot, garage
Parking place, church: pew
Parking space: berth,
Parking, type of: valet
Parks, Rosa: civil rights
Parliament, kind of: rump
Parliament member: lord
Parliamentary term: sine die
Parlor, beauty:
Parlor piece: sofa
Parmesan cousin: Romano (cheese)
Parmesan, prepare: grate
Parmesan pronoun: egli
Veal parmigiana
Parody: send up
Parolee, for one: ex-con
Paroxysm: spasm
Parquet feature: inlay
Parres: evades, fends
Parrot: echo
Parrot, large green: kea
Parroted: aped
Parrots: apes,
Parsimonious, be: stingy, frugal
Parsley serving: sprig
Parson, country: vicar
Parsons, Estelle: actress
Parson's expletive: amen
Part, bit: cameo
Part, essential: pith
Part man, part machine: bionic
Part of a dead man's hand: aces
Part of a famous soliloquy: not
Part of a rotating shaft: cam
Part of b & b: bed
Part of Iberia: Spain
Part of LA: los
Part of many a refrain: lala
Part of paba: amino,
Partakes of: uses
Parthenon goddess: Athena
Parthenon site: Greece
Partial refund: rebate
Partially, as a prefix: semi
Participates in the Hambletonian: trots
Particle, beta
Particle, minute: atom
Particle of matter: atom
Particle, tiny: mite
Particle, unseen: atom
Particular circumstance: specific,
Parties, wild: blast
Parting, word: adieu, bye, call me
Partly prefix: demi
Partly fermented grape juice: stum
Partner, neither: nor

Partner of all: one
Partner of marketing: sales
Partnership obstacle: ego
Party: fete, gala, soiree
Party after dark: soiree
Party appetizer: canape
Party, big: shindig, fete
Party centerpiece: cake
Party dishful: dip
Party, extravagant: bash, shindig, fete
Party offering: dip, keg
Party poopers: drags
Party spreads, some: paste
Party staple: dip
Party thrower plea: rsvp
Party, throws a: fetes,
Party to: abet, in on
Party to a deal: in on
Party tray cheese: brie
Party, wild: blast
Pascal, balise: math
Pascal essay: "Pensees"
Paschal symbol: egg
Paska: dyes
Pass along a cold: infect
Pass around: share
Pass at Indy: lap,
Pass, in Pirna: reichen (Germany)
Pass slowly: drag
Pass the bar: teetotal
Pass the deadline: late
Pass the word: tell
Pass through a semipermeable membrane:
        osmosis
Pass, tournament: bye
Passable: not bad
Passage, anatomical: iter
Passage between trees: allee
Passage for a sermon: text
Passage, opening: intro
Rite of passage
Passage of shops: arcade
Passage through a mine: stull, (a support)
"Passage to India" author: Forster, E. M.
Passages, featured: solos
Passageway: hall
Passageway, covered: arcade
Passé: old
Passed easily: aced
Passed with ease: aced
Passenger, extra: stowaway
Passerine birds: vireos
Passes along: relays
Passes, as a bill: adopts, enacts
Passes inferior goods: foists
Passes over tyrants: elides despots
Passes the buck: blames
Passing fancy: fad
Passing fashion: fad
Passing gossip: chin waggin
Passing remark: obiter dictum
Passing stats: tds
Passion: heat
Passion, blocks: impedes desire

Passion Sunday's period: Lent
Passionate: ardent
Passionate adherents: apostles
Passionate god: Eros
Passos, John Dos
Pass over: omit
Passover bread: matzo
Passover event: Seder
Passover feast: Seder
Passport: ID
Passport companion: visa
Passerine bird: wren
Past: ago, beyond, days of yore
Past or present: tense
Past de deux
Past due: unpaid
Past, long: yore
Past master: whiz, adept, maven, expert
Past, of the: olden
Past tense: preterit, preterite
Pasta alternative: rice
Pasta choice: ziti
Pasta cooking term: al dente
Pasta flavoring: anise
Pasta go-with: wine
Pasta piece: noodle
Pasta, prepare: boil
Pasta primavera: entrée
Pasta, rice-like: orzo
Pasta, short: ziti
Pasta topping: sauce
Pasta, tubular: penne, ziti
Pasta type: orzo
Pasta variety: penne
Pasta wheat: durum
Pasternak hero: Zhivago (Dr.)
        heroine: Lara
Pastel: soft
Pasteur portrayer: Muni
Pastime: game
Pastoral: rural, rustic
Pastoral deity: faun
Pastoral place: lea
Pastoral poem: idyll
Pastoral site: lea
Pastoral verse: idyl
Pastor's assistant: curate
Pastrami order: lean
Pastrami purveyor: deli
Pastrami supplier: deli
Pastry-enclosed eroquette: rissole
Pastry, fruit: pie, tart
Pastry place: bake shop
Pastry shell: crust
Pastry, tiny: tartlet
Pasture entrance: stile, gate
Pasture, idyllic: lea
Pasture, like a: grassy
Pasture locale: farm
Pat gently: dab,
Pat on the back: praise
Patches, they are found in: melons
Patchwork cat: calico
Pate de foie gras

Pate part: scalp
Pate topper: toupee
Pateete's island: Tahiti
Patella: kneecap
Patent medicine: tonic
Path, curved: arc
Path, Eastern: tao
Path of virtuous conduct: tao
Path to the altar: aisle,
Path with a perigee: orbit
Pathfinder's planet: Mars
Pathogenic bacteria: E coli
Pathway, kind of: neural
Patience, to a puzzle solver: asset
Patient care group: HMO
Patina: oxide
Patio: terrace, ter
Patio appliance: grill
Patio furnishing: lounger
Patio, Oahu: lanai
Patisserie output: aroma
Patois: cant, argot, dialect, lingo
Paton, Alan: novelist
Patrick's domain: Eire, Erin
Patriotic org.: DAR, SAR
Patriotic symbol: eagle
Patron of lost causes: Jude
Patronage: aegis
Patronage provider: pol
Patted on: dabbed,
Pattern, diagonal: twill
Pattern, recurring: cycle
Patty Hearst alias: Tania
Patty Hearst kidnapping org.: SLA
Paul Drake creator: Erle
Paul, Les: guitarist
Paul Revere's profession: coppersmith
Pauley, Jane: newscaster
Pauling, Linus: nobelist
Sao Paulo, Brazil
Pause: let up
Pause fillers: ers
Pause in a line of verse: caesura
Pause indicator: comma
Pavarotti piece: aria
Paved the way: eased
Pavement, pound the: job hunt
Pavements around a hangar: apron
Pavements, some: macadamize
        macadams
Pavilion, small: gazebo
Pavolv, Ivan: Russian physiologist
Pavlova, Anna: Russian ballet dancer
Pavlova of ballet: Anna
Pavlova's leap: jete
Paving stone: sett
Pawn taker: rook
Pawned: hocked
Pawnshop, take to a: hock
Pax rival: TNT
Pax vobiscum: "peace be with you"
Pay a brief visit: stop in, drop in
Pay a call on: visit
Pay attention: heed, hark

Pay by mail: remit, send
Pay chaser: ola
Pay dirt: lode
Pay, fails to: defaults
Pay for: own
Pay homage: kneel
Pay homage to: show reverence
Pay little attention to: gloss over
Pay one's share: chip in
Pay period: week
Pay the bill: foot, treat
Pay to hold hands: ante
Pay to play: ante
Pay with plastic: owe
Paycheck abbr.: hrs
Paying attention: alert
Paymaster's concern: hours
Payment, author's: royalty
Payment option: cash, plastic
Payment payment: dun
Payment status: past due
Payment, up for: due
Payne, John: actor
Pays attention: heeds, hearkens
Pays for a hand: antes
Pays for easily: affords
Pays for itself
Pays one's part: antes
Pays out: spends, remits
PBS founder: Nea
PBS funder: Nea
PBS kin: NPR
PBS series: NOVA
PC acronym: ROM
PC alternative: Mac
PC brain: CPU
PC button: Esc
PC fodder: data
PC gadget: mouse
PC image: icon
PC list: menu
PC media: CDs
PC memory unit: meg
PC monitor: CRT
PC monitor type: lcd
PC sign-on: log on
PC system, old: DOS, UNIX
PD dispatch: APB
RDP relative: ASAP, stat
Pea jacket: pod
Peabody, Amelia: fictional archeologist
Peace and quiet: order
Peace, conducive to: irenic
Peace in Russia: mir
Peace offering: sop
Peace pact of 1954: SEATO
Peace prize city: Oslo
Peace prize founder: Nobel
Peace symbol: doves
Peaceful: irenic, serene
Peaceful protest: sit-in
Peaceful relations: amities
Peacekeeping org.: NATO
Peach dessert: Melba

Peacock spots: eyes
Peacock's (Mrs.) game: Clue
Peak for Heidi: Alps
Peak near Bern: Alp
Peak of perfection: acme
Peaks: apexes
Peal of thunder: clap
Peale, Norman Vincent
Peanut: goober
Peanut, Mr., feature: monocle
Peanut shell: husk
Pear: pome
Pear, alligator: avocado
Pear, juicy: bosc
Pear, prickly: cacti
Pear type: bosc
Pearl buck heroine: olan
Pearl, kind of: seed
Pearl mosque site: Agra
Pearly gates tender: St. Peter
Pearly linen: nacre,
Pears and apples: pomes
Pear-shaped: pyriform
Pear-shaped instrument: lute
Peas or beans: legumes
Peasant, Indian: ryot
Peat source: bog
Peaty land, low: fen, bog
Peaty place: bog,
Peaty tract: moor, fen, bog
Pecan confection: praline
Peccadillo: sin
Pecking order: ladder, pyramid, hierarchy
Peckinpah namesake: sabers
Peckinpah, Sam: director
Peculiar, more: quirkier
Pedagogue: didact
Pedal: cycle
Pedal pusher: biker
Peddle: hawk, vend, sell
Pedestal: base
Pedestal part: dado, base
Pedestal, put on a: exalt
Pedicurist's concern: toe
Pedro's aunt: tia
Pedro's honorific: senor
Pedro's mom: madre
Pedro's mouth: boca
Pedro's pal: amigo
Peek, quick: gander
Peel corn: husk
Peel, Emma: actress
Peels backward: sleer
Peel's, Mrs., job: avenge
Peeping tom: voyeur
"Peer Gynt" composer: Grieg
Peer Gynt's mother: Ase, Aase
Peer of the realm: earl
Peerce, Jan: tenor
Peeress: wife, dame
Peerless example: paragon
Peers, some: earls
Peeve: irritate
Peeved mood: huff

Peeved, more: sorer
Peevish: testy
Peguod captain: Ahab
Pei, I. M.: architect
Pekoe packet: tea bag
Pekoe server: teapot
Peleg's father: eber
Peles tears: volcanic glass
Pellet: granular
Pellets: bbs, ammo
Pell-mell: chaos, snarl, muddle, rashly
Peloponnesian city: Argos
Pelota: jai alai
Pelted, severely: stoned,
Pelvic bone: ilia, sacrum, ilium
Pen name: anonym, pseudonym
Pen pals: pigs
Pen pals reply: oink
Pen points: nibs
Pen resident: con
Penalty caller: ref.
Penance, did: atoned
Pencil end: stub
Pencil holders, sometimes: ears
Pencil, kind of: eye brow
Pencil user: writer
Pencil (well-worn): nub
Pendaric (pindaric) penning: ode
Pendulous neck skin: dewlap
Penelope's father: Icarius
  husband: Ulysses, Odysseus
  mother: Periboea
Peneus's daughter: Daphne
  father: Oceanus
Penguin, Bloom County: opus
Penguin, kind of: emperor
Penguin's cousin: auk
Peninsula or nut: kola
Penitential period, of a: lenten
Penn zone: est
Penne alternate: ziti
Penniped: seal
Pennsylvania Dutch dish: screpple
Pennsylvania settler: Quaker
Penny ante
Penny or bowling: lane
Penny-pincher: miser, niggard, scrooge,
  tightwad, skinflint
Penny-wise: canny, tight, frugal, stingy,
  prudent, sparing, thrifty
Penguins, small: adelies
Pens: writes
Pension collector: retiree
Pension guarantee: vest, vesting
Pensioner's org.: AARP
Iambic pentameter
Pentateuch: Torah
Pentathlon event: epee
Penteconter mover: oars
Pentheus's grandfather: Cadmus
Pentheus, king of: Thebes
Pentheus's mother: Agave
Pentium producer: Intel
People: folk

People devourer: ogre
People, informally: guys, gals
People mover: tram, auto, train, bus, plane
Peeples, Nia: TV
People, of (pref.): socio, ethno
People of equal status: peers
People outside a profession: laity
People person: celeb
People with will-power: heirs
Pep: oomph
Pep meeting: rally
Pepe the toon: le Pew
Pepper: bombard
Pepper drink: kava
Pepper grinder: mill
Pepper, kind of: bell
Peppers, hot: Tabasco
Pequod's crew, e.g.: tars
          skipper: Ahab
Per capita: each
Per capita income
Perambulate: meander
Nez Perce tribe
Perceive: notice
Percent ending: -ile, -age
Perception: acumen
Perceptions plus speech
          and understanding: seven senses
Perceptive, acutely: keen
Perceptive, most: sagest
Perceptive, not at all: obtuse
Perch: sit
Perch, found a: alit, lit
Perchance: lest
Perched: alit, sat
Perched on: atop
Percheron's footfall: clop
Percolate: seep, leach
Percussion instrument: maraca
Perdita's father: Leontes
          mother: Hermione
Peregrine: falcon
Peregrine male: tercel, tiercel
Peremptory demand: ultimatum
Perennial candidate: Stassen
Perfect: ideal
Perfect game spoiler: hit
Perfect, just: ideal
Perfect or imperfect: tense
Perfect score: ten, ace
Perfection: utmost
Perfectly, do: nail, ace
Perfectly timed: on cue
Perform a canticle: intone
Perform without preparation: adlib
Performance, sort of: subpar
Performance that takes a second: duet
Performer, paid: pro
Performing animal: seal
Performs ballads: croons
Performs excessively: overdoes, hams
Perfume base: attar
Perfume essences: attar

Perfume extract: anise oil
Perfume, flowery: attar
Perfume label word: eau
Perfume, light: cologne
Perfume packet: sachet
Perfume purchase: elemi
Perfume quantity: dram
Perfumed bag: sachet
Pergola: arbor
Perigee: nearest point in orbit
Perignon, Dom
Peril at sea: gale, storm
Peril in the seas: reef
Period of comparative ease: let ups
Period of decline: ebb
Period of deployment: tour
Period of history: epoch, era
Period of history, important: era
Period of inactivity: calm
Period of rule: reign
Period of time: epoch, spell
Period of time (vast): eon, an eon
Period of watching: vigil
Period, recurring: cycle
Periodot's month: Aug
Peripatetic, is: roves
Periscope place: sub
Periscope site: sub
Perkin or samite: cloth
Perlman, Ron: actor
Permafrost region: tundra
Permanent con: lifer
Permanent place: salon
Permanent solution: cure
Permed hair, like: wavy
Permission, gives: lets, OKs, okays
Permit: license, let
Permit, entry: visa
Permitted: licit, legal
Pernod flavoring: anise
Peron, Eva: first lady
Peron, Signora: Isabel
Perpetually: ever
Perpetuity, in: ever
Perplexed: at sea, a sea
Perrin, lea &: steak sauce
Perry, Luke: actor
Perry White, emulate: edit
Perry's aide: Della
Perry's creator: Erle
Perry's penner: Erle
Persepolis's home: Iran
Perseus foe: Medusa
Perseus rescued her: Andromeda
Persia, modern: Iran
Persian, ancient: Mede
Persian elf: peri
Persian Gulf emirate: Qatar
Persian monarch: shah
Persian pavilions: kiosks
Persian ruler: shah
Persian's fairies: peris
Persist: last
"Persistence of memory" painter: Dali

Persistent worry, cause: gnaw
Person, awkward stupid: lout
Person, churlish: boor
Person, clumsy: cluts
Person, gentle: lamb
Person in an English class: noun
Person, mean: ogre
Person nobody knows: perfect stranger
Person, pretentious: snob
Person of prominence: nabob
Person of promise: phenom
Person, uncouth: oaf
Person, vain: snob
Person who writes memoir: biog,
          biographer
Person without a cause: rebel
Persona non grata
Personal appearance: mien
Personal atmosphere: aura
Personal identity: self
Personal preference: taste
Personal trio, one of a: ego
Personal viewpoint: slant
Personality: self
Personality, aggressive: type a
Personality part: ego
Personnel investigation: background check
Personnel, key: typist
Person's concern, cautious: risks
Person's natural height: stature
Person's nature: self
Persuade: coax, urge
Persuade to buy: sell
Persuaded gently: coaxed
Persuading: urging
Persuasion, use low-key: coax
Pert lass: minx
Pertaining to troy: ilian
Pertinent: apt
Pertinent in law: adrem
Perturb: nettle
Peruke: wig, periwig (archaic)
Peruses: reads
Perusing, keep: read on
Peruvian, ancient: Inca
Peruvian, early: Inca
Pervasive quality: aura
Pesci, Joe: actor
Peso unit: centavo
Pessimist, often: cynic
Pessimistic outlook: cynicism
Pessimist's word: can't
Pest control target: roach
Pestle, use a: mash
Pesto ingredient: basil, garlic, pine nut,
          cheese
Pesto seasoning: garlic
Pet adoption agency: SPCA
Pet, chatty: myna
Pet name: dear
Pet peeve: flea bite
Pet restraint: tether, leash, pen
Pet rock: fad
Petal essence: attar

Petal plucker word: not
Petards: fireworks
Peter Gunn's girl: Edie
Peter Nero: pianist
Peter or Nicholas: tsar
Peter Pan alternative: Jif, Jiffy
Peter Pan author: Sir James Barrie
Peter Pan dog: Nana
Peter Pan girl: Wendy
"Peter the Great" author: Massie
Petite, not: gras
Petite, plus: wee
Petition: plea, beg, sue, solicit
Petrarchan sonnet part: sestet
Petrarch's beloved: Laura
Petri dish stuff: agar
Petro measure: litre, liter
Petruchio's bride: Kate
       intended: Kate
Petruchio's job, do: tame
Petticoat, stiff: crinoline
Pettifoggers: shysters
Petty, be overly: split hairs
Petty crook: spiv
Petty, Lori: actress
Petty officer: yeoman
Petty officer, briefly,: bosn.
Petunia's suitor: Porky
Pew adjunct: kneeler
Pew location: nave
Pewter ingredient: tin
Pewter or steel: metal, alloy
PFC superior: cpl
Ph solution, high: alkali
Phaedra's father: Minos
       husband: Theseus
       mother: Pasiphae
       sister: Ariadne
       stepson: Hippolytus
Phaethon's father: Helios, Phoebus
"Phantom of the Opera"
Pharaoh amulet: scarab
Pharaoh beetle: scarab
Pharaoh charm: scarab, ankh
Pharaoh now: mummy
Pharaoh, well known: tut
Pharaoh's god: Osiris, Aten
Pharaohs, one of the: Seti, Tut
Pharaoh's textile: linen
Pharaoh's tomb: pyramid
Phaser blast: zap
Phaser setting: stun
Pheasants, brood of: nide, nye
Pheasant female: peahen
Phenomenon, endless: time
Pheromone quality: odor
Pheromones do, what: attract
Phi follower: chi
Philatelist's sheet: pane
Philemon, book after: Hebrews
Philippine city: Manila, Iloilo
Philippine island: Sulu, Archipelago, Cebu,
      Samar
Philippine native: Aeta

Philippine volcano: Apo
Phillips, Lou Diamond
Phillips, Sian: actress
Phillips University town: Enid
Philo, Vance: fictional detective
Philodendron: aroid
Philosopher, stoic: Cato
Philosopher's stone: key, elixir
Phlegm finish: atic
Phnom Penh
Phobia: fear
Phobias, having: neurotic
Phoenix cager: sun
Phoenician deity: Baal
Phoenician seaport, ancient: Tyre
Phonasthenia, suffering from: hoarse
Phone bug: tap, wire-tap
Phone button: nine, hold
Phone link, computer: modem
Phone playback: message
Phone, tied up the: yakked
Phone trio: def
Phonebook abbr.: res.
Phone-company nickname, old: Ma Bell
Phoned a letter: faxed
Phonetic symbol: agma, sch
Phony ducks: decoys
Phony operation: sham
Phony physician: quack
Phooey: fie, bah
Photo, trim a: crop
Photo color, old: sepia
Photo finish: matte
Photocopy: stat
Photograph, antique: tintype
Photographic shades: sepia, magenta,
      cyan
Photos, old style: sepias
Photosphere, it has a: sun
Photosynthesis factory, little: leaf
Phrase, common: idiom
Phrase, ultimatum: or else
Phraseology: locution
Phrases, set: idioms
Phrenologist's interest: bumps
Phrygian god: Atys, Attis
Phrygian goddess: Cybele
Phrygian king: Midas, Gordius
Physical ed.: gym
Physical love: eros
Physically delicate: frail
Physician, early: Galen
Physician, phony: quack
Physicist's prefix: astro
Physicist's study: energy
Physics calculation: mass
Physics impossibility: perpetual motion
Physics intro.: meta
Physics particle: muon, pion, quark
Physics particle, hypothetical: quark
Physics study: chaos
Physics topic: inertia
Physics unit: dyne
Physics unit of work: erg

Physique (slangy): bod
Pi, for instance: ratio
Piaf, Edith: musician
Pianist at Rick's: Sam
Pianist span: octave
Piano: spinet
Piano exercise: etude
Piano, like an old: tinny
Piano key wood: ebony
Piano name: Baldwin
Piano piece, pensive: nocturne
Piano rece: sonata, duet
Piano, small upright: spinet
Picard, Jean-Luc: Fr. astron.
Picard's predecessor: Kirk
Picador's target: toro
Picador's victim: toro
Picasso, Pablo: painter
Picasso's art movement: cubism
Picasso's year: ano
Piccadilly statue: eros
Piccadilly Circus statue: Eros
Piccolo kin: flute
Pisces or libra: signs
Pick the players: cast
Pick, type of: ice, nit
Picked from a deck: drew
Picked, just: fresh, ripe
Picked out of a lineup: fingered
Picket-line crosser: scab
Pickle relish: chow chow
Pickle serving: spear
Pickled or salted: cured
Pickler's need: alum
Pickling ingredient: alum
Pickling need: alum
Pickling solution: brine
Picks over: mulls
Pick up and go: move, leave
Pick-up, for: to go
Pick-up points, municipal: bus stops
Pickup stealthily: palm
"Picnic" author: Inge
Picnic basket: hamper
Picnic spoiler: rain, ants
Picnicked on: ate
Pictorial card: tarot
Picture holder: nail, frame
Picture, mind's: image
Picture of health: x-ray
Picture puzzle: rebus
Picture or sickness: motion
Picture (3D): hologram
Picturesque landscape: scenery
Pidgin, for one: lingo
Pie a la mode
Pie for presentation: chart
Pie crust: shell
Pie crust ingredient: lard
Pie holder, perhaps: deep dish
Pie maker: mom, oven, bakery
Pie pans: tins
Pie shell: crust
Pie slice: wedge

Piece de resistance: main dish, showpiece, centerpiece, chef d'oeuve
Piece for one: solo
Piece of advice: tip
Piece of cake: duck soap, easy
Piece of fencing: epee
Piece of hard candy: sourball
Piece of information: datum
Piece of lumber: board, plank
Piece of prose: essay
Piece of turf: divot
Piece of work: erg
Pieces, big: chunks
Pieces, in: apart
Pied horses: pintos
Pied piper city: Hamelin
Piedmont region: Asti
Piedmont wine city: Asti
Pier, in architecture: anta
Piers: quays, wharves, antae
Pierce with sharp stake: impale
Piercing: keen
Pierre's dad: pere
Pierre's date: ami, amie
Pierre's girlfriend: amie
Pierre's mother: mere
Pierre's weapon: arme
Pierre's word: mot
Pig, acted like a: oinked
Pig, movie: babe
Pig sound: grunt, oint
Pig sty: pen
Pig, type of: guinea
Pigeon dish: squab
Pigeon hawk: merlin
Pigeon pea: dal
Pigeon toed: squad
Pigeon, type of: pouter
Pigeon, young: squab
Pigeonhole: niche
Piggish, sound: oink
Miss Piggy word: oui, moi
Pigheaded: rigid, dogged, mulish, willful
Piglet, pal of: pooh, roo
Piglike animal: peccary, tapir
Pigment, earthy: ochre
Pike, Zebulon: explorer, general
Pike's Peak pass: Ute
Pilaf base: rice
Pilaster: anta
Pilchard relative: sprats
Pile driver weight: ram
Pile wood: alder, oak
Pile-up: amass
Pile-up, big: log jam
Pilgrimage site: Mecca, Lourdes
Pilgrims' interpreter: Squanto
Pill, phony: placebo
Pillaging: marauding
Pillar, inscribed: athel
Pillar of salt's mate: lot
Pillar, square: anta
Pillar, upright: stele
Pillboxes, some: hats

Pillow cover: sham
Pillow fabric: percale
"Pillow Talk" name: Doris
Pilot a ferry: ply
Pilot fish: remora
Pilot house: helm
Pilot, kind of: test, jet, airline
Pilotless plane: drone
Pilot's agreement: roger
Pilot's assent: roger
Pilot's fear: wind-shear
Pilot's ok: roger
Pilot's place: gas range
Pilot's problem: yaw
Pilot's test: solo
Pilsner alternative: ale
Pim, Mr., creator: Milne
Pimiento holder: olive
Pin down: nail
Zippy the Pinhead
Pin holder: etui
Pin location: lapel
Pin prompter: ATM
Pina colada
Pinafore: apron
Pinafore letters: HMS
Pinball no-no: tilt
Pinball palace: arcade
Pinball player's hangout: arcade
Pinball problem: tilt
Pince-nez part: lens
Pince-nez spectacles
Pinch: tweak, nip, iota, dab, nab
Pinch hitter: sub
Pinch into ridges: crimp
Pinch pennies: stint, skimp
Pinch off: nip
Pinching: tweaking
Pindar forte: lyrics, ode
Pindar's home: thebes
Pindaric poem, certain: ode
Pine cousin: fir
Pine exudation: resin
Pine, kind of: knotty
Pine leaf: needle
Pine or cedar: conifer
Pine paneling, kind of: knotty
Pine product: cone, resin
Pine relative: cedar
Pine, seed-bearing
Pine tree sap: rosin
Pine, type of: scrub
Pineapple island: maui
Pin-held scarf: ascot
Pinion partner: rack
Pink: damask
Pink lady ingredient: gin
Pink-slipped: fired
Pinnacles: apexes
Pinniped: seal, walrus
Pinocchio goldfish: Cleo
Pinocchio, often: liar
Pinochle term: meld
Pinochle combo: meld

Pinpoint: isolate
Pins and needles, on: antsy
Pins are made, where: mat
Pint fraction: ounce
Pinta's kin: Nina, Santa Maria
Pinto or garbanzo: bean
Pinza, Ezio: music
Pioneer: settler
Pioneer, legendary: Boone
Pious assent: amen
Pipe cleaner: drano
Pipe down: shh
Pipe dream: wish, chimera, fantasy
Pipe handle: stem
Pipe opening: intake
Pipe organ
Pipe pro: plumber
Pipe, repair: plumb
Pipe root: briar
Pipe type: PVC, corncob, copper, iron
Piper, Laurie: actress
Pied piper:
Pipsqueak, prankish: imp
Piquancy: zesty
Piquant: zesty
Pique: ire
Pique periods: fits
Piracy: theft
Pirandello, Luigi: playwright
Pirate: Jean Lafitte
Pirate at work: looter
Pirate, Barbary: corsair
Pirate base: lair
Pirate captain: Kidd
Pirate, fictional: Jack Sparrow
Pirate flag emblem: skull
Pirate, notorious: Kidd
Pirate rivals: Cubs
Pirate ship, swift: corsair
Pirate stashes: treasurers
Pirate "stop": avast
Pirate's base: lair
Pirate's quaff: rum
Pirate's swig: rum
Pirouette: twirl
Pisces successor: Aries
Pisa landmark: tower
Pisces follower: Aries
Pisces neighbor: Aries
Piscine school: shoal
Piscivore, flying: erne
Piscivorous bird: erne
Pismires: ants
Pistil top: stigma,
Pistol packing: armed
Pistol, thug's: Roscoe
Pit or stone: seed
Pita or dilo: tree
Pita sandwich: gyro
Pitch a tent: camp
Pitch dark: inky
Pitch suddenly: lurch
Pitch water: bail
Pitch-black: unlit

Pitched, as a vessel: rolled
Pitcher: ewer, hurler
Pitcher, famous: Cy Young
Pitcher handles: ears
Pitcher, one-armed: ewer
Pitcher, professional: ad man, pro
Pitcher's dream game: no hit
Pitcher's mound: slab
Pitches a tent: camps
Pitches: ads, throws, tars
Pitches, as a ship: rolls, lists
Pitching goof: balk
Pitching style: side arm
Pitchman's pitch: spiel
Pitfall: trap, snare
Pith helmet: hat, topi, topee
Pith helmet, Indian: topi
Pithy saying: gnome
Pits, removed: stoned
Pitt, brad: actor
Pitts, Zasu: actress
Pittsburgh pro: steeler
Pittsburgh river: Ohio
Pituitary hormone: ACTH
Pivot: slue
Pivotal: key
Pivotal point: crux
Pivoting: sluing
Pixels, essentially: dots
Pixie: sprite, imp, elf, dwarf
Pixie stick: wand
Pizarro's quest: oro, gold, Peru
Pizarro's foes: Inca
Pizazz: elan
Pizza herb: oregano
Pizza Hut alternative: KFC
Pizzeria buy: slice, pizza
Pizzeria sight: oven
Pizzicato, as opposed to: arco
Place: lieu, stead
Place for a pint: pub
Place for a run: hose
Place for an iris: uvea
Place for change: coin purse
Place for discussion: forum
Place for free spirits: open bar
Place for lunch: bag
Place for preconceived notions: sperm bank
Place for VJs: MTV
Place holder: book mark
Place, in combo: topo
Place in order: arrange
Place in proximity: appose
Place in storage: stow
Place, in the same: ibib
Place of bliss: cloud nine, Shangri-La
Place of control: helm
Place of exile: Elba
Place of privacy: retreat
Place of proximity: appose
Place of refuge: ark
Place of safety: haven, asylum
Place of trade: mart, store
Place on a list: enroll

Place side by side: appose
Place to get a peel: spa
Place to graze: meadow, pasture
Place to head-em off: pass
Place to hibernate: lair, den
Place to put all hands on: deck
Place to raise your spirits: pub, bar
Place to shoot from: hip
Place to surf: Web
Placed: put
Placed in order: ranked
Placed on a royal seat: throned
Places: locales, sets
Places of refuge: arks
Places of reverence: shrines
Placing in sequence: slotting
Plagiarize: copy
Plague: beset
Plaid, chieftain's: kilt
Plaid wearer: clan
Plain as day: overt
Plain, frozen: tundra
Plain, not: ornate
Plain people: Amish
Plain to see: overt
Plain view, in: overt
Plain wrong: all wet
Plainly: obviously
Plains home: tepee
Plains native: Oto
Plains tribe: Pawnee
Plaintiff: suer, litigant
Plaintive reed: oboe
Plan in detail: map out
Plan of action: idea
Ala plancha: (cooked on a griddle)
Plane, Orly, once: SST
Plane route: air line
Plane stabilizer: fin
Plane that flew only once: Spruce Goose
Planes, grounded: SSTS
Plane's electronic technology: avionics
Plane's milieu: midair
Planet, seventh: Uranus
Planet, sitcom: Ork
Planetarium, Chicago's: Adler
Planetary paths, of: orbital
Planet-finding grp.: SETI
Planet's movements: rotations
Plank curve: syn
Planks: wood
Plankton: brit, britt
Planner's woe: snag
Plano-concave, for one: lens
Plans, have: ideas, intent
Plant, aromatic: chia
Plant bristle: awn
Plant borders: hedges
Plant container: pot, urn, vase
Plant disease: ergot, smut, blight
Plant exudation: resin
Plant firmly: imbed
Plant growth, young: sprout
Plant in a swamp: reed

Plant, indigo: anil
Plant life: flora
Plant need: sun
Plant parasite: aphid
Plant parts: cyne, stem, pod
Plant pest: aphid
Plant, seedless: fern
Plant, small: bonsai
Plant stem: stalk
Plant sticker: bur
Plant study: botany
Plant, starchy: taro
Plant swelling: edema
Plant, tall: tree
Plant, tufted: moss
Plant, type: endogen
Plant variety, new: hybrid
Plant, voracious: flytrap
Plant with clover-like leaves: oxalis
Plantain lily: hosta
Plantation, fictional: Tara
Plantation drink: julep
Plantation machine: baler
Plantation, novel: Tara
Planted, as seed: sown
Planted items: seeds
Planter's concern: rotorage
Plant-form habitat: ecad
Planting guide: almanac
Planting tool: dibble
Plants, collectively: flora
Plants, like drooping: nutant, nutate
Plants of a region: flora
Plant-sucking insect: aphid
Plasm starter: ecto
Plaster: stucco
Plaster, apply: ceil
Plaster base: lath
Plasterboard: sheetrock
Plastered: lit, tanked, drunk
Plastic, clear: lucite
Plastic tube: straw
Plastic, used: owed, bought, paid
Plastic wrap: saran
Plastic Ono Band
Plat de jour
Plat du jour: plate of the day
Oro y plata
Plate armor, piece of: tasse, tassa
Plateau, high: mesa
Plateau, reach a: level off
Plateau, steep-sided: mesa
Platform: dais
Platform, chorus: riser
Platform, nautical: deck
Platform part: plank
Plating material: tin
Platitude: adage
Platoon setting: Nam
Plato's "a": alpha
Plato's "h": eta
Plato's mall: Agora
Plato's vowel: iota
Plato's "x": chi

Platters: lps
Platter spinner: DJ, dee jay
Platypus: duck bill
Platypus, like a: web-footed
Play area: yard
Play at full volume: blast, blare
Play back machine: VCR, TiVo
Play charades: mime
Play for a fool: uses,
Play for time: stall, stall tactic
Play group: cast
Play horseshoes: toss
Play, humorous: farce
Play in an alley: bowl
Play, mini: skit
Play on words: puns
Play part: role
Play prize: Obie
Play pro: dramaist, dramalist
Play, put on a: stages
Play, short: skit
Play the fink: rat on
Play to a crowd: pander
Play to the rafters: emote
Play type: drama
Play with idly: twiddle
Playboy: roue
Played a part: acted
Played a la Pan: piped
Played around: horsed
Played with: toyed
Player, bygone: hi fi
Player on the dealer's right: pone
Playful bite: nip
Playful pranks: capers
Playfully: in fun
Playfully shy: coy
Playground shout: whee
Playground time: recess
Play's anew: reruns
Plays for time: stalls
Plays the wrong suit: reneges
Plays wrap-up: epilog
Plaything: toy
Plaza Hotel resident: Eloise
Plaza imp: iambus
Plaza, town: square
Plea, cop a
Plead: ask, beg
Pleasant odor: aroma
Pleasantly warm: balmy
Pleasantness: amenity
"Please Don't Eat the Daisies"
Please greatly: tickle pink, elate
Please, in Spain: por favor
Please, in Vienna: bitte
Please, say: ask
Pleased as punch: elated, glad
Pleased person: happy camper
Pleasing to the ear: harmonic
Pleasure craft: yacht
Pleasure in, take: like, relish
Pleasure, like some: sensual
Pleasure, show: smile

Pleasure, small: treat
Pleasure trip: jaunt
Pleat: fold, tuck
Pledged fidelity: troth
Pleiades pursuer: Orion
Pleistocene period: ice age
Plexiglas: Lucite
Pliny bear: Ursa
Plinth: slab
Pliocene, for one: epoch
Plot element: acre
Plot inconsistency: hole
Plotting group: cabal
Plotting secretly: in league
Plover's abode: nest
Plow horses, like: shod
Plow (steel) inventor: Deere
Plow part: colter
Plow through: slog
Ploy: wile
Ploy, clever: ruse
Pluck: tweeze, mettle
Plucking, ready for: ripe
Plug add-on:adapter
Plug away: toil
Plug up: clog
Plugged in: aware
Plugs: ads
Plum, purple: damson
Plum shade: magenta
Plum, tart: sloe
Plum, wild: sloe
Plumed wader: egret
Plummer, Amanda: actress
Plummet, opposite of: soar
Plump & juicy: ripe
Plunderer's take: swag
Plunge about: thrash
Plural indicator: posit
Plus end: anode
Plutocratic backer: fat cat
Ply a gondola: pole
Plywood layer: veneer
Plywood, piece of: sheet
Plywood, sheet of: panel
Pneumonia type: viral
Poached edible: egg
Poacher's need: eggs
Poaching preventer: game keeper,
        game warden, warden
Pocahontas's husband: Rolfe
Pocket bread: pita
Pocket content: keys, coins, lint, bills
Pocket item: key ring
Pod member: whale
Pod-bearing tree: carob, locust, catalpa
Podded tree: cacao
Podium feature: mike, mic
Olla podrida: spicy stew
Poe, Edgar Allan: poet
Poe maiden: Lenore
Poe woman: Lenore
Poem, celebratory: ode
Poem division: canto

Poem, epic: epode, epos, epopee
Poem, fourteen-line: sonnet
Poem, heroic: epos
Poem, Homeric: Iliad
Poem, lyric: epode
Poem, medieval: lai
Poem, melancholy: elegy, elegm
Poem, mournful: lament, elegy
Poem of lament: elegy
Poem of praise: ode
Poem, obscure: rune
Poem, old norse: rune
Poem on a grand scale: epic
Poem, pastoral: idyll
Poem, praiseful: ode
Poem, religious: psalm
Poem, rustic: idyll
Poem, Shelley: ode
Poem, short: rhyme
Poems, of some: odic
Poe's "Annabel Lee"
Poe's night visitor: raven
Poet: bard, rhymer
Poet "above": oer
Poet "always": eer
Poet adverb: nigh
Poet, classical: Ovid
Poet contraction: o'er, tis, ne'er, een
Poet, humorous: Nash
Poet inspiration: muse
Poet laureate
Poet, national: bard
Poet, nonsense: Lear
Poet, romantic: Keats
Poet suffix: aster
Poet who helped Emerson: Mivnus
Poetic adverb: eer, yon, oft
Poetic door tapper: raven
Poetic dusk: een,
Poetic eternity: eer
Poetic eye: orb
Poetic foot: iamb, iambus, anapest
        trochee
Poetic grief: dolor
Poetic lines: verses
Poetic palindrome: ere
Poetic peeper: orb.
Poetic preposition: ere, oer
Poetic spheres: orbs
Poetic time: een
Poetic tribute: ode
Poetic twilights: eves
Poetic "your": thy
Poetically "dark": ebon
Poetry collection, ancient: epos
Poetry, inspired: odes
Poetry muse: Erato
Poetry term: ariso
Poet's new day: morn
Poet's soon: anon
Poet's spring: fount
Pogo: possum, opossum
Poi source: taro
Poindexter, like a: nerdy

Point apiece: one all
Point, came to a: narrowed, tapered
Point each: one all
Point fingers at: blame, name, accuse
Point, kind of: focal
Point, lowest: nadir
Point, main: nub
Point on a diamond: base
Point the finger: accuse, blame, name
Point, to the: terse
Pointed arch: ogee
Pointed part: tine
Pointed stick: goad
Pointed tool: awl
Pointed weapon: dagger
Pointer: tip
Pointers, high-tech: lasers
Pointillist Georges: Seurat
Pointless: inane
Point-of-view: angle, slant, outlook
Points in question: issues
Points of convergence: foci
Points on paper: nibs
Poise: aplomb
Poison: cyanid
Poison, arrow: curare, curari
Poison, deadly: bane
Poison ivy symptom: itch, rash
Poisonous plants: atis
Poisonous substance: toxin
Poltergeist: ghost
Poivre opposite: sel
Poivre's mate: sel
Poke fun at: tease, taunt, kid
Poke sharply: jab
Poker bet, met a: saw
Poker cynosure: pot
Poker declaration: I'm in
Poker game maneuvers: raises
Poker holding: hand
Poker, match in: see
Poker pack: deck
Poker payment: ante
Poker place: hearth
Poker player's declaration: I'm in
Poker player's last resort: IOU
Poker ploy: raise,
Poker pot, item in a: IOU, chips
Poker stack: bet,
Pokey, Liverpool: gaol
Polanski, Roman: director
Polar bear perch: floe
Polar buildup: ice cap
Polar chunk: floe, berg
Polar explorer: Scott, Peary
Polar feature: ice cap
Polar lights: aurora
Polar sight: ice cap, aurora
Pole, carved: totem
Pole for propulsion: oar
Polecat, domesticated: ferret
Poles connector: axis
Police alarm alert: APB
Police badge: shield

Police bust: raid
Police cars, like some: unmarked
Police dispatch: APB
Police procedure: line-up
Polish: rub, shin
Polish-born soprano: Raisa
Polishes: shines, refines
Polishes plank: sands
Polishing cloth: chamois
Polite: civil
Polite bloke: gent
Polite, far from: rude
Polite phrase: thank you
Polite query: may I
Political alliance: entente
Political concern: image
Political division: state
Political friend: crony
Political gathering: caucus
Political get-together: rally
Political grp.: bloc, nation
Political humor: satire
Political influence: clout
Political party principle: plank
Political science class: civics
Political sphere: arena
Political subdivision: state
Political takeover: coup
Political thaw: détente
Political tract: polemic
Political upheaval: coup de tat
Politician pickers: voters
Politics, dirty: sleaze
Polka dot
Poll maven: Elmo Roper
Poll, took a: canvassed
Pollack fish: sey, cod family
Pollen producer: anther, stamen
Pollen reaction: allergy
Polling subjects: voters
Hoi polloi
Pollster: Lou Harris
Pollster's discovery: trend
Polluted, not: pure
Pollution concern: ecology
Pollyanna's outlook: rosy
Polo, Marco: explorer
Polo stick: mallet
Polonius's daughter: Ophelia
          son: Laertes
Poltergeist: spirit, ghost
Poly to Tom: aunt
Polyester: Dacron
Polyester trademark: Dacron
Polygons, certain: isogons
Polygraph flunker: liar
Polygrapher's detection: lie
Polynesian banana: fei
Polynesian carving: tiki
Polynesian cookout: luau
Polynesian drums: lalis
Polynesian god: tane
Polynesian image: tiki
Polynesian king: alii

Polynesian pendant: tiki
Polynesian plants: tis
Polynesian screw-pines: Aras
Pommel horse
Pompeii art: fresco
Pompous fool: ass
Pompous language: bombast
Pompous sort: stuffed shirt
Ponce de Leon
Poncho Villa
Pond covering: algae, scum
Pond maker: dam
Pond near concord, mass: walden
Pond or lake: mere
Pond organism, tiny: alga, algae
Ponder silently: muse
Ponders: muse, weighs
Pong company: Atari
Pong maker: Atari
Pongo or wau-wau: apes, orangutans
Ponselle, Rosa: diva
Ponti, Carlo: director
Pontificate: orate
Ponti's homeland: Italia
Pontius: Pilate
Pony pad: stable
Pony up: pay
Pooh's creator: Milne
Pooh's pal: Roo
Pool, kind of: tidal, gene, lagoon
Pool division: lanes
Pool, enjoy the: swim, dive
Pool length: lap
Pool location: YWCA, YMCA
Pool measure: depth
Pool player's accident: miscue
Pool problem: algae
Pool prop: rack
Pool resources:
Pool shot, tricky: masse
Pool side changing rm.: cabana
Pool, type of: tidal
Pool user: natator
Pool with jets: spa
Pool worker: steno, temp
Pool-table rock: slate
Pool-table surface: baise
Pooped out: tired
Poor box donations: alms
Poor box filler: alms
Poor dog's portion: none
Poor loser, is a: sulks
Poor person: pauper
Poor Richard's book: almanac
Poor taste, in: tacky
Poorly made: shoddy
Pop: soda, dad, burst
Pop a question: ask
Pop back up: re-emerge
Popeye's foe: Bluto
Popeye's friend: Olive Oyl
Popeye's hi: ahoy
Popeye's tattoo: anchor
Iggy Pop: music

Pop quiz: test
Popcorn buy: tub,
Pope, Alexander: poet
Pope, of the: papal
Pope's representative: nuncio
Popeye's "stop": avast
Popinjay: fop
Poppy plant derivative: opiate
Pop's Teresa Brewer
Popular, become: catch on
Popular, commercially: hot
Popular dog's name: rex
Popular fur: lapin, mink, ermine
Popular lily: calla
Popular lunch order: BLT, burger
Popular mixer: seltzer
Popular movie: hit
Popular sofa: sectional
Popular shift: day
Popular, very: hot
Population count: census
Population survey: census
Pop-up item: toast, tissue
Pop-ups, program: adware
Porcelain: Chinese: lowest
     English: bow, derby, spode, minton
     French: sevres, limoges
     German: dresden, meissen
Porcelain, fine: limoges
Porch adjunct: steps, stairs
Porch, kind of: stoop,
Porcupine feature: quill
Porcupine quill: spine
Pore over: peruse, read
Porgy & bess
Porgy's love: Bess
Pork product: lard
Pork-barreling: patronage
Porous gem: pearl
Porpoise (freshwater): inia, emyd
Porpoise relative: orca
Porridge ingredient: pease
Porridge, thin: gruel
Port authority: wino
Port city: harbor
Portable dig: tent
Portable lodge: tent
Portable music player: iPod
Portal: door
Portal, prospector's: adits
Port-au-Prince native: Haitian
Portend: bode
Portent: omen, augury
Porter: red cap, ale
Porter, Cole: composer
Porter or stout: ales
Porter, William S.: O. Henry
Portfolio item: asset, stock, investment
Portfolio part, briefly: iras
Porthos and Athos, e.g.: amis
Portico: stoa
Portico feature: pillars
Portion, fixed: ration
Portion of: some

Portion out: mete, dole
Portion recipient: allottee
Portmanteau: carryall, suitcase
Portnoy's creature: roth
Portoferraio's island: elba
Portrait (kind of): self
Portrait, quickie: sketch
Portrait painter: artist
Portray: depict
Portrayer: actor, actress
Ports, between: a sea
Portuguese (old) coin: reis
Portuguese island: Azores
Portuguese lady: dona, donna
Portuguese title: dom,
Portuguese title of respect: senhor,
     senhores
Posada: inn
Pose a question: ask
Poseidon's spear: trident
Posers: enigmas
Posey, Parker: actress
Posh: elegant
Posing for Mr. Universe: flexing
Position, as troops: deploy
Positive aspect: upside
Positive market move: gain
Positive particles: protons
Positive post: anode
Positive potential: upside
Positive quantity: plus, surplus
Positive thing, it's a: anode
Positive, think: hope,
Positive thinker: Peale
Positive thinking: can-do
Posse dispatcher: sheriff
Posse picture: oater
Posse quarry: gang
Possession, valuable: asset
Possessive: zealous
Possessive pronoun: its
Possible binary digits: ones
Possible, made: enabled
Possible, quite: likely
Possibilities: ifs, maybe
Possibly, in Potsdam: etwa
Possum (comic): Pogo
Post: mail, send
Post a gain: earn,
Post box words: US mail
Post, deck: bitts, ship posts
Post, Emily
Post game discussion: recap
Post of employment: job
Post of propriety: Emily
Post office feature: flag pole
PO service: RFD
Post, sharp-ended: stack
Post, Wiley
Postage stamp, roll of: coil
Postal, go: rage
Postal machine: sorter
Postal meter unit: ounce
Postal purchase: stamps

Postal truck inscription: US mail
Postal work, do: sort
Posted: mailed, sent
Posted a parcel: sent
Poster paint: tempera
Post-fire task: reload
Postgraduate exam: oral
Posting, track: odds
Post-op stop, sometimes: ICU
Postpone action: wait
Postpone indefinitely: shelve
Postpones: buys time
Post-prandial chore: dishes
Postscript to a play: epilog
Post-Trojan War epic: "Odyssey"
Posture-perfect: erect
Pot: vessel, kettle
Pot-au feu (french stew)
Pot, cook's: olla
Pot filler: ante
Pot, large-mouth: olla
Potato: spud, tater, tuber
Potato alternative: rice
Potato au gratin
Potato farmer, ancient: Inca
Potato goody: chip, fries
Potato pancake: latke
Potato, purple: taro
Potato, russet: Idaho
Potato snack: chip, fry
Potent start: omni
Potential bed: sofa
Potential queen: pawn
Potential progeny: ova
Pother: ado
Potosi locale: Bolivia
Potpourri: olio
Potpourri piece: petal
Potpourri quality: scent
Pots & pans: cookware
Potsy or skittle, e.g.: game
Potter's field: magic, cemetery, God's
     Acre, graveyard
Potter's messenger: owl
Potter's need: kiln
Potters, noted: Hopi
Pottery, bake: fire,
Pottery chunk: shard
Pottery flaw: nick
Pottery fragments: shards
Pottery, glazed: delft
Pottery ovens: kilns
Pottery, well-made: feats of clay
Potts, Annie: actress
Pouched animal: pelican
Pouchlike part: sac
Poughkeepsie college: Vassar
Poultry farm: hennery
Poultry herb: sage
Pounce upon: assail
Pound resident: cur
Pound, Ezra: writer
Pound sounds: yelps, arfs
Pound the pavement: job hunt

Pounding instrument: pestle
Pounds (2.2): kilo
Pounds the keys: types
Pour forth: gush
Pourboire: tip
Poured out: emptied
Pourer's line: "say when"
Pours: teems, rains, decants
Pouting: sulky
Pouting grimace: moue
"Pow": wham
Powder base: talc
Powder container: keg
Powder, dusting: talc
Powder, fine: dust
Powdery: mealy
Powdery residue: ash
Powell, Eleanor: dancer
Power, absolute: tyranny
Power agency, since '33: TVA
Power, extraordinary: brute strength
Power failure: outage
Power here in granted
Power, kind of: atomic
Power loss: outage
Power move, aggressive: squeeze play
Power, seat of: throne
Power, seize: usurp
Power source: atom
Power units: mega watts, watts
Powerful auto engine: hemi
Powerful beam: laser
Powerful business man: baron
Powerful current: whirlpool
Powerful engine: turbo, jet, turbojet
Powerful industrialist: Adam Clayton
　　Powell
Powerful person: noble
Powerful raptors: eagle
Powerful ruler: emperor
Powerful, very: almighty
Powerless: unable
Powers, Mala: actress
Powers, Tyrone: actor
Power-train part: gear
Powwow drums: tomtoms
Powwow, has a: palavers, idle talk, empty
　　talk, conference
"A pox upon thee": fie
PR campaign: promo
PR, extreme: hype
Practical application: use
Practical, find: use
Practical joke: prank
Practice: rehearse
Practice a part: rehearse
Practice boxing: shadow box, spar
Practice, habitual: usage
Practice in the outfield: shag
Practice origami: fold
Practice, out of: rusty
Practice pugilism: spar
Practiced persistently: plied
Practiced Zen: sat

Practices, customary: usages
Prague resident: Czech
Prairie schooner: wagon
Praise: kudos
Praise, cries of: hosannas
Praise to the skies: exalt
Praise very highly: laud, extol
Praised too much: gushed
Praiser's using verse: odists
Praiseful poem: ode
Praline nut: pecan
Prance: sashay
Prank: dido
Prankish pipsqueak: imp
Pranks begin with, some: dares
Pranks, playful: capers
Prayer: orison
Prayer beads: rosary
Prayer book: missal, siddur, breviary,
　　hymnal
Prayer figure: orant
Prayer, formal: litany
Prayer leader: inman
Prayer, religious: novena
Prayer-wheel turner: Lama
Praying figures: orants
Preacher: like: pious
Preaching friar: Dominican
Preadult insect: pupa
Preassembled: pre-fab
Precable hookup: aerial
Precaution, as a: incase
Precede in time: antedate
Precedent, without: new
Preceding month: ultima
Pre-Christmas season: Advent
Precious item container: jewelry box
Precious, most: dearest
Precipitation, had some: rained, snowed
Precise, formally: prim
Precollege level: el-hi
Pre-Columbus Mexican: Aztec
Preconceived notions, place for: sperm
　　bank
Preconditions: ifs
Predator (tawny): lioness
Predatory dolphin: orca
Predatory group: gang
Pre-deal payment: ante
Predestine: ordain
Predetermine: ordain
Predicament: spot
Predictive card: tarot
Predominant part: yolk
Pre-Easter buy: dyes
Pre-eruption warning: tremor
Pre-euro currency: lira
Prefer charges: sue
Preferred evil: lesser
Prefix for pods: octo
Prefix meaning "heaven": urano
Prefix meaning "sun": helio
Prefix meaning "within": endo
"Pregame show"

Pre-historic creature: ape man
Prejudice: bias
Prejudicial: biased
Prejudicial person: bigot
Preliminary calculations: estimates
Preliminary text: draft
Premiere notables: stars
Premiere performance: debut
Premiered: opened
Premiers: first
Preminger, otto: director
Prentiss, Paula: comic, actress
Preoccupy: obsess, enrapt
Prep, get the: nab
Prepaid, not: cod, due
Prepare: get ready
Prepare, as dumplings: steam
Prepare cheese for pizza: grate
Prepare for next year's models: retool
Prepare for take off: taxi
Prepare parmesan: grate
Prepare pasta: boil
Prepare prunes: stew
Prepare the laundry: sort
Prepare to fire: aim, take aim
Prepare to take off: taxi
Prepared fish: boned
Prepared to shop: make a list
Prepared without meat or milk: par eve
Prepares a cue stick: chalks
Prepares flour: sifts
Prepares to drive: tees up, shifts
Prepares to sail: boards
Perplexed: a sea
Preprandial thank you: grace
Prerecorded: taped
Presage: omen
Prescribed amount: dose
Present occasion: nonce
"Present" start: omni
Present surrounding: wrapping paper
Presently: anon
Preservative, common: salt
Preside at a meeting: chair
President, silent: Cal Coolidge
Presidential prerogative: veto
Presidents:
　　Bush
　　Clinton:
　　Bush:
　　Reagan
　　Carter:
　　Ford:
　　Nixon:
　　Johnson:
　　Kennedy:
　　Eisenhower:
　　Truman:
　　F. Roosevelt:
　　Hoover:
　　Coolidge
　　Harding
　　Wilson
　　Taft

T. Roosevelt
Mckinley
Cleveland
Harrison
Cleveland
Arthur
Garfield
Hayes
Grant
Johnson
Lincoln
Buchanan
Pierce
Fillmore
Taylor
Polk
Tyler
Harrison
Vanburen
Jackson
Adams
Monroe
Madison
Jefferson
J. Q. Adams
Washington
President's address: my fellow Americans
Presides at tea: pours
Presley, elvis aron
Press agent: ironer
Press charges: accuse
"Press kit"
Presses potatoes: rices
Press on: advance
Pressure, experiencing: under the gun
Pressure, undue: duress
Pressure, unit of: torr
Pressure-packed period: crunch time
Pre-stereo: mono
Prestige: cachet
Preston, Robert: actor
Sgt. Preston's beat: Yukon, NWT
Prestorm condition: calm
Prestorm lull: calm
Presumptuousness: gall
Pretend: let on, put on, act, feign
Pretense: guise
Pretense, elaborate: charade
Pretense of courage: bravado
Pretentious: artsy
Pretentious, lack of: modesty
Pretentious talk: clap trap
Pretentious type: snob
Pretentiously cultured: arty.
Pretty good: fair,
Pretty, makes: adorns
Pretty new: recent
Prevail over: win
Prevail upon: urge
Prevailing tendencies: trends
Prevaricates: lies, fibs
Prevent legally: estop
Prevented: warded-off
Prevention unit: ounce

Preview, kind of: sneak
Previn, Andre: conductor
Previous: ere, pre
Previously cut: sawn
Previously owned: used
Prexy's assistant: veep
Prey upon: illuse
Priam: ruler of Troy
Priam ruled, where: Troy
Priam was its king: Troy
Priam's daughter: Creusa, Polyxena Cassandra
    father: Laomedon
    kingdom: Troy
    slain sister: Cilla
    subject: Trojan
    wife: Arisbe, Hecuba
Price before discounting: list
Price fixing group: cartel
Price, kind of: asking, sales
Price per unit: rate
Price reduction: rollback, sale
Price, sets a: asks,
Prices, at bargain: on sale
Prices, lower: slash
Prices may do it: soar
Pricing word: per
Prickly herb: teasel
Prickly pear: cacti
Prickly plant: thistle
Prickly seed: bur
Prickly sensation: itch
Prickly shrubs: bramble, gorse
Pride: ego
Pride, excessive: hubris
Pride or duty, word with: civic
Pride, show: walk tall,
Prie-dieu, used a: knelt (kneeling bench)
Priest's hat: beretta, miter, mitre
Priest, certain: jesuit
Priest, mosque: imam
Priestly: hieratic
Priest's hat: beretta, miter, mitre
Priest's flock: laity
Priest's scarf: orale
Priest's vestment: ephod
Prim: sedate, prissy
"Prim and proper"
Prima ballerina: etoile
Prima donna: diva, snob, star, artiste
    chanteuse, narcissist
Prima donna problem: ego
Prima donna's tune: aria
Prima facie: true, valid, apparent, self-evident
Primaries: caucuses
Primary blood carrier: aorta
Primary cell: zygote
Primate, extinct: ape man
Primate, semierect: ape
Prime minister: premier
Prime-time series: sitcom
Prime-time taboo: nudity
Primeval: old
Primitive abode: tepee
Primitive aquatic organism: algae

Primitive, often: tribal
Primitive reproduction body: spore
Primitive weapon: sling, spear
Primitive wind instrument: panpipes
Primordial slime: ooze
Primped: preened
Prince and the pauper
Prince Arn's mother: Aleta
Prince, Borodin: Igor
Prince Charles's sister: Anne
Prince Charming wannabes: toads
Prince, darkness: Satan
Prince Harry's alma mater: Eton
Prince, Indian: raja, bani
Prince of evil: Satan
Prince, petty: satrap
Prince, potential: frog
Prince Valiant's son: Arn
Prince Val's son: Arn
Prince wannabe: frog
Princely: regal
Princess, Asian: rani
Princess Di's niece: Bea
Princess disturber: pea
Princess, Indian: rajah, rani
Princess Leia's brother: luke
Princess of film: leia
Princess perturber: pea
Princess, spunky: leia
Princesse, father of a: roi (french)
Princeton athlete: tiger
Principle: axiom
Principle, guiding: credo
Principles, moral: ethics
Principles or rules, set of: code
Print measure: pica
Print options: fonts
Print, trial: proof
Print units: ems, ens
Printed matter: ephemera
Printed matter, sheet of: folio
Printemp follower: ete
Printemps month: Mai
Printer cartridge: ink
Printer mistakes: errata, erratum
Printer problems: jams
Printer type: laser
Printer's dagger: obelisk
Printer's flourish: swash
Printer's measure: ens, ems
Printer's order: stets
Printer's output: repro
Printer's word: dele
Printing process: off-set
Printing, second: re-issue
Printing unit: milline
Prints, check for: dusts
Prior to: ere
Prior to year 1: BC, BCE
Priority, high: urgent
Priors superior: abbott
Priscilla, proposer to: Elvis
Priscilla's John: Alden
Priscilla's suitor: Alden

Prism maker: geo
Prison or hospital division: ward
Pristine, no longer: used
Private agreement: yes sir
Private eye: sleuth
Private eye, slangily: tec
Private high school: academy
Private places: retreats
Privilege, feudal: soke
Privileged few: elite
Privy to: in on
Prize: award
Prize, coveted: Nobel
Prize fight: bout
Prize fight event: kayo, tko
Prize for Ferdinand: roses
Prize, kind of: door
Prized rug: Navaho
Prized sauterne: Yquem, white wine
Pro foe: anti
Pro, not: anti
Probably hungry: unfed
Probate concerns: estate
Problem, complex: acne
Problem, no: easy
Problem, unexpected: snag
Problem, unforeseen: snag
Proboscis: nose, snout, trunk
Procedure or method: system, process
Proceed easily: coast
Proceed on: wend
Proceed slowly but surely: plod
Proceeded along: wended
Proceeded onward: wended
Proceeds: wends
Process for sorting the injured: triage
Process, part of the: step
Procession head: hearse
Procession of matadors: paseo
Proclamations: edicts, banns
Proctor's announcement: time
Produce endorser: user
Produce pilsner: brew
Produce unit: peck
Product application: use
Product name: brand
Product symbol: logo
Production goal: quota
Profession: career
Professional pitcher: ad man, pro
Professor, retired: emeriti
Professor's goal: tenure
Professors, most: phds
Professor's talk: lecture
Proficiency: ease
Proficiency, with:ably
Profile (briefly): bio
Profound: deep, deepen
Profound, more: deeper
Profound, most: deepest
Profound respect, showing: reverent
Profuse: lavish
Progenitor: parent
Progeny, potential: ova.

Prognosticators: seers
Program that costs nothing: freeware
Program, weekly: series
Program with pop-ups: adware
Progress into: become
Progress, make slow: slog
Progress, slight: dent
Prohibit: forbid
Project for your dyeing days: batik
Project starter: idea,
Project, tentative: plan
Projected outward: jutted
Projectile track: arc
Projecting edge: flange
Projection: bulge, ledge
Projection, rounded: lobe
Projection, sharp: jag
Prolific auth.: anon
Prolonged account: litany
Prolonged attack: siege
Prolonged banishment: exile
Prom dates: teens, teenagers
Prom rental: limo
Prom sentry: chaperon
Prom, take to the: escort
Promenade, sheltered: stoa
Promenader, casual: stroller
Prometheus's brother: Atlas, Menoetius
      creation: man, mankind
      father: Iapetus
      gift: fire
      mother: Clymene
      rescuer: Heracles, Hercules
"Prometheus" muralist: Orozco
Prometheus or Atlas: titan
Prominent person: nabob
Promise, break a: renege,
Promise, solemn: vow, pledge, oath, word
Promised: assured
Promises: oaths,
Promising: rosy, apt
Promo tape: demo
Promontory: ness, cape
Promos: teasers
Promos, big: ballyhoos
Promote slowly: hype
Promoters, some: pr-men
Promotion basis: merit
Promotional connection: tie in
Promotional prose, brief: blurb
Prompt: speedy, cue
Prompt, in a way: urge
Prompted: cued
Prompting the hook: booing
Prompts, stage: cues
Ora pro nobis
Prone to: apt
Prone to sulking: moody
Prongs: tines
Pronoun, common: you
Pronoun, old: thy, thee
Pronoun, royal: our
Pronouncement: dicta
Pronto: ASAP, stat

Pronunciation mark: emlaut, tilde
Proof: evidence
Proof demander: skeptic
Proof ender: QED
Proof goof: erratum
Proof, math abbr.: QED
Proof of, give: attest
Proof word: ergo
Proofreader's find: error
Proofreader's mark: dele, stet, caret
Proofreader's "save": stet
Proofreading mark: caret
Propeller type: screw
Propelling force: impetus
Proper, they are often: nouns
Proper manner, in a: suitably
Proper manner, in the: duly
Proper one, overly: prig
Properly: duly
Property claims: liens
Property, landed: estate
Property marker: stake
Property receiver: a lienee
Prophecy: oracle
Prophet, female: seeress
Prophet: seer
Prophet, minor: Amos
Prophetic sign: omen
Proportions kin: ratio
Proposal: bid, idea
Proposal feature: ring
Proposal support: knee
Proposition in logic: lemma
Proposition, shortened: altho
Propulsion pole: oar
Prop-up: shore, brace
Prosciutto purveyor: deli
Prosciutto: ham
Proscribe: ban
Prose, piece of: essay
Prosecutor's entrant: misdemeanor
Prospector, maybe: miner
Prospector's portal: adit
Prospero's helper: Ariel
Protected, in a way: patented
Protecting shelter: lee
Protection: egis, aegis
Protective case: sheath
Protective coating: mastic
Protective embankment: berm
Protective glove: gantlet
Protective screen: grille
Protective trench: moat
Protein acid: amino
Protein model, hypothetical: biogen,
      biogenesis
Protein source: legume, meat
Protest, in a way: picket
Protest, mild: sit-in
Protest music name: Dylan
Protest, one way to: sit-in
Protest, peaceful: sit in
Protest participant, group: rioter
Protest sound, street: chant

Protest, strong: out cry
Protons, where are: nucleus, nuclei
Protractor measure: angle
Protruding metal edge: burr
Protuberance: node
"Proud Mary" grp.: CCR
"Aint too proud to beg"
Proust hero: swann
Prove false: belie, rebut
Prove innocent: clear
Prove useful: avail
Proven: teste
Proven reliable: tested
Proven thing: fact
Proverbial amount of brick: ton
Proverbial brick load: ton
Proverbial heirs: meek
Provide: endue
Provide a service: render
Provide bearings: orient
Provide capital: back, loan, fund, endow
Provide lodging for: take in
Provide money for: endow
Provide staff: man
Provide with: indue, endue, endow, imbue
Provide with clothes: tog
Provide with income: endow
Provide with property: endow
Provide with qualities: imbue, endue
Provide with work: take on, hire
Provided provender: led
Provided temporarily: lent
Providence: fate, care
Provider of small strokes: putter
Provides evidence: adduces
Provides food: caters
Provides funds: endows
Provides with interest: loans
Province, special: realm
Proviso word: unless
Provo school: byu
Provocative sort: riler
Provoke: pique, arouse
Provoke, as interest: pique
Prow opposite: stern
Prow, ship's: bow
Prowess:might
Prowl: lurk
Proximity, place of: appose
Prudent manner, in a: safely
Prudish (overly) one: prig
Prunes, prepare: stew
Pry open: force
Prynne, Hester: literature
Pryor, Rain: actress
Psalms word: selah
PS sequel: PPS
Pseudo: fake
Pseudonym letters: aka
Pseudopods, they have: amoebae
Pshaw: old oath
Psych out: rattle
Psyche: soul
Psyche component: ego

Psyche part: id, ego
Psyched up: agog
Psyche's beloved: Eros, Cupid
Psyche's suitor: Eros
Psychic may sense it: aura
Psychic sight: aura
Psychic's intro: I see
Psychics may see it: aura
Psychological blocks: hang-ups
Psychological disorders: neuroses
Psychology, kind of: Gestalt
Psychology pioneer: Jung
Ptarmigan: grouse
Pteridophyte plants: ferns
Pterodactyl terror in Tokyo: Rodan
Pub brew: lager, beer
Pub buddies: mates
Pub potables: ales
Pub serving: pint
Pub sign: on tap
Public address: speech
Public disorder: riot
Public encounter, ugly: scene
Public hall: lyceum
Public health weapon: vaccine
Public house: bar, inn, hostel, saloon,
     tavern, auberge, hospice
Public, made: aired
Public, make: air
Public meeting: forum
Public meeting place: fora
Public persona: image
Public prosecutor: d.a.
Public relations need: tact
Public sale: auction
Public sentiment: pulse
Public service: utility
Public show, large-scale: expo
Public spat: scene
Public square: plaza
Public standing: repute
Public tiff: scene
Public walking place: paseos
Public with, go: air
Publican's potable: ale
Publicity, excess: hype
Publicity, frenzy of: hype
Publicity info: bio
Publicized, over: hyped
Publicized showily: hyped
Publicly: openly
Publish: print, issue
Pucci, Emilio: designer
Puccini genre: opera
     heroine: Mimi
     piece: Aria
     murderess: Tosca
     work: Tosca, opera
Puck, chased the: skated
Puck, move the: pass
Puck's master: Oberon
Pudding, kind of: bread
Pudding starch: sago
Puddle, enjoy a: slosh

Puddle, made a: pooled
Puddle stuff: mud
Pueblo dweller: Zuni, Tiwa
Pueblo tribe: Keres
Puente, Tito: music, bandleader
Puff along: chug,
Puff of wind: gust
Puffed up: inflated
Puffin's kin: auk
Puffs along: chugs
Puget Sound city: Tacoma
Puget Sound port: Tacoma
Pugilism, practice: spar
Pugilist: boxer
Pugilist, legendary: Ali
Pug's seat: stool
Pulchritude, lacking: ugly
Pull a fast one: con, scam
Pull an all-nighter: cram
Pull apart: rip
Pull back: rein in, retreat, withdraw,
Pull down: earn, get, draw, raze, ruin,
     lower, wreck, reduce, depress
Pull in: nab, stop, check, pinch, arrest,
     collar, detain, pick up, inhibit
Pull off: attain, manage, achieve, succeed
Pull out: exit, quit, leave, depart, abandon
Pull the lever: vote
Pull through: rally, get over, recover,
ride out, survive
Pull up: heave
Pulled a pistol: drew,
Pulled a scam: fleeced
Pulled ahead: passed
Pulled, being: in tow
Pulled down: earned
Pullers at Henley: oars
Pullers, strong: oxen
Pulley: sheave
Pulley part: belt
Pullover: jersey, stop
Pullover raincoat: poncho
Pullover, skimpy: tank
Pull-ups, do: chin
Pulls away: wrests
"Pulp Fiction" name: Uma
Pulpit: ambo
Pulpy grapes: uvas
Pulse, split: dal
Pulsing with energy: vibrant
Pulverize: grind
Puma: cougar
Pumice source: lava
Pummel: pound, beat, hit
Pump choice: diesel, reg.
Pump, fix a: reheel
Pump fuel: gas
Pump part: sole
Pump, starts the: primes
Pumper's pride: abs
Pumpkin cousin: gourd
Pun feedback: groan
Punch: bop
Punch bowl: monteith

Punch card bit: chad
Punch ingredient: fist
Punch, quick: jab
Punches, trade: spar
Punch's partner: Judy
Punctilious professor, e.g.: purist
Pundit's interpretation: spin
Pungent: oniony
Pungent, bitterly: acrid
Pungent bulbs: onions
Pungent gas: ammonia
Pungent sauce: Tabasco
Pungent vegetable: onion
Pungent, very: acrid
Punic war soldier: roman
Punish by imposing a fine: amerce
Punjab capital: Lahore,
Punjab lord: raja
Punjab princess: rani
Punjabi monotheists: sikhs
Punk revival trio: Green Day
Punsters: wits
Punta del este
Pupa: chrysalis, cover
Pupil ring: areol
Pupil's award: star
Pupil's chores: lessons
Pupil's place: iris, eye
Puppet, Bergen: Snerd
Puppet, dragon: Ollie
Puppetry (dragon of): Ollie
Puppy love, expression of: arfs
Pup's pop: sire
Pups, undersize: runts
Purchase incentives: rebates
Purchase, made a: spent, bought
Purchase, thrifty: economy size
Pure and simple: utter
Pure bliss: utopia
Purfle: adornment
Purify metal: refine
Purify water: desalt, distill
Purim celebrant: Jew
Purim's month: Adar
Purloin: steal, swipe
Purple bloom: lilac
Purple, bluish: mauve
Purple, deep: dun
Purple, grayish: mauve
Purple hue: puce
Purple plum: damson
Purple red: maroon
Purple shade: puce, lilac, plum
Purple swallow: martins
Purplish red: claret
Purpose, to no: in vain
Purposeful: telic
Purposely burn: sear
Purposes: ends, aims
Purse material: leather
Purse, small: clutch
Purslane or tare: weed
Pursue: hound
Pursue relentlessly: hound

Pursued an academic specialty: majored
Purveyor of language lessons: Berlitz
Purview, ken
Pusan country: Korea
Pusan people: Koreans
Push aside: elbow
Push gently: nudge
Push pin: tack
Push to the limit: tax
Pushed gently: nudged
Pusher's customers: users
Pushes forcibly: thrusts
Pushes off: goes
Pushing ahead: nosing
Push-up muscle: pec
Pushy sport: sumo
Pussycat's mate: owl,
Pussy's, wood, defense: odor
Put: set, lay, place
Put a stop to: end
Put an end to: limit
Put another way: restate
Put aside for later: on ice
Put away: file, ate, stow, save
Put back in Washington: reelect
Put down: dis, slur, detract
Put down grass: sod
Put forth effort: exert
Put in a kiln: dry
Put in a snit: miff
Put in code: enciphed
Put in motion: activate
Put in order: file, tidy
Put in the lineup: use
Put into force: enact
Put into practice: use
Put into service: use
Put into words: speak, orate
Put money on: bet
Put off: defer, delay
Put oil on: anoint
Put on a pedestal: exalt, idolize
Put on a play: stages
Put on a production: stage
Put on board: lade
Put on guard: alert, alarm, warn
Put on display: array
Put on ice: clinch, chill
Put on solid foods: wean
Put on the back burner, maybe: heat
Put on the block: auction
Put on the airs: strut
Put on the back burner, maybe: heat
Put on the block: auction
Put one over on: dupe
Put out: exert, issue, use
Put out a candle: snuff
Put out a feeler: test
Put out a runner: tag
Put out bait: lured
Put restrictions on: limit
Put the finger on: name
"Put the kibosh on": nix, squash
Put through a sieve: strain

Put to flight: rout
Put to shame: abased
Put to work: hire, employ, take on
Put together: amass
Put together differently: redo
Put together hastily: rigged up
Put up a fight: resist
Put up food: can
Put up with: abided, abide, allow,
　　　endure, tolerate
Put you in your place, they: usher
Putnam, Israel: general
Puts at ease: calms
Puts below: stows
Puts forward: posits, proposes
Puts in a nutshell: sums up
Puts into motion: actuates
Puts money on: bets
Puts off: defers
Puts to a test: assays
Putting it all on black, e.g.: wagering
Putting on airs: snooty
Puzo, sao: novelist
Puzzle: vex
Puzzle direction: across
Puzzle out: solve
Puzzle, tough: poser, enigma
Puzzling buffalo kin: anoas
Pygmalion couple: Lunts
Pygmalion's beloved: Galatea
　　　father: Belus
　　　sister: Dido
Pygmy antelope: oribi
Pyle, Ernie: journalist
Pylon, traffic: cone
Pyramid builder: Mayan
Pyramid, essentially: tomb
Pyrenees native: Basque
Pyrenees republic: Andorra
Pyrite: ore
Pyromanic deed: arson
Pythia's friend: Damon
Python, Monty actor: Michael Palin
Pyxis, constellation near: Vela

Q

Qatar, for one: emirate
Qatar ruler: emir
QED: quod erat demonstrandum
Qom's country: Iran
Q-tip target: ear wax
Sine qua non
Quadrants: sectors
Quadrivium subject: music, geometry,
　　　astronomy, arithmetic
Quaff, festive: nog
Quaff, holiday: wassail
Quaff, minty: julep
Quaff, shipboard: grog
Quaff with cannelloni: vino
Quaff with sushi: sake, saki
Quaggy ground: mud

Quagmire: fen
Quahog: clam
Quail group: bevy, bevies
Quaint lodging: inn
Quaint oath: egad
Quake, mild: tremor
Quaker colonist: Penn
Quaker, famous: Penn
Quaker kid's cereal: Ohs
Quaker pronoun: thy, thee
Quaker "you": thou
Quaking trees: aspens
Qualifier, crucial: acid test
Qualifying races: heats
Qualifying test: tryout
Qualities, good: assets
Quality, candid: openness
Quality, lacks: junk
Quality, low: cheap, cheapo
Quality of being warm: hotness
Quality, pervasive: aura
Quality, subtle: aura
Quality that affects taste: sapor
Quality, unusual: oddness
Quality, useful: asset
Quantico initials: USMC
Quantity, absent of: zero
Quantity, small: drop
Quantity to be transported: shipment
Quark's home: atom
Quarrel, big: feud
Quarrel noisily: wrangle
Quarrel: dustup
Quarrelsome women: virago
Quarrier's quarry: stone
Quarrying: mining
Quarter halves: bits,
Quarter Pounder: pattie, patty
Quarter-round molding: ovolo
Quarterback's group: offensive line
Quarters, odalisque's: serai
Quartet member: tenor, alto
Quartet, minus one: trio
Quarts, eight: peck
Quartz or flint: silica
Quartz, variety of: jasper
Quash, as the opposition: quell
Quasimodo's creator: Hugo
Quatorze (half of): sept
Quatro preceder: tres
Quavering tone: trill
Quay: pier, levee, dock
"Que pasa", reply to: nada
Quebec peninsula: Gaspé
Quechua speaker: Inca
Quechuan Indian: Inca
Queeg's ship: Caine
Queen Anne's lace: carrot, wild carrot
Queen City athletes: Reds
Queen, comic strip: Aleta
Queen, Ellery: detective
Queen, fit for a: royal, regal
Queen Latifah, emulates: raps
Queen, long-reigning: Victoria

Queen, Nile: Nefertiti
Queen of Carthage: Dido
Queen of fairies: Mab
Queen of Scots: Mary
Queen of the Misty Isles: Aleta
Queenly: regal
Queens ballpark: Shea
Queen's followers: bees
Queens, many: bees
Queens park: Rego
Queen's quarters: hive
Queen's tar: limey
Queen's truck: lorry
Quell: stem
Quemoy's neighbor: Amoy, Matsu
Quench: slake, douse
Quenched ones thirst: slaked
Querier's interjection: ehs
Queries, short: ehs
Query: ask
Query starter: what
Query, polite: May I
Quest for innocent mischief: lark
Question intensely: grill
Question of time: when
Question, pop a: ask,
Question, pose a: Ask
Question, raised a: posed
Question, tough: poser
Question, type of: essay
Questionable: iffy
Questioning sounds: ehs
Questions: doubts
Queue: line
Queued up: in a line
Qui vive
Qui vive, on the: aware
Quick bite: nosh
Quick bread: muffin, biscuit
Quick breakfast: cereal,
Quick bucks: easy money
Quick call: snap decision
Quick drive: spin
Quick flashes: glints
Quick intelligence, having: clever
Quick kiss: peck
Quick letter: note
Quick lunch: sandwich
Quick pace: trot
Quick peek: gander
Quick pull: jerk
Quick punch: jab
Quick reminder: memo
Quick sketch: doodle
Quick takeover: coup
Quick to learn: apt.
Quick to the helm: yare
Quick view: glance
Quick-witted: keen, apt, acute, agile, alert,
    canny, ready, sharp
Quickie portrait: sketch
Quickly: pronto, presto
Quickly, briefly: ASAP, stat
Quickly, very: rapid

Quicksand: mire
Quid pro quo
Quien sabe
Quiescent: static
"Quiet life, fie upon this"
Quiet, period of: lull
Quiet sound: shh
Quiet time: lull, loll
Quilt, lightweight: eider
Quilt stuffer: eider
Quilt stuffing: batts
Quilt, fluffy: eider
Quilt, light-weight: eider
Quilting social: bee
Quinine water: tonic
Quinn, Aidan: actor
Quintuplets: Dionne
Quintus Horatius Flaccus: Horace
Quip: wisecrack, jest, mot, gag
Quires, twenty: ream
Quirky behavior: tic
Quit, so to speak: bail
Quit running: stalled, conked out
Quit stalling: act
Quite calm: serene
Quite grand: epic
Quite possible: likely
Quite ready: all set
Quite similar: akin
Quits raining: lets up
Quits wavering: opts, picks
Quitter's cry: uncle
Quiver carrier: archer
Quixote and Juan: Dons
Quiz answers: true, false
Quiz, kind of: pop
Qum native: Irani
"Quo Vadis" role: Nero
Quod erat demonstradum
Quoits peg: hob
Quorum: minyan
Quota: ration, limit
Quotation mark, French: guillemet
Quote: cite
Quote from: cite
Quote-book abbr.: anon
Quran deity: Allah (Koran)

R

Ra symbol: Aten
Rabat's country: Morocco
Rabbi Ben Ezra
Rabbi's reading: Torah
Rabbit: coney, cony, hare, lapin, novice
Rabbit coop: hutch
Rabbit dish: stew
Rabbit ears: antenna
Rabbit, fictional: Peter
Rabbit fur: lapin
Rabbit kin: hare
Roger Rabbit: toon character
Rabbit tail: scut

Rabbit, toon: Roger
Rabbit's burrow: warren
Rabbit's kin: hare
Raccoon faces: masks
Race by, (as clouds): scud, scuds
Race car embellishments: decals
Race car engine: turbo
Race: comb. form: ethno
Racehorse, famous: Man of War
Race, quick: sprint
Race site: track, Le Mans
Race to the finish: sprint
Racetrack boundary: rail
Racetrack character: tout
Racetrack, famous: Ascot
Racetrack numbers: odds
Race winning margin: nose
Racehorse, famous: Kelso
Races by, as clouds: scuds
Races, qualifying: heats
Racing automobile: dragster
Racing boat: scull
Racing shell: scull
Racing shell leader: coxswain
Racist: bigot
Rack and pinion
Rack up, as a debt: incur
Racket: noise: din
Racket, huge: din
Racket with a pouch: crosse (lacrosse stick)
Racy, beyond: lewd
Radames's love: Aida
Radar beam, uses a: scans
Radar meas.: mph
Radar or sonar: detectors
Radar screen image: pip, blip, spot, trace
Radar's favorite beverage: Nehi
Raddai's brother: David
        father: Jesse
Radial: tire
Radial filler: air
Radiance: light
Radiant: aglow
Radiant emanation: aura
Radiant quality: aura
Radiate: emit, exude
Radiate, as charm: exude
Radiation measure: roentgen
Radiation unit: rad, rem, rep, langley, sievert,
        roentgen
Radiator cover: grille
Radiator sound: hiss
Radii companion: ulna
Radio dial: tuner, volume
Radio enthusiast: ham
Radio hobbyists: hams
Radio, kind of: AM-FM
Radio sitcom surname: McGee
Radio station need: tower
Radio studio sign: On Air
Radio technique: fade-in
Radioactive decay components: gamma rays
Radioactive element: uranium
Radioactive element, unstable: astatine

Radioactive item: isotope
Radio-ers acknowledgement: ten-four
Radio's domain: airwaves
Radius companion: ulna
Radius neighbor: ulna
Radner, Gilda: actress
Rae, Charlotte: actress, comic
Raft, famous: Kon-Tiki
Raft, guide a: pole
Rafter: joist
"Rag Mop" brothers: Ames
Ragamuffin: waif, urchin
Rage, current: fad
Rage, kind of: road
Ragged, become: tattered
Ragged tear: snag
Ragout or burgoo: stew
Ragtime style: honky
Rag-to-riches author: Alger
Rah-rah: avid, enthusiastic
Raid, quick: foray
Raider (1066): Norman
Raids the fridge: eats, snacks
Pail securer: tie
Railroad car: sleeper
Railroad framework: trestle
Railroad, one of Gould's: Erie
RR state: ETA
Railroad switch: shunt
RR terminal: station, sta
Raiment: attire
Rain buckets: pour
Raincoat: slicker, mac, poncho
Rain cloud: nimbi
Rain forest feature: mist
Rain forest, like a: lush
Rain forest, tropical: sylvan, biome
Rain gear: mac
Rain hard: teem, pour, pelt
Rain in Spain: agua
Rain, lacking: arid
Rain or test: acid
Rainout proof: doomed
Rain parka: mac
Rain protector: tarp
Rain slicker: mac
Rainspout: gutter
Rainbow band: red, color, violet
Rainbow, for one: trout
Rainbow maker: prism
Rainbow sections: arcs
Rainbow shape: arc
Rainbows: irides, (iridescence)
Rained a bit: drizzled
Rainer, Luise: actress
Raines, Ella: actress
Rainfall, heavy: spate
Rains, Claude: actor
Rains, extremely heavy: torrential
Rainwater pipe: spout
Rainy weather system: low
Raise a red flag: warn
Raise cane: farm
Raise kids: parent, rear

Raise objections: demur
Raise up: elevate
Raised a brood: nested, reared
Raised design: emboss
Raised desk: ambo
Raised, in a way: bred
Raised, it's often: havoc
Raised places: ridges
Raised stripe: welt
Raises a bet: ups
Raises the lid: opens
Raises one's voice: yells
Raisin cake: baba
Raisin, seedless: sultana
Raison d'etat :political reason
Raison d'être : reason for living
Raitt, Bonnie: singer
Raj headquarters: Delhi
Rajah's consort: Rani
        spouse: Rani
        title: Sahib
        wife: Rani
Rake tooth: tine
Rake's look: leer, ogle
Rakish: dashing, jaunty
Rakish hat: fedora
Raleigh, for one: sir
Rally, kind of: pep
Ralph Lauren line: Polo
Ralph's wife: Alice
RAM and ROM, e.g.: storage
RAM counterpart: ROM
Ram in the sky: Aries
Rama worshiper: Hindu
Ramano, Ray: actor
Rama's wife: Sita
Ramble around: rove
Ramble on: natter
Rambler's protection: thorns
Ramblin' Wreck's school: Georgia Tech
Rammed earth: pisé
Ramp alternative: stair
Rampage, on a: amok
Rampant: rear up, rile
Ran a ferry: plied
Ran comfortably: loped
Ran up a tab: owed
Ranch butter: ram
Ranch quest: dude
Ranch ropes: lariat, riata, lasso, noose
Ranch segment: acre
Ranch work: roundup
Ranch worker: hand
Rancher, maybe: Texan
Ranchero's rope: riata,
Rancher's pal: pard, partner
Rancid: off, old
Rancor: enmity
Rand, Ayn: novelist
Rand, Sally: dancer
Randall, Tony: actor
Random number generator: dice
Rang: knelled
Rang up: called, phoned, sold

Rang up sales: clerked
Range: extent, scope
Range finder: telemeter
Range ridge: crete
Range rover: herd
Range, rugged: sierra
Rangy: lank, lanky
Rani garment: sari
Rani servant: amah
Rani wrap: sari
Ranier's realm: Monaco
Rani's mate: raja, rajah
Rank above species: genus
Rank, beginner: novice
Ranked, at the U.S. Open: seeded
Ran's husband: Aegir,
Ransacking, engage in: rifle
Ransom, king's: fortune
Rap session: séance, confab, parley, palaver,
    colloquy
Rap sheet letters: aka
Rapa Nui:Easter Island
Raphael's birthplace: Urbino
Rapid-fire: quick
Rapids, rides the: raft
Rapid's transit: raft
Rapier: epee
Rapper: Lil' Kim,
Rapper: Kool Moe Dee
Rapper: Tone Loc
Rapport, have: relate
Rapscallions: imps
Raptor: eagle
Raptor nest: aerie
Raptor, powerful: eagle
Raptor, immature: eaglet, owlet
Raptor, young: eaglet, owlet
Rapunzel's pride: hair
Rara avis: rare, something rare
Rare sports event: hole-in-one
Rarebit ingredient: cheese
Rarely seen animal: snow leopard
Rarin' to go: itchy, antsy, eager
Rash, have a: itch
Rasht resident: Irani
Raspberry: boo
Raspberry stem: cane
Rat, kind of: sewer
Rat poison: ANTU
Rate of speed: gait
Rathbone, Basil: actor
Rather: quite
Rather, Dan: TV
Rather old-fashioned: dated
Rather than, once: ere
Rathskeller container: stein
Rating, gives a: ranks
Rating range: one to ten
Ratite bird: emu
Rats, old style: fie
Rattan: cane
Ratter: cad, cat
Rattle, gourd-shaped: maraca

Rattled, it may be: saber
Rattletrap: crate
Raucous cry: caw
Raucous diver: loon
Raucous songbird: jay
Raucous sound: blare
Raul Julia: actor
Raunchy: lewd
Ravel classic: "Bolero"
Ravel favorite: "Bolero"
Raveling: fraying
Ravel's well-known composition: "Bolero"
"Raven" author: Edgar Allan Poe
"Raven" heroine: Lenore
Raven, what it did: quoth
Raven's call: croak
Ravi instrument: sitar
Ravine: arroyo
Ravine, shallow: coulee
Ravioli filler: meat
Raw cotton: bolls
Raw deal: bum rap
Raw or burnt: sienna
Raw rubber: latex
Ray gun blast: zap
Ray or skate: manta
Raye, Martha: comic
Razor sharpener: strop
Razorback: boar
RCA dog: Nipper
RCA Dome squad: Colts (NFL)
RCA TV innovation: color
RCMP rank: Sgt.
Re:: as to
Rea, Stephen: actor
Reach: attain
Reach a plateau: level off
Reach across: span
Reach an optimum: peak
Reach from end to end: span
Reach one's zenith: peak
Reached the runway: landed, alit
Reaches for rudely: grabs at
React to a scare: scream
React to an alarm: awake
React testily: bristle
Reaction, kind of: gut
Reaction promoter: catalyst
Read: peruse
Read a UPC: scan
Read at the table, it's: menu
Read hastily: scan
Read intently: pored
Read matter into film: photoset
Read to the class: recite
Reade, Charles: English
Reader in a church service: lector
Readiness, put in: prepare
Reading aid: lamp
Reading, heavy: tomes
Reading, stage: line
Ready and willing partner: able
Ready for eating: ripe
Ready for plucking: ripe

Ready, quite: all set
Ready to bake: risen
Ready to be plucked: ripe
Ready to fight: armed
Ready to ship: crated
Ready to streak: naked, nude
Ready to typeset: edited
Ready-to-use product, often: premix
Ready trio: aim, fire
Ready, willing, and able: eager
Reagan's library site: Simi Valley
Real estate agent: broker
Real estate event: open house
Real estate map: plat
Real estate ownership, type of: fee simple
Reality, bit of: dose
Reality, conforming to: true
Reality, like, at times: grim
Reality, not conforming to: illusory
Really: my word
Really angry: raving
Really bad: awful
Really bad move: folly
Really come down: pour
Really dreadful: dire
Really impress: awe, wow
Really enjoy: relish
Really hurry: fly
Really moved: sped, raced
Really not go for: dislike
Really relax: veg
Really skimps: ekes
Really sorry: rueful
Really steamed: irate
Really went for: adored
Realm, legendary: Atlantis
Realtor's favorite word: sold
Realtor's tactic: open house
Realty ad item: garage
Rearmost part: tail end
Rear, to Popeye: astern
Rearward: astern
Reason for imprisonment, once: debt
Reason for saving: rainy day
Reason's mate: rhyme
Reason out: infer
Reason to go to school: learn
Reason, valid: logic
Reasoner's word: ergo
Reasoning, science of: logic
Reasons: whys
Reassure: calm
Reassure Rover: pet
Rebate requirement: UPC code
Rebekah's son: Esau
He's a rebel
Rebellion: mutiny
Rebels: revolts
Rebounds: caroms
Reb's org.: CSA (Confederate States of
    America)
Rebuff: shun
Rebuffs: nos
Recall vividly: relive

Receipt, René's: reçu
Receive as a visitor: see
Received wisdom: lore
Recent (pref): neo
Recent, more: latter
Recent origin, of: new
Recently: of late, newly
Reception: tea
Reception aid: aerial, antenna
Reception, evening: soiree
Reception hall, large: sala
Reception room: salon, lobby
Reception supplier: caterer
Receptionist's directive: take a seat, have a seat
Receptive: open
Recess: niche
Recess, domed: apse
Recipe direction: sauté, mix, sift
Recipe yield: batch
Recipient, designated: heir
Reciprocal effect, have: interact
Recital extra: encore
Recital hall: odeum
Recital offering: duet
Recital piece: étude, solo
Recital, repetitive: litany
Recite from memory: reel off
Recite mantras: chant
Recite musically: intone
Reckless: madcap
Reckless impulsive: madcap
Reckless, more: hastier
Recline: lain, lie, lay
Recline indolently: loll
Recline lazily: loll
Reclined in a relaxed manner: loll
Recluse: hermit, eremite
Reclusive, very: eremitic
Recognition, sound of: ahs
Recognize: peg
Recognize and accept: canonic
Recognize the intention of: onto
Recognized to be: seen as
Recoil: kick
Recombinant letters: DNA
Recommend, heartily: swear by
Reconnoitered: scouted
Record (1950s): oldie
Record book: register, log, diary
Record, break the: top
Record, in a way: tape
Record mileage: log
Record, officials: acts
Record player: stereo
Recorded: taped
Recorder, modern: TiVo
Recording label, major: Arista
Recover quickly: bounce back
Recovery, step toward: rehab
Recreation room gear: VCR
Recreational shopper: browser
Rectangle: oblong
Recto counterpart: verso
Recurring, as wind: Etesian

Recurring intervals: cyclic
Recurring musical beat: ictus
Recurring pattern: cycle
Recurring period: cycle
Recurring wind: Etesian
Red army member: ant
"Red as a beet": simile
"Red as a rose": simile
Red cap: porter
Red color: crimson
Red cooperative: ARTEL
Red Cross supply: plasma
Red dye: eosin
"Erik the Red"
Red faced: florid
Red figure: debit
Red flag, raise a: warn
Red gem, dark: garnet
Red herring: ploy, smoke screen
Infra red
Red ink: debt
Red ink amount: loss
Red ink item: loss
Red inside: rare
Red pigment: henna
Red River city: Fargo
Red Sea canal: Suez
Red Sea peninsula: Sinai, Arabian
Red Sea republic: Sudan
Red Sea vessel: dhow
Red sign: stop
Red-spotted creature: newt
Red Square name: Lenin
"Red tape"
Red wine: Médoc, claret, pinot
Red Wing legend: Gordy Howe
Redding, Otis: music
Reddish dye: eosin
Reddish tint: henna
Reddish-brown: russet, auburn, henna, sepia
Reddish-brown chalcedony: sard
Reddy, Helen: music
Redeem, as a savings bond: cash in
Redemption money: ransom
Redgrave, Lynn: actress
Red-handed in India: flagrantly
Redhead's tint: henna
Redolent: odorous, aromatic
Red-tag event: sale
Reduce: bate
Reduce to junk: total
Reduce to wreckage: ruin
Reduced: on sale, dieted
Reduce sail: reef
Reduce to a fine mist: atomize
Redwood, California: sequoia
Reebok rival: Nike, Puma
Reed, Charles: English writer
Reed, Lou: music
Reed, Tex: critic
Reed, weaver's: sley
Reed, Willis: basketball
Reedlike grass: gama
Reef animal: coral

Reef former: coral
Reef polyps: corals
Reel in: land
Reese sonnet: "Tears"
Reeves, Keanu: actor
Referee, slangily: zebra
Referee's guidelines: rules
Reference: allusion
Reference book: almanac, atlas, bible, guide, manual, handbook, dictionary, encyclopedia
Reference book, famous: OED ("Oxford English Dictionary")
Reference book reference: see
Reference, repeat: idem
Refined, as skills: honed
Refined, not: coarse
Refinery word, do: smelt
Refit a factory: retool
Reflect: muse
Reflect deeply: mull
Reflect on: muse
Reflected sound: echo
Reflection: image
Reflective quality: albedo
Refluxed shores: mudflats
Reformer's target: ills
Refractive device: prism
Refrain: chorus`
Refrain from revealing: sit on
Refrain, jazzy: riff
Refrain start: tra la
Refrain syllables: las, lala, tra
Refrigerant: ethane, freon
Refrigerant trademark: dry ice
Refrigerator stick: oleo, butter
Refuge place: ark, haven
Refuge tunnel: burrow
Refugee, certain: émigré
Refuges: havens, asylum,Refund, partial: rebate
Refusal, Duma's: nyet
Refusal, rustic: naw, nope
Refusal, terse: nope
Refusal to buy: boycott
Refuse from the mill: slag
Refuse to go along: rebel
Regal dances: proms
Regal homes: castles
Regal reversal: lager
Regal symbols: orbs
Regard as: deem
Regard highly: esteem
Regard with covetousness: envy
Regard with devotion: adore
Regard with reverence: adore
Regarded as: deemed
Regarding, in re: as to
Regarding this point: hereto
Regatta entry: boat, yacht
Regatta gear, perhaps: oars
Reggae: Jamaican dance
Reggae cousin: ska (Jamaican dance music)
Region of Asia Minor: Ionia

Region of NE Spain: Aragon
Register for: enter, enroll
Register signer: enrollee
Registered on sonar: ping
Regret: rue, alas
Regretful word: alas
Regular lines of travel: routes
Regular routes: beats
Regular routine: habit
Regulations: canon
Reheats, in a way: nukes
Reimburse: pay
Rein in: limit
Reindeer: caribou
Reindeer herder: Lapp
Reiner, Rob: director
"Das Reinhold"
Reitman, Ivan: actor, director
Reject: spurn
Reject with contempt: spurn
Rejoiner, mild: egads
Rejuvenate: renew
Related: akin, told, family
Related grp.: fam., family
Related on mother's side: enate
Relating to a wedding: nuptial
Relating to office work: clerical
Relating to reality: factual
Relating to swine: porcine
Relating to the abdomen: celiac
Relations, peaceful: amities
Relationship, type of: casual
Relative: kinsman, kin
Relative of fie: tut
Relax: veg out, vex out
Relax, as rules: bend
Relax, order to: at ease
Relax, really: veg
Relax rules: bend
Relax, with "out": veg
Relaxation: ease
Relaxed, not: tense
Relay race portion: leg, lap
Relay team part: anchor
Release a safety latch: unlock
Release, conditional: parole
Release forcibly: spew
Release from an obligation: exempt
Release writers: PR men
Releasing mechanism: detent
Relevant, be: pertain
Relevant, in law: ad rem
Relevant, not: inapt
Reliable, proven: tested
Reliable, most: surest
Relief: succor
Bas relief
Relief carved gem: cameo
Relieve tension: ease
Relieved sound: sigh
Religion, like some: pagan
Religious devotee: oblate
Religious devotion site: shrine
Religious dissenters: heretics

Religious faction: sect
Religious grouping: cult
Religious holiday: Easter
Religious observance: rite, fast
Religious offshoots: cults, sects
Religious poem: psalm
Religious prayer: novena
Religious recluse: eremite
Religious repast: Seder
Religious song: hymn
Relinquish: unhand
Relinquish a claim: waive
Relish, hearty: gusto
Relish item: radish
Relish maliciously: gloat
Reluctant: averse, hesitant
Rely on: swear by
REM (part of): rapid
Remain on hold: wait
Remains: rests
Remark, clever: quip, bon mot
Remark, cutting: barb
Remark, disparaging: slur
Remark, incisive: mot
Remark, icy: brr
Remark, passing: obiter dictum
Remark, sarcastic: gibe
Remark, smart: quip
Remark, taunting: gibe
Remark, witty: quip
Remarkable person: oner
Remarks, nasty: digs
Rembrandt: Dutch painter
Rembrandt painting: oils
Remedy, old-time: nostrum
Remind too often: nag
Reminder, brief: memo
Reminder, quick: memo
Reminder, written: memo
Reminds too often: nags
Remnant: tag end, dreg San Remo
Remorseful one: ruer
Remote, use a: zap
Remote: far, aloof, afar
Remote button: pause
Remote in manner: aloof
Removal key: delete
Removal, unlawful: hoist, robbery
Remove: doff
Remove a hat: doff
Remove a stripe: demote
Remove all doubt: prove
Remove, as a cap: unscrew
Remove by melting: ablate
Remove chalk: erase
Remove from office: depose, oust, unseat
Remove glitches: debug
Remove graphite: erase
Remove in law: eloign
Remove one's hat: doffed
Remove one's self: bow out
Remove paint: strip
Remove the peel: pare
Remove water: wring, bail

Removed: doffed
Removed dishes: bused
Removed pits: stoned
Removed text: delete
Removes a hat: doffs
Removes a renter: evicts
Removes by melting: ablates
Remsen, Ira: chemist,
Renaissance artist: Titian
Renata Scotto solo, e.g.: aria
Render harmless: defuse
Rendezvous: trysts
Renege: weasel out
René's receipt: reçu
Renewal, type of: urban
Renewed, not get: lapse
Reno lake: Tahoe
Renoir contemporary: Monet
Renoir, Pierre-Auguste: painter
Renoir subject: nude
Renowned runner: Coe
Rent alternative: own
Rentable: leasable
Rentals: units, videos
Rentals, airport: autos, cars
Renter's document, perhaps: sublease, lease
REO contemporary: Essex
Repair a wrong: atone
Repair bill item: labor, parts
Repair costs: upkeep
Repast: meal, feed, feast
Repast, enjoy a: dine
Repayment reminder: IOU
Repeat: iterate
Repeat reference: idem
Repeat verbatim: quote
Repeated: echoed
Repeated rhythmic phrase: riff
Repent: rue
Repentance, opportunity for: sins
Repetitious sound: echo
Replace a button: sew,
Replicas, high-tech: clones
Reply: answer
Reply to a knock: it's open
Reply to "Que pasa?": nada
Report: info
Reporter often seeks one: quote
Reporter, rookie: cub
Reporters: press
Reporter's coup: scoop
Reporter's query: who
Reporter's recognitions: byline
Reports, unconfirmed: rumors, hearsay
Repressed: pent-up
Reprimanded: chided
Repro machine, obsolete: mimeo
Reproach oneself for: rue
Reproductions: images
Reproductive cell: gamete
Reptilian killer: asp
Republic: nation
Repugnance, deep: hate
Repulsive: rile

Repulsive (most): ugliest
Reputation, bad: infamy
Repute: name
Request: pray
Request, ernest: plea
Request, tearful: plea
Requiem, like a: dirgefull
Require: entail, need
Requiring immediate attention: urgent exigent
Reroute, as traffic: detour, divert
Rescue, comes to the: helps, aids
Rescue team, often: searchers
Rescued from harm: saved
Rescues: helps
Research paper: thesis
Resemble closely: mimic
Resembles another: ringer
Reserve: spare, reticence
Reserve a flight: book
Reserve, in: aside
Reserved: aloof, shy, taken, saved
Reservoir boundary: dam
Reservoir, liquid: tank
Reside: dwell
Residence, imposing: manor, estate, villa
Residence, taken up: moves in
Residences, imposing: villas
Residences, many NYC: apts.
Resident, future: intern
Resident, Sparks: Nevadan
Resides: dwells
Residue: dreg
Resin: gum
Resin, fossil: copal
Resin, hard: copal
Resin in paint: alkyds
Resin, incense-producing: myrrh
Resin, natural: lac
Resin-producing tree: arar
Resin, tropical: elemi
Resinous secretion: lac, lacquer
Resist authority: rebel
Resist boldly: defy
Resist, not: obey
Resistance, lots of: teraohm
Resistance, symbol of: omega
Resistance to change: inertia
Resistance, unit of: ohms
Resistant to: oppose
Resisting, boldly: defiant
Resolute: stiff, bold, steady
Resolve: determination
Resonance looking: tinny
Resort amenity: spa
Resort, Belgian: spa
Resort island: Curacao
Resort, restorative: spa
Resort, western: dude ranch
Resorts to: uses
Resound: echo
Respect: homage, esteem
Respect bow: salaam
Respectful amusement: awe
Respiratory noise: rale

Respiratory therapist's fee: airfare
Respond to a stimulus: react
Responder, 911: EMS, EMT
Response, bored: yawn
Response, faithful's: amen
Response from space: A-OK
Response on deck: aye
Response to a masher: slap
Response to a ring: I'll get it
Responsibility or burden: onus
Responsible (held): blamed, liable
Responsive, mentally: alert
Rest, intervals of: respites
Rest periods: Sabbaths
Restart a battery: jump, charged
Restaurant employee: maitre d
Restaurant, informal: bistro
Resting on: atop
Restitution, exact: avenge
Restitution, make: atone, redress
Restorative resort: spa
Restrain by judicial order: enjoin
Restrain with fetters: shackle
Restrained, as a flow: stemmed
Restraining element: kibosh
Restricted computer network: intranet
Restriction on, put: limit
Rests, British: lie down
Result: end
Result of action: karma
Result, yield a: pan out
Resulted in: led to
Resulting: ensuing
Resulting from: due to
Results getter: achiever
Results in: leads up to
Results of overexertion: ache
Résumé cousin: bio
Resumes: takes up
Retailer's ploy: bait and switch
Retainer: fee
Retaliate: avenge
Retaliatory move: countermeasure
Retina cell: rod, cone
Retinal structure: rod
Retired: abed
Retired fliers: SSTs
Retirement acct.: IRA
Retirement agency: SSA
Retirement allowance: SEP, pension
Retirement, closer to: older
Retirement options: annuities
Retirement plan: Keogh, IRA
Retiring: shy
Retort, salty: oath
Retort, snappy: riposte
Retort, witty: riposte
Retract (as claws): sheathe
Retractable tops: moonroofs
Retreat, victor's: winner sanctum
Retrieve a fish: reel in
Retrieves: gets back
Retrieves a DVD: ejects
Retro car: Beetle

Retton, Mary Lou: gymnast
Return, as chips: cash in
Return evil for evil: retaliate
Return mailer: SASE
Return of the Jedi
Return swing: fro
Return the favor: repay
Returnee question: miss me
Reuben bread: rye
Reuben purveyor: deli
Reunion attendee: alum, kin, aunt
Reunion crowd: alum, kin
Reunion members: alumni
Rev the engine: race, gun
Reveal: evince: unmask, tell
Reveal, as in verse: ode
Reveal or pretend: let on
Revel noisily: roister
Revenuer: Fed
Reverberate anew: re-echo
Reverberating: echoing
Revered expert: guru
Revered teacher: guru
Reverence: piety
Reverent one: adorer, admirer
Reverential fear: awe
Reverential salutation: ave
Reverie: dream, daydream
Reversal: U-turn
Reversal, complete: U-turn
Reverse: gear, undo
Reverse the effect of: undo
Review: bone up
Review, enthusiastic: rave
Review, four-star: accolade
Review harshly: pan
Review, lousy: slam, pan
Reviews, great: raves
Revise: emend
Revising: editing
Revival setting: tent
Revival shout: amen
Revoke: abolish
Revoke a law: repeal
Revolting person: rebel
RPM measurer: tach
Revolve the log: birl
Revolver, Wild West: colt
Rewrite: edit
Rex Stout detective: Wolfe
Rey, Alejandro: actor
Rey, Fernando: actor
Reykjavic's language: Icelandic
Reynardish looks: leers
Rhabdomancer's job: dowser
Rhadamanthus's brother: Minos
      father: Zeus, Jupiter
      mother: Europa
Rhadamanthus: judge
Rhapsodize: rave
Rhea kin: emu
Rhea's daughter: Hera
Rheims roast: roti
"Das Rheingold"

Rheostat: dimmer
Rhett: Butler of fiction
Rhett's hangout: Tara
Rhine port: Bonn
Rhine siren: Lorelei
Rhine River city: Bonn, Koln, Basel, Mainz,
    Covlenz, Cologne
Rhine temptress: Lorelei
Rhine whine: ach
Rhineland region: Saar
Rhinoplasty: nose job
Rhode Island motto: hope
Rhode Island Reds, some: hens
Rhone River city: Lyon, Arles, Lyons, Geneva,
    Avignon
Rhone source: Alps
Rhone tributary: Ain, Isère
Rhyme, jaunty: lilt
Rhyme maker: poet
"I got rhythm"
Rhythm, Rio: samba
Rhythmic cadence: lilt
Rhythmic phrase, repeated: riff
Rhythmical swing: lilt
Riboflavin: vitamin B_2
Ricci, Christina: actress
Ricci, Nina: fashion
Rice, Anne: writer
Rice cake: torte
Rice dish: pilaf
Rice for Ricardo: arroz
Rice wine: saki, sake
Ricelike pasta: orzo
Rice-shaped pasta: orzo
Rich: loaded
Rich and famous: celebs
Rich man: nabob
Rich, moderately: prosperous
Rich red: ruby
Rich soil: humus
Rich supply: lode
Rich tapestry, a: arras
Rich widow: dowager
Richly adorned: jeweled
Richthofen, von: Baron
Rickrack pattern: zigzag
Rickey ingredient: gin
Rickman, Alan: actor
Rick's pianist: Sam
Riddle: enigma
Riddle, Nelson: music
Riddle, Zen: koan
Riddles, obscure: enigmas
Ride a bike: cycle
Ride, free: lift
Ride, ready to: saddled
Ride, Sally: astronaut
Ride the rapids: raft
Ride the waves: surf
Rides freely: coasts
Rider's handhold: mane, rein
Rider's shout: whoa
Ridge, broad-topped: loma
Ridge, saw-toothed: Sierra

Ridge, sharp: Hogback
Ridges or crests, to a zoologist: crista, cristae
Ridiculous failure: fiasco
Riding academy: manege
Riding outfit: habit
Rife with vegetation: lush
Rig a match: fix
Riga native: Leti, Latvian, Lett
Rigatoni kin: ziti
Rigel's constellation: Orion
Rigg, Diana: actress
Rigged the dice: loaded
Rigging support: spar
Right after: upon
Right angle to a ship: abeam
Right away: now, at once, pronto
Right for, was: suited
Right, not: left, wrong
Right, not quite: amiss
Right notes, hitting the: on key
Right now: stat
Right of passage: easement
"Right off the bat"
Right on: bingo, amen
Right on a map: east
Right size, is the: fits
Right to decide: say
Right, yeah: as if
Right-angle shape: ell
Righted a wrong: atoned
Righteous indignation: wrath
Right-eyed flatfish: sole
Right-handed page: recto
Right-handed person: aide
Right-hooked man: Smee
Rightmost column: ones
Rights movement word: lib
Rights org.: ACLU
Rights regarding usage: dibs
Rights, slang: dibs
Rigid: ironclad
"Rigoletto" composer: Verdi
Rigorous: strict
Riis, Jacob: reformer
Rijksmuseum site: Amsterdam
Riled up: mad
Rim: edge, lip
Rimrock locale: Mesa
Rimrock neighbor: Mesa
Ring around a planet: orbit
Ring around the pupil: areola
Ring around the middle: flab
Ring around the moon: halo
Ring, bright: halo
Ring count: ten
Ring duo: tag team
Ring, kind of: signet
Ring of color: areola
Ring out: peal
Ring rhymer: Ali
Ring, rubber: gasket
Ring thing: gem
Ring up sales: clerk
Ringed planet: Saturn

Ringlet: lock, curl
Rings: annuli
Rings of light: halo
Rings solemnly: knell
Ring-shaped cake: bundt,
Ring-shaped coral reef: atoll
Ring-shaped island: atoll
Ring-shaped surface: toroid
Ringside shout: ole
Rink event: ice show, hockey
Rink leap: axel,
Rink machine: Zamboni
Rink official: ref
Rinse: lave
"Rio Bravo"
Rio rhythms: samba
Riot subduing stuff: mace
Rio's warm month: Enero
Riotous confusion: mayhem
Rip: jag
Rip angrily: rend
Ripe, get: age
Ripley's statement: believe it or not
Ripped apart: asunder
Ripple pattern: moiré,
Rippled-surface fabric: moiré
Rise abruptly: soar
Rise and shine: awaken
Rise partner: shine
Rise rapidly: soar
Rises from within: upwells
Risk a ticket: speed
Risk, as a guess: venture
Risk, not at: safe
Risky: dicey
Risky, more: diceier, dicier
Risky place to live: edge
Risky situation, in a: on thin ice
Ristorante order: ziti
Ritchard, Cyril
Rite answer: I do
Rite place: altar
Rite sight: altar
Ritual, court: oath
Ritzy spread: estate
Rival rival: Alpo
Rival, unbeatable: nemesis
Rival, without: peerless
Rivalry, engage in: vie
Rivals, were: vied
River, Aberdeen: Dee
River, African: Niger, Nile, Uele
River, Alexandria's: Nile
River, Amiens: Somme
River, Arizona: Gila
River, Asian: Amur, Ural
River, Avignon's: Rhone
River, Basel's: Rhine
Riverbed, dry: wadi
River, Belgium: Yser, Oise
River, Bismarck's: Missouri
River bottom: bed
River, Brazilian: Amazon, Rio Negro
River, Budapest: Danube

River, Burns's: Afton
River, Cairo: Nile
River, Canadian: Ottawa
River, China: Chang, Tarim
River crosser: ferry
River crossing: ford
River deposit: silt, delta
River, dots in the: islets
River, Durham-Yorkshire: Tees
River, Egyptian: Nile
River embankment: levee
River, England: Avon
River, European: Volga
River feature: delta
River, Florence: Arno
River, France: Oise, Aisne, Rhone, Isere,
    Somme, Seine
River, Germany: Oder, Elbe, Rhone
River, Giza's: Nile
River, Grenoble: Isere (French)
River hazard: snag
River, Honduras: Ulua
River horse: hippo, hippopotamus
River impounder: dam
River in a Christie title: Nile
River in Hades: Styx
River, India: Ganges
River, Indiana: Wabash
River, Ireland: Erne
River island: ait
River, Italian: Arno, Tiber, Liri
River, Koblenz's: Mosel, Mosell
River, Left Bank: Seine
River, London: Thames
River, Lorelei's: Rhine
River, Manhattan: East
River, Missouri: Osage
River, Mongolian: Herlen Gol
River mouth deposit: silt, delta
River movement: flow, current
River, Nebraska: Platte
River, Nefertiti's: Nile
River, Niagara source: Erie
River, Nigerian: Donga
River of Metz: Mosell
River of song: Swanee
River of Tuscany: Arno
River, Opole's: Oder
River or wine: Rhine
River, Oxford: Thames
River part: delta
River, Peru: Ucayali
River, Pittsburgh: Ohio
River rapids: sault
River, Rouen's: Seine
River, Russian: Ural, Ufa, Volga, Dvina,
    Belaya
River, Scottish: Dee
River, Shakespeare's: Avon
River, Siberian: Ural, Amur
River source: head, headwaters
River, Spain: Ebro
River, Strafford's: Avon
River, Swiss: Aare, Aar

River, Swiss Alps: Rhone
River tamer: dam
River, Tiverton's: Exe
River to the Caspian: Ural
River to the Humber: Ouse
River to the Rio Grande: Pecos
River to the Seine: Oise
River, Ucayali location: Peru
River under the Ponte Vecchio: Arno
River waltz: Danube
River, Venezuela: Orinoco
River, Yorkshire: Ure
River, Zimbabwe: Sabi, Limpopo, Zambez
Rivera, Chita: actress
Rivera, Guido: painter
Riverbank clown: otter
Riveria, Diego: painter
Riverine mammal: otter
Rivers, Joan: comic
Riviera nation: Monaco
Rivulet: brook, stream
Roach, Hal: film producer
Road atlas info: distance, location,
Road divider: median
Road junction: fork
Road movie locale: Rio
"Road" picture name: Hope
Road shoulder: berm
Road show grp.: USO
Road sign, triangular: yield
Road surface: asphalt
Road, uneven: bumpy
Road, urbane: street, st.
Roadie gear: amp
Roadside alerts: flares
Roadside marker: cone
Roadside warning: flares
Roadster creation: rumble seat
Roast beef au jus
Roast, center of a: honoree
Roast, Rheims, (Reims): roti
Roasted, on le menu: roti
Roasting chamber: oven
Robards, Jason: actor
Robbery at sea: piracy
Robbins, Tim: actor
Robe (desert nomad): aba
Robe, long white: Ibo
Robe, loose: caftan
Robe of office: toga
Roberts, Nora: novelist
Robin Cook book: "Coma"
Robin Hood's home turf: Sherwood Forest
"Robinson Crusoe" writer: Defoe
Robinson, Edward G.: actor
Robocop, for one: cyborg
Robust: hale
Robustness: vigor
Rochester's beloved: Eyre
Rochester's Jane: Eyre
Rock band member: roadie
Rock blaster: amp, TNT
Rock bottom: nadir
Rock cavity: vug

Rock clinger: limpe
Rock "cushion": moss
Rock, fluid: magma
Rock formation: sial (rock forming the
    continents)
Rock, fossil: shale
Rock fungus: lichen
Rock, glittery: mica
Rock, gray igneous: syenite
Rock group, Aussie: AC/DC
Rock, hard: slate
Rock, hollow: geode
Rock, igneous: basalt
Rock, jagged: crag
Rock, kind of: gneiss
Rock, layers of: strata
Rock, light porous: pumice
Rock, metamorphic: gneiss, slate
Rock, molten: magma
"Rock of Ages"
Rock of Gibraltar, of yore: Calpe
Rock or country: genre
Rock outcropping, of a sort: inliers
Rock, pet: fad
Rock plant: sedum, lichens
Rock, rugged: tor, crag
Rock salt: halite
Rock shop curiosities: geodes
Rock similar to granite: gneiss
Rock, steep: crag
Rock tumbler stone: agate
Rock video award: Ava
Rock concert purchase: T-shirt
Rocked: swayed
Rockers, down under: AC/DC
Rocket deviation: yaw
Rocket, first-stage: booster
Rocket house: silo
"Rocket Man": Elton John
Rocket motion: yaw
Rocket section: stage
Rocket type: retro
Rockets on a rocket: retros
Rockfish: rena
Rock hound find: geode
Rockies ridge: arête
Rockne, Knute: coach
Rock's Bon Jovi
Rock's cushion: moss
Rock's Fleetwood: Mac
Rock's Foo Fighters
Rocks (loose) at base of slope: scree
Rock's Los Lobos
Rock's Pink Floyd
Rocky hill: tor
Rocky ledge: crag
Rocky Mountain park: Estes
Rocky Mountain people: Utes
Rocky Mountain tree: aspen
Rocky Mountain tribe: Ute
Rocky peak: tor, crag
Rococo: ornate
Rodent: rat, agouti
Rodent, burrowing: agouti, mole

Rodent genus: mus
Rodent, large: nutria
Rodent, S. America: paca
Rodeo gear: lariat, riata, noose
Rodeo venue: arena
Rodin, Auguste-René: sculptor
Rodin creation: statue
Rodin sculpture: "Adam"
Rodnina, Irina: skater
Rod-shaped disease carrier: E coli
Roe producer: shad
Roe, Tommy: singer
Roentgen relative: rad
Rogaine alternative: hairpiece
Rogation: prayer,
Roger Rabbit: toon
Rogers, Ginger: dancer
Rogers, Mimi: actress
Roget, Peter Mark: Eng. scholar
Roguish: arch
Role model: dad
Role model, be a: inspire
Role, type of: title
Role-played: acted, acted out
Rolex rival: Omega
Roll call list: roster
Roll call response: here
Roll, crusty: kaiser
Roll, hard: bagel
Roll in the mud: wallow
Roll of postage stamps: coil
Roll, onion-flavored: bialy
Roll tightly: furl
Roll up, as a sail: reef
Roll with a hole: bagel, donut
Rolle, Esther: actress
Rolled up (flag): furled
Roller coaster feature: loop
Roller, typewriter: platen
"Rollerball" star: Caan
Rolling in: rich
"Rolling stones don't collect moss"
Rolls, soft: brioches
Rolls the dice: casts
Rolls up: furls
Rolodex numbers: tele, telephone
Rolvaag, Ole: novelist (Norwegian)
Roma Christmas: Natale
Romaine: cos, lettuce
Roman army: legion
Roman "au revoir" ciao
Roman "bad day": ides
Roman boxing glove, early: cestus
Roman bronze: aes
Roman burial stone: stelae, stele
Roman censor: Cato
Roman cloak: toga
Roman cuirass: lorica
Roman dates: ides
Roman deck of cards: LII (52)
Roman deity: faun
Roman eight: octo
Roman emperor after Galba: Otho
Roman Empire: Marcus Aurelius

Roman Empire invader: Goth
Roman eros: amor
Roman farewell: vale
Roman fire god: Vulcan
Roman foe: Goth, Celt
Roman founder: Aeneas
Roman fountain: Trevi
Roman friend: amici
Roman galley: trireme, trirene
Roman garment: toga
Roman god of fire: Vulcan
Roman god of sea: Neptune
Roman goddess of plenty: Ops
Roman goddess of the health: Vesta
Roman gods: Penates
Roman grain goddess: Ceres
Roman guardian spirit: Lar
Roman headband: vitta
Roman "hello": ave
Roman Hera: Juno
Roman highway: iter
Roman hill count: VII
Roman historian: Cato, Livy
Roman household god: Lar
Roman "I": ego
Roman "I am": sum
Roman "I came": veni
Roman invader: Goth
Roman "it was": erat
Roman language: Latin
Roman "law": lex
Roman leader: Caesar
Roman legion: army
Roman lyric poet: Horace
Roman magistrate: aedile, praetor
Roman marketplace: fora
Roman "Mediterranean": Mare Nostrum
Roman natural historian: Pliny
Roman "now": nunc
Roman official: edile
Roman orator: Cicero
Roman poet: Ovid
Roman poet, exiled: Ovid
Roman province, old: Gaul
Roman road: via
Roman robe: toga
Roman route: iter
Roman sacker: Goth
Roman satirist: Horace
Roman sculpture: bust
Roman ships: galleys
Roman Sistine Chapel
Roman "soon": anon
Roman soothsayer, ancient: augur
Roman statesman: Cato, Cicero
Roman theater, ancient: odea
Roman "this": hoc, Roman "to be": esse
Roman to Celt: foe
Roman troops: legion
Roman "was": erat
Roman worst day: ides
Roman wrecker: Hun
Roman year: anno, ano
Roman year, weeks in a: Lll

Romance, brief: affair
Romance, secret: amour
Romance, shipboard: idyll
Romance, Spanish: amor
Romance, Venice: amor
Romania city: Iasi,
Romanoff, once: tsar
Romanov title: tsar
Roman's worst day: ides
Romantic: dreamy
Romantic appointment: tryst
Romantic ballad: serenade
Romantic corner: nook
Romantic deity: Eros
Romantic duo: lovers
Romantic exploit: gest
Romantic interlude: idyll
Romantic island: Bali
Romantic old city: Khartoun
Romantic poet: Keats
Romantic sight: castle
Romany: Gypsy
Rome: apple, capital city
Rome moniker: Eternal City
Rome's AraCoeli church
Romeo kills him: Tybalt
Romeo's girl: Juliet
Romeo's surname: Montaque
Alfa Romeo: car
Rome's remains: cores
Rommel, Erwin: Ger. general
Romp about: frolic
Romulus's brother: Remus
    father: Mars
    mother: Rea Silvia
    victim: Remus
Roncesvalle's hero: Roland
Ronstadt, Linda: music
Roods, four: acre
Roof angles: hips
Roof ornament: epi
Roof overhang: eave
Roof rooster's: pigeons
Roof slope: mansard, gambrel
Roof support: rafter
Roof topping: slate
Roof, under the: indoors, inside
Roof worker: slater
Roofing material: terne
Rookery cacophony: cawing
Rookie reporter: cub
Room & board: keep
Room at the top: attic
Room in a seraglio: oda
Room price: rate
Room, small: cell
Room style: décor
Room to maneuver: space, leeway
Roomiest: widest
Roomy sleeve: raglan
Roomy vehicle: van
Roosevelt, Eleanor: first lady
Roosevelt, Teddy's daughter: Alice
Roost, found a: alit

Rooster, at the store: capon
Rooster's crest: comb
Root, fragrant: orris
Rootbeer seller, famed: A and W
Rootbeer treat: float
Root or Yale: Eli
Rooted: based
Rootless water life: alga, algae
Rootlessness: anomie
Roots: origin
"Roots" author: Haley
Rope fiber: oakum, sisal, jute, coir
Rope, interlacing of: know
Rope off: reserve
Rope, ranchero's: riata
Rope, thick: cable
Roper of polls: Elmo
Roper's job: poll
Reporter's angle: slant
Roquefort hue: blue, bleu
Rorem, Ned: composer
Rorschach creation: blot
Rorschach test ingredient: ink
Rosalind's beloved: Orlando
Rosaries, string of: novena
Rosary bead: ave
Rose Bowl feature: parade
Rose Bowl org.: NCAA
"Rose by any other name"
Rose, deep: damask
Rose distillation: attar
Rose dramatically: soared
Rose fruit: hips
Rose Noble: Ryal
Rose petal oil: attar
"Rosie the riveter"
Rosebud and others: sleds
Rose-colored dye: eosin
Rosemary: potherb
"Der Rosenkavalier" (opera)
Roses grow, where: trellis
Roses, pertaining to: floral
Ross, Betsy
Ross, Diana: singer
Roster: line up
Rostrum: dais
Roswell visitor: UFO, alien
Rosy glow: flush, blush
Rosy, less: paler
Rosy, not: pale
Rotary tool: reamer
Rotary-phone user: dialer
Rotatable knob: dial
Rotate on an axis: revolve
Rotating mechanism: cam, gyro
Rotating neutron star: pulsar
Rotating shaft, part of a: cam
Rotation, in: pivoting
Rotation, line of: axis
Rote, Kyle: NFL
Roth, Philip: writer
Rotters: cads
Rouen's river: Seine
Rough cut: hewn

Rough fabric: burlap
Rough homes: hue
Rough weather: squall
Roughen from cold: chap
Roughhewn: rude
Roughly: circa
Roulette bet: even
Roulette color: noir
Round about way: detour
Round building: yurt, silo
Round gem: pearl,
Round number: zero
Round of applause: hand
Round of four: semifinals
Round platter: dish, disc
Round starter: bell,
Round stopper: TKO
Round Table knight: Kay
Round Table quest: grail
Round Table titles: sirs
Round-trip, took a: orbited
Rounded roof: dome, cupola
Rounded roof, having a: domical, domed
Rounded up: herded
Roundish: oval
Rounds of applause: ovation
Roundup: herd
Rouse to action: bestir
Rouse up: woken
Roused up: woke
Rousseau classic: Emile
Route, direct: beeline
Route follower: bus
Route, jet: lane
Route, slow: detour
Route, the long: detour
Router connection: uplink
Routes: ways
Routine: norm, habit, usual
Routine, dull: rut
Routine duties: chores
Routine, exhausting: rat race
Routine monotony: daily grind
Routine, regular: habit
Routine, tiresome: rut
Rover's pal: Fido
Rover's planet: Mars
Roves like knights: errant
Row of seats: tier
Row of shrubs: hedge
Skid row
Rowan, Carl: columnist
Rowboat seat: thwart
Rowdier: noisier
Rower's blade: oar
Rowing team: crew
Rowlands, Gena: actress
Rowling character: Harry Potter
Roy Roger's real last name: Slye
Royal address: sire
"RCMP" rank: Sgt
Royal chair: throne
Royal crown: diaderm
Royal decree: edict

Royal digs: palaces
Royal domain: realm
Royal emblem: regalia
Royal furs: ermine
Royal guardsman: Exon
Royal headdress: tiara
Royal honorific: sire
Royal house: dynasty
Royal initials: HRH
Royal Leamington feature: spa
Royal order: decree
Royal pronoun: our
Royal prop: scepter
Royal residence: palace
Royal seat, placed on a: throned
Royal symbol: orb
Royal with a golden touch: King Midas
Royalty top: diadem, crown, jeweled
Royalty headband: tiara, coronet
RPM gauge: tach
RR stat: ETA
RSVP: répondez s'il vous plaît
R2D2 owner: Leia
Rub against: abrade
Rub hard: scrub
Rub it in: gloat
Rub out: efface, erase
Rub the right way: massage
Rub the wrong way: rile, irk, chafe
Rubaiyat author: Omar
Rubbed against: abraded
Rubbed it in: gloated
Rubbed out: effaced, erased
Rubbed the wrong way: callus
Rubber, kneaded: eraser,
Rubber-making substance: styrene
Rubber match, needing a: tied
Rubber ring: gasket
Rubber stamp: OK
Rubber-stamp word: void
Rubber, toughen: vulcanize
Rubber tree: ule, oboe
Rubber tree sap: latex
Rubberneck: stare, eye, gape, gawk, gaze,
        snoop, stare, goggle
Rubber stamp: approve, certify, endorse
Rubbing alcohol: ethanol
Rubbish, certain: detritus
Rubble: debris
Rubble maker: TNT
Rubens character: cherub
Rubens models: nudes
Rubik's Cube maker: Ernö Rubik
Rubicon crosser: Caesar
Rudder: helm
Ruddish: reddish
Ruddy opposite: wan
Rude, be too: dis, snub
Rude one: boor
Rude person: boor
Rudely assertive: pushy
Rudely ignores: snubs
Rudiment: ABCs
Rudimentary shelter: tent

Rudner, Rita: comic
Ruffle: frill, ripple
Ruffle hair: tousle
Ruffle some feathers: rile
Ruffles, with: frilly
Ruff's mate: ree
Rug coverage: area
Rug exporter: Iran
Rug, kind of: area, throw
Rug maker: weaver
Rug material, natural: sisal
Rug pile: nap
Rug, prized: Navaho
Rug rat: tot, toddler
Rug, shaggy: rya
Rug texture: nap
Rugby formation: scrum, scrummage
Rugged cliff: crag
Rugged mountain feature: arête
Rugged range: Sierra
Rugs: wigs, toupees
Ruhr Valley city: Essen
Ruin: gum up
Ruin a birdie: par
Ruin, bring to: undo
Ruin source: nemesis, bane
Ruin the secret: blab
Ruing loudly: lamenting
Rule: govern
Rule breaker: defier
Rule, established: axiom
Rule of conduct: precept
Rule of thumb: norm
Rule opposed by Gandhi: Raj
Ruled out in advance: preclude
Ruler, deposed: Shah
Ruler sequence: dynasty
Ruler, substitute: regent
Ruler's length: foot
Ruler's, bygone: shahs
Ruler's realm: empire
Rules, hard and fast: laws
Rules often, he: Hoyle
Rum cake: baba
Rum drink, hot: grog
Rum mixer: Coke
Rum source: cane
Rumba band instrument: maracas
Rumble, happy: purr
Rumble in the jungle winner: Ali
Ruminant, antlered: deer
Rummage sale: bazaar
Rummy combo: meld
Rummy, win at: gin
Rumor perhaps: lie, gossip
Rumor propagator: mill
Rumor, spread by: noised
Rumor squelchers: facts
Rumors, spreads: gossips
"Rumpelstiltskin" raw material: straw
Rumple: muss
Rumpus: melee
Run amok: riot
Run around: gad

Run-in: spat
Run in neutral: idle
Run in the raw: streak
Run into problems: hit a snag
Run Lola run
Run, make a: score
Run, not quite a: triple
Run of luck: streak
Run of the mill: usual, dull, so-so, common, normal
Run, one way to: scared
Run out of steam: flag
Run out on: abandon
Run the gauntlet:
Run to mom about: tell on
Run up a tab: owe
"Runaway Bride" co-star: Gere
Rundgren, Todd: artist
Rundown area: slum
Rundown hotel: fleabag
Rundown, more: seedier
Runic letter: wen
Runner, distant: miler
Runner, put out a: tag
Runner, renowned: Coe
Runner's concern: pace
Runner's rate: pace
Runners support it: sled
Running mate: veep
Running, stop: stall
Running wild: amok
Runs easily: lopes
Runs its course: ends
Runs nude: streaks
Runs smoothly: hums, purrs
Runway: tarmac, ramp
Runway displays: fashions
Runway material: tarmac
Runway participant: model
Runway, reached the: landed, alit
Runway surface: tarmac
Runway walker: model
Rupee fraction: paisa
Rupee, ten million: crore
Rural address: rte
Rural emporium: general store
Rural landmarks, some: silos
Rural necessity: well
Rural or suburban residence, large: villa
Rural outing: hayride
Rural structure: silo, bar, shed
Rural verse: idyll
Ruse: wile
Rush away: scurry
Rush furiously, as a river: rage
Rush off: hie, scoot
Rush order: ASAP
Rush past: hurtle,
Rush, sudden: gust
Rush-hour pace: crawl
Russel, Bertrand: philosopher
Russian blue or rex: cat
Russian chess master: Tal
Russian co-op: artel

Russian despot: tsar
Russian doll, like: nested
Russian edict: ukase
Russian epic hero: Igor
Russian export: vodka
Russian first lady: Raisa
Russian grandmother: babushka
Russian guilds: artels
Russian hunting dog: borzoi
Russian industrial center: Omsk
Russian info. source: Tass
Russian island: Kurils
Russian "John": Ivan
Russian law: ukase
Russian money: ruble
Russian mystic, famed: Gregory Rasputin
Russian news agency: Tass
Russian "no": nyet
Russian or pole: Slav
Russian pancake: blinis
Russian plains: steppe
Russian range: Ural, Alai
Russian royals: tsars
Russian satellite: Sputnik
Russian space station: Mir
Russian spirit: vodka
Russian urn: samovar
Russian wagon: telega, troika
Russian word " peace": mir
Russian-born artist: Erté
Russo, Rene: actress
Rust: oxide
Rust and patina: oxide
Rust component: iron
Rust or laughing gas: oxide
Rustic: rural
Rustic digs: cabins
Rustic negative: nary
Rustic poem: idyll
Rustic refusal: naw, nope
Rustic step: stile
Rustle (as silk): swish
Rutabaga relative: turnip
Ruth, George Herman "Babe": baseball
Ruth's 714: homeruns, homers
Ruth's son: Obed
Ruth's surpasser: Maris
RV connector: stu
RV haven: KOA
Rwanda natives, some: Tutsi
Rx directive: dose, dosage
Rx monitor: FDA
Rx watchdog: FDA
Rx recommendation: dose, dosage
Rya: rug
Ryan, Jack: Clancy hero
Ryan, Nolan: baseball
Ryan, Tim: sportcaster
Ryder, Winona: actress
Rye fungus: ergot
Rye grass: darnet
Ryuku island: Okinawa

S

Saarinen, Eero: architect
Sabastian Coe: runner
Saber kin: epee
Sable antelope: sasin
Sac: cyst
Sacagawea's craft: canoe
Sachet: freshener
Sachet component: petal
Sackcloth companion: ashes
Sacked out: abed
Sacramental rite: penance
Sacred anthem: motet
Sacred chest: ark
Sacred image: iconic, icon
Sacred, more: holier
Sacred music: hymn
Sacred song: motet, psalm
Sacrifice site: altar
Sacrifice, willing: martyr
Sad, pensively: wistful
Sadat, Anwar: Egypt ruler
Saddle horses: mounts
Saddle strap: girth
Safari: trek
Safari leader: bwana, hunter
Safari member: bearer
Safdie, Moshe: architect (Israeli)
Safecracker: yegg
Safe haven: refuge
Safe place: haven
Safe product org.: FDA
Safe subject: weather
Safe to drink: potable
Safe to eat: edible
Safe to proceed signal: all clear
Safeguard: defense
Safer, Morley: TV
Safety agency: OSHA
Safety installation: rail
Safety, place of: haven
Saffron (flavored sp. dish): paella
Sagacity: wisdom
Sagan, Carl: astrophysics, astronomer
Sagebrush state: Nevada
Saguaros: cacti
Sahara area: erg
Sahara mountains: atlas
Saharan nomadic tribe member: Tuareg
Saharan sanctuary: oasis
Sahib's place: India
Sahib's rule: Raj
Sahl, Mort: comic, satirist
Said again: iterated, repeated
Said explicitly: stated
Said further: added
Said hoarsely: rasped
Said over & over: iterated
Said to be: rumored
Sail: jib
Sail insert: gore
Sail material: canvas

Sail, triangular: jib, genoa
Sailboat, Arabian: dhow
Sailed: boated
Sailed through: aced
Sailing ships: xebex, xebec
Sailing vessel, small: lugger
Sailor: tar, gob, swabby, sea dog
Sailor, inexperienced: lubber
Sailor, obsessive: Ahab
Sailor's drink: grog
Sailor's footwear: sea boots
Sailor's patron: St. Elmo
Sailor's patron saint: St. Elmo
Saint Anthony's cross: tau
Saint Elmo's fire: corposant
Saint Francis town: Issisi, Assisi
Saint Laurent: Yves (designer)
Saint Lawrence Seaway
Saint Vitus dance: chorea
Saint's insignia: halo
Saint's picture: icon, ikon
Saison, a: ete
Sake: behalf
Saks, Gene: actor
Sal ammoniac
Sal soda
Salaam: bow
Dares Salaam (Dar es)
Salad with apples: Waldorf
Salad bowl wood: teak
Salad days: youth
Salad dressing cheese: bleu, brie
Salad dressing ingredient: vinegar
Salad follower: entrée
Salad green: cress, endive
Salad in shreds: coleslaw
Salad, kind of: tuna, taco
Salalah residents: Omani, Omanis
Salamander: eft, newt
Salamander (lake): mud puppy
Salami type: genoa
Salchow relative: axel
Sale, big: red tag
Sale caveat: as is
Sale, kind of: garage, red tag, bake, year-end
Sale, of a sort: auction
Sales disclaimer: as is
Sales enticement: rebate
Sales pitch: spiel
Sales slip holder: spindle
Sales tag words: as is
Salesman, type of: door to door
Salesperson: vendor, rep
Saline septet: seas
Salk, Jonas: medicine (polio)
Sallow: wan
Salmon, young: parr
Salmon, small: coho
Salmon, smoked: lax, lox, nova
Salmon, three-year-old: mort
Salome's father: Herod
        husband: Zebedee, Aristobulus
        mother: Herodias
        son: John, James

    stepfather: Herod
Salon job: coif (short for coiffure)
Salon request: set, dye job
Salon styles: do's
Salon tints: rinses
Salonika's former name: Therma
Salsa go-with: nacho
Salt: NACL
Salt base: sodium
Salt cellars: shakers
Salt element: sodium
Salt Lake City player: Ute
Salt, medical: epsom
Salt or smoke: cure
Salt solution: brine, saline
Salt to a chemist: NACL
Salt, trace element in: iodine
Salt tree: atle
Salta locale: Arg
Salten creation: Bambi
Salt's cry: avast,
Salts, curative: epsom
Salty: briny
Salty droplets: tears
Salty liquid: brine, saline
Salty retort: oath
Salutation, reverential: ave
Salutation, Sydney: g day
Salute, tug: toot
Salvage to use again: recycle
Salve, apply: rub
Salver: dish, tray, bowl
Salves, soothing: unguents
Sam I am
Samaritan's act: good deed
Same: idem
Same as before, in foot notes: idem
Same: combo form: iso
"Same here": ditto
Same as before: idem
Same old grind: rut
Same old thing: rut
Same time, at the: together
Samite or perkin: cloth
Samms of "general hospital": Emma
Sammy Davis book: "Yes I Can"
Samoan capital: Apia
Samoyed: dog
Samoyed syllables: arfs
Sampan dwellers: Asians
Sample invitation: have some
Sample, kind of: DNA
Sample recording: demo
Sample specimen: taste, try
Sampras, Pete: tennis
Samson's betrayer: Delilah
        birthplace: Zorah
        death place: Gaza
        father: Manoah
        pride: hair
Samuel's teacher: Eli
Samurai code: bushido
Sans anxiety: calmly
San Francisco hill: Nob

San Francisco newspaper: Examiner
San Francisco transit system: BART
San Juan Capistrano
San Juan Hill locale: Cuba
San Luis Obispo
San Raphael's country: Marin
San Simeon castle: Hearst
"San Simeon" owner: Hearst
Sanctified state: bliedni
Sanctify a second time: rededicate
Sanctimonious and formal: churchy
Acta sanctorum
Sand and such: grit
Sand hill: dune
Sand mandala builder: lama
Sandals, some: thongs
Sandalwood, burned: censed
Sandarac tree: arar
Sandbags, maybe: levee
Sandberg, Carl: poet
Sandhurst weapon: sten
Sandler, Adam: comic
Sandler, Eric: actor
Sandstone deposit: flysch
Sandwich, crunchy: BLT
Sandwich, large: hoagie
Sandwich, long: hero, sub
Sandwich man?: Earl
Sandwich shop: deli
Sandwich, triple-layer: club
Sandy's sound: arf
Sanford, Isabel: actress
Sang without moving lips: hummed
Sanskrit dialect: Pali
Santa in Calif.: Anna
Santa (what he makes): a list
Santa's revenge: coal
Santiago's summer month: Enero
Sao Tome (an island republic)
Sap sucking insect: aphid
Sapphira's husband: Ananias
Sappho's birthplace: Lesbos
Sappho's verse: ode
Sapporo sport: sumo
Sarah Orne Jewett
Sarajevo combatant: Serb
Sara's husband: Abraham
          son: Isaac,
Saratoga events: races
Sarawak locale: Borneo
Sarcasm: irony
Sarcasm, dripping with: snide
Sarcastic remark: gibe
Sarcastic retort: hah
Sardine-factory worker: canner
Sardines are packed, how: in oil
Sardonic: wry
Sardonic, more: wrier
Sargasso: sea
Sargasso swimmer: eel
Sarge's pooch: Otto
Sari wearer: emir, ranee, rani
Sarnoff's (David) co: RCA
Sartre, Jean Paul: poet

SAS competitor: KLM
Sash, kimono: obi
Sash, Kyoto: obi
Saskatchewan's capital: Regina
Sasquatch cousin: yeti
Sass: dis
Sassy talk: lip
Sat down: rested
Sat idly by: loafed
Satan: Beelzebub
Satan's disguise, in Mexico: serpent
Satellite: orbiter, moon
Satellite connection: uplink
Satellite launcher: NASA
Satellite of Jupiter: Europa
Satellite, scientific: ogo
Satellite task, for short: recon
Satellite, weather: tiros
Satellites, e.g.: orbiters
Satiate: cloy, sate, pall, glut
Satie, Erik: composer
Satire magazine: Mad
Satirical, maybe: ironic
Satirical work: farce
Satisfied sound: aah
Satisfied to excess: sated
Satisfy: suit
Satisfy fully: sate, sati
Satisfy, more than: sate
Satisfy thirst: assuage
Satori, way to: Zen
Satre, Jean Paul: writer
Saturate deeply: imbue
Saturday night special: bath
Saturn feature: ring
Saturn moon: Helene, Dione, Rhea, Titan
Saturnalia: orgy
Saturn's largest moon: Titan
Sauce, hot: Tabasco
Sauce in a wok: soy
Sauce pan: boiler, pot
Sauce, pungent: Tabasco
Sauce source: soy
Sauce with basil: pesto
Saucer without cups: UFO
Saucer-shaped bell: gong
Saucily: pertly
Saucy: pert
Saucy seasoning: herb
Saud and others: ibns
Saudi Arabia capital: Riyadh
Saudi Arabia money: riyal
Saudi vessel: oiler
Saul, ibn: king
Saul's successor: David
Sauna wood: cedar
Sausage: wurst
Sausage, batter-coa: toad in the hole
Sausage in Soho: banger (England)
Sausage, seasoned: bologna
Sausage, type: vienna
Sausage, vienna: wiener
Sausalito's county: Marin
Sauterne, prized: white wine

Savant, idiot: offensive term
Save for later: put by
"Save your breath"
Saving account record: passbook
S & L account: customer
S & L deposit: acct
S & L offering: IRA
S & L protector: FDIC
Saving, reason for: rainy day
Savoir faire: tact, grace, poise, aplomb,
          address, dignity, finesse
Savory jelly: aspic
Savory smell: aroma
Savvy about: onto, upon
Savvy's etymon: sabe
Saw: beheld
Saw the sights: toured
Saw things: teeth
Sawfly saw: serra
Sawhorse: trestle
Saw-like part: serra, serrat
Saw-tooth mountain: sierra
Saw-toothed: serrate, serried, serrated
Saw-toothed ridge: sierra
Sawyer, Diane: TV host
Sawyer's, Tom, half-brother: Sid
Saxifrage: fern, herb
Saxony native: Saxon
Say another way: reword, amend
Say by heart: recite
Say "cheers": toast
Say clearly: enunciate
Say frankly: avow, aver
Say further: add
Say harshly: rasp
Say I do: wed
Say in fun: joke, jest
"Say it isn't so": deny
Say it's so: aver
Say likewise: echo
Say please: ask
Say "tsk tsk": chide
Say what: huh
Say with certainty: aver
Say with conviction: aver
Say with gestures: mime
Say yes: assent, accept
Say "yeth": lisp
Saying, familiar: adage
Saying likewise: echoing
Saying, simple: adage
Saying, widely accepted: axiom
Says clearly: enounces
Says decidedly: avers
Says likewise: echoes
Says with gestures: mimes
Says without thinking: blurts
Scabbard: sheath
Scalawags: knaves
Scale button: tare
Scale notes: fas, las
Scalia garment: robe
Scallion kin: leek
Scaloppini base: veal

Scam: rip off
Scam, pulled a: fleeced, conned
Scamp: rogue, rascal, imp
Scamper: dart
Scan, hi tech: MRI
Scandalous gossip: libel
Scandinavian: Norse
Scandinavian airline: SAS
Scandinavian gods: bure
Scandinavian navigator: Eric
Scandinavian rug: rya
Scandinavian sagas: edda (Norse edda)
Scandinavians, ancient: Norse
Scaphopoid: tusk
Scarcest: rarest
"Scarecrow and Mrs. King"
Scare off: daunt
Scare silly: petrify
Scared stiff, looking: ashen
Scared-looking: ashen
Scarf or snake: boa
Scarf, neck: ascot
Scarf, pin-held: ascot
Scarlett's home: Tara
        love: Rhett
        mother: Ellen
Scarum's partner: harum
Scary feeling: fear
Scary yell: boo
Scat, first lady of: Ella
Scat queen: Ella
Scatter about: strew
Scatter freely: strew
Scatter hay for drying: ted
Scattered fragments: debris
Scavenger, slope-backed: hiena, hyena
Scene of a miracle: Cana
Scene of William Tell legend: Uri
Scenery: vista
Scenery chewer: ham, emoter
Scenes: tableaus
Scenic view: vista
Scent carrier: petal
"Scent of a Woman"
Scent, shower: bath oil
Scented bag: sachet
Scented ointment: pomade
Scents, it makes: attar
Scepter: shaft, rod
Scepter go with: orb
Scepter, wields the: reigns
Sched. question mark: TBA
Schedule: agenda, slate
Schedule position: slot
Schedule question mark: TBA
Scheduled: slated
Scheduling concern: lead time
Scheherazade's milieu: harem
Scheldt feeder: Lys
Scheme, deceptive: scam
Scheme, ensnaring: scam
Schiaparelli, Elsa
Schifrin, Lalo: composer
Schlep: hail, tote

Schmidt, Ole: conductor
Schmo: jerk
Schmooze, hobnob, gab, chat, talk
Schmooze with: hobnob
Schneider, Romy: actress
Schnitzel meat: veal
Schnoz-related: nasal
Wiener schnitzel
Danke schoen
Scholar, stuffy: pedant
Scholarly bore: pedant
Scholarly notation: sic
Scholarly org.: inst
Scholarship basis: need
Scholarship relative: grant
Scholastic prig: pedant
School assignment: lesson
School club, kind of: glee
School event, monitored: exam
School for Francois: ecole
School founded in 1440: Eton
School, kind of: prep
School letters: grades
School near Windsor Castle: Eton
School objectives, certain: obedience
School of thought: ism
School on the Thames: Eton
School paper: term, theme, essay
School session: term
School year: grade
Schoolhouse clanger: bell
Schools of thought: isms
Schooner fillers: ales
Schooner, prairie: wagon
Schorr, Daniel: jounalist
Schrew, acts like a: nags
Schubert rece: sonata
Schuss: ski
Schussing need: ski pole
Science class: botany
Science, environmental: ecol, ecology
Sci-fi award: Hugo
Sc-fi doctor: Who
Sci-fi, father of: Verne
Sci-fi gofer: droid
Sci-fi good guy: Jedi
Sci-fi knight: Jedi
Sci-fi psychic: empath
Sci-fi regular: robot
Sci-fi "The Omega Man"
Sci-fi weapon: phaser, ray gun
Sci-fi writer: Asimov
Science guy: Bill Nye
Science of reasoning: logic
Scientific law: principle
Scientific principle: law
Scientific question: why
Scientific satellite: ogo
Scintilla: atom, iota, whit
Scissor hands portrayer: Depp
Scissors, big pair: shears
Scissors sound: snip
Scoffed: sneered
Scolding: earful, reproof

Scone: tea cake
Scoop: dip
Scoop holder: cone
Scoop out water: bail
Scope: reach
Score early in the set: one all
Score entry: triads
Score finales: codas
Score of zero: nil
Score make-up: music
Scored well: aced
Scorn, express: sneer
Scorn, show: sneer
Scorpio star: Antares
Scorpio's neighbor: Ara
Scot, a: dreb
Scot of rank: thane
Scot "one": ane
Scot snow: sna
Scotland inlet: loch
Scotland island: iona
Scotland yard?: metre
Scotland Yard division: CID
Scotland's king: Macbeth
Scot's gaelic: erse,
Scottish accent: burrs
Scottish biscuit: scone
Scottish bread: oatcake
Scottish cap: tam
Scottish child: bairn
Scottish dance: reel
Scottish explorer: rae
Scottish family: clan
Scottish gaelic: erse
Scottish goblet: tass
Scottish hillside: brae
Scottish hymnist: bonar
Scottish island: iona
Scottish John: Ian
Scottish king: Macbeth
Scottish municipal officer: bailie
Scottish "no": nae,
Scottish "one": ane
Scottish "own": ain
Scottish philosopher: Hume
Scottish plaid: tartan
Scottish queen: Mary
Scottish refusal: nae
Scottish "swift": cran
Scotto, Renata
Scotty beamed him up: Kirk
Scoundrel, like a: maddish
Scourge of god: Attila,
Scout collection: badges
Scout's discovery: talent
Scrabble blocks: tiles
Scrap the mission: abort
Scrape aftermath: scab
Scrape off: abrade
Scraped one's shins: barked
Scrapes: rasps
Scrapes a knee: skins
Scraps of cloth: rags
Scratch: abrade

Scratch for scratch: forage
Scratch mark: dele
Scratch worthy, most: itchiest
Scrawny one: scrag
Scream and shout: rave
Screecher, young: owlet
Screen dots: pixels
Screen material: mesh
Screen, protective: grille
Screw up: flub
Screwball: kook
Screwdriver type: phillips
Scribble: doodle
Scribble down: jot
Scribble in: pencil
Scribes supplies: inks
Script lines: dialogs
Script, written in old: unical
Scripting, bit of: line
Scripts, mostly: dialog
Scroll, ancient: papyri
Scroll cabinet: ark
Scroll holder: ark
Scroll temple: Toran
Scrooge's nephew: Fred
Scrubbed mission: no go
Scrubs for surgery: preps
Scruff: nape
Scruggs, Earl: blue grass
Scruples, without: amoral
Scuba diving safety measure: buddy system
Scuba diving site: reef
Scuff at: gibe
Scull implement: oar
Scullery cloth: dish rag
Sculptor: carver
Sculptor, thinking man's: rodin
Sculpture in St. Peters: pieta
Sculpture media: jade
Sculpture, Roman: bust
Scum on molten metal: dross
Scurried along: hied
Scurrilous chap: cad
Scurry: hie
Scurry along: hie
Scut work, do: toil
Scuttles: hods
Scythe handle: snath, snathe
Scythe, use a: mow, reap
Scythe wake: swathe
Sea barrier: dike
Sea bird: solan, petrel, gannet
Sea dog: gob, tar, sailor
Sea duck: eider, scaup, scoter, merganser
Sea eagle: erne, ern, osprey, fish hawk
Sea flyer: tern, petrel
Seafood dish: clam, crab, squib, mussel, oyster,
　　shrimp, lobster, scallop, calamari
Seagull: mew
Sea hawk: osprey
Sea inlet: estuary
Sea lettuce: laver
Sea, like the: briny
Sea of Galilea

Sea pheasant: smee
Sea product: iodine
Sea raider: Viking
Sea rocks: skerries
Sea (to Yves): mer
Seafarer's luggage: steamer trunk
Seafood serving style: amandine
Seagel, Steven: actor
Seal a package: tape
Seal a tub: caulk
Seal of approval: cachet
Seal, type of: eared
Sealed: airtight
Sealed a deal: iced
Sealing a deal: clinching
Seam sample: ore
Seamy matter: ore
Sean Astin: actor
Séance holder: medium
Séance sound: rap
Search, as for talent: scout
Search deeply: delve
Search engine address: URL
Search engine find: URL
Search, kind of: strip
Search party: posse
Search the riverbed: dredge
Search thoroughly: scour
Search, type of: house to house
Seashell: conch
Seashell seller: she
Seashore: coast
Seasickness: mal-de-mer
Sea-saw necessity: two
Seascape hue: aqua
Season song: carol
Seasons: ages
Seasonal drink: nog
Seasoned dish: olla
Seasoning add: salt
Seasoning, in savoie: sel
Seasoning, saucy: herb
Seat, as a jury: impanel
Seat at a barn dance: bale
Seat, cozy: lap
Seat, elevated: perch
Seat formally: usher
Seat, hard: pew
Seat of learning
Seat of power: throne
Seat on the aisle: pew
Seating, Sunday: pews
Seatless sign: sro (standing room only)
SEATO counterpart: NATO
Seats, find: usher
Seats for services: pews
Seats, like some: taken
Seat-section separator: aisle
Seawall: levee
Seawater: brine
Seaweed: alga, kelp,
Seaweed, brown: kelp
Seaweed, edible: ulva
Seaweed extract: agar

Seaweed substance: agar
Sebastian Cabot: explorer
Sebastian Coe: runner
Secluded: lone
Secluded corner: nook
Secluded vale: glen
Secluded valley: glen
Second after thought (abbr.): pps
Second banana: stooge
Second childhood: dotage
Second estate: nobles
Second of a series: beta
Second of two: latter
Second person in the trinity: son
Second point in tennis: thirty
Second printing: reissue
Second rate: shabby
Second son: Abel
Second story job: heist
Second story man: yegg
Second thoughts: qualms
Second to none: best
Second vending: resale
Secondary domicile: pied-a-terre,
Secondary lane: by road, byway
Secondary road: byway
Second-hand tire: re-cap
Second-hand transaction: resale
Second-story job: heist
Second-story man: yegg
Second-stringer: sub
Secret: arcane, under wraps, untold, inner
Secret base: lair
Secret doctrine: cabala
Secret group: cabala
Secret joint adventure, take part in: elope
Secret message: code
Secret moniker: code name
Secret observers: spies
Secret romance: amour
Secret, ruin the: blab
Secret scheme: cabala, cabal
Secret sign: wink
Secret society: tong
Secret store: cache
Secret writings: codes
Secretly: entre nous, sub rosa
Sect: cult
Section, kind of: conic
Section of a long poem: canto
Section of an org.: div., division
Sector: zone
Secular: laic
Secure a contract: land
Secure, most: safest
Secure the bike: padlock
Secure with lines: moor
Securely closed: sealed
Securely placed: ensconced
Secures: ties, laces
Secures a rope: belays (ship's fasten line)
Security check: patrol
Security for freedom: bail
Security org.: DOD

Sedaka, Neil: music
Sedan stopper: brake shoe, brake
Sedaris, Amy: comic
Sedated: numbed, calmed
Sedative: opiate
Sedgewick, Kyra: actress
Sedgwick, Edie: actress
Sediment: lees
Sedimentary material: silt
Sedimentary rock: shale
Seductive art: wiles
Seductive woman: vamp
See at a distance: espy
See fit: deign
See or hear: sense
See eye to eye: agree
Seesaw: yo-yo
See the point: get
Seed, aromatic: caraway
Seed: ovule, pit, pip
Seed catalog offering: hybrid
Seed container: pod, hull
Seed covering: testa, hull, aril
Seed, flavorful: anise
Seed grain: kernel
Seed protector: aril
Seed starter: peatpot
Seed, type of: sesame
Seed-bearing pine: pinon
Seedless plant: fern
Seedpod, clingy: bur
Seedy joint: dive
Seeger, Pete: folksinger
Seek a job: apply
Seek a tan: bask
Seek booty: maraud
Seeks alms: begs
Seeks ambitiously: aspire
Seeming: quasi
Seemingly forever: ages
Seer of myth: Cassandra
Seer, Trojan: Cassandra
Seer's cards: tarot
Sees: espies
Sees eye to eye: agrees
See-through: thin, sheer
Segal, Erich: author,
Segal, George: sculptor
Sego lily's state: Utah,
Segovai, Andres: guitarist
Seiji, Ozawa: conductor
Seine: net
Seine ait: ile
Seine, dots on the: iles
Seine feeder: Oise
Seine moorages: iles
Seine site: ill, ile
Seine vista: ile
Seis, half of: tres
Seismic event: quake
Seize: glom onto
Seize forcefully: wrest
Seize quickly: snatch
Seizes the throne: usurps

Selassie, Haile: Ethiopia ruler
Seldom ever: rarely
Seldom seen: rara, rare
Select a jury: impanel
Select group: a list
Selected, carefully: well-chosen
Selects the dramatis personae: casts
Selene's brother: Helios
    father: Hyperion
    mother: Thea
    sister: Eos
Seles, Monica: tennis
Self: ego
Self-aggrandizement: ego trip
Self-aggrandizing one: egoist
Self-annihilation: suicide
Self-appointed trier: kangaroo court
Self-assertive: bold, brash, pushy, forward
Self-assurance: aplomb, poise, coolness
Self-assured: poised, smug, sanguine,
    confident
Self-assured and bold: assertive
Self-centered: vain, selfish, conceited
Self-centered chatterbox: popin jay
Self-centered, journey for the: ego trip
Self-centered person: egoist
Self-composed: calm, poised, serene, assured,
    collected
Self-confidence: poise, ease, aplomb, assurance
Self-confidence, destroy one's: abash
Self-confidence, lacking, shy
Self-confident, overly: cocky, jaunty, poised,
    sanguine
Self-contained: closed, formal, built-in,
    composed, enclosed
Self-control: will
Self-defense art: aikido, karate, judo, kung fu,
    jujitsu, tai kwan do
Self-denying one: ascetic,
Self-destruction: suicide, felo-de-se, hari-kiri
Self-esteem: ego, vanity, conceit, dignity,
    egotism
Self-evident truths: axioms
Self-importance: ego, smug, vain, lordly
Selflessly: nobly, generous, charitable
Self-move firm: U-haul,
Self-pity, suffer from: mope
Self-reproach: disgrace, remorse
Self-respect: pride, dignity, amour, properSelf-
    righteous: pious, canting, preachy,
    unctuous
Self-satisfied: smug
Self-seeking: greedy, selfish, egoistic
Self-serve diner: automat
Self-starter: hustler, go-getter
Sell cheap: dump
Sell off divest
Sell out: betray
Sell to a customer: retail
Sell to consumers: retail
Seller, dealer: trader
Sellers, Peter: actor
Selling point: asset, store
Sell-out notice: SRO (standing room only)

Selves: egos
Semaphore features: arms
Semester: term
Semester ender: exam
Semesters, two: year
Semiconductor: cber
Semi, drive a: haul
Semicircular letter: cee
Semi-circular molding: torus
Semi-erect primates: apes
Semile center: ASA
Seminole chief: Osceola
Semiquaver, for one: note
Semitic language: Hebrew
Semper fi grp.: USMC
Senate airing channel: C-span
Senate attire: toga
Senator wear, once: toga
Send back: remand, return
Send, clicked: e-mailed
Send forth: issue
Send in a crate: ship
Send in the taxes: file
"You send me"
Send off: emit
Send packing: expel, rout, oust
Sends: posts, mails
Sends forth: emits
Sends out: issues
Seneca's student: Nero
Senegal capital: Dakar
Senescence: old age
Senhor: don
Senhora: dona
Senility: dotage
Senior, former: grad, alum
Senior lobby: AARP
Senior source of funds: IRAs
Senora: dona, madam, sra
Senora "this": esta
Senora's house: casa
Sens scent: arome
Sensation, prickly: itch
Sense: intuit
Sense of self: ego
Sense of taste: palate
Sense of unease: malaise
Sense, uncommon: ESP
Senseless: inane
Senseless, utterly: absurd
Sensible, more: wiser
Sensible, most: wisest
Sent a wire: cabled
Sent packing: shooed
Sent to Siberia: exiled
Sent via a click: e-mailed
Sent via phone: faxed
Sentence: clause
Sentence, analyze a: parse
Sentence, long: life
Sentence starter: noun
Sentence piece: clause
Sentimental drivel: goo
Sentimental singer: balladeer

Sentimental, overly: gushy
Sentry duty: on watch
Sentry watch: vigil
Seoul air carrier: KAL
Separate parts, into: asunder
Separation allowance: palimony
Sequel's sequel: iii
Sequence of rulers: dynasty
Sequence, placing in: slotting
Sequence verifier: collator
Non sequitur: (unrelated statement)
"que sera, sera"
Seraglio: harem
Seraglio room: oda
Serape: shawl
Seraph: angel
Serenade: woo
Serenaders' light source: moon
Serendipity, bit of: fluke
Serengeti herd: zebras
Serengeti youngster: lion cub
Serf's master: lord
Sergeant: NCO, noncom
Series parts: episodes
Series segments: episodes
Serigraph artist: erte
Serin relative: canary
Serious charge, most: gravamen, grievance
Serious, more than: dire
Serious offender: felon
Serious stories: drama
Serious, very: dire
Serious warning: red alert
Serpentine letter: ess
Serpentine swimmer: eel
Serra, Junipero (Sp.): missionary
Serum holder: ampule, vial
Serum in Sicily: siero,
Servant, eastern: amah
Servant, half-free: serf
Served a meal: fed
Served hash: slung
Served time: did
Server's burden: tray
Server's edge: ad in
Service ender: amen
Service, put into: use
Service station adjunct, maybe: carwash
Service station supply: gas, motor oil
Service street: alley
Servile flatterer: toady
Serving bowl: tureen
Serving dish: platter
Serving need: tea set
Serving of whip cream: dollop
Servitude, put in: enslave
Sesame: teel
Sesame plant: til
Sesame sauce: tahini
Sesame seed confection: halvah
Sesame Street grouch: oscar
Sesame Street network: PBS
Sesame Street regular: Ernie
Set against: pit, averse

Set apart: isolate
Set aside: save, devote, void, annul, discard,
    dismiss, reserve
Set back: mire, delay, detain, hang up, hinder,
    retard, slow up
Set by a runner: pace
Set down: place
Set fire to: torch
Set firmly: embed
Set forth authoritatively: ordain
Set in motion: initiate
Set one back: cost
Set of four: tetrad
Set of nine instruments: nonet
Set of nine voices: nonet
Set of principles or rules: code
Set of squares: grid
Set of steps: stile, stairs,
Set one's sights on: aim for
Set phrases: idioms
Set sail: embark
Set straight: align, orient
Set the dial: tune in
Set the dog on: sic
Set things right: atone
Seth's brother: Abel, Cain
       father: Adam
       mother: Eve
       son: Enos
Seton, Anya: novelist
Sets a price: asks
Sets, as a trap: lays
Sets free: unleashes, releases
Sets right: atones
Settle and steady: staid
Settle, as an issue: iron out
Settle by conciliation: mediate
Settle up: pay
Settle up in advance: prepay
Settled: alit, paid, resolved
Settler, early: puritan
Setting for ducks: ponds
Setup: lay out
Seuss character: Lorax
Sevareid, Eric: news cast
Seven and eleven: odds
Seven deadly sins
Seven, group of: heptads, septets
Seven hills, city of: Rome
Seven pedal instrument: harp
Seven veil dancer: Salome
"Seven Year Itch, The" actor: Ewell
Seventh inning stretch
Seventh planet: Uranus
Severe or harsh: stern
Severe setback: beating
Severely pelted: stoned
Severn feeder: Avon
Seville locale: Spain
Seville parent: madre
Seville stew: ragu
Seville wave: ola
Sew loosely: baste
Seward peninsula seaport: Nome

Sewing chore, do a: hem, darn, mend
Sewing machine inventor: Elias Howe
Sewing supplies: notions (small useful items)
Sewed up: iced
Sewn: basted
Sex appeal: oomph
Sexologist Shere: Hite
Sextant's precursor: astrolabe
Shabby joint: dive
Shacks: hovels
Shackle: gyve, fetter
Shade, in Salerno: ombra, ombre
Shade of difference: nuance
Shade of meaning: nuance
Shade provider: awning, tree
Shaded walkway: alameda
Shadow, cast a: shade
Shadow location: eyelid
Shadow: umbra, umbrae, tail
Shadow, type of: eye
Shadows are shortest, when: noon
Shadowy: dusky, dim
Shady place: arbor
Shady shelters: gazeboes, bowers
Shaft entrance: adit
Shaggy beast: yak
Shaggy flower: mum
Shaggy rug: rya
Shah's domain: Persia
Shake a finger: wag
Shake a leg: hurry
Shake awake: roust
Shake down cruise: test
Shake down, obtain via: extort
Shake hands on: agree
Shake slightly: joggle
Shake up: jar
Shakerism, e.g.: sect
Shakespeare (Lear's) daughter: Regan
Shakespeare "in love"
Shakespeare, Mrs.: Anne
Shakespearean court jester: Yorick
Shakespearean fuss: ado
Shakespearean offering: sonnet
Shakespearean hero: Othello
Shakespearean king: Lear, Oberon
Shakespearean oath: fie
Shakespearean queen: Titania
Shakespearean sprite: Ariel
Shakespearean title character: Cleopatra
Shakespearean tragedy: Macbeth, Othello
Shakespearean villain: Iago
Shakespeare's nickname: bard
Shakespeare's river: Avon
Shakespeare's villain: Iago
Shale extract: oil
Shales, Tom: journalist
Shallow: inane
Shallow area: shoal
Shallow body of water: lagoon
Shallow container: tray
Shallow depression: swale
Shallow lake: lagoon
Shallow ravine: coulee

Shallow-water flat: slob
Sham: pseudo
Shaman: priest
Shaman's findings: omens
Shaman's quest: omen
Shamash: sun god
Shamash's father: Sin
          wife: Aya
Shambles of, makes a: ruins
Shame: ignominy, fie
Shame, for: tut
Shamed offering: apology
Shampoo additive: aloe
Shamu, for one: orca
Shanghai houseboat: sampan
Shangri-la: eden, utopia
Shankar's music: raga
Shankar's instrument: sitar
Shank's mare: leg
Shannon, Del: music
Shape clay: model, mold
Shape in advance: preform
Shape or form: mold
Shape stone: sculpt
Shape up: tone
Shape with an axe: hew
Shaped like a star: stellate
Shapeless mass: glob
Share a border: abut
Share accommodations: double up
Share, not: hog
Share, won't: hogs
Shareholder's payment: dividend
Shares equally: halves
Shares, less than 100: odd lot
Sharjah's top man: emir
Shark: mako, white
Shark hitchhiker: remora
Shark tag along: remora
Shark, type of: loan
Shark, warm water: mako
Sharp as a tack: keen
Sharp comment: jab
Sharp counterpart: flat, dull
Sharp divide: schism
Sharp end: apex
Sharp ended post: stack
Sharp, make: whet, hone
Sharp, make less: blunt
Sharp mountain ridge: arete
Sharp pain: stab
Sharp projections: jags
Sharp ridge: hogback
Sharp sensation: pang
Sharp spine: thorn
Sharp tasting: tart
Sharp to the taste: acrid
Sharp tug: yank
Sharp turn: zig, veer
Sharp wit: salt
Sharp-billed wader: egret
Sharpener, belt-like: strop
Sharpening device, type of: oil stone,stone
Sharpens: whets, hones

Sharpens, as cheddar: ages
Sharper-edged: keener
Sharp-eyed: keen, alert, vigilant, watchful
Sharply criticizes: raps
Sharpshooters aim, like a: true
Sharp-witted: keen, acute, canny, quick,
          smart, astute, clever, shrewd
Shasta or gerbera: daisy
Shaved wood: planed
Shavian heroine, in brief: cleo
Shaw, Artie: band
Shaw, Bernard: CNN
Shawl: stole
Shawl, blanket-like: serape
Shawnee chief: Tecumseh, Tecumtha
"She gets what she wants": Lola
"She" in Seville: elle
"She loves you refrain": yeah
She, objectively: her
Shearer, Norma: actress
Sheaves, bring in the: reap
Sheba, today: Yemen
Shed: slough, rid
Shed feathers, as a bird: moult, molt
Sheehy, Gail: writer
Sheen: utter
Sheep: mutton
Sheep, bunch of: flock
Sheep coat: fleece
Sheep: herder: collie
Sheep pen: cote
Sheep, pertaining to: ovine
Sheepskin: mouton
Sheepskin, prepares: taws
Sheep, wild: auodad, arui, urin
Sheepcote matriarch: ewe
Sheepdog, Hungarian: Puli
Sheepfold: cote
Sheep-herding area: lea
Sheepish comment: baa
Sheer joy: ecstasy
Sheer, not: opaque
Sheet candy: bark
Sheet fabric: percale
Sheet, kind of: rap
Sheet music words: lyrics
Sheet of printed matter: folio
Sheet of stamps: pane
Sheets of glass, with: panes
Sheik or emir: arab
Sheik's bevy: harem
Sheik's cliques, sometimes: harems
Sheik's colleague: emir
Sheik's cousin: emir
Shekel spender: Israeli
Skeletons are kept, where some: closet
Shell, fare in a: taco
Shelley's offering: ode
Shelley's poem: ode
Shellfish: abalone
Shellfish eater: otter
Shellfish genus: oliva
Shells and such: ammo
Shells out: spends

Shelter a fugitive: abet
Shelter, conical: tepee
Shelter, leafy: bower
Shelter, park: gazebo
Shelter, protecting: lee
Shelter, rough: hut, lean to
Shelter, rudimentary: tent
Shelter, shady: bowers, gazebo
Shelter, twig: nest
Shelter, wayside: spital, lazaretto
Sheltered place, in a: alee
Sheltered promenade: stoa
Sheltered side: lee, alee
Sheltered spot: cove
Shelves, on the: unsold
Shepard's workplace: lea
Sherbets: ices
Sheridan, Ann: actress
Sherlock Holmes's address: Baker Street
Sherlock Holmes's creator: Doyle
Sherlock's find: clue
Sherlock's friend: Watson
Sherpa's sighting: yeti
Sherry, golden: oloroso
Sherwood Forest denizen: Robin Hood
Shiaparelli, Elsa: designer
Shield center: umbo
Shift or cope: fend
Shift, type of: late, night, day, second
Shilly-shally: vacillate, waver
Shim or wedge: cotter
Shin neighbor: ankle, knee, fibula
Shindig, well-publicized: bash
Shine brightly: radiate
Shine lustrously: glisten
Shine source: sun
Shining: agleam
Shinto temple: sha
Shiny: glossy
Shiny, not: matte, vapid, flat
Shiotz, aksel: tenor
Ship, aboard: asea
Ship, any: she
Ship attendant: steward
Ship, couples only: ark
Ship deck: poop
Ship deserter: rat
Ship direction: astern
Ship, 1492: Nina
Ship, fuel carrying: coaler, oiler
Ship girder: keelson
Ship kitchen: galley
Ship part: prow
Ship, rusted out: hulk
Ship-shaped clocks: nef
Ship sinker: berg, ice berg
Ship spar, end of: yard arm
Ship tilt: list
Ship to "remember": the Maine
Ship-to-shore vehicle: amtrac
Ship, Valdez: oiler
Ship worm: teredo, teredinidae
Ship wreckage: flotsam
Shipboard quaff: grog

Shipboard romances: idylls
Shipment: load
Shipping ban: blockade
Shipping lane: seaway
Shipping means: rail, ship, air, truck
Shipping stop: sea port
Ship's base: home port
Ship's boat: dinghy
Ship's boom: spar
Ship's canvas: try sail
Ship's clerk: purser
Ship's company: crew
Ship's crew: sailors, tars
Ship's curved planking: svy
Ship's deck: poop
Ships, fleet of: armada, argosi
Ship's load: cargo
Ship's lowest deck: orlop
Ship's need: lift raft
Ship's officer: purser, ens, captain
Ship's pole: mast, spar
Ship's prow: bow
Ship's refuge: port
Ship's rope: vang
Ship's tiller: helm
Ship's unloading site: wharvies
Ship's with lateen sails: tartans
Shipshape: neat, snug, tidy, trig, trim, orderly
Shipworm: teredo, teredinidae
Shire, Talia: actress
Shirks: slacks, neglects
Shirt or blouse: top
Shirt, stuffed: prig, prude
Shirt-maker's cotton: pima
Shirts, stuffed: prigs, prudes
Shish kebab holder: skewer
Shiva believer: hun
Shiva devotee: hindu
Shiva's consort: devi, diva, wife: kali
Shivering fit: ague
Shivers, the: ague
Shivery comments: brr
Shivery feeling: ague
Shoat's (piglets) home: sty
Shock, displaying: agape
Shock, emotional: trauma
Shock, nasty: jolt
Shock, sudden: jolt
Shock to the system: trauma
Shock, type of: culture
Shockers, sinuous: eels
Shocking: outre
Shocks: zaps
Shoe box word: size
Shoe lace tip: aiglets, aglets
Shoe, lady's: flat, heel, wedgie
Shoe part: vamp
Shoe repair item: heel tap
Shoe saver: tap
Shoe shade, popular: bone
Shoe, soft: moc
Shoe strip: welt
Shoe style: wedgie
Shoe uppers: vamps

Shoe with fringed lace: gillie
Shoe, woman's: flat, heel, wedgie
Shoemaker, Willie: jockey
Shoes, ankle high: gaiter
Shoes, beaded: moc
Shoes, dressy: heels
Shoes, heavy: brogan
Shoes, low-cut sports: gillies
Shoes, slotted: penny loafers
Shoes without high heels: flats
Shoestring: lace
Shoe-wiping place: mat, doormat
Shogun apparel: obi
Shogun capital: Edo
Shogun spy: ninja
Shogun warrior: ninja, samurai
Shogun yes: hai
Shook hands: met
Shoot forth: erupt
Shoot the breeze: gab, chat
Shooter, skilled: sniper
Shooting star: meteor
Shoots, new: sprigs, sprouts
Shop: mart
Shop class gripper: vice
Shop talk: argot
Shoppe, adjective for: olde
Shopper, comparison: pricer
Shopper, recreational: browser
Shopper's bag: tote
Shopping center: plaza, mall
Shopping excursion: spree
Shore bird: rael, stilt
Shore, Dinah: music
Shore eagle: ern
Shore event: ebb tide
Shore house: cottage
Shore scuttles: sand crabs
Shore up: brace
Short airplane trip: hop
Short article: item
Short break: breather
Short distance: step
Shortfall: need, deficit
Short flight: hop
Short haircut: bob
Short, heavy clubs: cudgels
Short-lived: ephemeral
Short moral stories: parables
Short operatic melody: arietta
Short pasta: ziti
Short play: skit
Short shot deliverer: hypo
Short sock: anklet
Short solo: arietta
Short stay: visit
Short story, final: obit.
Short term: interim
Short termer: temp
Short time, for a: awhile
Short time, in a: anon
Shortage solver: ATM
Shorten: cut, bob, abridge, alter
Shorten a skirt: rehem

Shorten an article: edit
Shorten, as a board: saw off
Shortened proposition: altho
Shortfall: need
Shorthand expert: steno
Shorthand taker: steno
Short-hop providers: air taxis
Short-lived things: ephemera
Short-sheeting a bed: prank
Shortly: anon
Short-spoken: curt, bluff, blunt, brief, terse, abrupt, crusty, snippy
Shortstop's asset: range
Short-tailed lemur: indri
Short-tailed weasel: stoat
Shoshone chief: Washakie, Pocatello
Shoshoneans: Otos
Shostakovich, Dmitry: composer (Russian)
Shot, for short: ammo
Shot one: aced
Shot up: grew
Shotgun sport: skeet, trap, hunting
Shots, small: bbs
Should: ought
Shoulder feathers, fowl's: cape
Shoulder garment: stole
Shoulder gesture: shrug
Shoulder muscles: delts, deltoids
Shoulder ornament: epaulet
Shoulder, road: berm
Shoulder warmers: shawls
Shout from a bridge: ahoy
Shout hurray: cheer
Shout of glee: yippee
Shout of surprise: hah
Shout of triumph: tada
Shout, sneak's: aha
Shouts, derisive: hoots
Shouts forth: blares
Shove off: git, went, left, leave, exit, blow, scoot, scram, split
Shove or push: jostle
Shove, upward: hoist
Shoving match: sumo
Show: exhibit
Show approval: clap
Show backer: angel
Show concern: care
Show disappointment: boo
Show disdain: sneer
Show displeasure: groan
Show distress: grieve
Show evidence: prove
Show fear: pale
Show flexibility: adapt, bend
Show gratitude to: thank
Show grief: sob
Show how: teach
Show impatience with: snap at
Show me state: Missouri
Show of hands: vote
Show off: brag, pose, flaunt, act big
Show plainly: evince
Show pleasure: smile

Show pride: walk tall
Show reverence: pay homage to
Show, sidewalk: raree
Show signs of life: stir
Show, slide: travelog
Show surprise: react
Show teeth: snarl, smile
Show uncertainty: teeter
Show up for duty: report
Showboater composer: Kern
Showcase: flaunt, parade, cabinet, exhibit
Showdown: duel
Showed attentiveness: sat up
Showed disapproval: sneered
Showed how: taught
Showed off: paraded
Showed the way: led, guided
Shower gift, baby: layette
Shower gel ingredient, often: aloe
Shower mats, like some: nonslip
Shower rooms planks: duckboards
Shower scent: bath oil
Showers, like some: tiled
Showers with love: adores
Showing expertise: adept
Showing good judgment: level-headed
Showing no emotion: stoic
Showing profound respect: reverent
Show-offs, of a sort: pedants
Shows contempt for: sneers at
Shows to be true: proves
Showtime rival: HBO
Showy feather: plume
Shredded cheese: grated
Shrek, for one: ogre
Shreve, Anita: author
Shrewd, more: slier
Shrewdly: cagily
Shrewdness: acumen
Shrill insect: cicada
Shrimp: prawn
Shrimp butter: nantua
Shrimp dish: scampi
Shrimp, tiny: krill
Shrine city in Iran: Meshed
Shrine, historic: Alamo
Shrink back in fear: cringe
Shrinkage, to a retailer: thief
Shrinking sea of Kazakhstan: Aral
Shrink's reply: I see
Shriver, Pam: tennis
Shrovetide dish: blini
Shroyer spin-off: enos
Shucked corn: husked
Feng shui
Shula, Don: coach NFL
Shut noisily: slam
Shut-down, end of: reopen
Shuteye session: nap
Shutterbug buy: film
Shuttle complement: crew
Shuttle course: orbit
Shy: coy
Shy of a full deck: loco, nuts

Shy, playfully: coy
Si (french): oui
Siam governess: Anna
Siamese native: Thai
Siamese now: Thai
Siamese set-to: cat fight
Siamese twin: adnate
Siamese visitor: Anna
Sibelius, Jean: composer
Siberian native: Kets
Siberian range: Ural (mnts)
Siberian treeless tract: steppe
Sibilants, suffers through: lisps
Sibilate: lisp, hiss
Sibilation, unconventional: lisp
Sibyl: oracle
Sibyl's deck: tarot
Sicily erupter: Etna
Sicilian attraction: Etna
Sicilian hothead: Etna
Sicilian landmark: Etna
Sicilian resort city: Etna
Sick & tired: fed up
Sickle-shaped: falcate
Sickly color: sallow
Side by side: compare, abreast, apposed
Side by side, place: appose
Side squared, for a square: area
Side step: skirt, evade
Sidelong: askance
Sidewalk show: raree
Sideways: askance, laterally
Sideways, go: slue
Siding: weatherboard
Sidle past: edge
Siegfried Sassoon: poet
Siegmeister, Elie: composer
Sierra Club founder: John Muir
Sierra _____: Ancha, Leone, Madre, Blanca, Nevada
Sierra Nevada lake: Tahoe
Sieved pulp: puree
Siezes the throne: usurps
Sif's husband: Thor
Sift through: cull
Sigh, contented: aah
Sigh or murmur: utter
Sighed with delight: aahed
Sight for a psychic: aura
Sight, type of: hind
Sight, unpleasant: eye sore
Sighted: aimed
Sighting, unexplained: UFO
Sights and sounds: stimuli
Sightseeing, go: tour
Sightseeing trip: tour
Sightseeing vehicle: tour bus
Sigma follower: tau
"Rho sigma"
Sigmoret, Simone: actor
Sigmund's daughter: Anna
Sign: omen, placard
Sign, bad: omen
Sign of a good reception: open arms

Sign of boredom: yawn
Sign of disuse: rust
Sign of impact: dent
Sign of late summer: virgo
Sign of the future: omen
Sign off on: OK, okay
Sign on: enlist, join
Sign or support: endorse
Sign, red: stop
Sign, secret: wink
Sign, the first: Aries
Sign up for: take, enroll, enlist
Signal fire: beacon
Signal to stop: wave down, wave off
Signature song: theme
Signet: official seal, seal
Signify: denote, mean
Signing ape: Koko
Signoff, letter: regards
Sign-off, southwestern: adios
Signora peron: isabel
Signpost information: mile, miles
Signs of life, show: stir
Signs off on: OKs, okays
Signs up: enlists, joins
Sigourney sequel: Aliens
Sigurd's steed: Grani
Sigyn's husband: Loki
Sikorsky, Igor
Silence: gag
Silence, sudden: hush
Silent acting, bit of: charade
Silent actor: mime
Silent flowers: mums
Silent flyer: eagle
Silent music: tacitSilent one: clam
Silent performer: mime
Silent symbol: clam
Silently, not: aloud
Silents are seen, where: nickelodeon
Silica mineral: quartz, opal, sand
Silicon valley city: Palo Alto
Silk fabric, thin: pangee, gros
Silk netting: tulle
Silk or satin: textile
Silk, watered: moire
Silk worm, assam: eria, eri
Silk-fiber binder: sericin
Silky envelope: cocoon
Silky sound: swish
Sillier: zanier
Silliness: bosh
Sills, (Beverly) solos: arias
Silly: inane, foolish
Silly comedy: farce
Silly talk: drivel
Silly trick: antic
Silo resident: ABM, CBM
Silt deposit: delta
Silver, old style: argent
Silver, Ron: actor
Silver salmon: coho
Silver type: sterling
Silverheels (Jay) role: Tonto

Silverstein, Shel: author,
Silver-tongued: glib, fluent, voluble
Silver-white element: cobalt
Silvery fish: shad
Silvery metal: nickel
Silvery (poetic): argent
Sim, Alistair: actor
Simba's retreat: den
Simeon's father: Jacob
    mother: Leah
    sons: Ohad, Nemuel
Simian: ape, chimp, lemur, loris, baboon,
    monkey, primate
Similar in kind: akin
Simile center: asa
Simious creature: ape
Simmer, make: heat
Simon, Neil: playwrite
Simone's summer: ete
Simon's brother: Jesus, Andrew
    father: Jonah
    new name: Peter
    son: Judas, Rufus, Alexander
Simoom: Samiel, dusty wind, wind
Simple: mere
Simple organism: monad
Simple saying: adage
Simpleton: noddy, oaf
Simplicity: easiness
Simply: mere
Simply awful: horrid
Simpson, Adele: designer
Simpson kid: Lisa
Simpson, Lisa: sax (music)
Simpson's bartender: Moe
Simpson's bus driver: Otto
Simultaneous firearm discharge: salvo
Sinatra's home town: Hoboken, NJ
Sinbad's bird: roc
Sinbad's transport: roc
Sincere, less: phonier
Sincere, was: meant
Sinclair, Upton: writer
Sine qua non: need, must, essential, necessary,
    condition
Sing: troll
Sing at Sing Sing: rat on
Sing in falsetto: yodel
Sing lustily: troll
Sing one's own praise: boast, brag
Sing softly: croon
Sing Swiss-style: yodel
Sing without words: hum
Sing-along, bar: karaoke
Singapore language: Malay
Singer, Lori: actress
Singer, one name: Enya
Singer, sentimental: balladeer
Singing brothers: Ames
Singing club, type of: glee
Singing grp.: octet (8), sextet (6)
Singing sound: tra
Singing syllable: tra
Single attempt: one shot

Single entity: unit
Single, new: exe (ex-spouse)
Single, no more: wed
Single part: unit
Single (pref): mono
Single time, a: once
Single-cell microbe: monad
Single-file: tandem
Single-handed: alone
Single-helix molecule: rna
Single-masted sailing vessel: cutter
Single-minded: rigid, dogged, driven, intent,
    adamant, devoted
Single-strand molecule: rna
Singletons: ones
Singly: one by one
Singular, most: rarest
Sinkhole: dip, sag, bowl, basin, hollow,
    cesspool, concavity
Sinuous shocker: eel
Siouan language: Dakota
Siouan speakers, certain: Osages
Sioux dwelling: tepee
Sioux tribe subdivision: brule
Sipped slowly: nursed
Sir Anthony of Avon: Eden
Sir counterpart: maam
Sir, in Delhi: Sahib
Sir opposite: madam
Sire: beget
Siren: vixen, vamp
Siren, alluring: lorelei
Siren, early: bara
Siren song: lure, decoy, snare, come on, wail
Siskel, Gene: critic
"Sister Act" role: nun
Sisters' superior: abbesses
Sistine Chapel artwork: fresco
Sit around: loaf
Sit on eggs: brood
Sitar accompaniment: tabla, (hand drums)
Sitar, kind of: lutes, ravi
Sitcom after-life: reruns
Sitcom ET: alf,
Sitcom planet: Ork
Sitcom waitress: Flo
Sit-down affair: meal
Sit-down occasion: meal
Sit-in, for instance: protest
Sits haphazardly: sprawls
Sitter's bane: brat, imp
Sitter's handful: brat, imp
Sitting Bull's tribe: Sioux
Sitting room: parlor
Sitting room, woman's: boudoir
In situ: (as found)
Six pointer: TD
Six to an inning: outs
Six-sided state: Utah
16.5 feet: rod
Sixth notes: las
Sixties radical: yippie
Sized up: cased
Skaldic work: edda

Skate on thin ice: borrow trouble
Skaters:
    Babilonia, Tai
    Baiul, Oksana
    Blair, Bonnie
    Boitano, Brian
    Fratianne, Linda
    Galindo, Rudy
    Henie, Sonja
    Heiden, Eric
    Ito, Midori
    Lipinski, Tara
    Rodnina, Irina
    Thomas, Debi
    Slutskaya, Irina
Skater's jump: lutz
Skating venue: rink
Skedaddle: vamoose, flee, scat
Skein of yarn: hank
Skeleton site: closet
Skeleton, walking: bag of bones
Skelter head: helter
Skeptic or cynic attachment: ism
Skeptical about: doubtful
Skeptical one: cynic
Skepticism: disbelief
Sketch: limn, draw
Sketch, tentative: draft
Sketcher's need: eraser, pad
Skewer meat: kebab, kabob
Skewer treat: kebab, kabob
Ski bump: mogul
Ski event: alpine
Ski fastener: binding
Ski jacket: parka
Ski lift: t-bar
Ski run: schuss
Ski run, fast: schuss
Ski slope bump: mogul
Ski turns: telemarks
Skid row garbs: rags
Skid row woe: dts
Skidded: slued
Skiers:moe, tommy
Skiers social hour: apres-ski
Skies over sorrento: cieli
Skiff, flat bottom: sampan
Skiff movers: oars
Skiing style: alpine
Skilled: apt, adroit
Skilled at, become: master
Skilled ones: adepts
Skilled persons: adepts
Skilled sailor: seadog
Skillful, more: adepter
Skills, special: knacks
Skim along: scud
Skimps, really: ekes
Skimpy top: tube
Skin: dermis
Skin ailment: acne, wen, mange
Skin bubble: blisters
Skin diving, did: snorkeled
Skin problem, itchy: tinea (ringworm)

Skin ridge: welt
Skin softener: lotion, bath oil, emollient
Skin spot (small): speckle, freckle
Skin-deep: shallow, trivial, superficial
Skinner, Cornelia Otis
Skinny, the: info, dirt
Skip a class: cut
Skip a turn: pass
Skip past: omit
Skip stones on water: dap
Skipjack: boat, fish, tuna, bluefish, sailboat
Skipper's bellow: avast
Skipper's place: helm
Skirl, they: pipers
Skirmish: fray
Skirt, calf-length: midi
Skirt, divided: culotte, culottes
Skirt feature: pleat
Skirt, kind of: dirndl
Skirt panel: gore
Skirt slit: vent
Skirt style: A-line
Skirts of tulle: tutu
Skit show: revue
Skittle or potsy, e.g.: game
Skosh: tad
Skulk about: lurk, sneak
Skulks: lurks
Skulks around: sneaks, lurks
Skull cap: beanie, tam
Skunk Le Pew: Pepé
Skunk-like animal: civet
Sky arch: firmament
Sky chart: zodiac
Sky, clear: ether
Sky color: azure
Sky hunter: Orion
Sky light: moon,
Sky lit interiors: atria
Sky pad: aerie, nest
Sky tint: azure, cerulean
Sky blue: azure, cerulean
Skydive: jump
Skyrocket: zoom, jump
Skyscraper feature: air shaft
Skyscraper part: girder
Skywalker's father: Vader
Skywalker's guru: Yoda
Skywalker's (Luke) sister: Leia
Slack, gives some: loosens
Slacked off: abated, eased
Slacken off: abate, ease
Slacker: idler
Slack-jawed: agape
Slacks material: chino
Slacks, tan: khakis
Slalom maneuver: ess
Slalom obstacle: gate
Slam dunk: cinch, setup, shoo-in, safe
        bet, sure thing
Slammer: jail, pen
Slander: asperse, malign
Slander kin: libel
Slang: argot

Slangy lady: dame
Slanted type: italic
Slanting: diagonal, inclining
Slap, deserving a: fresh
Slap on hastily: daub
Slap together: make
Slapdash: hit or miss, hasty, messy,
        random, sloppy, cursory
Slapped together: made
Slapstick missile: pie
Slat: lath
Slate: shale
Slaughter, widespread: carnage
Slaughterhouse: abattoir
Slaughterhouse waste: offal
Slav: Croatian, Serb
Slave: bondsman
Slave away: drudge
Slave Dred Scott
Slave galley tool: oar
Slavery: thrall
Sledgehammer: maul
Sleep: shut-eye
Sleep, deep: sopor, coma
Sleep like a log
Sleep on it, you may: sheet
Sleep phenomenon: REM
Sleep, restlessly: toss
Sleep stage: REM
Sleeper, den: sofa bed, daybed
Sleeper with sound effects: snorer
Sleepwalker: somnambulist
Sleepy, for one: dwarf
Sleepy, get: drowse
Sleepy, looks: nods, yawns
Sleepy, was: yawned
Sleet, covered with: icy
Sleeve, like some: set in
Sleeve, roomy: raglan
Sleeve, type of: dolman
Sleeveless apron-like dress: pinny
Sleeveless garment: vest
Slender, graceful women: sylphs
Slept like a log
Sleuth, orchid-loving: Wolfe
Sleuth's lead: clue
Slice: cut
Slice and dice: mince
Slice of cake: wedge
Slick: facile
Slick, in conversation: glib
Slick talker's glib
Slicker: oilier
City slicker
Slicker's place: city
Slid down: fell
Slide show: travelogue
Slide sideways: slue
Slide sight: ameba, amoeba
Slight amount: trace
Slightly drunk: tipsy
Slim: svelte
Slim winning margin: hair, nose
Slime: crude

Sliminess: ooziness
Sling mud at: smear, asperse
Slinkies: coils
Slip away, as support: erode
Slip back: lapse
Slip by: elapse
Slip into: don
Slip on: don
Slip one over on someone: fool
Slip setting: marina, pier
Slipknot, large: noose
Slipper, bedroom: mule
Slipper, kind of: mule
Slipperiness symbol: eel
Slippers, lounging: mules
Slippery, made: greased
Slippery objects: peels
Slips away: escapes
Slips up: errs
Slither actor: Caan
Slithery squeezer: boa
Slob-like: oafish
Sloop spar: mast
Slope contraption: T-bar
Slope, gentle: rise
Slope, gradually: glacio
Slope of a rampart: escarp
Slope, steep: escarp
Slopping center: sty
Sloppy landing sound: splat
Slot for letters: drop-box
Sloth: sin
Sloth, like a: torpid
Sloth, two-toed: unau
Sloth, three-toed: ais
Slot-machine fruit: lemon
Slotted shoes: penny loafers
Slouch: loll, sag
Slovenly place: sty
"Slow as molasses"
Slow, annoyingly: poky, plod
Slow burn, do a: seethe
Slow lane, the: right
Slow mover: sloth
Slow moving animal: sloth
Slow moving commodious craft: ark
Slow oven: warm
Slow route: detour
Slow tempo: adagio, lento
Slow train: local
Slow-cooking creation: stew
Slow down: brake, retard, let up
Slower than andante: adagio
Slowly, to Mehta: lento
Slowly, went: edged
Slowness, symbol of: snail
Slow-witted: obtuse
Slow-witted one: dunce
Slug, biblically: smite
Slug ending: fest
Sluggard: idler
Sluggish: logy
Slug's relative: snail
Slumbered: slept

Slumbering: asleep
Slumber wear: pj's
Slumberland, visit: doze,
Slumgullion or goulash: stew, meat stew
Slung mud: smeared
Slur over: elide
Slur together: blend, elide
Slurred over (syllables): elided, elision
Slushy, turn: thaw
Slutskaya, Irina: skater
Sly tactic: ruse
Sly trick: wile
Slyly disparaging: snide
Slyly malicious: snide
Small accident: mishap
Small amount: trace, dab
Small amount of straw: wisp
Small and pretty: mignon
Small, as a town: one-horse
Small attic: garret
Small axe: hatchet
Small barrel: keg
Small bottle: vial
Small bus: jitney
Small business magazine: Inc
Small case for a lady: etui
Small cave: grotto
Small combo: trio
Small dam: weir
Small deer: napu
Small drink portions: drams
Small finch: linnet
Small fry: pan fish
Small gift: treat
Small hole: eyelet, slit
Small hotel: inn
Small, in Dogpatch: lil
Small inlet: ria, cove
Small island: eyot, ait, islet
Small key: islet
Small mass: wad
Small matter: atom
Small mountain lake: tarn
Small natural hill: knoll
Small organism: zoa
Small ornamental knobs: knops
Small part: cameo
Small penguins: adelies
Small person: pigmy
Small piece: snip
Small, prefix for: micro
Small progress, so to speak: dent
Small quantity: iota, mite, drop
Small salmon: coho
Small shot: dram
Small shoot: sprig
Small silvery fish: smelt
Small space: areola
Small sphere: globule
Small stove: Etna
Small style: nattiness
Small talk, make: chat
Small time: rinky dink
Small tower: turret

Small urban plaza: mini-park
Small, very: micro
Small wave: ripple
Small wind instrument: ocarina
Small woodlot: copse
Smaller than mini: micro
Smaller than small: teensy
Smallest amount: least
Smallest number: fewest
Smart aleck: show-off, wise guy,
    wiseacre, know-it-all
Smart, get: wise up
Smart group: Mensa
Smart remark: quip
Smart set: elect, elite, bon ton, gentry
Smart, unusually: apt
Smash into: ram
Smeared: daubed
"Smell a rat"
Smell, good: aroma
Smell, savory: aroma
Smelly: olid
Smelter refuse: dross, slag
Smelter input: ore
Smelting residue: slag
Smelting waste: slag
Smidgen: iota, tad
Smile broadly: beam
Smile, conceited: smirk
Smile, nasty: smirk
Smile of contempt: sneer
Smile, toothy: grin
Smile widely: grin
Smirk's kin: leer
Smirnoff rival, informally: stolid
Smith, Adam: economist
Smith, Alexis: actress
Smith, Bessie: blues singer
Smithy work, did: shod
Smithy's block: anvil
Smog Monster: Godzilla foe
Smoke, billows: plumes
Smoke detector output: ions
Smoke or mist: vapor
Smoke, thin streak of: wisp
Smoke trail: wisp,
Smoked herring: kipper
Smoked meats: hams
Smoked salmon: Nova
Smokehouse hangers: hams
Smoker or diner: car
Smoker's smoke: pipe
Smoking evidence: gun
"Smoking or non"
Smooth and level: even
Smooth and silky: sleek
Smooth brandy, like: aged
Smooth feather: preen
Smooth, make: iron, sand
Smooth musical transition: segue
Smooth operator singer: Sade
Smooth over, in a way: iron
Smooth pated: bald
Smooth spoken: glib

Smooth style: legato
Smooth talking: glib
Smooth the way: ease
Smooth, too: oily
Smooth transition, makes a: segues
Smoothly courteous: urbane
Smooth-tongued: glib
Smorgasbord: hash, olio, buffet, jumble
Smudge: smear, blot, blur
Smug grin: smirk,
Smug, looked: smirked
Smyrna chambers: oda
Snack attack, late night: raid
Snack, cheesy: nacho
Snack, had a: noshed
Snack, more than a: meal
Snack, nutritious: granola bar
Snag: stumbling block
Snag or rip: jag
Snail mail alternative: fax, e-mail
Snail-paced: poky, slow
Snail's trail: slime
Snake, African: mamba
Snake charmers wear: turban
Snake dance tribe: Hopi
Snake, deadly: mamba
Snake eyes: aces
Snake, moved like a: slithered
Snake: pref.: ophi, ophis
Snake River location: ida, idaho
Snake shape: ess
Snake toxin: venom
Snake, tree: lora
Snaked around: wound
Snake-haired woman myth: Medusa
Snakeless land: Eire
Snakes do it: shed
Snap judgment, often: first impression
Snap, type of: ginger
Snap shot: pic, photo
Snapshots, many: close-ups
Snazzy: chic
Sneak a look: peek
Sneak attack: ambush
Sneaking suspicion: idea
Sneak's shout: aha
Sneeze inducer: allergy
Sneezy's pal: Dopey
Snellen chart procedure: eye test
Snert's master: Hagar
Snick and snee
Sniffed at: nosed
Sniggler's pursuit: eels
Snipe's abode: marsh
Snippets, dramatic: scenes
Snippets for Fido: orts
Snippy retorts, contents of: sass
Snit, put in a: miff
Snitch: filch
Sno-cone: summer treat
Snob, often: egoist
Snook: robalo
Snooker shot: masse
Snooping about: nosy

Snoopy: beagle
Snooze, afternoon: siesta
Snooze, spot for a: sofa
Snoozing, still: abed
Snorkeler's sight: coral
Snorri Sturluson opus: Edda
Snort: nip
Snort, derisive: hah, bah
Snort of disgust: ugh, bah
Snort with glee: chortle
Snout-nosed animal: tapir
Snouted mammal: aardvark
Snow apple: mushroom
Snow boot: pac
Snow boot liner: felt
Snow field, alpine: neve
Snow, granular: firn
Snow in scotland: sna
Snow, of: nival
Snow particles: pellets, flakes
Snow ride: ski mobile, snow mobile
Snow shelter: igloo
Snow veggie: pea
Snow White's sister: Rose Red
Snows or gulls: dupes
Snug, very: tight
Snugger: cozier, tighter
Snugly warm: toasty
Snugly warm, more: homier
Snyder, Jimmy: "The Greek"
Snyder, Tom: tv
So: aha
So far: yet, as yet
So long: ciao
So long (in Soho): ta-ta
So-so, they're: even, odd
"So what": big deal
Soak (flax): ret
Soak in the sun: basks
Soaked in salt water: brined
Soak-up: imbibe
Soap: serial
Soap, bar of: cake
Soap bowl: tureen
Soap box Derby home: Akron
Soap bubbles: suds
Soap opera: drama
Soap plant: amole
Soap serving: ladleful
Soap target: dirt
Soapbox, mount the: orate
Soapbox mounter: orator
Soapstone: steatite
Sobbing: teary
Sobriety org.: MADD
Sobriquet: name
Soccer great, Brazilian: Pelé
Soccer luminary: Pelé,
Soccer players: Mia Hamm, Pelé
Sociable, be: mix
Sociable, least: shyest
Sociable, not: shy
Social asset: poise
Social blunder: faux pas

Social, British: Matei
Social class: caste
Social climber goal: status
Social end: ist, ite, ism
Social entrance: debut
Social equal: peer
Social groups: castes, tribes
Social instability: anomie
Social insect: ant, bee
Social isolation, state of: solitude
Social misfit: nerd, dork
Social mores: ethos
Social peer: equal
Social position: status
Social position or status: caste
Social rank: caste
Social strata: caste
Social stratum: caste
Social studies section: civics
Social type: joiner
Social worker: bee
Socialite: deb
Socially inept one: nerd
Societal guidelines: ethos
Societal square peg: geek
Society: club
Society newcomer: deb
Pillar of society
Sock away: bank, save, stow, cache,
    hoard, stash
Sock filler: toe, foot
Sock holder: garter
Sock hop locale: gym
Sock, short: anklet
Sock, type of: crew, argyle
Socked in: foggy
Socked out: abed
Socks, sort: match
Socrates' birthplace: Athens
    forum: agora
    hangout: agora
    last of: omega
    poison: hemlock
    pupil: Plato
    wife: Xantippe, Xanthippe
Soda can opener: tab
Soda fountain (n. England): spa
Sal soda
Sodium hydroxide: lye
Sodom refugee: Lot
Sofa: divan
Sofa, kind of: sectional
Sofa, popular: sectional
Sofer, Rena: actress
Soft ball company: NERF
Soft cheese: Brie
Soft-coated terrier: wheaten
Soft consonants: lenes
Soft drink name: Coke, Pepsi, Nehi
Soft drink nut: kola
Soft food: pap
Soft, in Solingen: leise
Soft leather: suede, kidskin
Soft palate resonance: snore

Soft shoes: mocs
Soft, silky fleece: alpaca
Soft soggy mixture: glop
Soft to the touch: silken
Soft underfoot: squishy
"Soft watches" artist: Dali
Soft wool: angora, merino
Softball event: out, hit, run
Softball toss: arc, lob
Soften: relent, ease
Soften in temper: relent
Soften up: thaw, melt
Softened: toned down
Softening substance: emollient
Soft felt hat, London: trilby
Softly lit: aglow
Software buyer: user
Software, fix: debug
Software stages: betas
Software theft: piracy
Software, transferred: uploaded
Software version: release
Soggy ground: mud
Soho apartment: flat
Soho co.: ltd.
Soho resident: Londoner
Soho street car: tram
Soil: besmear, stain
Soil, rich: humus
Soil, windblown: loess
Soiree: bash
Solar design, common: sunburst
Solar disk: Aten, Aton
Solar god: Horus
Solar phenomenon: flare
Solar plexus: rete
Solar system model: orrery, planetaria
Solar wind component: ion
Solar-lunar year difference: eleven days
Solar-lunar year differential: epact
'Sold out' letters: SRO(standing room only)
Solders field crew: bears, the bears
Sole amandine
Solemn assent: amen
Solemn ceremony: rite
Solemn, overly: owlish
Solemn promise: vow, oath, word
Solicit brazenly: tout
Solid, become: set
Solid state, leave a: melt
Soliloquy, part of a famous: not
Solitaire: jewel
Solitary: lone
Solitary sorts: loners
Solitude enjoyers: loners, losers
Solo's beloved: Leia
Solo for Caruso: aria
Solo in space: Han
Solo state: stag
Solomon to David: son
Solstice month: Dec.
Solution, inelegant: kludge
Solution, permanent: cure
Solvent of fats: ether

Somalia-born model: iman
Somber evergreen: yew
Sombrero, go with: serape, poncho
Some are double: chins
Some are golden: eagles
Some are liberal: arts
Some exams: mid-term
Some lie about it: age
Some notes: e-mails
Some old rentals: videos
Some pavements: macadams, macadamize
Some peers: earls
Some pranks begin with: dares
Some, to Yvette: des
Some uncertainty: reasonable doubt
Some years back: once, ago, past
Someone prized: gem
Something close to the heart: aorta
Something cons do: time
Something else: other
Something extra: bonus
Something for nothing: free ride
Something given to pacify: sop
Something often bid: adieu
Something on the books: law
Something setaceous: bristle
Something that's struck: pose
Something to cast: ballot, lure, rod, die
Something to check: coat
Something to pump: iron
Sometimes, more than: often
Somewhat: poco, a bit
Somewhat cerulean: bluish
Somewhat liberal: leftish
Sommers, Elke: actress
Son of, Arabic: ibn
Son of Eric the Red: Leif
Son of gun: so and so
Sonar or radar: detectors
Sonar sound: ping
Sondheim's "Into the Woods"
Song like: arioso, lyrical
Song, lively: lilt
Song, half of a: lyrics
Song of joy: paean
Song of praise: ode
Song of triumph: paean
Song or gab ending: fest
Song, romantic: ballad
Song syllable: tra
Song words: lyrics
Songwriter group: ASCAP
Songbird, brownish: phoebe
Sonic bounce: echo
Sonic prefix: ultra
Sonnet: verse, Poe
Sonnet kin: ode
Sonnet, last 6 lines of a: sestet
Sonnet part: sestet, octet
Sonnet stanza: octet
Sonnet writer: poet
Sonnet's coda, Italian: sestet
Sonoma neighbor: Napa

Sonora Indians: Seri
Sonora sandwich: taco
Sonora shawl: serape
Sonora snack: taco, nacho, tamale
Soon: anon
Soon after, very: upon
Soon, to a poet: anon
Sooner state: Oklahoma
Sooner than anon: ere
Sooner than (poet): ere
Soothe: allay, hush
Soothed: lulled
Soothing balm: salve
Soothing phrase, half of a: there
Soothsayers: oracles, augur
Soph or jr: years, yrs.
Sophie to Carlo: wife
Sophie portrayer: Meryl
Sophisticated: urbane
Soprano increase: crescendo
Soprano's piece: aria
Soprano's rendition: aria
Sorbet: ice
Sorbonne season: été (French)
Sorbonne summer: été (French)
Sorcery: icy, magic
Sordid: base
Sorenstam rival: Ochoa (IPGA)
Sorority letter: eta, beta
Sorority member: co-ed
Sorority woman: co-ed
Sorrel: oxalis
Sorrento skies: cieli
Sorrow: regret, rue, woe
Sorrow of yore: ruth
Sorrow sound: moan
Sorrowful exclamation: alas
Sorrowful through loss: bereaved
Sorrowful wail: alas
Sorry for, feel: regret
Sorry, really: rueful
Sorry situation: ills
Sort of: in a way
Sort of order: tall
Sort of performance: subpar
Sort or type: ilk
Sorts: types
Sorvino, Mira: actress
So that's it: oho
SOS response: help, aid
Sot's involuntary sound: hic
Sotto voce: soft voice
"Sou wester"
Souchong: tea
Souffle ingredient: egg
Souffle-like: eggy
Sound: sonance, hale
Sound and healthy: hale
Sound defeat: rout
Sound from two directions: stereo
Sound, furtive: psst
Sound, impolite: burp
Sound, inquiring: ehs
Sound, makes a: utters

Sound, menacing: grr
Sound, of: tonal
Sound of admonition: tsk
Sound of amusement: tehee
Sound of annoyance: tut
Sound of body: hale
Sound of deep thought: hmm
Sound of derision: snort
Sound of disapproval: boo, Bronx cheer
Sound of recognition: ahs
Sound of relief: phew
Sound of the surf: rote
Sound of the tone: beep
Sound, quality of: aureole
Sound, repetitious: echo
Sound, séance: rap
Sound thinking: logic
Soundtrack: audio
Soundtrack (add): dub
Sound units: bels
Sound, unwanted: noise
Sound upstairs: sane
Sound wistful: sigh
Sounded: pealed
Soundness of mind: sanity
Sound off: orate
Soup: won ton
Soup container: tureen
Soup dish: tureen
Soup du jour
Soup holder: cup, bowl, tin can
Soup ingredient: leeks
Soup, kind of: lentil
Soup legumes: lentils
Soup or salad: course
Soup server: tureen
Soup serving bowl: tureen
Soup, Spanish: sopa
Soup, thin: broth
Soup, thin: puree
Soup type: lentil, barley
Sourball, like a: tart
Sour cream additive: chive
Sour cream creation: dip
Sourdough strike: ore
Source: font, fount
Source of ambergris: whale
Source of cash: ATM
Source of funds, seniors: IRAs
Source of illegitimate income: scam
Source or much family friction: in-law
Source of pany leche: tienda
Source of ruin: nemeses
Sousaphone kin: tuba
South African artiodactyls mammal: llama
South African Dutch: Taal, Boer
South African people: Xhosa
South African village: Adar, Stad
South American capital: La Paz
South American knife: machete
South American plains: pampas, llanos
South American range: Andes
South American rodent: paca, agouti
South American weapon: bola

South Bend team: Irish
South forty unit: acre
South Korea capital: Seoul
South Pacific island group: Samoa
South Pacific region: Oceania
South Sea locale: Fiji
South Sea's staple: poi
South Sea's starch: taro
South Wales, New capital: Sydney
Southeast Asia: Lao, Laos
Southern beauty: belle
Southern bread: pone
Southern constellation: Arg
Southern India native: Tamil
Southern vine: kudzu
South-of-the border cheers: oles
Southwest art colony: Taos
Southwest art mecca: Taos
Southwest cuisine: Tex-Mex
Southwest desert: Sonora
Southwest stewpot: olla
Southwest tribe: Paiute
Southwestern homes: adobes
Southwestern native: Apache, Ute
Southwestern resort: Taos
Southwestern sign-off: adios
Souvenir buy: T-shirt
Souvenirs: curios
Sovereignty: rule
Soviet labor camp: gulag
Soviet news agency: Tass
Soviet newspaper: Pravda
Soviet space station: Mir
Soviet symbol: red star
Sow bug or gribble, e.g.: isopod
Soy product: tofu
Spa amenity: hot tub
Spa facility: sauna
Spa hot spot: sauna
Spa, Lake Geneva: Avian
Spa or syndrome: China
Space: ether
Space beginning: aero
Space between Botts' dots: lane
Space, blank: gap
Spacecraft rockets: retro
Spacecraft, unmanned: drone
Spacecraft, U.S.: Apollo
Space heater: sun
Space lead-in: aero
Space mission, deep: probe
Space, poetically: ether
Space probes: orbiters
Space race acronym: NASA
Space shuttle path: orbit
Space simian: Enos
Space station docking: link-up
Space station, former: Skylab
Space station, leave the: undock
Space telescope: Hubble
Space-time continuum
Space traveler: comet
Space, unfilled: void, blank
Space vehicle: Apollo, LEM

Spacewalk (to Nasa): EVA
Space width: ens
Spacecraft, U.S.: Apollo
Spacek, Sissy: actress
Space-time continuum
Spacious: airy
Spacious window: oriel
Spade (detective): Sam
Spades: suit
Spades in bridge: major suit
Spaghetti seasoner: herb
Spain & Portugal: Iberia
Spain "hot air": solano
Spain rain: agua
Spain, region of ne: Aragon
Spain's peninsula: Iberia
Span in years: age
Span of time: period, era, eon
Spandex fiber: Lycra
Spaniard or Italian: Latino
Spanish abode: casa
Spanish-American shawl: serape
Spanish appetizer: tara
Spanish "are": esta
Spanish area: Aragon
Spanish article: los, una, las
Spanish architect: Sert
Spanish attack: asaltar
Spanish aunt: tia
Spanish boy: niño
Spanish bravo: ole
Spanish child: nino
Spanish city: Seville, Toledo, Avila
Spanish coin: doubloon, peseta
Spanish "come on": arriba
Spanish "crazy": loco
Spanish dance: bolero, fandango
Spanish day: dia
Spanish direction: este
Spanish epic: Cid
Spanish exit: salida
Spanish explorer: Cortes, Desoto
Spanish "for": por
Spanish for "more": mas
Spanish force of old: armada
Spanish "four seasons": año
Spanish friend: amigo
Spanish gentleman: don, grandee
Spanish girl: niña
Spanish gold: oro
Spanish "good": bueno
Spanish "guy": hombre
Spanish "Helen": Elena
Spanish hero: el cid, cid
Spanish "hold it": alto
Spanish "hot air": solano
Spanish house: casa
Spanish income: renta
Spanish "is": esta
Spanish king: rey
Spanish "know": sabe
Spanish lady: dona
Spanish legislator: senador
Spanish "love": amor, amore

Spanish "me": mi
Spanish "mlle": srta
Spanish "mom": madre
Spanish month: enero
Spanish "more": mas
Spanish mother: madre
Spanish mouth: baco
Spanish movie theater: cine
Spanish "mrs.": sra
Spanish mud: lodo
Spanish muralist: Sert
Spanish museum: Prado
Spanish noblemen: dons
Spanish "nothing": nada
Spanish "now": ahora
Spanish old kingdom: Aragon
Spanish one: una
Spanish painter: Joan Miro, Dali, Goya,
 Lucientes
Spanish pal: amigo
Spanish part of city: barrio
Spanish "Peter": Pedro
Spanish "please": por favor
Spanish poet: Garcia Lorca
Spanish, Portuguese: Iberian
Spanish priest: padre
Spanish pronoun: esta
Spanish region: Aragon
Spanish restaurant appetizer: tapa
Spanish rice entrée: paella
Spanish romance: amor
Spanish saffron-flavored dish: paela
Spanish serf: helot
Spanish shawl: serape
Spanish "she": ella
Spanish six: seis
Spanish soup: sopa
Spanish speaking area: barrio
Spanish spelunker spot: caverna
Spanish spicy stew: olio
Spanish state: estados
Spanish stream: ria
Spanish sun: sol
Spanish surrealist: Dali, Miro
Spanish "that": esa
Spanish "that girl": esa
Spanish "the": este
Spanish "this": esta
Spanish "three": tres
Spanish title: senor, dona, srta
Spanish "tomorrow": mañana
Spanish "tot": niño
Spanish two: dos
Spanish "ugly": fea
Spanish uncle: tio, senor
Spanish "very": muy
Spanish wave: ola
Spanish "wealthy": rico
Spanish "where": adonde
Spanish wife: senora
Spanish wolf: lobo
Spanish year: año
Spar: mast
Spar, diagonal: sprit

Spare time filler: hobby
Spare tire: paunch
Sparingly, use: eke
Spark coil output: arc
Spark, creative: idea
Sparking rock: flint
Sparkle: vim, pop, pep, flash
Sparkler: gem
Sparkling adornment: diadem
Sparkling vino: asti
Sparkling-wine town: Asti
Spark plug switch: ignition
Sparks, Ned: actor, comic
Spark's resident: Nevadan
Sparse: meager
Sparta site: Laconia
"Spartacus" author: Fast
Spartan governor: harmost
Spartan king: Agis
Spartan music hall: odeon
Spartan serf: helot
Spartan slave: helot
Sparta's instrument: lyre
Spasm of pain: throe
Spawner, upstream: shad, salmon
Speak agitatedly: rant
Speak at length: dilate
Speak back to: sass, lip, dis
Speak formally: orate
Speak irritably: snap
Speak ones mind: opine
Speak pompously: orate
Speak slowly: drawl
Speak to: address
Speak well of: compliment
Speak with involuntary pauses: stammer
Speakeasy risk: raid
Speaker, eloquent: orator
Speaker in Cooperstown: Tris
Speaker, Tris: baseball.
Speaker's digression: aside
Speaker's stand: dais, podium, rostrum
Speaks on the record: raps
Spear: gaff
Spear, fish: gig, trident
Special case: exception
Special delivery?: air drop
Special event: occasion
Special girlfriend: inamorata
Special influence: clout
Special interest group: lobby
Special knack: art
Special province: realm
Special skill: knack, forte
Special talents: knack, forte
Special time in history: era
Specialist: expert
Species group: genera
Specifically: namely
Speck, tiny: iota
Spectacular: epic
Specter: demon, ghost, phantom
Spectrum maker: prism
Speculate recklessly: plunge

Sped: hied
Sped off: hied
Speech, censorious: tirade
Speech copy: text
Speech, eloquent: oratory
Speech opener: intro
Speech, part of: gerund, noun
Speech problem: lisp
Speech, regional: idiom
Speech, wild: rant
Speechless: mum, mute, dumb, awe
Speechless, leave: stun
Speed along: zoom
Speed for Spock: warp
REO Speedwagon
Undue speed: haste
Up to speed
Speeder, write-up a: cite
Speeder's penalty: fine
Speedy: rapid, fast
Speedy gonzales remark: si si
Spell, cold: snap
Spellbound: rapt
Speller's phrase: "as in"
Spelling, Aaron: producer
Spelling error: typo
Spelling, not my: sic
Spelling, like some: var.
Spelunker's find: cavern, cave
Spelunker's haunt: cave
Spelunker's light: lamp
Spelunker's scene: cave
Spelunker's spot - French: caverne
   Latin: caverna
   Spanish: caverna
Spelunking: caving
Spend like crazy: splurge
Spend unwisely: blow
Spending limit: cap
Sphagnum moss: peat
Sphere, tiny: bead
Sphere of action: arena
Sphere of expertise: area
Sphere one moves in: milieu
Sphere, small: globule
Sphere, tiny: bead
Spherule: bead
Sphinx locale: Egypt
Spica locale: Virgo
Spice: mace, cardamom
Spice counterpart: herb
Spice for absinthe: anise
Spice grinder: pestle
Spice, pungent: curry
Spice things up: season
Spiced ade: wassail
Spicy: racy, hot, keen, acute
Spicy cuisine: Creole
Spicy dip: salsa
Spicy meat: salami
Spicy, not: bland, mild
Spicy sauce: salsa
Spicy stew: olla
Spider: arachnid

Spider defense: venom
Spiderman creator: Lee
Spiffy tires: radials
Spike a drink: lace
Spiked the punch: laced
Spiky hairdo style: punk
Spill hot coffee on: scald
Spill over: slop, slosh
Spill the beans: blab, fess up, divulge
Spillane, Mickey: of whodunit
Spin a floating log: birl
Spinach-like plant: orach (goosefoot family)
Spine: comb. Form: rachi, rachio
Spine, sharp: thorn
Spineless cacti: mescals
Spine-tingling: eerie, scary
Spinks, Leon: boxing
Spinneret product: web
Spinning machine part: wharve, pulley
   flywheel
Spinning motion in billiards: English
Spiny anteater: echidna
Spiny tree: greenbark, acacia
Spiral: nebula
Spirally threaded rod: screw, bolt,
Spire ornament: epi
Spirit, Aladdin's lamp: genie
Spirit lamp: Etna
Spirit: soul, elan
Spirit, high: gaiety
Spirit of Russia: vodka
Spirit of the people: ethos
Spirited horse: steed
Spirited session: séance
Spiritedness: elan
Spiritless: amort
Spiritless one: moper
Spirits, bottled: genies
Spirits measure: proof
Spiritual advisors: gurus
Spiritual enlightenment: satori
Spiteful, more: meaner
Spitting image: twin, clone, double,
   ringer, duplicate
Spitz, Mark: swimmer
Splash against: lap
Splash clumsily: slosh
Splash out: slop
Spleen: ire
Splendidly: royally
Splendiferous spread: feast
Splendor: pomp
Spliced, get: wed
Splinter's group: cult, sect
Split apart: sunder, riven, rived
Split city: Reno
Split in-half: bisect, cleave
Split in two: rend, bisect
Split pulse: dal
Split to join: elope
Split up: part
Split with sharp instrument: cleave
Splits: schisms
Splits to unite: elopes

Splotch: mottle, blob
Mr. Spock: Nimoy, vulcan
Mr. Spock's father: Sarek
       friend: McCoy
       mother Amanda
Spock's portrayer: Nimoy
Spode, Joseph: potter
Spoil, didn't: kept
Spoiled: rancid
Spoiler: bane
Spoiling: on dotting
Spoils: loot, booty
Spoils shares: cuts
Spoils taken: loot
Spoke pompously: orated
Spoken: aloud,
Spoken, not: unsaid
Spoken with ease: fluent
Sponge, bath: loofa, loofah
Sponge cloth: ratine
Sponge feature: pore
Sponge off of: bum
Sponge up: absorb, sop
Sponge, vegetable: loofa, loofah
Sponger: leach
Spongy football, type of: NERF
Sponsorship: aegis
Spontaneous remark: ad-lib
Spooky author: Poe
Spool: bobbin
Spoon, use a: stir
Spoon, king size: ladle
Spore production: fern
Sport, heavyweight: sumo
Sport, pushy: sumo
Sport with a mask: epee
Sported: wore
Sporting house: bagnio, brothel, bordello
Sports award: MVP
Sports biggie: home game
Sports coat: blazer
Sports division: league
Sports event, big: bowl game
Sports event, rare: hole-in-one
Sports figure: stat, RBI ERA
Sports group: league, team
Sports honoree: MVP
Sports jacket: blazer
Sports match: bout
Sports palace: arena, stadium
Sports prelims: trials
Sports shoe: gillie
Sports sock: argyle
Sports spot: arena
Sports transaction: trade
Sportscast, like most: live
Sportura watchmaker: Seiko
Sporty vehicle: ute
Sporty wheels: mags
Spot for a snooze: sofa
Spot in the ocean: islet, isle
Spot of light: blip
Spot on the tube: TV ad
Spot or streak: marking

Spot remover: acetone
Spots: espies
Spots between peaks: valleys
Spot's pal: Fido
Spotted, as a horse: pied
Spotted mount: pinto
Spotted rectangle: domino
Spotted saddle horse: appaloosa
Spouse: wife, mate
Spouse's siblings: in-laws
Spouses, some: wives, husbands
Sprain, treated a: iced
Sprawl: lie
Sprawl, kind of: urbane
Sprawl out: loll
Spray: aerosol
Spray dispenser: aerosol
Spray, wind driven: scud
Spread, big: estate, ranch
Spread by rumor: noised
Spread, classy: pates
Spread, creamy, savory: aioli
Spread, ritzy: caviar
Spread sheet contents: data
Spread sheet unit: cell
Spread sparingly: dab
Spread, splendiferous: feast
Spread thick: slather
Spreads on thickly: slathers
Spreads rumors: gossips
Spree: bender, jag
Sprightliness: elan
Sprightly tune: air
Spring: origin, emanate
Spring beer: bock
Spring formal: prom
Spring holiday: Easter
Spring locale: oasis
Spring sign: Aries, robin
Spring up: leap
Spring-like: vernal
Spring lock opener: latchkey
Springs for a vacation: spa
Sprinkle: dot
Sprinkle with flour: dredge
Sprinkled: strewn
Sprinkling: dotting
Sprite: elf
Sprite, mischievous: Puck
Sprite, peri: Persian folklore
Spruce: trim, trig
Spruce up: smarten
Spud masher: ricer
Asti spumante(sparkling wine)
Spun on an axis: gyrated
Spunk, full of: feisty
Spurts: bursts
Spy: infiltrator
Spy communique: code
Spy file: dossier
Spy in hiding: mole
Spy in the sky: satellite
Spy, sort of: mole
Spydom, name in: Mata, Hari

Spyri's heroine: Heidi
Spyri Johanna: writer (Heidi)
Spy's communiqué: code
Squabble: tiff, spat
Squabble, petty: spat
Squad, kind of: riot, vice
Squalid: seedy, dirty, horrid, sordid
Squalid area: slum
Squalid, more: mangier
Squalidness: sleaze
Squander, in slang: blow
Square dance: hoe down
Square dance call: do-si-do
Square dance move: do-si-dos
Square dance music: fiddle
Square dance violin: fiddle
Square footage: area
Square headed fastener: U-nut, nut
Square of glass: pane
Square one, from: anew
Square pegs: misfits
Square pillar: anta
Square things: atone
Square, updated: nerd
Square-built: boxy
Square-rigged vessel: brig
Squares, in St. Cyre: carres
Squares, set of: grid
Square-shaped: boxy
Squash, kind of: acorn
Squash necessity: racket
Squashed circle: oval
Squat: hunker, dumpy
Squawks: noises
Squeal: rat on
Squeal: oinks, tells, pats
Squeeze dry: wring, wrung
Squeeze in: shoehorn
Squeeze oranges: ream
Squeezed: juiced, hugged
Squeezed out: extruded
Squeezer, slithery: boa
Squelch: quash
Squib: item
Squib and sepia: cuttle
Squiggle (señor): tilde
Squint: peer
Squint at: peer,
Squirrel away: hoard, save, stash
Squirrel, female: doe
Squirrel-like monkey: marmoset
Squirter, garage: oil can
Squishy: wet
Sri Lanka coin: rupee
Sri Lanka garment: sari
Srta in Paris: mlle
S.S.# and license: ids
SSS category: a one
St. Benedict's recruits: monks
St. Elmo's fire
St. Francis's town: Assisi
St. Helen's flow: lava
St. Johns, Adela Rogers: writer
St. Mark's home: Venice

St. Moritz sight: alps
St. Peter's sculpture: pieta
St. Petersburg's sister city: Tampa
St. Vincent Millay: Edna
Stabilizer, plane: fin
Stable fare: oat, hay
Stable particle: oat
Stable scion: colt
Stable, type of: livery
Stable worker: ostler, groom, liveryman
Stable youngster: colt, foal
Stables, row of: mews
Staccato opposite: legato
Stack the deck: rig
Stadium access: ramp
Stadium entertainer: organ
Stadium spot, ritzy: sky box
Stadium walkway: ramp
Staff member: aide
Staff notations: rests
Staff, provides: mans
Staff symbols: rests
Stag attendees: he(s), males, guys
Stag's mate: doe
Stage a coup: usurp
Stage award: Obie
Stage backdrop: scenery
Stagecoach robber: outlaw
Stage comments: aside
Stage direction: enter, exit, exeunt
Stage, early: onset
Stage in a procedure: step
Stage light covering: gel
Stage objects: props
Stage of development: phase
Stage production: drama
Stage reading: line
Stage scenery: set
Stage set: décor, scene, scenery, backdrop,
    mise-en-scène
Stage shows: revues
Stage whisper: aside
Staggered: lurched
Stahl, Leslie: TV
Stain: imbrue
Stain or tear: flaw
Stained glass art: mosaic
Stair alternative: ramp
Staircase post: newel
Stalactite site: cave
Stalactite starter: drip
Stale, as bread: moldy, molded
Stalemate: tie
Stalk prey: hunt
Stall, cattle: crib
Stalling, quit: act
Stallone role: Rambo
Stamp backing: gum
Stamp holder: album
Stamp, invoice: paid
Stamp on a stamp: date
Stampede attraction: rodeo
Stampless correspondence: email
Stamps a check, e.g.: enfaces

Stamps, block of: pane
Stamps, roll of: coil
Stand behind: back
Stand for: represent, mean, abide
Stand for a sitting: easel
Stand in line: wait
Stand, in Stuttgart: stehe
Stand, let it: stet
Standard: ideal, norm
Standard charge: base rate
Standard, guiding: ethos
Standard, high: ideal
Standard, lofty: ideal
Standard of behavior: norm
Standard of perfection: ideal
Standard product: oil, gas
Standards: norms
Stand-in: proxy
Stand-in for a file: icon
Standing: rep, rank
Standing on: a top
Standing rule: by law
Standish stand-in: Alden
Standoff: tie, impasse
Standoffish: aloof
Stand-out: mvp
Standout standing: A-one
Standout testee: acer
Stand-up guy: comic
Standup to: defy, faces
Stanley's wife: Stella
Stanza bit: couplet
Staple and clip-on: attach
Staple, south sea: poi
Stapleton, Jean: actress
Star athlete may become: pro
Star (bright) in Lyra: Vega
Star cluster: nebula
Star, exploding: nova
Star, falling: meteor
Star, first-magnitude: Vega
Star in Cygnus: Deneb
"A star is born"
Star location: sky, space
Star of Cygnus: Deneb
Star of westerns: badge
Star on a map: capital
Star seekers: magi
Star shaped: stellate
Star, suddenly bright: nova
Star to look up to: idol
Star turn at scala: aria
Star type: binary
Star, variable: nova
Star Wars creature: Ewok
Star Wars crime lord: Jabba, Joba
Star Wars director: George Lucas
Star Wars furry ally: Ewok
Star Wars gangster: Jabba, Joba
Star Wars knight: Jedi
Star Wars mentor: Yoda
Star Wars princess: Leia
Star Wars rogue: Han Solo
Star Wars villain: Darth Vader

Starbuck order: latte
Starbucks drinks, some: lattes
Starbuck's large: venti
Starch source: taros
Starchy, less: limp
Starchy meal: salep
Starchy root: taro
Star-crossed: doomed, hapless, unlucky,
    ill-fated, luckless
Star-crossed lover: Romeo, Juliet
Star-seeing state: daze
Star-shaped: astral
Stare angrily: glare
Stare at: gaze, gape, gawk
Stare openly: gawk
Stare stupidly: gawk
Stared unpleasantly: leered
Starfish arm: ray
Starfish part: arm, ray
Starlet, to-be: aspiring actress
Starlet's dream: role
Starlet's quest: role
Starling, chatty: myna
Starr, kay: singer
Starr and simpson: bart
Starry eyed: enrapt, dreamy, unreal, utopian,
    ecstatic
Starry prefix: astro
Starry vista: sky
Stars: asterisks
Stars, bright: novae
Stars, where to see: sky
Star seekers: magi
Star shaped: astral
Start, a: toe-holder
Start a match: serve
Start eating: dig-in
Start for center: epi
Start of a bray: hee
Start of a business day: open
Start of a famous boast: veni
Start of a marching cadence: hut
Start of something big: mega
Start slowly: ease into
Start the bidding: open
Start the volley: serve
Start to a carol: adeste
Start to act: inter
Start to fall: tip
Start to finish: in order
Start up again: reopen
Starting gate: post
Starting point: threshold
Starting time: zero time
Startled cry: eek
Star Trek physician: McCoy
Star Trek speed: warp
Star Trek weapon: phaser
Starvation diet: fast,
Stash the bags: stow
Stat equivalent: ASAP
Stat start: rheo
State: aver
State as a price: ask, quote

State categorically: assert
State, first US: Delaware
State further: and
State of decline: ebb
State of misfortune: hardship
State of normlessness: anomie
State of social isolation: solitude
"State of the art: new
State of the union: Idaho
State of vigilance: alert
State of Xenia: Ohio
State-run game: lotto
State, second smallest : Delaware, Del.
State, unkempt: mess,
State with a panhandle: Texas
State with conviction: aver
State with the motto "Industry": Utah
Stated indirectly: implied
Stately dance: pavane
Stately display: pomp
Statement of belief: creed
Statement of obvious fact: truism
Statement, verifiable: fact
Statesman, elder: Cato
Static: inert, noise, at rest
Station, as troops: deploy
Stationed: based
Stationery name: Eaton
Statistical calculation: mode
Statistical ups & downs: trends
Statistician's concern: data
Statistician's fodder: raw data
Statue, huge: colossus
Statue of Liberty creator: Bartholdi
Statuesque model: Iman
Statuette, famed: Oscar
Statuette recess: niche
Status, had: ranked
Status, have lots of: rate
Status, having more: higher
Status, like some: gilt
Status quo:
Statutes: laws, acts
Statutes, unpopular: blue laws
Staub, Rusty: baseball player
Stave off: fend
Stay glued: holds
Stay in hiding: lie low
Stay out of sight: lie low
Stay to the finish: last
Stayed: abided
Stayed at the inn: lodged
Stayed away from: avoided
Stead: lieu
Steadfast: abiding
Steady look: gaze
Steak throwaway: gristle
Steal: cop, rob
Steal software: pirate
Steal steers: rustle
Steam engine inventor: watt
Steamed: irate, a la vapeur
Steamed, really: irate

Steamed up, get: fume
Steamer, food: wok
Steam-turbine wheel: rotor
Steamy spot: sauna
Steed, mighty: Arab, Arabian
Steel, Danielle: writer
Steel, fine: Toledo
Steel or pewter: metal, alloy
Steel plow inventor: Deere
Steel town, big: Gary, Indiana
Steele, Remington: actor
Steen, Jan: Dutch painter
Steep slope: escarp
Steeple top: spire
Steep-sided land formation: mesa
Steep-sided plateau: mesa
Steer, kind of: bum,
Steer or ram: male
Steering wheel, nautical: helm
Steering-system component: tie-rod
Steers: cattle
Steers a ship, one who: helmsman
Stefani, Gwen: vocalist
Stein: mug
Stein, Gertrude: writer
Steinbeck's surname: John
Steinen, Gloria: feminist
"Win Ben Stein's money"
Stele: pillar
"Stella Dallas" author: Olive Higgins Prouty
Stellar hunter: Orion
Stellar sight: comet
Stellar review:rave
Stem, plant: stalk
Stem's from: arises
Steno group: pool
Stentorian: loud
Step down: alit
"Go a step further"
Step in step: March
"Step to the Ganges": Ghat
Step toward recovery: rehab
Stephen King's dog: Cujo
Stephen Vincent Benet
Stepped on: trod
Steppe's wind: bsce,(Russian)
Steps on it: hie, speeds
Steps over a fence: stile
Steps, set of: stile, stairs
Stept, Sam: composer
Stereo, better than: quad
Stereo times two: quad
Stereotypical inducement: carrot
Sterile: barren
Steriod type: anabolic
Stern: austere,
Stern, Howard: radio host
Stern, Isaac: violinist
Stern opposite: prow, stem
Stern's (Isaac) instrument: violin
Sternward: abaft, aft
Sternwheeler: river boat
Sterope's father: Atlas
        mother: Pleione

sister: Pleiades
Stetson-wearing force: RCMP
Steve Austin, like: bionic
Stevedore's job: load, lade, stow
Stevedore's org.: ILA
"Even Steven"
Steven King novel:Cujo
Stevens, Connie: singer
Stevens, Stella: actress
Stew: olio
Stew flavor source: bouillon cube
Stew or coffee: Irish
Stew pot: olla
Stew with a crust: pot pie
Steward, Payne: golfer
Stewed chicken dish: fricassee
Stick, kind of: pogo
Stick in the mud: fogy, foggy, mire
Stick on: attach, affix
Stick out: jut, show
Sticker: seal, bur,
Sticker information: MPG
Sticker, natural: cactus
Sticking point: rub
Stickler for correctness: purist
Stick-on designs: decals
Sticks in the oven: bakes, heats
Sticks on: adds,
Stickum, gymnast's: rosin
Stick-up: rob, heist
Stick up for: help, defend
Sticky: gooey
Sticky attachment: post-it
Sticky situation, be in a: adhere
Sticky soil: clay
Sticky strip: tape
Sticky thing: wicket
Sticky-tongued hopper: toad
Stiff: wooden
Stiff bristle: seta
Stiff drink: belt,
Stiffly decorous: prim
Stifling, not: airy
Still: yet, idle
Still under cover: abed
Stiller, Ben
Still-life subjects: ewers
Stimpy's pal: Ren
Stimulates: whets
Sting a bit: smart
Sting operation item: bug
Stinger, darting: wasp
Stinging arachnid: scorpion
Stings: smarts
Stingy: tight wad, tight fisted, mean
Stipes, Michael grp.: REM
Stipulations: ifs
Stir about violently: thrash
Stir to action: incite
Stir-frying vessel: wok
Stirred up: roused
Stirrup setting: ear, saddle
Stir-up: roust
Stitch loosely: baste

Stitches, be in: laugh
Stitches, in: sewn
Stoat, in winter: ermine
Stock character: steer
Stock ending: ade
Stock figures: ratio
Stock holders: pens
Stock market pessimist: bear
Stock of goods for sale: line
Stock on hand: inv., inventory
Stock option: put, call,
Stock shares, top-rated: white chips
Stockaded African village: kraal
Stockholm airline: SAS
Stockholm suburb: Solna
Stoic founder: Zeno
Stoic philosopher: Cato
Stoker, Bram: writer
Stokely Carmichael, once: Black Panther
Stole: wrap
Stolen goods: loot
Stolen money: pelf
Stomach enzyme: pepsin
Stomach lining: tripe
Stomach, turning: icky
Stomp all over: trod
Stone Age weapon: arrow
Stone, crystal containing: geode
Stone, deep red: garnet
Stone formed below earth's surface:
   hypogene
Stone foundation, irregular: rip rap
Stone, grinding: emery
Stone, heavy: buhr, buhrstone
Stone, hollow: geode
Stone marker: stele
Stone monuments: stele
Stone or atomic: age
Stone or ice: age
Stone pillar, tapering: obelisk
Stone, reddish: jasper
Stone, R. L: writer
Stone, Rosetta: stone tablet
Stone, strike with: pelt
Stone, striped: agate
Stonehenge builders: Celts
Stonehenge frequenters: druids, Celts
Stonehenge priests: druids
Stonehenge worshippers: druids
Stones, banded: agates,
Stones, rock tumbler: agates
Stones throw, within a: near
Stone-sliding sport: curling
Stood in line: waited
Stood petrified: froze
Stool pigeon: fink, rat, narc, decoy,
   snitch, ratfink, tipster.
   narco
Stooped down: bent
Stoops: crouches
Stop: pull up
Stop a train: flag
Stop abruptly: balk
Stop dating: drop

Stop, nautical: avast
Stop running: stall, fail
Stop short: balk
Stop signal: red
Stop talking: hush
Stop, the flow of: stanch
Stop, to a pirate: avast
Stop, to Popeye: avast
Stop wondering, perhaps: ask
Stop working: conk out, retire
Stopped short: balked
Storable sacks: cots
Storage bin: crib, closet, shed
warehouse
Store fodder: insile, insilo
Store in a secret place: stash
Store, kind of: general
Store neatly: file
Store stock: mdse, goods, inventory
Store-bought hair: wig
Stored selfishly: hoarded
Storied mariner: Nemo
Storied painting: Mona Lisa
Stork cousin: ibis
Stork, type of: argala
Storm: tempest
Storm about: raged
Storm cellar need: lantern
Storm drain: sewer
Storm preceder: calm
Storm track: path
Storm trooper: brownshirt
Storm, violent: typhoon
Stormed: attacked
"Stormy Weather" singer: Lena Horne
Storybook bear: papa, mama
Storybook elephant: Babar
Story, continued: serial, series
Story, cover: alibi
Story, funny: joke
Story, handed down: lore
Story, kind of: sob, inside
Story, long: saga, novel
Storyline: plot
Story, never-ending: soap
Story points: nubs
Story, second: sequel
Story teller, famed: O. Henry
Story-telling dance: hula
Story-telling uncle: Remus
Story, top: attic
Story, traditional: myth
Stout: ale
Stout heart, with: bravely
Stout relatives: ales
Stout, Rex: author
Stove chamber: oven
Stove, small: etna
Stove top whistler: kettle
Stove, type of: pot belly
Stovepipe: silk hat
Stovepipe or panama: hat
Stow cargo: steeve, lade, load
Stow lifts: T-bars

Stowe character: topsy, little eva, legree
Stowe footwear: ski boots
Stowe, Harriet Beecher: "Uncle Tom" author
Stradivarius relative: Amati
Straight from the keg: on tap
Straight laced: prim
Straight line: row
Straight out: flatly
Straight up: erect
Straight up, at the bar: neat
Straight-arrow link: as an
Straighten: even, tidy, align, neaten
Straighten a maze: unravel
Straighten up: neaten
Strained, more: tauter
Strainer, bowl-shaped: colander
Strainers & drainers: colanders
Strait, kind of: dire
Strait lace: prim
Strait of Dover, French: Pas-de-Calais
Straits, dire: musical grp.
Straits, kind of: dire
Strand like Crusoe: en-isle
Stranger: eerier
Stranger from a strange land: alien
Stranger to truth: liar
Strap, four-in-hand: rein
Straphanger's lack: seat
Straphanger's train: local
Strapless top: tube
Strasbourg location: Alsace
Strasbourg school: ecole
Stratagem: ruse, trick, ploy, trap,
   wile, feint
Strategy plan, first: plan a
Strategy, preferred: plan a
Stratford's river: Avon
Stratum: bed, layer, seam, tier
Strauss, Levi: clothing designer
Stravinsky, Igor: composer
Straw, bit of: wisp
Straw bundle: sheaf
Straw hat: boater
Straw in the wind: omen
Straw item: hat
Straw pile: sam
Straw, use a: sip
Straw vote: poll
Strawberry tree, wild: arbutus
Straws in the wind: omens
Stray bawler: dogie (calf)
Stray dog: mutt
Stray from the subject: digress
Strays: curs
Stream: rill
Streamlined, more: sleeker
Beale Street Blues
Street car: tram
Street car line: tram way
Street car name: desire
Street, Della penner: Erle
Street, Montreal: rue
Street protest sound: chant
Street salutation: bro

Street sense: smarts
Street show: raree
Street, side: by road
Street talk: slang
Street urchin: gamin, goose egg
Street vernacular: slang
Street wise: hip
Streisand, Barbara: musician
Strength of character: mettle
Strength, lost: enervate
Strength-building place: gym
Stress: pressure
Stressful: taxing
Stretch beside the water: coast, beach,
    shore
Stretch for the stars: limo
Stretch injuriously: sprain
Stretch out, as a book: pad
Stretch the truth: lie
Stretched one's neck: craned
Stretchy clothing material: Lycra
Stretchy cord: bungee
Strict belief: dogma
Strict disciplinarian: ramrod
Strict teacher: pedant
Strictly speaking: literally
Stride, long easy: lope
Strike alternative: ball
Strike caller: ump, union
Strike force: union
Strike, on: idle
Strike out: fan, delete, erase
Strike sharply: smack
Strike to produce a loud noise: whang
Strike with force: ram
Strike worker: scab, mediator
Strikes, announced: umped, umpped
Strikes back: reacts
Strikes occur, where most: lane
Striking effect: éclat
Striking to the eye: bold
String quartet member: cello, viola
String ties: bolos
Stringed instrument: violin, viol, viola zither,
    lute
Stringed instrument (old): oud, lyre, zither
Stringent, not: lax
Strip of land: isthmus, isthmi
Strip of silk, narrow: maniple
Stripe, remove a: demote
Stripe, type of: pin
Stripes blubber: flenses
Stripes of plaster: screed
Strive for: seek
Strive successfully: cope
Strive to win: vie
Strode along: loped
Stroheim, Erich von: actor
Stroke, brilliant: coup
Stroke, gentle: putt,
Strokes, provider of small: putter
Stroll, go for a: amble
Strolled along: ambled
Strong and healthy: hale

Strong, as meat: gamy
Strong as venison: gamy
Strong brown paper: kraft
Strong coffee: expresso, espresso
Strong cotton thread: lisle
Strong emotion: passion
Strong fiber: bast, bast fiber
Strong haulers: oxen
Strong inclination: yen
Strong man of myth: Atlas
Strong opposition: flak
Strong point: virtue, asset
Strong pullers: oxen
Strong smelling: fetid, reek
Strong sort of evidences: DNA
Strong suggestion: urging
Strong suit: forte
Strong tasting: oniony
Strong willed: resolute
Strong-arm: impel, bully, hector, lean on,
    assault, browbeat, bulldoze
Stronger, make: beef up
Strongest tasting: gamiest
Stronghold: fort
Strophitus, for one: mussel, mollusk
Strove: vied
Struck by shock: aghast
Struck silent: awed
Struck with fear: alarmed
Structure: edifice, building
Structure, column: portico
Strug, Kerri: gymnast
Struggle, violent: throe
Strut along: bop
Strut-and-fretter: ham
Struts: preens
Strutter's mate: peahen
Strutting horses: prancers
Stubborn person: bulldog
Stubbornness symbol: mule
Stuck around: bided, stayed
Stuck, gets: jams
Stuck in the mud: mired
Stuck-up person: snob, snoot
Stud placement: lobe (ear)
Stud site: lobe, ear
Student need: desk
Student of Socrates: Plato
Student stat: GPAa
Student worry: finales
Student's choice: major
Studied over: pored
Studies: dens
Studio: atelier
Studio bed, perhaps: futon
Studio renter: artist
Studio, urban: loft
Studious-looking: owlish
Study: den, con, examine
Study, belatedly: cram
Study closely: examine
Study, field of: area
Study hard: cram, pore
Stuffed corn husk:tamale

Stuffed shirts: brigs, prudes
Stuffier: mustier
Stuffing piece: batting
Stuffy scholar: pedant
Stumble across: come upon
Stumble upon: find
Stumbling block: snag
Stun: awe
Stunted: dwarfed, scrubby
Stupefies: dazes
"Stupid is as stupid does"
Stupid one: dunce
Stupid person: oafish, oaf, boob
    goon, dolt, dunce
Sturgis visitor: biker
Sturluson compilation: Edda
Sturm und drang: angst, unease, unrest,
    anxiety, ferment, turmoil
Stutz contemporary: reo
Sty cry: oink
Sty matriarch: sow, pig, hog
Styles ('30s): deco
Styling center: salon
Stylish: retro, chic, mod
Stylish and jaunty: pert
Stylist goop: mousse
Stylist suit brand: Armani
Stymphalides's slayer: Heracles, Hercules
Styne, Jule: composer
Styptic: alum
Styptic pencil target: nick
Styron's revolver: Nat Turner
Styron's Teri Turner
Styx's counterpart: Lethe, Acheron, Cocytu
    locale: Henry
    father: Oceanus
    mother: Tethys
Suave: urban
Suave, too: oily
Sub, downed a: ate
Sub rosa: secretly
Sub seller: deli
Sub station: deli
Sub-artic forest: taiga
Subatomic particle: muon, quarks, pion,
    neutron
Subatomic particle with no charge: neutron
Subdivisions of subdivisions: lots
Subject: topic
Subject for Keats: urn
Subject matter: topic
Submarine: hoagy, U-boat
Submarine commander (fictional): Nemo
Submarine, maybe: hero
Submarine on sonar: blip
Submarine outlet: deli
Submarine part: fin, scope
Submarine system: sonar
Submarine weapon: ICBM, torpedo
Submarine's ears: sonar
Submerged rock or coral ridge: reef
Submission to a record exec: demo
Submissive: docile, meek
Submissive respect: kowtow

Submit: send, obey
Submitted: obeyed, sent
Subordinate bureaucrat: satrap
Subpoena: writ
Subscription term: year
Subsidiary building: annex
Substance, invisible: gas
Substantial: meaty
Substantial, as sums: tidy
Substitute, a poor: ersatz
Substitute for: fill in
Substitute, unnamed: et al
Subtle: deep
Subtle differences: nuances
Subtle distinction: nuance
Subtle emanation: aura
Subtle, not: broad
Subtle quality: aura
Subtle suggestion: hint
Subway: metro
Subway coin: token
Subway coin, illegal: slug
Subway entrance: stile
Subway fare: token
Subway hanger: strap
Subways opposite: els
Succeeded: made it
Succeeds: pans out, pan out
Success, critical: eclat
Successful show: sellout
Successful, very: boffo
Successor, designated: heir
Successor, immediate: heir
Succinct: terse
Succinct, more: shorter
Succor: aid, help, relief
Succotash bean: lima
Succotash ingredient: lima, corn
Succulent, healing: aloe
Suckers, it's for: straw
Sucre locale: Bolivia
Sudan language grp.: Nilotic
Sudden: acute
Sudden fear: alarm
Sudden foray: raid
Sudden impact: jolt
Sudden increase: surge
Sudden inundation: avalanche
Sudden jolts: starts
Sudden numbing dread: pall
Sudden ouster: coup
Sudden outpouring: spate
Sudden shock: jolt
Sudden silence: hush
Sudden thought: idea
Suds, get rid of the: rinse
Sud's opposite: nord
Peggy Sue
Suet-coated: tallowed
Suez Canal outlet: Red Sea
Suffer from: has
Suffer from self-pity: mope
Suffering from phonasthenis: hoarse
Suffering, intense: agony

Suffers through sibilants: lisps
Suffix for poets: aster
Suffix with major: ette
Suffrage: vote
Suffragist, American: Carrie Chapman Catt
Suffuse: imbue
Sufi belief: Islam
Sugar cane product: rum
Sugar in coffee, e.g.: solute
Sugar, kind of: maple
Sugar maker: refinery
Sugar or flour: staple
Sugar partner: spice
Sugar, piece: lump, cube
Sugar substitute: aspartame
Sugar, table: sucrose
Sugar, type: ketose
Sugarbush tree: maple
Sugarcane cutter: bolo
Sugarcane refuse: bagasse
Sugarloaf locale: Rio
Suggest for consideration: posit
Suggest, more than: urge
Suggested retail price: list
Suggestion: advice, idea
Suggestion, indirect: hint
Suggestion, strong: urging
Suggestive look: leer
Suggestive, more: racier
Suicidal emperor: Nero
Suicidal pilot: kamikaze
Suit, black: spade, club
Suit brand, stylish: Armani
Suit, fix a: adapt, tailor, alter
Suit material: serge
"Suit of lights" wearer: bullfighter
Suit pocket item: hanky
Suit, two-piece: bikini
Suit, type of: zoot
Suitable: apt, aptly
Suitable for sprat: fat free
Suitable material: serge
Suitcase: valise, bag
Suite amenity: wet bar
Suite, kind of: bridal
Suitor, another: rival
Sulk angrily: fume
Sulk in silence: pout
Sulking, prone to: moody
Sulky puller: trotter
Sullen: dour
Gilbert & Sullivan
Sultan cousin: emir
Sultan of swat: Babe Ruth
Sultana, for example: raisin
Sultanate citizen: Omani
Sultan's decrees: irades
Sultry west: mae
Sulu portrayer: Takei
Sum and substances: gist
Sumac: poison oak
Sumac souvenir: itch
Sumac, Yma: singer
Sumatra: island

Sumatran region, north: Achin
Sumerian sun god: Utu
Summary (quick): recap
Summaries: synopses
Summer, of: estival
Summer cooler: ade, iced tea, breeze
Summer games org.: IOC
Summer house: gazebo
Indian summer
Summer oppressor: heat
Summer outing: picnic,
Summer stock, did: acted
Summer TV: reruns
Summer top: halter
Summers, Donna: actress
Summon, as courage: muster
Summoned for jury duty: paneled
Summons, discreet: psst
Summons, issue a: cite
Summons to court: cite
Sumptuous: deluxe
Sun, eclipse of the:
Sun: sol, orb
Sun block additive: aloe
Sun Devils school: ASU
Sun don't shine, where the: shade
Sun, in combo: helio
Sun glasses: shades
Sun god, Sumerian: Utu
Sun hat: topee
Sun King: Louis
Sun King's number: XIV
Sun ring: corona
Sun Valley site: Idaho
Sun-baked: arid
Sunbathe: tan
Sundance Kid's girl: Etta
Sundance Kid's wife: Etta
Sunday seating: pews
Sunday wrap-up: amen
Sundial arm: gnomon
Sundries case: etui
Sundry: misc
Sunflower grower: Kansas
Sunflower relative: aster
Sunflower state: Kansas
Sunnism, e.g.: sect
Sunny side?: yolk
Sunnyside up, not: over
Sunrise serenade: aubade
Sunscreen letters: SPF
Sunset state: Oregon
Sunshine state: Florida
Sunspot phenomenon: aurora
Super deluxe: posh
Super market bars: UPCs
Super market wagon: cart
Super, not: okay
Super secret gov. Agency: NSA
Superabundant: riotous
Superficial cyst: wen
Superficial, not at all: deep
Superior, be: excel
Superior's inferior: Erie (lake)

Superlative ending: -est
Superman creator:Jerry Siegel, Joe Shuster
Superman foe: Lex Luthor
Superman's mom: Lara
Superman's symbol: ess
Supernova: star
Superstar: idol
Supervise: oversee
Supervision, kind of: adult
Supine opposite: prone
Supplant: oust
Supplement: add
Supplication end: amen
Supplied laboriously: eked
Supplied the eats: catered
Supply, reserve: store, cache
Support a cause: espouse
Support for a proposal: knee
Support group: staff
Support the economy: spend
Supported: braced
Supporters: fans
Supporting pieces: trusses
Supporting structure: buttress
Suppose: infer
Suppositions: ifs
Suppress completely: quash
Suppressed: pent up
"Supra", opposite of: infra
Supreme Court complement: nine
Supreme's label: Motown
Surcharge: tax
"Sure, let's": why not
Sure thing: fact
Sure winner: shoo-in
Surf maker: tide
Surf, place to: web
Surf sound: rote
Surf, where to: net
Surface: emerge
Surface a road: pave
Surface layers, fertile: top soil
Surface measure: areas
Surfboard skeg, e.g.: fin
Surfeit: sate, jade
Surfer wannabe: hodad
Surfer's journal: blog
Surfer's mishap: wipeout
Surfer's sobriquet: dude
Surfer's warning: fin
Surfing Mecca: Oahu
Surfing site: net, web
Surfing the net: online
Surfing the web: online
Surge: wallow, well-up
Surgeon, kind of: oral, vascular, gen.
Surgeon's insertion: stent
Surgeon's instrument: lancet, scapula
Surgery, kind of: elective, minor, major
Surgery or printer type: laser
Surgical beam: laser
Surgical knife: lancet, scapula, scalpel
Surgical probes: stylet

Surgical removal: ablation
Surgical saw: trepan
Surmountable barriers: hurdles
Surmounting: atop
Surpass: out do
Surprise attack: raid
Surprise greatly: amaze
Surprise looking: agape
Surrealist painter: Dali
Surrealist painting: Dali
Surrendered territory: ceded
Surreptitious: sly
Surrey trimming: frieze
Surround sound provider: stereo
Surrounded by: amid, amidst
Surrounding: milieu
Survey: map, poll
Survey chart: plat
Survey finding: area
Survey the enemy: recon
Surveyed: mapped
Survival: made it
Survivor, type of: sole
Susan Lucci vamp: Erica
Susann, Jacqueline: writer
Sushi bar eggs: roe
Sushi bar selection: eel
Sushi bar soup: miso
Sushi drink: sake
Sushi ingredient: kelp
Sushi, like: raw
Sushi morsel: eel
Sushi quaff: saki, sake
Suspect: fear
Suspect's answer: denials
Suspect's need: alibi
Suspected: feared
Suspense novel: chiller
Suspicion, inspiring: fishy
Suspicion, with: askance
Suspicious: fishy
Suspicious of: on to
Suspicious, more: leerier, fears
Suspicious smell, what's the: a rat
Suspiciously alert: wary
Suva's country: Fiji
Suzerainty: reign
Suzette namesake: crepe, crepes
Swab: Q-tip
Swabbie: gob, sailor, tar
Swab's swig: grog
Swagger: strut
Swaggering walk: strut
Swahili master: bwana
Swain: beau
SWAK: "seal with a kiss"
Swallow greedily: gulp, engulf
Swallow, tiny: sip
Swallow up: engulf
Swamis and fakirs: Hindus
Swamp: fen, morass
Swamp bird: sora
Swamp chorus: frogs
Swamp critter: gator

Swamp fever: malaria
Swamp fox: marion (francis)
Swamp gas: miasma
Swamp, like a: mirky, miry
Swamp matter, decayed: peat
Swamp plant: reed
Swamp sound: croak
Swamp tree: cypress
Swamp vapor: miasma
Swamped: awash
Swamper: handyman
Swampy ground: mire, bog
Swan, lady: pen
Swan Lake: ballet
Swan lake costume: tutu
Swan, male: cob
Swan, type of: mute
Swan, young: cygnet
Swank: tony
Swann, Lynn: football
Swap jobs: trade positions
Swarm: teem
Swarm around: mob
Swarm in: crowd
Swarms with: abounds, teems
Swayed, easily: amenable
Swear to: attest
No sweat: easy
Sweater letter: omega, eta, rho, beta
     phi, psi
Sweater makings: yarns
Sweater, soft: mohair
Sweater, type: V-neck
Swedish furniture chain: IKEA
Swedish import: Volvo, Saab
Swedish industrialist: Nobel
Swedish nightingale: Jenny Lind
Swedish physicist: Anders Angstrom
Swedish pop-rock group: Abba
Swedish singing group: Abba
Swedish ski resort: Are
"Sweet as Cider" girl: Ida
"Sweet" girl of song: Adeline
Sweet potato: ocarina
Sweet-smelling necklace: lei
Sweet square: fudge
Sweet, too: sugary
Sweet, very: angelic
Sweet wine: sauterne
Sweeten the pot: raise
Sweethearts: lovers, honeys
Sweetie pie: doll, dear, hon, honey,
     darling
Sweetsop: ates
Swell, as a river: rise
Swell out: billow , bulge
Swell outward: bulge
Swelled head: ego, pride, egoism, vanity,
     conceit, egotism, smugness
Swelling, plant: edema
Swelter: roast, sweat
Sweltering: torrid
Swenson, inga: actress
Swept away: seduced

Swift: satirist
Swift, not too: obtuse
Swift pirate ship: corsair
Swift traveler: Gulliver
Swift works, Jonathan: satires
Swift writing: satire
Swiftest animal: cheetah
Swiftly lazar, for ex.: agt.
Swig, swab's: grog,
Swim alternative: sink
Swim, quick: dip
Swimmer, bright: sun fish
Swimmer, invisible: amoeba
Swimmer, tiny: amoeba
Swimmer units: laps
Swimmer's aids: flippers
Swimmer's choice: stroke
Swimmer's routine: laps
Swimming: natant
Swimming:
 Ederle, Gertrude: swimmer
 Louganis, Greg: diving
Swimming stroke: crawl, dolphin, trudgen
 butterfly, dog paddle
Swimming pool location: YMCA, YWCA
Swim's antithesis: sink
Swimsuit: bikini
Swimsuit fabric: spandex
Swimsuit type: maillot
Swindle: bunco, rook, gouge
Swindler: thief
Swine, relating to: porcine
Swing around: pivot, slue
Swing locale: tree
Swing loose: dangle
Swing loosely: flap
Swing, make shift: tire
Swing off course: yaw
Swing on an axis: slue
Swing the camera: pan
Swing to & fro: flap
Swing vote: ind
Swirled around: eddied
Swirling around: eddying
Swirling current: eddy
Swirling effect: eddy
Swiss abstractionist: klee
Swiss artist: Klee
Swiss canton: Uri
Swiss capital: Bern, Berne
Swiss cheese hole: eye
Swiss financial hub: Zurich
Swiss girl, literary: Heidi
Swiss mathematician: Euler
Swiss miss: Heidi
Swiss peak: Alps
Swiss song: yodel
Swiss steak (make): braise
Swit's co-star: Alan Alda
Swit, Loretta: actress
Switch back?: eroo
Switch finish?: eroo
Switch partner: bait
Switchback curve: ess

Switzerland lake: Geneva
Swizzle stick, use a: stir
Swoboda, Ron: baseball
Swoon: faint, fad, torpor
Sword: estoc, epee
Sword, crossword: epee
Sword fighter: fencer
Sword handle: hilt, haft
Sword holder: scabbard
Sword, light: rapier,
Sword, one edge: saber
Sword, three-sided: epee
Sword, thrust & parry: epee
Sword, two-edge: rapier
Sword's superior: pen
Sword-shaped: ensiform
Swung around: slued
Sycamore: tree
Sycophant: minion, toady
Sycophant's answer: yes
Sycorax's son: Caliban
Sydney gem: opal
Sydney salutation: g'day
Sydow, Max von: actor
Syllable omission: apocope
Syllables, inquiring: ehs
Syllables (omit) in pronunciation: elides
Syllogism word: ergo
Sylvester or Tweety: toon
Symbol, kind of: status
Symbol of Ra: Aten
Symbol of bondage: yokes
Symbol of justice: scales
Symbol of prying: nose
Symbol of resistance: omega
Symbol of satiety: hilt
Symbol of servitude: yoke
Symbol of slipperiness: eel
Symbol of slowness: snail
Symbol of Wild West justice: noose
Symbolic figure of speech: metaphor
Symbolic staff: mace
Symbolic tale: allegory
Sympathize: relate
Symphony: opus
Symphony crasher: cymbal
Synagogue: temple
Synagogue chief: rabbi
Synagogue expert: roget
Synagogue item: torah
Synagogue leaders: rabbi
Synagogue scripture: torah
Synchronize: phase
Synopsis of a book: precis
Synthesizer ancestor: organ
Synthesizer inventor: Moog
Synthetic fabric: Arnel, Orlon
Syrian cursive script: Serta
Syrian leader: Assad
Syrian's blundering solder: Assad Sack
Syringe amount: cc
Syrup source: maple, sap
Syrup, sweet: molasses
Syrupy drink: julep

System of morals: ethics
System starter: eco
System, type of: binary, eco

T

Ta ta: ciao
Tab, run up a: owe
Tabbouleh complement: pita
Tabby: feline, cat
Table, at the: seated
Table: d'hôte
Table, fixed a: laid, set
Table land: mesa
Table linen fabric: damask
Table, Lord's: altar
Table protector: trivet
Table scrap: ort
Table spread: olio, meal
Table sugar: sucrose
Table, temple: altar
Tableau: scene
Tableau, like a: posed
Tablet: legal pad
Tablet, inscribed: stele
Tableware, Connecticut: Bristol Crystal
Tabloid abductor: alien
Tabloid aviator: ETs
Tabloid fare: scandals
Tabloid monster: Nessie
Tabloid topic: UFOs
Tabloid twosome: item
Taboo, echoing: no-no
Taboo item: no-no
Taboo, makes: bans
Taboo, not: null
Tabriz denizen: Iranian
Tabula rasa: clean slate
Tacit: unsaid
Tack: baste
Tack on: add, append
Tackiness: sleaze
Tackle: hoist
Tackle moguls: ski
Tackle's neighbor: end (football)
Taco filling: beef
Taconite: ore
Taconite yield: iron
Tactful maneuvering: finesse
Tactic, clever: ploy
Tactic, sly: ruse
Ta-da: voilà
Tabby treat: catnip
Tadpoles have them: gills, tails
Tae kwon do
TAE, part of: Alva
Taffy, like: chewy
Tag info: price, name
Tag sale site: DMV
Tags: labels
Tag-team member: wrestler
Tahini base: sesame
Tai chi chuan

Thai language: Lao
Taiga animal: elk
Tail ends: rears, rear ends
Tail flyer: kite, comet
Tail, like a: caudal
Tailgater's need: grill, cooler
Tailless amphibian: toad
Tailor's measure: inseam
Taiwan Strait island: Matsu
Taj Mahal site: Agra, India
Taj Mahal stopover: Agra
Take a beating: lose
Take a bow
Take a break, in a way: nap
Take a card: draw
Take a crack at: try
Take a firm stand: insist
Take a flier: risk
Take a glance at: see
"Take a hike"
Take a nap: snooze
Take a powder: bolt
"Take a tip from me"
Take a toll on: tax
Take a walk: stroll
Take a whiff: sniff, smell
Take advantage: avail
Take advantage of: use
Take advice: heed
Take aim: zero in
Take away: remove, minus
Take away by force: wrest
Take away, in law: adeem
Take back: recant, unsay, abjure,recall
Take back in battle: rewin
Take by force: storm
Take-charge type: doer
Take down: note, lower, write, record,reduce,
    deflate, dismount
Take effect: work, inure
Take for a ride: con, scam
Take for granted: assume
Take forcibly: seize
"It'd take forever"
Take fright: panic
Take hastily: grab
Take in: con, dupe, fool, furl, jail,arrest,
    accept, absorb, see
Take issue with: protest
Take it all off: unload, undress
"Take it on the lam"
Take long steps: stride
Take long stitches: baste
Take off: doff, exit, quit, leave, scram, deduct,
    depart, remove
Take off, certain: JATO
Takeoff, does a: apes, mimics
Takeoff, prepare for: taxi
Takeoff site: runway
Take offense: resent
Take on: adopt, don, face, hire, meet,annex,
    accept, append assume
Take out: delete, date, see
Take out for dinner: treat

Take out, in printing: dele, delete
Takeout words: to go
Take over: step in, seize, spell, usurp,assume,
    capture, relieve, oust
Take part in a hunger strike: fast
Take part in a secret joint adventure: elope
Take pleasure in: like, relish
Take potshots at: snipe
Take precedence over: preempt
Take steps: walk, act, act on
Take stock of: assess
Take tea: sip
Take the honey and run: elope
Take the wrong way: steal
Take to task: rebuke
Take to the air: aviate
Take to the cleaners: fleece, scam
Take to the prom: escort
Take turns: rotate, spell
Take up: use, fill, open, adopt, begin
Take up a leg: alter
Take up again: rehem
Take up, as a cause: espouse
Take vows: wed
Take wing: soar, aviate
"Take your time": no rush
Taken aback: stumped, surprised
Taken back: aghast, awed
Taken with: smitten
Takeover, political: coup
Takeover, quick: coup
Takes a chance: dares
Takes a curtain call: bows
Takes a turn: goes
Takes aback: fazes
Takes for a ride: cons, scams
Takes for granted: assumes
Takes here: brings
Takes off the skin: pares
Takes on: assumes
Takes over: usurps, ousts, adopts
Takes steps: acts
Takes the bait: bites
Takes the edge off: dulls
Takes to a higher power: cubes
Takes umbrage: resents
Takes up or lets out: alters
Tal, Mikhail: chess
Tale, adventure: yarn
Tale of adventure: gest
Tale of heroism: saga
Tale of woe: jeremiad
Tale, symbolic: allegory
Tale, tall: yarn
Tale, wild: yarn
Talent hunter: scout
Talent, natural: flair, forte
Talent scout's rave review: can't miss
Talent search: scout
Talent, special: knack
Talented enough: able
Tales, carry: tattle
Tales of two cities hero: Darnay
Talese, Gay: writer

Lex talionis: (law of retaliation or revenge)
Talisman: amulet, charm
Talk, absurd: bosh
Talk and talk: yak, jaw
Talk, foolish: prate
Talk idly: yak
Talk indistinctly: mumble
Talk informally: rap
Talk of Toledo: Español
Talk online: chat
Talk, pretentious: claptrap
Talk radio participant: phone-in
Talk rhythmically: rap
Talk, tech: argot
Talk to a beat: rap
Talk, trifling: prattle
Talk unclearly: slur
Talk up: sell
Talk wildly: rant, rave
Talk with one's hands: sign
Talk workers: Eds
Talkative, become: open up
Talked a blue streak: swore
Talked foolishly: prated
Talker's paradise: gabfest
Talking bird: myna, mynah
Talking, not: mum
Talking up: selling
Talks idly: prates
Talks to a beat: raps
Talks up: touts
Tall & lanky: rangy
Tall & thin: lanky
Tall grass stalk: reed
Tall topper: opera hat
Tallow source: suet
Tally mark: notch
Talon: nail
Tamandua feature: snout, (anteater)
Tamarisk salt tree: atle
Tame: dull, blah
Tame a horse: break
Tame carnivore: cat
Tame, less: wilder
Tamiroff, Akim: actor
Tamper resistant: sealed
Tamper with: doctor
Tampico cash: peso
Tampico pal: amigo
Tam-wearer tongue: Erse
Tan, Amy: writer
Tan, seek a: bask
Tan slacks: khakis
Tandy, Jessica: actress
Tang: biti, bity, bitter,
Tangelo, wrinkly: ugli, ugly
Tangle, in a: afoul
Tangled, get: mat
Tango number: two
Tango partner: dancer
Tangy: zesty
Tangy flavor: mint, lemon, bitter
Tank blaster: bazooka
Tankard: stein

Tankard's kin: stein
Tanker mishap: spill
Tanner, Roscoe: tennis
Tannery inventory: hides
Tannin source: sumac
Tanning lotion letters: SPF
Tantalus's daughter: Niobe
    father: Zeus
    son: Pelops
Tantrum, throw a: rage
Tanyu, Kano: Japanese painter
Tao Te Ching
Taoism founder: Lao-tse
Taos dwelling: adobe
Tap on the shoulder alternative: psst
Tape, audition: demo
Tape measure part: reel
Tape, not on: live
Tape over: erase
Tape, pieces of: strips
Taper off: wane
Tapered tuck: dart
Tapering stone pillar: obelisk
Tapestry: arras, arra
Tapestry, a rich: arras
Tapestry, did a: wove
Tapestry, made a: wove
Tapestry weave: arras
Tapioca-like food: salep
Tapped in, in golf: putted
Taproom sights: stools
Taps: knocks
Taps one's fingers: drums
Tar, in Tampico: brea
Tar pits: La Brea
Tara family name: O'Hara
Tarantino or Crisp: Quentin
Tarbell, Ida: muckraker
Tarboosh: fez, hat (Muslim)
Tarboosh feature: tassel
Tare or purslane: weed
Target amount: quota
Target, easy: sitting duck
Target, face the: aim
Target in the wild: prey
Target of fawning: idol
Target practice, does: aims
Target practice site: range
Tariff-raising exercise: trade war
Tarmac area: apron
Tarmac, touched the: alit, landed
Taro dish: poi
Taro paste: poi
Taro root: eddo
Taro with water: poi
Tarot indication: omen
Tar's saint: Elmo
Tart plum: sloe
Tartan: plaid
Tartan fabric: plaid
Tartan trousers: trews
Tarzan: Ron Ely
Tarzan, really: lord
Tarzan's chimp: Cheeta

Tarzan's conveyance: vine
Tarzan's counterpart: Sheena
Tarzan's mate: Jane
Tarzan's moniker: apeman
Tarzan's nanny: ape
Tarzan's Ron: Ely
Tarzan's title: earl
Tarzan's tot: Boy
Task, disagreeable: onus
Tasks (in London): labours
Task, mundane: chore
Task, simple: snap
Task, up to the: able
Tasman, Abel: explorer
Tasmanian peak: Ossa
Tasseled headgear: fez
Tasseled topper: fez
Taste, sense of: palate
Taste, zingy: tang
Tasteful, not: tacky
Tastes: palates
Tasting, foul: vile
Tatami: mat
Tatami material: straw
Tatamis: mats
Tati, Jacques: director
Tattered: ratty, ragged
Tattered cloth: rag
Tattered clothing: rags
Tatters: rags
Tattler's supply: tales
Tattoo word: mom
Taught, be: learn
Taunt: gibe
Taunt, ironic: sarcasm
Taunting remark: gibe
Taurus neighbor: Aries
Tautomeric compound: enol
Tavern near a tube station: pub
Tawny predator: lioness
Tax form: return
Taxpayer's dread: audit
Tax reform victim: IRA
Tax shelter, briefly: IRA
Taxes: levies
Taxes, send in: file
Te Kanawa, Kiri: diva
Tea, black: pekoe
Tea, brew: steep
Tea cake: scone
Tea clipper: boat
Tea holder: caddy
Teahouse attire: obi, kimono
Teahouse mat: tatami
Tea, Indian: Assam
Teakettle, Ivan's: samovar
Tea, kind of: herb, herbal
Tea leaf reader: seer
Tea leaves, interpret: read
Tea, preside at: pour
Tea source, major: Assam
Tea, tangy: mint
Teacher of one: tutor

Teacher, revered: guru
Teacher's plan: lesson
Teacher's tool: pointer
Team: side
Team building: arena
Team goal: win
Team list: roster
Teamwork obstacle: ego
"Teapot Dome" scandal
Teapot, emulates a: whistles
Tear gas target: rioter
Tear or stain: flaw
Tear, ragged: snag
Tear to pieces: shred
Tear violently: rive
Tearful request: plea
Tearoom: café
Tears: eye drops
Tears asunder: rends
Tears to your eyes, brings: onions
Teasdale, Sara: actress
Tease: twit, kid, bait
Tease to anger: rile
Teases: kids
Teasing taunt: jest
Tebaldi, Renata: soprano
Tech magazine: Byte
Tech talk: argot
Technical details: specs
Technical school: inst., institute
Technical word: term
Technical writer's guidelines: specs
Technique-teaching composition: etude
Teddy trim: lace
Teddy bear lookalike: koala
Tedious one: bore
Ted's (Turner) station: TBS, TNT
Tee preceder: ess
Tee shirt, wild: tie-dye
Teemed with: swarmed
Teen bane: adult
Teen catchphrase: as if
Teen escapade: joy ride
Teen fave: idol
Teen hangout: mall, arcade
Teen outcast: nerd
Teenaged: young
Teenagers, like: youthful
Tees, roomy: XLs
"Arm to the teeth"
Teeth chattering sound: brr
Teeth, having: dentate
Teetotaler's selection, perhaps: soda
Tel Aviv coin: shekel
Telecast component: audio
Telegram word: stop
Telemarketing danger: scam
Telepathy initials: ESP
Telephus's mother: Auge
Telescope lens: ocular, optic
Telescope, space: Hubble
TV adorner: set decorator
TV adjunct: antenna, remote, VCR, DVD,
    TiVo

TV band: UHF
TV control: knob, remote
TV equine: Mr. Ed
TV evaluator: Nielsen
TV frog: Kermit
TV from DC: C-SPAN
TV goof: blooper
TV hookup: VCR
TV planet: Ork
TV spots: ads
TV street: Sesame
TV teaser: promo
TV tube gas: xenon
TV warrior princess: Xena
Tell jokes: regale
Tell off: flay, rate, ream, chide, scold, berate,
    rebuke, chew out
Tell secrets: blab
Tell the teacher: snitch
Teller, midnight: ATM
Tells a story: narrates
Tell's home canton: Uri
Temp, end-of-year: Santa
Temper: mood
Temperature scale: Celsius
Tempest spirit: Ariel
Tempest in a teapot: ado
Tempest locale: teapot
Tempestuous: fiery
Temple: pagoda, taa
Temple action: incensing
Temple image: idol
Temple leader: rabbi
Temple scholar: rabbi
Temple scroll: Torah
Temple team: Owls
Temple, Thai: wat
Templeton, Alec: pianist
Tempo, lively: allegro
Temporal brinks: eves
Temporary: interim
Temporary car: loaner, rental
Temporary currency: script
Temporary delay: deferral
Temporary failure: lapse
Temporary job: gig
Temps: fill-ins
Temp's employer: agency
Tempt: entice
Tempting: luring
Tempting dangler: carrot
Tempting, very: seductive, alluring
Ten, group of: decade
Ten (prefix): deca
Ten Roman soldiers: decade
Ten million rupees: crore
Tenants, feudal: vassals
Tend carefully: nurture
Tendencies, prevailing: trends
Tender, offer: hire
Tenderfoot: dude
Tendon: bone cushion, bursa, sinew
Tendrils, use: climb
Tenement: slum

Tenet: ism, credo
Ten-four buddy: CBer
Ten-gallon hat: Stetson
Tennessee athlete: Vol
Tennessee gridder: Titan
Tennessee state flower: iris
TVA project: dam
Tennille, Toni: pop singer
Tennis call: let
Tennis match unit: set
Tennis players:
    Agassi, Andre
    Austin, Tracy
    Bjorn, Borg
    Chang, Michael
    Davenport, Lindsay
    Edberg, Stephen
    Evert, Chris
    Gibson, Althea
    Goolangong, Evonne
    Hingis, Martina
    King, Billy Jean
    Lendl, Ivan
    McEnroe, John
    Nastase, Ilie
    Navratilova, Martina
    Sampras, Pete
    Seles, Monica
    Shriver, Pam
    Tanner, Roscoe
    Williams, Serena
Tennis prize: Davis Cup
Tennis second point: thirty
Tennis situation: ad in
Tennis stadium: Ashe
Tennis surface: lawn
Tennis term: ad in, love, deuce
Tennis, the two for: ens
Tennyson, Lord Alfred: poet
Tennyson heroine: Enid
Tenor great: Caruso
Tenor, voice above: alto
Ten-penny item: nail
Tense: on edge
Tense and jumpy: wired up
Tense, become: tauten
1066 loser: Saxon
Tensor: muscle
Tent dweller: Arab, Bedouin
Tent, nomad: yurt
Tentacle: feeler, arm
Tentative project: plan
Tenterhooks, on: tense
Tenth part: tithe
Tentlike dwelling: yurt
Tenure: term
Tenzing, for one: Sherpa
Tenzing Norgay, e.g.: Sherpa
Tequila cactus: agaves, agave
Tequila plant: agaves, agave
Tequila source: agave
Terentia's husband: Cicero
Tereus's son: Itys
    wife: Procne

Terhune dog: Lad
Terhune's hero: Lad
Term of endearment: hon
Term of office: tenure
Term of respect: sir
Term paper: thesis
Term paper abbr.: ibid., et al.
Terminator, for one: cyborg
Termine: end
"Terminer" partner: oyer
Termite kin: ant
Terms, came to: agreed
Terms of endearment: hon, honor
Terpene solvent: pinene
Terpsichore, etc.: muse
Terra alba
Terra firma, far from: asea
Terra firma, on: ashore, on solidground
Terra incognita
Terrace: patio
Terrarium plants: ferns
Terre Haute college: ISU
Terrible things to waste: minds
Terrible twos, e.g.: phase
Terrier of film: Asta
Terrier, type of: cairn, Skye
Terrific bargain: buy
Territory, surrender: cede
Terrorist's prisoner: hostage
Terse affirmative: yep
Terse refusal: nope
Tersely cogent: pithy
Terza rima: (Italian rhyming verse)
Tesh, John: music
Tesla, Nikola: physicist
Test exercise: dry run
Test for fit: try on
Test or rain: acid
Test show: pilot
Test tapes: demos
Test, unwritten: oral
Test version: beta
Test venue: lab
Testee, standout: acer
Testify: depose
Testiness: ire
Testing site: lab
Tet Offensive: Vietnam war
Tête topper: beret
Tethys'sdaughter: Oceanides
    father: Uranus
    husband: Oceanus
    mother: Gaea, Terra
Tetley rival: Salada
Tetley temptation: tea
Tetra's home: tank
Teutonic trio: drei
Texas AFB: Reese
Texas billionaire: Perot
Texas oranges: Osage
Texas police group: Rangers
Texas tea: oil
Tex-Mex cuisine
Tex-Mex treat: fajita

Text book division: unit
Text mistake list: errata
Text of news story: copy
Textile component: fiber
Texture, lacking: limp
Thackeray's forte: prose
Thai king: Rama
Thai language: Lao
Thai temple: wat
Thailand bucks: bahts
Thailand monetary unit: baht
Thailand neighbor: Laos
Thailand once: Siam
Thalia, Urania, etc.: muses
Thames gallery: Tate
Thames puller: oars
Thames school: Eton
"Thank you" partner: please
Thanks, German: danke
Thanksgiving Day event: parade
Thanksgiving hymn: paean
Tharp, Twyla: choreographer, dancer
"That" alternative: this
Thataway: yonder
"That ain't hay"
"That Girl" girl: Ann Marie, Marlo Thomas
"That is," Latin: id est
"That is easy to say": namely
That muchacha: esa
"That" in Tjuana: esa, eso
That was close: phew
That way: thither, yonder
Thatch palm: nipa
Thatcher followers: Tories
Thatches, worker who: reeder
That's gross: ugh
That's right: amen
That's the ticket
The auld sod: Eire, Erin
"The Barber of Seville"
The behind behind you: derriere
"The Black Camel" gumshoe: Chan
The end of an era: legend's retirement
"The English Patient" setting: Sahara
The force was with him: Yoda
The fourth estate: press
"The Gift of the Magi"
The "going" rate: fare
"The Iceman Cometh" writer: O'Neill
The jig is up
"The Lady of the Lake"
The limit, they say: sky
"The Loco-Motion" girl: Eva
The lowdown: facts
"The Marriage of Figaro": opera
"The Merry Widow" composer: Lehar
"The Mummy" setting: Egypt
O'er the ramparts
The Old South: Dixie
"The Omen" boy: Damien
The one in charge: head, boss
The other woman: mistress
The others: them
The Plastic Ono Band

"The Prince of Denta"
"The Prisoner of Zenda"
"The Scarlet Pimpernel"
"The Seven Year Itch" actor: Ewell
The sixth is one: sense
"The Squire of Alsatia"
The stuff of legends: lore
The time being: nonce
The twins: Gemini
The two for tennis: ens
The very beginning: outset
The very essence: gist
"The way" to Confucius: Tao
"The Wreck of the Mary Deare"
Thea's daughter: Selene
      father: Uranus
      husband: Hyperion
      mother: Gaea
Theater (ancient): adeum
Theater audience: house
Theater award: Obie
Theater box: loge
Theater cheer: bravo
Theater company: troupe
Theater district: Rialto
Theater drop fabric: serim
Theater, Grecian: odea
Theater, Greek: odeon
Theater level: loge
Theater offering: scene
Theater part: aisle
Theater piece: prop
Theater section: loge
Theater sign: SRO
Theatrical lighting: neon
Thebes, neighbor of: Sparta
Thebes' legendary founder: Cadmus
Their boughs make a bow: yews
"Thelma and Louise"
Them there: those
Theme: motif
Theme park, California: Marine World
Themis's father: Uranus
      goddess of: law, justice
      husband: Zeus
      mother: Gaea
Then, in Touraine: alors
Theodosia's solicitors: barristers
Theorem ender: QED
Therapy, kind of: gene, chemo
There is always one at home: ump, umpire
Therefore: ergo, hence
Thermal unit: BTU, degree, calorie
Thermodynamic scale founder: Rankine
Thermometer base: bulb
Thesaurus compiler: Roget
Thesaurus entry: synonym, syn.
Thesaurus find: word
Thesaurus, challenge for: labyrinth
Thesaurus word: syn.
These, in Tulle: gore (French)
These may be growing: pains
Thespian, be a: act
Thespian, works as a: acts

Thespian's need: role
Thespian's quest: role
Thespian's road: Nathan Lane
Thessalonica letters: etas
Theta follower: iota
Theta preceder: eta
They are caught in pots: eels
They are found in patches: melons
They are found in pockets or seams: ores
They are given away: brides
They are good for openers: keys
They are inclined to brood: hens
They are made only at home: runs
They are not from around here: ETs
They are often burned: CDs
They are parallel to radii: ulnae
      parallel to radius: ulna
They are pitched: tents
They are required: musts
They begin in Juin: etes
They branch out: limbs
They break on shore: waves
"They Call the Wind Maria"
They can create highlights: dyes
They can't go home again: exiles
They come in shades: lenses
They could be split: ends, atoms
They cross the line: road hogs
They don't last long: fads
They are extras: frills
They frequent outlets: prongs
They garner a lot of interest: payday loans
They hang from branches: sloths
They have a chilling effect: cold snaps
They have catkins: willows
They have one horn: rhinos, unicorns
They have regrets: ruers
They have their pride: lions
They hold all the cards: dealers
They know the answers: oracles
They know the drills: dentists
They lack edges: spheres
They love their queen: bees
They make the cuts: shears
They may all be off: bets
They may be abuzz with activity: hives
They may be decked: halls
They may be filled with jets: spas
They may be left on doorsteps: mats
They may be multifaceted: gems
They may be pressing: needs
They may be read: lips, palms
They may be split: ends, atom
They may have contacts: eyes
They offer cold comfort: ice bags
They often clash: egos
They put you in your place: ushers
They remove moisture: dryers
They ring some necks: reatas
They seem to last forever: eons
They skirl: pipers
They swim with crocs: hippos
They take turns: rotors
They tie stories together: stairs

They troupe for the troops: USO
They try: litigators
They wrote in Latin: Romans
They're compared to fermions: bosons
They're found in a yard: feet
They're good for tricks: aces
They're hard on the joints: agues
They're produced by hives: itches
Thick: syrupy
Thick board: plank
Thick head of hair: mane
Thick mass of hair: mop
Thick mud: mire
Thick knap: shag
Thick of things: midst
Thick outer covering: rind
Thick piece: slab, chunk
Thick skulled: obtuse
Thick with cattails: reedy
Thick with trees: wooded
Thick-brick center: ASA
Thicken, as pudding: gel, set
Thickening agent: agar
Thickening mixture: roux
Thicket: coppice, copse
Thickness: ply
Thickset: burly, boxy, stout, beefy
Thickset horse: cob
Thief in the southwest: ladrón
Thief, Yiddish: ganef, ganof
Thief's job: heist
Thief's need: fence
Thieve: rob
Thigh muscles, in the gym: quads
Tiller, at the: aft
Thimblerig item, often: pea
Thin, become very: emaciate
Thin blooded: anemic
Thin coating: film
Thin covering: veneer
Thin heels: stilettos
Thin layer: veneer
Thin-layered mineral: mica
Thin, make too: emaciate
"The Thin Man" pooch: Asta
Thin material: voile
Thin metal: foil
Thin nail: brad
Thin necktie: bolo
Thin out: dilute
Thin, plain-weave fabric: batiste
Thin silk fabric: pongee
Thin slice of bacon: rasher
Thin slice of veal: cutlet
Thin streak of smoke: wisp
Thin, too: bony
Thing: entity
Thing in court: res
Thing, in Latin: res
Thing of little value: trifle
Thing to eat, unpleasant: crow
Things: phenomena
Things to consider: aspects
Things to rattle: sams, sabers

Thing unto itself: entity
Think: ideate, deem
Think about: ponder
Think ahead: plan
Think alike: agree
Think faster than: outwit
Think highly of: admire
Think logically: reason
Think over: ponder
Think positively: hope
Think tank output: idea
Think up: ideate
Thinker, creative: idea man
Thinking man's sculptor: Rodin
Thinking, way of: mind-set
Thinks fit: deigns
Thinly spread: sparse
Thinner, makes: dilutes, diets
Thinner, make: dilute
Third degree, one who's given the: PhD
Third dimension: depth
Third estate: plebs, people, plebes, populace
Third largest island, world's: Borneo
Third planet: Earth
Third power, in math: cube
Third rank (of the): tertiary
Third rate: lousy, poor
Thirds, cut in: trisect
Thirteen (13), now fifty (50): USA
Thirteen witches: coven
Thirteenth or the fifteenth: ides
35 mm setting: f-stop
"This Is Spinal Tap": movie
This and that: olio
This evening: tonight
"This", in Havana: esta, este
"This", in Tijuana: esta, este
This may be acute: accent
This or that: either
Thither and yon
Thole filler: oar
Thomas, Debi: skater
Thomas, Dylan: writer
Thomas Gray works: odes
Thomas, Isaiah: publisher
Thomas, Marlo: actress
Thomas of clocks: Seth
Thompson, Emma: actress
Thompson, Lea: actress
Thompson, Sada: actress
Thong: strap
Thoreau's pond: Walden
Thornfield Hall governess: Eyre
Thoroughfare, narrow: lane
Thorpe, Jim: Olympian
Thor's boss: Odin
    father: Odin, Wotan
    god of: thunder
    mother: Jorth
Those behind the times: fogeys
Those forcing expatriation: banishers
Thou: you
Thought: idea
Thought, brainy: idea

Thought, bright: idea
Thought, forms a: ideates
Thought, nice: idee(Fr.)
Thought on: mused
Thought, sudden: idea
Thought, vague: notion
Thought, without: rashly
Thoughtful murmur: hmm
Thoughtless: unkind
Thousand bucks: gee
Thousands of seconds: hours, hrs.
Thrash about: flail
Thrash soundly: drub
Thrash with a stick: cane
Thrashed: laced
Thread buy: spool
Thread, bits of: fibers
Threads, got: wore
Thread, heavy: lisle
Thread, hosiery: lisle
Thread of smoke: wisp
Thread unit: spool
Thread winding machine: reeler
Threadbare: shabby, worn
Threads, loose: lint
Threat: menace
Threat, familiar: or else
Threaten: menace
Threatening: ominous
Three before V: STU
"Three-card monte"
3-D scan: MRI
3-D shape: cube
Three dots, in Morse code: ess
Three element tube: triode
Three in Bolivia: tres
Three in Toledo: tres
Three in Torino: tre
Three in Tuscany: tre
Three lines of verse: tercet
Three Musketeer, a: Athos
Three oceans touch it: Asia
Three of a kind: drei
Three parts, it had: Gaul
Three parts, having: trinary
Three seater: sofa
Three sheets to the wind: lit
Three under par: double eagle
Three, up front: tri
Three-handed card game: skat
Three-in-one: triune
Three-lined verse: haiku
Three-wheeler: trike
Threshing refuse: chaff
Threw away: junked
Thrice dix: trente
Thrifty, is very: ekes
Thriftily, used: eked
Thrifty purchase: economy size
Throat features: tonsils
Throat tissue: tonsil
Throbs or beats: pulses
Throne, seized the: usurped
Throne, sits on the: rules, reign

Throng: army, cram, crowd, herd, host,mob
Throngs: mobs
Through: via
Throw: cast
Throw a rider: buck
Throw a tantrum: rage
Throw away: dump
Throw caution to the wind: dare
Throw for a loop: stun
Throw in: add
Throw in the towel: give in
Throw off heat: emit, radiate
Throw out the duds: cull
Throw over: jilt
Throw the blue book at: test
"Throw the book at"
Thrown-down gauntlet: dare
Throws a party: fetes
Throws away: dumps, discards
Thrush, type of: veery
Thrushes, white-crescent: ouzels
Thrust-and-parry sword: epee
Thrust forward: propel, obtrude
Thud: bam
Thuds: clunks
Thugs: hoods
Thug's pistol: Roscoe
Thumb through: skim, leaf
Thumb twiddler: idler
Thumbs down, give the: nix
Thumbs up, definite: rave
Thumbs through: riffles, leafs
Thumper's pal: Bambi
Thunder bolt hurler: Thor
Thunder, clap of: peal
Thunder god: Thor, Donar
Thunder, peal of: clap
Thunderhead: cloud
Thunderstruck: awed, aghast, amazed
Thurible: censer
Thurible, use a: cense
Thuringian territory: Saxe, Saxony
Thurmond, Uma: actress
Thus: ergo
Thus, in citations: sic
Thwack: conk
Thwarts a villain: foil
Thy: your
Thyestes's brother: Atreus
   daughter: Pelopia
   father: Pelops
   mother: Hippodamia
   son: Aegisthus
Thyme: herb
Tia Maria: coffee liqueur
Tiamat's husband: Apsu
Tiant, Luis: baseball
Tiara: coronet, crown, diadem, circlet
Tiara adornments: gems
Tiara inset: jewels
Tiberius's garb: toga
Tiberius's mother: Livia
Tiber's land: Italy
Tibetan gazelle: goa

Tibetan legend: yeti
Tibetan oxen: yaks
Tibiae and fibulae: leg bones
Tick kin: mite
Tick off: anger, rile
Ticked off: sore, mad, upset
Ticket bargain: twofer
Ticket, courted a: sped
Ticket, free: pass, comp
Ticket, give a: fine
Ticket info: tier, seat, row, aisle
Ticket, kind of: one way
Ticket office notice: SRO
Ticket remnant: stub
Ticket, risk a: speed
"That's the ticket"
Ticketed one: nominee
Tickle, things to: ivories
Tickled pink: glad
Tidal bore: eagre(19th century origin)
Tidal flood: bore
Tidal wave: eagre, tsunami
Tidal wave, high: eagre
Tide classification: neap
Tide, dangerous: rip
Tide, first quarter: neap
Tide, lowest high: neap
Tide over: help, aide
Tide, type of: neap
Tided over
Tidy loose ends: mop up
Tidy the lawn: rake, mow
Tie: cravat
Tie a turkey: truss
Tie down: tether, lash
Tie fabric: rep
Tie, high-class: ascot
Tie holder: pin
Tie print: paisley
Tie stories together, they: stairs
Tie, type of: clip-on, bow, bolo, ascot
Tie, wide: cravats
Tied up: busy, bound
Tied up the phone: yakked
Tie-dyed garment: tee
Tien Shan range: Alai
Tier: row
Tierney classic: Laura
Tierra Del Fuego
Tiff, public: scene
Tiger tooth: fang
Tigger's pal: Winnie the Pooh, Roo
Tight embrace: bear hug
Tight spot: scrape, fix
Tight-fitting: snug
Tightly packed: dense
Tightrope walker: acrobat
Tigon's kin: liger
Tijuana house: casa
Tijuana Ms.: Srta.
Tijuana Mrs.: Sra.
Tijuana parent: madre
Tijuana "that": esa, ese
Tijuana tike: niño

Tijuana time-out: siesta
Tijuana toms: gatos
Tijuana trio: tres
Tijuana "two": dos
Tikkanen, Esa: hockey
Kon Tiki
Tile floor material: PVC
Tile separator: grout
Tile worth ten points: zee
Till: unto
Tillable land: arable
Tiller, equipped with a: steerable
Tillers: helms
Tilly, Meg: actress
Tilted: leaned
Tilting matches between knights: jousts
Timber decay: dry rot
Timber, horizontal: sill, lumber, board
Timber, long: beam
Timber, nautical: spar
Timber problem: wet rot, dry rot
Timber tree: apa
Timbuktu's country: Mali
"Any time now"
Time at bat: inning
Time being: nonce
Time for festivity: holiday
Time for fools: April
Time gone by: age, past, yore
"Time in a Bottle"
Time in office: term
Time limit: deadline
"Time Machine" race: Eloi
Time, memorable: epoch
Time of one's life: age
Time of the mammals: eocene
Time of year: season
Time on the job: stint
Time or estate, kind of: real
Time period: era, eon, epoch
Time, play for: stall
Time preceding dusk: sunset
Times Square eatery: Sardis
Time, the whole: all along
Time to beware: ides
Time to celebrate: eve
Time to crow: sunup, sunrise
Time, unlucky: ides
Timetable stat: ETA
Timing signal light: strobe
Timeless, in olden times: eterne
Timeline indication: era
Times, anticipatory: eves
Timely blessing: boon
Timely question: when
Timely windfall: boon
Timex rival: Casio
Timid type: milksop
Timpanist's tool: mallet
Tin, like: rust proof
Tin source: ore
Tina Turner's ex: Ike
Tinker Bell: fairy
Tinker with: tamper, putter

Tin-lead alloy: solder
Tinseltown idol: Oscar
Tint, salon: rinse
Tinted window prevents it: glare
Tinware, decorated: tole
"Tiny Alice" playwright: Edward Albee
Tiny amount: iota
Tiny bit: mite
Tiny margin: whisker
Tiny particle: mote
Tiny pond organism: alga, algae
Tiny space: areola, areolar
Tiny speck: iota
Tiny Tim's dad: Bob
Tiny Tim's pudding: plum
Tip, helpful: hint
Tip, located at the: apical, distal
Tip, nautically: list
Tip one's hat: doff
Tip over: keel, upend
Tipped off: alerted
Tipple: drink
Tippy, not: stable
Tips off: alerts
Tire center: Akron
Tire maintenance, do: rotate
Tire nut: lug
Tire pattern: tread
Tire problem: flat
Tire, second-hand: recapped
Tire trouble: flat
Tire, trunk: spare
Tired, get: flag
Tired, got: flagged
Tired out: all in, bleary
Tired, very: all in, bleary
Tires, adj.: aligned
Tiresome, get: wear thin
Tiresome event: drag
Tiresome noise: din
Tissue: tela (Latin for web)
Tissue box word: ply
Tissue layer: tela, ply
Tissue paper art: collage
Titania's spouse: Oberon
"Titanic" message: SOS
Tither's amount: tenth
Title holder: champ, owner
Title, type of: italic
Title with a tilde: señor
Titled: named, ennobled
Titled woman: dame
Titles like Tarzan's: earl
Title-shot hopeful: top contender
Titmouses, like some: tufted
Tito, Josip Broz: ruler
Titularly: in name
Tiverton's river: exe
TiVo predecessor: VCR.
Tizzy: snit, stew
TLC provider: RN, nurse
TNT ingredient: amatol
TNT (part of): tri
To a greater extent: more so

"To a man"
To be, exactly: nicety
To be, in Burgundy: etre
To be, to Balzac: etre
To be, to Brutus: esse
To be, to Caesar: esse
To be, to Tiberius: esse
To date: yet
To do: ruckus
To love, in Toulouse: aimer
To some extent: in part
To such a degree: insomuch
To the hilt: fully
To the point: terse
To the side: lateral
Toads, group of: knot
Toady: fawn
Toady answer: yes
Toast, Cancun: salud
Toast, dry: rusk
Toast, Norwegian: skoal
Toast, offer a: propose
Toast starter: here's
Toast topper: jelly, oleo, jam
Toaster type: pop up
Tobacco chew: quid
Tobacco kiln: oast
Tobacco pipe: corn cob
Tobacco-curing chamber: oast
Toby contents: ale
Today's paper: news
Toddler's jumpsuit: romper
Toddy base: rum
Toe covering: nail
Toe problem: bunion
Toe-out stance: pronated
Toes the line: behaves
Tofu base: soy, soy bean, bean curd
Tofu constituent: soy
Tofu source: soy bean
Toga party delivery: keg
Toga party site: frat
Together: en masse, in mass
Togo's neighbor: Ghana
Toil wearily: slog
Toity's companion: hoity
Token amount: sop
Token move: gesture
Tokyo, once: Edo
Told to go: sent
Toledo lady: señora
Toledo view: Erie
Tolerates: lets
Tolkien beasts: orcs
Tolkien character: Frodo
Tolkien folk: hobbit
Tolkien hobbit: Frodo
Tolkien trees: ents
Toll road: pike
Toll unit for trucks: axle
Tolled: rung
Tolls: peals
Tolstoy, Leo: writer
Tolstoy heroine: Anna

Tolstoy title word: War
Tolstoy's Karenina: Anna
Tom, Dick, and Harry: anyone
Tom Sawyer's half-brother: Sid
Tomato container: can
Tomato jelly: aspic
Tomato product: paste
Tomato type: Roma
Tomb raider: Lara Croft
"Tomb Raider" heroine: Lara
Tomfoolery: escapades
Tombstone figure: Earp
Tombstone lawman: Wyatt Earp
Sao Tome: capital of Sao Tome andPrincipe
Tome: opus, book
Tomei, Marisa: actress
Tomkat member: Holmes
Tomlin, Lily: actress
Tomlin, Lily, character: Edith Ann
Tomorrow: mañana
Tom's cry: meow
Tom's turf: alley
Tone down: mute, soften, sober, low-key,
    mellow, subdued
Tone Loc: rapper
Tone, quavering: trill
Tones, neutral: taupe
Tongs: forceps
Tongue clicking sound: tsk
Tongue, old: Erse
Tongue-tied: speechless, silent
Tongue-in-cheek: ironic
Tongue-lash: rail, chide, scold, berate, rebuke,
    revile
Tongue-tied: mum, shy, mute, silent,bashful,
    speechless
Tonic partner: rum, gin
Tonsorial target: hair
Tonsorial work: trim
Tonto's friend, like: lone
Tony's cousin: Obie (theater award))
Too bad: tsk
Too compliant: meek
Too exacting: fussy
Too impulsive: rash
Too much, in Toulouse: trop
Too too: ultra
Tootle-oos: byes
Took a flier: risk
Took a load off: sat
Took a poll: canvassed, surveyed
Took a round trip: orbited
Took advice: heeded
Took aim: zeroed in
Took an apartment: rented, leased
Took back: recanted
Took cover: hid
Took from the top: redid
Took in: fooled, booked
Took it easy: lounged, rested
Took off: absconded
Took off a winter coat: deiced
Took out: deled
Took the lead: starred

Took the point: led
Took the wrong way: stole
Took to the cleaners: bilked
Took to the ice: skated
Took over: ousted
Tool handle wood: ash
Tool repository: shed
Tool, unwitting: cat's paw
Tool with a bubble: level
Tool with jaws: vise
Tool with teeth: saw
Tools, box of: kit
Toon clownfish: Nemo
Toon flapper Betty: Boop
Toon rabbit: Roger
Toon skunk: Le Pew
Toon troublemaker: Bart
Tooth anchor: root
Tooth, front: incisor
Tooth layer below enamel: dentine, dentin
Tooth tissue: dentine, dentin
Toothed, botanically: dentate
Toothed music maker: saw
Toothed tool: saw
Toothy smile: grin
Toots one's horn: brags
Tootsie attire: drag
Top banana
Top choices: A list
Top clock number: XII
Top dog: boss
Top drawer: A one
Top grade: A plus
Top honors, made: aced
Top level: loft, attic
Top of the morning: one a.m.
Top of the world: Everest, poles
Top off: fill
Top seed benefit: bye
Top seed reward: bye
Top story: attic
Top, strapless: tube
Topaz or opal: jewel, gem
Topic of dispute: issue
Topknot doll: Kewpie
Top-notch vocalist: diva
Topographical necks: isthmi
Top-rated stock shares: white chips
Top-Sider: shoe
Top-up: refill(British term)
Topsy turvy: messy, upside down
Torah enclosure: ark
Torah reciter: rabbi
Torah section: maftir
Torch, flaming: brand
Torch's misdeed: arson
Toreador's vest: bolero
Tori's dad: Aaron
Torme, Mel: singer
Torn: rent
Torn, Rip: actor
Tornado finder: radar
Tornado origin: funnel cloud
Torte: cake

Tortellini topping: pesto
Tortilla dip: salsa
Tortilla snack: nacho, fajita
Tortoise-and-hare name: Aesop
Tory's foe: Whig, Whit
Tosca: opera
Tosca highlight: aria
Toscanini, Arturo: conductor
Toshiba rival: Sony
Toss: cast, throw, lob, sling
Tostada's cousin: taco
Tot watcher: nanny
Tot of whiskey: dram
Total: sum, amount, ruin
Total, as a bill: ring up, run
Total disorder: chaos
Total vocabulary: lexis
Totally dark: unlit
Totally lacking: out of
Totals: adds, wrecks
Tot up: add
"Toto" creator: Baum
Toto's home: Kansas
Tot's perch: knee, lap
Tot's spot: nursery, lap, knee
Toucan feature: beak
Touch: abut
Touch and go: unsafe, risky
Touch-and-go game: tag
Touch base: tag up
Touch, just: abut
Touch lovingly: caress
Touch up: enhance, edit
Touché provokers: epees
Touched the tarmac: alit, landed
Touches lightly: dabs, pats
Touching at a single point: tangent
Tough cookie, like a: stale
Tough fiber: hemp
Tough phrase for foreigners: idiom
Tough problem: poser
Tough puzzle: poser, enigma
Tough question: poser
Tough, not that: chewable
Tough spot: bind
Tough to outwit: astute
Toughen: anneal, inure
Toughen rubber: vulcanize
Toughs it out: endures
Toulouse or Chinese chaser: goose
Toulouse-Lautrec, Henri: artist
Toupee: hairpiece
Tour de force: feat
Tour de France: race
Tour guide: cicerone
Tour guide, museum: docent
Tour of duty: stint
Tour outline: itinerary
Tourist need: visa
Tourist staple: camera
Tourist tote: camera
Tournament favorite: seed
Tournament pass: bye
Tournaments, some: opens

Tourniquet, use a: tie off
Tousle: muss
Tout: spy on horse racing info
Tout's concern: horse racing
Tow along: drag
Tow-away zone
Toward a higher position: upward
Toward sunset: west
Toward the center: into, entad
Toward the future: ahead
Toward the mouth: orad
Toweling: terry
Towel's place: rod, bar
Tower, bell: steeple
Tower, biblical: Babel
Tower builder: Eiffel
Tower ice: serac (Swiss, nineteenth century origin)
Tower designer: Eiffel
Tower, leaning, city: Pisa
Tower over: loom, dwarf
Tower, small: turret
Tower structure: spire
Towering over: dwarfing
Town: burg
Town near Karnak: Luxor (Egyptian village)
Town, small: burg
"Our Town"
Town meeting: forum, fora
Town plaza: square
Town square: plaza
Townsend, Pete: guitarist
Townspeople: villagers
Toxic emanation: radon
Toy boat locale: pond
Toy, old fashion: rag doll
Toy on a string: kite, yoyo
Toy person: doll
Toy racers: slot cars
Toy soldier: G.I. Joe
Toyed with: flirted
Toyota, old: Tercel
"Toys in the Attic" playwright: Hellman
Trace element of salt: iodine
Trace, leave no: vanish
Trace mineral: zinc
Tracery design, intricate: moresque
Traces, faint: tinges
Track down: trace
Track event: race, relay, meet
Track and field:
　　　Devers, Gail: track
　　　Lewis, Carl: runner
　　　Owens, Jessie: track
　　　Sabastian, Coe: runner
　　　Zatopek, Emil: runner
Track best: record time
Track competition: meet
Track event: race, dash
Track figures: odds
Track intersection: grade crossing
"One track mind"
Track postings: odds
Track tipster: tout

Track transaction: wager, bet
Tracked down: traced, found
Tracking device: radar
Tracking dog: bloodhound
Tracking system: radar
Tracks crossbrace: railroad tie, tie
Tracks down: hunts
Tracks, made: hied
Tracts of wasteland: heaths
Mrs. Dick Tracy: Tess
Tracy's true-heart: Tess
Trade: swap
Trade center: mart
Trade item: tool
Trade, make a: swap
Trade, prohibited: embargo
Trade punches: spar
Trade show: expo
Trade has, what a: tricks
Trader, certain, for short: arb. (short for arbitrageur)
Trade in: redeem
Trading center: mart
Trading place: mart, market
Tradition, kind of: oral
Traditional: age old
Traditional learning: lore
Traditional story: myths
Traffic circle: rotary
Traffic jam: tie-up
Traffic jam sounds: beeps, honks, blares
Traffic problem: gridlock
Traffic signal: green, amber, red
Tragedy by Euripides: Medea
Tragic footwear: buskins
Tragic king: Lear
Trail, kind of: nature
Trail mix: gorp (snack food)
Trailing: last, lagging, behind, losing
Trails behind vessels: wakes
Train accommodations: berths
Train bed: berth
Train for the ring: spar
Train, gravy
Train mail station: RPO
Train of thought: tenor
Train, slow: local
Train stop:depot
Train, stop a: flag
Train, straphanger's: local
Trainee, perhaps: new hire
Training program, intense: crash course
Training units, for short: reps
Train's current carrier: third rail
Traipse: roam, gad
Traipse about: gad
Trait carrier: gene
Trait determinant: gene
Tram contents: ores
Tramp: slog
"As if in a trance": dazedly
Tranquility, conducive to: restful
Tranquility, state of: repose
Transactions, like some: cash

Transaction, track: wager, bet
Transcript fig.: GPA
Transfer design: decal
Transfer paper design: decal
Transfer sticker: decal
Transform: alter
Transgresses: errs
Transgression: sin
Transgressor: sinner
Transistor's electrode: emitter
Transit type: rapid
Translucent ceramic ware: porcelain
Translucent mineral: mica
Transparent: clear, pellucid
Transparent linen: toile
Transparent optical device: lens
Transport, chief: canoe
Transport, fast: jet
Transport, kind of: rapid
Transport system, underground: metro
Transported: rapt
Transported kids: bused
Transported with delight: rapt
Transvaal settler(S. African province)
Trap, sets a: lays
Trap trigger: trip wire
Trapper's commodity: fur, pelt
Trappings, etc.: harness
Trapshooting, type of: skeet
Trash collector: bin
Trash hauler: scow
Trattoria entrée: calamari
      order: ravioli, penne
      sauce: pesto
      soup: minestrone
      tubes: penne
Trauma aftermath: scar
Travel around: tour
Travel about: tour
Travel agent offering: tour, cruise
Travel bag: valise, suitcase
Travel by boat: at sea
Travel choice: air, rail, car
Travel, course of: route
Travel downer: jet lag
Travel effortlessly: coast
Travel guide: map
Travel on powder: ski
Travel quickly: zoom, speed
Travel reference: atlas
Travel reservation, online: e-ticket
Travel shots: photos
Travel stops: layovers, inns
Traveler, Swift: Gulliver
Traveler's check: itinerary
Traveling actors: troupe
Traveling bag: valise
Traveling library: bookmobile
Traveling show: circus
Traveling urges: wanderlusts
Traveller's rider: Lee
Travis, Randy: singer
Trawler gear: seine, nets
Trawler's haul: shad

Trawler's net: seine
Trawling need: net
Treadmill unit: mile
Treasure: dear
Treasure box: chest
Treasure chest: arca, cista, kiste
Treasure, family: album
Treasure find: trove
Treasure guardian: gnome
Treasure hunter's aid: sonar
"Treasure Island" topic: piracy
Treasure State: Montana
Treasurer, university: bursar
Treasured: dear
Treasure's hiding place: cache
Treasures, like some: sunken
Treasury Dept. Div.: IRS
Treat badly: ill use, misuse, abuse
Treat shabbily: use
Treat with disdain: scorn
Treated a sprain: iced
Treated with a beam of light: lase
Treater's phrase: It's on me
Treater's words: on me
Treatises: theses
Treats unjustly: wrongs
Treats steel: anneals
Treaty: pact
Treaty assn.: OAS
Treaty, joined by a: allied
Treaty, old: SEATO
Treaty signer: ally
Tree anchors: roots
Tree digs: nests
Tree-dwelling animal: loris
Tree, fallen: log
"If a tree falls"
Tree, flowering: mimosa
Tree, former: stump
Tree, fragrant: fir, oleander
Tree frog: peeper
Tree giant: sequoia
Tree, graceful: weeping willow
Tree grafted site: node
Tree growth: moss
Tree house: nest
Tree knot: gnarl
Tree limb: bough
Tree, miniature: bonsai
Tree, nut: beech, walnut, hickory, pecan
Tree of Life locale: Eden
Tree or vase, kind of: Ming
Tree, quaking: aspen
Tree, Rocky Mountain: aspen
Tree snake: lora
Tree, spreading: banyan
Tree sprite: nymph
Tree that symbolizes sorrow: yew
Tree timber: apa
Tree topper: angel
Tree trimmer: tinsel
Tree trunk: bole
Tree trunk cover: moss, bark
Tree with catkins: willows

Tree with pods: cacao
Tree with smooth bark: beech
Treehouse underpinning: limb
Treeless plain: steppe
Tree-lined walk: alley, lane
Trees, of: arboreal
Tree-shaded walkway: alameda
Trekker: hike
Trekkie idol: Nimoy
Trellis: arbor, lattice
Tremble with fear: quake
Trembles: quakes
Trench, protective: moat
Trencherman's activity: eating
Trends: vogues
Trendy apartment: loft
Tres elegant: chic
Tresses, luxuriant: manes
Trevi fountain coin: lira, lire
Trevi fountain site: Rome
Trey's neighbor: deuce
Trial balloon: test
Trial print: proof
Trial run: prep
Trial setting: venue, court
Trial site: venue, court
Trial venue of note: Salem
Trials and tribulations: woes
Triangle corner: vertex
Triangle parts: sides, angles
Triangle sides: legs
Triangle tip: apex
Triangle tone: ting
Triangle, type of: acute, right, obtuse, scalene,
    isosceles, equilateral
Triangular cloth insert: gore
Triangular road sign: yield
Triangular sail: lateen, jib, Genoa
Triangular wall: gable
Triathlete vehicle: bike
Tribal adviser: elder
Tribal magician: witch doctor
Tribe or helicopter: Apache
Tribe, southwest: Paiute
Tribulations: woes, crosses, trials, ordeals
Tribute, facetious: roast
Tribute, final: eulogy
Tribute in verse: ode
Tribute, poetic: ode
Trick: ruse, wile
Trick alternative: treat
Trick, sly: wiles
Tricked: foxed
Trickery: deceit
Trickier: wilier
Trickle down: drip
Tricky, more: cagier
Tricky pool shot: massé (curving billiards
    shot)
Trident features: tines
Trident prong: tine
Trident-shaped letter: psi
Tried and true: tested, proven, secure, trusty,
    reliable, dependable

Tried out: tested
Tried to catch: ran for, ran after, paged
Trifled with: toyed
Trifling: mere
Trifling amount: mite, sou
Trifling talk: prattle
Trig function: secant
Trig terms: sine, cosine, secant, tangent
Trig units: radians
Trigger lock: safety
Trilled: sang
Trilling works, Lionel: essays
Trillion, comb. form: tera, treg, trega
Trillion, prefix for: tera
Trim back: clip, pare
Trimming, gaudy: glitz
Trinidad partner: Tobago
Trinity member: father
Trinket: bauble, gaud, gewgaw, doodad
Trinket stealer: magpie
Trio of goddesses: fates, furies, graces
Trip, honey-do: errand
Trip interruption: layover
Trip, pleasure: jaunt
Trip of a sort, short: errand
Trip segment: leg
Triple crown event: derby
Triple decker, some: BLT
Triple flip, e.g.: feat
Triple-layer sandwich: club
Tripod relative: easel
Tripoli ruler, former: Deys
Trippet: cam, wiper
Trireme mover: oars
Tristan's love: Isolde
     wife: Isolde
Tri-Star Pictures
Trite: banal, corny
Trite phrase: cliché (overused expression)
Triumph, song of: paean
Trivet part: leg
Trojan seer: Cassandra
Trojan seer, unheeded: Cassandra
Trojan war cause: Helen
Trojan war counselor: Nestor
Trojan war epic: Iliad
Trojan war figure: Nestor
Trojan war hero: Ajax, Aeneas
Trojan war saga: Iliad
Trojan war warrior: Ajax
Trojan's tailor: Sartor
Trombone slide: valve
Troopers, young: BSA
Troops, position: deploy
Trophies, tube (TV): Emmys
Trophy handles: ears
Trophy, often:cup
Trophy, wild west: scalp
Tropical basket fiber: istle
Tropical constrictor: boa
Tropical cuckoo: ani
Tropical disease: sprue
Tropical disease, chronic: sprue
Tropical eel: moray

Tropical fish: bigeye, tetra
Tropical flowering shrub: oleander
Tropical flowering tree: mimosa
Tropical fruit: ates, mango, guava
Tropical grass: bamboo
Tropical nut: kola
Tropical nut tree: kola
Tropical rain forest: biome
Tropical resin: elemi
Tropical starch: cassava
Tropical tree: banyan, eboe
Tropical ungulate: tapir (mammal)
Tropical vine: liana
Trot or gallop: ride, gait, stride
Trotsky, Leon
Trotters, had: dined (pig feet)
Troubadour prop: lute
Trouble afoot: bunion
Trouble brewing: unrest
Trouble, expecting: in for it
Trouble partner: toil
Troubled condition: unrest
Troubles (to Hamlet): ills
Troubleshoot: debug
Troublesome joint: knee
Troublesome one: twit
Trouser fabric: twill
Trouser halves: legs
Troy (Latin): Ilium
Troy mountain: Ida
Troy, NY, college: RPI
Troy, pertaining to: Ilian
Troy warrior: Ajax
Truant GI: AWOL
Truce result: peace
Truck driver: hauler
Truck floor: bed
Truck, queen's: lorry
Truck, ore: tram
Truck, sporty: Ute
Truck stop sight: semi
Truckee city: Reno
Trucker's concern: tare
Trucker's truck: rig
Trucks, all-purpose: Utes
Trudge: plod
True, name that means: Vera
Trueheart, Tess: comic
True's companion: tried
Trudge through sludge: slog
Truism: adage
Truly: really
Truman's birthplace: Lamar, MO
     wife: Bess
     instrument: piano
Trumped up: false
Trumpet muffler: mute
Truncate, as a branch: lop
Trunk: bole
Trunk content: spare, tool kit, tire iron
Trunk in a trunk: aorta
Trunk outgrowth: burl
Trunk possessor: tree
Trust account: escrow

Trusted: relied
Trusting, least: leerier
Trusting, overly: naïve
Truth, abandon the: lie
Truth stretcher: liar
Truthful: honest
Try: assay
Try, as a case: hear
Try for an ace: serve
Try out: audition, demo
Try to find: seek
Try to find out: ask
Trying experience: ordeal
Trying to lose: on a diet
Tryst keeper: lover
Tsar: czar
Tsar, terrible: Ivan
Tub ritual: bath
Tubby, too: obese
Tube (kind of): triode
Tube (TV) award: Emmy
Tube (TV) trophy: Emmy
Tuber (type of): taro
Tuber (South Seas): taro
Tube-shaped bead: bugle
"Friar Tuck"
Tucked in: snug
Tuck's title: friar
Tuffet, uses a: sits
Tug salute: toot
Tug sharply: yank, jerk
Tugboat's cable: tow rope
Tugs hard: yanks, jerks
Tukkanen, Esa: hockey
Tulle skirt: tutu
Tumble the wash: dry
Tumbler of rhyme: Jill, Jack
Tumbler's protection: mat
Tummy flattener: sit-ups
Tummy tightener: sit-ups
Tumor, fatty tissue: lipoma
Tumult: stir, din, ado
Tuna relative: bonito
Tuna salad ingredient: celery
Tuna, type of: ahi
Tune (happy): lilt
Tune (vintage): oldie
Tuned in: aware
Tunesmith's org.: ASCAP (American Society
     of Composers, Authors, and Publishers)
Tunic, full-length: caftan
Tunisian seaport: Sfax
Tunisian ruler:dey
Tuni's pasha: dey
Tunnel: dig
Tupelo phenom: Elvis
"Turandot" composer: Puccini
Turbid, make: roil
Turbulent: roiling
Tureen utensil: ladle
Turf accountant's friend: bettor
Turf area: lawn, yard, sward
Turf grabber: cleat
Turf, piece of: divot

Turf occupier: gang
Turf warriors: gang
Turgenev, Ivan: novelist
Turgenev heroine: Elena
Turgenev's birthplace: Orel
Turin term of endearment: cara mia
Turing, Alan: science
Turk, high-ranking: pasha
Turkey club: NATO
Turkey feature: wattle (loose skin hanging
     from the throat of bird or lizard)
Turkey, moisten a: baste
Turkey, on Broadway: flop
Turkey or dog: trot
Turkey or fox chaser: trot
Turkey side dish: yams
Turkey's capital: Ankara
Turkey's highest point: Ararat
Turkey's wattle: dewlap
Turkic tribesman: Tatar
Turkish bath decoration: tile
Turkish city on the Seyhan: Adana
Turkish coin: asper
Turkish dignitaries: beys
Turkish flag: olem, alem
Turkish hospice: imaret
Turkish jambalaya: pilaf
Turkish official: agha
Turkish pound: lira
Turkish speaking person: Tatar
Turkish title: pasha, aga, agha
Turkish title, old time: pasha
Turn: obvert
Turn abruptly: swerve
Turn aside: parry
Turn away: avert
Turn back: reverse
Turn down: nix, refuse
Turn down a page: dogear
Turn inside out: evert, invert
Turn left: haw
Turn off: alienate, exit
Turn on a pivot: plie, pique
Turn on the dramatics: emote
Turn on the waterworks: weep
Turn out: evict
Turn over: obvert, cede
Turn, quick: jerk
Turn right: gee
Turn signal: arrow
Turn slushy: thaw
Turn the page: PTO (please turn over), leaf
Turn toward: face
Turn yellow: ripen
Turndown: refusal
Turned chicken: ran
Turned down: vetoed, denied, refused,
     rejected
Turned off course: slued
Turned outward: everted
Turned over: ceded
Turned pale: blanched
Turned sharply: veered, zigged
Turner, Lana: actress

Turner, Nat: abolitionist
Turner, Tina: music
Turner, Tina's ex: Ike
Turning part of a dynamo: rotor
Turning point: crisis, cusp, pivot,
     climax,landmark, climacteric
Turnip: rutabaga
Turnip-shaped: napiform
Turnip-shaped root vegetable: jicama
Turnpike rumbler: semi
Turnpike stop: plaza
Turnstile: gate
Turtle to be: egg
Tuscans, certain: Sienese
Tuscany city: Siena
Tusked animal: boar
Tusker, wild: boar
Tutelage, give: instruct
Turelary deities: genii
Tutor: coach, drill, teach
Tutor, Oxford: don
Tut's sacred beetle: scarab
TV adorner: set decorator
TV adjunct: antenna, remote, VCR
TV band: UHF
TV control: knob, remote
TV equine: Mr. Ed
TV evaluator: Nielsen
TV frog: Kermit
TV from DC: C-SPAN
TV goof: blooper
TV hookup: VCR
TV planet: Ork
TV spots: ads
TV street: Sesame
TV teaser: promo
TV tube gas: xenon
TV warrior princess: Xena
Twain, Mark: Samuel Clements
Twain's "Eve's Diary"
Twangs and drawls: accents
Twangy: nasal
Tweak: nip
Tweak the memory: jog
Tweed, kind of: Harris
Tweed, like: nubby
Twelfth Hebrew month: Elul
Twelfth letter: ell
"Twelfth Night" character: Olivia
"Twelfth Night" heroine: Olivia
Twelve: comb. form: dodec, dodeca (Greek:
     dodecahedron)
Twelve points: pica
Twenty chessmen: set
Twenty, comb. form: icos, icosa, icosi (Greek:
     icosahedron)
Twenty-one or sometimes eighteen: of age
Twenty-four horas: dia
Twenty-four hours, lasting: daylong
Twenty quires: ream
Twenty-six fortnights: year
Twice: bis
Twig juncture: node
Twig shelter: nest

Twilight, poetic: eve
Twilight's dark side: dusk
Twilled cloth: serge, silesia
Twin, biblical: Esau
Twin, hairy: Esau
Twin of 90210: Brenda, Brandon
Twining shoot: bine
Twinkle: flash
Twins share them: genes
Twins, sign of: Gemini
Twist: wind, skew
Twist about: slew
Twist in pain: writhe
Twist of fate: irony, ironies
"A Twist of Fate"
Twist, Oliver
Twist out of shape: gnarl
Twist the truth: lie
Twist together: entwine
Twist, unwelcome: sprain
Twist violently: wrest
Twisted, got: kinked
Twisted: wrung
Twisted, most: wriest
Twisted treat: pretzel
Twisting and turning: snaking, restless
Twist-offs: caps
Twitch, nervous: tic
Twitch, recurring: tic
Twitches: jerks
Twittered: cheeped
Two-bedroom unit: apt
Two cents worth: input
Two cubed: eight
Two evils, one of: lesser
Two-footed animal: biped
Two, group of: diad, dyad
Two hundred fins: gee, mil
$200 monopoly properties: RRs, railroads
Two identical things: pair
Two in a row: oars
Two of a kind: set, pair
Two oxen: yoke
Two-piece part: bra, top
Two-piece suit: bikini
2.2 pound units: kilos
Two striper: NCO
Two tablets, maybe: dose
Two to two: even, tied
2000 was its year: dragon
Two-timer: rat, cad
Two-digit sign: vee
Two-edged sword: saber
Two-fold: binate, binary
Two-horse bet: exacta
Two-masted craft: ketch
Twosome: diad, dyad, duo, pair
Two-seater bicycle: tandem
"2001" author: Arthur C. Clark
Two under par score: eagle
Two-way: dual
Two- wheel farm cart: tumbrel
Two-year-old sheep: teg
Tybalt's killer: Romeo

Tyler, Anne: novelist
Tyler, Liv: actress
Tympanic membrane site: ear
Tympanum: ear drum
Tynan portrayer: Alda
Type faces: fonts
Type measures: quads
Type of appeal: snob
Type of auto insurance: no-fault
Type of barrier: sonic
Type of bear or cap: polar
Type of charge: negative, positive
Type of chord: triad
Type of collar: flea
Type of cracker: oyster
Type of deal: done
Type of diving: sky
Type of eagle: erne, bald
Type of interest: self
Type of model: role
Type of moment: senior
Type of navigation system: inertial
Type of package: care
Type of pine: scrub
Type of sight: hind
Type of stable: livery
Type of stove: potbelly
Type of survivor: sole
Type of van: mini
Type of wave or bore: tidal
Type of wit: nit
Type of wrench: allen, crescent, box-end
Type size: pica, elite, point
Type size for fine print: agate
Type style: font
Type type: pica, elite
Typed in: keyed
Types: ilks
Typesetting mistakes: errata
Typewriter bar: space
Typewriter roller: platen
Typewriter setting: tab
Typos, check for: proof
Typos, list of: errata
Tyrant: autocrat, czar, tsar, despot
Tyrant, cruel: Nero
Tyrant's comeuppance: revolt
Tyrol ending: ean
Tyrolean tunes: yodels
Tyros must learn, what: ropes
Tyr's father: Odin, Othin
Tyson, Cicely: actress
Tzara's movement: dada
Lao-tzu: philosopher

U

UAE members: emirates
U-boat movie: "Das Boot"
Ucayali River location: Peru
UCLA Bruins
UFO shape, common: disk
Uggams, Leslie: actress

Ugh: ick, yuck
Ugly, in Madrid: fea, feo
Ugly public encounter: scene
Ugly old woman: hag
Uh-huh: I see
Uh-oh: oops
Uhlan's weapon: saber
Uh's cousin: ers
Uhura's crewmate: Sulu
Ukraine capital: Kiev
UK broadcaster: BBC
UK media initials: BBC
UK part: Eng., N. Ire.
UK time: GMT, GST
"Ulalume" author: Poe
Ullmann, Liv: actress
Ulm's river: Danube
Ulterior motive: angle
Ulterior motive, without an: sincere
Ultimate aim: ideal
Ultimate cause: root
Ultimate conclusion: end-all
Ultimatum phrase: or else
Ultimatum word: or else, else
Ultra: very
UV blocker: ozone
Umbra: shadow
Umbrage: ire
Umbrage, takes: resents
Umbrella part: rib
Um-hmm: I see
Umpire guidelines: rules
Ums' kin: ers
Unable to decide: torn
Unable to flee: at bay
Unable to move: inert
Unable to react, as helium: inert
Unabridged: entire
Unaccompanied efforts: soli, solos
Unadorned: plain
Unadulterated: pure
Unaspirated: lene, unannounced
Unassuming: meek
Unaus, kin of: Ais
Unbalanced: alop
Unbeliever, pagan: infidel
Unbounded joy: glee
Unburden: free, ease, rid, confide
Uncanny: eerie
Uncanny, more: eerier
Uncaptured: at large
Uncategorized: miscellaneous
Unceasingly: ever
Uncertainty, fraught with: risky
Unchain: free
Unchangeable, to a poet: errata, e'er
Unchanging: stable, static
Unclaimed mail dept: DLO
Uncle, French: eme
    Spanish: tio
Uncle Remus character: Brer Fox, Brer Rabbit
Uncle Remus creator: Harris, Joel
"Uncle Tom's Cabin" author: Harriet Beecher
    Stowe

Uncle, well-known: Sam
Uncles and nephews: kin
Uncomfortable neckwear: noose
Uncommon: rare, rara, rara avis
Uncommon occurrence: rarity
Uncommon sense: ESP
Uncompromising: stern
Unconfirmed report: rumor, hearsay
Unconquerable opponents: nemeses
Unconscious state: coma
Uncontrollable, it may be: urge
Unconventional: outre
Unconventional, beyond: outre
Unconventional, extremely: weird
Unconventional sibilation: lisp
Uncool one: nerd, dweeb
Uncouple: detach, unhitch
Uncouth: crass, rude
Uncouth one: boor, oaf, lout
Uncouth person: oaf, boor, lout
Uncouthly, most: rudest
Unctuous: oily
Unctuous, more: suaver, oilier
Uncultured one: oaf
Uncultivated land: heath
Uncultivated plant: weed
Undecided, be: pend
Undelivered mail: nixie
Under: nether, below
Under any circumstances: at all
Under cover, still: abed
Under ideal conditions: at best
Under, in verse: neath
Under par: ill
Under the roof: indoor, inside
Under the table: covert, hidden, secret, sneaky, furtive, subrosa
Under wraps: secret
Undercover, go: spy
Underestimated: lowball
Undergarment, flexible: girdle
Undergo change: mutate
Underground access: manhole
Underground, in London: subway
Underground place: basement
Underground transport system: metro
Underground villain: mole
Underground work: mining
Underhanded: sly
Underline: stress
Undermine: sap, weaken
Underscore: stress
Undersized: puny
Undersized pups: runts
Understand: get it, see, get
Understand, easy to: clear
Understand, least likely to: densest
Understandable: clear, lucid
Understanding: empathy
Understood by only a few: arcane
Understood without being expressed: tacit
Undertake: try
Undertake something superficially: dabble
Undertow, to Hans: sog

Underwater weapon: depth charge
Underway, get: go, leave, start, begin
Underworld river: Styx
Underwriter: insurer, angel
Undesirable condition: malady
Undeveloped nations: Third World
Undisguised: overt
Undistinguished crowd: ruck
Undoes: ruins
Undoes a dele: stets
Undone, wished: rued
Undressed, may come: salad
Undue pressure: duress
Undulating: wavy
Unduly: too
Une, _deux_
Unearth: dredge, excavate
Uneasiness, unfocused: malaise
Uneasy feeling: malaise
Uneaten morsel: ort
Unescorted male: stag
Uneven: spotty
Uneven, as if gnawed: erose
Unevenly edged: erosed
Unexpected benefit: manna
Unexpected defeat: facer, upset
Unexpected help: manna
Unexpected win: upset
Unfamiliar: alien
Unfavorable: adverse
Unfettered: loose
Unfilled slot, abbr.: TBA (to be announced)
Unfilled space: void, blank
Unfired brick: adobe
Unflinching: stoic
Unfocused uneasiness: malaise
Unfold (to a poet): ope
Unforeseeable event: act of God
Unforeseen problem: snag
Unfortunate: unlucky
Unfounded reports: rumors
Unfrequented: lone
Ungentlemanly chap: cad, lout
Ungentlemanly one: lout, cad
Unglued, come: rage
Ungulate, long-nosed: tapir
Unhearing: deaf
Unhip one: nerd
Unhurried gait: lope
Unicellular organism: amoeba, ameba
Unicellular plant: diatum, diatom
UFO shape: disk
Uniform: equal
Uniform color: olive
Uniform fabric: chino
Uniform ornament: epaulet
Uniform segment, WWII: puttee
Uniformity, relieve of: vary
Unimaginative: stale
Uninteresting: dry
Union branch: local
Union flouter: scab
Union, kind of: credit
Union man: yankee

Union members: yankees, workers
Union oath: I do
Union pariah: scab
Unique person: rara avis
Uni relative: mono
Unisex attire: tee, slacks, sarong
Unisex wear: tee, slacks
Unison, in: as one, sync
Unit: one, module
Unit equal to 15.432 grains: gram
Unit of inductance: henry
Unit of light: pyr
Unit of loudness: sone
Unit of pressure: torr
Unite securely: weld, solder
United: allied
UAE group: emirates
United group: bloc
UK broadcaster: BBC
UK fliers: RAF (Royal Air Force)
UK media initials: BBV
UK time: GMT, GST
United Nations loaner: IMF
United Nations Kofi _Annan_
USAF unit: sac
U.S. leader: pres.
USS Arizona locale: Oahu
Universal competitor: MGM
Universal time, abbr.: GMT
Universe, like the: vast
Universe, of the: cosmic
University acquisition: degree
University board member: regent
University numbers: GPAs
University prof: don
University treasurer: bursar
University VIP: prexy
Unkempt: ragtag
Unkempt state: mess
Unkind, extremely: harsh
Unknown author: anon.
Unknown factors: ifs
"Unknown" surname: Doe
Unlace: loosen, untie
Unlawful removal: hoist, robbery
Unless: nisi
Unless, in law: nisi
Unlimited credit: blank check
Unload or put off fraudulently: fob off
Unloaded, in a way: sold
Unlock: open
Unlucky consequence: tough break
Unlucky gambler: loser
Unlucky time: ides
Unmanned aircraft: drone
Unmanned spacecraft: drone
Unmatched: odd
Unmeasured amount: any
Unmoving: inert
Unnamed person: someone
Unnatural aura: eeriness
Unnatural, frighteningly: eerie
Unnerve: unman, upset, rattle, alarm
Uno doubled: dos

Uno plus one: dos
"Numero uno"
Uno plus duo: tre
Uno y dos: tres
Unorthodox belief: heresy
Unpaid autoworker, type of: robot, mechanical robot
Unpaid debt: arrears
Unpen: release
Unpleasant: nasty
Unpleasant look: leer
Unpleasant thing to eat: crow
Unpolished: coarse
Unpopular statutes: blue laws
Unpowered craft: glider, sled
Unprecedented: novel
Unpredictable: erratic
Unprincipled one: cad, evil
Unproductive: otiose
Unqualified: utter
Unravel: fray
Unreal: illusory
Unrefined: crude, raw
Unrestrained revelry: riot
Unrewarding: hard scrabble
Unruffled: sedate
Unruly bunch: mob
Unruly do: mop
Unsaid: tacit
Unsaid but understood: tacit
Unsalted: bland
Unsatisfactory: off
Unsavory: sordid
Unseal (to a poet): ope
Unseeded, left: fallow
Unseemly: improper
Unseen emanation: aura
Unseen particle: atom
Unseld, Wes: basketball
Unsettled: stormy
Unskilled person: peon, dub
Unsmiling: doom, dour
Unsolicited script, an, e.g.: spec
Unsophisticated: naive
Unsophisticated person: cornball, naif, yokel, rube
Unspoiled locales: Edens
Unspoken: tacit
Unspoken but understood: tacit
Unstable radioactive element: astatine
Unsubstantial, more: wispier
Unsuitable: inapt
Unsullied: pure
Untamed: wild, savage
Untidy one: slob
Untidy person: sloven, slob
Until now: to date
A law unto itself
Untold centuries: eons
Untrained, as a recruit: raw
Untrue, declare: deny
Untrustworthy sort: rogue
Unused portion: rest
Unusual collectible: curio

Unusual, in Caesar's day: rara, rara avis
Unusual, most: rarest
Unusual quality: oddness
Unusual thing: rara avis
Unusual, to Pliny: rara
Unusually smart: apt
Unvarnished: raw
Unwanted guests: bores, ants, pests
Unwanted sound: noise
Unwary: naive
Unwavering: rigid
Unwelcome email: spam
Unwelcome expression: leer
Unwelcome kind of wicket: sticky
Unwelcome mail: bills
Unwelcome obligation: onus
Unwelcome twist: sprain
Unwelcome visit: invasion
Unwholesome vapor: miasma
Unwilling: loath
Unwilling, be: demur
Unwilling to negotiate: adamant
Unwind: relax
Unwitting accomplice: pawn
Unwitting one: pawn
Unwitting tool: cat's paw
Unwrap: open
Unwrap eagerly: rip open
Unwritten test: oral
Unyielding: firm, rigid
Unzipped, come: gape
Up a creek: in a jam
Up above: atop
Up and about: astir
Up and running: alive
Up-and-up, on the: legit, legal
Up, ante: pay
Up for payment: due
Up in the air: iffy
Uplifted: edified
Up next: on deck
Up to: until, til, till
Up to date: modern, modish, timely, trendy, abreast, current
Up to date, most: newest
Up to now: as yet, yet
Up to the job: able
Up to the task: able
Upbeat outlook: optimism
Update, as a license: renew
Uphill battle, it has an: coho
Upholstery fabric: poplin, velour, damask
Uplifting element: helium
"Fie upon this quiet life"
Upper body: torso
Upper class: rank, elite, gentry, peerage, quality, society, affluent
Upper crust: elite
Upper left key: esc
Upper hand: edge
Upper house: senate
Upper or lower, it may be: case
Upper part: top
Uppity one: snob

Uppsala resident: Swede
Upright and slender: reedy
Upright pillar: stele
Uproar: riot, din, ruckus, to-do
Uproar, wild: bedlam
Ups and downs, statistical: trends
UPS delivery: package
UPS units: lbs.
Upscale: tony
Upscale cheese: brie
Upscale cookie: scone
Upscale neighborhood: exurb
Upscale wheels: Mercedes, BMW
Upset the money market: devalue
Upset, very: irate
Upsilon follower: phi
Upsilon preceder: tau
Upswept hairdo: pouf
Uptight, more: uneasier
Uraeus feature: asp, serpent
UR locale: Iraq
Uranium decay product: astatine
U-235: isotope
Uranus moon: Ariel
Urban: suave, debonair
Urban blight: slum, smog, gang
Urban concern: zoning
Urban cruiser: taxi
Urban eyesore: slum
Urban grocery store: bodega
Urban ill: smog
Urban map: plat
Urban nuisance: pigeons
Urban people movers: Els
Urban plaza, small: minipark
Urban roads: Streets
Urchin: waif
Urchin, street: gamin, waif
Urdu speaker: Asian
Urey, Harold: chemist
Urgency: haste
Urgency initials: ASAP
Urgent: dire
Urgent acronym: ASAP
Urgent appeal: plea
Urgent notation: ASAP
Urgent request: plea
Urges: yens
Urges on: spurs
Uris hero: Ari
Uris, Leon: writer
Uris novel: The Haj
URL beginning: http
"URL" piece: slash, com
"URL" punctuation: dot
"URL" suffix: org, com, gov
Urn homophone: erne
Uruguay monetary unit: peso
"Us", in Bonn: uns
        in Essen: uns
"Us," to Popo: enemy
"USCG" officer: ensign, ens.
Use a diapason: tune
Use a hand shuttle: tat

Use a remote: zap
Use a straw: sip
Use a swizzle stick: stir
Use a whetstone: hone
Use a whisk: whip
Use, as traverse: ply
Use intimidation: coerce
Use sparingly: eke
Use the overhead: show
Use tendrils: climb
Used a foot pedal: treaded
Used a hawser: roped, towed, cabled
Used car transaction: resale
Used car worry: rust
Used eyelets: laced, tied
Used, not being: idle, on ice
Used plastic: owed, paid, bought
Used to be: was, inured
Useful, be: avail
Useful hint: tip
Useful, prove: avail
Useful quality: asset
Useful things: assets
Useful word processing feature: undo
Useless: otiose, worthless
Users drop it: acid
Uses an abstergent: laves
Uses a curling iron: crimps
Uses a fork: stabs, eats
Uses a parachute: bails
Uses a radar: scans
Uses a tuffet: sits
Uses an auger: bores
Uses bath powder: dusts
Uses cosmetics: makes up
Uses, has 1001
Uses jointly: shares
Uses up: expends
Ushers: sees in
Usher in: herald
Usher's beat: aisle
USMA: U.S. Military Academy
USN bigwig: admiral, adm.
USO offering: road show
U.S. Open rank: seed
USPS has one: creed
USPS rival: email
Ustinov, Peter: actor
Usual practice: habit
Usurp forcefully: wrest
Utah Beach vessel: LST
Utah dam: Flaming Gorge
Utah feature: salt flats
Utah mountains: Uinta
Utah range: Uinta
Utah resident, longtime: Ute
Utah ski resort: Alta
Utah state flower: sego lily
Utility gauge: gas meter
Utility measure: kwh
Utilize, fail to: waste
Utmost: nth
Utopia Planitia setting: Mars
Utopian visions: ideals

Utter a dismal cry: yowl
Utter aloud: read
Utter an orison: pray
Utter chaos: havoc
Utter deliriously: rave
Utter disorder: chaos
Utter failure: bust
Utter indistinctly: slur
Utterly defeat: thrash, romp
Utterly inattentive: out to lunch
Utterly senseless: absurd
Uxmal resident: Mayan
Uxorial: wifely

V

Vacation acquisition: tan
Vacation option: cruise
Vacation plus: suntan
Vacation spot: spa
Vacation spot, exotic: Bali
Vaccaro or Lee: Brenda
Vaccinated: immune
Vaccine amount: cc's
Vaccine measure: cc's
Vaccine vials: ampules, ampoules
Vacillating, without: firmly
Vacillate: yoyo
Vacuum attachment: wand
Vacuum tube: diode, triode, tetrode
Vacuum's lack: air
Vader, once: Jedi
Vade mecum: guide, manual, baedeker,
    handbook, guidebook
Vader's domain: Empire
Vader's side: Empire
Quo vadis
Vagabond: bum, hobo
Vagrant: hobo
Vague: hazy
Vague amount: some
Vague feeling: sense
Vague impression, have: sense
Vague rumors: on-dits
Vague thought: notion
Vail amenity: ski tow, T-bar
Vain dude: fop
Vain one: fop
Vain bird's mate: peahen
Val and Aleta's son: Arn
Vale, Jerry: music
Valedictorian, name, e.g.: honor
Valentine: heart
Valentine figure: cherub
Valhalla honcho: Odin
Valhalla host: Odin
Valid reasoning: logic
Validate: stamp
Vallée from Vermont: Rudy
Valletta locale: Malta
Valletta's place: Malta
Valley, hidden: glen
Valley known for its wines: Napa

Valley, secluded: glen
Valley, small narrow: ravine
Valley where Goliath met death: Elah
Valley, wooded: glen, dell
Value, without: null, worthless
Valuable fur: ermine, mink
Valuable glacial deposit: placer
Valuable mineral: gem
Valuable possession: asset
Valuable quality: asset
Valuable stash: trove (collection of valuables)
Valuable things: assets
Valve attachment: tappet
Vamoosed: fled
Vamp (act like a): seduce, tempt
Vamp, movie: Theda Bara
Vampire: lamia (classical monster of Greek
    and Roman mythology)
Vampire, female: lamia
Vampire, famous: Dracula
Vampire repellent: garlic
Vampire vanquisher: stake
Vampires, some: bats
Vamp's wrap: boa
Van Ark, Joan: actress
Van der Rohe, Mies: architect
Van der Waal's equation
Van der Waal's force
Van Gogh flower: iris
Van Gogh painted here: Arles
Van Gogh painting: Irises
Van Gogh setting: Arles
Van Gogh, Vincent
Van Gogh's city: Arles
Van Gogh's medium: oils
Van Pelt, Lucy
Vance, Cyrus: Secretary of state
Vancouver island native: Kwakiutl
Vandal: Hun
Vane bird's mate: peahen
Vanessa's sister: Lynn
Vanilla source: bean
Vanisher (1937): Earhart
Vanity: ego
Vanity case kin: etui
Vanna's cohost: Pat
Vanquish: defeat
Vanquish a dragon: slay
Vanquished one: loser
Von Sydow, Max: actor
Vapor, unwholesome: miasma
Vaporous: gaseous
Variable studies: algebra
Variations, slight: nuances
Varied collection: olio
Varieties: ilks
Variety, of a: typal
Variety of corundum: emery
Variety of topics: miscellany
Variety show: revue
Various functions: uses
Varnish ingredient: elemi, resin, laq, lac
Varnished truth: lie
Varsity: A team

Varsity, made: lettered
Vasco de Gama: explorer
Vase: urn
Vase, footed: urn
Vase handle: ansate
Vase or tree: Ming
Vase, porcelain: Ming
Vase, type of: bud
Vase, valuable: Ming
Vase with pedestal: urn
Vases, often: jars
Vase-shaped pitcher: ewer
Vassal: serf
Vassal oath: fealty
Vassal's land: fief
Vassar grads, most: alumnae
Vast number: slew, myriad
Vat, large: tun
Vatican ambassador: nuncio
Vatican surrounding: Roma, Rome
Vatican related: papal
Vaudeville bit: skit
Vaudeville prop: cane
Vaughan, Sarah: vocalist
Vault, underground: crypt
Vaulted recess: apse
Vaya con dios: adios
VCR button: mute
VCR, early: Beta
VCR needs: TVs
Veal marsala: entrée
Veal, thin-sliced: scallop
Veblen, Oswald: math
Vedic intonation: mantra
Vedder, Eddie: rock music
Veer: yaw
Veer off course: slue
Veer out of control: skid
Veg out: relax, laze around, loll
Vega's astral home: Lyra
Vega's constellation: Lyra
Vegan's staple: tofu
Vegan's taboo: red meat, meat
Vegas lead-in: Las
Vegas sevens: naturals
Vegetable, Bourbon Street: okra
Vegetable, green: kale
Vegetable oil type: canola
Veggie, orange: yam
Veggie sponge: loofah
Vehement argument: heated
Vehicle, gravity-powered: sled
Vehicle, off-road: Jeep, ATV
Vehicle owner's document: title
Vehicle, roomy: van
Vehicle, versatile: Ute
Vehicle with a checkered past: taxi
Veiling material: tulle
Vein content: ore
Vein network: rete
Veldt: grassland
Veldt grazer: gnu
Velvet ending: een
Velvet Fog, The: Torme

Velvety plant: moss, gynura
Velvety surface: knap
Omnia venat amor: love conquers all
Vendetta: feud
Vending, second: resale
Veneer: façade
Venerable advisor: elder
Venerable scholar: Bede
Venerated object: relic
Venetian boat: gondola
Venetian boatman: gondolier
Venetian bridge: rialto
Venetian evening: sera
Venetian honcho: doge
Venetian magistrate: doge
Venetian or Florentine: Italian
Venetian product: glass, glassware
Venetian ruler: doge
Venetian school: Titian, Bellini, Teipolo,
     Veronese, Giorgione
Venetian street: canal
Venezuela, island near: Aruba
Venezuelan Indians: Caribs
Veni, vidi, vici: I came, I saw, I conquered
Venice of the East: Bangkok, Udaipur
Venice of the North: Bruges, Brugge
     Amsterdam, Stockholm
Venice's old ruler: doge
Venice's principal waterway: Grand Canal
Venom carrier: fang
Venom's toxic substance: venin
Vent ending: ure
Ventilated, better: airier
Ventura, Jesse: governor
Venue: site
Venue for thousands: arena
Venus de Milo
Venus de Milo's lack: arms
Venus, son of: Amor
"Venus of Urbino" painter: Titian
Aloe vera lotion
Veracruz capital: Jalapa
Veranda, Hawaiian: lanai
Verb, Dogpatch: ain't
Verb finish: ose
Verb preceder: noun
Verbal abuse: flak
Verbal attack, launch a: lash out
Verbal blows, exchange: spar
Verbal defiance: lip, sass
Verbal stumble: stammer
Verbalized an ache: moaned
Verbally acidic: sharp of mouth, sharp
     tongued
Verbose: wordy
Verbose, hardly: terse
Verdant: lush, green
Verdi classic: Aida
Verdi creation: opera
Verdi heroine: Aida
Verdi masterpiece: Il Trovatore
Verdi opera: Il Trovatore, Aida
Aider by verdict
Verdigris: patina

Verdi's princess: Aida
Verdon, Gwen: dancer, actress
Verdugo, Elena: actress
Verges: rims
Verifiable statement: fact
Vermicelli: pasta
Vermont granite center: Barre
Verne captain: Nemo
Verne hero: Nemo
Verne, Jules: writer
Versailles agreement: oui
Versatile vehicle: Ute
Verse: sonnet, poem
Verse (fourteen lines): sonnet
Verse having three measures: trimeter
Verse, laudatory: ode
Verse lead-in: uni
Verse prefix: uni
Verse, three-lined: haiku
Verse, tribute in: ode
Versed in: up on
Verses, make: rhyme
Version, first: draft
Version in process: beta
Versus: against
Vertex: apogee
Vertical metal strip: stave
Vertical position: apeak, upright
Verve: elan (vigor and enthusiasm)
Very: ultra
Very angry: livid
Very close ending: photo finish
Very cold temperature: absolute zero
Very funny person: riot
Very heavy: leaden, ponderous
Very hot: boiling
Very important: value, valued
Very, in France: tres
Very in music: assai
Very in Vera Cruz: muy
Very, informally: real, really
Very old car gadget: crank
Very or too: adverbs
Very popular: hot
Very precious: golden
Very reclusive: eremitic
Very soon after: upon
Very soon now: any day
Very sweet: angelic
Very tired: bleary, all in
Very upset: irate
Very, very: ultra
Very well known: famous
Vespid: wasp, hornet
Vespucci, Amerigo: navigator
Vessel, small sailing: lugger
Vessel, two-mast: ketch
Vessel used for boiled breakfast item: egg cup
Vessel's curved planks: sny
Vest: weskit, waist coat
Vestibule: hall
Vestige: shred, trace, mark, sign
Vestment: robe, alb
Vestment, ancient: ephod

Vestment, linen: alb
Vestment, liturgical: alb, amice
Vesuvian flow: lava, ash
Vesuvius flow: lava, ash
Vex greatly: plague
Vexation: ire
Vexed: plagued
VHS predecessor: Beta
Via Appia: iter
Vial warmer, chemist's: etna, bunsen
Vibrant, hardly: drab
Vibrate: whir
Vibration, nervous: tremor
Vicar's helper: curate
Vicinity, in the: around, near
Vicious criminal: thug
Vicious old woman: hag
Vicksburg fighter: Reb
Victim: goat
Victim, early: Abel
Victim, initial: Abel
Victim of Genesis: Abel
Victim one of murder one: Abel
Victim, Vesuvius's: Pompeii
Victorian: era, prissy
Victorian garment: corset
Victorian interjection: egad
Victorian oath: egad
Victorian or Napoleonic: era
Victorian outburst: egad
Victorian sort: prig
Victor's retreat: winner sanctum
Victor's wreath: laurel
Victory sign: vee
Victrola maker: RCA
Vidal, Gore: writer
Video companion: audio
Video game classic: Pac-Man
Video game Hedgehog: Sonic
Video game movie: Tron
Video game pioneer: Atari
Video partner: audio
Video store offering: rental
Vienna sausage: wiener
Vienna-based cartel: OPEC
Viennese analyst: Freud
Viennese dessert: torte
Veni, vidi, vici
Vidi: I saw, see
View as: deem
View flirtatiously: ogle
View from an oasis:
View from Everest: Nepal
View, coming into: emergent
View, kind of: bird's eye
"A Room with a View"
View with approval: admire
Viewed with alarm: feared
Vigilance, state of: alert
Vigilant, in Vichy: alerte
Vigoda, Abe: actor
Vigor, assured: elan
Vigor, enthusiastic: elan
Vigor, full of: lusty

Vigor, lacking: enfete, effete
Vigor partner: vim
Vigorous: robust
Vigorous, make: animate
Viking, noted: Erik
Viking, comic strip: Hagar
Viking letters: runes
Viking name: Olaf, Erik
Viking, perhaps: raider
Villa d'Este
Village: dorp (s. African village)
Village figure: idiot
Village, South African: dorp
Villain, classical: Iago
Villainous expression: sneer
Villainous visages: sneers
Villain's foe: hero
Villain's lament: foiled
Vincent, Fay: baseball
Vincit omnia veritas
Vine, climbing: wisteria
Vine, jungle: liana
Vine product: melon, grape
Vine, southern: kudzu
Vine, woody: liana
Vine-covered recess: arbor
Vinegar acid: acetic
Vinegar based: acetic, acetum
Vinegar bottle: cruet
Vinegar holder: cruet
Vinegar mixer: oil
Vinegary: acid, acetic, acidic
Vineyard unit: acre
Vintage: old
Vinton, Vobby: music
"Violà": ta-da
Viola clef: treble
Viola's brother: Sebastian
           husband: Orsino
Violent change: upheaval
Violent storm: typhoon
Violet lead-in: ultra
Violin kin: fiddle
Violin knob: peg
Violin maker, noted: Amati
Violin middle: waist
Violin part: bow, peg
Violin relative: cello
Violin, valuable: Amati
Violin virtuoso: Menuhin
Violinist's heirloom, perhaps: Amati
Violinist's need: rosin
Violin's curved heads: scrolls
Violist's clef: treble, bass
Viper, European: adder
Viperides members: adders
Virago: shrew
Virgil's epic:Aeneid
Virgil's epic hero: Aeneas
Virgil's Trojan hero: Aeneas
Virgin goddess: Diana, Hestia, Artemis
Virginia dance: reel
Virginia caverns: Luray
VMI student: cadet

Virgo's neighbor: Libra
Virtual page: website
Virtuoso: ace
Virtuous: moral
Visage: face
Visage, villainous: sneers
Visayan island: Leyte (Philippines)
Viscera: innards
Viscid exudates: gums
Viscosity symbol: eta
Viscount's superior: earl
Viscous substance: goop
Vise grip
Vice versa
Vishnu avatar: Rama
Vishnu, incarnation of: Rama
Visibility, lessened: fogged
Visibly frightened: ashen
Visigoth king: Alaric
Vision, defective: anopia, myopia
Visit often: haunt
Visit slumber land: doze
Visit, unwelcome: invasion
Visitor from Melmac: ALF
Visitor, receive as a: see
Visitor to Siam: Anna
Visitor, weekend: house guest
Visitors, frequent: habitués
Visitor's opposition: home team
Visored helmet: armet
Visual aid: graph, chart
Visual ailment: myopia
Vital fluid: plasma
Vital force: soul
Vital sign: pulse
Vitality: life, élan
Vitamin amts.: RDAs
Vitamin B: niacin
Vitamin extra: iron
Vitamin info.: RDA
Vituperation: abuse
Viva Las Vegas
Viva voce: oral, orally, spoken
Vivacity: élan
Viva Zapata
Bon vivant
Vive le roi
Vive's opposite: abas
Vivid images: eidetic
VJ's channel: MTV
Vladimir Ulyanov: Lenin
Pax vobiseum
Vocabulary (specialized): argot
Vocabulary, total: lexis
Vocal sound: tone
Vocalist, top-notch: diva
Sotto voce (soft voice):
Viva voce: word of mouth
Vodka and lime juice drink: gimlet
"Vogue" rival: Elle
Voice above tenor: alto
Voice box: larynx
Voice, low: alto
Voiceless consonants: surbs

Voigt, Jon: actor
Volatile liquid: nitro
Vol-au-vent: French menu item
Volcanic dust: ash
Volcanic flow: magma, lava
Volcanic glass: obsidian
Volcanic rock:basalt, pumice
Volcano cracks: vents
Volcano detritus: ash
Volcano, famous: Etna
Volcano fissure: vent
Volcano, Mexican: Popocatepetl
Volcano mouth: crater
Volcano output: magma
Volcano shape: cone
Volcano top: cone
Deo volente
Volition: will
Volley, start the: serve
Volleyball player: striker
Volstead act opponents: wets
Volts or watts: units
Volume: tome
Volume, heavy, large: tome
Volume, huge: tome
Volume measure: cubic
Volumnia's son: Coriolanus
Volunteers: offers
Voluptuous: sensual
Von Bismarck, Otto
Von Richthofen's title: baron
Von Braun, Wernher: rocket inventor
Vonnegut Jr., Kurt: novelist
Vontrier, Lars: director
"Voodoo" singer: D'Angelo
Voodoo slave: zombie
Voracious mouth: maw
Voracious plant: flytrap
Vortex: eddy
Vote, declines to: abstains
Vote, swing: independent
Voter: citizen
Votes: ayes
Votes against: nos
Voting district: ward
Voting group: bloc
Voting number: quorum
Vouch for: attest
Voucher: chit
Vouchsafe: award, favor, deign, give
S'il vous plait
Vowel sequence: AEI
Vowel topper: umlaut
Vows venue: altar
Maiden voyage: first trip
Voyager 1 destination: Saturn
Déjà vu
Vulcan's forge: Etna
Vulgate's language: Latin
Vulpine abodes: dens

W

Wabash locale: Indiana, Ind.
Wabe's, Ashea, stage Name: Little Egypt
Wacky: zany
Wacky, most: zaniest
Wad, tobacco: quid
Wading birds: plover, egret, ibis, rael
Wade through puddles: slog, slosh
Wader: boot
Wader, long-billed: ibis
Wader, majestic: egret
Wader, plumed: egret
Wader, sharp-billed: egret
Wader, showy: egret
Wadi: oasis, dry river bed
Wafer-like, amazingly: paper-thin
Wage receipt: pay slip
Wager: bet, ante
Wager, match a: see
Wagner forte: opera
Wagner opera: Lohengrin
Wagon, large farm: wain
Wagon, primitive: ox cart
Wagon puller: horses, oxen
Wagon train direction: west
Wagon train team: mules
Wags words: quip
Wahine's welcome: aloha, lei
Wail: ululate
Wail, sorrowful: alas
Wailed: keened
Wailed in lamentation: keened
Wailing instrument: sax
Wailing woman of yore: banshee
Wails: keens
Waist band: sash
Waist material: sash
Waistcoat: vest
Waistline, high: empire
Wait: bide
Wait awhile: bide
Wait in concealment: lurk
Wait nearby: hover
Wait patiently for: abides
"Wait until dark"
Waiter's check: tab, bill
Waiter's handout: menu
Waiter's helpers: bus boys
Waiting in the wings: on tap
Waiting one's turn: on deck, in line
Waiting room: lobby
Waka and banca: canoes
Wake, toward the: astern
Wake-me-up: coffee
Waken: call
Waker upper: alarms
Wake-up call: alarm, reveille
"Waking Ned Divine"
Waldheim, Kurt: United Nations
"Where's Waldo"
Walesa, Lech: Poland leader
Walk a long distance: hike

Walk, a way to: on air, on water
Walk all over: traipse
"Walk Away Renee"
Walk, carefree: amble
Walk childishly: toddle
Walk heavily: plod, tramp
Walk laboriously: plod
Walk on eggs: tip-toe
Walk, shaded: mall
Walk slowly: amble
Walk softly: pad
Walk tall: stride
Walk the beat: patrol
Walk tiredly: plod
Walk unsteadily: totter
Walk with vigor: strides
Walked from bank to bank: waded
Walker, easy: ambler
Walker, Alice: writer
Walker, Greg: cartoonist
Walker, in a liquor cabinet: Hiram
Walker, wobbly: dodderer
Walking skeleton: bag of bones
Walking, started: toddled
Walking stick: cane
Walkman accessory: adapter
Walkman brand: Sony
Walk-on: bit, role
Walks: treads
Walks barefoot: pads
Walks imperiously: strut
Walks laboriously: trudges
Walkthrough: rehearsal
Walkway: aisle
Walkway, sloping: ramp
Walkway, tree-shaded: alameda
Wall border: dado
Wall bracket: sconce
Wall columns: antae
Wall covering: paint, mural, wallpaper
Wall décor: mural
Wall hanging: art, arras
Wall hanging, modern: HD TV
Wall, off the
Wall painting: fresco
Wall recess: niche
Wall section: panel
Wall Street concern: economy
Wall Street debut: IPO
Wall Street director: Stone,
Wall Street index: S and P
Wall Street jump: rally
Wall Street landmark: NYSE
Wall Street name: Dow
Wall Street optimist: bull
Wall Street skeptic: bear
Wall Street watchdog: SEC
Wall Street worker: arb.
Wallach, Eli: actor
Walled city, once: Berlin
Wallet filler: cash, one's
Walleye fish: pike
Wallpaper, etc.: décor
Wallpaper, roll of: bolt

Walls, without: open
Walrus cousin: sea lion
Walrus hunter: aleut
Walrus tooth: tusk
Walt Kelly comic strip: Pogo
Walt Kelly possum: Pogo
Walton daughter: Erin
Waltz city: Vienna
Wampum: peag
OBI Wan Kenobi
Wand: rod
Wand wielder: fairy
Wander: gad, roam
Wander about: gad
Wanderer: nomad
Wanderlust, one with: nomad
Wane, on the: ebbing
Wanes in intensity: sags
Wang, Vera: designer
Wankel's wonder: nngine
Wanly: palely
"All I want"
Want ad abbr.: EEO
Want badly: desire
Wanted poster depiction: felon
Wanted poster initials: AKA
Wanted poster offer: award, reward
Wanted poster word: reward
Wanting: needy, needing
Wanting it all: greedy
Wapiti: elk
Wapiti relative: moose
Boer War
War, engaged in: waged
War mementos: scars
War of the Roses house: York
Warbuck's, Daddy, servant: Asp
Ward healer: doc, medic
Ward off: avert
Ward, Sela: actress
Warden: jailer
Warden fear: riot
Wardrobe: armoire
Wardrobe, large: armoire
Warehouse: depot,
Warehouse worker: stock keeper
Warfare: strife
Warhol, Andy: writer
Warhol subject: can
Warhol's genre: pop art
Warm and cozy: toasty
Warm and humid: muggy
Warm and pleasant: balmy
Warm greeting: embrace
Warm over: reheat
Warm up: prep
Warmhearted: nice, kind
Warming beverage: cocoa
Warmly comfortable: snug, cozy
Warmonger god: Ares
Warms up: heats
Warning: omen
Warning float: buoy
Warning, old-time: alarum

Warning, surfer's: fin
Warped: bend, bent
Warranted, not: undue
Warranty, without: as is
Warren dweller: rabbit
Warren report name: Oswald
Warrior at Troy: Ajax
Warrior, fierce: Maori
Warrior, fearsome: Zulu
Warrior princess: Xena
Warrior, Shogun: Ninja
Warrior woman: Amazon
Warrior's horse: steed
Warship: frigate, carrier
Wary, more: leerier
Was an omen of: augured
Was concerned about: cared
Was driven: rode
Was fooled: bit
Was in front: led
Was in store for: awaited
Was in the red: owed
Was more inventive: lied
Was over-fond: doted
Was the cause of: led to
Was, to Livy: erat
Was, to Ovid: erat
Was willing: would
Wash: lave
Wash ashore: beach
Wash down: hose
Wash out with solvent: elute
Wash, tumble the: dry
Wash Vigorously: Scour
Washboard abs
Washed down:hosed
Washed out: faded, eroded, beat, all in,
　　　spent, weary, bushed
Washed up: beat, done, kaput, spent,
　　　done in, defunct
Washer companion: dryer
Washing machine phase: cycle
Washing machine units: loads
Washington, Dinah: singer
Washington waterway: Puget
Washout: dud
Washroom, for short: lav
Washroom, London: loo
Washroom tub: basin
Washstand item: ewer
Wasn't colorfast: bled
Wasn't enough: ran short
Wasn't forthright: lied
Wasn't merely mad: rage
Wassail alternative: nog
Wasserstein, Wendy: Playwright
Waste allowance: tret
Waste away: fade, fail, molder, shrink
　　　atrophy, decline, dwindle
Waste away gradually: erode
Waste maker: haste
Waste material: slag
"Waste not, want not," e.g.: adage
Waste site: dust bin

Waste time: dally
Wasted: ill-spent
Wasted no time: sped
Wasted, not: used
Wasteland, heath-covered: moor
Wasteland, tract of: heath
Wasting time: idling
Watch chain: fob
Watch for a special purpose: observe
Watch from the bleacher: spectate
"Watch it, buster": hey
Watch out: beware, make way
Watch pocket: fob
Watch secretly: spy
Watch winder: stem
Watchdog breed: akita
Watched the birdies: posed
Watching period: vigil
Watchmaker, Sportura: Seiko
Water: oxide
Water, after vaporization: steam
Water and alcohol: solvents, solutions,
　　　liquid
Water and rust: oxide
Water bottles: carafes
Water buffalo: arna, bovid, oxen,
　　　carabao (female)
Water carrier: pipe
Water chestnut: saligot
Water closet, British: loo
Water container, circular: basin
Water conveyance: boat
Water coolers: ice cubes
Water-covered: awash
Water cow: dugong, manatee
Water down: thin
Water holder: pail, bucket, tank
Water, in combo: hydro
Water, in Baja: agua
Water in the Seine: eau
Water, lazy: bayou
Water lily: lotus
Water lily leaves: pads
Water lily painter: Monet
Water, look for: dowse
Water nymph: lily, naiad, mayfly
Water or oil: resource
Water oscillation: seiche
Water partner: soap
Water pipe: main
Water place: spa
Water plant: lotus
Water plants: tend, lilies
Water power org.: TVA
Water ski locale: lake
Water slide: chute
Water softener: borox
Water source: well, tap, hydrant
Water spirit, female: nixie
Water sport: polo,
Water, supply: hydrate
Water surface movement: seiche
Water tank: cistern
Water under the bridge, like: past

Water wheel: noria
Watercourse, dry: wadi
Watercraft: raft, boat, ship
Watered silk: moire
Waterfall sound: roar
Waterfront event: tide
Waterfront sight: quay
Waterless: bone dry
Water-level control: sluice gate
Waterlogged: sodden, soaked
"Waterloo" pop group: Abba
Waterloo's location: Belg (Belgium)
Waterproof, make: seal
Water's edge: shore
Waters, Ethel: music
Waterson, Sam: actor
Waterspout, grotesque: gargoyle
Waterway, narrow: strait
Waterworks, turn on the: weep
Watery: runny, thin,
Watery blood component: sera, serum
Wats, part of: area
Wattle, turkey's: dewlap
Waugh, Alec: novelist
Wave: roller, flutter
Wave away: shoo
Wave, catch a: surf
Wave crest: white cap
Wave cutter: prow
Wave down: flag, hail
Wave down a taxi: flag, hail
Wave foam: spume
Wave hello: greet, welcome
Wave in Seville: ola
Wave maker: sea
Wave of applause: round
Wave on le lac: onde
Wave peak: crest
Wave preceder: tidal
Wave prefix: micro
Waved the white flag: called it quits
Wavelet: ripple
Waves, big: rollers
Waves, small: ripples
Waves, where to make: salon
Wavy dagger: kris
Wavy pattern: moiré, squiggle, undulation
Wax: cere
Wax melodramatic: emote
Wax opposite: wane
Waxed: cerated, grew
Waxes theatrical: emotes
Wax's antithesis: wane
Waxy content in cork: cerin
Waxy ointment: cerate
Waxy-patterned fabric: moire
Way: mode
Way back when: ages, ago, long ago
Way cool: rad
Way in or out: door, egress
Way of old Rome: iter
Way of the freighter: shipping lane
Way of thinking: mind-set
Way off: afar

Way off yonder: afar
Way out, easy: door
Way out: radical, rad.
Way to cook fish: pan broil, pan fry
Way to cook pasta: al dente
Way to go: route
Way to satori: zen
Way to the top: steps, stairs
Way up the hill: T-bar
Way up there: high
Way with words: tact
Wayfarer's refuge: inn
Wayside inn: motel
Wayside shelter: spital, lazaretto
Wayne's World word: not
WB competitor: Fox
WB network symbol: frog
WCTU member: dry
We all do this: age
"Lest we forget"
"Ain't We Got Fun"
We have, what: ours
We hope they meet: ends
We try harder: avis
Weak: puny
Weak brew: near beer
Weakening: dilution
Weaker: punier
Weaker, as an excuse: lamer
Weakest, as an excuse: lamest
Weak-kneed: timid, wobbly, gutless,
    cowardly, wavering
Weakness: vice, bias
Weakness, minor: vice
Wealth: comb. form: plut
Wealth, excess desire: greed
Wealthy entrepreneur: tycoon
Wealthy in Madrid: rico
Wealthy place: El Dorado
Wealthy, Spanish: rico
Weapon, long-pointed: spear
Weapon, nonlethal: taser
Weapon, primitive: sling, spear
Weapon, quaint: dirk
Weapon right at hand: fist
Weapon, sci-fi: ray gun
Weapon since 1952: H-bomb
Weapon, Star Trek: phaser
Weapon, underwater: depth charge
Weapon, whaler's: harpoon
Weapon, whirled: bola
Weapons, check for: frisk
Wear away by erosion: ablate
Wear away by friction: abrade
Wear away, tending to: erosive
Wear down: tire
Wear down slowly: corrode
Wear (forum): toga
Wear out: over use
Wear, type of: men's
Wearing flats: shod
Wearisome task: drag
Weary, becomes: jades
Weary, grow: sag, tire

Weasel: ermine
Weasel, short-tail: stoat
Weasel, white-coated: ermine
Weasel-like carnivore: marten
Weasels out of: evades, reneges, shirks
Weather affecting current: La Niña, El Niño
Weather balloon, kind of: radiosonde
Weather factor: stationary front
Weather map lines: isobars
Weather person's adjective: severe
Weather phenomenon: El Niño
Weather, rough: squall
Weather systems: fronts, high, low
Weather systems, rainy: lows
Weatherboard: siding
Weatherworn: eroded
Weave on a straight course: yaw
Weaver frame: loom
Weaver, Sigourney: actress
Weaver's craft: basketry
Weaver's reed: sley
Weaving defect: scob?
Web abbr.: URL
Web address, for short: URL
Web address starter: http
Web designer: spider
Web habitué: user
Web help list: FAQs
Web journal: blog
Web marketplace: eBay
Web page feature: hot line
Web picture format: gif
Web search engine: Yahoo, Google
Web suffix: org, com, net
Webber musical: Cats
Webbing: mesh
Weber, Max: German sociologist
Web-master's creation: site map
Web Site clutter: ads
Web Site language: Java
Web Site unit: page
Webster, Noah: dictionary
Webster's unabridged, e.g.: tome
Web-surfer's device: modem
Web-surfer's suffix: org
Webzine: E-mag
Wed economically: elope
Wedding announcement: bann
Wedding cake, like a: tiered
Wedding focal point: altar
Wedding keepsake: album
Wedding proclamation: bann, banns
Wedding, relating to a: nuptial
Wedding rental: tux, limo
Weddings: unions
Wedge, carpenter's: shim
Wedge, for one: iron
Wedge in: jam
Wedge or shim: cotter
Wedge placed beneath a wheel: sprag
Wedge up: shim
Wedge-shaped: cuneate, cottered,
    sphenoid, cuneiform
Wedge-shaped piece: gib, shim

Wedgewood, Josiah: English potter
Wednesday's god: Odin
Wednesday's kin: Itt
Wednesday's namesake: Odin
Wee drinks: drams
Wee hour, a: one
Wee in Dundee: sma
Weed out: screen, cull
Weed preventer: mulch
Weed whacker: hoe
Weekend event, often: sale, yard sale
Weekend visitor: house guest
Weekly message, some: sermons
Weekly program: series
Weeks in a Roman year: Lll
Weep over: rue, bemoan
Weepier: tearier
Weigh, as evidence: sift
Weigh on the mind: ponder
Weighed down: laden
Weight: heft
Weight allowance: tare
Weight, container: tare
Weight deduction: tare
Weight, height, etc.: stat
Weight, kind of: kilo, troy, gram, dram,
  pound, ounce
Weight lifter's pride: torso
Weight lifting maneuver: jerk
Weight of an empty truck: tare
Weight of packaging: tare
Weight rebate: tare
Weight reduction: tare
Weight, tested: hefted
Weighty work: tome
Weil, Simone: philosopher
Weiner: hot dog, red hot, frankfurter
Weiner schnitzel base: veal
Weir: dam
'Weird Al': Yankovic
Weird way, in a: eerily
Weirder: eerier
Weird-sounding bird: loon
Welch, Raquel: actress
Welchman: Celt
Welcome benefit: boon
Welcome loudly: applaud
Welcome, nonverbal: open arms
Welcome warmly: ask in
Weld, Tuesday: actress
Weldon, Fay: British novelist
Well aware of: onto
Well care: HMO
Well chosen: apt
Well, deep: artesian
Well dressed: natty
Well fed: sleek
Well mechanism: pump
Well partner: alive
Well publicized shindig: bash
Well put: apt
Well versed: fluent
Well worn: old
Well worth having: valued

Well-bred: genteel
Well-bred chap: gent
Well-groomed: soigne, natty
Well-informed: onto
Well-known: famous, famed
Well-founded: sound, valid, cogent,
  rational, justified,
  convincing
Well-made pottery: feats of clay
Well-mannered: polite
Well-practiced: adept
Well-read: erudite
Well-read individual: literati
Well-worn: old
Weller, Peter: actor
Wellingtons: boots
Welles's blond race: Eloi
Welles, Orson: director
Welsh emblem: leek
Welsh festival of music: Eisteddfod
Welsh form of John: Evan
Welty, Eudora: writer
Wends or Sorbs: Slavs
Went around: skirted
Went back over: retraced
Went down: sunk
Went first: led
Went for, really: adored
Went for the gold: vied
Went forward: headed
Went into the air: flew up
Went like heck: tore, sped
Went on the lam: absconded
Went one better: topped
Went slowly: edged
Went south: wintered, migrated
Went straight: reformed
Went too far: over-did
Went toward: headed
Wepner whipper: Ali
Wept over: rued
"We're Off to See the Wizard"
Were rivals: vied
Wertmuller, Lina: film director
West, Adam: actor
West Coast giants: sequoias
West End attraction: theatre
West highland: terrier
West Indies belief: Obeah
West Indies dance: limbo
West Indies music: reggae
West Indies native: Carib
West Indies religious belief: Obeah
West Mongolian border mountains: Altaic
West Point greenhorn: plebe
West, Shelly: western music
West Texas peak: Ord
Wester, Sou
Western Alaska: Aleutian
Western buddy: pardner, pard
Western contest: rodeo
Western defense org.: NATO
Western farewell: adios
Western hemisphere native: Amerind

Western hemisphere org.: OAS
Western hemisphere pact: OAS
Western native: Ute
Western omelet ingredient: ham, eggs
Western party: posse
Western resort: dude ranch, tahoe
Western spread: ranch
Western's star: badge
Westheimer's topic,: sex
Westinghouse rival: Amana
"Westworld" name: Yul
Wet and chilly: dank
Wet behind the ears: downy-cheeked
Wet down: hose
Wetlands: fens
Wet noodle, like a: limp
Wet soil: mud
Wet thoroughly: douse, soak
Whacks hard: bashes
Whale: orca
Whale bones: baleens
Whale diet: krill
Whale, female: cow
Whale, free willie: orca
Whale group: gam, pod
Whale, order of: cete
Whale school: gam
Whale seeker, noted: Ahab
Whaler, obsessed: Ahab
Whaler of fiction: Ahab
Whaler's weapon: harpoon
Whale's diet: krill
Wham: Pow
Wharf: quay
Wharf denizen: rat
Wharton alums, perhaps: MBAs
Wharton's Frome: Ethan
Wharves: quays
What a mendicant does: begs
What a shame: too bad
What a trade has: tricks
What arabesques are performed on: one
  leg
What buffalos do: roam
What cold winds do: bite
"What did i tell you?": see
What eternity has: no end
What fuel provides: energy
What has to be: karma
What have-nots have: need
What hoboes ride: rails, train
What hubbard's dog had: none
What hudson's guzzle: gas
What "I" is: vowel
What i.e. means: id est
"What" in Oaxaca: que
"What" in Seville: que
What is more: also
What it all comes out in: wash
What models need: glue, agent
What Munchhausen spun: yarns
What one isn't: even
What person: who
What pheromones do: attract

What results may do: vary
What sentence components should do: agree
What the suspicious smell: a rat
What this may take: awhile
What to hazard: guess
What tyros must learn: ropes
What was that?: huh
What we eat: diet
What we have: ours
What winter hats cover: ears
Whatever way, in: how
What's cooking: menu
What's in: trend
"What's in a name"
What's more: plus
"What's My Line" host: Daly
What's that?: huh
Wheat, cracked: bulgur
Wheat protein: gluten
Wheaties box adorner: athlete
Wheedle: coax, lure, con, cajole,
    finagle
Wheel: honcho
Wheel bolts: lugs
Wheel buy: an "A", "E", "I", "O", "U"
Wheel hubs: naves
Wheel lock: boot
Wheel type: mag
Wheeled around: spun
Wheeler, Ella: writer
Wheels for nanny: pram
Wheels, sporty: mags
Wheels, temporary: rental, loaner
When eggs roll: Easter
When mammal's flourished: escene
When pigs fly: never
When there's a will: testate
"When We Was Fab"
Whence the Pishon flowed: Eden
Where the King marched: Selma
Where acrobats might meet: midair
Where Adam's apple came from: Eve
Where amahs serve: Orient
Where American day begins: Guam
Where David hid from Saul: Engesi
Where IKEA began: Sweden
"Where" in Madrid: donde
Where Greek met Greek: agora
Where kine (cows) dine: lea
Where LaRusso finds relief: bull pen
Where lions roar: MGM
Where many exes are made: Reno
Where most strikes occur: lane
Where pins are made: mat
Where silents are seen: Nickelodeon
Where some skeletons are kept: closet
Where the caballeros roam: llanos
Where the sun don't shine: shade
Where to find a hero: deli
Where to get off: exit, ramp
Where to hear Farsi: Iran
Where to make waves: salon
Where to read contracts: between the lines
Where to see stars: sky

Where to surf: net
Where X marks the spot: map
Where you are on a map: here
"Where's the beef" lady: Clara
Wherewithal: funds, moola, means,
    money
Wherewithal, with the: able
Wherry adjuncts: oars
Wherry equipment: oars
Whetstone, use a: hone
"Whew" feeling: relief
Whey opposite: curd
Whey-faced: wan
Whichever: any
Which is more: also
Which person: who
While away: idle
While beginning: erst
Whilom: bygone, former, onetime,
    quondam, formerly, previous
Whim: urge, vagary
"On a whim"
Whimp: sissy
Whimper: mewl
Whims: urges, vagaries
Whimsical: droll
Whimsical, more: droller
Whine: yammer
Whine tearfully: snivel
Whining noise: zing
Whinnies: neighs
Whip: lash
Whip, use a: flog
Whip, rider's: crop
Whipped up: make
Whipping boy: goat, patsy, fall guy,
    scapegoat
Whipple wagger: tail
Whips up: makes
Whirl: gyrate
Whirled weapon: bola
Whirlpool: eddy, vortex, hot tub
Whirlpool outlet: jet
Whisk: beater
Whisker, by a: barely
Whiskey, blended: rye
Whiskey bottle size: fifth
Whiskey chaser: a-go-go
Whiskey, cheap: Red Eye
Whiskey cocktail: Rob Roy
Whiskey drink: sour
Whiskey Manhatten: Rob Roy
Whiskey measure: jigger, shot
Whiskey, tot of: dram
Whisper, furtive: psst
Whisper loudly: hissed
Whisper, not in a: aloud
Whisper, stage: aside
Whistle blower: cop
White alternative: rye
White cliffs locale: Dover
White collar work: stae, stay
White flag: truce
White hat wearer: chef

White house cat: socks
White House office: Oval
White House section: West Wing
White lightning: hooch, bootleg, whiskey,
    moonshine, bathtub gin,
    mountain dew
White plumed bird: egret
White poplar: abele
White symbol: peace
White wine: soave
Whitecaps: foam
White-coated weasel: ermine
White-faced: pallid
White—sheet connector: as a
Whitewash component: lime
White-water craft: raft, canoe, kayak
Whitney's business partner: Pratt
Whiz: ace
Whiz kids: brains
Whiz leader: gee
Whizzes: adepts
Whodunit: novel
Whodunit award: Edgar
Whodunit herring: rod, red
Whodunit MacDonald: Ross
Whodunit musts: bodies
Whodunit name: Erle
Whodunit poison: cyanide
Whodunit suspect: butler, heir
Whodunit terrier: Asta
Whodunit writer: novelist
Whole: intact, entire
Whole, as a: in toto, in total
Whole bunch: gob
Whole enchilada: all
Whole extent: gamut
Whole gale classification: Beaufort number
Whole number of: all
"The whole shebang"
Whole thing: shebang
Wholesale: at cost
Wholesale-retail spread: markup
Wholesome: oneness
Wholly absorbed: enrapt
Whoop it up: revel
Whorl: volute
Whorl member: petal
Who's who entry: bio
Why: how so
Wicker work materials: rattan
Wicket: hoop
Wicket, unwelcome kind of: sticky
Wide awake: alert
Wide destruction: havoc
Wide divergence: gap, parting, deviation,
    digression, gulf
Wide-eyed: naive
Wide inlet: sound
Wide neckwear: ascot
Wide spread: rife
Wide spread confusion: havoc
Wide spread damage: havoc
Wide-spread slaughter: carnage
Widely accepted saying: axiom

Widen: dilate, expand
Widen a hole: ream
Widening of market venues: ad creep
Wider, get: flare, expand
Wider in scope: grander
Wide-eyed with wonder: in awe
Widely known: famous, famed
Wide-spouted mantel piece: ewer
Widest part: beam
Widow's dower: thirds
Wiedersehen, auf
Wield a hammer: nail
Wield an axe: hew
Wielded: plied
Wields: plies
Wields a brush: paints
Wields the scepter: reigns
Wiener schnitzel base: veal
Wiesel, Elie: writer, Nobel Prize
Wiest, Dianne: actress
Wife of Paris: Oenone
Wife of the Bard: Anne
Wight as an example: Isle
Wigwam: tent, wickiup
Wilbur, Richard, product: verse
Wilco's partner: Roger
Wild about: into
Wild ass: onager
Wild blue yonder: sky, ether
Wild buffalo: arna
Wild cards, sometimes: deuce
Wild cat: ocelot
Wild cat strike: oil
Wild country: bush
Wild fancy: vagary
Wild, go: run, riot, on a tear
Wild goat: ibex
Wild goose: brant
"Wild goose chase"
Wild horse: bronco
Wild, no longer: tamed
Wild ox: gaurs
Wild party: orgy
Wild plum: sloe
Wild sheep: arui, aoudad, urial,
    argali
Wild sheep, African: arui
Wild sheep, Asian: argali, urial
Wild shrubs: sumac
Wild speech: rant
Wild strawberry tree: arbutus
Wild tale: yarn
Wild T-shirt: tie-dye
Wild time: spree
Wild uproar: bedlam
Wild West justice, symbol of: noose
Wild West peacekeeper: posse
Wild West revolver: Colt
Wild West show: oater, rodeo
Wild West showman: Cody
Wild West trophy: scalp
Wildcat, forest: lynx
Wildcat strike: oil
Wildcatter's find: oil

Wildebeest: gnu
Wilde, Cornet: actor
Wilde, Oscar: writer
Wilder, Alec: songwriter
Wilder, Gene: actor
Wilder, Ingalls, Laura: writer
Wilderness rarity: road
Wildflower habitat: meadow
Wildlife protector: warden
Wildlife refuge: den, lair
Wildlife shelter: nest, den, lair
Wildlife staple: acorn
"Will it play in Peoria"
Will, made a: testate
Will power, she has: heiress
Willamette River city: Salem
Willard sequel: Ben
Willard's pet: rat
William of Occam: philosopher
William, S. Porter: O' Henry
Williams, Andy: music
Williams, Doug: QB NFL
Williams, Edy: actress
William's mother: Diana,
Williams, Serena: tennis
Williams, Ted: baseball
Willie Wonka creator: Nash
Willies-inducing: eerie
Willing, more than: eager
Willing sacrifice: martyr
Willing to try: game
Willingly: gladly
Willow flower: catkin
Willow twig: osier
Willow, virginia: itea
Willow shoot: osier
Willow, water: osier
Willows: osier, itea
Willowy: slim, svelte
Wilson, Mara: actress
Wilson of cars: Owen
Wilson, Rita: actress
Wily maneuver: ploy,
Wily manner, having a: sly
Wilier: Cagier
Wimbledon's game: tennis
Wimple-sporter: nun
Wimple-wearer: nun
Win, easy: romp
Win four of four: sweep
Win, just barely: nip
Win narrowly: nose out
Win over: endear
Wind around: meander
Wind catcher: kite, sail
Wind, cold Adriatic: bora
Wind direction, determiner of: Coriolis force
Wind ensemble member: oboe
Wind flower: anemone
Wind indicator: vane
Wind instrument: vane
Wind instrument (small ovoid): ocarina
Wind into loops: coils
Wind, kind of: trade

Wind machine: fan
Wind of, got: heard
Wind, puff of: gust
Wind resistance: drag
Wind, southeast: Eurus
Wind spirally: coil
Wind storms: gales
Windblown soil: loess
Wind-borne item: spore
Wind-driven mist: scud
Windfall, timely: boon
Windflower: anemone
Windhoek's continent:Afr, Africa
Windjammer, ride a: sail
Windjammer sheet: main sail
Windmill blades: vanes
Window alternative: Unix
Window, attic: dormer
Window covering: blind, shade
Window grating: grill
Window on a corbel: oriel
Window on the bay: oriel
Window or arch style: lancet
Window purchaser: user
Window shopper: browser
Window side post: jamb
Window, spacious: oriel
Window sticker: decal
Window style: lancet
Window, type of: dormer
Windows alternative: UNIX
Windows ancestor: Dos
Wind-powered vessel: sailer
Windshield adjunct: visor
Windshield device: wiper
Wind toy: kite
Winds-up: cranks
Windy and cold: raw
Windy city sobriquet: chi
Windy day flier: kite
Wine: vino
Wine, amber: Madeira
Wine and dine: regale, woe, fete
Wine barrel: tun
Wine, Bordeaux: claret
Wine bottle feature: cork
Wine cabinet: cellaret
Wine cask: tun, vat
Wine, cassi-flavored: Kir
Wine category: sec, red
Wine city, Piedmont: Asti
Wine, clarify: decant
Wine, cooking: sherry, marsala
Wine cooler: ice
Wine, dessert: sauterne, Madeira
Wine, dry: sec, zinfandel
Wine, dry Italian: Soave
Wine, dry White: Rhine
Wine, French: vin
Wine, German white: Rhine, Moselle
Wine glass: goblet
Wine grape: pinot
Wine, Greek: retsina
Wine, honey: mead

Wine hot drink: negus
Wine, Hungarian: Tokay
Wine, in Cannes: Aile
Wine, Italian: Soave,
Wine jug, ancient: olpe
Wine juice drink: cooler
Wine label information: year
Wine, light pink: rose
Wine lover study: oenology, enology
Wine made from honey: mead
Wine, made with: vinous
Wine makers aboveground storage: chai
Wine making area: Napa
Wine, monsieur's: vin
Wine, of: vinous
Wine press residue: marc
Wine purchase: jug
Wine region, California: Sonoma
Wine, red: claret, modoc, merlot
Wine, red dry: merlot
Wine, rice: saki, sake
Wine sediment: lee
Wine served warm: saki
Wine server: carafe
Wine, spiced: wassail
Wine, sweet: port, sauterne
Wine, type of: blush
Wine valley: Napa, Sonoma
Wine vessel: flagon
Wine, warm: saki
Wine, white: Moselle, Soave
Wine-making process stage: aging
Winery cask: tun, vat
Winery storage: cask
Winery word form: oeno. oenology
Wine's partner: dine
Wing: annex
Wing: comb. form: pter
Wing it: ad-lib
Wing shaped: ular, alula
Wing, spurious: alula
Winged horse: Pegasus
Winged monster of Greek myth: harpy
Winged victory: Nike
Winged wonder of myth: Roc
Wing-footed: aliped
Wing-like: alar, alate
Wings:alate
Wings for Amor: Alate
Wingtip, fix a: re-sole
Wingtip-to-wingtip dimension: span
Winner for sure: shoo-in
Winner spot: first place
Winner's award: medal
Winner's take: all, pot
Winnie the Pooh'sfriend: Piglet
Winning big: on a roll
Winning margin: nose, hair
Winningham, Mare: actress
Winnow: sift
Wins four of four: sweeps
Win's over: disarms, endears
Winslet, Kate: actress
Winsome: cute

Winsome, more: cuter, charming
Winter accessory: scarf
Winter apple: russet
Winter bug: flu,
Winter coat: parka
Winter coat, took off: de-iced
Winter constellation: Orion
Winter games org.: IOC
Winter hats cover, what: ears
Winter jacket: parka
Winter melon: casaba
Winter Olympics event: biathlon
Winter overshoe: galosh
Winter, place to: den
Winter resort wear: apresski
Winter shower: sleet
Winter time sound: brr
Winter warmer: cocoa
Wintry: hiemal
Wintry autobahn hazard: Eis, (ice)
Wintry coating: frost,
Wintry region: frost belt
Wipe out: eradicate
Wipe out a file: erase
Wipe out entirely: efface, erase
Wipe the woodwork: dust
Wire cousin: telex
Wire, sent a: cabled
Wire tap, remove a: debug
Wire measure: mil
Wire mesh: screen
Wire stringers: linesmen
Wired: hyper
Wireless set: radio
Wisconsin iron range: Gogebic
Wisconsin native: badger
Wisconsin state flower: violet
Wisdom, bit of: axiom
Wisdom, received: lore
Wise: sage
Wise counselor: nestor
Wise lawgiver: solon
Wise men: magi, sages, guru, magus,
     savant
Wiser: sager
Wise ones: oracles
Wise person: magi, sage
Wise saying: adage
Wise teacher: mentor, guru
Wisecrack: quip
Wisely: sagely
Wisest: sagest
Wish and hope: dream
Wish grantor: genie
Wish, improbable: dream
Wish nullified: rue
Wish otherwise: rue
Wish things otherwise: rue
Wish undone: rue, regret
Wished undone: rued, regretted
Wishes and hopes: dreams
Wishes otherwise: rues
Wishes undone: rues, regrets
Wishful words: i hope

Wispy clouds: cirrus
Wister, Owen: writer, novelist
Witch: hag
Witch concoction: brew
Witch eye, like a: evil
Witch group: coven
Witch town: salem
Witch vessel: caldron
Witchcraft goddess: Hecate
Witches band: coven
Witches, not place for: salem
Witches, thirteen: coven
Witch's bestowal: curse
Witch's brew ingredient: newt
Witch's concoction: brew
Witch's job: hexing
Witch's stock in trade: hexes
Witchy woman: crone
With a clean slate: anew
With all one's heart: dearly
With conviction: adamantly
With defects and all:as is
With full force: amain
With full attention: raptly
With great skill: adroitly
With icing: frosted
With it: hip, hep
With little formality: casual
With no strings attached: freely
With respect to: in re
With ruffles: frilly
With the wherewithal: able
"With," to Fifi: avec
With us now: here
Withdraw: opt out, secede
Wither: sere
Withered and dry: sere
Withered, most: serest
Witherspoon, Cora: actress
Witherspoon, Reese: actress
Withhold: deny, keep, retain
Within a stone's throw: near
Within reach: near
Within sight: near
Without: sans, lack
Without a care in the world: blithe
Without a choice in the matter: fated
Without a connection: apart
Without a mixer: neat
Without adornment: bare
Without an ulterior motive: sincere
Without assistance: solo, alone
Without, be: lack
Without delay: ASAP
Without doubt: by far
Without effort: easily
Without equal: peerless
Without further delay: now
Without ice: neat
Without ice, drink: neat
Without imagination: aridly
Without melody: tuneless
Without much energy: wanly
Without precedent: new

Without purpose: idly
Without repairs: as is
Without results: vainly
Without rival: peerless
Without scruples: amoral
Without stopping: no end
Without thought: rashly
Without value: null
Without walls: open
Without warranty: as is
Witness: notary
Witness, bear: attest
Witness, false: liar
"Witness" group: Amish
Witness might view: line up
Witness phrase: I saw, I do
Witness vow: I do
Wits, one lacking: dolt
Witticism: mot, quip
Witty one: wag
Witty remarks: mots, epigram, jest
       quip, bon mot
Witty retort: riposte
Wizard, famous: Merlin
Wizened: sere, dry, dried, wrinkled
Woadwaxen and others: dye stuffs
Wobble: teeter, reel, sway, totter
Wobbles, as a rocket: yaws
Wobbly: unsafe
Wobbly walker: dodderer
"Woe is me": alas
Wok, cook in a: stir-fry
Wok sauce: soy
Wolf, at times: ogler
Wolfe, Nero: Sleuth
Wolfe, Nero: Orchid Loving
Wolf, gray: lobo
Wolfpack unit: U-boats
Wolf, prairie: coyote
Wolf, spanish: lobo
wolf, type of: lone
Wolf, young: cub
Wolf's look: ogle
Wolf's pastime: ogling
Wolfish: lupine
Wolfish look: leer
Wolfgang's thanks: danke
Wolfman Jack: Deejay
Wolfman portrayer: Lo
Wolverine state: Michigan
"Dances with Wolves"
Woman graduate: alumna
Woman, a Little: Amy
Woman admired by Sherlock: Irene
Woman characteristics: feminine
Woman hat: toque, tuque
Woman, Hispanic: Latina
Woman on campus: coed
Woman, overbearing: battle ax
Woman, seductive: vamp
Woman, the Bionic
Woman, witchy: crone
Womanish (old): anile
Womanizer: roue

Women, alluring: siren
Women, ill-tempered: shrews
Women on campus: coeds
Women's magazine: Cosmopolitan, Cosmo
Women's patriotic society: D.A.R.
Women's quarters: harem, oda
Women's sitting room: boudoir
Won ton soup
Wander: gad, roam
Wonder aloud: ask
Wonder, stevie: music
Wonder woman's friend: etta
Wonka's creator: Dahl
Won't share: hogs
Wood ash product: lye
Wood insect: tick
Wood knot: burl
Wood, Natalie: actress
Wood nymphs: napaea
Wood, of durable: oaken
Wood pattern: template
Wood pile: alder, oak
Wood protector: varnish, finish
Wood pussy's defense: odor
Wood, Ron: guitarist
Wood shaving tool: adz
Wood shavings: excelsior
Wood sorrel: oxalis, oca
Wood strips: lath
Woodchuck: rodent
Wooden: sylvan
Wooden container: barrel, vat
Wooden footwear: sabots
Wooden horse saga: Iliad
Wooden peg: dowel
Wooden pin, carpenter's: dowel
Wooden rods: dowels
Wooden shoe: sabot, clog
Wooden tub: soe, vat
Woodland deity: faun, satyr
Woodlot, small: copse
Woodpecker, cartoon: Woody
Woods: forest
Woodsy: sylvan
Woodward, Joanne: actress
Woodworking tool: adz, adze
Woody: xyloid
Woody hill: holt
Woody vine: liana
Woody's ex: Mia
Woody's son: Arlo
Woof: yap
Woofer's partner: tweeter
Wool coat: fleece
Wool, course: abby
Wool fabric: tweed
Wool fiber: nep
Wool hue, raw: ecru
Wool on clay sheep: chia
Wool, raw: fleece
Wool, resembles: lanate
Wool, soft: Angora, Merino
Wool substitute: Orlon
Wool washing residue: sud

Woolen cap: tam
Woolen fabric: worsted
Woolen fabric, heavy: melton, twill, tweed
Woolen fabric, light: kersey
Wooly: lanate
Wooly animal: mammoth
Wooly clothing: sweater
Wooly mammoth time: ice age
Wooly quadruped: ram
Doo-wop: 50s music
Word blindness: alexia
Word diviser: coiner
Word feminizer: ette, ettes
Word finders: thesauri
Word for word: verbatim, literal
Word form for "ancient": paleo
Word from the pew: amen
Word groups: phrases
Word guessing game: Jotto
Word in an octagon: stop
Wordlessly: mutely
Word of advice: tip
Word of commitment: I do
Word of contempt: pish
Word of honor: oath
Word of inquiry: who, when, what
Word of mouth: viva voce, parol, oral,
       spoken, verbal, unwritten
Word of woe: alack
Word on pennies: unum
Word play: pun
Word processor concern: text
Word processing feature, useful: undo
Word processing function: tab set
Word processor command: save, delete
Word processor, one time: steno
Word separator: space
Word spoken in court: honor
Word suggesting options: else
Word to the wise: advice
Word with crazy or clockwork: like
Word with pad or worthy: note
Word with pride or duty: civic
Words: id est
Words at the pump: octane
Words for songs: lyrics
Words from the wise: sayings
Words from Wordsworth: odes
Words heard after a veronica: ole
Words, man of many: Roget
Words of agreement: so am I
Words of approximation: or so
Words of befuddlement: your guess is
       as good as mine, only God knows,
       I have no idea
Words of concession: I lose
Words of wisdom: adage
Words relating to Jewish Diet: pareve
Words to a backstabber: et tu
Words to an audience: aside
Words to Brutus: et tu,
Words to live by: credo
Words with a ring to them: I Do
Words, without: tacitly

Wordsworth's words: odes
Work antithesis: play
Work, as clay: knead
Work at getting in shape: train
Work, assigned: task
Work clothes: Levi's
Work crew house: wanigan
Work doggedly: slog
Work dough: knead
Work environment: milieu
Work force: crew, staff
Work gang: crew
Work, gives: assigns
Work, line of: trade
Work on a score: notate
Work, paid: job
Work part-time: temp
Work, physical: labor
Work place extra: perk
Work place posting: memo
Work shop: atelier
Work shop objects: idols
Work the fields: plow, till
Work together: cooperate
Work unit: ergs
Work well together: mesh
Workable: viable
Workaholic, like a: driven
Worked at a trade: plied
Worked out, not: failed
Worked up: agog
Worker, new: trainee
Worker who thatches: reeder
Worker's assn.: ILO, UAW, CIO, IWW
Worker's extra benefit: perk
Worker's home: ant hill
Worker's incentives: bonus, raises
Workers, some unpaid: interns
Workers with acid: etchers
Worker's with green cards: legals
Worker's with twomasters?: tars
Worker's with wheels: potters
Working cat: mouser
Working order: useable
Working stiff: peon
"Working without a net"
Workout garb: sweats
Workout results: aches
Workout target: biceps, abs
Workout units: reps.
Workplace overseer, govt's.: OSHA
Works: labors
Works by Shelley: odes
Works for the accused: defends
Works of art: oeuvres
Works on a cartoon: animates
Works on "US": Adits
Workweek ending: TGIF
World bank org.: IMF
World book: atlas
World Cup score: goal
World Cup sport: soccer
World fair: expo
World org. based in Paris: UNESCO

WW I poet: Poe
WW II address: ETO
WW II correspondent: Pyle (Ernie)
WW II sea menace: U-boat
WW II uniform segment: Puttee
World's biggest hold-up man: Atlas
World's largest desert: Sahara
World's third largest island: Borneo
World-weary: blasé
Worldwide crop: rice
Worm container: can
Worn: haggard
Worn away: erose, erosion, eroded
Worn like a book: dog-eared
Worn-out: shabby, overused
Worn, well: old
Worn frazzle link: to a
Worried: uneasy
Worried, act: pace
Worry: fret, stew, agonize
Worshipper, nonclergy: laity
Worshipper's section: nave
Worse than bad: evil
Worshiped ones: idols
Worst case scenario
Worth, Irene: actress
Worthless bit: ort, dross
Worthless material: dross
Wotan: Odin
Would rather:prefer
Wouldn't obey: defied
Wound around: snaked
Wound deeply: lacerate
Woven product: web
Wraith: spooky
Wrap around: entwine
Wrap, graceful: sari
          exotic: sari
Wrap, it's a: finished, done, ended
Wrap, light: cardigan
Wrap, Malay: sarong
Wrap, shiny: foil
Wrap with feathers: boa
Wrapped headdress: turban
Wrapping, food: foil
Wrap up, condense: re-cap
Wray, Vina Fay: actress
Wreath: anadem, diadem, garland
Wreath for the head: anadem
Wreath, kanaka's: lei
Wreath, victor's: laurel
Wreck: mess, ruin, raze
Wreck a car: total
Wreck and ruin: havoc
Wreck, as a train: derail
Wreck, completely: total, ruin
Wrecked ship: derelict
Wrecker: tow truck
Wrecker's job: tow
Wrecking ball alternative: TNT
Wrench away: tear
Wrench, British: spanner
Wrench, type of: allen, crescent, box end
Wren's Beau: Geste

Wrestler, defeats a: pins
Wrestler's grip: hold
Wrestling, form of: sumo
Wretched: sordid, bad
Wriggled in pain: writhed
Wrigley's adornment: ivy
Wrinkle: line
Wrinkled: seamy
Wrinkle-free: ironed
Wrinkles, get rid of: iron, press
Wrist movement: flick
Wrist, of the: carpal
Writ of execution: elegit
Write back: answer, reply
Write hastily: jot
Write hurriedly: scrawl
Write, mediocre: hack
Write off: cancel, dismiss, expense,
          amortize, discount, eliminate
Write up a speeder: cite
Writer, mediocre: hacker
Writer's best friend, maybe: editor
Writer's credit: byline
Writer's concern: plot
Writer's enclosure: SASE
Writer's inspiration: muse
Writes down: jots, records
Writing end: pen point,
Writing pad, old: blotter
Writing, ordinary: prose
Writing, slanted: italic
Writing, set down in: indite
Writing master: penman
Written after: adscript
Written composition: essay
Written order: prescription
Written record: log, journal, diary
Written reminder: memo
Written with ease: fluent
Wrong, actionable: tort
Wrong key, hit the: err, typo
Wrong, morally: evil
Wrong move, make a: err
Wrongdoing, assist in: abet
Wrongdoing, charge of: accusal
Wrongful act: tort
Wrongheaded: mulish, forward, contrary,
          perverse, obstinate
Wry: ironic
Wry face: moue
WWW address: URL
WWW language: HTML
WWW part of: Web, Web address
Wyatt's cohort: Doc
Wyeth, Andrew: painter
Wyeth's subject: Helga
Wyle, Noah: actor
Wyman, Jane: actress
Wynn, Keenen: actor
Wynonna's mother: Naomi
Wynter, Dana
Wyoming range: Tetons

X

"X" marks the spot, where: map
X and O game start: Tic
X or Y, in geometry: axis
Xanadu group: ELO
Xanadu builder: Khan
Xanthippe, reputedly: shrew
Xenophobe's fear: alien
Xenophobe's nightmare: alien
Xerography powder: toner
Xerox competitor: Canon
Xerxes ruled here: Persia, Iran
X-File topic: UFO
XKE, for one: Jaguar
X-rated: lewd
X-ray kin: MRI
Xylophone striker: mallet
Xylophone's cousin: marimbas

Y

"Y" beneficiary: son
Yacht basin site: mast
Yacht mooring: berth
Yacht pronoun: her, she
Yada yada: etc.
Yahtzee need: dice
Yakking, keep: prate
Yale graduate: Eli
Yale grounds: campus, quad
Yale, Mr.: Elihu
Yales vine: Ivy, Ivies
Yalta conferee: Stalin
Yalta conference site: Crimea
Yank from the ground: uproot
Yin Yang
Yard enclosure: fence, hedge
Yarn, coil of: hank, skein
Yarn, quantity: skein
Yarn unit: hank
Yawn, make: bore
Yawn, wide: gape
Ye Olde Shoppe
Yeah, right: as If
Year 1, Prior to: BC, BCE
Year in school: grade
Year, Spanish: año
      French: an
Year book: annual, annal
Year of school: grade
Years and years: ages, eons
Years past, from: olden, ago
Yearned: pined
Years on end: eon
Yeast: leaven
Yeats, William: writer
Yegg's preferred name: alias
Yegg's job: heist
Yegg's target: safe
Yek: Ugu
Yell, scary: boo

Yellow bugle: iva
Yellow, dark: ocher, ochre
Yellow element: sulfur
Yellow fever mosquito: aedes
Yellow, pale: flaxen, straw
Yellow parts of eggs: yolks
Yellow pigment: ocher
Yellow sea country: Korea
Yellowstone sight: geyser
Yellow-brown gem: tigereye
Yellowhammer: finch, bunting, flicker
Yellowknife Prov.: NWT (Northwest
      Territory)
Yells insults: jeers
Yeltsin, Boris: Russian leader
Yemen city: Aden
Yemen monetary unit: rial
Yemen native: Adeni
Yemen seaport: Aden
Yeomen of the English Royal Guard: beef-
      eater
Yens: urges
Yerkish, communicators using: apes
"Yes" in Japan: hai
"Yes" in Kyoto: hai
"Yes" in Yokohama: hai
Yes-man: toady
Yes, ma'am
Yes to Miss Piggy: oui
Yes, monsieur: oui,
Yes on the Riviera: oui
Yes to Angus: Aye
Yes to Rob Roy: Aye
Yesteryear: past
Yesterday to Yvette: hier
Yesterday tomorrow: today
Yesterday's news, like: old-hat, passé
Yet to come: ahead
Yeth, say: lisp
Yiddish thief: ganef
Yield by treaty: cede
Yield territory: cede
Yield to: obey
Yield to fatigue: sat, sit
Yield to gravity: sag
Yield via treaty: cede
Yikes: egad
Yin complement: Yang
Ymir's defeater: Odin
Yo: hey
Yoda's student: Luke
Yodeler's locale: Tyrol
Yodeler's home: Chalet
Yodeler's place: Alps
Yoga class need: mat
Yoga position: lotus
Yoga Postures: Asanas
Yoga principle: prana
Yoga type: hatha
Yogi Bear's pal: Boo Boo
Yogurt, like some: fat free, no fat
Yokel: rube
Yokel, country: rube
Yoko's son: Sean

Yokum, Daisy Mae
Yokum creature: Capp
Yokum lad: Abner
Yom Kippur (Kipper)
Yon maiden: She
Hither and yon
Yore, exclamation of: egad
Yorkshire city: Leeds
Yosemite toon: Sam
Yosemite, Sam
You bet: sure
You can say that again: amen
You don't say: do tell, duh
You, formerly: thee
You get a charge out of it: credit card
You, girl: missy
You got that right: I'll say
You homophone: ewe
You may do it with the sun: rise
You may sleep on it: sheet
You might give the business: son
You of yore: thou
You, once: thou
You, Quaker): thou
YouTube cofounder: Steve Chen
"You wish": dream on
Young chicken: fryer
Young dolphin: calf
Young haddock: scrod
Young hen: poulet
Young louse: nit
Young man, beautiful: adonis
Young oyster: spat
Young pigeon: squab
Young screecher: owlet
Young socialite: deb
Young troopers: BSA
Young upstart: turk
Youngster, mischievous: scamp
Youngsters: tykes
Your choice: any
Your first may be blind: date
"You're in a heap of trouble"
Your majesty: sire
Your, old style: thy
Yours and mine: ours
Yours in Tours: à toi
Yours may be checkered: past
Yours may be saved: seat
Youth: lad
Youth org.: BSA
Yo-Yo Ma plays it: cello
Yo-yo part: spool
Yucatan native: Mayan
Yuck: ugh
Yucky: icky
Yucky residue: gunk
Yukon garb: parka
Yukon hauler: sled
Yuletide trio: magi
Yuletide visitors: magi
Yul's film realm: Siam
Yvette's head: tête
Yvette's home: chez

Yves girl: amie

Z

Zadora, Pia: actress
Zahn, Paula: TV
Zaire, now: Congo
Zanjan's locale: Iran
Zany quality: nuttiness
Zapata, Viva
Zappa, Moon Unit
Zatopek, Emil: runner
Zealous, beyond: rabid
Zebulon Pike: Gen., explorer
Zedong, Mao: premier
Mao Zedong
Zellweger, Renee: actress
Zen follower: Stoic
Zen goal: satori
Zen practiced: sat
Zen poem: haiku
Zen question: koan
Zen riddle: koan
Zen Verse: Haiku
Zenana cubicle: oda
Zenith opposite: nadir
Zenith, reach one's: peak
Zeno followers: Stoics
Zeno's birthplace: Elea
Zeno's home: Elea
Zephyr: west wind
Zephyrus's father: Astraeus
        mother: Eos, Aurora
Zeppelin: blimp

Zero: nil
Zero in sports: zip
Zero, it's left of: star
Zero-star meal: slop
Zero thru nine: digits
007 alma mater: Eton
O07 first movie: Dr. No
007 foe: Odd-job, Dr. No
Zest for life: élan
Zetterling, Mai
Zeus: god
        brother: Hades
        consort: Hera
        daughter: Athena
        father: Cornus
        mate: Metis
        messenger: Hermes
        mother: Rhea
        mount: Olympus
        realm: sky
        son: Apollo, Ares, Hermes, Minos
        wife: Hera
Zeus' lachrymose daughter: Niobe
Zeus, to Romans: Jove
Zhivago's love: Lara
Ziegfeld nickname: Flo
Zigzag edge, cut a: pink
Zigzagged at sea: tacked
Zilch: nada, nil, zero, naught, squat
Zinger: Barb
Zip: nada, nil
Zip or area: code
Ziploc competitor: Glad
Zipped by: flew
Zipped through: aced

Zippy the Pinhead's word: yow
Zither cousin: lute
Zodiac animal: crab, lion
Zodiac fish: Pisces
Zodiac scales: Libra
Zodiac sign: Leo (lion), Aries (ram), Libra
        (balance), Virgo (virgin), Cancer (crab),
        Gemini (twins), Pisces (fish), Taurus
        (bull), Scorpio (scorpion), Aquarius
        (water-bearer), Capricorn (goat),
        Sagittarius (archer)
Zodiac symbol: scales
Zodiac twins: Gemini
Zola, Emile: writer
Zola courtesan: Nana
Zola heroine: Nana
Zone, of a: area
Zoo barrier: moat
Zoo building: aviary
Zoo denizen: lion
Zoologist's foot: pes
Zoologist's study: fauna
Zoom: rip
Zoom on runners: ski
Zoom past: whiz
Zoomed: tore, sped
Zorba portrayer: Quinn
Zoroastrian text collection: Avesta
Zorro's mark: Z
Zorro's first name: Diego
Zoysia or fescues: grasses
Adm. Elmo Zumwalt
Zwei, half of: Eins
Zwieback: rusk (Crisp bread)

Printed in the United States
136545LV00001B/23/P

9 781604 941722